ACSAC'98

Proceedings

14th Annual Computer Security Applications Conference

December 7–11, 1998

Phoenix, Arizona

Sponsored by

Applied Computer Security Associates

in cooperation with

ACM Special Interest Group on Security, Audit, and Control

IEEE COMPUTER SOCIETY

Los Alamitos, California

Washington • Brussels • Tokyo

IEEE Computer Society Order Number PR08789
IEEE Order Plan Catalog Number 98EX217
ISBN 0-8186-8789-4
ISSN 1063-9527

Additional copies may be ordered from:

IEEE Computer Society
Customer Service Center
10662 Los Vaqueros Circle
P.O. Box 3014
Los Alamitos, CA 90720-1314
Tel: + 1-714-821-8380
Fax: + 1-714-821-4641
E-mail: cs.books@computer.org

IEEE Service Center
445 Hoes Lane
P.O. Box 1331
Piscataway, NJ 08855-1331
Tel: + 1-908-981-1393
Fax: + 1-908-981-9667
mis.custserv@computer.org

IEEE Computer Society
Asia/Pacific Office
Watanabe Bldg., 1-4-2
Minami-Aoyama
Minato-kuTokyo 107-0062
JAPAN
Tel: + 81-3-3408-3118
Fax: + 81-3-3408-3553
tokyo.ofc@computer.org

Editorial production by Lorretta Palagi

Cover art design and production by Joseph Daigle

Printed in the United States of America by Technical Communication Services

IEEE COMPUTER SOCIETY

IEEE

Table of Contents

14th Annual Computer Security Applications Conference—ACSAC'98

TRACK A: Information Infrastructure

Chair: L. Notargiacomo, Trusted Computer Solutions

TRACK B: Internet Technologies

Chair: D. Thomsen, Secure Computing Corporation

THURSDAY MORNING, DECEMBER 10

Plenary Panel Session: Computer Security and the Millieunnium

Moderator: F. C. Smith, Santa Fe Attorney

TRACK A: Electronic Commerce

Chair: K. Keus, German Information Security Agency

TRACK B: Architectures
Chair: J. Heaney, The MITRE Corporation

THURSDAY AFTERNOON, DECEMBER 10

TRACK A: Panel Session—Opening the Doors, Selectively, to the Big Ten Virtual Library
Moderator: D. Brink, Gradient Technologies

TRACK B: High-Speed Networks
Chair: A. Friedman, National Security Agency

TRACK A: Cryptography
Chair: E. Siarkiewicz, Rome Labs

TRACK B: Intrusion Detection
Chair: C. Schuba, Sun Microsystems Laboratories

Message from the Conference Chair

Welcome to the 14th Annual Computer Security Applications Conference. When I started working with this conference in the publicity area in 1988, I never expected that I would have the opportunity to be your Conference Chair. I'm happy to be here and look forward to getting some feedback from you about the conference this year.

I'm excited to be bringing you so many new things this year. First, the conference is being held in a new city, Phoenix/Scottsdale. I hope you will enjoy the location and the hotel. Second, we made a small change to the conference Advance Program brochure to give it a new look. Please provide us with your comments and suggestions on these changes. Third, we changed the flavor of our Vendor Track to Case Studies.

As the week progresses, I hope you find the conference everything you expected it to be. My committee and I are dedicated to bringing you the best we have to offer such that the conference provides *practical solutions to real security problems*. Take a moment during the week to let us know how we are doing and how we could improve the conference to truly be *the technical exchange meeting for the next millennium*!

Dee Akers, The MITRE Corporation

Conference Chair

Conference Committee

Conference Chair

Dee Akers, The MITRE Corporation

Panel/Forum Chair

Jody Heaney, The MITRE Corporation

Program Chair

Klaus Keus, German Information Security Agency

Web Advisor

Robert Hobbes Zakon, The MITRE Corporation

Tutorial Chair

Daniel Faigin, The Aerospace Corporation

Publicity Co-Chairs

Art Friedman, National Security Agency
Vince Reed, The MITRE Corporation

Photo not available

Student Paper Chair

Dr. Matt Bishop, University of California–Davis

Case Studies Chair

Steve Rome, National Security Agency

Registration Chair

Jim Litchko, Integrated Management Services, Inc.

Multimedia Chair

Dr. Frank Sledge, TRW Corp.

Special Events Chair

Noelle Hardy, Nichols Information Technology

Photo not available

Treasurer

Steve LaFountain, National Security Agency

Recording Secretary

Dan Gambel, Mitretek Systems

ACSA Chair

Dr. Marshall Abrams, The MITRE Corporation

Photo not available

ACSA Vice Chair

Dr. Ron Gove, SAIC

Photo not available

ACSA Member-at-Large

Dr. Dixie Baker, SAIC

ACSA Treasurer

Ann Marmor-Squires, TRW Corp.

Program Committee

Klaus Keus, German Information Security Agency, *Program Chair*
Art Friedman, National Security Agency, *Program Co-Chair*
Matt Bishop, University of California–Davis, *Student Paper Chair*
Jeremy Epstein, Network Associates, Inc.
Virgil Gligor, University of Maryland
Noelle Hardy, Nichols Information Technology
Jody Heaney, The MITRE Corporation
Patrick Horster, University of Klagenfurt
Steven LaFountain, National Security Agency
Teresa Lunt, Defense Advanced Research Projects Agency
John McDermott, Naval Research Laboratory
LouAnna Notargiacomo, Trusted Computer Solutions
Steve Rome, National Security Agency
Ron Ross, National Institute of Standards and Technology
Christoph Schuba, Sun Microsystems Laboratories
Dan Thomsen, Secure Computing Corporation

Tutorial Committee

Daniel Faigin, The Aerospace Corporation, *Tutorial Chair*
Frank Belvin, The MITRE Corporation
Patricia Daggett, Data General Corporation
Jeremy Epstein, Network Associates, Inc.
Cynthia Irvine, Computer Science Department, Naval Postgraduate School
Klaus Keus, German Information Security Agency
Vincent LeVeque, SAIC
Barbara Mayer, Computer Sciences Corporation
Stuart Schaeffer, The Aerospace Corporation
Gaurang Shah, Raytheon Systems Company

Reviewers

Marshall Abrams, The MITRE Corporation, USA
John Adams, Network Associates, Inc., USA
Gene Bacic, TEXAR, USA
Dave Bailey, Galaxy Computer Services, USA
David Bell, Mitretek, USA
Matt Bishop, University of California-Davis, USA
Aaron Cohen, JOTA System Security Consultants Inc., Canada
Edward J. Coyne, Science Applications International Corporation, USA
Mary Denz, Air Force Research Laboratory, Rome Research Site, USA
Gerd Enste, Debis IT-Security Services, Germany
Jeremy Epstein, Network Associates, Inc., USA
Daniel Faigin, The Aerospace Corporation, USA
Ellen Flahavin, National Institute of Standards and Technology, USA
Simon Foley, University College, Cork, Ireland
Art Friedman, National Security Agency, USA
Daniel W. Gambel, Mitretek, USA
Thomas Gast, German Information Security Agency, Germany
Virgil Gligor, University of Maryland, USA
Noelle Hardy, Nichols Information Technology, USA
Jody Heaney, The MITRE Corporation, USA
Patrick Horster, University of Klagenfurt, Austria
George Jelen, G-J Consulting, USA
Mike Joyce, EDS, USA
Klaus Keus, German Information Security Agency, Germany
Peter Kraaibeek, Competence Center Informatik, Germany
Helmut Kurth, Industrie Anlagen Betriebsgesellschaft, Germany
Steven LaFountain, National Security Agency, USA
Carl Landwehr, Naval Research Laboratory, USA
Steven B. Lipner, Mitretek, USA
Teresa Lunt, Defense Advanced Research Projects Agency, USA
John McDermott, Naval Research Laboratory, USA
Mike Nash, Gamma Secure Systems Ltd., UK
Patrick Nilson, Defence Material Administration, Sweden
LouAnna Notargiacomo, Trusted Computer Solutions, USA
Rolf Oppliger, Bundesamt für Informatik, Switzerland
Guenther Pernul, Universität GH Essen, Germany
Reinhard Posch, University of Technology, Austria
Steve Rome, National Security Agency, USA
Ron Ross, National Institute of Standards and Technology, USA
Bernard Roussely, NATO NC3A, Belgium
Bruce Schneier, Counterpane Systems, USA
Qi Shi, John Moores University, UK
Christoph Schuba, Sun Microsystems Laboratories, USA
Roland Schützig, Swiss Security Service Laboratory, Switzerland
Dan Thomsen, Secure Computing Corporation, USA
Gene Troy, National Instute of Standards and Technology, USA
Rayford Vaughn, Mississippi State University, USA
Jean Viale, SCSSI, France
Jeremy Wilde, SYNTEGRA, UK
Paul Williams, Admiral Management Services Limited, UK
Ed Wojciechowski, National Security Agency, USA
Petra Wohlmachern, University of Klagenfurt, Austria

Track A

Network Intrusion Detection

Chair

M. Bishop, University of California–Davis

How to Increase Security in Mobile Networks by Anomaly Detection

Roland Büschkes, Dogan Kesdogan, Peter Reichl
Aachen University of Technology - Department of Computer Science
Informatik 4 (Communication Systems)
D-52056 Aachen, Germany
{roland, dogan, peter}@i4.informatik.rwth-aachen.de

Abstract

The increasing complexity of cellular radio networks yields new demands concerning network security. Especially the task of detecting, repulsing and preventing abuse both by in- and outsiders becomes more and more difficult. This paper deals with a relatively new technique that appears to be suitable for solving these issues, i.e. anomaly detection based on profiling mobile users. Mobility pattern generation and behavior prediction are discussed in depth, before a new model of anomaly detection that is based on the Bayes decision rule is introduced. Applying this model to mobile user profiles proves the feasibility of our approach. Finally, a special emphasis is put on discussing privacy aspects of anomaly detection.

1. Introduction

Cellular radio networks gain more and more popularity and the amount of mobile communication will increase dramatically in the near future. Mobile users will no longer be restricted to the use of mobile phones. New network architectures like UMTS will place enhanced multimedia communication at the user's disposal. One major concern for the present and future cellular radio networks is security. But with increasing complexity of the networks the task of detecting, repulsing and preventing abuse by out- and insiders becomes more and more difficult. Obviously it is not possible to make any system absolutely secure with the currently known security techniques like e.g. authentication and encryption. This is related to the fact that a lot of attacks are simply based on software flaws and design errors, which may often be intelligently combined in order to open the door to any system under attack. One recent example is the cloning of GSM cards [4].

Additional countermeasures are therefore needed. One possible technique is anomaly detection based on the profiling of mobile users. Anomaly detection tries to detect the abnormal use of a system, i.e. a behavior which is significantly different from the usual behavior of a user. It is not restricted to any specific network environment. As a matter of fact, an anomaly detection component is a major building block within most available intrusion detection systems (IDS).

In this paper we focus on the application of anomaly detection techniques to mobile networks, an issue which has its own specific security requirements and user characteristics. We introduce a new model of anomaly detection which is based on the Bayes decision rule. A special emphasize is put on the privacy protecting aspects, and it is shown that, while a profiling function may seriously offend the privacy of one user, it can add value to another user.

Our paper is subdivided into seven sections. After this introduction we give a general outline of different anomaly detection models. Thereafter we introduce our own model based on the Bayes decision rule. In section 4 we apply this rule to generate a profile for a mobile user and prove its feasibility. Based on these results we continue with the description of general application scenarios and respective protocols. In this context we discuss privacy related issues. Afterwards we compare our approach with related work from other researchers and conclude with an outlook on future work.

2. Anomaly Detection

The first work in the field of anomaly detection has been done over a decade ago, focusing on main frame scenarios. With the rise of more complex data- and telecommunication networks like the Internet and mobile networks the designers of anomaly detection systems have to face new challenges resulting from the more distributed nature of these networks.

[23] lists three main statistical models currently used for anomaly detection:

- operational model

0-8186-8789-4/98 $10.00 © 1998 IEEE

- mean and standard deviation model
- time series model

The operational model is based on thresholds, i.e. an alarm is raised if a variable observed (e.g. the number of login attempts) reaches a certain threshold. The mean and standard deviation model raises an alarm if an observation does not lie within a given confidence interval. The time series model takes the time at which an event takes place into account. If the probability for that event at that particular time is too low an alarm is raised.

Anomaly detection systems have major advantages compared to other intrusion detection approaches (see e.g. [23]) as they:

1. do not require any a priori knowledge of the target system, and
2. provide a way to detect unknown attacks.

But there also exist serious disadvantages which have to be considered before applying any of these techniques:

1. Not all users actually have a normal or standard behavior.
2. A user can slowly change his behavior over time from "good" to "bad", i.e. fool the system by slow long-term attacks.
3. The privacy of the users can be seriously injured.

We will come back to discuss these disadvantages and their relevance to mobile networks later. First of all we introduce our general approach towards anomaly detection, which is based on the Bayes rule.

3. The Bayes Decision Rule

Our approach towards anomaly detection is based on the Bayes decision rule and can therefore be classified as a statistical approach.

The Bayes decision rule is widely used in statistical pattern recognition [6]. A pattern recognition problem can be described in the following way: A set of objects can be divided into a number of classes. For each of these objects we measure a couple of observable characteristics and combine them to a vector. This observation vector will be different for each object, thus we can interpret this vector as a random variable X. To classify a new object, we have to learn the probability distribution of X for each class. If we know these distributions, we can calculate the probability that an object with observation vector x belongs to class c, namely $P(c|x)$. Therefore we can classify a new object in the following way:

1. Measure the observation vector for the object.
2. Calculate the class probabilities $P(c|x)$ for every class.
3. Choose the class with the highest probability as the object's class.

This decision rule is called the *Bayes decision rule for minimum error rate*. It can be shown that every other decision rule yields even higher error rates than the Bayes rule.

The so-called *a-posteriori* probability $P(c|x)$ can be expressed as:

$$P(c|x) = \frac{P(c)p(x|c)}{p(x)}$$

$p(x|c)$ is the *class conditional* probability density of observing a vector x, $P(c)$ is the *a-priori* probability for class c, and $p(x)$ is the probability density of observing a vector x. Because $p(x)$ is constant for every class c for a particular observation vector x, all we have to do is to learn the class conditional probability density $p(x|c)$ and the a-priori probability $P(c)$. $P(c)$ can be calculated as the relative frequency of observing a vector of class c. E.g. if we observe n vectors and n_1 vectors of them are of class c_1, the empirical probability $\hat{P}(c_1)$ can be calculated as

$$\hat{P}(c_1) = \frac{n_1}{n}$$

$p(x|c)$ is more difficult to learn. A simple technique is the use of histograms: We divide the vector space into intervals, count the number of vectors falling into every interval and then estimate the probability of vectors within this interval as the proportion of the number of vectors within this part compared to the number of all vectors. This technique only works if the number of intervals is small compared to the number of vectors (e.g. low dimension of the vector space).

4. Mobile User Profile Generation

We have applied the Bayes decision rule towards the generation of user profiles within GSM mobile networks.

4.1. The User and the Network

The network of GSM [12] is distributed in order to allow the reuse of transmission frequencies. Several *Mobile Switching Centers* (MSC) and local databases (*Visitor Location Register*, VLR) are distributed in the system serving their respective local areas (*MSC-areas*). The MSC-area in turn is subdivided into several *Location Areas* (LA), and an LA is subdivided into several cells, which are actually the smallest unit of the cellular network. Within a cell the mobile subscriber is able to call anyone and is reachable for everyone. As the subscribers are free to go everywhere in the service area, it is obvious that they will enter and leave cells. Therefore, location information must be managed. Taking into account some performance considerations, the location information maintained in the network is in terms of LAs. Currently management of such data is organized using a central database, the *Home Location Register* (HLR). A centralized HLR stores data on subscribers and mobile stations. When a subscriber enters a new LA served by a new MSC, only the relevant data is downloaded to the VLR.

If a mobile terminated call from the public switched telephone network to a GSM subscriber has to be established, the call is routed to a gateway, called *Gateway MSC* (GMSC). GMSC interrogates with the called mobile user's HLR. The HLR requests the currently serving VLR to find out the routing number of the visited MSC. After receiving the mobile subscriber's number, the GMSC forwards the call to the terminating MSC. The MSC initiates the transmission of a paging message, i.e. the MSC pages the *Mobile Station* (MS) with a paging broadcast to all cells of the location area, as the exact cell of the user is unknown.

Location Update (LUP) and paging procedure are the basic operations for tracking and finding a user. Both procedures work with the same granularity of location information, e.g. five cells in an LA. Therefore mobile networks already provide the basic functionality which is necessary to track and profile users. With the use of more adaptive and dynamic tracking and paging algorithms, i.e. the collection and computation of more information about the users, it is possible to define individual mobility and behavior patterns. This additional knowledge about the users can be used to protect them and the network providers, because the availability of user profiles allows applying anomaly detection techniques.

Actually the first commercial versions of software which provide a certain degree of user protection through the GSM functionality itself have shown up on the market [3]. These systems physically hide a GSM terminal within a vehicle, which transmits a signal for localization purposes. The intended use is fleet management, vehicle tracking, vehicle recovery, rental services, emergency services and insurance.

Our approach goes one step further. We do not restrict ourselves to single positions a user takes during a trip, we also consider the different routes he normally takes over a longer period of time. This provides us with an elaborate user profile.

Take e.g. the following scenario into account: The mobile phone card of user A has been cloned by attacker X. If the GSM network is able to learn the routes user A normally takes in the sense that it can predict the time at which he is passing through single cells, the user can be tracked. In case of any anomaly, i.e. major deviations from the route, longer residence times or unusual cells, the user can be checked for its current status. Thereby misuse through the cloned phone card by attacker X can be detected by comparing the time and place of the call with the user's standard behavior.

One of the main questions is how the GSM network can learn the routes of the user, i.e. predict which is the most probable cell for a mobile station at a certain time, and what prediction level can be achieved. The next section proposes two algorithms for this learning process.

4.2. Decision Algorithms for Mobile Networks

The Bayesian Algorithm. If we interpret the time of day as the observation vector and the cells as classes, we can solve our problem of finding the most probable cell for a mobile station at a certain time of day with the Bayes rules as follows:

We divide the time axis into intervals (e.g. one second) with length δt. Using the movement patterns we generate a sequence of observation vectors $t_{1,c_1}, t_{2,c_2}, \ldots, t_{n,c_n}$ with $t_{i+1,c_k} - t_{i,c_l} = \delta t$. Using these vectors we estimate the distributions $P(c)$ and $p(x|c)$ by the respective empirical distributions $\hat{P}(c)$ and $\hat{p}(x|c)$ and calculate with the help of these distributions the most probable movement profile.

In the following the location algorithm using the Bayes decision rule will be called *Bayesian algorithm.*

Mean Residence Times. A simpler but efficient technique is the calculation of the mean residence times for each cell. Here we first have to find out the different movement patterns of a mobile station. Then we can use the residence times of the samples of each movement pattern to calculate the mean residence time for each cell. According to these times we can construct a movement profile.

We consider this simple algorithm, which we call the *Average algorithm*, as an example of a domain specific algorithm, while the Bayesian algorithm is universally applicable.

4.3. Evaluation Modeling

The predictability of the position of a mobile station depends on several factors such as:

- the number of movement patterns, and
- the variability of residence times in cells.

Even if the correct profile is chosen from the number of profiles (movement patterns), the residence times can degrade the performance of a prediction algorithm. Therefore two basic models have been developed for the performance evaluation of our approach:

- a model of the simulation surface and the routes of the mobile station, and

- a model of the residence times of the mobile station in the cells.

Surface and Route Model. For the surface model we have divided the surface into equally wide squares. Every square models one cell, and every location area contains the same number of cells. Every cell has got one unique number for identification. By varying the density of the cells different scenarios can be modeled (town, motorway). The routes which were used for the simulation were derived from the following real routes in Germany:

Scenario	Route	Distance	Mean Speed	Cell Size
town	Köln-Longerich Köln-Hochkirchen	19 km	40 km/h	1 km
motorway	Aachen-Europaplatz Köln-Longerich	74 km	100 km/h	3 km

In reality the base stations are located beside the roads to save signalling costs for LU and handover. Therefore we modified the routes on the simulation surface so that the mobile station crosses a cell only in vertical or horizontal direction. Thus a cell sequence can be found by the coordinates of the starting point and the endpoint and the sequence of points at which the movement direction changes.

Residence Times. The modeling of the residence times of a mobile station in the cells is more difficult. Instead of being fixed they vary around a certain mean. These variations can be caused by a lot of different factors like the actual traffic situation, the weather or the driver himself. Nonetheless, the driving time regarding a given route cannot fall below a minimal value because of the maximum speed of a vehicle and the speed limits.

To derive a model for the residence times, we need statistics of the behavior of individual users. Unfortunately such statistics do not exist. So we decided to use an investigation about driving time variations of bus routes [5]. In this investigation the driving times of the busses of three bus routes in Dortmund (Germany) have been measured. One main result was that the variations of the driving times between two bus stations can be described by an Erlang-k-distribution. The Erlang-k-distribution is zero in the origin, increases to its maximum and approaches zero again for infinity. For $k = 1$ the Erlang distribution is equivalent to the exponential distribution, for large k to the normal distribution. So, if we assume that the driving times of a car from cell border to cell border are comparable to the driving times of a bus from bus station to bus station, we can model the residence times for a mobile station in a cell by an Erlang-k-distribution.

This assumption is also backed by other research in this field [16].

We can motivate the use of an Erlang-k-distribution by the following rationale: As a participant mostly uses the same route through a cell, we can estimate a minimal residence time T_{min} by

$$T_{min} = \frac{S_{cell}}{V_{max}}$$

and the actual driving time T as

$$T = T_{min} + \Delta T$$

with S_{cell} being the length of the route through the cell, V_{max} the maximal speed of the user and ΔT the variation of the driving time which is restricted by $0 \leq \Delta T \leq \infty$. As a first approximation we can then model the time ΔT as an exponentially distributed random variable [2, 13, 17].

This simple model can be refined if we consider the fact that a route through a cell is not completely uniform, but consists of many small pieces with different driving conditions. So we can find a better approximation to reality if we model the run through a cell as a sequence of runs through smaller cells with i.i.d. exponentially distributed ΔT_{sub_i} (with rate λ, resp.). Put it in other words: The run through a cell may be inhomogeneous, i.e. the delay may vary for different parts of the cell. Therefore the cell is divided into subcells of such a respective size that identical delays are experienced while crossing each of these subcells. This may be modelled by a Poisson process X with arrival rate λ. Then the time between two arrivals in the Poisson process is equivalent to the time which is necessary for crossing one of the k subcells. Hence, the probability that crossing the whole cell takes longer than t equals the probability that it takes longer than t until k arrivals have taken place, i.e. the probability that there are less or equal $k - 1$ arrivals between 0 and t [10]:

$$\begin{aligned}
P(\Delta T > t) &= P(X \leq k-1) \\
&= \sum_{j=0}^{k-1} \frac{(\lambda t)^j}{j!} e^{-\lambda t} \\
F_{\Delta T}(t) &= P(\Delta T \leq t) \\
&= 1 - P(\Delta T > t) \\
&= 1 - \sum_{j=0}^{k-1} \frac{(\lambda t)^j}{j!} e^{-\lambda t}
\end{aligned}$$

$F_{\Delta T}(t)$ is the distribution function of the trip time for the cell which is equal to the Erlang-k-distribution function.

4.4. Metrics

To evaluate the performance of the prediction algorithms we use the *Mean Prediction Level* as a metric.

The Mean Prediction Level (MPL) is the empirical probability that a mobile station is actually in the expected cell. This has to be verified by the verification function of the anomaly detection system, which compares the actual cell of the user with the expected cell(s). Let hit be the number of successful verifications and $miss$ the number of unsuccessful verifications. Then the MPL can be calculated as

$$MPL = \frac{hit}{hit + miss}$$

4.5. General Results

The following subsections present the MPL values and the 90% confidence intervals, which are obtained for different precision (different number of cells in an LA), for both prediction algorithms (Bayesian and Average algorithm) and the following verification strategies:

- Verification based on LA
  The most probable cell is taken from the profile and the corresponding LA is compared with the actual LA of the user.
- Verification based on an $2n$-minute interval
  The actual cell of the user is compared with the cells which fall into the time interval $(T-n, T+n)$ around the most probable cell.
- Verification based on n cells
  The actual cell of the user is compared with the n cells surrounding the most probable cell.

These different verification strategies define the sensitivity of the anomaly detection system concerning anomalous behavior. The first strategy accepts the highest degree of variance in the user's behavior, while the other two strategies are more stringent.

The results for each of the strategies are given in the following subsections.

Verification based on LA. Fig. 1 presents the MPL for the motorway scenario. We can notice the same evolution of the MPL for both algorithms. The stability of the system, i.e. a state for which new data do not improve the learning result, is reached after 15 days (in the following this state will be called *convergence state*). From this point the curve varies in a convergence interval of width 0.003, i.e. between 0.952 and 0.955. This also means that at least 15 dates must be collected to guarantee an efficient prediction and localization.

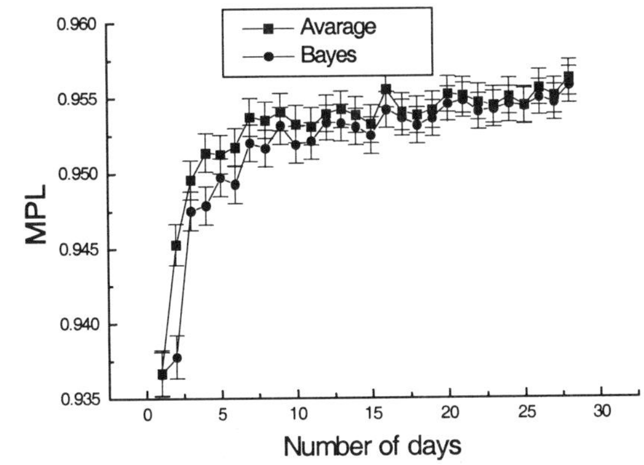

Figure 1. MPL - Verification based on LA for the motorway scenario.

We can notice that this strategy obtains a very good result, because the probability of a successful verification (for this type of user) reaches a value above 90% (0.936) at the second day.

Fig. 2 presents the result of this strategy for a city. At the convergence state, which is reached for both algorithms after 15 days, the MPL is 0.835. This value is 20% lower than the MPL value on the motorway. The reason for this is the small cell size in the city (1 km diameter) and the resulting small LA size.

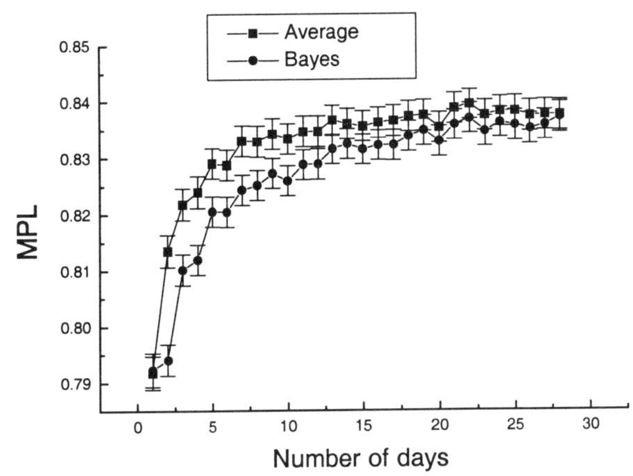

Figure 2. MPL - Verification based on LA for the city scenario.

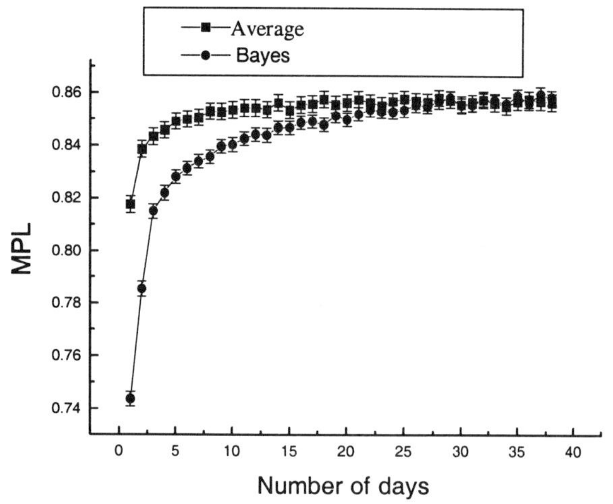

Figure 3. MPL - Verification based on 3 **cells.**

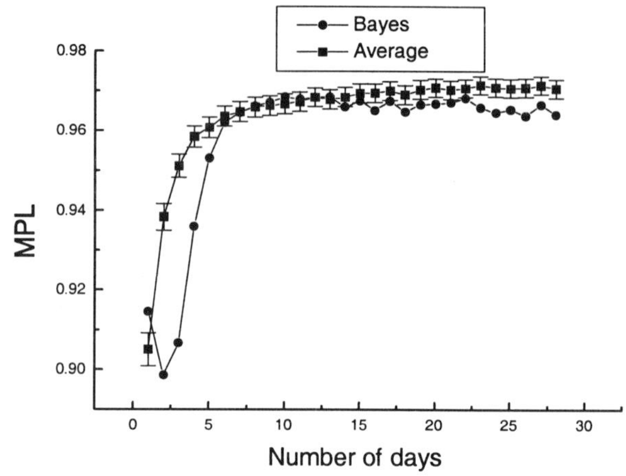

Figure 4. MPL - Verification based on a $2n$**-minute interval (city).**

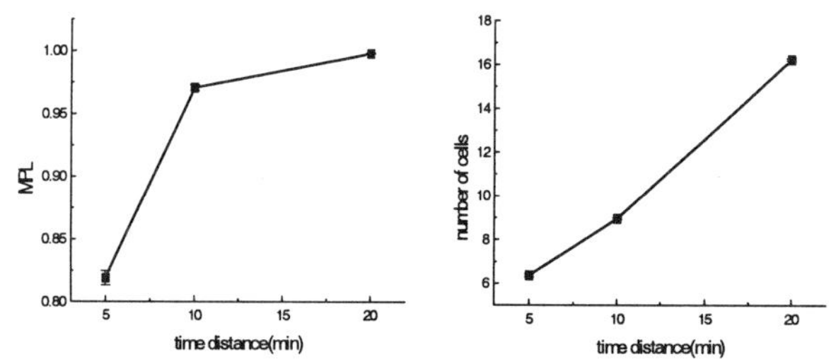

Figure 5. The effect of the time interval on the MPL (left) and the number of cells (right).

Verification based on 3 **cells.** Fig. 3 presents the results for the motorway scenario with a verification strategy based on three cells. The estimation of the three cells is performed for both algorithms in different ways. The Average algorithm estimates for the time of the incoming call (T) the most probable cell and its direct neighbors from the profile matrix. The Bayesian algorithm can estimate directly the three most probable cells. At the convergence state, which is reached with 22 days, the MPL varies around 0.85. For the Bayesian algorithm the first value is located around 0.74, so the gradient of the learning curve is 11% there. Considering the first value we can notice that the same value can be achieved if we try to locate the user in one cell. This is because, if we use only one day for estimating the profile, then only one most probable cell exists.

Verification based on an $2n$**-minute interval.** For the verfication strategy we estimate the cells at time (T) which lie in the (T-n;T+n) interval. The investigation of this strategy is done for $n = 20$ minutes and for the city model. Both curves start with 0.91, after the 10th day they converge at 0.97 (see Fig. 4).

With this strategy we obtain nearly the same results as by the verification based on LA. In both cases the probability of a successful verification is above 95%. The advantage of this strategy is the possibility of a dynamic estimation of the LA size for each user. If a user is called seldomly we can choose a big time interval, for a user who is called often the time interval is small. The size of the interval determines the number of cells in a search area. The question is, how many cells should be included into an interval, if we consider e.g. a city with the cell size of 1 km. The answer is presented in Fig. 5 (right). On the abscissa the different time intervals ($n = 5, 10, 20$ minutes) are spread. The investigations are performed for the convergence state (based on 30 dates for estimating a profile). We can see that for $n = 5$ minutes the number of cells is about 6.5, for $n = 10$ minutes 9 and for $n = 20$ minutes 16. Fig. 5 (left) presents the dependence between time interval and MPL. For intervals longer than $n = 8$ minutes the user can be located with a probability of more than 95%.

The number of cells was determined not only for the driving time but for the whole observation period. In reality an observation period has a duration of one day. In the simulation the subscriber moves around half of the time, and the other time he stays at the same place. That means, if a user stays at the same place for a long time (e.g. at work), then the average number of cells converges to 1, because most of the calls are routed to the same cell. For the investigations

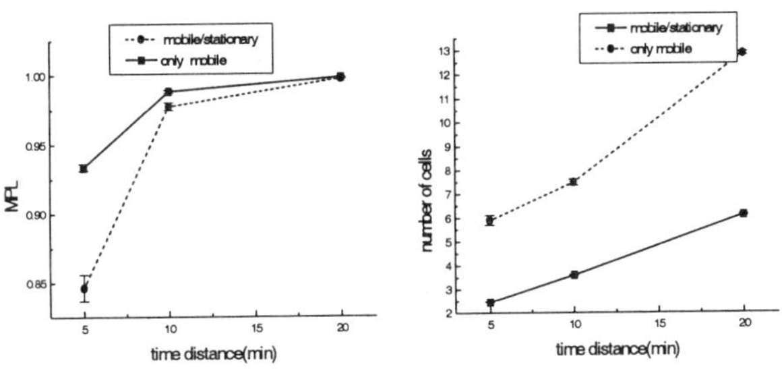

Figure 6. The effect of the length of the stationary state on the MPL (left) and the number of cells (right) in dependence of the time interval.

above we have assumed that the subscriber spends a part of the observation period at the same place. The next figure (Fig. 6) shows how the MPL rates and the number of cells (which were used for paging) change if the investigations are limited to the period where the subscriber moves.

These results refer to the motorway and are presented together with the results (mobile/stationary). The values for the five minute time interval are different, the values for the ten and twenty minute time intervals are approximately the same. The reason for this is that for big time intervals the user can be located anyway. For small time intervals it is more difficult to locate the user during the trip. This long duration of immobility influences the result.

Hence we need a classificator which indicates if a subscriber is only mobile or mobile and stationary to choose the appropriate time interval.

Notice that our current approach does not include a dynamic learning process in the sense that it considers already verified actual user positions. In that sense our simulation is a worst-case analysis and the result can be improved by introducing the described level of dynamic learning.

5. Application Scenarios and the Privacy of the Users

The results described above prove that it is possible to profile certain kinds of mobile user with a high quality concerning precision, speed and stability. Two general questions arise:

- Which kind of users can actually be profiled?
- Which of these users would like to be profiled?

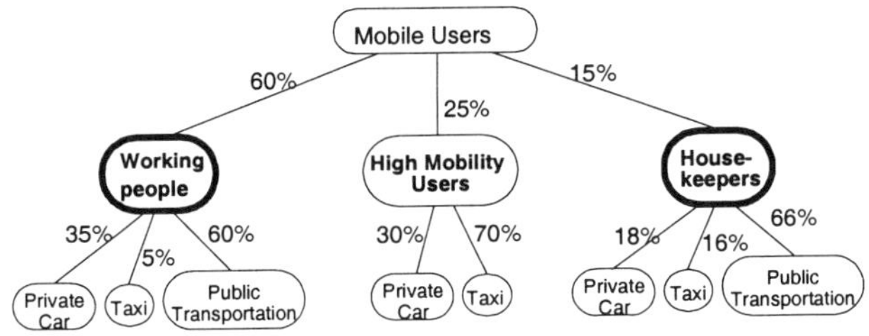

Figure 7. Categorization of mobile users according to their mobility behavior.

5.1. UMTS User Categories

The answer to the first question leads us to a basic observation, which actually provides the main base for our work. The UMTS RACE specification dealing with mobility management explicitly takes the different mobility behavior of the users into account. For this reason the model considers different user classes, environments, geographical areas like e.g. workers, driving in a bus from the rural to the metropolitan area[1]. The classification is done according to the statistics taken from different conurbations: London (UK), Randstad (Netherlands) etc. A categorization of mobile users considering their mobility behavior is shown in Fig. 7 [11][2].

In a further investigation UMTS discusses the different aspects of user mobility. There the mobility is defined as a movement from one geographical location to another. The categorization of the roaming area is made according to the frequency the user visits these areas. The area with the highest frequency is the daily used access domain. Within this domain the user roams daily, for instance the trip of a worker from his home to his working place. Statistics about the starting point (generation model), the endpoint (attraction model), movement duration, time of day or day of week versus percentage of user types (e.g. car driver) can be found in the RACE specification.

The general conclusion for our work must be that the classification shows that approximately 75% of the users can be considered as potential candidates for the successful application of anomaly detection techniques. Only the high mobility users, for which it must be expected that they establish much more chaotic behavior patterns, are not directly suited for our approach. The other user groups can be expected to behave according to more stringent behavior patterns, simply because of their social environment.

[1] RACE considers the following areas starting from the center of the city: metropolitan, urban, suburban and rural.

[2] To avoid any conflict with ETSI, we took a publication that follows the work of RACE and was partly written from the same authors of the RACE document.

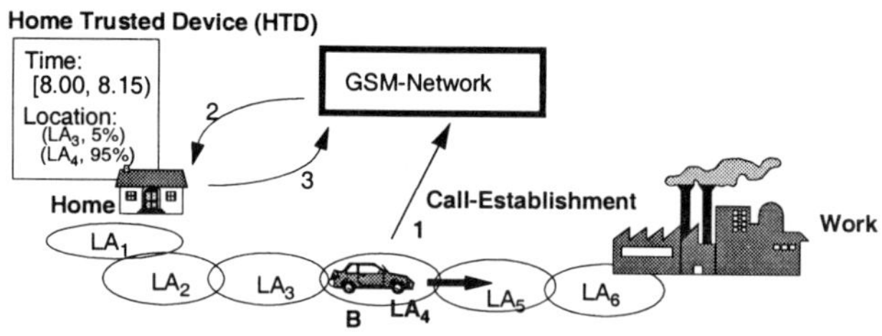

Figure 8. Trustworthy maintenance of mobility profile in a HTD.

5.2. Profiling and Privacy

While this classification and the related numbers answer the question what kind of users can actually be profiled, the second question remains to be answered: Which of these users would like to be profiled? For the mobile network scenario depicted above the profiling adds an additional level of security to specific groups of users. Other users will not be too enthusiastic about the possibility of profiling their behavior. In order to protect this sensitive information the control over the profiling and anomaly detection algorithms must obviously be located at a unit that the user trusts and/or controls. No potential communication partner or third party (including the network operator) should be able to have access to the users profile.

An approach to store profiles in conformity with these security requirements is to keep them in a trustworthy environment. [14], [20] and [21] propose to store confidential information in a personal digital assistant or "personal communication bodyguard". A *Home Trusted Device* (HTD) is the most common realization of such a trusted and private environment. In the following we explain the role it can play in profile management and anomaly detection in a mobile network (see Fig. 8).

The above scheme of a learning, predicting and controlling HTD, which supplements the classical GSM network, can be realized as a modular extension. User B repeats his daily movement from home to work and back. The MS continues to use the classical GSM location tracking algorithm and collects the daily repeated moving data. This information is transmitted to the HTD every day in a secure way by connecting the MS directly with HTD_B. Secret key and authentication procedures guarantee the integrity of the data. After this initial phase the HTD generates a user specific profile. The profile is stored in the HTD.

If a call has to be established (1), the GSM location tracking algorithm sends its current location information to the HTD (2). The HTD compares the location of the user with his stored profile. If the location information given by the GSM net corresponds to the stored profile, i.e. the verification results in a positive answer, the call can be established. Otherwise special measures, which we leave unspecified here, have to be taken. The HTD sends its answer back to the GSM net[3] (3). This request/response signalling should be protected using a symmetric cryptographic system.

The measure taken in case of a deviation from the stored profile and the sensitivity of the deviation must also be controlled by the user. In general the mobile network scenario is not that sensitive to certain attacks like other networks. Recalling the argument that a general anomaly detection systems can be fooled by a user, which slowly changes his behavior over time from "good" to "bad", does not apply to our scenario, because we do not have to deal with these kinds of internal attacks. In case of a slow shift of the behavior pattern the profile must be updated, because it can be considered to be a valid change of the user's behavior. An attacker must either steal a mobile device or clone the card. In the first case only one user with a specific ID actually uses the network, in the second case two users are present in the net. Both attacks do not give the attacker the time to slowly modify the stored profiles.

6. Profiling and Anomaly Detection - Related Work

Work related and relevant to our own approach comes from two fields:

- Network Oriented Location Management, and
- Anomaly Detection.

Concerning the network oriented location management several investigations make the assumption that the mobility of the users can be foretold [15], [18], [22].

The network in [15] observes the mobility of every user and generates a profile for an individual user with the following content: for each period $[t_i, t_j)$ the network handles a set of location area identifiers $a_1, ..., a_n$ combined with $\alpha_1, ..., \alpha_n$. α_i is the probability that the user is in the respective location area a_i. Having this information in the network "memory", the network does not need to explicitly track the user's mobility if the user follows the known mobility pattern. If a call has to be established, the appropriate set of a_i's and α_i's will be chosen considering the calling time. The network will then broadcast in the different a_i's according to their probabilities. Having this profile a first check will be the calculation of the predictability level of the user. Therefore Tabbane defines in [22] the mobility predictability level as $MPL := \sum_{i=1}^{N} \frac{\alpha_i}{i}$. This parameter is a measure of how predictable the pattern of the users

[3] This check can be performed in parallel to the connection setup in order to accelerate the call establishment.

are. In the subsequent work he evaluates his prediction by using the MPL as an input parameter. He concludes that using a mobility profile results in a "great amount of resource (radio as network)" savings especially for users with high MPL values.

Our approach follows these dynamic location management concepts (especially the work of [22]) and we have also shown that this approach, like the one mentioned above, can be used to reduce the location update and paging costs [9]. Nonetheless the focus in these works has been put on cost aspects and not on security aspects. To use these profiles in the sense of an anomaly detection system for a mobile network has to our knowledge not been considered before.

The second branch of relevant work is the general research in the field of anomaly detection, especially as a building block of a broader IDS. Examples are the IDES Statistical Anomaly Detector [7], which monitors a computer system and adaptively learns what is normal for individual users and groups of users. Based on these data it identifies potential intrusions. For the profiling the so-called multivariate method is used (see also [8]). Statistical profiles and their generation can also be found in many other systems and publications (see e.g. [1] [19]). However, to our knowledge, no work exists so far which bases its learning mechanism on the Bayes decision rule. In addition the currently known anomaly detection mechanisms have not been applied to the mobile network scenario depicted above.

7. Conclusions and Outlook

In this paper we have proposed a new algorithm for the profiling of mobile users, which is based on the Bayes decision algorithm. It has been shown that this approach can successfully be applied in order to provide advanced security features for mobile network users. One of our main concerns has been the discussion of privacy problems related to the profiling of users.

Our future work will concentrate on the adaptation of our profiling technique to standard data communication networks like the Internet. We will investigate the performance of the Bayesian algorithm for Intranet and LAN scenarios, the classical application fields of intrusion detection systems.

Further investigations will extend our approach to provide additional security to a mobile agent environments, as obviously there exists a straightforward mapping between the mobile network scenario (users moving from cell to cell) and an mobile agent scenario (agents moving from server to server).

References

[1] D. Anderson, T. Lunt, H. Javitz, A. Tamaru, and A. Valdes. Safeguard final report: Detecting unusual program behavior using the NIDES statistical component. Technical report, Computer Science Laboratory, SRI International, Menlo Park, CA, December 1993.

[2] P. Camarda, G. Schiraldi, and F. Talucci. Mobility modeling in cellular communication networks. In *21st IEEE Conference on Local Computer Networks*, Minneapolis, Minnesota, October 1996.

[3] Cellpoint Systems AB, http://www.cellpt.com/. *GSM Positioning*.

[4] Computer Science Division, University of California, Berkeley, http://www.isaac.cs.berkeley.edu/isaac/gsm-faq.html. *Internet Security, Applications, Authentication and Cryptography (ISAAC) Research Group*.

[5] F. Dauber. *Einflußgrößen auf die Bedienqualität von Buslinienverkehren unter besonderer Beachtung von Fahrplan- und Folgezeitenabweichungen*. PhD thesis, RWTH Aachen, Germany, 1986.

[6] R. O. Duda and P. E. Hart. *Pattern Classification and Scene Analysis*. J. Wiley, New York, 1973.

[7] H. Javitz and A. Valdes. The SRI IDES statistical anomaly detector. In *Proceedings of the IEEE Symposium on Research in Security and Privacy*, pages 316–326, May 1991.

[8] H. Javitz and A. Valdes. The NIDES statistical component description and justification. Technical report, Computer Science Laboratory, SRI International, Menlo Park, CA, March 1994.

[9] D. Kesdogan, M. Zywiecki, and K. Beulen. Mobile user profile generation - a challenge between performance and security. In *Proceedings of the 2nd Workshop on Personal Wireless Communications (Wireless Local Access)*, Frankfurt am Main (Germany), December 1996.

[10] H. J. Larson. *Introduction to the Probability Theory and Statistical Interference*. Wiley Series in Probability and Mathematical Statistics. J. Wiley & Sons, New York, 1982.

[11] J. Markoulidakis, G. Lyberopoulos, D. Tsirkas, and E. Sykas. Evaluation of location area planning scenarios in future mobile telecommunication systems. In *Wireless Networks 1*, 1995.

[12] M. Mouly and M.-B. Pautet. The GSM system for mobile communications. ISBN 2-9507190-0-7, 1992.

[13] S. Nanda. Teletraffic models for urban and suburban microcells: Cell sizes and handoff rates. In *Wireless Communications, Future Directions*, Dordrecht, Boston, 1993.

[14] A. Pfitzmann. Technischer Datenschutz in öffentlichen Funknetzen. *Datenschutz und Datensicherheit (DuD)*, pages 451–463, August 1993.

[15] G. Pollini and S. Tabbane. The intelligent network signalling and switching costs of an alternate location strategy using memory. In *IEEE 43th VTC*, 1993.

[16] S. Rappaport. Blocking, hand-off and traffic performance for cellular communication systems with mixed platforms. In *IEEE Proceedings-I, Vol. 140, No. 5*, October 1993.

[17] S. Rappaport and L. Hu. Microcellular communication systems with hierarchical macrocell overlays: Traffic performance models and analysis. In *Proceedings of the IEEE, Vol. 82, No. 9*, September 1994.

[18] C. Rose and R. Yates. Ensemble polling strategies for mobile communication networks. In *IEEE 46th VTC*, 1996.

[19] M. Sebring, E. Shellhouse, M. Hanna, and R. Whitehurst. Expert systems in intrusion detection: A case study. In *Proc. of the 11th National Computer Security Conf.*, Baltimore, MD, October 1988.

[20] M. Spreitzer and M. Theimer. Scalable, secure, mobile computing with location information. *Communications of the ACM*, 36(7), 1993.

[21] M. Spreitzer and M. Theimer. Architectural considerations for scalable, secure, mobile computing with location information. In *Proceedings of the 14th International Conference on Distributed Systems*. IEEE, 1994.

[22] S. Tabbane. An alternative strategy for location tracking. *IEEE Journal on Selected Areas in Communications*, 13(5), June 1995.

[23] A. B. Tucker Jr., editor. *CRC Computer Science and Engineering Handbook*. CRC Press, December 1996.

An Architecture for Intrusion Detection using Autonomous Agents*

Jai Sundar Balasubramaniyan, Jose Omar Garcia-Fernandez,
David Isacoff, Eugene Spafford, Diego Zamboni†
COAST Laboratory
Purdue University
West Lafayette, IN 47907-1398

E-mail: {balasujs,jgarcia,isacoff,spaf,zamboni}@cs.purdue.edu

Abstract

The Intrusion Detection System architectures commonly used in commercial and research systems have a number of problems that limit their configurability, scalability or efficiency. The most common shortcoming in the existing architectures is that they are built around a single monolithic entity that does most of the data collection and processing. In this paper, we review our architecture for a distributed Intrusion Detection System based on multiple independent entities working collectively. We call these entities Autonomous Agents. This approach solves some of the problems previously mentioned. We present the motivation and description of the approach, partial results obtained from an early prototype, a discussion of design and implementation issues, and directions for future work.

1. Background and motivation

We start by introducing some concepts that are used throughout this paper, as well as describing the limitations that we see in existing Intrusion Detection Systems, and why a distributed approach using autonomous agents can help in overcoming those limitations.

1.1. Intrusion Detection

Intrusion detection (ID) is defined [16] as "the problem of identifying individuals who are using a computer system without authorization (i.e., 'crackers') and those who have legitimate access to the system but are abusing their privileges (i.e., the 'insider threat')." For our work, we add to this definition the identification of *attempts* to use a computer system without authorization or to abuse existing privileges. Thus, our definition matches the one given in [9], where an intrusion is defined as "any set of actions that attempt to compromise the integrity, confidentiality, or availability of a resource."

We also use the broad categorization of models of intrusion detection described in [16]:

Misuse detection model: Detection is performed by looking for the exploitation of known weak points in the system, which can be described by a specific pattern or sequence of events or data.

Anomaly detection model: Detection is performed by detecting changes in the patterns of utilization or behavior of the system. This is the type of intrusion detection described in [5]. It is performed by building a model that contains metrics derived from system operation and flagging as intrusive any observations that have a significant deviation from the model.

An Intrusion Detection System (IDS) is a computer program that attempts to perform ID by either misuse or anomaly detection, or a combination of techniques. An IDS should preferably perform its task in real time [16].

IDSs are usually classified [16] as host-based or network-based. Host-based systems base their decisions on information obtained from a single host (usually audit trails), while network-based systems obtain data by monitoring the traffic of information in the network to which the hosts are connected.

Notice that the definition of an IDS does not include preventing the intrusion from occurring, only detecting it and reporting the intrusion to an operator.

1.2. Desirable characteristics of an IDS

In [4], the following characteristics are identified as desirable for an IDS:

*Portions of this work were supported by contract MDA904-97-6-0176 from the Maryland Procurement Office, and by sponsors of the COAST Laboratory.

†Main author and contact person for questions concerning this paper.

- It must *run continually* with minimal human supervision.
- It must be *fault tolerant* in the sense that it must be able to recover from system crashes and reinitializations.
- It must *resist subversion*. The IDS must be able to monitor itself and detect if it has been modified by an attacker.
- It must impose a *minimal overhead* on the system where it is running.
- It must be able to be configured according to the security policies of the system that is being monitored.
- It must be able to adapt to changes in system and user behavior over time.

As the number of systems to be monitored increases and the chances of attacks increase we also consider the following characteristics as desirable:

- It must be able to *scale* to monitor a large number of hosts.
- It must provide *graceful degradation of service* in the sense that if some components of the IDS stop working for any reason, the rest of them should be affected as little as possible.
- It must allow *dynamic reconfiguration*, this is, the ability to reconfigur the IDS without having to restart it.

1.3. Limitations of existing IDS

Many of the existing network- and host-based IDSs [10, 9] perform data collection and analysis centrally using a monolithic architecture. By this we mean that the data is collected by a single host, either from audit trails or by monitoring packets in a network, and analyzed by a single module using different techniques. Other IDSs [11, 22] perform distributed data collection (and some preprocessing) by using modules distributed in the hosts that are being monitored, but the collected data is still shipped to a central location where it is analyzed by a monolithic engine. A good review of systems that take both approaches is presented in [16].

There are a number of problems with these architectures:

- The central analyzer is a single point of failure. If an intruder can somehow prevent it from working, the whole network is without protection.
- Scalability is limited. Processing all the information at a single host implies a limit on the size of the network that can be monitored. After that limit the central analyzer becomes unable to keep up with the flow of information. Distributed data collection can also cause problems with excessive data traffic in the network.
- It is difficult to reconfigure or add capabilities to the IDS. Changes and additions are usually done by editing a configuration file, adding an entry to a table or installing a new module.
- Analysis of network data can be flawed. As shown in [20], performing collection of network data in a host other than the one to which the data is destined can provide the attacker the possibility of performing Insertion and Evasion attacks.

Other IDSs have been designed to do distributed collection and analysis of information. A hierarchical system is described in [24], and [29] describes a cooperative system without a central authority. These systems solve some of the problems mentioned.

1.4. Autonomous Agents

A software agent can be defined as [1]:

> ... a software entity which functions continuously and autonomously in a particular environment ... able to carry out activities in a flexible and intelligent manner that is responsive to changes in the environment ... Ideally, an agent that functions continuously ... would be able to learn from its experience. In addition, we expect an agent that inhabits an environment with other agents and processes to be able to communicate and cooperate with them ...

In our context, we define an *autonomous agent* (henceforth *agent*) as a software agent that performs a certain security monitoring function at a host.

We term the agents as *autonomous* because they are independently-running entities (i.e., their execution is scheduled only by the operating system, and not by other process). Agents may or may not need data produced by other agents to perform their work, but they are still considered to be autonomous. Additionally, agents may receive high-level control commands from other entities. This high-level control does not interfere with our definition of agent autonomy.

An agent may perform a single very specific function, or may perform more complex activities.

1.4.1. How the use of Autonomous Agents can improve the characteristics of an IDS

Because agents are independently-running entities, they can be added and removed from a system without altering other components, therefore without having to restart the IDS. Furthermore, agents may provide mechanisms for reconfiguring themselves without having to restart. Additionally, agents can be tested on their own before introducing them into a more complex environment. An agent may also be part of a group of agents that perform different simple functions but that can exchange information and derive more complex results than any one of them may be able to obtain on their own.

Thus, we argue that an IDS whose data collection and analysis elements are agents solves all the problems mentioned in Section 1.3:

- If an agent stops working for any reason, one or two things may happen:
  - If the agent is independent and produces results on its own, only its results will be lost.
  - If the data produced by the agent was needed by other agents, that group of agents may be impeded from working properly.

  In any case, the damage is restricted to at most a set of agents.
- By organizing the agents in a hierarchical structure with multiple layers of agents reducing data and reporting it to the upper layers, the system can be made scalable. This idea is proposed in [3] and is also used in [24].
- The ability to start and stop agents independently of each other in the systems that are being monitored adds the possibility of reconfiguring the IDS (or parts of it) without having to restart it. If we need to start collecting a new type of data or monitoring for a new kind of attacks, the appropriate agents can be started without disturbing the ones that are already running. Similarly, agents can be stopped or reconfigured without having to restart the whole IDS.
- If an agent collects network information related to the host where it is running, we reduce the possibility of being subject to insertion and evasion attacks by reducing the number of mismatched assumptions that can be made.

Additionally, using agents as data collection and analysis entities provides the following desirable features:

- Because an agent can be programmed arbitrarily, it can obtain its data from an audit trail, by probing the system where it is running, by capturing packets from a network, or from any other suitable source. Thus, an IDS built from a collection of agents can cross the traditional boundaries between host-based and network-based IDSs.
- Because agents can be stopped and started without disturbing the rest of the IDS, agents can be upgraded to new versions, and as long as their external interface remains unchanged (or backward-compatible), other components need not even know that the agent has been upgraded.
- If agents are implemented as separated processes on a host, each agent can be implemented in the programming language that is best suited for the task that it has to perform.

1.5. Related Work

The ideas of doing distributed intrusion detection and of having different functions performed by different modules of the IDS are not new. The GrIDS project at UC Davis [24] employs modules running in each host to report information to engines that build a graph representation of activity in the network and use it to detect possible intrusions. GrIDS also provides mechanisms to allow third-party security tools to be used as data sources.

The NADIR system [11] performs distributed data collection by employing the existing *service nodes* in Los Alamos National Laboratory's Integrated Computer Network (ICN) to collect audit information, which is then analyzed by a central expert system.

Another approach is presented in [29], in which Cooperative Security Managers (CSM) are employed to perform distributed intrusion detection that does not need a hierarchical organization or a central coordinator. Each CSM performs as a local IDS for the host in which it is running, but can additionally exchange information with other CSMs. The architecture also allows for CSMs to take reactive actions when an intrusion is detected. Unclear aspects are the mechanisms through which CSMs can be updated or reconfigured, and the intrusion detection mechanisms that are used locally by each CSM.

The idea of employing widely distributed elements to perform intrusion detection, by emulating to some extent the biological immune systems, and by giving the system a sense of "self", has also been explored [8].

A distributed sensor system that performs central processing and that can be organized in a hierarchical fashion is described in [12]. This paper proposes a system that is almost identical to the original design of our system as done in [3]. It appeared several years later in the same conference, but [12] has little in the way of detail, and no citations to related work that would enable us to determine how their work may relate to ours.

The EMERALD project [19] proposes a distributed architecture for intrusion detection that employs entities called *service monitors* which are deployed to hosts and perform monitoring functions. They define several layers of monitors for performing data reduction in a hierarchical fashion. Monitors can be programmed to perform any function. The EMERALD project is work in progress, and we expect it to provide some interesting results.

The approach for using Autonomous Agents in ID that was the foundation for our work was proposed in [4, 3].

These papers introduced the idea of lightweight, independent entities operating in concert for detecting anomalous activity, prior to most of the approaches mentioned previously.

2. System architecture

We propose an architecture (which we call AAFID for *Autonomous Agents For Intrusion Detection*) for building IDSs that uses agents as their lowest-level element for data collection and analysis and employs a hierarchical structure to allow for scalability as described in Section 1.4.1.

2.1. Overview

A simple example of an IDS that adheres to the AAFID architecture is shown in Figure 1. This figure shows the three essential components of the architecture: agents, transceivers and monitors. We refer to each one of these components as AAFID entities or simply *entities*, and to the whole IDS constituted by them as an *AAFID system*.

An AAFID system can be distributed over any number of hosts in a network. Each host can contain any number of *agents* that monitor for interesting events occurring in the host. All the agents in a host report their findings to a single *transceiver*. Transceivers are per-host entities that oversee the operation of all the agents running in their host. They exert control over the agents running in that host, and they have the ability to start, to stop and to send configuration commands to agents. They may also perform data reduction on the data received from the agents. Finally, the transceivers report their results to one or more *monitors*. Each monitor oversees the operation of several transceivers. Monitors have access to network-wide data, therefore they are able to perform higher-level correlation and detect intrusions that involve several hosts. Monitors can be organized in a hierarchical fashion such that a monitor may in turn report to a higher-level monitor. Also, a transceiver may report to more than one monitor to provide redundancy and resistance to the failure of one of the monitors. Ultimately, a monitor is responsible for providing information and getting control commands from a user interface. This logical organization, which corresponds to the physical distribution depicted in Figure 1, is shown in Figure 2.

All the components export an API to communicate with each other and with the user.

In the following section we describe each component in greater detail.

2.2. Components of the architecture

2.2.1. Agents

An agent is an independently-running entity that monitors certain aspects of a host, and reports abnormal or "interesting" behavior to the appropriate transceiver. For example, an agent could be looking for a large number of **telnet** connections to a protected host, and consider the occurrence of that event as suspicious. The agent would then generate a report that is sent to the appropriate transceiver. The agent does not have the authority to directly generate an alarm. Usually, a transceiver or a monitor will generate an alarm based on information received from one or more agents. By combining the reports from different agents, transceivers build a picture of the status of their host, and monitors build a picture of the status of the network they are monitoring.

Agents do not communicate directly with each other in the AAFID architecture. Instead, they send all their messages to the transceiver. The transceiver decides what to do with the information based on agent configuration information.

Notice that the architecture does not specify any requirements or limitations for the functionality of an agent. Thus it may be a simple program or a complex software system (for example, an instance of IDIOT [2]). As long as the agent produces its output in the appropriate format and sends it to the transceiver, it can be part of the AAFID system.

Internally, agents are also allowed to perform any functions they need. Some possibilities are:

- Agents may learn or evolve over time using genetic programming, as suggested in [3], or other machine learning techniques.
- Agents may employ techniques to retain state between sessions, allowing them to detect long-term attacks or changes in behavior. Currently, the architecture does not specify any mechanisms for maintaining persistent state.
- Agents could migrate from host to host by combining the AAFID architecture with some existing mobile-agent architecture.

Agents can be written in any programming language. Some functionalities (e.g., reporting and communication) are common to all the agents, and can be provided through shared libraries or similar mechanisms. Thus, a framework implementation can provide most of the tools and mechanisms necessary to make writing new agents a relatively simple task.

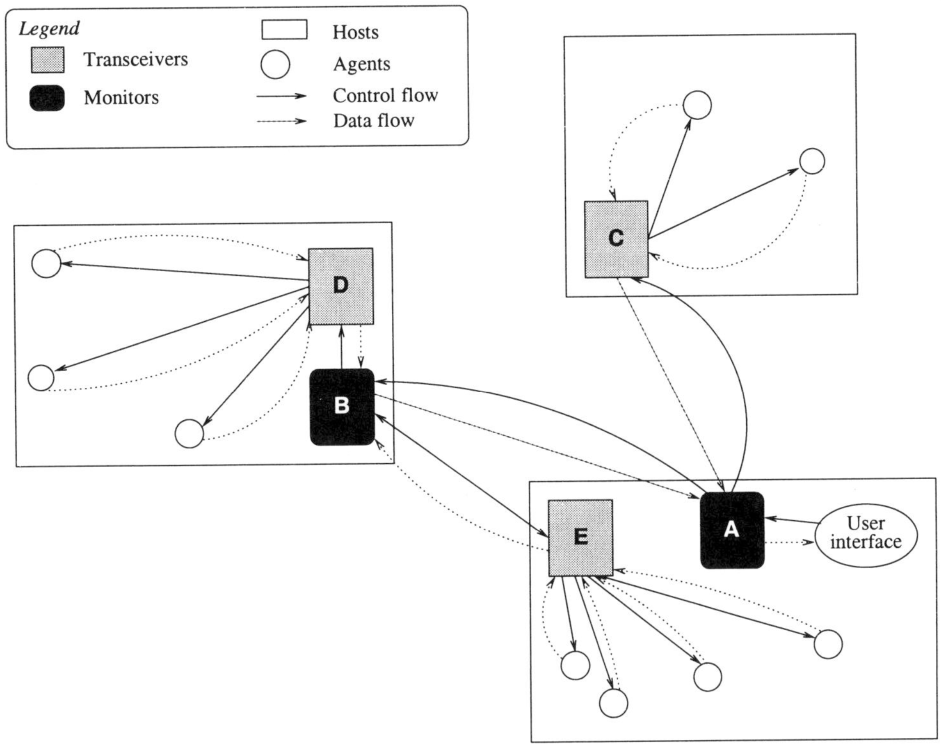

Figure 1. Physical layout of the components in a sample AAFID system, showing agents, transceivers and monitors, as well as the communication and control channels between them.

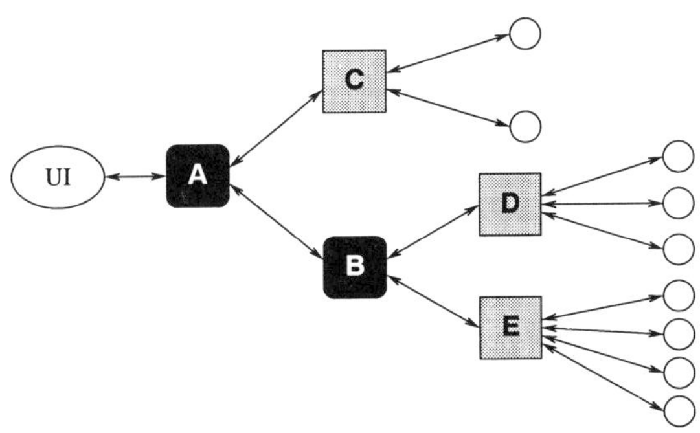

Figure 2. Logic organization of the same AAFID system showing the communication hierarchy of the components. The bidirectional arrows represent both the control and data flow between the entities. Notice that the logical organization is independent of the physical location of the entities in the hosts.

2.2.2. Transceivers

Transceivers are the external communications interface of each host. They have two roles: control and data processing. For a host to be monitored by an AAFID system, there must be a transceiver running on that host.

In its control role, a transceiver performs the following functions:

- Starts and stops agents running in its host. The instructions to start and stop agents can come either from configuration information, from a monitor, or as a response to specific events
- Keeps track of the agents that are running in its host.
- Responds to commands issued by its monitor by providing the appropriate information or performing the

requested actions.

In its data processing role, a transceiver has the following duties:

- Receives reports generated by the agents running in its host.
- Does appropriate processing on the information.
- Distributes information to other agents or to a monitor, as appropriate.

2.2.3. Monitors

Monitors are the highest-level entities in the AAFID architecture. They also have control and data processing roles that are similar to those of the transceivers. The main difference between monitors and transceivers is that a monitor can control entities that are running in several different hosts whereas transceivers only control local agents.

In their data processing role, monitors receive the reduced information from all the transceivers they control, and thus can do higher-level correlations, and detect events that involve several different hosts. Monitors have the capability to detect events that may be unnoticed by the transceivers.

In their control role, monitors can receive instructions from other monitors and they can control transceivers and other monitors. Additionally, monitors have the ability to communicate with a user interface and provide the access point for the whole AAFID system.

If two monitors control the same transceiver, mechanisms have to be employed to ensure consistency of information and behavior. The AAFID architecture does not currently specify the mechanisms for achieving this consistency.

2.2.4. User interfaces

The most complex and feature-full IDS can be useless if it does not have good mechanisms to allow users to interact with and control it. We have not looked in full detail into the user interface problem, although some issues are mentioned in Section 4.4.

The AAFID architecture clearly separates the user interface from the data collection and processing elements. A user interface has to interact with a monitor and it has to use the API that the monitor exports to request information and to provide instructions.

This separation allows different user interface implementations to be used with an AAFID system. For example, a Graphical User Interface (GUI) could be used to provide interactive access to the IDS, while a command-line based interface could be used in scripts to automate some maintenance and reporting functions.

2.3. Communication mechanisms

The transmission of messages between entities is a central part of the functionality of an AAFID system. Although the AAFID architecture does not specify which communication mechanisms are to be used, there is a minimum set of characteristics that we consider desirable. A more detailed discussion of the tradeoffs that have to be made can be found in Section 4.1.

We consider the following to be some important points about the communication mechanisms used in an AAFID system:

- Appropriate mechanisms should be used for different communication needs (for example, communication within a host versus inter-host communication).
- The communication mechanisms should be efficient and reliable in the sense that they should not add significantly to the communications load imposed by regular host activities, and provide reasonable expectations of messages getting to their destination quickly and without alterations.
- The communication mechanisms should be secure in the sense that they should be resistant to attempts of rendering it unusable by flooding or overloading, and provide some kind of authentication and confidentiality mechanism.

The topics of secure communications, secure distributed computation and security in autonomous agents have been already studied [6, 13], and possibly some previous work can be used in AAFID implementations.

2.4. Other ideas and possible components

In the course of designing our system architecture, we explored some alternate architectural components. We briefly discuss two such components. These components are not currently part of the AAFID architecture.

2.4.1. The Simple Network Management Protocol (SNMP)

The Simple Network Management Protocol (*SNMP*) [21] is a protocol designed to facilitate the exchange of management information between network devices. The SNMP model comprises a *Network Management System* (NMS) and *Managed Devices*. An SNMP Agent runs in each managed device, and an SNMP Manager operates in the machines from which the network is going to be monitored. The Management Information Base (MIB) is a database that specifies variables that are maintained by the agents, and that the manager can query or set [26].

The SNMP model can be used to implement the AAFID architecture. The transceivers can be implemented as SNMP agents, while the functionality of the monitor can be achieved by the SNMP NMS. The autonomous agents (not to be confused with the SNMP agents) can be given unique identifiers in a specially designed MIB. These object identifiers can provide access to a set of parameters within the MIB whose values represent the state of the autonomous agent and that can be retrieved or set by the NMS. The transceivers could communicate with the monitor by raising SNMP traps. The autonomous agents communicate with the transceiver by setting their corresponding data values.

Using SNMP to implement the AAFID architecture might be an interesting possibility. However, there are a number of significant issues that would have to be further investigated, including security, fault tolerance and ease of extension and deployment of the implementation.

2.4.2. Audit Router

System audit trails are an essential source of information for an IDS. However, there are problems that arise when many different entities try to access them simultaneously. It may be useful to have a mechanism that helps in distributing the information to the entities that need it.

The first and simplest scheme is to pass all the audit records to all the agents. The problem with this scheme is that every agent must process the whole audit trail, which is probably a waste of processing resources.

Another possibility is to embed the agents within a central audit server that passes appropriate records to appropriate agents. A version of this approach has successfully been used in the IDIOT IDS [15, 2]. One problem is that this model only supports the push mechanism of client-server interaction. This means that the server sends events to the agents as they become available. If an agent is not ready to receive events, those events are lost.

We propose the use of another mechanism that uses a central *audit router*. The central audit router maintains a database of agents and the audit classes that they require, and implements support routines such as buffer management. Agents need to register with the router and give it information regarding the types of audit records that they require. When doing so they receive a handle in return. The agent can then simply read from the handle whenever it is ready to receive new events. This technique implements the pull model of computing. The downside is that the audit router becomes more complex because of the need to manage buffers and other associated tasks.

This model could also support the push model by allowing agents to specify a callback function that can be invoked by the audit router when certain types of data are received.

2.5. Disadvantages of the AAFID architecture

We have identified several shortcomings in the AAFID architecture that we propose.

- In their control role, monitors are single points of failure. If a monitor stops working, all the transceivers that it controls stop producing useful information. This can be solved through a hierarchical structure where the failure of a monitor would be noticed by higher-level monitors, and measures would be taken to start a new monitor and examine the situation that caused the original one to fail. Another possibility is to establish redundant monitors that look over the same set of transceivers so that if one of them fails, the other can take over without interrupting its operation.
- If duplicated monitors are used to provide redundancy, mechanisms have to be used to ensure that redundant monitors will keep the same information, will obtain the same results, and will not interfere with the normal operation of the IDS.
- The AAFID architecture currently does not specify access-control mechanisms to allow for different users to have different levels of access to the IDS. This is an issue that will need to be addressed at the monitor, transceiver and agent levels as well as in the user interfaces.
- Detection of intrusions at the monitor level is delayed until all the necessary information gets there from the agents and transceivers. This is a problem common to distributed IDSs.

3. Implementations

We have developed two prototypes based on the AAFID architecture, and we are currently in the process of improving those implementations as well as developing new ones.

3.1. First prototype

The first prototype we built was programmed in a combination of Perl [28], Tcl/Tk [18] and C [14], and was intended as a proof of concept for the architecture. In this implementation, which we call $AAFID_1$, much of the behavior of the components was hard-coded and it was not extremely configurable. It used UDP as the inter-host communication mechanism and Solaris message queues as the intra-host communication mechanism. This prototype allowed us to:

- Show that the AAFID architecture could work for doing distributed detection of anomalous events.

- Gain some experience in writing agents that allowed us to identify important functionality that is needed for all agents.
- Identify some design issues that had to be improved. For example, this first prototype integrates the monitor and the GUI in a single program, which proved to be a limitation because it does not allow to organize monitors in a hierarchical fashion.

3.2. Second prototype

Drawing from the experiences obtained with the first prototype we developed a second one from scratch, which we call $AAFID_2$. This prototype is written exclusively in Perl, which has the advantage of making it easy to port to other architectures at the expense of some performance loss. The main objective of this implementation is to allow for extensive testing of the architecture, therefore emphasis has been made in its ease of use, configurability and extensibility. Some of the major contributions of this new implementation are:

- Increased portability because it is written completely in Perl.
- Implementation of an infrastructure that provides all the base services necessary for developing new entities.
- Definition of an internal API for developing new agents.
- Clear separation of communication mechanism internals and other platform-dependent elements.
- Clear definition of each entity as an object, and of the relationships between the different classes of objects.
- Different execution modes for entities, which facilitate developing, testing and debuggging new entities.
- Definition of an extensible message format that can be extended to represent different types of information.
- Separation of the monitor and the user interface.

This implementation is our current test bed for the architecture and is the one under which we are developing new agents and exploring new communication and data-reduction mechanisms. A much more detailed description of $AAFID_2$ can be found in [23].

3.3. Low-level implementations

The first two prototypes have helped us in refining the architecture as well as identifying needs and problems that have to be solved. However, not much emphasis has yet been placed in performance issues because the prototypes have been mostly implemented in high-level scripting languages such as Perl, which have large memory and CPU footprints. For this reason, as the architecture design starts to stabilize, we have started to work in porting the architecture to lower system levels. In particular, we are currently working on integrating components of the AAFID architecture into the Unix kernel. We are currently working on incorporating additional auditing and monitoring capabilities into the Linux kernel, and will possibly work also with Solaris, BSD/OS and Windows NT.

4. Experiences, comments and design issues

Through the experiences obtained with the design and implementations of the AAFID architecture (see Section 3 and [23]), we have identified a number of issues that should be subject of future work. They are discussed in this section.

4.1. Communication and Scalability

To reduce the overhead imposed by the IDS, the communication mechanisms employed have to be as efficient as possible.

We can classify the communication needs of the IDS in two major groups: intra-host communication (between processes inside a single host) and inter-host communication (between processes running in different hosts).

4.1.1. Intra-host communication

Although the general inter-host communication mechanisms may be used for communication within the same host, we think that intra-host communication should be optimized to make use of the fact that the entities involved are in the same host.

For our IDS architecture, we have identified two main types of intra-host communication that will take place:

- One-to-many communication, as in the case of the transceiver sending a message to several agents.
- Many-to-one communication, as when the agents send information to the transceiver.

Keeping these needs in mind, we have considered several different intra-host communication schemes:

Message queues. This mechanism makes use of the System-V IPC facilities for establishing message queues.

The primary shortcoming of message queues is that the maximum number of messages that can exist in the system at a given time is usually fairly low. A consequence of this resource limitation is that this method is vulnerable to denial-of-service attacks. Additionally, these restrictions place a practical limit on the number of agents that may be running simultaneously in the system.

An advantage of this approach is that this is fairly straightforward to implement and it also provides a mechanism to prioritize the messages so that agent messages can be processed immediately.

This approach was used for the first prototype, but it will most likely not be used in future versions of our system, mainly because of the lack of scalability and its vulnerability to attacks.

Shared memory. This scheme provides an efficient means of sharing data between two processes because data is not actually copied between processes.

This scheme is vulnerable to the same flavor of denial-of-service as the message queues, because the size of the shared memory space is fixed. This scheme also introduces a practical limit on the number of agents that can be run simultaneously in a system.

The shared memory scheme seems to be adequate for one-to-many communication. Given this perspective, a new problem would be how to implement reliable signaling for the transceiver to notify the agents that there is new information that they should receive.

Pipes. In traditional Unix implementations , a pipe is a unidirectional, first-in first-out, unstructured data stream of fixed maximum size [27]. Data is written to the end of the pipe and read from the front of the pipe. The data is removed from the pipe after it is read.

Another common type of pipe is a named pipe or FIFO (first-in, first-out) file. Although they behave very similar to a traditional pipe they differ in the way that they are created and accessed. One major difference is that a FIFO is bidirectional.

Either type of pipe could be used for communication between entities running on the same host. One of the disadvantages of either type of pipe is that there is an internal limit on the volume of data that can be put into a pipe if the reading process does not extract it.

Using pipes as a communication device also has several benefits. They are relatively simple to implement and every modern version of UNIX implements both types of pipes. Because pipes are accessed through file handles they have extreme flexibility in how the components of a distributed system can be used and interconnected.

Independently of the communication scheme used, the IDS needs access control in the communication channels. All the mechanisms mentioned have the ability of performing access control by the following means:

- For message queues and shared memory, the process that sets up the structure establishes its access modes.
- For regular Unix pipes, the pipe is only accessible to the process that creates it and its children.
- For named pipes, the access control is performed by the Unix file permissions.

In conclusion, although some of the schemes show some promise, they still have to be studied carefully before deciding on a particular one. It may be feasible to use more than one different communication scheme depending on the situation. The one-to-many and many-to-one distinctions are clear examples of where this may be possible.

4.1.2. Inter-host communication

The main characteristics that we would like to achieve in a communication scheme for an IDS are performance, reliability and security.

Performance. For the IDS to operate in real time, messages must be delivered as quickly as possible from one part of the system to another, but without overloading the network when many agents are running.

Reliability. Whether the messages sent from one host to another arrive correctly, in order and on time may be a major concern in an IDS, or it may not. The question is: can a single missing message from an agent make a drastic difference, such as the one between an intrusion being detected or not? If we can estimate the maximum amount of lost messages, we might also be able to give an acceptable estimate of the degradation in the service.

Security. Privacy and authentication are important needs for an IDS because some of the messages generated by the IDS may contain sensitive data about the hosts being monitored, and unauthorized entities should not be able to generate messages that are accepted by monitors and transceivers. Usually, cryptography is the solution to both problems. However, cryptography comes at a cost in performance and in overhead imposed to the systems.

The communication protocol used may also be subject to denial-of-service attacks in which an attacker makes it impossible or difficult for messages to get delivered.

The issues mentioned raise a number of questions on whose answers depend the specific approach that should be followed. Currently, we see two possible solutions:

- Use an existing protocol (such as UDP or TCP) in a way that takes into account its weaknesses to provide the functionality we need.
- Design a new protocol with the needs of the IDS in mind. Such a protocol may provide reliable transmission, low overhead, and security mechanisms.

After expressing our concerns regarding inter-host communication, particularly those related to performance and scalability, we come to a more fundamental question: do we really need to worry? In particular, will we ever get to a point when we have thousands of hosts communicating? It can be argued that if an appropriate hierarchical organization is used that may never happen. For example, if the system is structured such that only one subnetwork reports to a single monitor and those monitors in turn report to higher level monitors, the problem may not be as relevant as the previous discussion suggested. In this case, secure and reliable communication would be the priority.

Finally, the level of efficiency required from the communications protocol depends on the level of data reduction that can be achieved. If the data-reduction schemes are such that the amount of information that is actually sent through the network is limited, then efficiency may become a secondary concern.

4.2. Impact on host performance

In the first implementations of the AAFID architecture, all the entities are implemented as separate processes. However, much of the data that are being collected and analyzed are generated in the kernel (for example, user login information, process accounting and network connection establishment). This means that every time a system action has to be logged or analyzed, the information has to be transferred from kernel space to user space, causing a context switch, and increasing the load imposed on the system by the IDS. As the number of agents running on a host increases, the load overhead caused by them may start to impact normal use of the host.

One approach to reduce the overhead caused by the IDS is to write all the components in a compiled language, such as C, instead of in an interpreted language such as Perl. This would reduce the memory and CPU usage, but would not solve the context-switching problem, or the overhead derived from having many separate processes running.

A further step would be to use a language that supports multithreading, and implement each agent as a separate thread instead of a separate process. This may further reduce the per-agent overhead, but still would not address the context-switching problem.

The lowest level that we could achieve would be to integrate some of the components in the Unix kernel. Doing this would have several benefits:

- A context switch is prevented, because the agent would be running within the kernel itself.
- The information is registered and processed very close to where it is produced, reducing the possibility of it being modified by an attacker before it gets to the agent.
- It becomes harder for an intruder to tamper with the agents.

The transceivers could also be built into the kernel. This way, the data would never have to be transferred outside the kernel until the transceiver decides to send them to a monitor for further processing, or for making a notification.

The approach just described also has the following disadvantages:

- Building entities as kernel components essentially destroys the portability of the agents.
- An entity that misbehaves can do much more damage if it is running in the kernel.
- Entities in the kernel can have a large impact in the host behavior by slowing down fundamental operations (e.g. accesses to disk, memory and kernel data structures) or by disrupting timing in critical low-level operations (such as disk accesses).
- The resources that are available for entities in the kernel are very limited and may be insufficient for performing useful actions. For example, an agent that monitors IP packets may need a large amount of memory to be able to to keep enough state information to monitor all of the events necessary to detect a SYN-flood attack. Preliminary work indicates that it is probably not possible to develop distinct independent kernel agents that will perform any complex tasks unless they are tightly coupled into the kernel code itself.

4.3. Data processing and reduction

To make the agents as lightweight as possible, they should be little more than a forwarding element that sends data to the transceiver, which in turn merges the data coming from all the agents and forwards them to the appropriate monitor where everything is processed and the appropriate actions are taken. However, this technique can create a high amount of network traffic, which limits the scalability of the system.

The counterpart is to move computation load from the monitor to the transceivers and agents. This can be taken to the extreme of making each transceiver a local ID system on its own which communicates to the monitors as part of a larger global ID system. Unfortunately, this has an impact on the hosts being monitored because local computation will take away computing cycles from the real applications of the hosts.

A related problem is to decide where the state of the IDS is kept. In the centralized approach, all state is kept in the central monitor. Therefore, if that host is taken down or somehow compromised or destroyed, the state of all the hosts that depend on that monitor may be lost. On the other hand, if each host has its own processing engine, the state information is distributed in different hosts, making its complete loss much more difficult. The disadvantage is that building a consistent picture of the state of the whole IDS becomes more difficult.

We think that the best approach is to try to find a balance between the two extremes. More detailed performance studies may help in making a decision about how the computational load can be distributed between the agents, transceivers, and monitors to maximize the throughput and scalability of the system without imposing and excessive load on the hosts and the network.

4.4. User interface

Any IDS can be rendered useless if it does not have good mechanisms to allow users to control and monitor it. In our case, the user interface has to deal with a common problem: how to interface a high-speed, distributed, continuous-running computer system with the human user, which cannot quickly analyze large volumes of data and cannot be on-guard 24 hours a day. It is a problem that involves issues ranging from data formats and storage to GUI design, including communication, security and consistency.

We think that some of the fundamental issues are:

1. What data do the IDS entities need to provide to give the user a clear picture of the system.
2. How to efficiently, reliably and consistently get the information to the user.
3. How to present the information in a useful way. The interface has to be able to provide the user with multiple levels of detail in a manner that is as easy to use as possible.
4. How to allow the user to provide feedback and to control the entities in the system. Ideally, this has to be done in a way that is efficient, reliable, secure, auditable and manageable.
5. How to make the interface responsive. The user will want to be able to immediately see the effects of any changes made and to be told immediately when something of interest happens.
6. How to keep enough state to provide meaningful information to the user.

The issue of user interface is one that we have not studied in detail yet, and it is likely to be considered for future work.

5. Future work

These are some of the specific points we have identified as relevant for future work:

- Developing agents.
- Low-level implementations:
- Communication mechanisms.
- Developing transceivers and monitors.
- Semantics of the communication.
- Data reduction.
- Porting to other platforms.
- Deployment and testing.
- Global administration and configuration.
- Reliability and fault tolerance.

6. Conclusions

We propose an architecture for Intrusion Detection Systems called AAFID, which is based on independent entities called Autonomous Agents for performing distributed data collection and analysis. Centralized analysis is done on a per-host and per-network basis by higher-level entities called Transceivers and Monitors. The architecture allows for computation to be performed (and thus, for Intrusion Detection to happen) at any point where enough information is available.

We have demonstrated the feasibility of this architecture by the implementation of working prototypes.

The AAFID architecture allows data to be collected from multiple sources, thus being able to combine the best characteristics of traditional host-based and network-based IDSs. It apparently also allows to build IDSs that are more resistant to insertion and evasion attacks [20] than existing architectures, although no tests have been performed to support this claim.

Furthermore, the modular characteristics of the architecture allow it to be easily extended, configured and modified, either by adding new components, or by replacing components when they need to be updated. For example, it should be possible to modify the system to produce messages in CIDF format [25].

The AAFID architecture faces many of the problems that have been traditionally in the realm of distributed systems research, such as scalability, performance and security. Tradeoffs between efficiency, resource consumption and security have to be made, and although we may be able to use results from previous research to implement the mechanisms that AAFID needs, finding the appropriate balance in the ID context between the different factors is still an open area for research.

User interface is a big issue for future work. Most of the work that has been done in Intrusion Detection over the last few years focuses on how to perform the detections, but very little has been done in the way of presenting the information to the user, as well as how to allow the user to specify policies such that the IDS can understand and therefore enforce them.

References

[1] J. M. Bradshaw. An introduction to software agents. In J. M. Bradshaw, editor, *Software Agents*, chapter 1. AAAI Press/The MIT Press, 1997.

[2] M. Crosbie, B. Dole, T. Ellis, I. Krsul, and E. Spafford. *IDIOT—Users Guide*. COAST Laboratory, Purdue University, 1398 Computer Science Building, West Lafayette, IN 47907-1398, September 1996. Available at `http://www.cs.purdue.edu/coast/coast-library.html`.

[3] M. Crosbie and E. Spafford. Defending a computer system using autonomous agents. In *Proceedings of the 18th National Information Systems Security Conference*, Oct 1995.

[4] M. Crosbie and G. Spafford. Active defense of a computer system using autonomous agents. Technical Report 95-008, COAST Group, Department of Computer Sciences, Purdue University, West Lafayette, IN 47907-1398, Feb 1995.

[5] D. E. Denning. An Intrusion-Detection Model. *IEEE Transactions on Software Engineering*, 13(2):222–232, Feb. 1987.

[6] W. M. Farmer, J. D. Guttman, and V. Swarup. Security for mobile agents: Issues and requirements. In *Proceedings of the 19th National Information Systems Security Conference*, volume 2, pages 591–597. National Institute of Standards and Technology, October 1996.

[7] S. Forrest, S. Hofmeyer, A. Somayaji, and T. Longstaff. A sense of self for Unix processes. In *Proceedings of the 1996 IEEE Symposium on Security and Privacy*. IEEE, IEEE Computer Press, 1996.

[8] S. Forrest, S. A. Hofmeyr, and A. Somayaji. Computer Immunology. *Communications of the ACM*, 40(10):88–96, Oct. 1997.

[9] R. Heady, G. Luger, A. Maccabe, and M. Servilla. The Architecture of a Network Level Intrusion Detection System. Technical report, University of New Mexico, Department of Computer Science, Aug. 1990.

[10] L. Heberlein, G. Dias, K. Levitt, B. Mukherjee, J. Wood, and D. Wolber. A Network Security Monitor. In *Proceedings of the IEEE Symposium on Research in Security and Privacy*, May 1990.

[11] J. Hochberg, K. Jackson, C. Stallings, J. F. McClary, D. DuBois, and J. Ford. NADIR: An automated system for detecting network intrusion and misuse. *Computers and Security*, 12(3):235–248, May 1993.

[12] W. Hunteman. Automated information system — (ais) alarm system. In *Proceedings of the 20th National Information Systems Security Conference*. National Institute of Standards and Technology, October 1997.

[13] IEEE Journal on Selected Areas in Communications, May 1989. Special issue on Secure Communications.

[14] B. W. Kernighan and D. M. Ritchie. *The C Programming Language*. Prentice-Hall, Englewood Cliffs, NJ 07632, USA, second edition, 1988.

[15] S. Kumar. *Classification and Detection of Computer Intrusions*. PhD thesis, Purdue University, West Lafayette, IN 47907, 1995.

[16] B. Mukherjee, T. L. Heberlein, and K. N. Levitt. Network intrusion detection. *IEEE Network*, 8(3):26–41, May/June 1994.

[17] "intrusion". Merriam-Webster OnLine: WWWebster Dictionary. `http://www.m-w.com/dictionary`, 1998. Accessed on May 16, 1998.

[18] J. K. Ousterhout. *Tcl and the Tk Toolkit*. Addison-Wesley, Reading, MA, USA, 1994.

[19] P. A. Porras and P. G. Neumann. EMERALD: Event monitoring enabling responses to anomalous live disturbances. In *Proceedings of the 20th National Information Systems Security Conference*. National Institute of Standards and Technology, 1997.

[20] T. H. Ptacek and T. N. Newsham. Insertion, evasion, and denial of service: Eluding network intrusion detection. Technical report, Secure Networks, Inc., January 1998.

[21] M. Rose. *The Simple Book: an introduction to management of TCP/IP based internets*. Prentice Hall, NJ, 1993.

[22] S. R. Snapp, J. Brentano, G. V. Dias, T. L. Goan, L. T. Heberlein, C. Ho, K. N. Levitt, B. Mukherjee, S. E. Smaha, T. Grance, D. M. Teal, and D. Mansur. DIDS (Distributed Intrusion Detection System) - Motivation, Architecture, and an early Prototype. In *Proceedings of the 14th National Computer Security Conference*, pages 167–176, Oct. 1991.

[23] E. Spafford and D. Zamboni. A framework and prototype for a distributed intrusion detection system. Technical Report 98-06, COAST Laboratory, Purdue University, West Lafayette, IN 47907-1398, May 1998.

[24] S. Staniford-Chen, S. Cheung, R. Crawford, M. Dilger, J. Frank, J. Hoagland, K. Levitt, C. Wee, R. Yip, and D. Zerkle. GrIDS: A graph based intrusion detection system for large networks. In *Proceedings of the 19th National Information Systems Security Conference*, volume 1, pages 361–370. National Institute of Standards and Technology, October 1996.

[25] S. Staniford-Chen et al. Common intrusion detection framework. WWW page at http://seclab.cs.ucdavis.edu/cidf/.

[26] W. R. Stevens. *TCP/IP Illustrated*, volume Volume 1—The Protocols of *Professional Computing Series*. Addison-Wesley, 1994.

[27] U. Vahalia. *UNIX Internals: The New Frontiers*. Prentice-Hall, Englewood Cliffs, NJ 07632, USA, 1996.

[28] L. Wall, T. Christiansen, and R. L. Schwartz. *Programming Perl*. O'Reilly & Associates, Inc., second edition edition, September 1996.

[29] G. B. White, E. A. Fisch, and U. W. Pooch. Cooperating security managers: A peer-based intrusion detection system. *IEEE Network*, pages 20–23, January/February 1996.

NetSTAT: A Network-based Intrusion Detection Approach

Giovanni Vigna and Richard A. Kemmerer
Reliable Software Group
Department of Computer Science
University of California Santa Barbara
[vigna,kemm]@cs.ucsb.edu

Abstract

Network-based attacks have become common and sophisticated. For this reason, intrusion detection systems are now shifting their focus from the hosts and their operating systems to the network itself. Network-based intrusion detection is challenging because network auditing produces large amounts of data, and different events related to a single intrusion may be visible in different places on the network. This paper presents NetSTAT, a new approach to network intrusion detection. By using a formal model of both the network and the attacks, NetSTAT is able to determine which network events have to be monitored and where they can be monitored.
Keywords: *Security, Intrusion detection, Networks.*

1. Introduction

Network intrusions have become common and sophisticated. Attacking a system through a network provides the attacker with advantages that are not available when attacking a host. For example, network attacks often do not require any previous access to the attacked system and may be totally invisible from the audit trail produced by the attacked host. In addition, the use of firewalls to protect enterprise networks from the external Internet has often supported the design of open, efficient, and *insecure* internal networks. These networks are open to insider attacks. Although networks give the attacker additional advantages, networks, by their very nature, have some characteristics that intrusion detection systems (IDSs) can take advantage of. For instance, networks can provide detailed information about computer system activity, and they can provide this information regardless of the installed operating systems or the auditing modules available on the hosts. In addition, network auditing can be performed in a non-intrusive way, without notching the performance of either the monitored hosts or the network itself, and network audit stream generation cannot be turned off. Finally, network traffic has more precise and timely timing information than the audit records produced by the standard OS auditing facilities.

Network-oriented intrusion detection systems can be roughly divided into distributed IDSs and network-based IDSs. A survey of network-oriented IDSs is given in [7]. Distributed IDSs are an extension of the original, single-host intrusion detection approach to multiple hosts. Distributed IDSs perform intrusion detection analysis over audit streams collected from several sources, which allows one to identify attacks spanning several systems. Examples of this kind of systems are IDES [4] and ISOA [12]. Network-based IDSs take a different perspective and move their focus from the computational infrastructure (the hosts and their operating systems) to the communication infrastructure (the network and its protocols). These systems use the network as the source of security-relevant information. Examples of this kind of systems are NSM [2], DIDS [10], and EMERALD [9].

NetSTAT is a tool aimed at real-time network-based intrusion detection. The NetSTAT approach extends the state transition analysis technique (STAT) [3] to network-based intrusion detection in order to represent attack scenarios in a networked environment. However, unlike other network-based intrusion detection systems that monitor a single subnetwork for patterns representing malicious activity, NetSTAT is oriented towards the detection of attacks in complex networks composed of several subnetworks. In this setting, the messages that are produced during an intrusion attempt may be recognized as malicious only in particular subparts of the network, depending on the network topology and service configuration. As a consequence, intrusions cannot be detected by a single component, and a distributed approach is needed.

Network-level monitoring and distribution pose some new requirements on intrusion detection systems:

- Networks produce a large amount of data (events). Therefore, a network-based intrusion detection system (NIDS) should provide mechanisms that allow the Net-

0-8186-8789-4/98 $10.00 © 1998 IEEE

work Security Officer (NSO) to customize event "collectors" so that they listen for only the relevant events.

- Relevant events are usually visible in only some parts of the network (especially in the case of large networks). Therefore, a NIDS should provide some means of determining where to look for events.

- A NIDS should generate a minimum amount of traffic over the network. Therefore, there should be some local processing of event data.

- A NIDS needs to be scalable. At a minimum, "local" NIDS should interoperate with other NIDSs (possibly in a hierarchical structure).

- For maximum effectiveness, NIDSs should be able to interoperate with host-based IDSs so that misuse patterns include both network events and operating system events.

The NetSTAT tool presented in this paper addresses the aforementioned issues. The NetSTAT approach models network attacks as state transition diagrams, where states and transitions are characterized in a networked environment. The network environment itself is described by using a formal model based on hypergraphs, which are graphs where edges can connect more than two nodes [1]. By using a formal representation of both the intrusions and the network, NetSTAT is able to address the first three issues listed above. The analysis of the attack scenarios and the network formal descriptions determines which events have to be monitored to detect an intrusion and where the monitors need to be placed. In addition, by characterizing in a formal way both the *configuration* and the *state* of a network it is possible to provide the components responsible for intrusion detection with all the information they need to perform their task autonomously with minimal interaction and traffic overhead. This can be achieved because network-based state transition diagrams contain references to the network topology and service configuration. Thus, it is possible to extract from a central database only the information that is needed for the detection of the particular modeled intrusions. Moreover, attack scenarios use assertions to characterize the state of the network. Thus, it is possible to automatically determine the data to be collected to support intrusion analysis and to instruct the detection components to look only for the events that are involved in run-time attack detection. This solution allows for a lightweight, scalable implementation of the probes and focused filtering of the network event stream, delivering more reliable, efficient, and autonomous components.

In order to address the remaining issues, namely scalability and integration with other IDS, NetSTAT is designed to be *interoperable*. A NetSTAT instance protecting a network can interact with other NetSTAT instances in an integrated way and it can interact with other IDS. Although the interoperability of NetSTAT is an important and interesting issue, due to space limitations it will not be discussed in this paper.

The remainder of this paper is structured as follows. Section 2 presents the NetSTAT architecture. Section 3 describes NetSTAT at work on an example attack scenario. Finally, Section 4 draws some conclusions and outlines future work.

2. NetSTAT Architecture

NetSTAT is a distributed application composed of the following components: the network fact base, the state transition scenario database, a collection of general purpose probes, and the analyzer. A high level view of the NetSTAT architecture is given in Figure 1. In the following subsections the design of the main NetSTAT components is presented.

2.1. Network Fact Base

The network fact base component stores and manages the security relevant information about a network. The fact base is a stand-alone application that is used by the Network Security Officer to construct, insert, and browse the data about the network being protected. It contains information about the network topology and the network services provided.

The network topology is a description of the constituent components of the network and how they are connected. The network model underlying the NetSTAT tool uses *interfaces*, *hosts*, and *links* as primitive elements. A network is represented as a hypergraph on the set of interfaces [11]. In this model, interfaces are nodes while hosts and links are edges; that is, hosts and links are modeled as sets of interfaces. This is an original approach that has a number of advantages. Because the model is formal, it provides a well-defined semantics and supports reasoning and automation. Another advantage is that this formalization allows one to model network links based on a shared bus (e.g., Ethernet) in a natural way, by representing the shared bus as a set containing all the interfaces that can access the communication bus. In this way, it is possible to precisely model the concept of network traffic eavesdropping, which is the basis for a number of network-related attacks. In addition, topological properties can be described in an expressive way since hosts and links are treated uniformly as edges of the hypergraph.

The network model is not limited to the description of the connection of elements. Each element of the model has

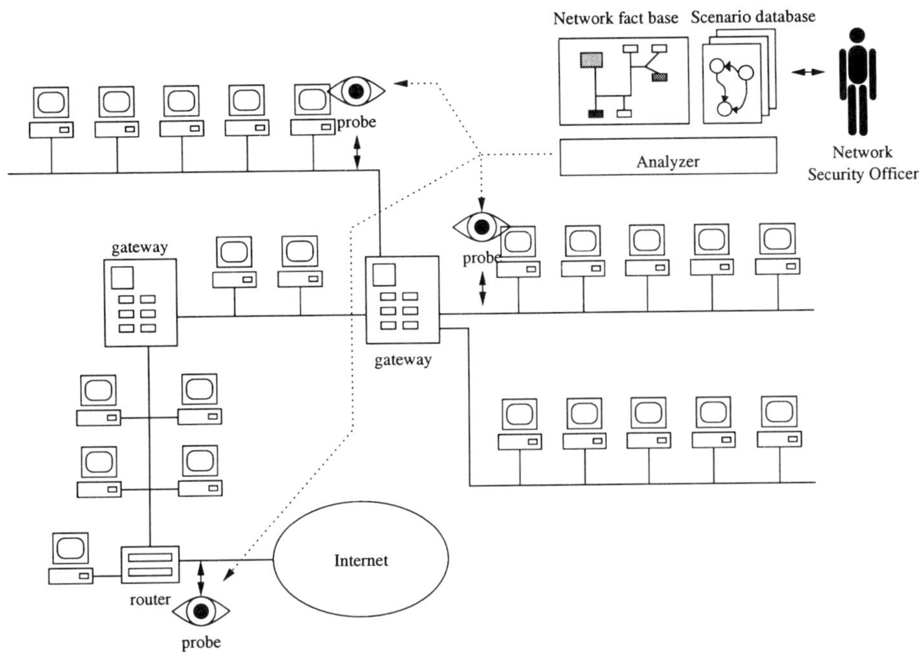

Figure 1. NetSTAT architecture.

some associated information. For example, hosts have several attributes that characterize the type of hardware and operating system software installed. The reader should note that in this model "host" is a rather general concept. More specifically, a host is a device that has one or more network interfaces that can be the (explicit) source and/or destination of network traffic. For example, by this definition, gateways and printers are considered to be hosts. Links are characterized by their type (e.g., Ethernet). Interfaces are characterized by their type and by their corresponding link- and network-level addresses. This information is represented in the model by means of functions that associate the network elements with the related information.

The network services portion of the network fact base contains a description of the services provided by the hosts of a network. Examples of these services are the Network File System (NFS), the Network Information System (NIS), TELNET, FTP, "r" services, etc. The fact base contains a characterization of each service in terms of the network/transport protocol(s) used, the access model (e.g., request/reply), the type of authentication (e.g., address-based, password-based, token-based, or certificate-based), and the level of traffic protection (e.g., encrypted or not). In addition, the network fact base contains information about how services are deployed, that is how services are instantiated and accessed over the network.

Figure 2 shows an example network. In the hypergraph describing the network, interfaces are represented as black dots, hosts are represented as circles around the corresponding interfaces, and links are represented as lines connecting the interfaces. The sample network is composed of five links, namely L_1, L_2, L_3, L_4, and L_5, and twelve hosts. Hereinafter, it is assumed that each interface has a single associated IP address, for example interface i_7 is associated with IP address a_7. The outside network is modeled as a *composite host* (the double circle in the figure) containing all the interfaces and corresponding addresses not in use elsewhere in the modeled network. As far as services are concerned, host `fellini` is an NFS server exporting file systems `/home` and `/fs` to `kubrick` and `wood`. In addition, `fellini` is a TELNET server for everybody. Host `jackson` exports an *rlogin* service to hosts `carpenter` and `lang`.

The Network Security Officer can access the network fact base through a graphic interface. The interface provides functions to design the network topology and to define the service infrastructure, as well as to browse the network-related information. Note that while the model is a complex, formal system, the interface used to manage the network fact base is intuitive and user-friendly.

NetSTAT is intended to represent large networks containing a large number of hosts that provide diverse services. For this reason, as an alternative to the graphic interface, all the information can also be inserted and retrieved by using ASCII-based tools. As a result, scripting languages like Perl or the Bourne Shell can be used to automate the retrieval of information from the network hosts, by querying the network information services (e.g., yellow pages, DNS) or by examining the configuration files of the involved hosts (e.g., `inetd.conf` on UNIX sys-

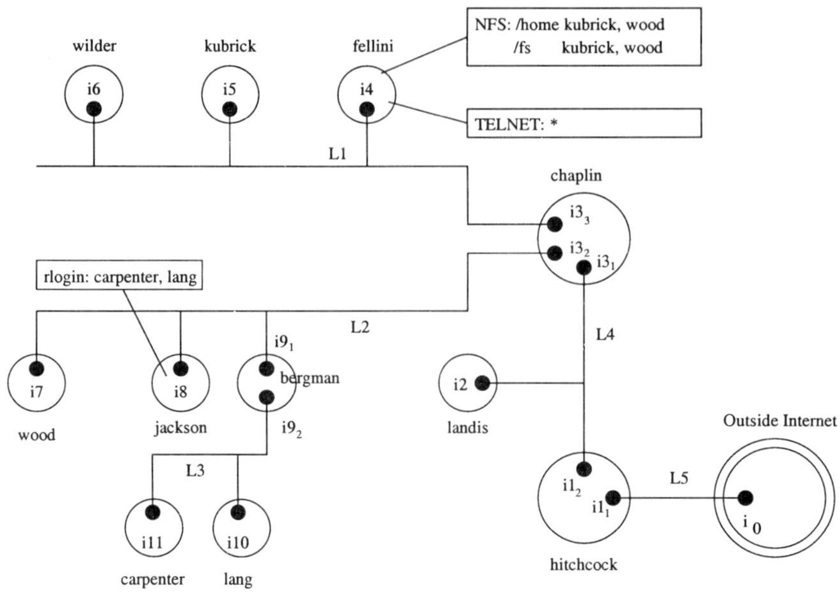

Figure 2. An example network.

tems). Large networks by their very nature are also subject to changes. Thus, the network fact base component will provide procedures that allow the Network Security Officer to verify the internal representation of the network against the actually deployed infrastructure in order to identify inconsistencies and incomplete or outdated information.

2.2. State Transition Scenario Database

The state transition scenario database is the component that manages the set of state transition representations of the intrusion scenarios to be detected. The state transition scenario database can be executed as a stand-alone application that allows the Network Security Officer to browse and edit state transition diagrams using a friendly graphic interface.

The state transition analysis technique was originally developed to model host-based intrusions [3]. It describes computer penetrations as sequences of actions that an attacker performs to compromise the security of a computer system. Attacks are (graphically) described by using *state transition diagrams*. *States* represent snapshots of a system's volatile, semi-permanent, and permanent memory locations. A description of an attack has a "safe" starting state, zero or more intermediate states, and (at least) one "compromised" ending state. States are characterized by means of *assertions*, which are functions with zero or more arguments returning boolean values. Typically, these assertions describe some aspects of the security state of the system, such as file ownership, user identification, or user authorization. *Transitions* between states are indicated by *signature actions* that represent the actions that, if omitted from the execution of an attack scenario, would prevent the attack from completing successfully. Typical examples of host-based signature actions include reading, writing, and executing files. For a complete description of the state transition analysis technique see [8]. For NetSTAT the original STAT technique has been applied to computer networks, and the concepts of state, assertions, and signature actions have been characterized in a networked environment.

States and Assertions

In network-based state transition analysis the state includes the currently active connections (for connection oriented services), the state of interactions (for connectionless services), and the values of the network tables (e.g., routing tables, DNS mappings, ARP caches, etc). For instance, both an open connection and a mounted file system are part of the state of the network. A pending DNS request that has not yet been answered is also part of the state, such as the mapping between IP address `128.111.12.13` and the name `hitchcock`. For the application of state transition analysis to networks the original state transition analysis concept of assertion has been extended to include both *static assertions* and *dynamic assertions*.

Static assertions are assertions on a network that can be verified by examining the network fact base; that is, by examining its topology and the current service configuration. For example, the following assertion:

```
service s in server.services|
  s.name == "www" and
  s.application.name == "CERN httpd";
```

identifies a service s in the set of services provided by host server such that the name of the service is www and the application providing the service is the CERN http daemon[1]. As another example, the following assertion:

```
Interface i in gateway.interfaces|
  i.link.type == "Ethernet";
```

denotes an interface of a host, say gateway, that is connected to an Ethernet link.

These assertions are used to customize state transition representations for particular scenarios (e.g., a particular server and its clients). In practice, they are used to determine the amount of knowledge about the network fact base that each probe must be provided with during configuration procedures.

Dynamic assertions can be verified only by examining the current state of the network. One examples is NFSMounted(filesys, server, client), which returns true if the specified file system exported by server is currently mounted by client. Another example is ConnectionEstablished(addr1, port1, addr2, port2), which returns true if there is an established virtual circuit between the specified addresses and ports. These assertions are used to determine what relevant network state events should be monitored by a network probe.

Transitions and Signature Actions

In NetSTAT, signature actions are expressed by leveraging off of an *event model*. In this model events are sequences of messages exchanged over a network.

The basic event is the *link-level message*, or *message* for short. A link-level message is a string of bits that appears on a network link at a specified time. The message is exchanged between two directly connected interfaces. For example the signature action:

```
Message m {i_x,i_y}|
  m.length > 512;
```

represents a link-level message exchanged between interfaces i_x and i_y whose size is greater than 512 bytes.

Basic events can be abstracted or composed to represent higher-level actions. For example, IP datagrams that are transported from one interface to another in an IP network are modeled as sequences of link-level messages that represent the intermediate steps in the delivery process. Note that the only directly observable events are link-level messages appearing on specific links. Therefore, the IP datagram "event" is observable by looking at the payload of one of the link-level messages used to deliver the datagram. For example, the signature action:

```
[IPDatagram d]{i_x,i_y}|
  d.options.sourceRoute == true;
```

represents an IP datagram that is delivered from interface i_x to interface i_y and that has the source route option enabled. This event can be observed by looking at the link-level messages used in datagram delivery along the path(s) from i_x to i_y. It is also possible to write signature actions that refer to specific link-level messages in the context of datagram delivery. For example, the signature action:

```
Message m in [IPDatagram d]{i_x,i_y}|
  m.dst != i_y;
```

represents a link-level message used during the delivery of an IP datagram such that the link-level destination address is not the final destination interface (i.e., the message is not the last one in the delivery process).

Events representing single UDP datagrams or TCP segments are represented by specifying encapsulation in an IP datagram. For example, the signature action:

```
[IPDatagram d [TCPSegment t]]{i_x,i_y}|
  d.dst == a_y and
  t.dst == 23;
```

denotes the sequence of messages used to deliver a TCP segment encapsulated into an IP datagram such that the destination IP address is a_y and the destination port is 23.

TCP virtual circuits are higher-level, composite events. A virtual circuit is identified by the tuple *(source IP address, destination IP address, source TCP port, destination TCP port)* and is composed of two sequences of TCP segments exchanged between two interfaces. Each of these two sequences defines a byte stream. The byte stream is obtained by assembling the payloads of the segments in the corresponding sequence, following the rules of the TCP protocol (e.g., sequencing, retransmission, etc.). The streams are denoted by streamToClient and streamToServer.

For example, the signature action:

```
TCPSegment t in
          [VirtualCircuit c]{i_x,i_y}|
  c.dstIP == a_y and
  c.dstPort == 80 and
  t.syn == true;
```

denotes a segment that has the SYN bit set and belongs to a virtual circuit established between interfaces i_x and i_y and that has destination IP address a_y and destination port 80.

Events at the application level can be either encapsulated in UDP datagrams or can be sent through TCP virtual circuits. In the former case, the application-level event can be referenced by indicating the corresponding datagram and specifying the encapsulation. For example, the signature action:

[1]The only (possibly) non-standard notation used in the assertions is the use of "|" for "such that".

```
[IPDatagram d
     [UDPDatagram u
          [RPC r]]]{i_x,i_y}|
   d.dst == a_y and
   u.dst == 2049 and
   r.type == CALL and
   r.proc == MKDIR;
```

represents an RPC request encapsulated in a UDP datagram representing an NFS command.

In the TCP virtual circuit case, application-level events are extracted by parsing the stream of bytes exchanged over the virtual circuit. The type of application event determines the protocol used to interpret the stream. For example, the following signature action:

```
[c.streamToServer [HTTPRequest r]]|
  r.method == "GET";
```

is an HTTP GET request that is transmitted over a TCP virtual circuit (defined somewhere else as `c`), through the stream directed to the server side.

2.3. Probes

The probes are the active intrusion detection components. They monitor the network traffic in specific parts of the network, following the configuration they receive at startup from the analyzer, which is described in the following section. Probes are general purpose intrusion detection systems that can be configured remotely and dynamically following any changes in the modeled attacks or in the implemented security policy. Each probe has the structure shown in Figure 3.

The *filter* module is responsible for filtering the network message stream. Its main task is to select those messages that contribute to signature actions or dynamic assertions used in a state transition scenario from among the huge number of messages transmitted over a network link. The filter module may be configured remotely by the analyzer. Its configuration can also be updated at run-time to reflect new attack scenarios, or changes in the network configuration. The performance of the filter is of paramount importance, because it has strict real time constraints for the process of selecting the events that have to be delivered to the inference engine. In the current prototype the filter is implemented using the BSD Packet Filter [5] and a modified version of the *tcpdump* application [6].

The *inference engine* is the actual intrusion detecting system. This module is initialized by the analyzer with a set of state transition information representing attack scenarios (or parts thereof). These attack scenarios are codified in a structure called the inference engine table. At any point during the probe execution, this table consists of snapshots of penetration scenario instances (instantiations), which are not yet completed. Each entry contains information about the history of the instantiation, such as the address and services involved, the time of the attack, and so on. On the basis of the current active attacks, the event stream provided by the filter is interpreted looking for further evidence of an occurring attack. Evolution of the inference engine state is monitored by the *decision engine*, which is responsible for taking actions based on the outcomes of the inference engine analysis. Some possible actions include informing the Network Security Officer of successful or failed intrusion attempts, alerting the Network Security Officer during the first phases of particularly critical scenarios, suggesting possible actions that can preempt a state transition leading to a compromised state, or playing an active role in protecting the network (e.g., by injecting modified datagrams that reset network connections.)

Probes are autonomous intrusion detection components. If a single probe is able to detect all the steps involved in an attack then the probe does not need to interact with any other probe or with the analyzer. Interaction is needed whenever different parts of an intrusion can be detected only by probes monitoring different subparts of the network. In this case, it is the analyzer's task to decompose an intrusion scenario into subscenarios such that each can be detected by a single probe. The decision engine procedures associated with these scenarios are configured so that when part of a scenario is detected, an event is sent to the probes that are in charge of detecting the other parts of the overall attack. This simple form of forward chaining allows one to detect attacks that involve different (possibly distant) subnetworks.

2.4. Analyzer

The analyzer is a stand-alone application used by the Network Security Officer to analyze and instrument a network for the detection of a number of selected attacks. It takes as input the network fact base and a state transition scenario database and determines:

- which events have to be monitored; only the events that are relevant to the modeled intrusions must be detected;
- where the events need to be monitored;
- what information about the topology of the network is required to perform detection;
- what information must be maintained about the state of the network in order to be able to verify state assertions.

Thus, the analyzer component acts as a probe generator that customizes a number of general-purpose probes using

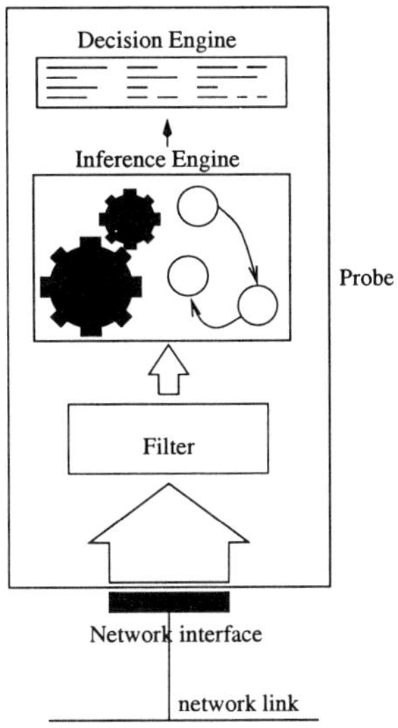

Figure 3. Probe architecture.

an automated process based on a formal description of the network to be protected and of the attacks to be detected. This information takes the form of a set of probe configurations. Each probe configuration specifies the positioning of a probe, the set of events to be monitored, and a description of the intrusions that the probe should detect. These intrusion scenarios are customized for the particular subnetwork the probe is monitoring, which focuses the scanning and reduces the overhead.

The analyzer is composed of several modules (see Figure 4). The network fact base and the state transition scenario database components are used as internal modules for the selection and presentation of a particular network and a selected set of state transition scenarios. The *analysis engine* uses the data contained in the network fact base and the state transition scenario database to customize the selected attacks for the particular network under exam. For example, if one scenario describes an attack that exploits the trust relationship between a server and a client, that scenario will be customized for every client/server pair that satisfies the specified trust relationship[2]. This customization allows one to instantiate an attack in a particular context. Using the description of the topology of that context it is then possible to identify what the sufficient conditions for detection are or if a particular attack simply cannot be detected given the current network configuration.

Once the attack scenarios contained in the state transition scenario database have been customized over the given network, another module, called the *configuration builder*, translates the results of the analysis engine to produce the configurations to be sent to the different probes. Each configuration contains a filter configuration, a set of state transition information, and the corresponding decision tables to customize the probe's decision engine.

[2]Thus, state assertions are treated as if they were universally quantified.

3. Example

The architecture of NetSTAT supports a well-defined configuration and deployment process. Firstly the Network Security Officer builds a database of attack scenarios. This database may include pre-modeled well-known scenarios or may be extended by the Network Security Officer following his/her perception of what an attack is and conforming to the local security policy. The attack scenario database is created and maintained using the state transition scenario database as a stand-alone application. Next, the Network Security Officer builds a network fact base describing the network to be protected. This task can be achieved by a combination of methods ranging from manual data introduction to automated information retrieval. This operation is performed by using the network fact base as a stand-alone application. In the next phase, the Network Security Officer invokes the analyzer. Using the integrated network fact base and state transition scenario database modules the Network Security Officer selects a particular network description and a set of scenarios that have to be detected. Again, this choice is dictated by the particular level of security that has to be achieved and by the network security policy. The Network Security Officer then starts the analysis and customization process. This process will be mostly automated, but in some circumstances it may require some interaction with the Network Security Officer, for example in order to manage situations where some attack scenarios cannot be detected. When the analysis is completed, the probe configurations will be created and sent to the probes installed

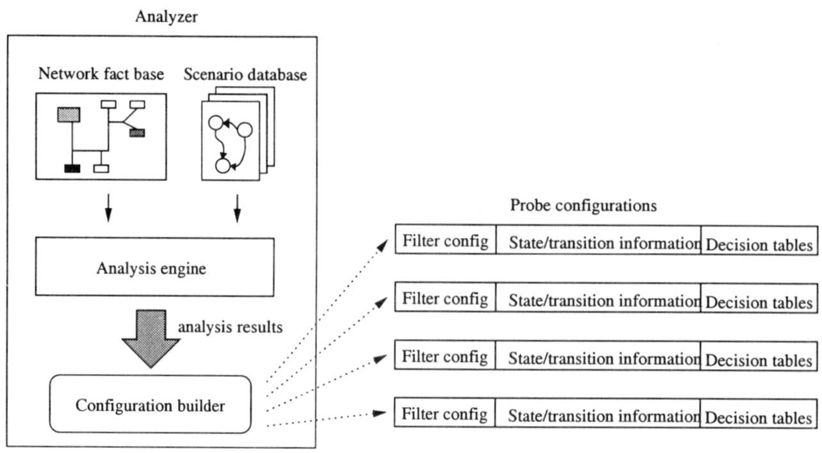

Figure 4. Analyzer architecture.

across the network.

The example attack considered is an active UDP spoofing attack. In this scenario an attacker tries to access a UDP-based service exported by a server by pretending to be one of its trusted clients, that is, by sending a forged UDP-over-IP datagram that contains the IP address of one of the authorized clients as the source address. The receiver of a spoofed datagram is usually not able to detect the attack. For this example, consider the network presented in Figure 2 and assume that host `lang` is attacking host `fellini` by providing an NFS request that pretends to come from `wood`, who is a trusted, authorized client. Host `fellini` receives the request encapsulated in a link-level message from `chaplin`'s interface i_{3_3} to `fellini`'s interface i_4. Host `fellini` has no means to distinguish this message from the final link-level message used to deliver a legitimate request coming from `wood`. Therefore, `fellini` cannot determine if the datagram is a spoofed one. The spoofing can be detected, however, by examining the message on link L_2. In this case, since the link-level message comes from `bergman`'s interface i_{9_1} while it should come from `wood`'s interface i_7, the datagram can be recognized as spoofed. In general, if one considers a single link-level message that encapsulates a UDP-over-IP datagram, the datagram may be considered spoofed if there is no path between the interface corresponding to the datagram source address and the link-level message source interface in the network obtained by removing the link-level message source interface from the corresponding link.

This attack scenario is described in Figure 5 using a state transition diagram. The scenario assumes that two networks have been defined, `Network` and `ProtectedNetwork`. `Network` is a reference to the network modeled in the fact base; `ProtectedNetwork` is a subnetwork that contains the hosts that must be protected against the attack.

The starting state (S_1) is characterized by assertions that define the hosts, interfaces, addresses, and services involved in the attack. The first assertion states that the attacked host `victim` belongs to the protected network. The second assertion states that there is a service `s` in the set of services provided by `victim` such that the transport protocol used is UDP, and service authentication is based on the IP address of the client. The third assertion states that `a_v` is one of the IP addresses where the service is available. The fourth assertion says that `a_t` is one of the addresses that the service considers as "trusted". The following assertions characterize the attacker. In particular, the fifth assertion states that there exists a host `attacker` that is different from `victim` and that doesn't have the trusted IP address. The sixth assertion states that `i` is one of the `attacker`'s interfaces.

The signature action is a spoofed service request. That is, a UDP datagram that pretends to come from one of the trusted addresses, although it did not originate from the corresponding interface. Actually the signature action is a link-level message `m` that belongs to the sequence of messages used to deliver an IP datagram from interface `i` to the interface associated with the address of the attacked host. The IP datagram enclosed in the message has source address `a_t` and destination address `a_v`. The IP datagram encloses a UDP datagram, whose destination port is the port used by service `s`. In addition, the message is such that, if one considers the network obtained by removing the message source interface from the corresponding link (i.e., `Network.detachFromLink(m.src)`), there is no path between the interface corresponding to the datagram IP source address and the link-level message source interface. For example, consider a link-level message exchanged between `bergman`'s interface i_{9_1} and `chaplin`'s interface i_{3_2}. The message is an intermediate step in the delivery of a UDP-over-IP datagram to `fellini`; the IP source address of the datagram is `wood`'s a_7. Intuitively, it

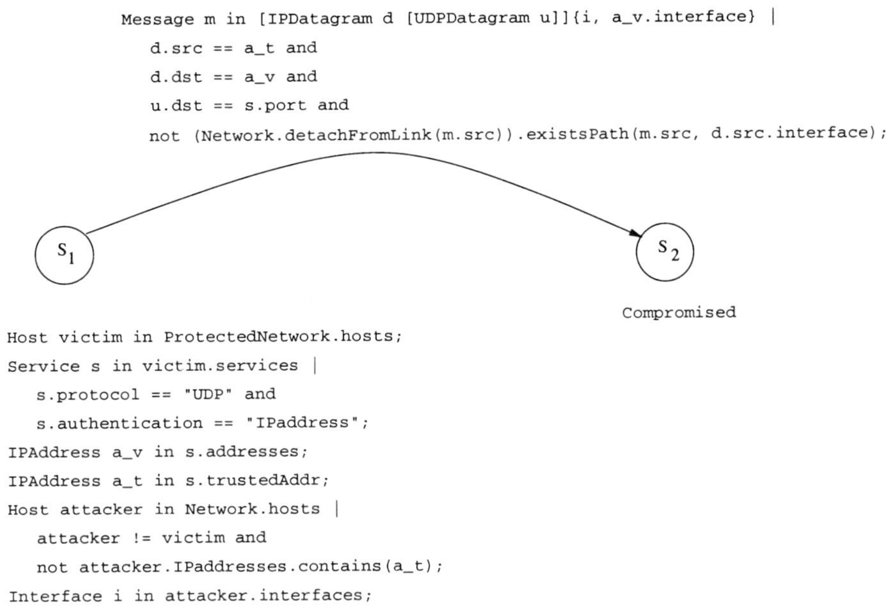

Figure 5. UDP spoofing attack scenario.

is clear that a message originated by wood and intended for fellini cannot come from one of bergman's interfaces, because there is no path in the network that would require bergman to act as a forwarder of the datagram. One way to check for this is by removing the source interface of the message (i_{9_1}) and checking whether or not there still exists a path from the host whose IP address is the source of the datagram (wood) to the host that contains the interface that was removed (bergman). The second state (S_2) is a "compromised" state.

The analysis of the attack starts by identifying the possible scenarios in the context of a modeled network. Thus, the analysis engine determines all the possible combinations of victim host, attacked service, spoofed address, and attacker in a particular network. A subset of the scenarios for the network in Figure 2 is presented in Table 1. In all scenarios fellini is the attacked host, NFS is the service exploited, and the spoofed address can be kubrick's or wood's.

The next step in the analysis is to determine where the events associated with the signature action can be detected. For each of these scenarios, the analysis engine generates all the possible datagrams between the interface of the attacker and the interface of the victim. In practice, the engine finds all the paths between the interfaces defined by the scenario and, for each path, generates the sequence of messages that would be used to deliver a datagram. For each message the predicate contained in the clause of the signature action is applied. The messages that satisfy the predicate are candidates for being part of the detection of the scenario. For example, consider the scenario where carpenter is attacking fellini by pretending to be wood. In this case, the spoofed datagram is generated from interface i_{11} and delivered through three messages to fellini's interface i_4. The first message is between carpenter and bergman, the second one is between bergman and chaplin, and the third one is between chaplin and fellini. Of these three messages only the first two satisfy the predicate of the signature action. Therefore, to detect this particular scenario one either needs a probe on L_3 looking for link-level messages from carpenter's interface i_{11} to bergman's interface i_{9_2}, or a probe on L_2 looking for messages from bergman's interface i_{9_1} to chaplin's interface i_{3_2}. In both cases, the IP source address is a_7, the destination IP address is a_4, and the destination UDP port is the one used by the NFS service. By analyzing all the scenarios, one finds that in order to detect all possible spoofing attacks it is necessary to set up probes on links L_1, L_2, and L_4.

4. Conclusions and Future Work

State transition analysis has proved to be an effective approach to host-based intrusion detection. This paper presents a further application of the state transition analysis approach, namely to detect network-based intrusions. The approach is based on formal models of attack scenarios (state transition diagrams) and of the network itself (network hypergraphs). These two models have been composed in order to determine the configuration and positioning of intrusion detection probes. The resulting architecture is distributed, autonomous, and highly customized towards the target network. In this way probes are more focused and the high volume event streams generated by networks can

victim	s	a_v	a_t	attacker	i
fellini	NFS	a_4	a_5	Outside	i_0
fellini	NFS	a_4	a_7	Outside	i_0
fellini	NFS	a_4	a_5	hitchcock	i_{1_1}
fellini	NFS	a_4	a_7	hitchcock	i_{1_1}
...	...	...	...	...	...
fellini	NFS	a_4	a_5	lang	i_{10}
fellini	NFS	a_4	a_7	lang	i_{10}
fellini	NFS	a_4	a_5	carpenter	i_{11}
fellini	NFS	a_4	a_7	carpenter	i_{11}

Table 1. Possible scenarios for the UDP spoofing attack.

be filtered resulting in decreased overhead.

The current prototype of the NetSTAT tool allows the Network Security Officer to define a network and the state transition diagrams describing the attacks. A number of sample networks have been constructed using the prototype network fact base component. In addition, network-based state transition representations for different flavors of UDP/TCP spoofing attacks, UDP race attacks, CGI-based attacks, remote buffer overflows, and denial of service attacks have been defined using the prototype state transition scenario database component. The analyzer is in a very initial stage of development. It provides a limited, *ad hoc* set of analytic capabilities, mostly related to topological analysis of network hypergraphs. Currently, the analyzer is not able to produce actual probe configurations and, although several configurations have been generated manually using the existing algorithms, it has not yet been tested on real networks.

Future work will focus on completion of the first prototype and on the refinement of its architecture. In addition, preparations are being made to test the prototype on a real network, containing several interconnected subnetworks, composed of heterogeneous hosts (PCs with Linux and Windows NT, SPARCstations with different versions of SunOS and Solaris, and IBM workstations with AIX).

Acknowledgments

This research was supported by the Defense Advanced Research Projects Agency of the Department of Defense under contract F30602-97-1-0207.

References

[1] C. Berge. *Hypergraphs*. North-Holland, 1989.

[2] L. T. Heberlein, G. Dias, K. Levitt, B. Mukherjee, J. Wood, and D. Wolber. A Network Security Monitor. In *Proceedings of the IEEE Symposium on Research in Security and Privacy*, pages 296 – 304, Oakland, CA, May 1990.

[3] K. Iglun, R. A. Kemmerer, and P. A. Porras. State Transition Analysis: A Rule-Based Intrusion Detection System. *IEEE Transactions on Software Engineering*, 21(3), March 1995.

[4] H. S. Javitz and A. Valdes. The SRI IDES Statistical Anomaly Detector. In *Proceedings of the IEEE Symposium on Security and Privacy*, May 1991.

[5] S. McCanne and V. Jacobson. The BSD Packet Filter: A New Architecture for User-level Packet Capture. In *Proceedings of the 1993 Winter USENIX Conference*, San Diego, CA, January 1993.

[6] S. McCanne, C. Leres, and V. Jacobson. Tcpdump 3.4. Documentation, 1998.

[7] B. Mukherjee, L. T. Heberlein, and K. N. Levitt. Network Intrusion Detection. *IEEE Network*, pages 26–41, May/June 1994.

[8] P. Porras. STAT – A State Transition Analysis Tool for Intrusion Detection. Master's thesis, Computer Science Department, University of California, Santa Barbara, June 1992.

[9] P. Porras and P. Neumann. EMERALD: Event Monitoring Enabling Responses to Anomalous Live Disturbances. In *Proceedings of the 1997 National Information Systems Security Conference*, Baltimore, MD, October 1997.

[10] S. Snapp, J. Brentano, G. Dias, T. Goan, T. Heberlein, C. Ho, K. Levitt, B. Mukherjee, S. Smaha, T. Grance, D. Teal, and D. Mansur. DIDS (Distributed Intrusion Detection System) – motivation, architecture, and an early prototype. In *Proceedings of the 14th National Computer Security Conference*, Washington, DC, October 1991.

[11] G. Vigna. A Topological Characterization of TCP/IP Security. Technical Report TR-96.156, Politecnico di Milano, November 1996.

[12] J. Winkler. A Unix Prototype for Intrusion and Anomaly Detection in Secure Networks. In *Proceedings of the* 13th *National Computer Security Conference*, Washington, D.C., October 1990.

Track B: Panel Session

Can Internet Commerce Be Secure?

Moderator

E. Appel, CertCo

If not for the lack of security and the high risk of loss, the Internet would be a ready platform for high-finance business-to-business electronic commerce on a global scale. But deliberate acts of costly computer crime—insider and outsider data theft and corruption, embezzlement, fraud, sabotage, viruses, service disruption and abuse—can effectively crush the Web's potential. Risk must be minimized or Internet commerce will not take the next step toward a truly global trading host. Can a public key infrastructure (PKI) minimize risk, ensuring the authentication, privacy, and validity of high-value electronic transactions? This forum will attempt to answer that question.

A PKI linking organizations and individuals to each other for secure worldwide transactions over open networks using public key cryptography is a high priority of business and government. Can PKC provide sufficient security to satisfy business and government needs over the Internet? Experts in the risks, threats, and solutions for government and business PKI provide an up-to-the-minute view, from government and financial institution pilots to computer crime and security issues.

PKI trust institutions are creating a global trust infrastructure that guarantees and insures transactions. Despite the residual perception that the Internet is inherently insecure, financial institutions and governments are finding ways to adopt the technology and provide the services to make public key cryptography an effective part of the PKI so as to ensure the success of electronic business-to-business commerce on a global scale.

The following forum members will discuss these issues: *Moderator:* **Edward J. Appel,** Vice President, CertCo (former FBI security and counterintelligence expert), who retired as Director, Counterintelligence Programs, National Security Council, The White House (and Co-Chair, Interagency Working Group on Cryptography Policy) in May 1997. CertCo's efforts to enable financial institutions to create a global Internet PKI extend beyond technology to law, business and sophisticated risk management. Mr. Appel will set the stage for this discussion of risk management on the Web: "Can Authentication and Encryption Secure the Web?"

Patricia Edfors, GTE Internetworking. Ms. Edfors recently left the Treasury Department, where she served as Champion for Security, Government Information Technology Services Board, and previously served the Justice Department as information systems security director. As coordinator of the U.S. government pilots testing PKC and key recovery encryption, and consultant to business, she has unique insights into what works securely for government and business on the Internet. She has evaluated products, systems and PKI models end to end for effectiveness, security, and interoperability. She will discuss "Going from Closed to Open Networks and Systems."

Kenneth Geide, FBI, Critical Infrastructure Protection Center. In coordinating computer crimes investigations and critical infrastructure protection, the FBI has gained unique insights into the dangers on the Web, for government and business. The types of threats from both inside and outside attacks are rapidly growing. The FBI itself must protect one of the nation's most sensitive databases from these threats. Despite the growth of computer crimes, some organizations are containing cyber threats and succeeding with PKI implementations. Supervisory Special Agent Geide will discuss what we should know about "Crimes on the Web."

Richard Guida, Champion for Security, Government Information Technology Services Board, Department of the Treasury. Mr. Guida, formerly with the Defense Department, has the mission of providing both secure and effective technology for government use as he coordinates PKC pilots. The government, a large-scale business itself, has a commitment to extend more services, at lower cost, to both business and public. Can Internet services be delivered to the public securely and efficiently? In their second year, over a dozen government pilots suggest that they can. Mr. Guida will speak on "Your Secure Web Link to Government."

Track A

Security Administration

Chair

J. Litchko, Integrated Management Services, Inc.

The RRA97 Model for Role-Based Administration of Role Hierarchies

Ravi Sandhu and Qamar Munawer
Laboratory for Information Security Technology and ISE Department
George Mason University—Mail Stop 4A4, Fairfax, VA 22030
sandhu@isse.gmu.edu, www.list.gmu.edu

Abstract *Role-based access control (RBAC) has recently received a lot of attention due to its flexibility, expressive power and simplicity in administration. In RBAC permissions are associated with roles and users are made members of roles thereby acquiring the associated permissions. Centralized management of RBAC in large systems is a tedious and costly task. An appealing possibility is to use RBAC itself to facilitate decentralized administration of RBAC. The recently proposed ARBAC97 (administrative RBAC '97) model identifies components called URA97, PRA97 and RRA97 for administration of user-role, permission-role and role-role assignments respectively. URA97 and PRA97 have already been described in detail in the literature, whereas RRA97 has so far not been defined.*

The central contribution of this paper is to give a complete and formal definition of RRA97, thereby completing the ARBAC97 model. The effect of role-role assignment is to construct a role hierarchy (that is, a partial order) in which senior roles inherit permissions from junior roles. Modifications to the role hierarchy can have drastic impact on the effective distribution of permissions to roles. At the same time we would like to decentralize this aspect of RBAC administration so that, for example, it should be possible for project security officers to rearrange roles within a project without impacting other role relationships within the department in which the project exists. RRA97 shows how this goal can be achieved.

1 Introduction

Role-based access control (RBAC) has recently received considerable attention as a promising alternative to traditional discretionary and mandatory access controls. In RBAC permissions are associated with roles, and users are made members of appropriate roles thereby acquiring the roles' permissions. This greatly simplifies management of permissions. Roles are created for the various job functions in an organization and users are assigned roles based on their responsibilities and qualifications. Users can be easily reassigned from one role to another. Roles can be granted new permissions as new applications and systems are incorporated, and permissions can be revoked from roles as needed. Role-role relationships can be established to lay out broad policy objectives.

In large enterprise-wide systems the number of roles can be in the hundreds or thousands, and users can be in the tens or hundreds of thousands. Managing these roles and users, and their interrelationships is a formidable task that often is highly centralized in a small team of security administrators. Because the main advantage of RBAC is to facilitate administration, it is natural to ask how RBAC itself can be used to manage RBAC. We believe the use of RBAC for managing RBAC will be an important factor in the long-term success of RBAC. Decentralizing the details of RBAC administration without losing central control over broad policy is a challenging goal for system designers and architects.

There are many components to RBAC [SCFY96]. RBAC administration is therefore multi-faceted. In particular we can separate the issues of assigning users to roles, assigning permissions to roles, and assigning roles to roles to define a role hierarchy. These activities are all required to bring users and permissions together. However, in many cases, they are best done by different administrators or administrative roles. Assigning permissions to roles is typically the province of application administrators. Thus a banking application can be implemented so credit and debit operations are assigned to a teller role, whereas approval of a loan is assigned to a managerial role. Assignment of actual individuals to the teller and managerial roles is a personnel management function. Assigning roles to roles includes aspects of user-role assignment and role-permission assignment, but more significantly role-role

0-8186-8789-4/98 $10.00 © 1998 IEEE

relationships establish broad policy. Control of these relationships would typically be relatively centralized in the hands of a few security administrators.

Sandhu et al [SBC+97] recently introduced a model for role-based administration of RBAC. This model is called ARBAC97 (administrative RBAC '97). It consists of three components called URA97, PRA97 and RRA97 for administration of user-role, permission-role and role-role assignments respectively. URA97 and PRA97 have already been described in detail in the literature [SB97, SBC+97, SB98], whereas RRA97 has so far not been formally defined. Sandhu et al [SBC+97] describe some of the requirements and intuitive goals of RRA97, but leave many issues open. Modifications to the role hierarchy can clearly have drastic impact on the effective distribution of permissions to roles. The intuitive idea of RRA97 is to decentralize role-role assignment so that, for example, project security officers can rearrange roles within a project without impacting other role relationships within the department in which the project exists. A fundamental assumption in RRA97 is that there is a single global hierarchy of roles which is known to all administrators.

The central contribution of this paper is to give a complete and formal definition of RRA97, thereby completing the ARBAC97 model. The effect of role-role assignment is to construct a role hierarchy (that is, a partial order) in which senior roles inherit permissions from junior roles. RRA97 shows how this goal can be achieved. It is the first attempt in the literature to give a comprehensive model for decentralized management of role hierarchies.

The rest of this paper is organized as follows. In section 2 we review the ARBAC97 model and, particularly, its URA97 and PRA97 components. We also briefly discuss the RBAC96 models on which ARBAC97 is based. Section 3 gives a formal definition of the RRA97 model and rationale for the design choices made here. Section 4 concludes the paper.

2 RBAC96 and ARBAC97 Models

This section gives a brief review of the RBAC96 and ARBAC97 models.

2.1 The RBAC96 Model

The well-known RBAC96 model [SCFY96, San97] is summarized in figure 1. The top half of the figure shows the regular roles and permissions that regulate access to data and resources. The bottom half shows the administrative roles and permissions to regulate the administration of users, roles and permissions. A user is a human being, a role is a job function and a permission is an approval of access to some objects or a privilege to carry out a particular task. Sessions are related to one user and possibly to many roles for which the user is a member. The management of permissions and roles is greatly simplified by associating permissions to the roles and assigning the users to roles. In this way the users acquire the associated permissions. Roles are created for various job functions in an organization. The permissions required to carry out the job are associated to the roles. New permissions can be granted to roles as new applications and systems are incorporated. Unnecessary permissions can be revoked from the roles. Users are assigned to the roles depending on the responsibilities and qualifications and can be reassigned from one role to another. Role-role relationships can be established to lay out broad policy objectives of the organizations.

2.2 The ARBAC97 Model

Sandhu et al [SBC+97] have outlined a comprehensive model for administration of RBAC in context of RBAC96. The model is called ARBAC97 and consists of three components which we describe briefly below. As stated earlier the RRA97 component of ARBAC97 is defined for the first time in this paper in the next section. A complete definition of the URA97 and PRA97 components, and the intuitive motivation for these models,is given in [SB97, SB98, SBC+97].

2.2.1 URA97 for user-role assignment

URA97 was developed by Sandhu and Bhamidipati [SB97]. It is concerned with the administration of user-role assignments. The basic idea is that administrative roles have authority to modify the UA relation of RBAC96. For example the administrative roles in figure 2(b) are authorized to modify the memberships of the roles in figure 2(a). In these diagrams senior roles are shown at the top and junior ones at the bottom. Permissions are inherited upwards in the hierarchy. The power of a administrative role extends over some range of regular roles—identified by giving the top and bottom of the range, and indicating whether the top and bottom are themselves included in the range. Familiar interval notation is used for this purpose. Thus [E1, PL1]={E1, PE1, QE1, PL1} and [E1, PL1)={E1, PE1, QE1}. A novel aspect of URA97

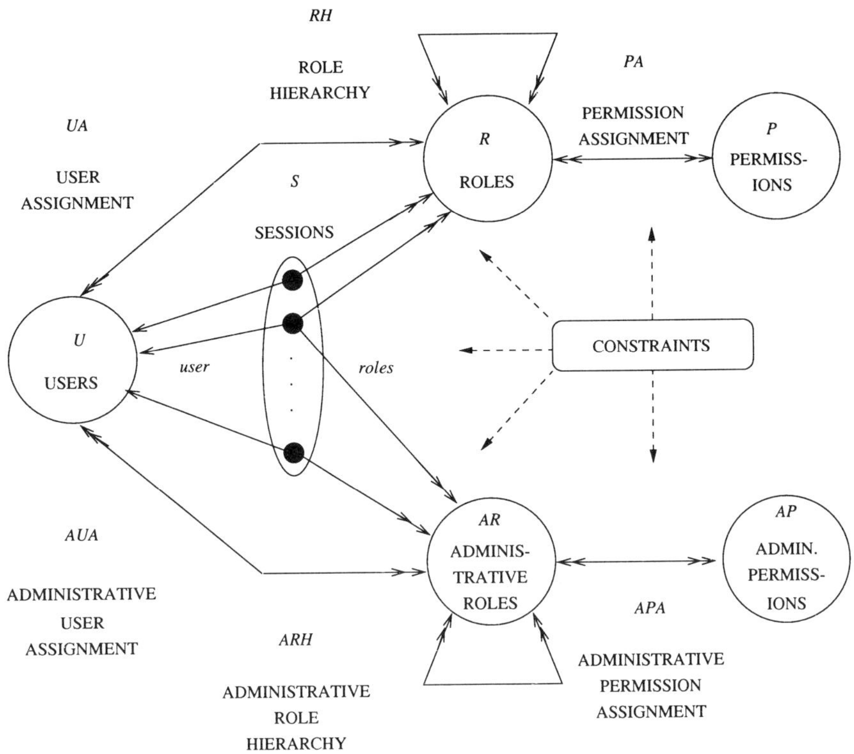

- U, a set of users
  R and AR, disjoint sets of (regular) roles and administrative roles
  P and AP, disjoint sets of (regular) permissions and administrative permissions
  S, a set of sessions

- $UA \subseteq U \times R$, user to role assignment relation
  $AUA \subseteq U \times AR$, user to administrative role assignment relation

- $PA \subseteq P \times R$, permission to role assignment relation
  $APA \subseteq AP \times AR$, permission to administrative role assignment relation

- $RH \subseteq R \times R$, partially ordered role hierarchy
  $ARH \subseteq AR \times AR$, partially ordered administrative role hierarchy
  (both hierarchies are written as $\geq$ in infix notation)

- $user : S \rightarrow U$, maps each session to a single user (which does not change)
  $roles : S \rightarrow 2^{R \cup AR}$ maps each session s_i to a set of roles and administrative roles $roles(s_i) \subseteq \{r \mid (\exists r' \geq r)[(user(s_i), r') \in UA \cup AUA]\}$ (which can change with time)
  session s_i has the permissions $\cup_{r \in roles(s_i)} \{p \mid (\exists r'' \leq r)[(p, r'') \in PA \cup APA]\}$

- there is a collection of constraints stipulating which values of the various components enumerated above are allowed or forbidden.

Figure 1: Summary of the RBAC96 Model

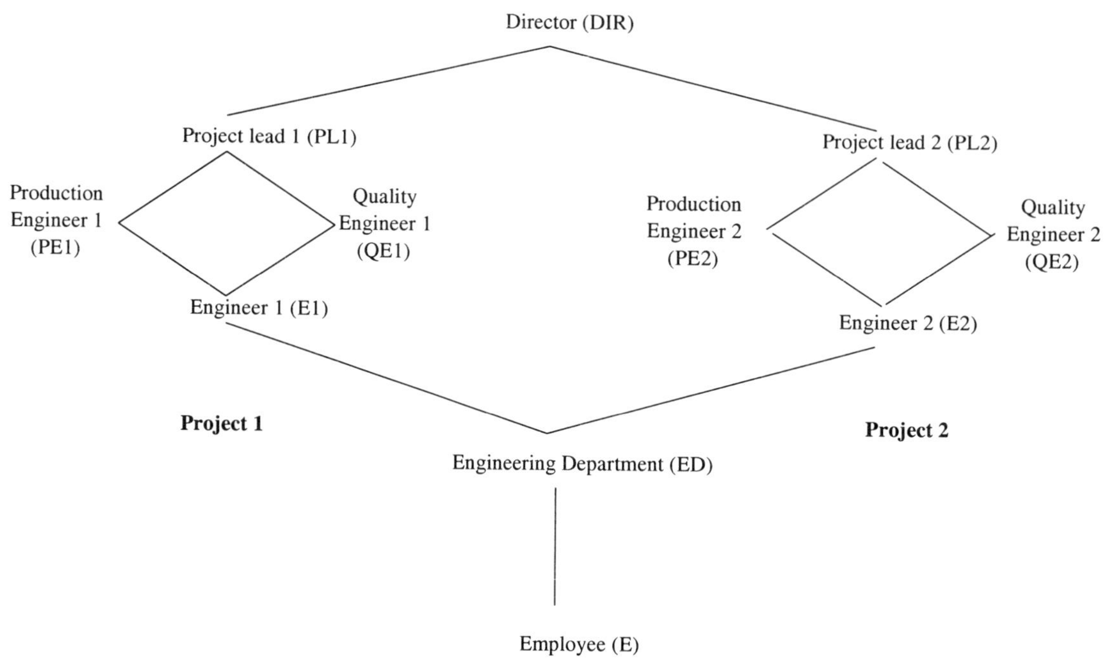

(a) Roles

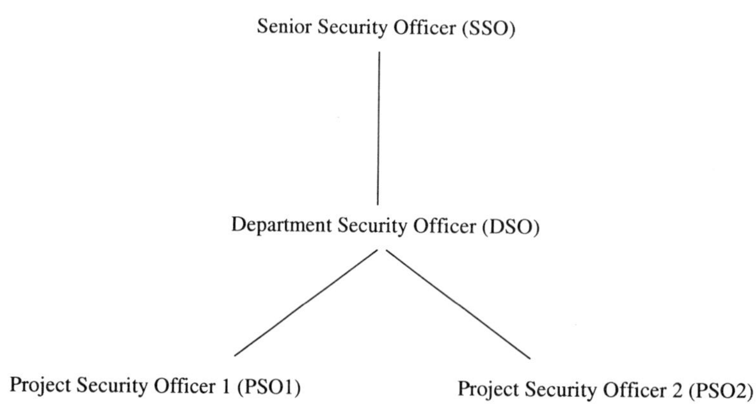

(b) Administrative Roles

Figure 2: Example Role and Administrative Role Hierarchies

is that the user population that can be assigned by an administrative role to such a range is specified by means of prerequisite conditions as follows.

Definition 1 A prerequisite condition is a boolean expression using the usual $\wedge$ and $\vee$ operators on terms of the form x and $\overline{x}$ where x is a regular role (i.e., $x \in R$). For a given set of roles R let CR denotes all possible prerequisite conditions that can be formed using the roles in R. A prerequisite condition is evaluated for a user u by interpreting x to be true if $(\exists x' \geq x)(u, x') \in UA$ and $\overline{x}$ to be true if $(\forall x' \geq x)(u, x') \notin UA$. □

The simplest example of a prerequisite condition is simply a prerequisite, for example, the prerequisite condition ED requires membership in ED. The more complex condition ED$\wedge\overline{\text{E2}}$ specifies users from the engineering department who are not assigned to project 2.

Definition 2 User-role assignment and revocation are respectively authorized in URA97 by the following relations, *can-assign* $\subseteq AR \times CR \times 2^R$ and *can-revoke* $\subseteq AR \times 2^R$ (with subsets of R identified by the range notation). □

For example *can-assign*(PSO1, ED, [E1,PL1)) authorizes members of the administrative role PSO1 to assign users who are already members of ED to the roles E1, PE1, QE1. Similarly, *can-revoke*(PSO1, [E1,PL1)) authorizes members of the administrative role PSO1 to revoke users from the roles E1, PE1, QE1. The exact semantics of revocation in this context is somewhat subtle and is discussed at length in [SB97, SB98, SBC+97].

2.2.2 PRA97 for permission-role assignments

This component of ARBAC97 deals with the assignments of permissions to roles. From a role-based , users and permissions have a similar character so PRA97 is an exact analog of URA97. The notion of a prerequisite condition is identical to that in URA97 except the boolean expression is now evaluated for membership and non-membership of a permission in specified roles. Analogous to URA97 we have the following two relations to control permission-role assignment and revocation.

Definition 3 Permission-role assignment and revocation are respectively authorized in PRA97 by the following relations, *can-assignp* $\subseteq AR \times CR \times 2^R$ and *can-revokep* $\subseteq AR \times 2^R$. □

3 RRA97 Model for Role-Role Assignment

In this section we develop the RRA97 model, which is the central contribution of this paper.

3.1 Abilities, Groups and UP-Roles

For role-role assignment we distinguish three kinds of roles, roughly speaking as follows.

- **Abilities** are roles that can only have permissions and other abilities as members.
- **Groups** are roles that can only have users and other groups as members.
- **UP-Roles** are roles that have no restriction on membership, i.e., their membership can include users, permissions, groups, abilities and other UP-roles.

The term UP-roles signifies user and permission roles. We use the term role to mean all three kinds of roles or to mean UP-roles only, as determined by context. The three kinds of roles are mutually disjoint and are identified respectively as A, G, and UPR.

The main reason to distinguish these three kinds of roles is that different administrative models apply to establishing relationships between them. The distinction was motivated in the first place by abilities. An ability is a collection of permissions that should be assigned as a single unit to a role. For example the ability to open an account in a banking application will encompass many different individual permissions. It does not make sense to assign only some of these permissions to a role because the entire set is needed to do the task properly. The idea is that application developers package permissions into collections called abilities which must be assigned together as a unit to a role.

The function of an ability is to collect permissions together so that administrators can treat these as a single unit. Assigning abilities to roles is therefore very much like assigning permissions to roles. For convenience it is useful to organize abilities into a hierarchy (i.e., partial order). Hence the PRA97 model can be adapted to produce the very similar ARA97 model for ability-role assignment.

Once the notion of abilities is introduced, by analogy there should be a similar concept on the user side. A group is a collection of users who are assigned as a single unit to a role. Such a group can be viewed as a team which is a unit even though its membership may change over time. Groups can also be organized in a hierarchy. For group-role assignment we adapt the URA97 model to produce the GRA97 model for group-role assignment.

This leads to the following models.

Definition 4 Ability-role assignment and revocation are respectively authorized in ARA97 by *can-assigna* $\subseteq AR \times CR \times 2^A$ and *can-revokea* $\subseteq AR \times 2^A$. □

Definition 5 Group-role assignment and revocation are respectively authorized in GRA97 by *can-assigng* $\subseteq AR \times CR \times 2^G$ and *can-revokeg* $\subseteq AR \times 2^G$. □

For these models CR is interpreted as the collection of prerequisite conditions formed using roles in UPR, and the prerequisite conditions are interpreted with respect to abilities and groups respectively. Membership of an ability in a UP-role is true if the UP-role dominates the ability and false otherwise. Conversely, membership of a group in a UP-role is true if the UP-role is dominated by the group and false otherwise.

Assigning an ability to an UP-role is mathematically equivalent to making the UP-role an immediate senior of the ability in the role-role hierarchy. Abilities can only have UP-roles or abilities as immediate seniors and can only have abilities as immediate juniors. In a dual manner, assigning a group to an UP-role is mathematically equivalent to making the UP-role an immediate junior of the group in the role-role hierarchy. Groups can only have UP-roles or groups as immediate juniors and can only have groups as immediate seniors. With these constraints the ARA97 and GRA97 models are essentially identical to the PRA97 and URA97 models respectively. This leaves us with the problem of managing relationships between UP-roles. We use the term role to mean UP-roles in the rest of the paper.

3.2 The can-modify relation

Decentralization of administrative authority requires that members of different administrative roles should have authority over different parts of the hierarchy. Authority over a part of the role hierarchy implies autonomy in modifying the internal role structure of that part. That includes the creation and deletion of roles as well as the alternation of role-role relationships by adding or deleting the edges. For example in figure 2 we would like the DSO to configure changes in the role hierarchy between DIR and ED. The PSO1 would manage the hierarchy between PL1 and E1, whereas PSO2 would manage the part between PL2 and E2. This leads to the following notion of a can-modify relation.

Administrative Role	UP-Role Range
DSO	(ED, DIR)
PSO1	(E1, PL1)
PSO1	(E2, PL2)

Table 1: Example of can-modify

Definition 6 Role creation, role deletion, edge insertion and edge deletion are all authorized by the relation, *can-modify* $\subseteq AR \times 2^{UPR}$ (with subsets of R identified by the range notation but limited to open ranges that do not include the endpoints). □

Table 1 illustrates an example of can-modify relative to the hierarchies of figure 2. The meaning of *can-modify*(x, Y) is that a member of the administrative role x (or a member of an administrative role that is senior to x) can create and delete roles in the range Y and can modify relationships between roles in Y. The examples in the rest of the paper are all in context of figure 2 and table 1. For purpose of our example we have ignored PSO2 in this table and have instead authorized PSO1 to manage the roles of both projects. This illustrates how a single administrative role can be authorized to control multiple pieces of the role hierarchy.

The semantics of the four operations—create role, delete role, insert edge and delete edge—are described in subsequent subsections. Some of the important intuitive ideas are mentioned here in anticipation. In particular none of these operations is allowed to introduce a cycle in the hierarchy.

Creation of a new role requires the specification of its immediate parent and child in the existing hierarchy. Thus PSO1 can create a new role with immediate parent PL1 and immediate child E1, or a new role with immediate parent PL1 and immediate child PE1. Generally the immediate parent and immediate child must fall within the range or be one of the endpoints as specified in can-modify. Since creation of a role also introduces two edges in the hierarchy, it is not possible to use any two roles as the immediate parent and immediate child. Clearly we do not want this operation to introduce a cycle in this manner. As we will see we also impose additional restrictions to prevent undesirable side effects of role creation.

Deletion of a role leaves relationships between the parents and children of the deleted role unchanged. So if DSO deletes E1, PE1 and QE1 continue to be senior to ED after deletion of E1. As such deletion does not pose a problem. However, deletion of E1 will leave dangling references in table 1, since the range (E1, Pl1) no longer exists. In general, some roles are referenced in various relations in URA97, PRA97 and RRA97. If these roles are actually deleted we will have dangling references. Our approach is to prohibit deletion that would cause a dangling reference. Roles that cannot be deleted due to this reason can be deactivated so that they can be phased out later by adjusting the references that prevent deletion. Furthermore, when a role is deleted we need to do something about the users and permissions that are directly assigned to this role.

Insertion of an edge is meaningful only between incomparable nodes. Thus insertion of an edge from PL1 to E1 has no meaning, whereas insertion of an edge from PE1 to QE1 does. As well see there are edges that should not be inserted because they can lead to anomalous side effects later.

Likewise deletion of an edge is meaningful only if that edge is not transitively implied by other edges. For example, deletion of the edge PL1 to E1 is meaningless and has no impact on the hierarchy. Deletion of the edge QE1 to E1 will change the hierarchy. Edge deletion only applies to a single edge and does not carry over to implied transitive edges. For example, deletion of the edge QE1 to E1 makes QE1 and E1 incomparable, but QE1 continues to be senior to ED.

More sophisticated forms of these operations can be constructed out of the basic ones defined here. In these basic operations roles and edges are created and destroyed one at a time. This approach is analogous to the definition of weak revocation in URA97 and PRA97 [SBC+97] from which various forms of strong revocation can be constructed. Similarly, in RRA97 more complex operations can be constructed in terms of these basic ones.

3.3 Restrictions on can-modify

The relation can-modify confers authority to administrative roles to change the role hierarchy. We would like to restrict this authority so as to maintain global consistency of authorization. The issue of dangling references has already been raised and RRA97 will not allow dangling references to occur. But this is not enough.

Consider the example of figure 3. Now if PSO1 who has authority over the range (E1, PL1) makes PE1 junior to QE1 by introducing an edge the effect is to indirectly introduce a relationship between X and Y roles. The role PSO1 does not have the authority to create this relationship, so this is an anomalous side effect. We should either restrict the authority of the administrative role (in our example DSO) that introduced X and Y roles in the first place, or PSO1 should be prevented from introducing relationships that makes PE1 junior to QE1 (and indirectly Y junior to X). In general administrative roles are given autonomy within a range but only so far as the global side effects are acceptable.

To formally state these restrictions on the authority of the administrative roles we introduce the concepts of authority range, encapsulated authority range and create range.

3.4 Concept of Range

The concept of range is very important in RRA97. It is formally defined as follows.[1]

Definition 7 A range of roles is defined by giving lower bound x and upper bound y, where y > x. Formally $(x, y) = \{z : R \mid x < z < y\}$. We say x and y are the end points of the range. □

Note that a range, as defined here, does not include the end points. In figure 2, (E1, PL1), (E2, PL2) and (ED, DIR) are different ranges. The range (ED, DIR) contains the roles which constitute ranges (E1, PL1) and (E2, PL2). We say ranges (E1, PL1) and (E2, PL2) are junior to range (ED, DIR).

Definition 8 For two ranges Y and Y' if $Y \subset Y'$, then Y is a junior range to Y' and Y' is a senior range to Y. □

Here Y is a proper subset of Y'. This eliminates the possibility of a range to be junior or senior to itself. This makes later definitions more convenient.

[1]We understand there is existing mathematical terminology for this concept and others to be introduced below. We have chosen to develop our own terminology motivated by administrative RBAC.

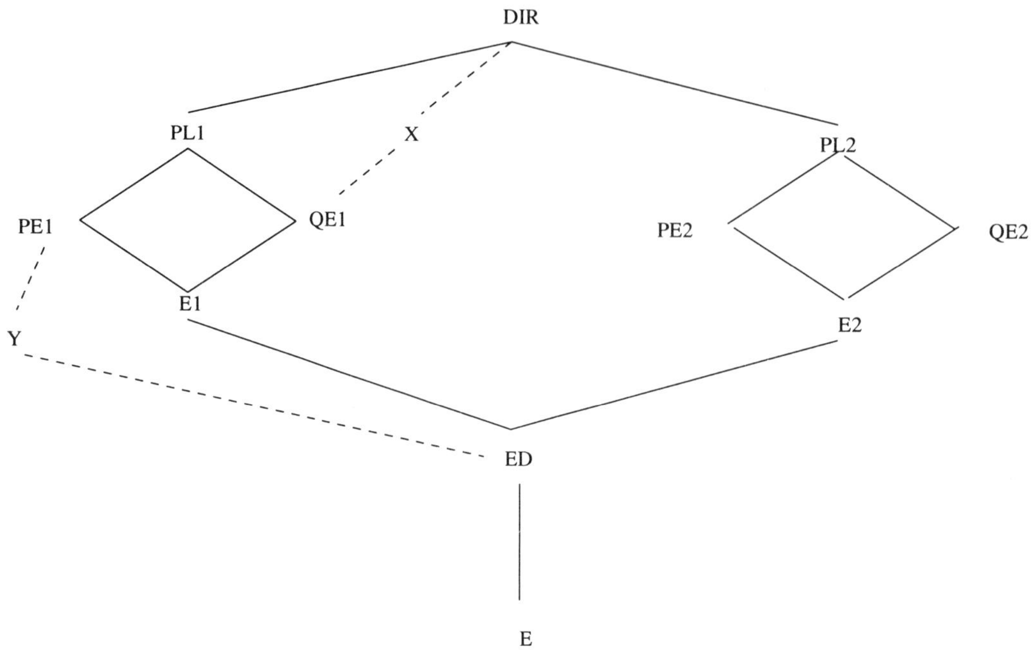

Figure 3: Out of Range Impact

If two ranges Y and Y' in the role hierarchy are such that one is not junior to the other then they are either incomparable or partially overlapping. Formal definitions of partially overlapping and incomparable ranges are as follows.

Definition 9 Ranges Y and Y' partially overlap if $Y \cap Y' \neq \phi$ and $Y \not\subset Y'$ and $Y' \not\subset Y$. Ranges Y_1 and Y_2 are said to be incomparable if $Y_1 \cap Y_2 = \phi$. □

Note that incomparable ranges may have one common end point.

3.5 Authority Range and Encapsulated Authority Range

The members of an administrative roles are authorized to modify certain range of roles in role hierarchy. These ranges are called authority ranges.

Definition 10 Any range referenced in the can-modify relation is called an authority range. □

To ensure that administrative authority over authority ranges does not overlap, we introduce the following restriction.

Definition 11 In RRA97 authority ranges do not partially overlap. □

Note that an administrative role may have more than one authority range. Table 1 shows that DSO has authority over the range (ED, DIR). In figure 2 the authority range (ED, DIR) has two junior authority ranges, (E1, PL1) and (E2, PL2). Since these junior authority ranges are completely contained within the authority range for DSO, DSO has authority over these junior authority ranges as well. In other words DSO has inherited the authority over the ranges (E1, PL1) and (E2, PL2).

Our model allows an administrative role to have authority over more than one incomparable authority range. Table 1 shows that PSO1 has authority over two incomparable authority ranges namely (E1, PL1) and (E2, PL2).

Let us consider figure 3 again. To maintain consistency we observed that either DSO should not be allowed to create roles X or Y in the role hierarchy or PSO1 should not be allowed to make PE1 junior to QE1. In the latter case the autonomy of PSO1 to manage its authority range is interfered by DSO's actions. While this is a possibility we pursue the former case here. Decentralization of authority and autonomy requires that all inward and outgoing edges from an authority range should only be directed to and from the end points of the authority range. The concept of

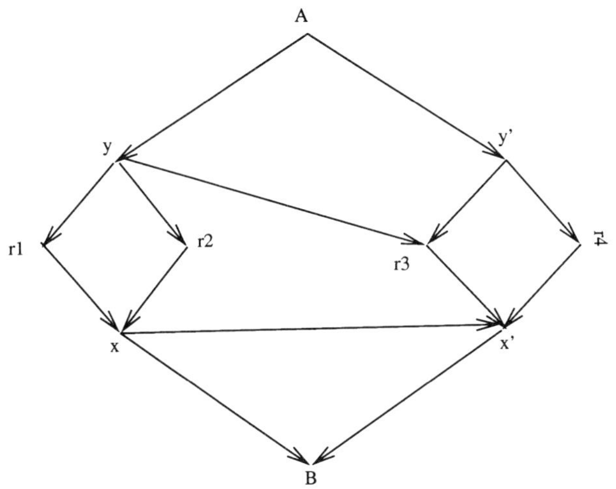

Figure 4: Encapsulated Range (x, y)

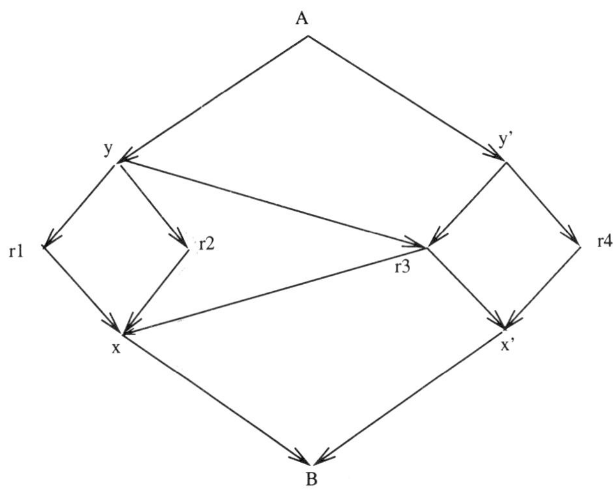

Figure 5: Non-Encapsulated Range (x, y)

encapsulation of authority range serves this purpose.

Definition 12 A range (x, y) is said to be encapsulated if $\forall r1 \in (x, y) \wedge \forall r2 \notin (x, y)$ we have $r2 > r1 \Leftrightarrow r2 > y$ and $r2 < r1 \Leftrightarrow r2 < x$. □

Intuitively an encapsulated range is one in which all roles have identical relation to roles outside of the range. The intuition in RRA97 is that an encapsulated range is the correct unit for autonomous management of role-role relationships within the range. All authority ranges in RRA97 are required to be encapsulated. Figure 4 and 5 respectively show examples of encapsulated and non-encapsulated range (x, y).

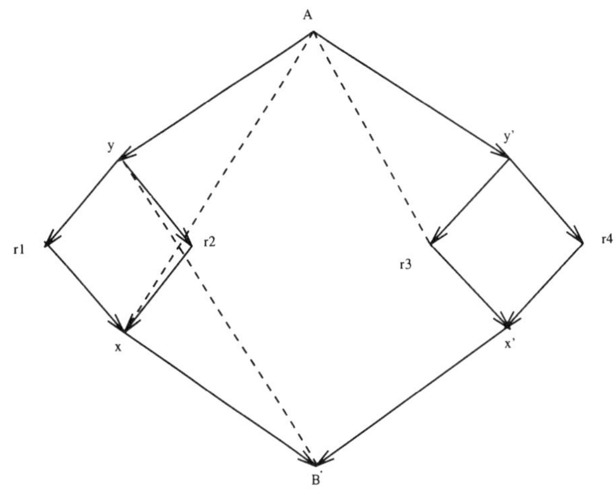

Figure 6: Create Range

3.6 Role Creation

As discussed earlier creation of a role requires specification of the new role's immediate parent and child. If the immediate parent and child are the end points of an authority range, there is no difficulty. More generally we wish to allow creation of a new role such that its immediate parent and child are within the authority range rather than being at the end points. Thus PSO1 can create a new role with parent PL1 and child PE1. However if DSO exercises this power we can end up with up the undesirable situation illustrated in figure 3. To prevent this from happening we introduce the following notions.

Definition 13 The immediate authority range of role r written $AR_{immediate}(r)$ is the authority range (x, y) such that $r \in (x, y)$ and for all authority ranges (x', y') junior to (x, y) we have $r \notin (x', y')$. □

Definition 14 The range (x, y) is a create range if $AR_{immediate}(x) = AR_{immediate}(y)$ or x is an end point of $AR_{immediate}(y)$ or y is an end point of $AR_{immediate}(x)$. □

Note that only comparable roles constitute a create-range.

Consider figure 6. Let (B, A) and (x, y) be authority ranges whereas (x', y') is not an authority range. The ranges marked by the dotted lines, i.e., (r3, A), (x, A) and (B, y) are create ranges. However (r1, A) or (r2, A) do not satisfy the conditions and thereby are not create ranges.

In RRA97 we require that the immediate parent and child of a new role must be a create range in the hierarchy prior to creation of the new role.

Roles can be created outside the authority ranges or without a parent or child only by the chief security officer. In general the chief security officer can do arbitrary modifications.

3.7 Role Deletion

Deletion of roles in a hierarchy is a complicated process. Our assumption is that a role in an authority range can be deleted by the administrator of that range. It does not matter how this role got there.

ARBAC97 defines some authorization relations such as can-assign, can-revoke and can-modify. If the roles specified as end points of the role ranges of these relationships are deleted, we will leave dangling references to non-existing roles. The ranges with these deleted end points will become meaningless. To avoid this problem RRA97 provides two alternatives.

1. Roles referred in can-assign, can-revoke and can-modify relationships cannot be deleted. Though it is a more restrictive constraint but it is required to keep the range referential integrity intact.
2. Roles referred in 1 above can be made inactive (explained in the next paragraph) whenever it is needed to delete them. The advantage of deactivating roles is that it avoids references to non-existing roles and at the same time achieves the purpose of deletion.

A role is said to be inactive if a user associated to it cannot activate it in a session. The edges to and from the inactive role, its associated permissions and assigned users remain unchanged. While a user assigned to an inactive role cannot activate it, the permissions associated with that role are still inherited by senior roles. In this way the hierarchy is not changed but at the same time a partial effect of deletion is achieved.

RRA97 allows both of the above alternatives. Regular users cannot invoke inactive roles, but administrators can revoke users and permissions from these roles. These roles can be made empty but cannot be deleted from the hierarchy until the references preventing deletion are suitably adjusted. Other roles in the role hierarchy can be deleted.

In case of deletion of a role we need to preserve the permissions and users assigned to the role. RRA97 provides two alternatives for deletion of roles.

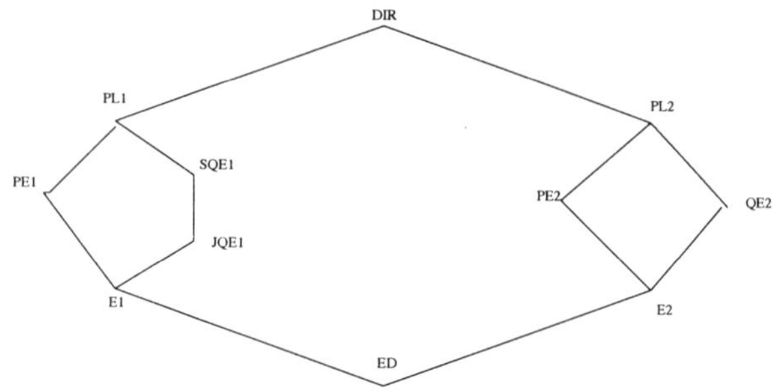

Figure 7: Before Deletion of edge from SQE1 to JQE1

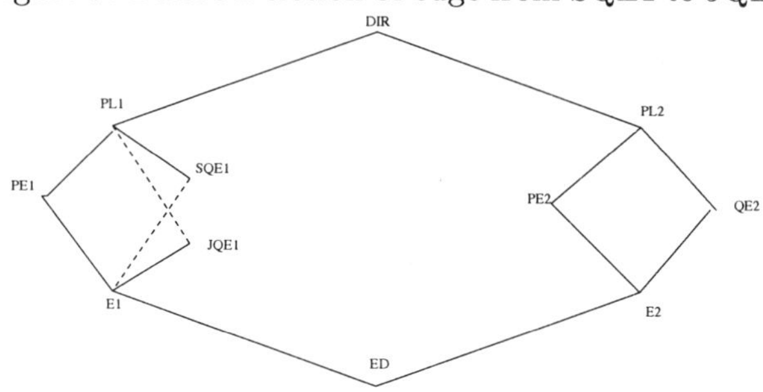

Figure 8: After Edge Deletion

1. Roles can be deleted only if they are empty.
2. Delete role but at the same time take care of the assigned permissions and associated users as follows: assign permissions to the immediate senior roles and assign users to immediate junior roles.

3.8 Edge Insertion

Now let us explain how the model deals with the insertion of edges in the role to role relationships. The insertion of transitive edges has no effect so we only consider edges inserted between incomparable roles. When an edge is inserted we must ensure that encapsulation of authority range is not violated. We have the following rules.

- The roles between which the edge is inserted must have same immediate authority range, or
- if the new edge connects a role in one authority range to a role outside the range encapsulation of the authority range must not be violated.

For example in figure 5 assume edges (y, r3) and (r3, x) are initially not present, and that (x, y) and

(B, A) are authority ranges. Insertion of the edge (y, r3) does not pose any problem. However in presence of this edge, insertion of edge (r3, x) violates encapsulation of authority range (x, y), hence it must not be allowed. Similarly in the presence of (r3, x) the edge (y, r3) would not be allowed. This leads to the following formal definition for insertion of an edge.

Definition 15 A new edge AB can be inserted between incomparable roles A and B

- if $AR_{immediate}(A) = AR_{immediate}(B)$ or
- if (x, y) is an authority range such that $(A = y \wedge B > x) \vee (B = x \wedge A < y)$ then insertion of AB must preserve encapsulation of (x, y). □

3.9 Edge Deletion

The deletion of a transitive edge does not change the hierarchy, so their deletion is meaningless. In RRA97 we consider only those edges for deletion that are in transitive reduction of the hierarchy. If edge AB is not in the transitive reduction then it is not a candidate for deletion.[2] For example in figure 7 deletion of the edge SQE1 to JQE1 will change the hierarchy. Edge deletion only applies to a single edge and does not carry over to implied transitive edges. As discussed in the general rules for edge deletion RRA97 keeps intact transitive edges after deletion. For example, deletion of the edge SQE1 to JQE1 makes SQE1 and JQE1 incomparable, but SQE1 continues to be senior to E1 and JQE1 junior to PL1 shown in figure 8.

There is one special case that needs to be considered. If the edge being deleted is between the end points of an authority range, deletion of the edge will disrupt the authority range and cause inconsistency in the model. Hence this operation is disallowed.

4 Conclusion

This paper defines the RRA97 model thus completing the definition of ARBAC97 started in [SBC+97]. RRA97 is very different from the URA97 and PRA97 components of ARBAC97 which have been previously reported in the literature. RRA97 provides for decentralized administration of role hierarchies. This desire is to give administrative roles autonomy within a range but only so far as the side effects of the resulting actions are acceptable. To do so we need to disallow some operations authorized by the authority range, thereby tempering the administrative role's authority. We have formally identified these restrictions in the paper and have provided their motivations. RRA97 is the first model to deal with these issues.

[2]Other models and applications do not have this restriction. For example, Oracle allows insertion and deletion of transitive edges [KL95].

5 Acknowledgment

This work is partially supported by grant CCR-9503560 from the National Science Foundation at the Laboratory for Information Security Technology at George Mason University.

References

[KL95] George Koch and Kevin Loney. *Oracle The Complete Reference.* Oracle Press, 1995.

[San97] Ravi Sandhu. Rationale for the RBAC96 family of access control models. In *Proceedings of the 1st ACM Workshop on Role-Based Access Control.* ACM, 1997.

[SB97] Ravi Sandhu and Venkata Bhamidipati. The URA97 model for role-based administration of user-role assignment. In T. Y. Lin and Xiaolei Qian, editors, *Database Security XI: Status and Prospects.* North-Holland, 1997.

[SB98] Ravi Sandhu and Venkata Bhamidipati. Role-based administration of user-role assignment: The URA97 model and its Oracle implementation. *The Journal Of Computer Security*, 1998. in press.

[SBC+97] Ravi Sandhu, Venkata Bhamidipati, Edward Coyne, Srinivas Ganta, and Charles Youman. The ARBAC97 model for role-based administration of roles: Preliminary description and outline. In *Proceedings of 2nd ACM Workshop on Role-Based Access Control*, Fairfax, VA, November 6-7 1997. ACM.

[SCFY96] Ravi Sandhu, Edward J. Coyne, Hal L. Feinstein, and Charles E. Youman. Role-based access control models. *IEEE Computer*, 29(2):38–47, February 1996.

Role Based Access Control Framework for Network Enterprises

Dan Thomsen, Dick O'Brien, and Jessica Bogle
Secure Computing Corporation
2675 Long Lake Road
Roseville, MN 55113
thomsen@securecomputing.com

Abstract

A business's success depends on its ability to protect valuable business assets in an increasingly hostile environment. Protecting information requires a cost, not only in purchasing security components, but also in ensuring that those security components are properly managed. Role Based Access Control (RBAC) shows promise for making security administration easier, thus reducing the cost of managing security components.

RBAC provides a convenient layer of abstraction by describing access control patterns. This paper presents an RBAC framework comprised of seven abstract layers. Multiple layers allow users to work with a layer they understand. Thus a balance can be struck between fine grained access control and ease of management. The goal is to provide easy security management for a wide variety of network applications. The NAPOLEON tool which implements parts of the framework is also described.[1]

1. Introduction

Administrating security systems is a complex task. In order to enforce a tight security policy many security constraints must be expressed. Security constraints can be classified into two broad categories, those required by the application, and those required by the local security policy. The RBAC framework presented here is broken down into seven abstract layers. The first four layers deal with the application specific constraints. The remaining layers focus on the site specific constraints.

This approach applies the divide and conquer principle to the tough problem of security management. Rather than place all the burden of security management on a system administrator in the field, the application developers share the burden by creating basic security building blocks. These building blocks capture complex application specific security constraints, freeing the local system administrators from configuring the many detailed constraints. The application developers are the people who best understand the application and can best describe the application security constraints.

Only the local administrators know the local security policies, thus they are the only ones who can describe their security constraints. The application designers cannot create security policies that apply to all sites. Thus the local system administrators must have the capability to create their own building blocks, should those prepared by the application developer be insufficient.

The goal of the RBAC framework is to centrally control access to a wide variety of network resources. This means incorporating diverse applications on a variety of hosts, legacy applications, and applications with unsophisticated security mechanisms. Incorporating these diverse resources into a consistent framework for security specification and enforcement creates many challenges that are discussed throughout the paper.

The remainder of this section discusses how network resources and applications are modeled in the framework. Section 2 discusses the layers in the RBAC framework, Section 3 describes the NAPOLEON policy tool based on the framework, and Section 4 summarizes the paper.

1. This work was supported by DARPA under contract F30602-97-C-0245.

0-8186-8789-4/98 $10.00 © 1998 IEEE

1.1. Modeling the application

Before access to network resources can be granted those resources must be understood. This means that the network applications must be incorporated into the model. Applications are written in different languages and run on a variety of hosts with different security mechanisms. A universal description of applications is needed that is independent of their implementations.

Currently there are two widely accepted frameworks for developing distributed network applications: CORBA and Microsoft's COM/DCOM [1], [2]. Both frameworks use an interface definition language (IDL) to describe how an application can be accessed. The IDL definition expresses the application in an object oriented framework by listing each object's publicly available methods. Thus an object oriented approach provides a good foundation for the RBAC framework. Access is either granted to an object method or it is denied.

Creating this object oriented model of the application is simple in the CORBA and COM/DCOM environments. The IDL file that describes an object's publicly available methods can be parsed and automatically incorporated into a security management tool.

To incorporate a legacy application into the framework, an IDL file must be created. This involves defining the legacy application in terms of objects and object methods. This is similar to how applications can be wrapped with a CORBA interface for the CORBA environment. However, the interface does not have to connect to the legacy application. The concern for the RBAC framework is, IF a method can be accessed not HOW. As you will see in the next section a component can be created to translate between the RBAC framework and the legacy applications enforcement mechanism.

1.2. Enforcing the RBAC framework

This section provides an overview of how the RBAC framework is enforced in a heterogeneous network environment.

Making access control decisions centrally for the entire enterprise would likely create a performance bottleneck. Centralized decision making also leads to a single point of failure that could shutdown the entire network. While these performance problems could be mitigated by duplicate security servers, performance would still lag local enforcement. So we prefer centralized management of the policy, with the security decisions being enforced as close as possible to the application.

The centralized management tool grants users access to objects. Once a change is made the tool translates the security policy from the RBAC framework to the target's native security mechanism, which is then transported to the target.

For example, if a user was given access to the Internet via the security management tool, the tool translates that request into a number of modifications to a firewall Access Control List (ACL). These modifications are then communicated to the firewall, which implements the changes.

The location of each application is known. The tool must push the security information out to the application making the access control decisions. Since we are assuming a heterogeneous network the central security policy must be translated into security mechanisms for each host making up the enterprise. If the target host already has an understanding of roles, or has a unified access control mechanism like CORBA, the translation process is easy. If the host does not understand roles the translation of the policy becomes more difficult.

For legacy applications the translation from the RBAC framework to the legacy application's security mechanisms is harder still. For example, protecting an FTP server on a Unix host first requires describing the FTP server in object oriented terms. For enforcement the policy must be translated to the equivalent user accounts and file permissions. While this translation is difficult, the important point is that the legacy applications can be included into the centralized policy management, albeit at a higher cost.

1.3. Divide and conquer

There are two primary users of the RBAC framework, application developers and local system administrators. The hard problem of creating a security policy must be divided between these two groups. The approach is for the application developers, using their in-depth knowledge of the application, to create generic security components. These security components serve to hide the application specific details. The local system administrators use these security components as the security building blocks to customize the security policy for their organization.

Just as it is important to document software design to facilitate application maintenance, it is important to document the security components of the application. When the application developers create the security building blocks not only are they creating tools for the local system administrators, but they are also documenting security design and usage. Permanent documentation is critical for the long term maintenance of an application, since application developers may leave or not remember details.

In the RBAC framework described in the next section there are two role hierarchies, one for the application developers, and one for the local system administrators. This allows each type of user to express the constraints they understand best.

Local System Administrator	• 7. Enterprise constraints • 6. Key chains • 5. Enterprise keys
Application Developer	• 4. Application keys • 3. Application constraints • 2. Object handles • 1. Objects

Figure 1. Abstract layers in RBAC framework

2. RBAC framework layers

One difficulty with any security enforcement mechanism is to ensure that the policy is accurately expressed, in an easily understood manner. Even with tools, describing a consistent security policy is a huge task. Each system administrator has a different understanding of the security mechanisms available to them. The RBAC framework provides seven abstract layers of security policy specification. This allows an administrator to quickly implement a course grained security policy, or precisely specify a fine grained policy. As their understanding of the enterprise grows, they can further customize the policy using the more detailed layers of abstraction.

At the highest layer users perform simple operations that are easy to understand. At this layer administrators hand out sets of predefined access rights. If this layer does not provide them with enough detailed security control, they can proceed to the next layer down where they have finer control of the access rights.

Figure 1 shows the abstract layers of the model. Each layer is described in detail below, starting with the finest security control to the broadest security control. The first four layers are the responsibility of the application designer. The final three layers are the responsibility of the local system administrator.

It is important to note that the first four layers are designed to be used by the application developers to create generic solutions for most sites. This means that at each layer there is documentation describing the rational for the security constraint and its intended use. This provides crucial guidance for local system administrators and application owners should they need to customize the security policy.

2.1. Layer 1 - Objects

The basic building block of this RBAC framework is an object. An object is an abstract description of some kind of data in the system. An example of an object might be a patient record or an ftp proxy.

Each object has a name and a set of public methods that can be used to access the object. The object can only be accessed through the public methods. Object attributes and private methods are hidden and cannot be accessed.

Since the methods are the only way to interact with the application, controlling access to the methods is sufficient to control access to the application [4]. The RBAC framework supports a mechanism for grouping methods into sets that can be assigned to roles. Thus the security policy is built up out of layered sets of methods. Read or write permissions are not associated with objects. A role can either access a method or it cannot.

Method parameters do not need to be included in the access control decision. It is the responsibility of the method creator to ensure that the parameters are valid. For example suppose a parameter value of "DANGER" must only be entered by a supervisor. To capture this in the framework an additional method is created. The new method is identical to the first except that it checks the parameter to ensure it is not "DANGER". The original method can then be assigned to supervisors, while only the new method can be assigned to others.

Each CORBA object is described in an Interface Description Language (IDL) file. The IDL file describes the name of the object and its publicly accessible methods. The Network Application POLicy EnvirONment (NAPOLEON[1]) tool was created to read in IDL files to specify application specific security policy. The NAPOLEON tool is described further in Section 3. DCOM has an object description language similar to IDL.

Organizing objects. The goal of the RBAC framework is to provide enterprise wide security. For an entire enterprise there can be thousands of objects. Thus the objects must be presented to the application developers via some structure.

Clearly the first step is to organize the objects into the applications to which they belong. If an object belongs to more than one application, the object can be treated as a separate application, or service.

Once grouped by application, the objects can be organized by the software modules that contain them. However, to system administrators in the field, organizing objects by

1. NAPOLEON is named after the layered dessert rather than the historical figure.

module does not make much sense, since that is a software engineering construct rather than an administration construct. Thus the objects need to be organized differently based on who is using the framework.

Cascading objects. There is an issue of how the user's identity is used to make access control decisions on secondary objects. Consider a distributed application where one object (*A*) calls another object (*B*) to calculate an answer. *B* may have different access constraints. The RBAC framework requires that object *A*, be aware of any access constraints of any object it uses. *A* is responsible for making sure that object *B* has all the information needed to make its access control decisions. Object *A* must also handle the case where *B* denies access. This approach is in line with good software engineering practices.

2.2. Layer 2 - Object handles

Usually an object has several methods that are often accessed in conjunction. Rather than having to assign each method to a role individually, the methods can be grouped into a set. The set provides a convenient handle for granting access to an object. The object handle has a text description indicating the kind of access represented by this set of methods and how it should be used.

For example, suppose a medical health application has a patient record object that contains the following methods

- getPrimaryPhyscian()
- getDiagnosis()
- setDiagnosis()
- getBloodPressure()
- setBloodPressure()

There may be many roles on the system that need to access all the "get" methods listed above. Thus the methods can be grouped into an object handle called *Read-Only*, with the following description, "Give the user read access to the patient record".

The object handle captures the way the object is used. It is important to make a distinction between an object handle and the methods needed by a particular role. Here is an example of an incorrect use of an object handle. Suppose a handle called *Doctor* was created for a patient record. If the hospital Administrator role needed the same access as the doctor role it would be very confusing to give the Administrator role the *Doctor* handle. A better object handle name would be *Maintainer* or, if the handle contained all the methods, *All* would be a good descriptive name.

2.3. Layer 3 - Application constraints

Roles accurately describe which types of people need access to certain types of objects. However, a complete policy needs to also express which individuals have access to specific object instances. For example, just because the doctor role has a set of accesses to a patient record does not mean the doctor role should access all patient records. A doctor can only access the patient records for those people currently assigned to the doctor.

There have been several approaches for creating an instance level policy for roles [5], [6], [7]. To encompass these approaches we propose that a set of conditions can be specified when an object handle is assigned to a role. These conditions must be satisfied before access is granted to the methods in the handle set.

The scope of the conditions is broad. The conditions can be based on any combination of the following

- attributes of the user accessing the object
- attributes of the object itself [5]
- other records, such as the current emergency room team in a hospital [6]
- time based constraints
- user's history of accesses

Together these constraints can express most security policy conditions.

Complex constraints. Many of the complex constraints discussed in other RBAC models are described in the application constraints layer. For example, consider a dynamic separation of duties policy where the clerk issuing a check cannot be the same clerk who made the check request. An application constraint is placed on the *issueCheck* method to ensure that the user executing the method is not the person listed as the requestor. Other complex constraints, such as time based, or history based constraints can be captured as well.

Most complex constraints are application specific and can be expressed by the application designer. However, the application designer cannot levy any constraints on specific users, or constraints that span several applications. Those constraints are addressed in layer 6 - enterprise constraints.

There are several an open issues regarding the complexity of the constraints. Should the complexity be limited so that the constraint is easy to understand? Should the application developer be allowed to put in arbitrary code? Is there a limit on the complexity of policy that can be enforced? More research is required in this area.

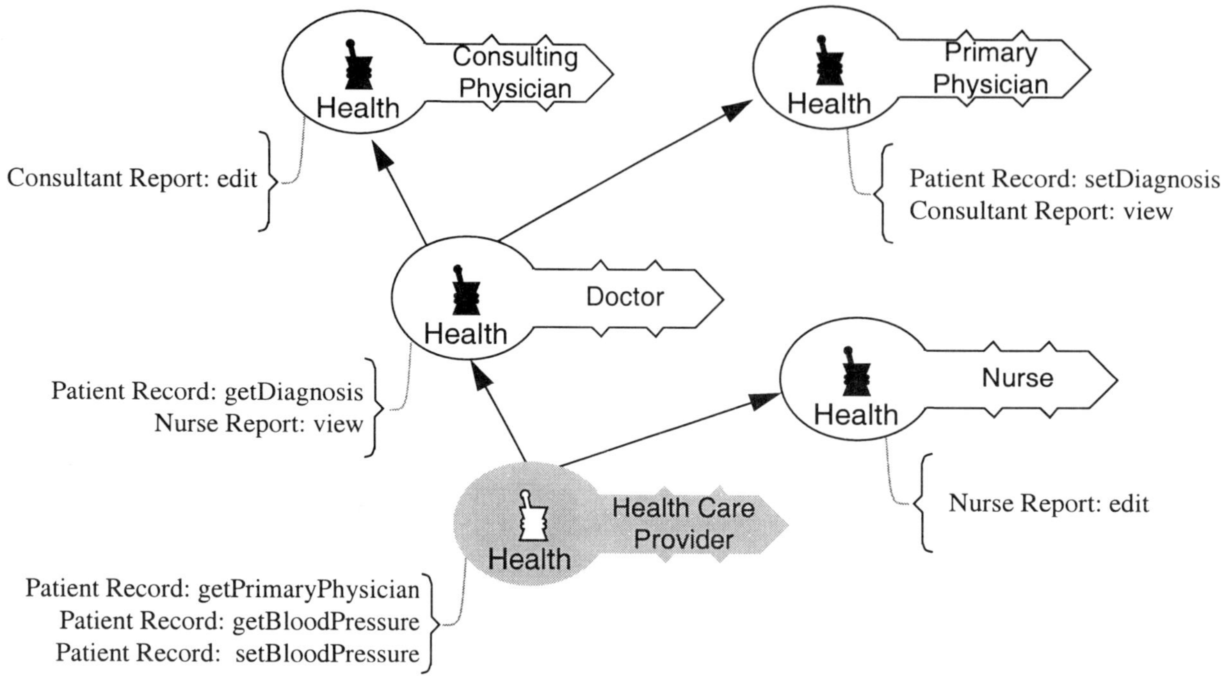

Figure 2. A sample Application key hierarchy showing how methods are inherited, Patient Record, Nurse Report and Consultant Report are objects

2.4. Layer 4 - Application keys

The security information encoded by the application developer needs to be put in an easy to use form for the local system administrator. This collection of security information is an application key. An application key is much like a door key. When a key is given to a user they can access the resources represented by the key. In the RBAC framework application keys are a set of methods and application constraints on those methods. An application key can be considered an application specific role.

A common theme in many RBAC approaches is to have a role hierarchy that is used to capture relationships between roles [3]. The role hierarchy also describes constraints. As mentioned earlier there are two role hierarchies. The first hierarchy is used by the application developer to show the relationship between application keys, and is called the application key hierarchy.

For example in a medical application you might have role relationships similar to Figure 2. The figure indicates that the doctor role has all the privileges of the health care provider, plus privileges unique to the doctor role. Both the consulting and primary physicians have more, but different permission than the doctor.

The application developer must include each method of the application in at least one key, otherwise users would not be able to access that method

Abstract roles. The role hierarchy is similar to an object oriented class hierarchy and has all the benefits and drawbacks of that approach. One example is the concept of abstract roles. Abstract roles are the equivalent of abstract classes in object oriented languages. It is intended that no users be assigned to an abstract role. The abstract role serves as a description of some permissions that other roles can inherit.

For example, a doctor may not inherit all the permissions of a nurse. A nurse may prepare reports that doctors can read but not write. If the doctor role inherited from the nurse role, the doctor role would have the extra permission. Instead an abstract role called health care provider is created that has all the inheritable permissions. No users can be assigned to the health care provider role. Abstract roles provide a way of indicating information about the structure of the role hierarchy.

Multiple inheritance. Another major problem that a object oriented hierarchy faces is multiple inheritance. For the application key hierarchy multiple inherence does not cause a problem.

First consider an application that does not have any application constraints. Each application key consists of a set of methods. If a key inherits from two different keys the two methods sets are combined. This is because if a method is inherited multiple times, there is no ambiguity, since the user can either access the method or not. It does not matter which key the method was inherited from.

If a key inherits from two keys with application constraints there are two possibilities. The first is that the methods do not overlap. In this case the methods and conditions can be combined with no ambiguity. If however, the two keys contain the same method with different constraints, the constraints are logically ORed together. Thus a user may satisfy either constraint to gain access to the method.

2.5. Layer 5 - Enterprise keys

When an application is installed into a network, a description of all its objects and an initial set of application keys are installed in the management tool. This is the first layer in the framework in which users are incorporated. There is a one to one mapping between application keys and enterprise keys, except for abstract keys which do not appear as enterprise keys. Enterprise keys can be assigned to users.

Local system administrators grant access by assigning the enterprise keys to users, see Figure 3. Once assigned the user has access to the object methods listed in the key as long as any application constraints associated with the key are satisfied. Note that keys are not capabilities, and cannot be passed between users.

2.6. Layer 6- Key chains

As the application developers create a role hierarchy to describe the constraints of the application, the local administrators describe their constraints with their own role hierarchy. In keeping with the key theme local system administrators group keys into sets called key chains.

A key chain is simply a collection of enterprise keys. A key chain may contain other key chains. As a result the local system administrator is able to build up a complex hierarchy that fits the needs of their site. For example, if the basic user at the site has access to three applications, those enterprise keys can be group into a single key chain, see Figure 4.

Key chains express the local security policy constraints. The local system administrator can build a policy as complex or as simple as they like by proper structuring of the key chains.

Multiple inheritance for key chains is resolved the same as multiple inheritance in the application key hierarchy.

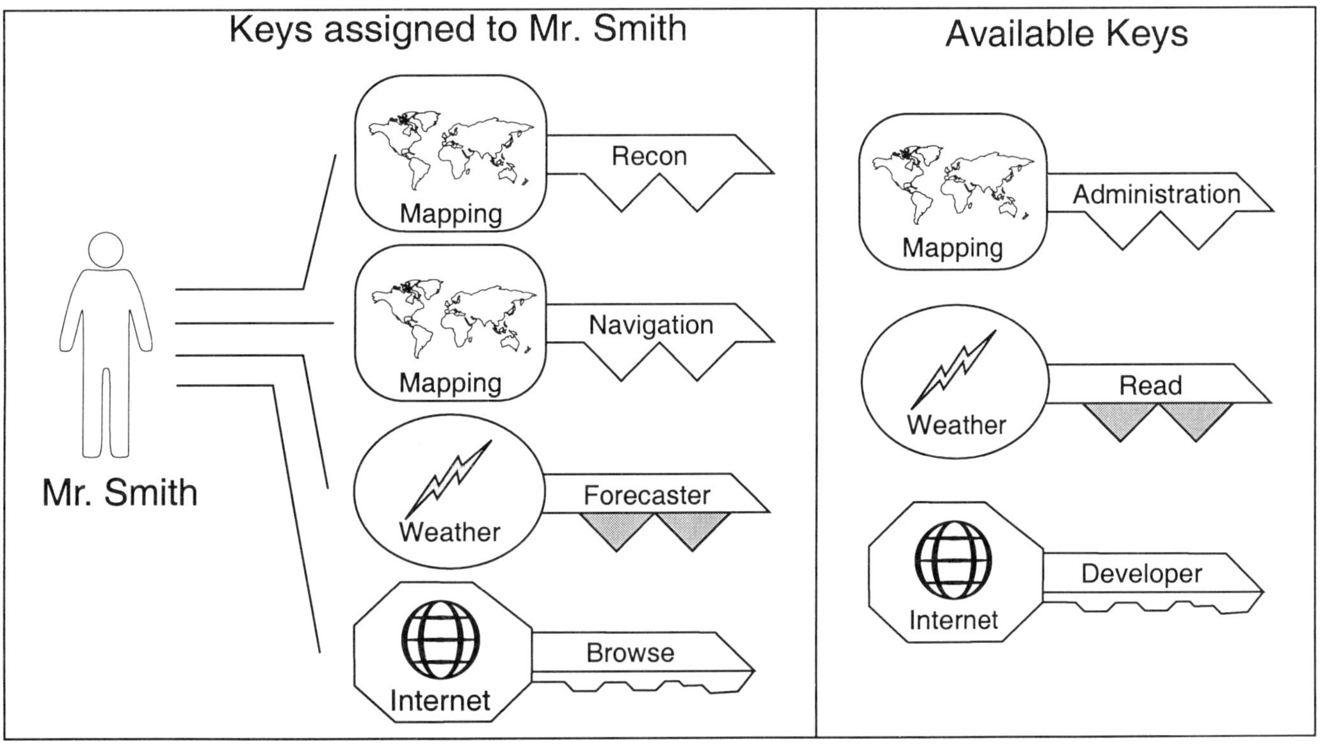

Figure 3. Assigning users access by giving them keys

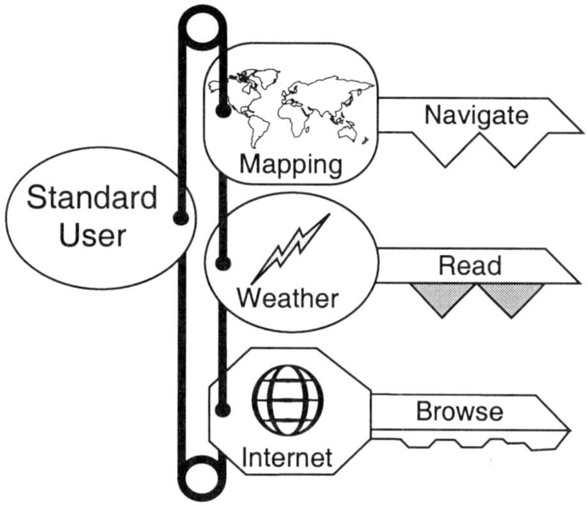

Figure 4. Local system administrators can group keys into key chains

Access to an object is granted as long as one complete set of access constraints is satisfied.

2.7. Layer 7- Enterprise constraints

There are complex enterprise security constraints that only the local system administrator knows. Unlike application constraints that are applied to application keys, enterprise constraints can only be applied to key chains. This is because the enterprise keys are the basic building block, shipped with the application. Allowing constraints to be associated with enterprise keys would confuse later system administrators.

Since enterprise constraints are applied to key chains, the constraints can span several applications. If constructed and managed properly the constraints can span the entire enterprise.

This completes the basic description of the RBAC framework. The next section discuss the NAPOLEON tool that implements portions of the framework.

3. NAPOLEON policy tool

The previous sections discussed a general RBAC framework for providing consistent roles across an enterprise. The NAPOLEON tool implements the portion of the framework used by the application developer.

3.1. NAPOLEON implementation

The current implementation focuses on CORBA applications. NAPOLEON serves as an IDL reader that allows the user to create new application policies, specify and store the policy, and translate the policy into a security enforcement mechanism.

Creating new policies. A new application policy is created by the user selecting an IDL file and assigning it to an application. In CORBA an object is called an interface. Each interface has a description of the publicly accessible

- methods
- read only attributes
- read-write attributes
- inherited interfaces

The RBAC framework only includes methods, so accessing attributes has to be modeled as methods based on the attribute name with read or read-write appended to it. Inherited interfaces basically include methods from other objects with unique names. There is no method overloading in CORBA.

When reading in an IDL file the tool automatically creates an object handle called *ALL* for each object/interface. The *ALL* handle contains all the accessible items in the interface.

Specifying policy. Once the IDL file is loaded the user can start specifying the policy. The user can

- create new object handles (see Figure 5)
- create application keys
- assign object handles to keys

The application keys are the equivalent of application specific roles. However, NAPOLEON does not provide an interface to show the role's hierarchical nature to each other as described in Figure 2. A hierarchy is a convenient design tool, but so far in the examples we have considered the number of application specific roles is small. Thus little benefit is gained by showing the hierarchical relationship between application keys.

Currently the application constraint layer is not implemented. In the future when application constraints are implemented they will be associated with the binding between the object handle and the application key. As the user creates policy components they are stored permanently in a relational database.

Translating the policy. To see the impact of having the application developer design policy pieces, the NAPOLEON prototype was integrated with the Open Group Research Institute's Adage policy tool. Adage provides command line and GUI interfaces for specifying security

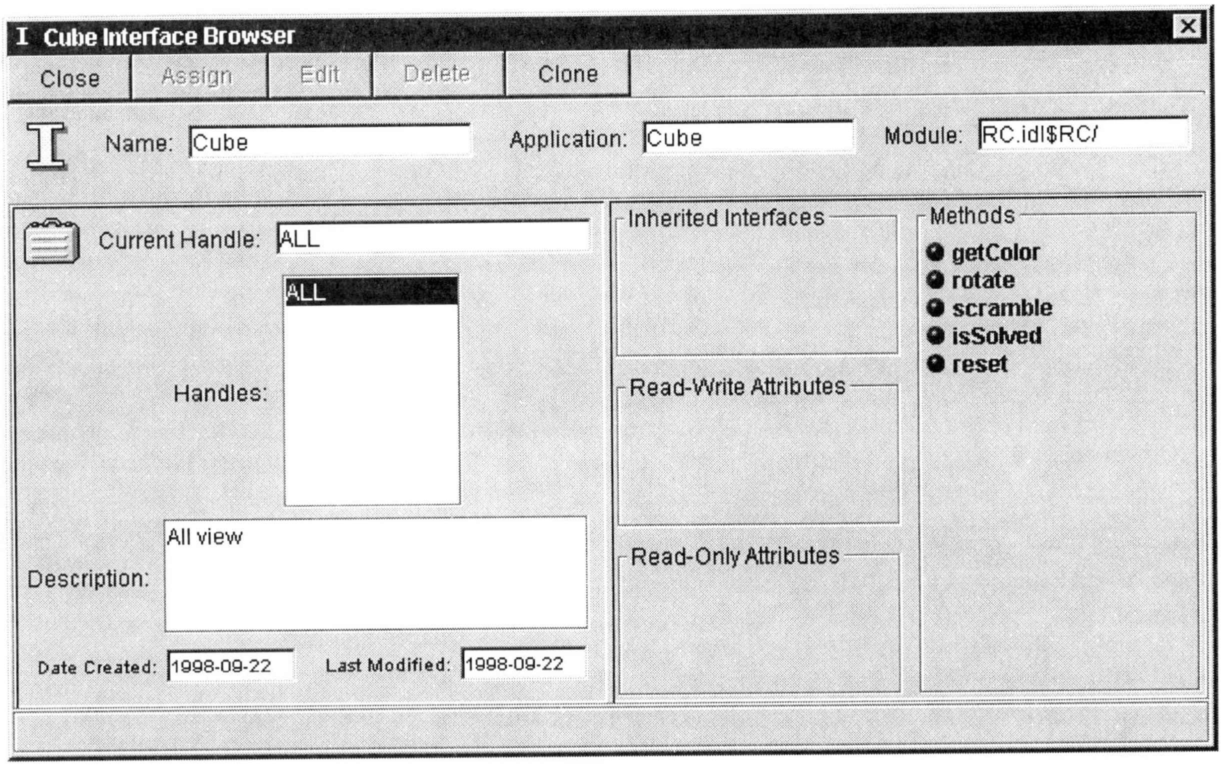

Figure 5. Using the NAPOLEON tool to create object handles.

policies [9]. The application keys created by the developer were translated into Adage rules using the command interface. Then using Adage the local system administrator added users and groups to the NAPOLEON created rules.

Adage also has a decision engine that returns yes/no answers to requests for resources. The decision engine was the target enforcement mechanism. By intercepting CORBA request and rerouting them to the decision engine, we were able to dynamically control access to CORBA object methods.

The NAPOLEON prototype showed that it was extremely useful for portions of the security policy to be designed with the application. The local system administrator was able to implement a fine grained policy in minutes, without having to analyze the application.

3.2. Future prototype work

The most challenging layers of the RBAC framework are the constraint layers. Our next task will be to implement constraints so we can better understand the complexity and challenges placed on the users. We hope to create classes of constraints that make trade-offs between fine grained security and performance. One of the first areas we will look at is having the application designer specify workflow semantics as information flows through the system.

Another area that must be explored is the mapping of security policy to different mechanisms. A complex policy involving history constraints could be expressed in the tool, but could not be enforced by a number of platforms. Handling the loss of fine grained security by translation, must be researched further.

4. Summary

The RBAC framework described in this paper allows for the creation of tight access control policies for the entire enterprise. It allows the incorporation of a wide variety of applications on different hosts with different access control mechanisms.

The approach simplifies the security administration for the enterprise by taking a divide and conquer approach. Security policy managers can focus at the level of detail they are familiar with, modifying details only as necessary. The Napoleon prototype has demonstrated the value of well designed, layered, security building blocks, indicating that the RBAC framework provides a means of balancing the complexity of administrating a large network with the need for controlling security access at a fine level of detail.

References

[1] Orfali R., and Harkey D., "Client/Server Programming with Java and CORBA," Wiley, New York, 1998.

[2] Sessions R., "Com and Dcom: Microsoft's Vision for Distributed Objects," Wiley, New York, December 1997.

[3] Sandhu R.S., Coyne E.J., Feinstein H.L, and Youman C.E. "Role-Based Access Control Models," *Computer*, 29:38-47, Feb 1996.

[4] Barkley J., "Implementing Role-Based Access Control Using Object Technology", *Proc. of the First ACM Workshop on Role-Based Access Control*, pp. II93-II98, November 1995.

[5] Thomsen D. J., "Role Based Application Design and Enforcement," *Database Security, IV Status and Prospects*, edited by S. Jajodia and C.E. Landwehr, pp. 151-168, North Holland, New York 1991.

[6] Thomas R., "Team-Based Access Control (TMAC)," *Proc. Second ACM Workshop on Role-Based Access Control*, pp. 13-22, November, 1997.

[7] Thomas R. K. and Sandhu R. S., "Task-Based Authorization Controls (TBAC): A Family of Models for Active and Enterprise-oriented Authorization Management," Proc. Eleventh Annual IFIP WG 11.3 Working Conference on Database Security, Fall 1997.

[8] Thomsen D. J., "Integrity Issues in Secure Systems," May 1991, Master Thesis, University of Minnesota.

[9] Zurko M. E. and Simon R. T., "User-Centered Security," *New Security Paradigms Workshop*, September 1996.

Concentric Supervision of Security Applications: A New Security Management Paradigm

Philip C. Hyland
TASC, Inc., Ph.D. Candidate, George Mason University
4801 Stonecroft Blvd., Chantilly, VA 20151
Phone: (703) 633-8300 (W), Fax: (703) 449-1080
E-Mail: pchyland@tasc.com, http://mason.gmu.edu/~phyland

Dr. Ravi Sandhu
Professor, Department of Information and Software Systems Engineering
George Mason University, Fairfax, VA 22030-4444
Phone: (703) 993-1659 (W), Fax: (703) 993-1638
E-Mail: sandhu@gmu.edu, http://www.list.gmu.edu/~sandhu

Abstract

This paper questions the status quo regarding Security Management (SM) tools that function in an isolated, monolithic fashion. People work best by interacting with others and with their systems to see the "big picture" to interpret individual events. Our view of SM called Concentric Supervision of Security Applications (CSSA) is a continuous cycle of information flow. CSSA processing of status information and control of security features does not replace existing notions. It serves to enhance the existing ad hoc and segmented "engineered" solutions so that SM systems support "the way people work".

We divide management functions into three phases: administration, operations, and assessment. Different skills, authority, and data are needed to perform tasks in each phase, but some information must flow for efficient and effective functionality. We give suggestions on some linkages by describing typical SM scenarios and how they might function. Parallels are drawn with related issues in network management systems and relationships to current management approaches are discussed.

1. Introduction

Business managers today recognize information system security as a major corporate requirement. Significant research and development effort has produced a variety of security technologies. However, security is not strictly a technology problem; system developers and operators need complete lifecycle solutions that permit reliable implementation of a single, consistent *security policy*. A critical part of a complete security solution — along with security policies and mechanisms — includes *assurance* methods to ensure that security designs and implementations continuously meet the objectives of the security policy.

Assurance spans activities from prevention of design errors and configuration errors during deployment to detection of anomalies during operations and rational recovery from the effects of a security event after it has occurred. A complete security assurance plan would address all phases; however, we confine our discussion here to Security Management (SM) activities after system deployment. We define SM to include the activities to configure, monitor, and control the security services that a system provides. We also shall consider how the administration, operations, and assessment phases of SM can be viewed as analogs of similar functions in the network management community. The great strides in recent years by network managers to actively plan, monitor and control suggests there is a considerable potential for equivalent systemic improvements for management of system and network security.

Current security tools, for the most part, take a very narrow view of SM. Most focus on configuring or controlling particular security mechanisms such as single sign-on, Intrusion Detection Systems (IDS) or key management. Security management must ensure that organizational security responsibilities match up with resources and rules to implement the defined security policy while not inhibiting the normal way people work. The framework we propose, called Concentric Supervision of Security Applications (CSSA), is an end-to-end SM concept that leverages related functions and data in the *administration*, *operations*, and *assessment* phases of management. However, we first consider what components make

0-8186-8789-4/98 $10.00 © 1998 IEEE

up the management of security and how they relate to each other.

2. SM Notions—New and Old

2.1. Assessing Administrative and Operational SM

As technology becomes more complex, we must refine terminology and re-partition problems to understand the issues better and focus attention on solvable pieces. In 1987, the OSI Security Architecture (ISO 7498-2) [**1**] identified three categories of SM — system security management, security service management, and security mechanism management — plus security of management itself. System SM is concerned with overall policy management, interaction with other OSI and SM functions and with general security functions such as event handling, auditing and recovery. Security service management deals with interactions with particular security services such as negotiation of protection levels and mechanisms. Security mechanism management includes management of keys, encipherment, digital signatures, access controls, integrity, authentication, traffic padding, routing control and notarization. Security of management (the main area SNMPv3 [**2**] deals with) defines methods and structures to ensure vital status and control functions are protected.

Although the OSI functional breakdown is useful as a reference model, it does not recognize the typical division of duties between system administrators, security managers, and systems operators. In contrast, we postulate three major phases of SM that distinguish the desirable characteristics of a management framework, namely administration, operations and assessment of security. In CSSA, we further consider SM from the view of *who* is involved, the *purpose* of their activities, and the *types of information* affected. Our intent is to indicate that different assumptions, rules-of-thumb and tools are applicable in each phase, thus justifying our subdivision of the discipline.

As a starting point, **Figure One** shows one view of the essential SM components. All systems function under a security policy (even if it is null). From the security policy, a security administration process defines configuration *rules* that specify security subsystem behavior. This process supports operational SM (represented by the traffic light labeled "Control Entities") which controls one or more security mechanisms. These mechanisms provide on-line security services that actually affect security clients. The feedback path from status sensors to the control entity provides operational health and anomaly detection information. This feedback is a resource that enables the value-added tools of security assessment.

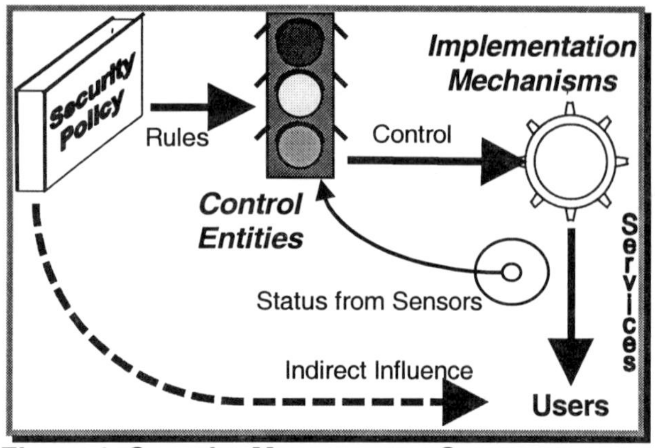

Figure 1. Security Management Components

The assessment phase is not visible in **Figure One** because it has largely been an off-line, human process due to the time and processing demands. The important concept is to use dynamic feedback to modify the security posture as events occur and the perceived security threats change.

In fact, there are two major shortfalls with this initial view of SM. First, nothing in **Figure One** integrates the management of security mechanisms together into a unified, coordinated capability. In other words, each mechanism might have its own parallel rules, configuration process and control structure that does not interact or benefit from others. Second, there is no lifecycle view of the SM process that ensures configuration data, operational data and historical audit/performance data can all be accessed and assessed to support continuous improvement. The security policy should be the starting point of a spiral of dynamic rules that adjust and improve the security posture based on current conditions, the time of day or week, and the perceived vulnerability. We believe a common SM framework will help resolve these data management issues and thereby bring more effective and mutually supporting management to security devices and applications.

The objective of assurance is effectiveness. SM tries to ensure that the security services delivered are adequate and compliant with the organization's security policy while minimizing the administrative overhead. As **Figure Two** depicts, CSSA consists of three phases with data in the middle. It operates in a repeated cycle, always seeking a secure management state.

Administrative SM can include pre-operational system development and testing, but we focus here on the *user-driven* configuration activities of system installation, setup, and maintenance. Administration minimizes system vulnerabilities by opening system access enough to meet users' needs while purposely constraining certain activities to satisfy the applicable security policy. Administrative activities are often done in a batch mode since immediate response time is not expected. Adminis-

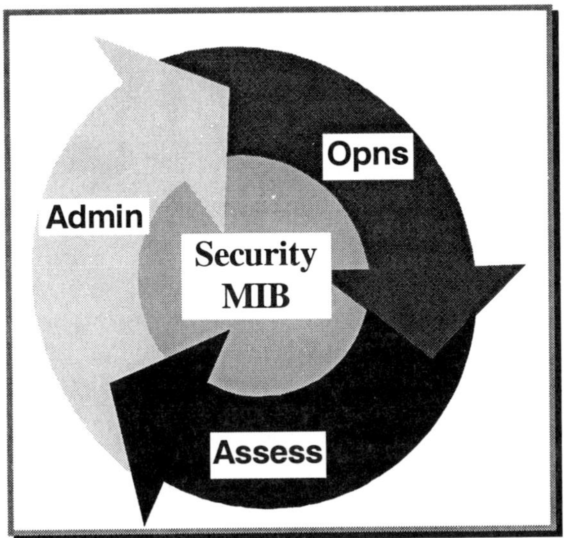

Figure 2. Concentric Supervision Cycle

trative security actions may be stopped or interrupted for a period without degrading security. In other words, administrative SM is relatively routine and part of the normal day-to-day functioning of the enterprise.

Differences between administrative SM and operational SM are evident especially in their purposes. Operational SM is a more active, *event-driven* component of assurance that is concerned with detection and reaction to current conditions applicable to security mechanisms. Operational SM consists of real-time interactions between the security *service providers* (mechanisms), *status sensors* and *control entities.*

Tools should be designed to monitor and maintain security posture at levels defined by the established security policy. As the desired protection level increases, the corresponding management functions must become more stringent (see **Table One**). For example, at level C, access control defined by Ad3 would be more restrictive than for level B and below. Likewise, operational thresholds may be tighter and assessment responses more conservative. Operational SM exists to detect noncompliance with security policy; thus, operational management tools must be sensitive and continuously available to reliably track and respond to unpredictable security events.

Table 1. Security Protection Levels

Security Level	Administration	Opns	Assessment
A	Ad1	O1	A1
B	Ad2	O2	A2
C	Ad3	O3	A3

The assessment phase of SM is *performance-driven*; that is, it is concerned with measuring whether objectives are met and how potential changes may affect the security system. Evaluation of audit trails and pattern matching are assessment activities. Such assessments may have short-term or long-term scope. Short-term, quick response assessments generally support reaction to imminent threats detected during the operations phase. Based on other events correlated in time, space, or modus operandi, an appropriate response is initiated or recommended to an operator. Long-term assessment may support security policy planning, trend analysis of threats, or quality of protection issues. A simulation tool may test a proposed administration state against a range of operational conditions to assess its desirability.

2.2. Existing Management Architectures and Related Work

The foregoing concepts do not detract from the work that has been done in many areas of the security management challenge. IDS research has been a major thrust while configuration-checking tools such as COPS, and SATAN have improved the security position of many sites. Several major commercial products such as CA Unicenter TNG, Sun Security Manager, and Tivoli TME10 do support SM functions within their management architectures, but none view management as a continuous cycle of activities as we have suggested. The OSI Security Architecture has little sense of temporal issues or sharing data between administration, operations, and assessment functions. Other more generic management models such as SNMPv3, the DCE security management framework [**3**], and two European research projects (SAMSON [**4**] and SMCN [**5**]) focus mostly on protocols and operational tools for a few security mechanisms. Notably, the "Security Mechanisms for Computer Networks" project (1985-1990) included security management in its Comprehensive Integrated Security System (CISS) design. CISS emphasizes use of existing mechanisms and APIs for common security functions. Of the ten functional agents identified in CISS, two are devoted to security administration functions, two provide general support to all components, and six support operational SM.

3. Elements of CSSA

We organize management functions into three phases because similar data, processing, and skills are used in each phase. In this section, we present details of how CSSA phases mutually support each other.

3.1. Administration

The administration phase includes both initial configuration of security services and routine updates to add, delete, or modify user and resource information. The authority for such actions must be carefully controlled and audited. Before updates are applied, crosschecks for compliance with security policy should occur. This implies a security policy that has been tuned to a set of guiding principles. If the security policy is defined as a set of management rules, this process may be automated. Otherwise, a manual checklist procedure can verify consistency of changes.

Some configuration parameters apply widely (e.g. current security level) while others are relevant only to specific security mechanisms (e.g. key expiration date). In many cases, important data for user authentication, key distribution, access control, security filters, and directory services will be stored in one or more databases. The CISS model calls the aggregation of all security management data the Security Management Information Base (SMIB). **Figure Three** shows the types of SMIB access during each management phase. Administration involves mostly writing of data, while operations phase is equally read-write and assessment is mostly read-only. Some assessment results may be passed to administration for action or saved for future use.

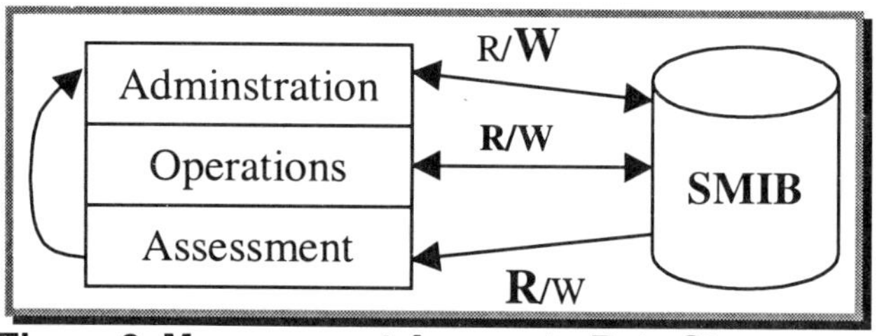

Figure 3. Management Access to Data Store

A common means to access and update configuration data is important. Security mechanisms that do not implement a structured data store like the SMIB and a secure means of access must use a local configuration file for vital management data. This leads to inconsistency among applications and requires a proxy to interface with the control entity using standard protocols.

Suitable control over the integrity and correctness of security configuration information is vital to compliance with a security policy. Delegation of authority to make changes needs to be very fine-grained. Senior security administrators may need full authority to update configuration, operational and assessment roles and privileges while delegating local tasks, such as user account updates and modification of access lists for local resources to subordinate security managers. *Least privilege* facilitates decentralization without giving too much power to any individual.

Administrative management also may be viewed as a workflow problem. A sequence of steps and crosschecks can be designed to ensure proper authority and compliance with policy rules. Although space prevents full details here, the process can be reduced to a set of Integration Definition (IDEF) diagrams. Relationships become complex if the security policy requires special measures such as two-person authorization (i.e. for database updates) or Chinese wall access controls. Separation of duties permits independence while enforcing integrity checks for roles in which one person could have undue authority.

3.2. Operations

Operational SM is characterized by real-time interaction with security components that provide security services to end-users. Management tools for security operations need several capabilities such as real-time interactive control, detection and alarm mechanisms, event logging and correlation, and graphical display systems. In addition, limited access to configuration and historical data would make trouble-shooting and problem prevention easier. For example, a system operator should have read access to contact information for any user within their domain and should have write access to certain configuration data within their responsibilities. Consequently, the operator would be able to notify the user of an alert from a certification authority that their certificate is near expiration.

The driving force in design of operational SM is dealing with active or suspected security threats. Like the performance and fault management functions within the field of network management, operational SM has a strong temporal factor. Monitoring the real-time status of performance and component health, along with tracking of security events is necessary to permit active responses to changing conditions. For example, in a benign security environment, an indication from a network component sensor of a performance bottleneck might result in the control element setting a more permissive filtering stance (i.e. reduced logging). This would improve performance until the backlog is reduced. On the other hand, exceeding a security monitoring threshold (such as number of repetitive logon failures) that might signal an attack may justify increased event logging, alarms to system operators, or automated responses to deter damage to system integrity.

3.3. Assessment

In many ways, the assessment phase is the most critical in creating an effective management system. It is the essence of intrusion detection research. It is the chief feedback loop to modify system attributes based on current conditions. Events that are detected and recorded during operations need to be matched against known patterns, related targets, or even similar times of occurrence. Depending on the danger and uncertainty of an event, immediate or long-term configuration changes may be effected. Context is significant. Certain threats may trigger pre-determined responses such as session termination, increased monitoring, or deception mechanisms. Unfamiliar or uncertain events should result in more cautious and conservative actions. Artificial intelligence methods are helpful in correlating similar situations. A major benefit of a centralized management approach is the capability to evaluate individual events against a broader system view and more sophisticated software on higher performance systems than possible with many dispersed nodes. On the other hand, an assessment approach with a distributed correlation database may provide needed redundancy and scalability.

Assessment is not necessarily a static process. As was indicated in **Table One**, the security level may drive a more aggressive stance as perceived vulnerability grows (i.e. before a new product release or during sensitive negotiations). In this way, the SM system becomes more proactive, in contrast to its traditional reactive style.

4. SM Notions in Action

Why is a distinction between management of security administration, operations, and assessment important? Different people and priorities are involved, but sharing and evaluating common data can vastly improve overall management. To achieve the goal of an integrated SM architecture, both the administrative and operational environments must be understood and supported. Finally, the role of assessment in the context of configuring and monitoring security mechanisms to comply with an overall security policy is vital.

Now we present a few examples to highlight the difficulties of trying to integrate security management. We consider some simple, but practical applications that justify our Concentric Supervision of Security Applications (CSSA) concept. We will determine where sharing data between the configuration, operational, and assessment phases is currently possible and where it is problematic.

4.1. Virus Alert

Our first scenario begins with a security incident detected by a security mechanism during normal operations. At 3:40 PM, an automated virus checker identifies and reports a virus imbedded in an email message sent to Alice from the XMU.edu domain. As an active security mechanism, the virus checker supports the operations component of CSSA by generating a notification to the control entity as shown in **Figure Four**.

In the first stage of reaction to a notification, the event manager (dispatcher) module logs pertinent information (see **Table Two**) and starts an audible alarm at the network operator's console. The network operator, if on

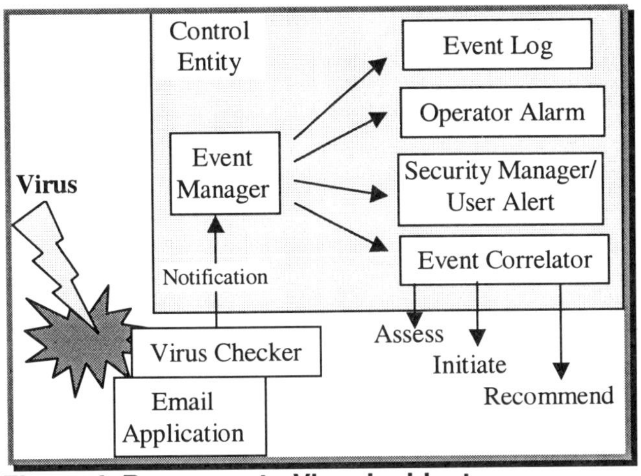

Figure 4. Response to Virus Incident

duty, reacts according to the severity of the alert and the importance of other on-going activities. In addition, the event manager alerts the security officer via email (or pager) to review whether current actions are appropriate and whether executive management needs to be informed.

In a cooperative environment, peer monitoring sites may be alerted about information that could represent a low-key, but broad-scale attack. Optionally, application users (email sender and recipient) may be notified. In some cases, this notification may be undesirable because it may reveal more than desired about the response capabilities.

Lastly, but most importantly, the event manager signals the event correlator to evaluate the incident. The signal to the correlator represents transition into the next phase of CSSA cycle, security assessment. The event manager forwards data from the initial notification. The event correlator uses this data and information extracted from the event log, including alerts from peer control entities, to evaluate and recommend a course of action congruent to the desired security level.

The correlator may initiate some protective measures automatically through interim configuration updates. It leaves recommendations for weightier policy or configuration changes for human action. Automated updates may include damage mitigation that requires immediate action

Table 2. Event Notification/Logging Format

Name	Value
Source Address	IP Address of reporting entity
Type of Alarm	Security Event
Date/Time Stamp	Date Time Group (DTG)
Severity Level	(Critical, Major, Immediate, Warning, Minor, Informational)
SubEvent Type	Virus detection
Suspected Source	IP Address, Domain, USERID
Comment Field	Additional event-specific details

to prevent further damage. Examples of conservative responses might include disabling email from the suspected source address or isolating an infected disk volume. Care is needed to ensure protective measures do not cause unintentional denial of service that is more harmful than the original incident.

When the correlator recommends a particular operator action, the operator may not respond promptly or at all. Based on operator history, the security level, and the event severity, the response may be automated. Suppose another virus originated 3 months earlier from the same XMU.edu domain. In this case, changes to the security policy or baseline configuration may be appropriate. Since XMU.edu is not a vital business partner, the event correlator chooses to block all traffic from that domain. At this point, the relevant commands and information pass from the assessment phase into the administration phase of the CSSA cycle.

In the administration phase, a security administrator typically sets and updates parameters that control the operations of security mechanisms to match the security policies of the organization. In the CSSA concept, all security events can potentially result in configuration changes. An automated configuration change initiated in the assessment phase may bypass the manual process when necessary. Non-urgent changes are reviewed by the security management and implemented by the security administrator. All changes are logged as an internal security event. Since internal security events are not assessed by the event correlator, this completes the scenario. **Figure Five** shows the sequence of processing through all phases of our model.

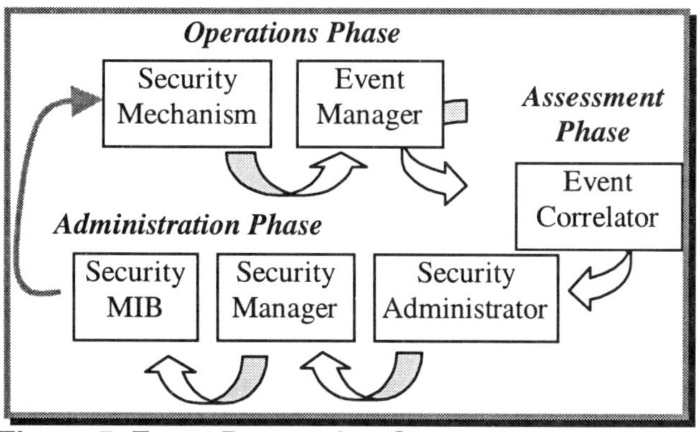

Figure 5. Event Processing Sequence

4.2. Remote Site Firewall

In scenario two, Bob is configuring the firewall component for a new remote office LAN as outlined in **Figure Six**. Proxy services need to be implemented based on the corporate security policy specified in **Box 1**.

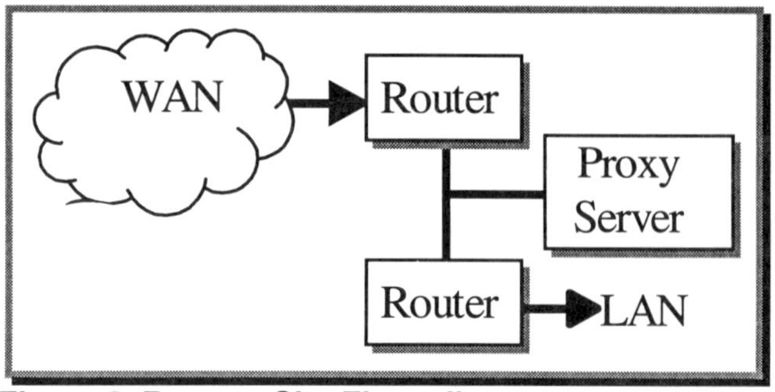

Figure 6. Remote Site Firewall

Typical Internet and Intranet services will include a local Email server, internal FTP to the corporate FTP server, outgoing HTTP and Telnet, and Domain Name Services (DNS). Because of the small size of the branch office and a desire to minimize costs, the firewall setup will use router-based packet filtering and the TIS Firewall Tool Kit (FWTK).

Design of packet filtering rules and implementation of appropriate proxy services is a daunting task, even for an experienced network engineer. Although some vendors have delivered configuration tools to simplify definition of rules, consistency across vendors is low. This leads to errors, inconsistencies, and vulnerabilities without a reliable means of verification. Existing tools do not use common conventions and all store their configuration data in different formats.

Given that an initial security configuration has been developed, the next step is to install and test it. This

Box 1. Security Policy

1. All services not specifically required for operations will be disabled.
2. All email and ftp traffic to/from government sites will be encrypted.
3. Strong authentication is required for dial-up remote access service (RAS).
4. Incoming TELNET and FTP is prohibited except for FTP to the FTP server on the bastion host.
5. Passwords and user keys must be updated at least every six months, must be at least 8 characters and be of medium randomness.
6. System administrators must re-validate all accounts at least every six months.
7. No auto forwarding of email is permitted to external accounts.
8. All outgoing email will be checked for security releasability (dirty word check).
9. All incoming email, ftp and http traffic will be virus checked
10. No site access is permitted from non-US domains.
11. More than three security events from a single domain will require explicit authorization for continued access.

process opens new possibilities for errors and undiscovered faults due to limited testing rigor. While a number of vulnerability testing tools such as COPS, Tiger, and SATAN have been useful to detect configuration problems, they are static and do not test configurations against local security policies. In addition, none uses local security events as input to dynamically tailor assessments. That would require standardized security policy formats, common event and configuration parameter definitions, and new verification tools.

Another approach for validating security configurations is simulation of the operational environment using modeling tools. A simulation environment for security management comparable to those that exist for network modeling would permit the effect of changes to be considered under a broad range of assumptions about the threats and vulnerabilities. Mechanisms could be evaluated under increasing levels of stress to determine performance and points of failure. Such a simulation environment has not been attempted yet and would require modules to simulate each category of security mechanism. Standard parameters must be created to define critical performance capabilities and measurables.

Once the validation of a newly developed security configuration is complete, approval and deployment can proceed. Audit records must capture who makes each change, when, why and how secondary approval (i.e. the security manager) was accomplished. This information becomes a permanent part of the site security log for future reference.

4.3. Security Guard

In our final scenario, a government agency is planning for management of a security device that will provide a trusted interface between systems at two different security levels. **Figure Seven** shows the main components of a security guard. Active supervision of the information security guard function will minimize risk, but minimal human interaction is also desired. Typically, a semi-automated review process may include automated checks

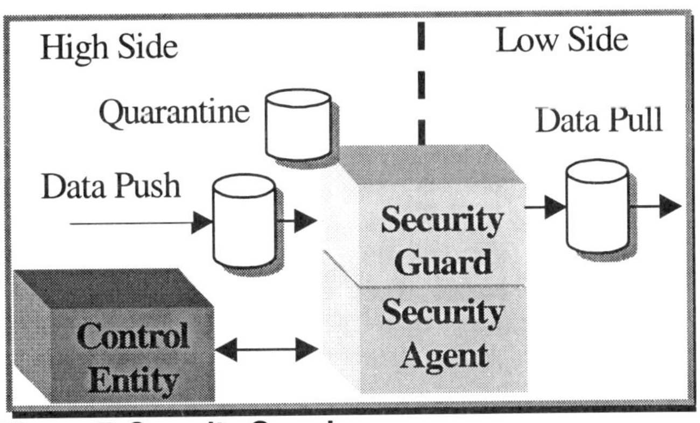

Figure 7. Security Guard

for data integrity, template matching and filtering for unreleasable words or phases, followed with a final human review of images or graphics.

In the present case, a security guard with highly advanced releasability evaluation software will operate to permit only properly marked, formatted, and signed data items to pass from the higher security domain to the lower domain. The guard will operate independently given a proper configuration, but will generate status and alarm information to indicate its operational health and any abnormal conditions. To minimize the logic required within the security guard, the CSSA monitoring actions will be initiated by the control entity except for security event notifications.

The first task before beginning operations of the security guard is to configure required parameters. There are two types of parameters-mechanism configuration data and user data. The first type of data determines how the security device will communicate and operate. User data is used in the basic guard functions to validate releasable data. **Table Three** lists some representative data items. Configuration data that is unique to the security guard may be stored locally for immediate access. Since user data may be used by several mechanisms besides the guard, it is stored in the SMIB and accessed on demand. The list of authorized releasers and their public keys helps to document an audit trail of release actions using digital signatures.

Table 3. Configuration Parameters

Performance Data	User Data
Notification Destination(s)	Authorized Releasers
Control Entity Public Key(s)	Public Keys of Releasers
Agent Private Key	Approved Destinations
Throughput Threshold	Custom Filter Data
Input Buffer Threshold	Template Value Data

Once configured, the security guard can be tested and placed into operations. To monitor the guard operations for maximum benefit, two measures of quality are paramount. The first priority in security applications is effectiveness of the solution. Therefore, the number of false negatives (releases allowed that should not have been) should be nearly zero (fewer than a human would allow). This prevents catastrophic failures that negate all potential benefits of the system. The number of false positives (releases prevented that were okay) should be low also. This factor determines how efficient the system is. If too many releases are stopped when subsequent manual review shows no problem, it indicates inadequate intelligence in evaluation algorithms. Manual review results in lower efficiency and slower payback. Once accredited as effective and certified as efficient, system operations can begin.

The configuration data defined above is used during operations to guide how the security guard functions. If a buffer for data nears capacity, an alert may be generated to the control entity to slow input. If the throughput of the guard and the security threat are low, then less restrictive processing may be set. For example, if several files are backlogged while waiting processing, time-consuming steps may be skipped to speed things up.

Other events may signal the control entity of problems like quarantined files that fail security screening and requiring human intervention. Reasons for flagging files and the results of manual evaluations can be logged and translated into revised configuration data that will permit better processing in the future. Even if tools to implement the cyclic processing of security management data are not highly automated, the process of continuous feedback and rule enhancement should improve responsiveness and quality of operations over time. The critical factor for enhancing system performance is to use assessment results to update configuration parameters or relevant security policies. While the feedback process may occur manually, synergies can grow as automation permits better linkages between CSSA phases and security applications.

4.4. Network Management Parallels

Since SM is considered a component of the network management framework, there are bound to be some similarities between them. The increasing number of security devices in need of integrated management tools can be compared to the state of network management several years ago. SM implementation is fragmented and proprietary, much like network management was prior to emergence of the standards-based SNMP and CMIP [**6**] communities.

Since then, network management has advanced hugely within three development areas. SNMP and CMIP still deal mainly in operational network management, along with some aspects of network administration (i.e. accounting and configuration). Although fault management is a big part of network management, standards do not define administrative aspects such as trouble ticket systems. The third part of network management is network engineering and performance assessment. Recent efforts have enabled use of operational network performance data as input to design analysis and performance modeling tools. In a way, this provides a feedback path like the one we suggest for SM whereby operational data can influence the initial configuration. From these trends in network management, we can argue that SM needs to move toward standards to spur more development of integrated tools for administration, operations, and assessment/planning.

Both security and network management involve troubleshooting to determine cause-effect relationships of events of unclear origin. Just as good configuration and asset management helps network managers during troubleshooting, operational SM stands to gain from better security administration. Security administration is a necessary investment in user and resource identification, privilege assignment, and system security configuration. In an environment of partial knowledge, both network and security management need the ability to sift through events in the past or in other parts of the network to detection patterns in audit trails and event logs. This enables full exploitation of computer-assisted SM by using feedback to update configuration data.

Security and network management processes both must allow human operators to view current status in the context of past actions and related configuration information to guide operators toward rational changes. To do so, operational SM systems may use secure components of an existing network management system to perform data collection/display and support assessment and decision support functions. Below we discuss the supporting components and functions that are necessary to deliver the features of CSSA.

5. CSSA Infrastructure

The CSSA concept requires a number of support capabilities, some of which exist and some which do not. **Figure Eight** is an overview of the required components.

5.1. Components

Administration functions are located in the upper left corner of **Figure Eight.** This is where the administration manager adjudicates access to the security policy, authentication data and access rights, etc. This data may be stored centrally in a SMIB or secure directory, at distributed security mechanisms, or both. Existing network management standards do not specify MIB modules for security applications (e.g. a Firewall MIB) or how MIB data is physically stored. The SMIB may comprise access control lists and security policies, as well as active security status information. Our work indicates MIB definitions must be closely aligned with application functionality; however, a standard data access API and certain core parameters for the SMIB could simplify development of SM development by enabling use of common modules. Wide availability and open standards should be the main drivers of any choice.

The core of the operational management function is the security event manager. This module makes first-level decisions on how to handle notifications of security events and mechanism status. Next to the event manager in **Figure Eight** is the Management Protocol Interface

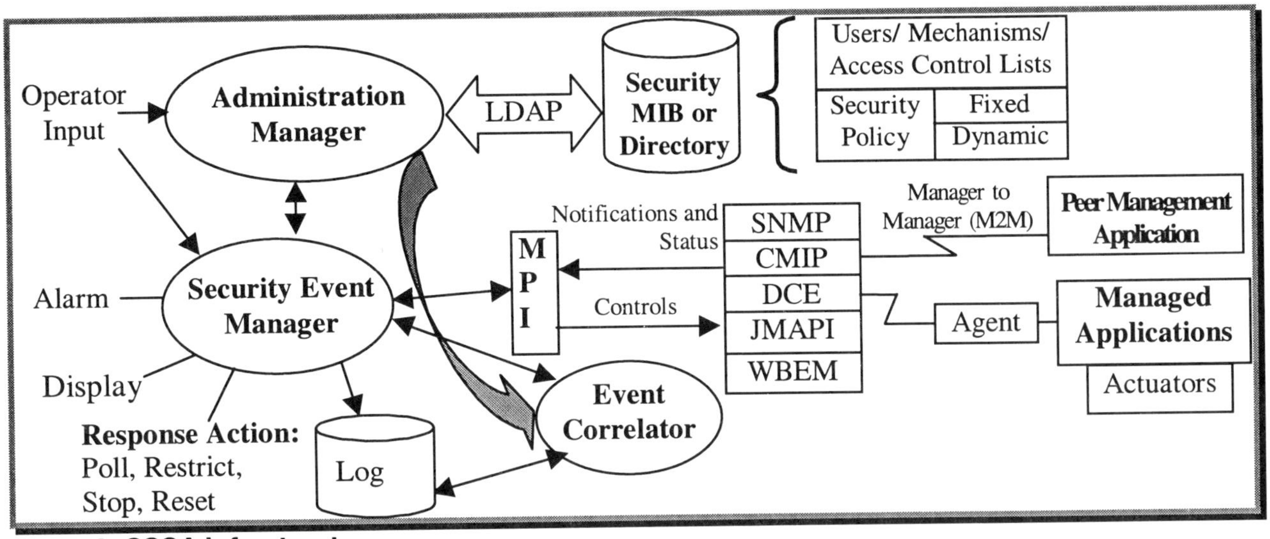

Figure 8. CSSA Infrastructure

(MPI) module. The MPI translates to/from selected management protocols that generate commands (controls) and receive notification and status information from external applications or peer management nodes. The X/Open Management Protocol (XMP) [7] was developed to provide similar functions for SNMP and CMIP.

Assessment functions are represented by the event correlator module. It uses current event data, SMIB data, and historical information from security logs to determine complex patterns and trends. Ongoing work on pattern-matching engines and intrusion detection methods [**8**] fit into this role nicely. The bi-directional arrow to/from the correlator implies that it generates recommendations based on its analysis of incoming events and the current security posture. Recommendations may involve policy updates, mechanism configuration changes, or access control actions.

A fundamental need for the CSSA is a means of secure transactions between many security mechanisms and one or more control entities. In **Figure Eight**, we show several candidate interface protocols (e.g. SNMPv3, CMIP, DCE etc.). More than one may be used to operate in a mixed environment. Below we describe some possible sequences.

5.2. Secure Transactions

A typical transaction sequence such as associated with the virus checker scenario would begin with the managed application signaling an event to its local agent (see **Figure Nine**).

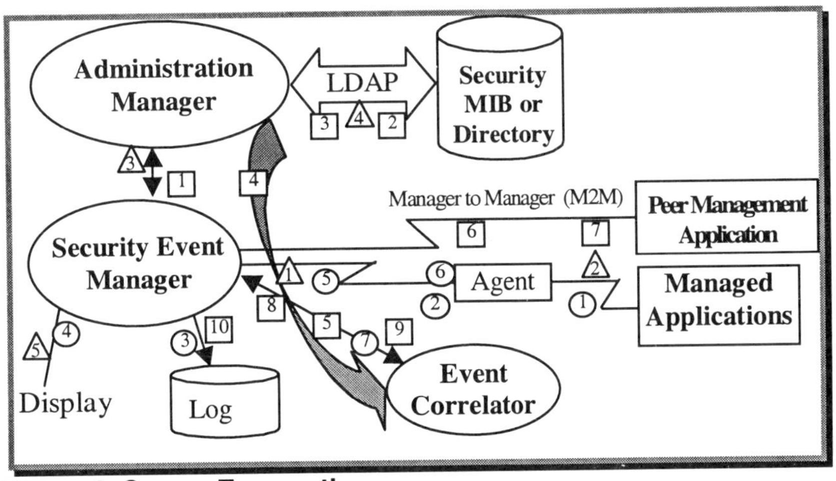

Figure 9. Secure Transactions

The steps listed below in three groupings are keyed to **Figure Nine**. They comprise actions to share data in support of the operations, assessment, and (re)configuration phases.

Operations Phase:

① **Signal**: Managed Application > Device Agent
② **SNMP Trap**: Device Agent >MPI >Event Mgr
③ **Log Record**: Event Mgr > Log
④ **Display Status Change**: Event Mgr >Display
⑤ **SNMP Poll**: Event Mgr >MPI >Device Agent
⑥ **SNMP Bulk GET**: Agent > MPI >Event Mgr
⑦ **Event Data**: Event Mgr > Event Correlator

Note that steps ① through ④ represent the initial alert. Steps ⑤ and ⑥ are actions by the event manager to gather additional details of the event that are not in the alert message. Such actions are typical of many network management systems.

Assessment Phase:

1. **Data Request**: Event Correlator > Admin Mgr
2. **LDAP Access**: Admin Mgr > SMIB
3. **LDAP Response**: SMIB > Admin Mgr
4. **Configuration Data**: Admin Mgr > Correlator
5. **Data Request**: Event Correlator > Event Mgr
6. **CMIP GET**: Event Mgr > MPI >CMIP Agent
7. **CMIP Response**: CMIP Agent >MPI >Event Mgr
8. **External Data**: Event Mgr > Correlator
9. **Assessment Result**: Correlator > Event Mgr
10. **Log Record**: Event Mgr > Log

In the assessment phase, the event correlator first initiates a request for similar data from the SMIB. Steps 6 and 7 represent an optional request to an external management node for related event information. This data could show evidence of a distributed, but coordinated probe or attack. The correlator passes assessment results back to the event manager for logging and possible action.

Configuration Phase:

1. **SNMP SET**: Event Mgr >MPI >Device Agent
2. **Local Change**: Device Agent > Managed Appl
3. **Configuration Update**: Event Mgr > Admin Mgr
4. **LDAP Write**: Administration Mgr > SMIB
5. **Display Status Change**: Event Mgr > Display

If configuration changes are deemed necessary, data is sent to the managed application using a SNMP SET operation and to the administration manager to update the SMIB. Not shown above are possible steps for operator or administrator interactions to control specific changes.

5.3. Areas with Good Research Potential

Several topics related to SM and CSSA need further development to attain the critical mass seen in network management. One weakness that strains system administration resources is ease of configuration and upkeep. Lack of consistency, common tools, and shared services (e.g. directory services) contribute to this problem. Standardized SMIB definitions for key applications (e.g. firewalls) would help vendors to move toward standard interfaces and interoperable tools.

The SMIB (or secure directory) repository enables structured data sharing. Common methods for storing SMIB data would enable better interoperability. Direct access to the SMIB is restricted to the trusted administration module; however, role-based access could be useful. A unified SMIB access module might use the Lightweight Directory Access Protocol (LDAP) or other distributed data archive.

A third area that may benefit from additional research is use of simulation methods to assess a potential security system for adequate protection. Virtual security systems could be tested at various threat levels and traffic conditions to determine processing loads and reaction to high stress situations. Integration with operational systems may lead to real-time feedback.

6. Conclusion

The increasing need for SM is clear as the number of security devices and applications grow. Current methods of manual access control and system security configuration are labor intensive and error-prone. To support the needs of organizational policy and operational SM, closely integrated tools for security administration and real-time operations are needed. Increasing complexity and sophisticated attacks make better assessment methods a priority.

As a contribution toward a cohesive security management framework, we proposed a three-phase CSSA lifecycle. While some pieces do exist, further work is required to refine the specific data needs in each phase, design the structure of SMIB data to be shared, and establish a standard data management API for information distributed among modules. Our proposed feedback process should lead to significantly enhanced security levels as developers adapt tools to share information between the SM phases more effectively.

7. References:

[1] International Standards Organization, Information Processing Systems – OSI Reference Model. Part 2: Security Architecture, ISO/TC 97 7498-2, 1988.

[2] Harrington, D., Presuhn, R., and Wijnen, B., "An Architecture for Describing SNMP Management Frameworks", Request for Comments: 2271, SRI International, Ravenswood, CA, January 1998.

[3] Common Security: CDSA and CSSM, ISBN 1-85912-194, The Open Group, 1997.

[4] Lechner, S., "SAMSON: Management of Security in Open Systems", `Computer Communications, July 1994.

[5] Muftic, Sean, et al, Security Architecture for Open Distributed Systems, Wiley and Sons, New York, 1993.

[6] International Standards Organization, Information Processing Systems – Common Management Information Protocol Specification, ISO/IEC 9596, 1989.

[7] Systems Management: Management Protocols API (XMP), The Open Group, ISBN 1-85912-027-X, 1994.

[8] Lunt, T., et al, A real-time Intrusion Detection Expert System (IDES) - Final Report, SRI International, Menlo Park, CA, February 1992.

Track B: Panel Session

The Common Criteria and Protection Profiles

Moderator

M. Abrams, The MITRE Corporation

Track A

Information Infrastructure

Chair

L. Notargiacomo, Trusted Computer Solutions

Application-Level Isolation to Cope With Malicious Database Users*

Sushil Jajodia[1,2] Peng Liu[2] Catherine D. McCollum[1]

[1]The MITRE Corporation
McLean, VA 22102-3481
{jajodia, mccollum}@mitre.org

[2]Center for Secure Information Systems
and
Department of Information and Software Engineering
George Mason University
Fairfax, VA 22030-4444
{jajodia, pliu}@isse.gmu.edu

Abstract

System protection mechanisms such as access controls can be fooled by authorized but malicious users, masqueraders, and misfeasors. Intrusion detection techniques are therefore used to supplement them. The capacity of these techniques, however, is limited: innocent users may be mistaken for malicious ones while malicious users stay at large. Isolation is a method that has been applied to protect systems from damage while investigating further. This paper proposes the use of isolation at an application level to gain its benefits while minimizing loss of resources and productive work in the case of incidents later deemed innocent. We describe our scheme in the database context. It isolates the database transparently from further damage by users suspected to be malicious, while still maintaining continued availability for their transactions. Isolation is complicated by the inconsistencies that may develop between isolated database versions. We present both static and dynamic approaches to identify and resolve conflicts. Finally, we give several examples of applications in which the isolation scheme should be worthwhile and be able to achieve good performance.

*Jajodia and McCollum were supported by Air Force Research Laboratory/Rome under agreement number F19628-94-C-0001E.

1 Introduction

Recently there has been increasing emphasis on supplementing protection of networks and information systems with intrusion detection [7, 10]. Recognizing that access controls, filtering, and other protection mechanisms can be defeated or bypassed by would-be attackers who take advantage of remaining vulnerabilities, intrusion detection systems monitor system or network activity to discover attempts to disrupt or gain illicit access to systems. Intrusion detection must be concerned both with attempts by external penetrators to enter or interfere with the system and by authorized users to exceed their legitimate access or abuse the system in some way. The latter case also includes seemingly authorized users, such as masqueraders operating under another user's id and password, or outside attackers who successfully gained system access but eluded detection of the method of entry.

Two general approaches are taken. In the first, sniffer logs, audit data, or other data sources are examined for evidence of operations, sequences, or techniques known to be used in particular types of attacks. Intrusion detection methods that look for these kinds of indicators are known as signature-based methods. In the second approach, relevant data are compared by statistical or other methods to representative profiles of activity on the system or network. These profiles may be of normal, expected system activity, in which case deviations indicate suspicious behavior, or they may be characteristic of activity associated with attacks, in which case matches indicate suspicious behavior. Both signature-based and profile-based approaches can be used to detect external penetration attempts as well as some kinds of malfeasance by authorized users. While these methods are generally applied at the level of operating system and network services, some types of system abuse or disruption will be distinguishable from normal activity only with knowledge of application-level semantics. Thus, there is increasing recognition that similar detection strategies will be necessary at the level of applications and databases, and some initial efforts are exploring this area.

When a suspicious thread of activity is discovered, the intrusion detection system or a system administrator must decide how to react and whether to allow continued access by the associated process, user, or host. If an entity B comes under suspicion for some reason, the system can let B continue to access the system, risking further damage, or take action to deny B continued access to the system, which may also be undesirable, for a couple of reasons. Further investigation may show that what looked suspicious was actually unusual but legitimate activity. If this is the case, denying B access could result in unwarranted denial of service. It is even possible that an attacker is intentionally spoofing B to provoke a denial of service response against B. On the other hand, if B proves guilty, immediately denying access to the system may mean losing the opportunity to gather more information that would help identify the attacker and the objectives of the attack. Experience with system and network penetrations has shown the usefulness of another alternative: *isolation*.

Isolating B transparently into a separate environment which still appears to B to be the actual system allows B's activities to be kept under surveillance without risking further harm to the system. An isolation strategy that has been used in such instances is known as *fishbowling*. Fishbowling involves setting up a separate lookalike host or file system and transparently redirecting the suspicious entity's requests to it. This approach allows the incident to be further studied to determine the real source, nature, and goal of the activity, but has some limitations, particularly when considered at the application level. First, the substitute host or file system is essentially sacrificed during the course of the suspected attack to monitor B, consuming significant resources that may be scarce. Second, since B is cut off from the real system, if B proves innocent, denial of service could still be a problem. While some types of service B receives from the substitute, fishbowl system may be adequate, in other cases the lack of interaction with the real system's resources may prevent B from continuing to produce valid results. On the other hand, if the semantics of the application are such that B can continue producing valid work, this work is lost when the incident is concluded even if B is deemed innocent and reconnected to the real system. The fishbowling mechanism makes no provision for re-merging updates from the substitute, fishbowl system back into the real system.

In this paper, we offer an application-level isolation strategy that, while in some sense a counterpart to fishbowling, takes advantage of application semantics to avoid some of these limitations. In this isolation approach, as in the case of fishbowling, when B comes under suspicion, we let B continue working while we attempt to determine whether there is anything to worry about. At the same time, we isolate the system from any further damage B might have in mind. However, we provide this isolation without consuming duplicate resources to construct an entirely separate environment, we allow options for partial interaction across the boundary, and we provide algorithms for smoothly merging B's work back into the real system should B prove innocent.

Consider a supermarket repricing application. The database contains prices for different kinds of merchandise, and the price tag for each merchandise is generated based on the information stored in the database. Assume there are several clerks in charge of submitting transactions to reprice merchandise periodically based on the decisions made by managers. Suppose now that the system administrator discovers that clerk B is repricing merchandise anomalously (for example, she is repricing too often or repricing too many items of merchandise). The system administrator can reject changes made by B if he is sure that B is malicious. However, if he is not certain of this, rejecting changes made by B would cause the loss of B's productive work even if further investigation showed B not be malicious after all. On the other hand, allowing B to continue repricing may cause further loss if B turns out to be either a misfeasor or a masquerader. In this situation, isolating B is a good solution. It ensures that B cannot cause any further damage and at the same time B can continue working productively.

We illustrate our approach in the context of a database system, and consider the following attack scenario: Suppose a user B of the database comes under suspicion for some reason (perhaps the system administrator noticed that some of B's updates seem to be out of the usual range). To let B continue working and at the same time to isolate the database from any further damage from B, we propose to create an on-the-fly "separate database version" for the user B we are concerned about. All transactions submitted by B are then directed only to the separate suspicious database version, while transactions from other users are applied to the main database version. The two versions may become inconsistent over time. Any inconsistency can be resolved when a determination is reached about whether the suspicious user B is actually malevolent or is innocent after all. If B turns out to be malicious, the suspicious database version can be discarded to protect the main database from harm. If B turns out to be innocent, B's updates in the suspicious version are merged back into the main database version; conflicting transactions are identified so that conflicts can then be resolved.

The benefit of this scheme is that work can continue while the investigation is in progress. Disruption of the database's operations is kept to a minimum if B is innocent, but B would have been prevented from doing further damage to the database if B is guilty.

This work has relevance to information warfare (IW) defense [1, 5, 8, 9]. As pointed out by Ammann, et al. [1], IW defense does everything possible to prevent attacks from succeeding, but it also recognizes that attempting to prevent information attack is insufficient; attacks that are successful to some degree must be recognized as unavoidable, and comprehensive support for identifying and responding to attacks is required.

The rest of the paper is organized as follows. Section 2 discusses related work. We present our isolation system architecture in Section 3, and the isolation protocol in Section 4. Section 5 presents our static conflict resolution methods. In Section 6 we propose a method to resolve conflicts dynamically. Section 7 extends our isolation protocol to deal with multiple suspicious users. Section 8 concludes the paper.

2 Related Work

There is a substantial body of work in intrusion detection [7, 10], based on either detecting deviations from expected statistical profiles or pattern-matching against known methods of attack. The detection, however, primarily focuses at the operating system level. Although work is ongoing to extend it to networks of distributed systems, it does not yet provide any help with intrusion detection at the level of applications such as the database management system (DBMS). In a DBMS, the problem can be particularly difficult, since it involves detecting that data inserted into the database is unreasonable or incorrect.

Although the area of IW defense is new, there is some relevant work. Graubart et al. [5] identify a number of aspects of the management of a DBMS that affect vulnerability with respect to information warfare. McDermott and Goldschlag [8, 9] identify some techniques for defending against data jamming that, while primarily intended for detection, could also help deceive the attacker and confuse the issue of which data values are critical.

Finally, Ammann et al. [1] take a detailed look at the problem of surviving IW attacks on databases. They identify a number of phases of the IW process and describe activities which occur in each of them. To maintain precise information about the attack, they propose to mark data to reflect the severity of detected damage as well as the degree to which the damaged data has been repaired. They define an access protocol for normal transactions and show that transactions following the protocol maintain database consistency even if part of the database is damaged.

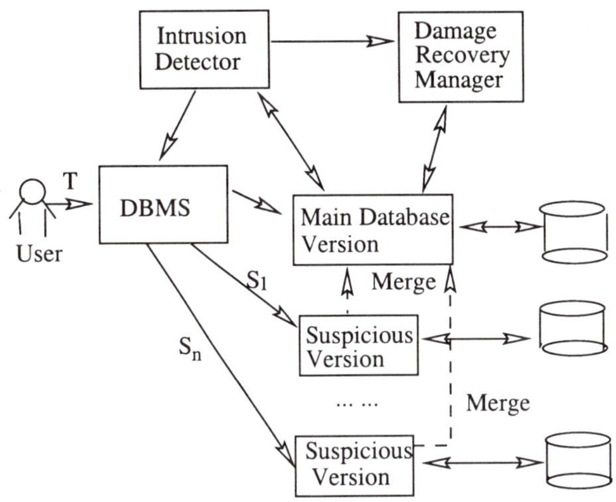

Figure 1. Architecture of the Isolation System

3 System Architecture

Data in database systems are operated upon by transactions. We assume that the DBMS employs a concurrency control that produces serializable histories [3]. For simplicity, we assume also that the read set of a transaction always contains its write set. We assume that there are three kinds of users of a database system: *trustworthy* users, *suspicious* users and *malicious* users. The architecture of the isolation system, shown in Figure 1, has following components.

The *DBMS* enforces the access controls in accordance with the system security policy on every access request in the form of transaction execution. We assume no data access can bypass it.

The *Intrusion Detector* seeks to identify users who are either definitely malicious or suspicious. When a malicious user is detected, the Intrusion Detector notifies the Reference Monitor to reject any further malicious transactions, transactions submitted by the malicious user. At the same time, the Intrusion Detection notifies the *Damage Recovery Manager* to undo any changes made by the malicious user's past transactions. Trusted damage recovery, however, is outside the scope of this paper. Interested readers are referred to [2], where a family of read-write dependency-based damage recovery algorithms has been proposed. From the viewpoint of isolation, we can assume that there is no damage caused by malicious transactions in the current history.

When a suspicious user is detected, first we need to examine the effects that the user has already had on the current history, because, if the user proves malicious, any damage already done may spread. Several strategies are available. At one extreme, if we think all the changes are erroneous, we can let the Damage Recovery Manager remove them all. At the other extreme, if we do not think any of the changes can cause any serious damage, we can accept them all. Strategies between these extremes are also possible.

The Intrusion Detector then notifies the Reference Monitor to direct subsequent transactions submitted by the suspicious user, i.e., suspicious transactions, to a separate database version. Since we are focusing in this paper just on isolation, we assume that the Damage Recovery Manager has already removed any changes considered harmful before isolation of the suspicious user begins. The main database version is assumed to be sound; that is, it reflects only the effects of trustworthy transactions.

Note that there can be several different suspicious users, i.e., $S_1, \ldots, S_n$, being isolated at the same time. Therefore, multiple suspicious database versions can exist at once. We explain how the isolation is done in detail in the next section.

If a suspicious user turns out to be malicious, the corresponding suspicious history (a history generated on a suspicious database version) can be discarded to protect the main database from harm. If, on the other hand, the user turns out to be innocent, the corresponding suspicious history is merged with the main history (a history generated on the main database version), and isolation of the user's transactions to a separate version ceases.

Over time, as suspicious transactions are executed in a separate database version, the suspicious database version and the main database may become inconsistent. For example, a trustworthy transaction and a suspicious transaction may update the same data item x; thus, neither the main database version of x nor the suspicious database version of x is known to be correct when the suspicious history is merged into the main history.

In this paper, two approaches are proposed for identifying and resolving conflicts between suspicious transactions and trustworthy transactions. Static resolution, described in Section 5, allows both the main history and the suspicious histories to grow without restriction, then identifies the conflicts when a suspicious history is merged into the main history, and resolves them by backing out some committed transactions. Dynamic resolution, described in Section 6, in contrast, does not allow either the main history or the suspicious histories to grow unless mutual consistency is guaranteed.

4 Isolation Protocol

In the normal course of events when all users are believed to be trustworthy, the database has only one version, namely, the main database version; any updates by a user are seen by all other users of the database and vice versa. When a suspicious user S_1 is detected, there are several different types of data flow to consider:

Complete Isolation Updates by S_1 are not given to other users, and any updates by other users are not given to S_1.

One-way Isolation Updates by S_1 are not given to other users, but any updates by other users are given to S_1.

Partial Isolation Some updates by S_1 are given to other users, and vice versa.

In this paper, we assume that complete isolation is the strategy chosen by the system administrator. One-way isolation and partial isolation are also reasonable strategies in some situations, but are outside the scope of this paper.

There is one other complication that we need to consider. Unless all other trustworthy or suspicious users are forbidden to update a data item that has already been updated by a suspicious user S_i, it is possible to have two independent updates to an item x. Since we consider this restriction unreasonable, we will take the approach that conflicting updates can be made independently by S_i and other users. As a result, there can be four states associated with each data item (let **S** denote the set of suspicious users; **G** denote the set of trustworthy users):

1. The data item has not been updated by either **S** or **G**.
2. The data item has been updated by **S**, but not by **G**.
3. The data item has been updated by **G**, but not by **S**.
4. The data item has been updated by both **S** and **G**.

Based on the complete isolation strategy, the following two rules must be obeyed:

Isolation Rule A suspicious history can never read the value of a data item updated by another suspicious history; a suspicious transaction can never read the value of a data item updated by any trustworthy transaction which commits during the isolation, and vice versa.

Read Rule For each data item x, the original value of x in a suspicious database version should be the same as that in the oldest suspicious database version, that is, all the active suspicious database versions should have the same original database state (the *state* is determined by the values of the data items in the database); and the original value of x in the first suspicious database version should be the same as the main database version value of x just before the first suspicious history was isolated. We show the reason for this rule in Section 7.

Our isolation protocol works as follows.

- At the beginning of the main history each data item x is associated with the same version number $MAIN$, denoted $x[MAIN]$.

- When data item x is read or updated by a trustworthy transaction T, $x[MAIN]$ is given to T, and after $x[MAIN]$ is updated by T, if the version includes other version numbers (we show the reason below), then a new version $x[MAIN]$ associated with only one version number $MAIN$ is generated which denotes the value that has been updated by T, and the old value with the same set of version numbers except that $MAIN$ is excluded remains.

- When the first suspicious user S_1 is identified, we attach the specific version number $INIT$ to each data item. As a result, a version of x may be associated with several version numbers, for example, $x[MAIN][INIT]$ denotes the value of x which should be the original value of x for each following suspicious database version, and can be updated by a trustworthy transaction.

- When a suspicious user S_i is identified (including the first one), a unique version number, for example, the time stamp t_i, is attached to the $INIT$ version of x. $x[INIT][t_i]$ denotes the value of x which has not been updated by S_i but can be updated by a suspicious transaction submitted by S_i.

- When x is read or updated by a suspicious transaction submitted by S_i, the version of x which includes the version number t_i will be given to S_i. After the version is updated by S_i, if the version includes the version number $INIT$, then a new version $x[t_i]$ is generated which denotes the value that has been updated by S_i, and the old value with the same set of version numbers except that t_i is excluded remains.

Theorem 1 The isolation protocol ensures that both the isolation rule and the read rule are satisfied.

Proof: *(Sketch)* It is easy to see that when a data item x is updated by a suspicious user S_i, the following updates of S_i can only be performed on $x[t_i]$ which is unique to S_i and will not be updated by other suspicious users. Therefore, suspicious users are isolated from each other. During the isolation of S_i, if x is updated by a trustworthy transaction, then $x[MAIN]$ will have a new value different from $x[INIT]$ which is the version S_i will work on. Thus trustworthy transactions and suspicious transactions are isolated from each other. Therefore, the isolation rule holds. When a suspicious user S_i is identified the version number t_i is attached to the $INIT$ version of every data item, so each suspicious database version has the same initial version value, namely, the $INIT$ version. Therefore, the read rule holds. □

5 Static Identification and Resolution of Conflicts

As we mentioned before, trustworthy transactions and suspicious transactions can conflict with each other during isolation. In this section, we propose the static conflict resolution method, adapted from Davidson's optimistic protocol [4], which is used in partitioned distributed database systems. For simplicity, we restrict our discussion to allow only one suspicious database version. The protocol which incorporates multiple suspicious database versions is discussed in Section 7.

In partitioned distributed database systems, Davidson's optimistic protocol [4] allows transactions to be executed within each partitioned group independently with communication failures existing between partitioned groups. As a result, serial history H_i consisting of all transactions executing within group P_i is generated. Using the serial histories of P_1 and P_2, H_1 and H_2, a specific *precedence graph G* is constructed, and Davidson proved that if there is no cycle in G, then H_1 and H_2 can be merged without conflicts. The merging is done by forwarding updates from transactions in H_1 to P_2 or H_2 to P_1

Here, we can view the suspicious history and the corresponding main history (the trustworthy history which begins with the same initial database state as the suspicious history, it is usually a sub-history of the main history; here, we call it "the main history" for short) as two partitioned histories because our isolation protocol can assure that they are completely isolated. Then we can construct a similar precedence graph using both the suspicious history and the main history as follows:

- Let T_i and T_j be two suspicious transactions that perform conflicting operations on a data item. There is a directed edge $T_i \rightarrow T_j$ if T_i precedes T_j.

- Let T_i and T_j be two trustworthy transactions that perform conflicting operations on a data item. There is a directed edge $T_i \rightarrow T_j$ if T_i precedes T_j.

- Let T_g be a trustworthy transaction that reads the main version of a data item that has been updated by a suspicious transaction T_s(thus the data item has also a suspicious version), then there is a directed edge $T_g \rightarrow T_s$.

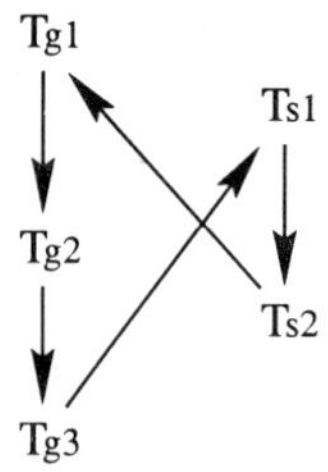

Figure 2. The Precedence Graph for the History in Example 1

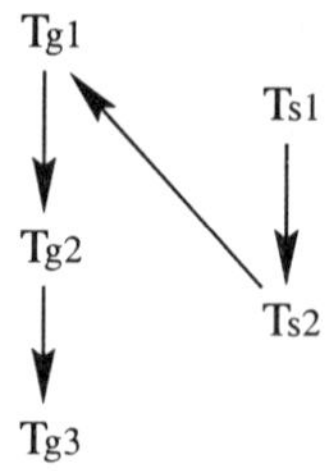

Figure 3. The Precedence Graph for the History in Example 2

- Let T_s be a suspicious transaction that reads a data item that has been updated by a trustworthy transaction T_g, then there is a directed edge $T_s \rightarrow T_g$.

Example 1 *Consider the five transactions given below:*

$READSET(T_{g1}) = WRITESET(T_{g1}) = \{d_1, d_2\}$
$READSET(T_{g2}) = \{d_2, d_3\}$, $WRITESET(T_{g2}) = \{d_3\}$
$READSET(T_{g3}) = \{d_3, d_4, d_5\}$, $WRITESET(T_{g3}) = \{d_4\}$
$READSET(T_{s1}) = WRITESET(T_{s1}) = \{d_5\}$
$READSET(T_{s2}) = \{d_1, d_5\}$, $WRITESET(T_{s2}) = \{\}$

Assume that the trustworthy history is: $H_g = T_{g1}\ T_{g2}\ T_{g3}$; the suspicious history is: $H_s = T_{s1}\ T_{s2}$. The precedence graph G is shown in Figure 2. Since the graph has a cycle, conflict exists among the transactions. Note that since T_{s2} read the item d_1 which is then updated by T_{g1}, T_{s2} should precede T_{g1}; since T_{g1} should precede T_{g3}, T_{s2} should precede T_{g3}; however, since T_{g3} read the item d_5 which is then updated by T_{s1}, T_{g3} should precede T_{g1}, since T_{s1} should precede T_{s2}, T_{g3} should precede T_{s2}, yielding a contradiction.

Example 2 *Suppose we change the read set of T_{g3} to $\{d_3, d_4\}$. Suppose further that the database executes the transactions in the following order: $T_{g1}T_{s1}T_{g2}T_{s2}T_{g3}$.*

The resulting conflict graph, shown in Figure 3, is acyclic, denoting that there are no conflicts among these transactions. Clearly the history $H = T_{s1}\ T_{s2}\ T_{g1}\ T_{g2}\ T_{g3}$ is an equivalent merged history which can generate the same database state as the state generated by merging H_s into H_g. However, is should be noticed that the initial executing order of the transactions cannot generate the same state in most circumstances.

The correctness of the approach is shown in the following theorem, which is similar to Theorem 2.2.2 in [4].

Theorem 2 Given H_g and H_s, the precedence graph $G(H_g, H_s)$ is acyclic if and only if H_s and H_g are serializable (i.e., equivalent to some merged history H).

In order to build the precedence graph, we keep track of read and write sets of each transaction T in H_g or H_s. We can get the write set of T from the log where every write operation of T is recorded; we can get the read set of T by several ways, such as augment the write log with read information (read records); extract read sets from the profiles of transactions; extract read information from physical or logical logs, etc. The discussion on these approaches is out of the scope of the paper.

After some conflicts are identified, we have to back out enough committed suspicious or trustworthy transactions (actually, we know at this point that these suspicious transactions are trustworthy) so that the conflicts could be resolved. Unfortunately, it is shown in [4] that just minimizing the number of transactions to be backed out is NP-complete, let alone minimizing the total back-out cost, i.e., assigning each transaction a weight or back-out cost and then minimizing the total back-out cost. Although this result discourages attempts to minimize the total back-out cost, the simulation results of [4] show that in many situations where the size of transactions is small and there is a relatively small number of transactions, a relatively large number of data-items in the database and large percentage of read-only transactions, several back-out strategies, in particular breaking two-cycles optimally, can achieve good performance. Interested readers can refer to [4] for more details on these back-out strategies.

6 Dynamic Identification and Resolution of Conflicts

The static resolution approach has several drawbacks:

- During the period of time when H_s is merged into H_g and the conflicts between these two histories are identified and resolved, the performance of normal transaction processing can be seriously degraded because the resolution and recovery will spend a substantial amount of system resources, although after the common data items which are updated by either H_s or H_g are identified, transactions accessing other data items may safely execute.

- The *back-out problem*, that is, minimizing the number of transactions backed out (or minimizing the total back-out cost), is an NP-complete problem. This means the cost of minimizing the total back-out cost is exponential to the number of transactions in H_s and H_g.
- Although under some conditions several back-out strategies with polynomial complexity can be used to achieve good performance, in most cases when a transaction T is backed out to break a cycle in the precedence graph all the transactions that are affected, directly or indirectly by T, have to be backed out at the same time. For example, in Example 1 if T_{g1} is chosen to be backed out, then T_{g2} needs to be backed out since it reads the item d_2, which has been updated by T_{g1}. Furthermore, T_{g3} needs to be backed out also since it reads the item d_3, which has been updated by T_{g2}.

In this section, we adopt a dynamic approach to identify and resolve conflicts. The basic idea of *dynamic resolution* is that neither a trustworthy transaction nor a suspicious transaction is allowed to commit unless we can ensure that the transaction will not cause a new cycle in the corresponding precedence graph. Compared with static resolution, dynamic resolution can support flexible strategies in resolving conflicts and can give users more availability and less service delay. For simplicity, we assume that there exists only one suspicious database version. Dynamic resolution methods that address multiple suspicious database versions are discussed in Section 7.

Dynamic resolution works as follows:

1. We build an online precedence graph based on both the trustworthy history H_g and the suspicious history H_s as they are growing. To achieve this, we keep track of the read set and write set of each ongoing transaction. The precedence graph is built in the same way as in Section 5.
2. When a suspicious transaction T_s is going to commit, we first check if T_s will introduce a cycle to the precedence graph, the check is done by detecting if there is any cycle in the precedence graph built from $H_g \cup H_s \cup \{T_s\}$.* If so, then T_s is rolled back; if not, then T_s is committed, and T_s is added to H_s.
3. When a trustworthy transaction T_g is going to commit, we first check if T_g will lead to a cycle to the precedence graph. If not, then T_g is committed and appended to the precedence graph; if so, then whether or not T_g can commit is decided as follows:
    - Assume the set of suspicious transactions with the minimum total weights that can be backed out to remove all the new cycles caused by T_g is $\mathbf{TS}$.
    - Assume the *suspicion factor* of H_s, a real number between 0 and 1 which indicates the measure of the suspicion that the system has on H_s, is α.
    - Let $Weight(T_g)$ denote the weight of T_g, then if $Weight(T_g) \geq (1-\alpha)Weight(\mathbf{TS})$, that is, the cost of rollbacking T_g is greater than or equal to the cost of backing out TS, then TS is backed out; otherwise, T_g is rollbacked.

To illustrate, assume that in Example 1 the database executes the transactions in the following order: T_{g1} T_{s1} T_{g2} T_{s2} T_{g3}, when T_{g3} is going to commit, we will find that T_{g3} will create a cycle in the precedence graph (shown in Figure 2). At this point, we can either roll back T_{g3} or back out T_{s1} and T_{s2} to remove the cycle. Assume the weight for each transaction is 1. If the suspicion factor of H_s is less than 0.5, then T_{g3} will be rolled back; otherwise, T_{s1} and T_{s2} will be backed out.

Compared with static resolution, dynamic resolution builds the precedence graph on the fly instead of doing it after H_s is found innocent. Although dynamic resolution may introduce extra costs when H_s turns out to be malicious, for example, the cost of maintaining the precedence graph for H_s, the merge of H_s into H_g can be done with almost no delay, and transactions can be processed with almost no wait when H_s is innocent. In addition, the complexity of static methods in conflict identification and resolution can be dramatically decreased, since in dynamic resolution, when a potential cycle is detected it can be removed in a very simple way, for example, roll back the transaction that causes the cycle.

It should be noticed that dynamic resolution cannot be enforced in [4] because in partitioned distributed database systems data on each partition group are physically isolated, that is, the coordinator on one partition cannot have the knowledge of the data on another partition. However, in our isolation scheme, the suspicious database version and the main database version are just logically isolated, that is, both the main database version and the suspicious database version are known to the isolation manager.

For two serializable histories H_g and H_s, the cost of backing out, i.e., the total number of transactions which have been backed out to merge these two histories, in either static resolutions or dynamic resolutions, depends on

*There are well-known algorithms for detecting and enumerating all cycles in a directed graph. See, for example, [6].

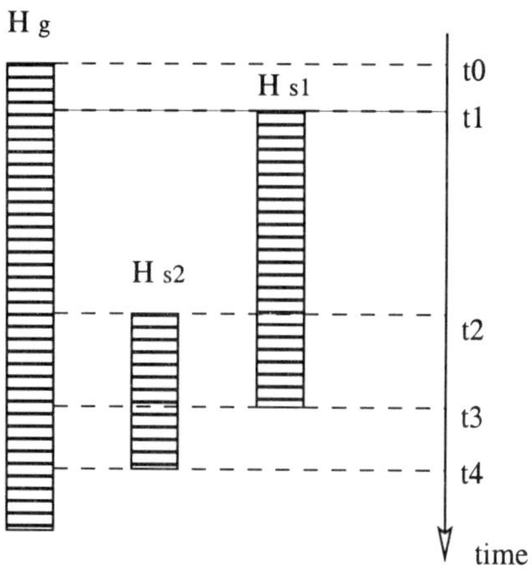

Figure 4. The Relation Between Multiple Suspicious Histories

the access property of the transactions in H_g and H_s and the interleaving of the trustworthy transactions in H_g and the suspicious transactions in H_s. For example, if the transactions which may cause cycles are executed earlier in each history, then dynamic resolution may back out less transactions; however, if there are many situations where several transactions are responsible for one cycle, then the static method may get better result.

7 Dealing with Multiple Suspicious Users

As we mentioned in Section 3, there can be several different suspicious users, i.e., S_1, ..., S_n, being isolated at the same time. Although our isolation protocol is proposed based on this assumption, and as a result, multiple suspicious database versions are correctly maintained and completely isolated from each other, we still have not considered the influence of a merge on other suspicious histories, and how to deal with it. These are the topics of this section.

7.1 Extension of Static Resolution

In static resolution, assume there are n active suspicious histories at time t, namely, H_{s1}, ..., H_{sn}. These histories might start to be isolated at different points in time, for example (see Figure 4), the main history H_g began at time t_0, suspicious history H_{s1} began and ended at time t_1 and t_3 respectively, suspicious history H_{s2} began and ended at time t_2 and t_4 respectively, and both H_{s1} and H_{s2} were active during the period of time from t_2 to t_3. We assume that both H_{s1} and H_{s2} are innocent.

Two possible isolation strategies may be applied here. Strategy 1 is to let suspicious histories, i.e., H_{s1} and H_{s2}, take different main database states as the original states for their suspicious database versions. For example, H_{s1} takes the main database state at time t_1 as its original suspicious database state, and H_{s2} takes the main database state at time t_2 as its original suspicious database state. Since the main database version value of some data item x may change during the period of time from t_1 to t_2, different values of x can be given to H_{s1} and H_{s2}.

Strategy 1 can cause serious problems when there is more than one suspicious history. Suppose data item x was updated by H_{s1} and read by H_{s2}, suppose further that x had not been updated by H_g from t_1 to t_2, then after H_{s1} was merged into H_g at time t_3, the transaction in H_{s1} which updated x could be merged into H_g in a position between $p(t_1)$ and $p(t_2)$ ($p(t)$ denotes the position of the latest committed transaction in H_g at time t). In this situation, the value of x in the main database version at $p(t_2)$ would be changed, and the new value of x should have been given to H_{s2} when it read x. However, since H_{s2} might read x before the merge, there can be inconsistencies between the main database version and the suspicious database version for S_2 after the merger. In other words, when H_{s2} is going to be merged into H_g, we may fail to find a subhistory of H_g into which can H_{s2} be merged.

Strategy 2 is to let all suspicious histories take the same main database state as their original suspicious database state, namely, the main database state just before the first suspicious history was isolated. This will work for multiple suspicious histories, because no matter how other suspicious histories will update data item x which is read by H_{si}, H_{si} can always get the right value of x, that is, the value of x in its version; and no matter how other merges will take place, H_{si} can always find a proper main history to merge into, that is, the main sub-history which begins with the same database state as H_{si}. This is also the reason why we took this strategy in our isolation protocol.

One performance issue of strategy 2 is that the backout cost of merges will increase substantially as the main history grows longer and longer. Although different suspicious histories usually will be merged into different main histories if they are found innocent, all these main histories begin with the same main database state. As a result, the longer the main history, the more the conflicts between the main history and the suspicious histories exist. Therefore, it is desirable to find shorter main histories for suspicious histories to be merged into, and to avoid the inconsistency problem we have mentioned in strategy 1 at the same time.

In Figure 5, H_{s1} and H_{s2} should take the same main database state as their original suspicious database state since H_{s1} may update a data item between t_1 and t_2 which is then read by H_{s2} between t_2 and t_3. In this situation, inconsistency between H_{s2} and H_g may happen after H_{s1}

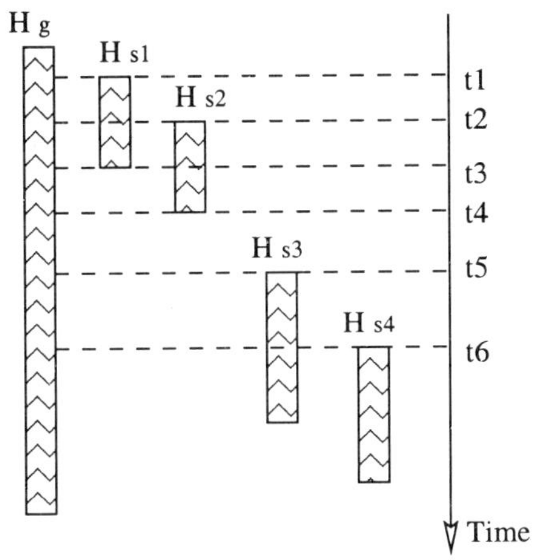

Figure 5. Isolation Reset

is merged into H_g if H_{s2} takes a main database state after t_1 as its original database state. For the similar reason, H_{s3} and H_{s4} should take the same main database state as their original suspicious database state. However, H_{s3} need not have the same original suspicious database state as that of H_{s1} and H_{s2}, because H_{s3} is isolated after both H_{s1} and H_{s2} terminate. Hence no matter how H_{s1} and H_{s2} would change the main database version if they were merged into H_g, their effect has already been reflected on the main database version and turns out to be a part of the main database version. So H_{s3} can take the main database state at time t_5 as its original database state without the danger of causing any inconsistences. The observation is summaried by the following theorem. For limited space, the proof is omitted.

Theorem 3 The isolation of multiple suspicious users is *correct*, in the sense that at any time there are no inconsistences between the main database version and any suspicious database version if and only if any overlapping suspicious histories (two suspicious histories are overlapping if their durations are overlapping) take the same main database state as their initial suspicious database state, and the main database state is generated when they begin to be isolated.

The above optimization to strategy 2 can be easily incorporated into our isolation protocol. For simplicity, only the modification is specified.

- Whenever there are no active suspicious histories in the database, the value of a specific signal variable $RESETABLE$ is set to be $TRUE$ if it has not been set yet.
- When a suspicious user S_i is going to be isolated, if the value of $RESETABLE$ is $TRUE$, then we first set the value of $RESETABLE$ to be $FALSE$, then attach both the $INIT$ and the t_i version number to the current main database version, namely, data items associated with the $MAIN$ version number and remove the old $INIT$ database version.

7.2 Extension of Dynamic Resolution

Dynamic resolution shares the similar problem with static resolution when overlapping suspicious histories take different main database states as their original suspicious database states because when a suspicious history is found innocent it will be merged into the main history and the merge will affect other overlapping suspicious histories.

Assume that all overlapping suspicious histories take the same main database state as their original database state. In order to resolve conflicts on the fly, we maintain an online precedence graph for each suspicious history. When a merge is done, several strategies can be taken to deal with the influence of the merge on other suspicious histories:

1. Modulate all of the online precedence graphs correspondingly and resolve the conflicts caused by the merge before any new transaction is processed. Notice that the main history after the merge may bring new cycles to these precedence graphs. Note that the modulation should be done one by one unless no trustworthy transactions are allowed to be backed out. Under this condition, trustworthy transactions can be concurrently executed during the modulation.
2. Modulate all of the online precedence graphs. If some cycles are found in precedence graph G_i, leave them alone until the time when H_{si} is decided to be merged or discarded.
3. Modulate all of the line precedence graphs, but only remove part of their cycles.

Strategy 1 may suspend normal transaction processing when a merge is done, however it can ensure that every emerge can be done with almost no delay. Strategy 2 may allow transactions to be executed continuously after a merge is done; however, at the time when a suspicious history is merged into the main history, there can be cycles in the precedence graph. Thus the identification and resolution of these cycles may cause un-neglectable service delay. Strategy 3 is a trade-off of strategy 1 and 2.

Compared with static resolution, in dynamic resolution a merge seems to have a more serious effect on other suspicious histories. However, dynamic methods still can enhance the performance of static methods to some extent, since usually most of the cycles in a precedence graph will be removed during normal processing of transactions.

8 Conclusion

In this paper, we proposed a novel security mechanism, namely, application-level isolation, to increase the security (integrity and availability) of information systems vulnerable to authorized malicious users. We developed an isolation scheme in the database context that isolates databases from any further damage caused by malicious users and at the same time gives suspicious users the ability to continue running transactions transparently, when we suspect that some damage is done. Isolation is complicated since it may create inconsistencies between isolated database versions. We presented both static and dynamic approaches to identify and resolve the conflicts. Static resolution is easy to perform, but may cause suspension in normal transaction processing; dynamic resolution needs to maintain an online precedence graph for each suspicious history, but it can support flexible strategies in resolving conflicts and gives users more availability and causes less service delays. Corresponding performance issues are also well discussed.

The isolation scheme could prove worthwhile for many applications. If the suspicion factor of each suspicious history is relatively large and the back-out rate for innocent histories is sufficiently small, the inconvenience of occasionally having to reexecute a suspicious or trustworthy transaction is offset by the increased security (integrity) and availability of the system. Examples of such applications are:

Repricing system: This example has already been mentioned. Based on the assumption that different clerks will reprice different categories of merchandise during most circumstances, the conflict rate between each suspicious history and the main history will be very low. Since an innocent clerk's work output will not be lost, the supermarket would benefit by using isolation.

Banking system: In a bank, since different customers access different accounts in most cases, the conflict rate between the histories of different customers can be very low. Since innocent customers would not be irritated by possibly being denied access to their accounts, the bank would benefit by using isolation.

Airline reservation system: The underlying database of flight information is fairly large, and references to flights are probably pretty evenly distributed. Many transactions are read-only, for example, "Is there a flight connecting flight #188 in Washington?", "Is flight #488 arriving at 4:18 in New York on time ?", etc. People wishing to book seats could be told that their reservations were conditional; backed-out transactions could be automatically reexecuted and confirmed, unless the flight became overbooked, in which case the customer could be consulted.

In our future research, we will discuss one-way isolation and partial isolation, for example, consider the following scenarios:

1. The isolation of the main database from the suspect's updates could be partial. If his updates on some data items are not considered risky, they could be selectively propagated to the main database, while anything else he attempts to update are confined to the suspicious version.
2. Disclosure of updates from the main database version to the suspicious version could be partial. If some of the updates by other users are considered sensitive, they could be selectively withheld from being propagated to the suspicious version where they would be divulged to the suspicious user.
3. Remerging of the database versions could be partial. Even if the user was found to be a malefactor, it might be desirable to accept certain of his updates into the main database version (for example, after being examined, or those on particular data items) rather than discarding them all outright.

References

[1] P. Ammann, S. Jajodia, C. McCollum, and B. Blaustein. Surviving information warfare attacks on databases. In *Proceedings of the IEEE Symposium on Security and Privacy*, pages 164–174, Oakland, CA, May 1997.

[2] P. Ammann, P. Liu, and S. Jajodia. Trusted recovery from malicious transactions. Technical report, George Mason University, Fairfax, VA, 1997. http://isse.gmu.edu/faculty/pammann/papers/recovery.ps.

[3] P. A. Bernstein, V. Hadzilacos, and N. Goodman. *Concurrency Control and Recovery in Database Systems.* Addison-Wesley, Reading, MA, 1987.

[4] S. B. Davidson. Optimism and consistency in partitioned distributed database systems. *ACM Transactions on Database Systems*, 9(3):456–581, September 1984.

[5] R. Graubart, L. Schlipper, and C. McCollum. Defending database management systems against information warfare attacks. Technical report, The MITRE Corporation, 1996.

[6] D. Johnson. Finding all the elementary circuits of a directed graph. *SIAM J. Comput.*, (4):77–84, 1975.

[7] T. Lunt. A Survey of Intrusion Detection Techniques. *Computers & Security*, 12(4):405–418, June 1993.

[8] J. McDermott and D. Goldschlag. Storage jamming. In D. Spooner, S. Demurjian, and J. Dobson, editors, *Database Security IX: Status and Prospects*, pages 365–381. Chapman & Hall, London, 1996.

[9] J. McDermott and D. Goldschlag. Towards a model of storage jamming. In *Proceedings of the IEEE Computer Security Foundations Workshop*, pages 176–185, Kenmare, Ireland, June 1996.

[10] B. Mukherjee, L. T. Heberlein, and K. Levitt. Network intrusion detection. *IEEE Network*, pages 26–41, June 1994.

Maintaining Security in Firm Real-Time Database Systems

Quazi N. Ahmed and Susan V. Vrbsky
Department of Computer Science
The University of Alabama
Tuscaloosa, AL 35487-0290
U.S.A.

Abstract

Many real-time database systems, such as military institutions and government agencies, are contained in environments that exhibit restricted access of information, where mandatory access control for security is required. Hence, in addition to timing constraints, real-time database systems have security constraints. Conventional multi-level secure database models are inadequate for time-critical applications and conventional real-time database models do not support security constraints. The objective of this work is to incorporate security constraints in real-time database systems in such a way that not only is security achieved, but achieving security does not degrade real-time performance significantly in terms of deadlines missed. We propose a new optimistic concurrency control algorithm for secure firm real-time databases. Results show that the algorithm performs fairly well in terms of security and timeliness compared to a non-secure algorithm. We argue and show that achieving more security does not necessarily mean more sacrifice in real-time performance.

1. Introduction

Real-time database systems [3,4], such as military command control, communication, avionics, radar tracking, and managing automated factories, have timing constraints. These timing constraints are typically in the form of deadlines that require a transaction to be completed by a specified time. In such environments, multiple users share the same database, and some of the users can have restricted access to information from the database. Hence, it is necessary to provide database security for real-time databases. Conventional database security models are not adequate for time-critical applications [5]. A model for database security in real-time databases must address satisfying the timing constraints and security constraints. Major efforts to design secure databases have focused on databases without timing constraints. It is only recently that work [2,5,6] has been reported in the area of database security for real-time databases. The objective of this work is to study the factors involved in secure concurrency control, develop a suitable concurrency control algorithm, implement and study the performance of the algorithms with a real-time database system simulation.

Mandatory access control is implemented by multilevel secure (MLS) databases [7,8,9] and can be used in many environments that exhibit hierarchical propagation of information, such as military institutions, government agencies, hospitals, etc. Many real-time database systems are contained in such environments, and, hence, are considered for this study. Mandatory access control is applicable on large amounts of information that requires firm protection in an environment where the subjects are grouped into clearances and objects are grouped by their classifications. In a multilevel secure database model objects have security levels and subjects have clearance levels. According to the Bell-LaPadula simple property [7], a subject can read a certain data object if the subject's clearance level dominates the object's security level. According to the Bell-LaPadula star-property [7], a subject can write to an object if the subject's clearance level is dominated by the object's security level. The two Bell-LaPadula properties prevent the direct flow of information from objects and/or subjects at a higher security clearance level to subjects at a lower level, and are the basis for all MLS models. However, the concurrent execution of transactions results in contention for data objects, and as a result, it is possible to have an indirect flow of information from objects at higher levels to subjects at lower levels due to a covert channel [13].

A secure real-time database system has to simultaneously satisfy two goals, provide security and ensure that the deadline miss percentage is minimized. In many occasions, these two goals conflict and to achieve one goal is to sacrifice the other. For example, suppose we have a high priority transaction at a high security level and a low priority transaction at a low security level, and

0-8186-8789-4/98 $10.00 © 1998 IEEE

there is a data conflict between them. (Priority is based on deadline, where a higher priority means an earlier deadline.) If the high priority transaction gets the data and blocks the low security transaction, then although the priority is maintained, a covert channel is introduced. The lower security level can determine there are transactions at higher levels and may even be able to receive information from the length of the delay. If the reverse is allowed to happen, security will be maintained but the priority will be violated. Whether to maintain security or priority is dependent upon the system. If the system requires that security be maintained regardless of the deadline of the conflicting transactions, then conflict must be resolved in favor of security. If the system allows a compromise between security and priority, then the goal is to maintain as much security as possible without raising the deadline miss percentage significantly.

In firm real-time database systems transactions are removed as soon as they miss their deadlines. In this paper, we study security for firm real-time database systems. Our main investigation is to identify how to minimize the number of missed deadlines for real-time transactions while avoiding covert channels wherever possible. Our main contributions in this paper can be summarized as follows:

- We present a new concurrency control algorithm in this study. The algorithm recognizes the security as well as the priority of real-time transactions. The algorithm can be used for systems where security can be compromised for priority and vice versa.
- We introduce two metrics to measure the level of security maintained in secure real-time database systems.
- We show that by using our algorithm, it is possible to achieve an almost 100% covert channel free system without a great deal of sacrifice in real-time performance in terms of missed deadlines.

The rest of the paper is organized as follows. In section 2, we discuss related work in secure real-time concurrency control and the secure real-time factor. In section 3, we present the secure concurrency control algorithm and metrics for security maintenance, and in section 4 we describe the simulation model and the results. In section 5 we present our conclusions.

2. Secure real-time concurrency control

Real-time transactions can have soft, hard or firm deadlines [3,10]. A transaction with a soft deadline may miss its deadline, yet the result produced still has some value (although the value monotonically decreases with time after the deadline). Soft transactions are allowed to complete even if a deadline is missed. On the other hand, if a hard deadline of a transaction is missed, the consequence can be catastrophic. The value assigned to a result when a deadline is missed is negative. For a firm deadline, the consequences of missing a deadline are less severe than a hard deadline, but a result produced after a deadline is useless, and is assigned a value of 0. For both firm and hard deadlines, if a deadline is not met, the transaction is discarded as soon as the deadline is missed.

2.1 Related work

Few works that address the security of real-time databases are described in [2, 5, 6]. In [5] a concurrency control strategy is presented which trades off security for improved timeliness if the system does not provide the desired deadline miss percentage. They use a measure called "capacity" to adjust the covert channel to get better real-time performance. In [6] a secure two-phase locking algorithm is used to allow partial violations of security for improved timeliness. Decisions are made concerning the trade off between security and meeting deadlines by comparing two measures to resolve conflicts: the security factor and the deadline miss factor. This comparison is used to determine if a lower level transaction should be aborted or proceed when it conflicts with a higher level transaction. If the security properties are more important, then any conflict is resolved in favor of the lower level transaction, otherwise if meeting deadlines is more important, then the higher priority transaction is given precedence. Our work also considers the need to tradeoff between security and timeliness but shows that security can be achieved with negligible sacrifice in timeliness.

In [2], security of firm real-time databases is addressed. In this study, security is viewed as a correctness criterion, and the number of missed deadlines as a performance issue. They do not trade off between missed deadlines and security, but instead propose to minimize the number of missed deadlines without compromising security through the choice of concurrency control strategy. They examine the performance of such strategies as a two-phase locking priority scheme, a prioritized optimistic concurrency control algorithm and a new approach, called the dual approach. The dual approach utilizes different concurrency control strategies depending on whether transactions are at the same security level or at different security levels. In contrast, our algorithm is capable of handling transactions both at the same and different security levels.

2.2 Secure real-time factor

The concurrency control algorithm for a secure real-time database system must use security levels of transactions as well as their deadlines to resolve data conflicts. Not only that, the difference in security levels of transactions also needs to be considered when a security conflict is to be resolved. If one transaction is at the highest security level and the another one is at the lowest and a covert channel is introduced between them, then the severity of the covert channel will be higher than the one where transactions are at adjacent security levels. None of the previous works discussed in section 2.1 recognizes the difference in security levels as a measure to resolve a security conflict. In secure real-time database systems, where timeliness is one of the goals to be achieved, one cannot afford to sacrifice it for some covert channel not severe enough to be concerned about. Thus, we believe that difference in security level is an important issue for determining whether a covert channel has to be closed by possibly sacrificing timeliness. To be able to determine the severity or consequences of security violations, we introduce the following "covert channel property" for secure real time database systems.

Covert Channel Property: The greater the difference of security levels between two transactions at data conflict, the greater the severity or the consequence if a covert channel is introduced.

The covert channel property indicates that consequence is proportional to the difference in security or access levels. In other words, the greater the difference in access levels, the more important it is to maintain security and close the covert channel. If two conflicting transactions are at two extreme security levels, the consequence of opening a covert channel is the maximum. If the two conflicting transactions are at two adjacent security levels the consequence is the minimum. Of course, if the two transactions are at the same security level, there is no covert channel, and hence no consequence. We introduce a metric to measure the consequence of introducing a covert channel, to be known as the *Covert Channel Factor* (CCF). The CCF is obtained by normalizing the difference of access levels between the two conflicting transactions:

$$\text{CCF} = \frac{\text{Difference in access levels}}{\text{Maximum difference possible}} = \frac{\text{Difference in access levels}}{\text{\# of access levels - 1}}$$

The maximum value of CCF is 1 when the two transactions are at two terminal access levels. The minimum value of CCF is $\frac{1}{\text{\# of access levels} - 1}$ when the two transactions are at two consecutive security levels. Of course, if two transactions are at the same security level, CCF is obviously zero meaning no covert channel.

Sometimes, security levels have a partial ordering instead of a complete ordering and, as a result, not all the security levels are comparable to each other. For example, assume we have 5 security levels namely, TOP SECRET, SECRET1, SECRET2, UNCLASSIFIED1 and UNCLASSIFIED2 and, the ordering is TOP SECRET > SECRET1, TOP SECRET > SECRET2, SECRET1 > UNCLASSIFIED1 and SECRET2 > UNCLASSIFIED2. In this case, certain levels are not directly comparable, e.g., SECRET1 and SECRET2, SECRET1 and UNCLASSIFIED2 etc. In order to be able to compute the CCF, the ordering between every possible pair of security levels needs to be known. This can be achieved by converting the partial order to a tree structure. For each ordering A > B, we create a parent node A and a child node B. If one of the nodes already exists, we only create the new one and make the appropriate hierarchy with the existing one. In this example, this can be done by having TOP SECRET as the root, SECRET1 and SECRET2 as the root's two children, UNCLASSIFED1 as the child of SECRET1 and UNCLASSIFIED2 as the child of SECRET2. Security levels at same depth of the tree can be considered as same levels and hence no covert channels exist between them. The difference between two security levels will be equal to the difference in their depths. Assuming the root has the minimum depth and the leaves have the maximum depth, one security level, A will be considered higher than another security level, B if depth(A) < depth(B). This work assumes that a partial ordering under MLS model is convertible to a single tree. Any ordering that leads to more than one tree is out of the scope of this paper.

3. Secure concurrency control algorithm

As mentioned earlier, secure real-time database systems have to satisfy the security constraints in addition to the timing constraints. Security can be considered as a correctness criteria where security must be enforced. It can also be thought of as a compromising criteria with timeliness where security can be sacrificed to achieve fewer deadline misses. The algorithm we present here supports the latter type. Although, the algorithm can achieve 100% covert channel free system, it can not guarantee that this is the case always. Later we will discuss why it is not possible to provide such a guarantee. Before describing our algorithm, we give a brief introduction to the existing non-secure algorithm upon which our algorithm is based. The existing algorithm is the Optimistic Concurrency Control (OPT) [11]. This algorithm and our algorithm, to be called the Secure OPT, are described in the following sub-section.

3.1 Secure OPT

In a traditional optimistic algorithm, transactions are allowed to read and update data items without any restriction. All data updates are made permanent during the commit time before which a transaction must pass a validation test where it tests that there is no currently executing conflicting transaction [11]. The validating transaction restarts if the test fails. The main goal of real-time optimistic algorithms is to prevent low priority validating transactions from committing one-sidedly when they conflict with higher priority transactions. There are two different optimistic strategies for real-time transactions, priority sacrifice and priority wait. In priority sacrifice, known as the OPT-SACRFICE, the validating transaction restarts if any higher priority transaction exists in the conflicting set (the set of currently executing transactions that conflict with the validating transaction.) In the priority wait, known as the OPT-WAIT, the validating transaction waits if there is any higher priority transaction in the conflicting set. These algorithms do not check the security levels in the transactions and there can be covert channels when a validating transaction commits and aborts the transactions in the conflicting set. For example, in the priority-sacrifice algorithm, if the validating transaction's access level and priority are higher than those of any of the transactions' in the conflicting set, a covert channel is introduced when the validating transaction commits aborting all in the conflicting set. Similarly, in the priority wait algorithm, if the validating transaction is blocked and there exists a transaction of a higher access level in the conflicting set, a covert channel is also introduced. We examine the different conflicts that can occur between a validating transaction (VT) and those in the conflicting set (CS) and present their resolutions in the following.

1. *∀ T∈CS if deadline(T)>deadline(VT) and ∀ T∈CS if access level(T)>access level(VT) then commit VT and abort all T in CS.* Since VT is at the highest priority and lowest security level, both the priority and the security are maintained.
2. *∀ T∈CS if deadline(T)<deadline(VT) and ∀ T∈CS if access level(T)<access level(VT) then block VT.* VT is at the lowest priority and highest security level. Again priority is maintained and no covert channel is introduced.
3. When none of the above conditions are met, a covert channel will be introduced no matter which side is aborted or blocked unless the size of the conflicting set is 1. Hence, using the optimistic strategy the system cannot be made 100% covert channel free if some validation phase falls in this case (case 3) and there are more than one transactions in the conflicting set. We want to resolve this case such that CCF is minimized and priority is also recognized whenever possible.
    a) *Minimize the CCF.* For this, we calculate the CCF when the validating transaction is aborted and also calculate the CCF when the conflicting set is aborted. The two CCFs are compared to see which option introduces more of a covert channel.
    b) *Consider the priority.* We need to consider the priority of the transactions in the conflicting set in order not to lose real-time performance. To do this we simply check if there is any transaction in the conflicting set with a higher priority than the VT.

Considering the above two cases, a conflict can be resolved in several ways. However, we want to minimize the CCF and also to recognize the priority. Thus, if one of the above conditions (a or b) are in favor of the VT, VT is allowed to commit.

If (CCF for aborting CS <CCF for aborting VT)
OR
(no high priority transaction exists in CS)
Then
Commit the VT and abort the CS.
Else
Abort the VT.

For example, assume that {T1 = (4, 10.40), T2 = (5, 11.57), T3 = (2, 12.67)} is the conflicting set where each member is a transaction presented as an ordered pair (access level, deadline). Assume also that the validating transaction is VT=(3,10.54). If the total number of access levels is 6 then the CCF for aborting the conflicting set is =(3-2)/5=1/5 due to the only security conflict with T3. Aborting T1 and T2 will not cause any covert channel as they are at higher security levels. The CCF for aborting the VT is =(4-3)/5 +(5-3)/5=1/5+2/5 =3/5. The first *if* condition is satisfied and VT commits. This option recognizes both security and priority, and if either the CCF is minimized (case a) or the priority is considered (case b), a VT is allowed to commit. The objective of this option is to have as many commits as possible and increase real-time performance. Maintaining security is not of prime importance here. By considering both the CCF and the priority, this option maximizes the number of commits and therefore, it is an *optimal* option. However, if only security is of concern, we use only the first *if* condition (case a) above) to see which side to abort. We call this the *secure option.*

If (CCF for aborting CS<CCF for aborting VT) Then
Commit the VT and abort the CS
Else
Abort the VT

3.2 Metrics of security maintenance

We now introduce two metrics or security factors to measure the security maintenance of a system. One metric keeps track of the number of times security has been maintained. The other one recognizes the differences between the access levels.

$$\text{Security factor 1} = \frac{\text{\# of times security is maintained}}{\text{Total number of security conflicts}}$$

Security factor 2

$$= \frac{\text{Sum of the difference in access levels for conflicts having security maintained}}{\text{Sum of the difference in access levels in all security conflicts}}$$

Both the metrics are suitable for measuring the performance of the system. Depending upon the system, one metric might be more appropriate than the other. If only the number of conflicts maintained is of concern the first factor is appropriate. The second factor is appropriate in systems where difference in access-levels is crucial. In this study, we choose the security factor 2.

3.3 Metric of priority maintenance

In order to express the level of priority maintenance in a system, we use the following priority maintenance factor.

Priority maintenance factor =

$$= \frac{\text{\# of times priority is maintained}}{\text{Total number of data conflicts}}$$

This metric is used to determine how priority maintenance affects the real-time performance.

4. Simulation model

This section outlines the structure and details of our simulation model used to evaluate the performance of our concurrency control algorithms for real-time database systems. Central to our simulation model is a single-site main memory database system operating on a single processor. The database is modeled as a collection of data pages in memory. The simulation consists of three main components: a Transaction Manager (TM), a CPU Manager (CM), and a Log Manager (LM). The TM is responsible for issuing lock requests, CM for granting CPU access, and LM for log disk access. The service discipline used for the queues is Earliest Deadline First (EDF) [12] without preemption. Each transaction consists of multiple operations each of which can be either read or write. If the operation is read, then the accessed page is not updated. The write operation updates the accessed page and an entry is written into the log buffer.

When an operation of a transaction makes a data access request, i.e., lock request on a data object to the TM, the request goes through concurrency control to obtain a lock on the data object. If the request is granted, the transaction requests CPU access to the CM. If the CPU is free, the request is granted and the transaction does the CPU computation. After the CPU computation, if there are any more operations left, the transaction proceeds with the next operation and makes a lock request to the TM. If all operations are done, the transaction requests log disk access to the LM and if access is granted, it writes the log buffer to the log disk and commits.

If the request for the lock is denied, the transaction will be placed into a block queue. The blocked transaction will be awakened when the requested lock is released.

Table 1: System Resource Parameters

Parameter	Explanation	Value
DBSIZE	Number of data pages in the database	400
CPU_TIME	CPU time for processing a data page	5 msec
WRITE_PROB	Probability that an operation is write	0.5
MAXACCESS	# access levels	6

4.1 Parameters of simulation model

Table 1 gives the system resource parameters. The parameter CPU_TIME is the time to process a page by a CPU. The simulation does not explicitly take into account the time required for accessing the transaction manager, the CPU manager, and the log manager. It is assumed that those times are included in the time required to access the resources, i.e., the CPU, and the log disk.

Table 2 summarizes the workload parameters that characterize the transactions and the system workload. Transactions' inter-arrival rates are exponentially distributed. The *Rate* parameter specifies the mean rate of transaction arrivals. The *TransSize* determines the mean number of operations in the transactions determined from a normal distribution with mean of *TransSize*. The actual data objects or pages accessed by each operation are uniformly distributed across the whole database. The *LogDelay* is the time required for writing a log buffer to the log disk. The *RestartDelay* is the overhead for roll back when a transaction is aborted. The parameters *MinSlack* and *MaxSlack* are used to set the lower and upper bound of transactions' deadlines. The following deadline assignment formula is used to assign the deadline to the arrived transaction.

$$Deadline = Arrival\ time + Uniform(MinSlack, MaxSlack) * Execution\ time$$

The *Arrival time* is the time of arrival of each transaction. The execution time of a transaction is calculated from the data requirements in all the operations using *TranSize*, *CPU_TIME*, and *LogDelay*.

Table 2: Workload Parameters

Parameters	Meaning	Value
Rate	Arrival rate of the transactions	[5,50]
TransSize	Average transaction size	6
LogDelay	Overhead for writing log buffer to the log disk	5 msec
RestartDelay	Overhead for restarting	5 msec
MinSlack	Minimum slack factor	2
MaxSlack	Maximum slack factor	8

4.2 Experiments and results

The simulation program is written in C++ using the next event simulation strategy and is run for 5000 transactions. Different random seeds are used for different calls to the random number generator to make sure that the arrived transactions are exactly the same for different algorithms. In order to simulate the firm real-time system, at the beginning of each event, the system is checked to see if there is any transaction that has missed its deadline and if so, it is removed from the system. We do a detailed simulation study on firm database systems using our proposed algorithm and compare them with the existing non-secure algorithm. We discuss the effectiveness of our algorithms in terms of maintaining security and minimizing deadline miss. We also study restart ratios for both the algorithms.

Figure 1 illustrates the deadline miss percentage for the non-secure OPT and the Secure OPT algorithm with *secure* option. We use the OPT-SACRIFICE as the non-secure OPT algorithm in this study. OPT-SACRIFICE is priority cognizant and hence has a better performance over the secure OPT algorithm. The non-secure algorithm does not have any deadlines missed with arrival rates below 20. On the other hand, in the secure algorithm transactions start to miss deadlines around an arrival rate of 15 but has a low deadline miss percentage if the arrival rate is below 20. The main difference between the performance of the two algorithms is prominent between arrival rates 15 and 25, after which a majority of the transactions start to miss their deadlines in both the algorithms.

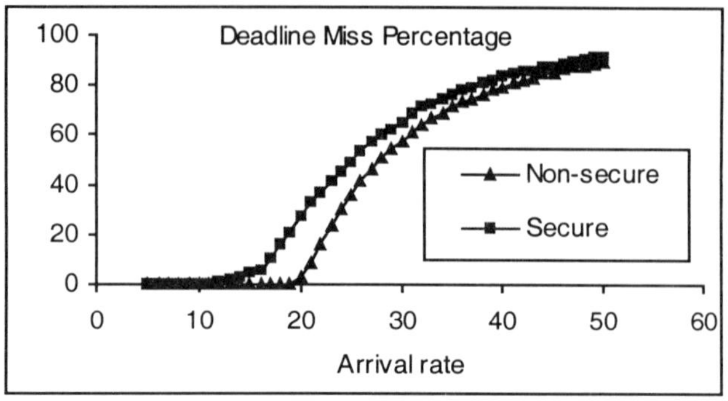

Figure 1 Comparison of Deadline Miss Percentages

The Secure OPT algorithm recognizes covert channels and, therefore, the security factor of a system is improved when the algorithm is used. This result is illustrated in the figure 2, which compares the security factors for the secure and non-secure algorithm. In the secure algorithm, the security factor is very close to 1; in contrast, in the non-secure algorithm, it is inconsistent and remains around 0.5. It is interesting to notice in Figure 1 that although we enforce security with the Secure OPT, we do not necessarily have to sacrifice the real-time performance a great deal. This is because there are many data conflicts for which security enforcement does not violate priority based on deadline. Increasing security means more data conflicts resolved in favor of lower security transactions, irrespective of their deadlines. If a lower security transaction has a later deadline, enforcing security means loss of priority. However if it happens to have an earlier deadline, then priority is maintained as well. Therefore, achieving high security (e.g. security factor close to 1) does not mean that we lose all the priority.

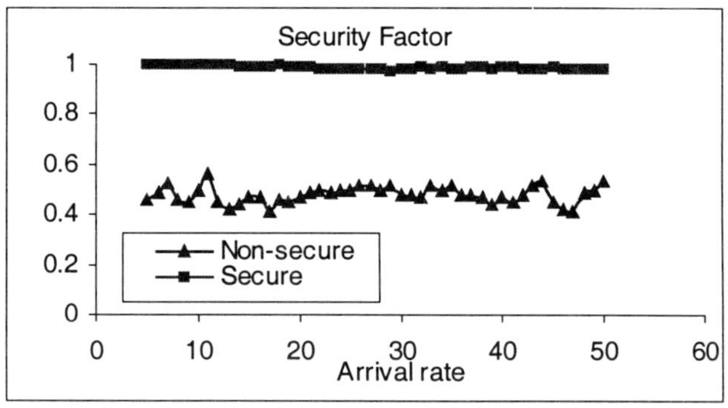

Figure 2 Comparison of Security Factors

Figure 3 shows the priority maintenance factor when the security factor is very close to 1.0. In this case priority maintenance factor is not zero but instead varies between 0.15 to 0.35. That is the reason why the real-time performance with the Secure OPT in Figure 1 is similar to the non-secure OPT. This is a very important feature of our algorithm.

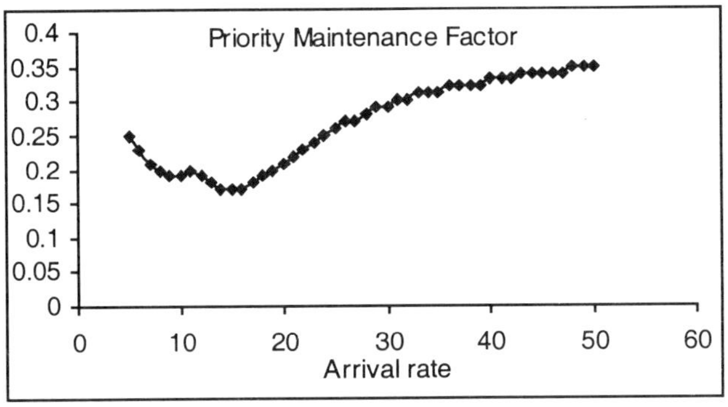

Figure 3 Priority Maintenance Factor for Secure OPT

Figure 4 shows a comparison of the restart ratios between the non-secure and the Secure OPT algorithms. For each algorithm, the restart ratio rises with the increase of arrival rate and starts to decrease after a certain arrival rate, e.g., 15-16 for secure and 21-22 for non-secure case. This can be explained as follows. Most of the transactions meet their deadlines until the arrival rate exceeds 15-16 for the secure case or 21-22 for the non-secure case. If the arrival rate is low, there are fewer conflicts and consequently fewer restarts. However as the transactions start to miss the deadlines, some of the aborted transactions may be already late and hence may not even restart because they are removed from the system as soon as they miss their deadlines. With an increased arrival rate, the number of late aborted transactions increases, which in turn decreases the number of restarts. Thus, the restart ratio increases with the increase in arrival rate until the system starts missing deadlines, after which the restart ratio starts decreasing and it continues to decrease with the subsequent increase in arrival rate.

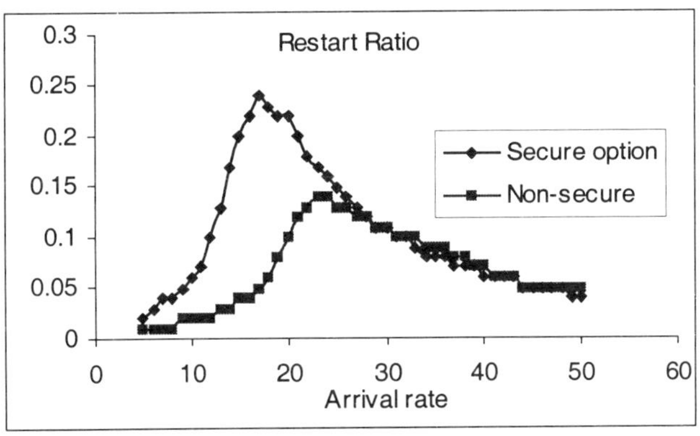

Figure 4 Comparison of Restart Ratios

5. Conclusion

In this paper we have identified the covert channel property of secure real-time databases and, we have proposed a new secure optimistic concurrency algorithm based on this property. We have implemented the secure algorithm and a non-secure algorithm and studied their performance in detail using a real-time database system simulation model. Our study covers firm real-time database systems. We have also introduced metrics to measure security in real-time database systems. Results clearly show that our algorithm performs fairly well in terms of security and timeliness compared to the non-secure algorithm. We also have shown that achieving security does not necessarily mean a great deal of sacrifice in real-time performance. A system can be made almost 100% covert channel free, but can still have a low deadline miss percentage for an arrival rate as high as 20. In the future we will examine temporal consistency, design suitable concurrency control algorithms and study their performance.

References

[1] Abbott, R. and H. Garcia-Molina, "Scheduling Real-Time Transactions: A Performance Evaluation" *ACM Transactions on Database Systems* 17, 1992, pp. 513-560.

[2] George, B. and J. Haritsa, "Secure Transaction Processing in Firm Real-Time Database Systems," *Proceedings SIGMOD*, Phoenix, AZ, 1997, pp. 462-473.

[3] Ozsoyoglu, Gultekin, and Richard T. Snodgrass, "Temporal and Real-Time Databases: A Survey," *IEEE Transactions on Knowledge and Data Engineering*, vol. 7 no. 4, Aug. 1995, pp. 513-532.

[4] Ramamritham, Krithi, "Real-Time Databases," *International Journal of Distributed and Parallel Databases*, 1993, pp. 199-226.

[5] Rasikan, David, Sang H. Son and Ravi Mukkamala, "Supporting Security requirements in Multilevel Real-Time Databases," *Proceedings IEEE Symposium on Security and Privacy*, Oakland, CA, May 1995, pp. 199-210.

[6] Son, Sang H., Rasikan David and Bhavani Thuraisingham, "An Adaptive Policy for Improved Timeliness in Secure Database Systems," *Proceedings of Annual IFIP WG 11.3 Conference of Database Security*, Aug. 1995.

[7] Bell D. E., and L. J. LaPadula, "Secure Computer Systems: Mathematical Foundations and Model," *Technical Report*, MITRE Corporation, 1974

[8] Denning, Dorothy E., "The Sea View Security Model," *Proceedings IEEE Symposium on Security and Privacy*, Oakland, Ca, April, 1988.

[9] Jajodia, Sushil and R. Sandhu, "Toward a Multilevel Secure Relational Data Model," *Proceedings ACM SIGMOD*, Denver, Colorado, May, ACM, New York, 1991, pp. 50-59.

[10] Wolfe, V. F. and L. C. DePippo. "Real-Time Database Systems" in *Database Systems Handbook*, (Paul J. Fortier, ed.), McGraw Hill Publishers, 1997.

[11] Haritsa, J. R., M. J. Carey and M. Livny, "Data Access Scheduling in Firm Real-Time Database Systems", *The Journal of Real-Time Systems*, 4, 203-241 (1992).

[12] Liu, C. L. and J. W. Layland, "Scheduling Algorithms for Multiprogramming in a Hard Real-Time Environment," *Journal of the ACM*, vol. 20, no. 1, Jan 1979, pp. 46-61.

[13] Moskowitz, I. S. and Allen R. Miller, "Simple Timing Channels", *Proceedings of the IEEE Symposium on Security*, 1994, pp.56-64.

[14] Qian, Xialoei, "Inference Channel-Free Integrity Constraints in Multilevel Relational Databases", *Proceedings of the IEEE Symposium on Security*, 1994, pp. 158-167.

Towards an Infrastructure for MLS Distributed Computing

Myong H. Kang, Judith N. Froscher, and Brian J. Eppinger

Naval Research Laboratory
Information Technology Division
Washington, DC, 20375

Abstract

Distributed computing owes its success to the development of infrastructure, middleware, and standards (e.g., CORBA) to support interoperability. The computing community has slowly recognized the need to protect information and has begun to develop commercial security infrastructures and standards. The US Government must protect national security information against unauthorized information flow. To support MLS distributed computing, a MLS infrastructure must be built that enables information sharing among users at different classification levels. This infrastructure should provide MLS services for protection of classified information and use both the emerging distributed computing and commercial security infrastructures, when possible. The resulting infrastructure will enable users to integrate commercial information technology products into their systems.

In this paper, we examine the philosophy that has led to successful distributed computing among heterogeneous, autonomous components and propose an analogous approach for MLS distributed computing. We identify some services that are required to support MLS distributed computing, argue that these services are needed regardless of the MLS architecture used, present an approach for designing these services, and provide design guidance for a critical building block of the MLS infrastructure.

1. Introduction

The goals of distributed computing have not been achieved painlessly. The 80's and early 90's witnessed not only the reengineering of corporate business processes to compete in global markets, but also the migration of those corporations' legacy information technology (IT) assets to widely distributed, interoperable components. This journey has been difficult and many wrong turns were taken. The development of a distributed computing infrastructure, middleware, and standards by industry have resulted in the promise of true interoperability among globally distributed users. These standards have also made it possible for many different vendors to build IT products that are interoperable. IT users, developers, and businesses, generally, have benefited from interoperable products. The US Government policy is to reap these benefits and enjoy similar productivity increases by harvesting COTS products.

In particular, the use of COTS products promises the warfighter global access to open resources. However, the use of COTS products introduces additional risk to national security because COTS products do not address the secure handling of classified information. To allow secure access to both open and classified resources, the DOD must provide multilevel secure (MLS) services to ensure that only properly cleared users access classified national security information. The confidentiality, integrity, and availability of national security resources must be protected both from hacker attacks and from attacks mounted by national intelligence organizations. In a distributed system, lots of data, even code, move from system to system. How to restrict access to the data and system resources is an important problem. Commercial security services (e.g., CORBA security services [6] and Java security [3]) attempt to address secure information sharing in a single-level distributed system. These security services are designed to work in a heterogeneous environment while preserving other properties such as autonomy and location independence. The DOD should make appropriate use of these services to protect single-level information.

A multilevel secure (MLS) service allows users with different clearances to access all and only the data their clearances authorize them to see. MLS distributed systems must satisfy functional, distribution, and single-level security requirements as well as

- enforce strict separation among classification domains and
- control the flow of information across classification boundaries.

MLS-specific requirements for distributed system design hinge on prevention of unauthorized information

0-8186-8789-4/98 $10.00

flow and require convincing evidence (i.e., assurance) that no high information is released to unauthorized systems and users and, that low cannot adversely affect the operation of high systems. High-assurance MLS systems are extremely difficult and expensive to build because the software must satisfy rigorous development standards, must undergo an extensive evaluation and certification process by an independent party, and must be protected against the insertion of malicious code throughout the entire lifecycle. As a result, almost no MLS systems are in operational use today. MLS systems are just not tractable in the current fast-paced development of new technology. Just as distributed computing only became feasible after industry developed infrastructures, middleware, and standards to support it, MLS distributed computing needs an infrastructure, middleware, and standards to make it tractable for operational use. The MLS infrastructure must co-exist with industry standard infrastructures for distributed computing and security, and must provide standard MLS services to support MLS computing.

The role of multilevel security engineers includes devising approaches that can make MLS distributed computing tractable. One way to achieve this goal is

- to develop a distributed system design approach that separates MLS protection from the design of other required functionality,
- to build a MLS distributed computing infrastructure
  - to hide the complexity of the required MLS mechanisms from system designers as much as possible,
  - to separate application specific security requirements from MLS enforcement mechanisms (i.e., MLS infrastructure provides MLS enforcement mechanisms),
  - to allow system designers to use commonly accepted distributed computing services and applications (i.e., a purpose of the MLS infrastructure is to extend single-level security services, distributed computing infrastructures and applications across classification domains), and
  - to standardize the approval process for using MLS distributed computing systems,
- to offer cost effective, reusable, and easy to maintain security devices.

In this paper, we propose an infrastructure for MLS distributed computing, and identify some necessary services and critical MLS building blocks for the proposed MLS infrastructure.

2. MLS Distributed Computing

Today's system designers and users have higher expectations than ever for usability and functionality of computer systems. Distributed object computing standards, like CORBA and DCOM, have made a basic level of interoperability possible. For example, in today's distributed object-oriented computing environment, lots of client and server objects reside in many different hosts (i.e., *heterogeneity*). Designers and users of globally distributed objects cannot be expected to know whether server objects are located in the same machine or at a remote host (i.e., *location independence*). Users and organizations want to manage their own data and computing resources (i.e., *autonomy*), but at the same time they expect sharing of information among different organizations across many systems (i.e., *information sharing*). Keeping servers active all the time hogs system resources and can be exploited to deny service to legitimate users. On the other hand, users expect a client object to be able to send a request to a server at any time and receive the reply right away (i.e., *performance and usage of system resources*). To satisfy these high expectation, standards and infrastructures for distributed computing have been built (e.g., CORBA).

What makes MLS protection different from single level security? MLS mechanisms ensure that principals can access all and only the information they are authorized to see. No protection mechanism is perfect. Flaws can be introduced in the lifecycle from the concept stage through implementation and maintenance. Any flaw in a protection mechanism can become a means for illegally leaking information or for inserting false information or malicious code. MLS protection identifies and restricts insecure information flow, for example the flow of more sensitive information to less sensitive users. An assurance argument must be developed to demonstrate that the mechanism is effective, is correctly implemented, and lastly has been so thoroughly evaluated and analyzed that there is high confidence that we have found all the exploitable vulnerabilities. The development of this assurance evidence and independent evaluation have made MLS products very costly, outmoded, difficult to use and, therefore, not really tractable in today's computing environment.

2.1 A Design Principle

Despite the difficulties that we mentioned above, when we design MLS systems, we must be concerned with assurance as well as functionality. Our prime principle for designing a MLS infrastructure and critical MLS building blocks is separation of concerns (e.g., trust and functionality). The separation of concerns principle does not provide solutions for MLS problems; however, the principle certainly makes the assurance argument easier and the solution tractable. That is because the systems that were designed based on this principle are easier to understand and allow people to concentrate on the parts that they are responsible for and familiar with.

Let us examine some lessons learned from a few successful single-level security-related technologies. Two security technologies have become commonplace in today's distributed computing environment. The first is cryptography, which can provide sender-to-receiver authentication, non-repudiation, and ensure the integrity and privacy of data in transit through a network. The second example is firewall-related technology that can isolate a community of interest from unwanted outsiders. The two main reasons for the success of these security technologies are

1. they satisfy the needs of users reasonably well,
2. their use is independent of system functionality, and therefore, almost transparent to system designers and end users (e.g., a system designer does not have to worry about whether the software will be used inside the firewall or not).

Distributed computing infrastructures have made it much easier for developers of distributed systems to practice the software engineering design discipline: *separation of concerns*. They must understand and correctly use the infrastructure and its services. When designing a system, the infrastructure allows distributed computing concerns to be addressed separately from functional issues, and makes the development of distributed systems tractable. Similarly, single-level security services must be easy to use and their use should be independent of the desired application functionality.

There are many requirements that MLS system designers have to consider. Some of them are depicted in figure 1. Functional and distribution requirements are not much different from those for single-level distributed systems. Example requirements include supporting heterogeneity, autonomy, location independence, and transparency of the distributed application in the development process (i.e., developing applications for a distributed system should not be too different from developing applications for a standalone system). Additionally, MLS distributed systems can use some single-level security mechanisms (e.g., authentication, privacy, integrity).

The MLS infrastructure should provide the services and MLS functionality to allow MLS system designers to practice an engineering discipline that is similar to that used for distributed single-level systems. The MLS infrastructure should enable system functionality to be separate from MLS enforcement and distributed computing concerns. To be successful, MLS enforcement must also be tractable. We believe that being able to reason about security independently makes tractability more attainable.

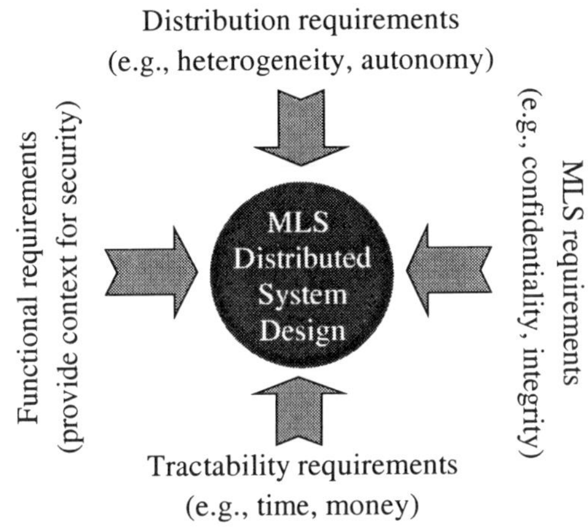

Figure 1: Requirements for MLS distributed system design

In the following subsection, we examine a few high-level requirements for a MLS distributed infrastructure.

2.2. A Few Services for a MLS Distributed Computing Infrastructure

MLS distributed computing is still in its infancy. For widespread use of MLS distributed computing, the MLS infrastructure should provide equivalent services and programming paradigms to the single-level distributed computing infrastructure. Learning from the past 20 years of MLS computing history, it is not practical to expect that MLS distributed computing will depend only on a MLS distributed computing infrastructure, which is built from scratch. What we need is a MLS infrastructure that

- seamlessly works with the single-level distributed computing infrastructure,
- operates in a heterogeneous environment while preserving other properties such as autonomy and location independence, and
- provides similar services to those available in a single-level distributed computing infrastructure across classification boundaries.

From these requirements, we derive a few important principles and identify MLS services that the MLS distributed infrastructure should provide. When we derive and design MLS services for the MLS infrastructure, we want to make sure that the MLS system designers can apply widely used design principles and paradigms. Only then will security become an "enabling technology" rather than an "encumbering technology." In this context, we set out the goals in designing the MLS distributed infrastructure.

- The infrastructure should facilitate and encourage system engineers to concentrate on system functionality. This is possible only when the MLS infrastructure faithfully carries out its "behind-the-scenes" support. This is extremely important because system functionality gives the context in which the security solution has to live and be used.
- The infrastructure should support a sound architecture and consist of well-defined functional units so that the MLS system designer makes the correct choice and can easily show that the MLS distributed architecture is secure. This principle provides a basis for using the appropriate assurance techniques to build different trusted components.
- The infrastructure should support a flexible architecture so that users and designers can place the right functions at the right place. It is important because today's user wants to manage his own computing resources and is responsible for maintaining his own resources (i.e., autonomy).
- The infrastructure should be as transparent as possible in terms of usability, performance, and the consumption of system resources.

Based on the above design goals and recent developments in single-level distributed systems, the following services extend a single-level capability across the classification boundaries:

1. *MLS server activation*. There may be many servers that expect requests from clients at different classification domains. Requiring these servers to be active all the time places an extra burden on the systems. Hence, a MLS activation service that can activate the server when requests from other classification domains arrive is needed.
2. *MLS request/reply coordination*. When a client and a server are located in different classification domains, the client's request and server's reply may not go through the same channel. For example, a client's request from a high domain to a lower domain may go through a downgrader, but the server's reply from the lower domain to the high-level client must be upgraded. However, at the same time, we do not want client software to behave differently when the servers are located in the same classification domain. Hence, there may be a need for a coordinator that can associate the corresponding reply to client's request and direct the reply to the correct client.
3. *MLS cryptography*. A MLS cryptographic infrastructure that can provide authentication and non-repudiation of the senders, and the integrity and privacy of network messages from a sender at one classification domain to a receiver at different classification domain is needed. This infrastructure should provide secure extensions of single-level cryptography across classification boundaries.

The MLS services that are described are not specific to a particular MLS architecture. Rather, they are needed in all MLS distributed systems although the implementation details may vary depending on the MLS distributed architecture.

3. Proposed Infrastructure for MLS Distributed Computing

In this section, we propose an infrastructure for MLS distributed computing. We then analyze classification boundary controllers that are the cornerstones of the proposed MLS infrastructure. In that process, we identify a generic flow controller and present a potential logical design of the flow controller.

Throughout this section, we use the multiple single level (MSL) approach [2,4] as our target architecture. The idea is that applications run at system high on physically or logically separated system high networks. Information is shared across classification levels through classification boundary controllers. This architecture allows the smooth insertion of new technology as well as the use of legacy systems. The architecture with all its security can provide a basic level of MLS interoperability through client-server interactions. Even though we use MSL architecture, it is not difficult to modify the proposed solutions to work with other architectures.

Throughout this section, we consistently apply the same guiding principle, separation of concerns (e.g., trust and functionality). We strongly believe that applying this principle to design the MLS infrastructure is important because separation of concerns enables the system designer to produce tractable solutions.

3.1. MLS Service Solutions

In this subsection, we closely look at each of the services for a MLS distributed infrastructure, as identified in section 2.2, and propose solutions. We believe the solutions should meet the following requirements.

- Proposed solutions should be independent of the MLS architecture.
- Proposed solutions should work with security unaware software, COTS or no COTS.
- Proposed solutions should have efficient system resource utilization (e.g., 10% performance penalty) pay as little performance penalty as possible, and be easy to manage.

3.1.1. MLS Server Activation Service

In today's distributed computing environment, a lot of server objects are required in order to provide appropriate system functionality and flexibility. It is not practical for all these resource servers to always be active and thereby wasting system resources. What we need is a server activation scheme across classification boundaries, which will augment the current single-level services. Figure 2 shows our proposed solution.

Our proposed solution involves the use of MLS activation daemons, which are designed to listen to boundary controllers for service requests. Servers (i.e., proxy servers in our case) that need to be started must first be registered with the MLS activation daemon. After a server has been registered, a (proxy) client can use that server by passing the desired server name to the MLS activation daemon. When the MLS activation daemon receives a request, the daemon will activate the target server and redirect the message traffic to that server.

The approach that we have described thus far is similar to single-level activation services such as Orbix's Orbixd daemon or Java's remote object activation daemon. Single-level clients and servers can talk to each other either through Internet Inter-ORB Protocol (IIOP) or Java's Remote Method Invocation (RMI) protocol. The difference in the MLS case is that those protocols have to pass through a classification boundary controller. One potential solution is to make the classification boundary controllers aware of the IIOP and RMI protocols. The drawbacks of this approach are:

- Whenever a new protocol appears, the classification boundary controllers have to be expanded and may need to be re-evaluated, re-certified, or re-accredited.
- Boundary controllers, in general, do not provide a good programming environment as we will explain in section 3.3.
- Some protocols may require feedback from the server that can not be accommodated through a boundary controller.

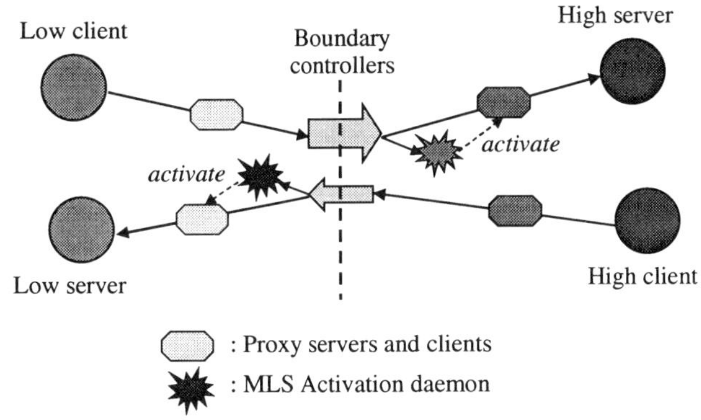

Figure 2: MLS server activation service

There is another way to provide the same capability. Rather than having boundary controllers be aware of all the protocols that potentially pass through them, boundary controllers can communicate with other software through their own protocol. The translation of application specific protocols to a boundary controller protocol is handled by *proxies*, which we sometimes call *wrappers* that wrap boundary controllers from applications. For example, when a high CORBA client requests some service from a low CORBA server, the high client activates the high proxy through a single-level activation service such as a CORBA activation daemon. The high proxy translates the IIOP request to the information release boundary controller protocol. The information release boundary controller then activates the low proxy through the MLS activation daemon to deliver the request. The low proxy translates the request that is in the form of the information release boundary controller's protocol into an IIOP request. It then can activate the real server through Orbixd. Note that two daemons, MLS and single-level activation daemons, were involved in the above server activation scenario. Also note that we could have one proxy per application protocol.

3.1.2. MLS Request/Reply Coordination Service

Usually in single-level distributed systems, the request and reply paths are through the same logical connection (e.g., a connection-oriented protocol). However, requests from clients and replies from servers may not pass through the same logical connection in MLS distributed systems. To provide an illusion to the client and server objects that they have a bi-directional connection, MLS coordination services are needed. The object or process that provides such a service is called a "coordinator" in this paper. The main responsibilities of the coordinator include:

- Act as a fake server/client so that the real client/server can establish a connection through a coordinator within the same classification domain to send requests and receive replies.
- Make use of proper classification boundary controllers.
- Coordinate replies for the proper requests.

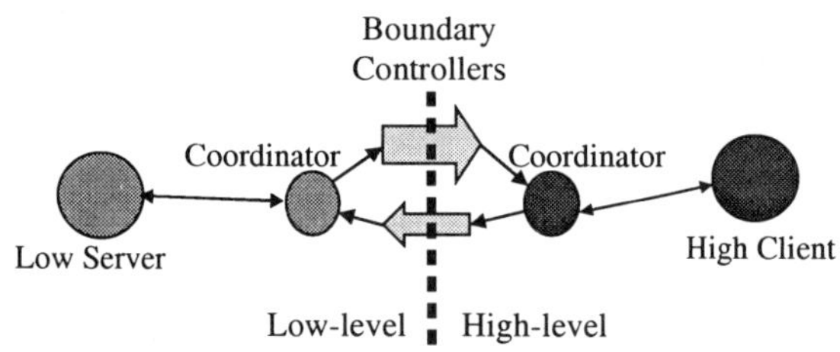

Figure 3: MLS coordination service

Figure 3 depicts an architecture for MLS coordination services. If a high client wanted a connection-oriented communication channel with a low side server, then the coordinators would be required to act as proxies to provide that connection. The coordinators would also be required to route traffic from various clients and servers to the correct destinations.

3.1.3. MLS Cryptography

In today's distributed systems, users are interested in the full range of cryptographic services. These services include privacy, authentication, integrity, and non-repudiation. MLS distributed systems, where senders and receivers may reside in different classification domains, require the same security properties. A MLS infrastructure requires a comprehensive solution to provide an equivalent security service across classification levels due to:

1. each classification domain probably has different sets of principals and
2. each classification domain may use different cryptographic infrastructures (e.g., one classification level uses a Kerberos-based cryptographic infrastructure and another classification level uses SSL-based cryptographic infrastructure).

These two factors are not unique to MLS distributed computing. However, solutions to those problems are more difficult than for single-level distributed computing due to MLS information flow restrictions.

When a MLS cryptographic infrastructure is designed, it should

- accommodate a variety of applications and cryptographic infrastructures in different classification domains,
- minimize encryption and other overhead, and
- accommodate multiple cryptographic mechanisms and Internet standards.

Figure 4 illustrates our proposed solution. This approach involves low-side and high-side cryptographic proxies. A low-side proxy that acts on behalf of a high-side sender or receiver understands the low-side cryptographic infrastructure. On the other hand, a high-side proxy that acts on behalf of a low-side sender or receiver understands the high-side cryptographic infrastructure.

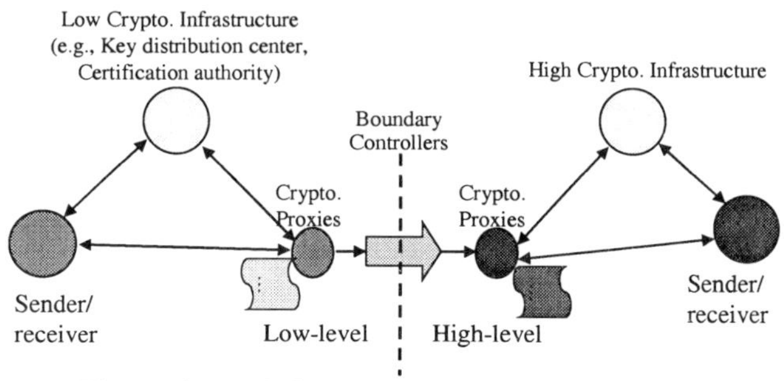

Figure 4: MLS Cryptographic services across classification domains

Consider a scenario where a low sender transmits messages to a high receiver. The high receiver needs to know if the messages come from a legitimate low source. Let's also assume that boundary controllers can use their own cryptographic algorithms that may be different from the low-side and high-side cryptographic algorithms. Let's also assume that the low-side proxy knows the set of low senders who can send messages to known high receivers. When a low sender sends a message with his own signature, that message is delivered to a low proxy. The low proxy validates the sender, through a low-level cryptographic infrastructure, that the message actually originated from the legitimate sender and is destined to a legitimate high receiver. The low proxy then relays the message to a high proxy through a boundary controller. If the high classification domain knows the low sender, the high proxy may relay the message with the low sender's signature. If the high classification domain does not know the low sender, the high proxy may relay the message with its own signature. Hence, in this case, the authentication of a low message to the high receiver is based on the trust between a low sender and a low proxy, the trust between a low proxy and a high proxy, and the trust between a high proxy and a high receiver.

As illustrated in the above scenario, cryptographic proxies can behave as if they were the endpoints (sender/receiver). The proxies perform two major roles:

- translation of the cryptographic protocol of one classification domain to the cryptographic protocol of another classification domain, and
- translation or replacement of principals so that the principal is known to the proper classification domain.

If the original message is encrypted then the problem becomes more complex. We can consider two possibilities:

- ♦ The cryptographic infrastructure of the sender's domain is replicated to the receiver's domain. In this case, encrypted messages can be passed all the way to a receiver. The receiver can decrypt the message using the replicated infrastructure.
- ♦ If the receiver's domain knows nothing about the cryptographic infrastructure of the sender's domain, then the cryptographic proxies at the sender side may have to decrypt the message. When the message reaches a receiver-side proxy, it may re-encrypt the message using the cryptographic infrastructure of the receiver's domain. Note that the message from a sender-side proxy to a receiver-side proxy may be encrypted depending upon the boundary controller and its configuration.

3.1.4. Putting It All Together

In this subsection, we have introduced many servers, coordinators, and proxies. One may wonder how we can manage all these proxies. However, it is not difficult to see that some proxies can be combined to carry out multiple functions. Consider a scenario where a high client sends a request to a low server and expects a reply. In this case, one may want to combine a high proxy server with a high request/reply coordinator and a high cryptographic proxy as one server that deals with the boundary controllers. If each proxy that participates in the merger requires cryptographic authentication in the system design, then the duplicate function can be streamlined. *It is up to the security system designer to mix and match many different techniques and functions for their needs.* The system designers have to consider all requirements (see figure 1) and come up with a reasonable solution that is clean and simple.

3.2. Anatomy of Classification Boundary Controllers

We have introduced the need for three MLS services for the MLS infrastructure in section 2. In section 3.1, we proposed solutions for the MLS infrastructure using the MSL distributed system architecture. In this section, we analyze the core functions of classification boundary controllers (CBCs) that are the key components of the proposed MLS infrastructure. Different MLS distributed architectures may have different ways to implement CBCs. However, the core functions of CBCs do not change. It is important to analyze the core functions of CBCs because it provides the basis for satisfying the MLS design goals that we described in section 1.

CBCs are, in general, high-assurance devices that have to follow rigorous development processes and go through extensive and long evaluation, certification, and accreditation processes. Hence, it is not practical to build a CBC for each specific application. Instead what we want is a high-assurance multipurpose device that can be reused in many situation, no matter what the application or the data.

To find whether it is possible to build a high-assurance multipurpose device, A few basic design questions need to be answered.

- What basic functions does a CBC perform?
- Where does each function belong? Is the function specific to each organization or is it common to all organizations that have needs to release or receive information.
- How can we organize CBCs so that they are flexible enough to add and change functionality without affecting their trustworthiness? In other words, CBCs may consist of many building blocks that perform different functions. Do all building blocks have to be trusted to the same degree? Is there any room for a different assurance strategy for different building blocks?

There are roughly three functional units through which information may have to pass when it goes across classification boundaries. They are a *release-policy server*, *flow controller*, and *receive-policy server*. An information releaser (sender) may have a specific policy to release information. An information receiver may have another policy for receiving information. The policies may differ based on the relationship between different information senders and receivers. The flow controller makes sure that information flows only in the intended direction. Let us concentrate on each functional unit one section at a time and analyze information flow across a classification boundary in terms of functionality and policy that has to be supported.

3.2.1. Information Release

Information may pass through several functional processes before it is actually released. One process may enforce the organizational and/or application-specific release policies. A release-policy server determines if the information to be released complies with the application and organizational release policies. If there is a need to sanitize information, that process has to be performed before the information reaches a release-policy server. The flow controller enforces information flow direction (i.e., no bad message or code flows from the other side). The flow controller also makes sure that all messages it receives have been authorized by the release-policy server (i.e., all information that needs to be released has to go though a valid information release-policy checker). Figure 5 shows these three functions.

In some special situations, the releaser may consider the domain to which the information is destined to be more highly protected than his domain. For a domain to be more highly protected requires that it is only accessible by more trustworthy personnel and computing resources than the releaser's domain. In this situation, the releaser's information may not need to be sanitized and the release-policy server may only have to provide an acknowledgement to the flow controller for the information's release.

Note that the answer to "which classification domain is higher (better protected) than the other?" could be very subjective. If domain A considers domain B to be accessible by suspicious personnel or computing resources, then domain A may consider itself as a higher domain than domain B. However, domain B may believe that the opposite is true (i.e., mutual suspicion).

3.2.2. Information Receive

Information receive policy depends on the trust relationship between the information sender and receiver. The receive-policy server may enforce integrity, labeling and other policies that the receiving domain wants to enforce. For example, if the receiving organizations have specific policies such as checking for viruses or adding labels to information received from another domain, then they can implement those policies in their receive-policy servers. The flow controller makes sure only authorized information flows to the receiver's classification domain and that neither information nor bad software flows from the receiver's classification domain to the sender's classification domain. Figure 5 shows this concept.

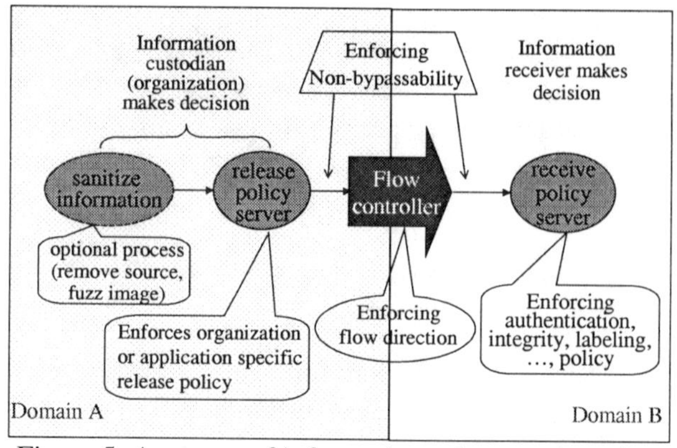

Figure 5: Anatomy of information release and receive

Note that if the receivers of information consider their domain a more highly classified domain than the senders' domain, then they may want to deploy a flow controller that can prevent covert information leakage such as the NRL Pump [5]. We would like to emphasize again that the strength and mechanism of policy servers and flow controllers depends on the trust relationship between releasers and receivers.

3.2.3. Implementation Issues

There are many ways to realize the functions and components in figure 5. One obvious way to implement these components is to host everything on a trusted machine or device. One advantage of this approach may be its footprint. However, we think this approach violates the MLS design principles proposed earlier in this paper. This approach may force every organization that has a need to release or receive information to maintain its own trusted machines that are usually very expensive in terms of hardware, software, and maintenance. Otherwise, this approach may create an organization whose sole purpose is to manage classification boundary controllers. This approach violates the autonomy principle and creates bureaucracy.

We propose another way to organize components in figure 5. Since each organization may have different release and receive policies, release-policy and receive-policy servers have to be updated and maintained by each organization that needs to release and receive information. The flow controller protects information in a classification domain rather than a specific organization. In addition, the policy that the flow controller enforces is a simple, invariant policy. Hence, the flow controller can be shared by many organizations in the same classification domain. To enforce the non-bypassability property among the flow controller and policy servers, a cryptographic algorithm could be used to provide authentication and non-repudiation services. Release-policy and receive-policy servers are managed by each organization while the flow controller is shared by many organizations.

The flow controller has to be either a trusted device or trusted software on a MLS platform because it is located at a classification boundary. The release-policy and receive-policy servers should be trusted software, where trusted means that the software will do what it is supposed to do. The question is "do we have to run a policy server on a MLS platform?" If an organization does not have to run the policy server on a MLS platform, it may save hardware and maintenance costs. We believe the policy server can be run on a single-level platform with modest trust. This trust is a little different from the TCSEC [1] multilevel trust in the sense that a designer does not have to worry about covert channels and so on. The reasons for single-level platform are as follows:

- Since policy servers are not actually located at classification boundaries, MLS platforms do not add any additional value over single-level platforms.
- If a bad process tries to smuggle information without approval from a policy server, it must prove that the information passes the test of a policy server to a flow controller. To do this the bad process must circumvent the non-bypassability channel between a policy server and the flow controller, since a flow controller will only release information from that channel.

Therefore, what needs to be protected is access to the flow controller's communication channel. In the example above, we proposed that cryptographic algorithms be used to establish this channel. In this case, what needs protection is the cryptographic key for the user who operates the policy server. Since protecting a key on a computer is not a multilevel problem, we believe a well-engineered single-level system should do the work as effectively as a MLS system.

From the description of information release and receive, it is clear that we need a high-assurance building block, a flow controller, that is flexible enough to incorporate various mechanisms for providing a trusted communications channel without affecting the assurance argument of the device.

3.3. A Logical Design of Flow Control Devices

In section 3.2, we analyzed the classification boundary controllers that are the core components in the proposed MLS infrastructure. In that process, we identified the need for a multipurpose high-assurance flow controller that is independent of a specific application to avoid repeated evaluation and certification.

In this section, we investigate the requirements of such devices. We can summarize the requirements of high-assurance flow controllers as follows.

- A flow controller should levy as little overhead as possible in terms of performance.
- They need to be network devices that can support many different network protocols (e.g., TCP/IP on Ethernet, Token ring, ATM) and simultaneous connections.
- They may need to incorporate cryptographic-based algorithms to support authentication and non-repudiation of policy servers, and the integrity and privacy of messages.
- They should have their own flexible protocol, which may be independent of network or application-level protocols, to avoid frequent changes of the device but, at the same time, support various network protocols.
- A flow controller should be structured so that it does not require new evaluation and certification every time a new network protocol, a new cryptographic algorithm, or even the direction that they are used is changed (i.e., upward or downward).

Figure 6 shows a configuration of the flow controller that can meet the above requirements. One of the most important guiding principles for the following configuration is "separation of function and trust" (which is the same principle that was applied to the analysis of boundary controllers), so the different components can be trusted in a different way and to different degrees. The MLS component should be small and generic to avoid repeated evaluation and the single-level components should be versatile, so they can adapt to many different environments.

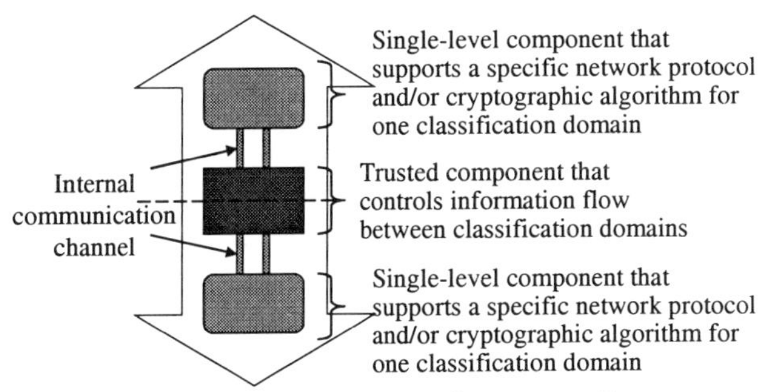

Figure 6: A multipurpose flow controller

In figure 6, the MLS middle component enforces the direction of information flow between classification domains. Two other components that are located on either side of the trusted component are single-level components that communicate to the trusted component through internal communication channels. The main functions of those two components are supporting low-level network protocols and possibly some cryptographic algorithms for the authentication of policy servers and the integrity and privacy of messages. Note that the single-level components in figure 6 can be modified without affecting the trustworthiness of the device (from the MLS point of view). Also note that there are direct paths between the MLS component and the single-level components in the device.

4. Conclusion

For widespread use of MLS distributed computing, a MLS infrastructure that provides equivalent services and programming paradigm to the single-level distributed computing infrastructure is needed. In this paper, we examined several services for the MLS distributed infrastructure. They were MLS server activation, MLS coordination, and MLS cryptographic services. We then examined classification boundary controllers that are core pieces of the MLS infrastructure. Traditional classification boundary controllers contain many functions. In this paper, we propose to distribute organization-specific functions to policy servers where the organization can update and maintain them. This approach

1. promotes autonomy and reuse,
2. is more flexible and tractable than the traditional classification boundary controller approach, and
3. saves time and money by not forcing the same level of assurance for all components.

Finally, we examined the logical structure for a multipurpose flow controller, which may be a building block of classification boundary controllers. One of the most important aspects of such devices is separation of trust and functions. The MLS component should be as small and generic as possible to avoid repeated evaluations and the single-level components should be able to adapt to as many environments as possible.

We believe this paper is a step in the right direction for MLS distributed computing in terms of trust, functionality, tractability, and usability.

References

1. Department of Defense, "Trusted computer system evaluation criteria," DoD5200.28-STD, 1985.
2. Defense Advanced Research Projects Agency, Information Systems Office, "Security Architecture for the AITS Reference Architecture," Draft document, 1998.
3. Gong, L. "Java Security Architecture (JDK1.2)," Draft document, 1998.
4. Kang, M. H., Froscher, J. N., and Moskowitz, I. S. "An Architecture for Multilevel Secure Interoperability," Proceedings of 13th Computer Security Applications Conference, San Diego, CA, 1997.
5. Kang, M. H., Moskowitz, I. S. and Lee, D. C. "A network Pump," IEEE Transactions on Software Engineering, vol. 22, no. 5, pp. 329 - 338, 1996.
6. Object Management Group "CORBA Security," OMG document 97-02-20, 97-02-21, 1997.

Track B

Internet Technologies

Chair

D. Thomsen, Secure Computing Corporation

Protecting Web Servers from Security Holes in Server-Side Includes*

Jared Karro Jie Wang
Division of Computer Science
University of North Carolina at Greensboro
Greensboro, NC 27402, USA
Jared_Karro@uncg.edu, wang@uncg.edu

Abstract

This paper first investigates and analyzes security holes concerning the use of Server-Side Includes (SSI) in some of the most used Web server software packages. We show that, by exploiting features of SSI, one could seriously compromise Web server security. For example, we demonstrate how users can gain access to information they are not supposed to see, and how attackers can crash a Web server computer by having an HTML file execute a simple program. Such attacks can be made with no trace left behind. We have successfully carried out all the attacks described in this paper on dummy servers we set up for this investigation. We then suggest several practical security measures to prevent a Web server from such attacks.

1. Introduction

Computer and network security has been studied intensely for many years and a number of defense tools, such as various encryption techniques [15] and firewall technologies [4], have been developed and put in use. World Wide Web is a new Internet application; it offers new concepts and technologies for a large scale, on-line, multi-media repository of information, which has created many new ways for conducting business and has greatly influenced the daily life of many people. But the use of World Wide Web has also interjected a new set of security problems at the same time. For example, while new programming languages such as Java and JavaScript have made it easy to produce active Web documents, some of the new programming techniques introduced in these new languages have also created new security flaws. The study of Web security has therefore become an important issue. Previous research of Web security has been primarily focused on security flaws in Java [11], ActiveX [1], and other Web programming environments [10]. The integrity and security of Web server software packages, however, have not seemed to attract much attention. To make things worse, one could use the World Wide Web without having to use a Java or an ActiveX environment, but one is forced to use Web server software. Hence, the issue on the security of Web server software deserves serious consideration.

Web servers offer certain features that ordinary network servers do not allow. Such features are useful for users to create dynamic Web documentations. For instance, a Web server may provide certain mechanisms that allow users to automatically update the "date last modified" information of their Web pages. Such features, however, may also unknowingly give away certain valuable information to unauthorized Web users. Information about server computers obtained through Web servers may be used by a malicious user to harm the Web server in a number of ways, including crashing the Web server computer. Thus, investigating what type of information is obtainable from a Web server and what harm can be made by obtaining such information becomes interesting and important, particularly to universities, Internet service providers, and other organizations where a variety of users are allowed (and often are encouraged) to create their own home pages.

Most Web servers support Server-Side Includes (SSI), which can be used to execute CGI (Common Gateway Interface) scripts and echo valuable information to Web browsers. The ability to do SSI is independent from the Web browsers, making it particularly convenient in the multi-browser world we currently live in. Thus, SSI may serve as a powerful tool to obtain information and perform

*This work was supported in part by the University of North Carolina at Greensboro under grant 3-19612 and by NSF under grant CCR-9424164.

other tasks. In this paper, we will discuss flaws and areas of security concerns on SSI in many of the major Web server software packages used on the Internet. We show that, by exploiting features of SSI, a user can gain valuable information about a Web server computer as well as do harm to the server. For instance, a user can obtain information about the server computer configuration and what processes are currently in running on the server computer and by whom; he can kill a process that does not belong to him; and he can even crash the server computer. He can do so from a client computer without having access log into the actual server computer.

We investigate several Web server software packages for computers running UNIX, Windows 95, and Windows NT operating systems. We restrict our discussion to Web server software packages that are available either free of charge; or as free, fully functional, evaluation copies. We do not intend to cover all Web server software packages in this paper, nor do we intend to include all of the versions for the Web servers we do discuss. Certain security holes found in an early version of a particular Web server software package may have already been corrected in a newer version; but we found that a number of organizations, including our own, were/are still using an early version of certain Web servers, and so we feel that we are obligated to publishing our findings. Findings of this sort may also help server software developers and server administrators to identify some of the gray areas of security that might have been overlooked.

For convenience, in what follows, we will use "Web server" to denote "Web server software package" and "Web server computer" to denote the computer that runs the server software. We will use "Web viewer" to denote the individual who is viewing the Web pages and "Web user" to denote the individual who is creating the pages. The "Web facilitator" refers to the UNIX user ID under which all the Web server processes are executed. Depending on the Web server, the Web facilitator does not need to be an actual user on a UNIX system. In other words, the Web facilitator may simply be a fictitious user who does not own a directory nor have explicit rights (in fact, as we will discuss later, it may be safer to use a fictitious user rather than a real user). For simplicity, we sometimes omit the word "Web".

This paper is organized as follows. In Section 2, we show that one can exploit SSI loop holes to accomplish certain useful tasks on one hand, and to compromise the security of the underlying Web server on the other hand. Since most published works that deal with Web security (e.g., [14], [7], and [2]) have only briefly, if at all, mentioned the possible hazards of SSI, we demonstrate several examples of attacks that we have devised and carried out on dummy servers we set up for this investigation. These examples of attacks include methods to crash Web server computers, to kill other users' processes, and to have the Web server automatically send out e-mail messages to selected individuals. Such attacks can be made with no trace left behind. In Sections 3 and 4, we show and discuss how to obtain the necessary rights to execute those harmful SSI feature even though the user may be denied such rights by the default setting of SSI. We analyze the following Web server software packages on the UNIX platforms in Section 3: Apache, Stronghold, Netscape Fast-Track 3.0, Zeus Server; and we analyze the following software packages on the Windows platforms in Section 4: Netscape Fast-Track 2.0, Netscape Enterprise (NT only), and O'reilly WebSite Professional (NT only). The Apache server, according to a recent survey [12], is the most used Web server under UNIX platform. In Section 5 we offer several security measures, based on our investigation and analysis of security holes in SSI, to protect Web servers from the attacks we describe in this paper. We hope that this paper will serve as a useful tool to help the reader in choosing a suitable Web server and Web environment, as well as a guide for securing his Web server from attacks of these types.

2. SSI and security holes

We will first show in this section how SSI can be used to perform certain useful things when users are denied access to CGI scripts. We will then show how SSI can be used to compromise the security of the underlying Web server. We assume that the user has rights to execute the exec and include directives. This opens a door for users to create their own scripts (programs), which could be used to do useful things such as setting up counters, or could be used to do harmful things such as crashing the server computer.

2.1. Useful Exploitation of Loop Holes

Depending on the server environment, it may become necessary for the users to exploit loop holes in SSI to accomplish certain useful tasks. For instance, the Web server at our university does not allow users to execute their own CGI scripts, and it only provides a CGI script for mailmerge. This means that if we want to set up a counter of visits in our pages, we have to use a service provided by other Web servers outside of the campus. This will slow down the loading of our pages and we cannot guarantee that the counter will always work.

To get around this problem, we wrote a C++ program to look at a log file, count the number of hits on the given page periodically, and output the result with a graphic image. The program needs to know the current time for the counting purpose, which is done by executing the date system call. The CGI variable $REMOTE_HOST or $REMOTE_ADDR provides information on which location the viewer was hitting the page.

2.2. Examples of attacks

We describe five possible attacks using SSI in this subsection, which have all been carried out successfully in our experiments.

Example 1: Crashing the Web server computer. A malicious user can crash a Web server computer by running a CGI script that runs the following simple C program.

```
for (;;) malloc(1024);
```

Using an SSI line to execute this C program will use up all available RAM of the Web server computer in a matter of seconds, yielding a system crash. Moreover, while the Web server computer is completely unfunctional, it is still able to respond to pings. This means that common administrative programs which ping network servers periodically to ensure that servers are up and running will not notice anything wrong. However, the computer will not be able to allocate memory to create any new process. Hence, all connection requests will be refused. Any connections that were already established will lock. As a consequence, unsaved data may be lost.

Example 2: Starting a daemon process. Users can write an SSI file to start a daemon process (e.g., another server) from the Web server computer. For instance, although our Web server does not allow user logins on the server, we were able to start an ftp server on the server computer. It is interesting to note that the Web server could not tell who actually caused the ftp server to start. The Web server thought that the Web facilitator (which did not even exist) started the process. This means that user activities are covered (or shielded) from the Web server. The Web server log files, which we will discuss later in Section 2.3, are also of no use. Attackers could possibly write their own server program so that it contained flaws, which could then be used to further exploit the server. If the attacker made the program appear to be a legitimate process that normally runs on the server (by making the name look similar to httpd or some other common process), the system administrator may not notice the attackers' program. If the program is served as a back door into the system, the attacker could get control the entire system. The ftp server that we started, for instance, did not require logins; thus, the ftp client had gained access equivalent to the Web facilitator.

Example 3: Killing a process. An attacker can kill a process generated by the Web facilitator. This means that the attacker could kill all of the other children processes started by the Web facilitator. Even if the original process were to re-generate the children process (as in the case of the most Web servers), a program could be written to continuously kill these processes as soon as they are created. Thus, all Web processes created to answer requests would be killed before requests could be answered. Since the processes generated by the Web facilitator can be killed by the attacker, the attacker can kill any process on the Web server computer if the root of the Web server is also the Web facilitator.

Example 4: AutoMail. Users can write a program that would in turn connect to other computers and do certain things. These activities would appear to be generated by the Web server rather than by the users. For instance, the user could have the Web server send out fake e-mail to random recipients or to particular persons (e.g., the chancellor of a university or a state senator). Since the Web server creates the message, there would be no information in the e-mail headers showing that it was the user's computer that was responsible for generating the message.

Example 5: Probing Web server computers. We describe below steps that could be used to probe a Web server computer. The idea is consistent for either the UNIX or the Windows operating system, but the syntax and the process is slightly different. As a result, knowing what operating system the Web server is running is the first issue that must be resolved. This can be done with the following SSI lines:

```
<!--#echo var="SERVER_SOFTWARE"-->
<!--#echo var="PATH"-->
```

Executing an SSI file that contains these two lines will display the Web server software and the path for the Web facilitator. This should give the user enough information to figure out which operating system the Web server is running. In some cases, only one of these may be necessary.

In an UNIX system, one can use a series of the SSI lines below to probe a system. For a Windows 95/NT system, one must use a batch file containting the equivalent DOS commands.

```
<!--#exec cmd="pwd"-->
```

```
<!--#exec cmd="ls <directory>
                   <switches>"-->
<!--#exec cmd="rm <file>"-->
<!--#exec cmd="more <file>"-->
```

2.3. Logging of SSI

All of the Web servers we have tested appear to generate similar logs, and so we will discuss the logging of SSI in a general framework. We will show how to make the attacks we described above with no trace left behind.

If the execution of an SSI file does not generate an error, there will be no special entry in the Web server's log file. As usual, the Web document that was requested is entered into the access log, but there is no mentioning of SSI execution. If someone tries to execute an SSI file, but the execution is denied by the server for the directory containing the SSI file, then the URL will be logged as illegally attempting to perform execution.

The lack of logging successful SSI execution means that if someone runs a program that crashes the server computer, the server administrator would be unable to see exactly what happened or who did it. Chances of catching the perpetrator would be reduced even more if the attacker had the program wait for sufficiently long time before executing the deadly functions. In this way, although the access of the SSI file that runs the attacker's program was entered into the access log, this entry might have already been deleted after the actual attack was initiated. The attacker could also have the program altered the SSI file after the file was parsed, thus removing the line that dealt the deadly blow.

3. Web servers on UNIX platforms

We analyze the following Web servers for UNIX operating systems: Apache 1.2.0, Stronghold 2.0, Netscape Fast-Track 3.0, and Zeus Server. The Apache server, according to a recent survey by Netcraft [12], was the most used Web server. It was used by almost 44% of about 1.2 million sites that responded to the Netcraft survey. Stronghold is an enhanced commercial version of Apache, which, according to Netcraft [12], is the second most popular commercial Web server. We will discuss how a user may obtain rights to execute SSI directives exec and include, even though the user may be denied such rights by the default setting of the Web server. Once the user obtains such rights, then the attacks we described in Section 2 can be carried out.

3.1. Apache 1.2.0

The Apache server is the result of the joint work of many independent programmers, which is based on the NCSA Web server. Apache 1.2.0 has two basic configuration files: access.conf and httpd.conf. Some versions of Apache also have a srm.conf file, but in recent versions of Apache the srm.conf file can be included at the end of httpd.conf. The httpd.conf file stores the basic Web server configuration information, including things such as the port to listen to, the server administrator, the user directory path, the server namespace, and the AccessFileName variable (which will be described later). The access.conf file tells the server what type of services is allowed and where the requests for these services can be made from.

We find that with Apache, users are allowed to override the settings that have been set by the server administrator. This can be done by creating a file named .htaccess in the user's directory, which is, by default, the access override file that does the overriding job. The administrator can change the file name .htaccess to some other file names by editing the AccessFileName entry in the httld.conf file. But the server administrator cannot simply remove this line to prevent the user from using access overriding file because if this line is removed, or the filename is actually a directory followed by a file (i.e. `<directory>/<file>`), then the default, .htaccess will be used. While overriding the server settings for the server's root directory is turned off by default, access overriding is allowed for user directories. This means that even if the administrator does not intend for users to parse or execute CGI scripts, users can still give themselves access rights to do so, unless specifically denied.

As a default setting, Apache does not allow users to parse SSI files. This feature may seem secure enough to prevent users from running the attacks we described in Section 2. However, if overriding settings is permitted, the user can activate the Web server to parse SSI files using one of the following Apache configurations: ExecCGI, Includes, and IncludesNOEXEC. The user can also have the Web server parse any extensions they desire. The following is an example of a .htaccess file:

```
Options Indexes FollowSymLinks Includes
AddType text/x-server-parsed-html .html
AddType text/x-server-parsed-html .htm
```

The first line turns on all SSI features so that SSI files can be parsed and executed. The other three lines tell the Web server to parse files with extensions .cgi, .html, and .htm. Files with other types of extensions could also be added if desired.

When the Web server finds a .htaccess file (such as the one described above) in any of the parent directories of the directory where the requested HTML file is located, the server will use the settings in that file unless the server is explicitly told to ignore the access override file. By adding "AllowOverride NONE" to the section of the access.conf file for the directory where overriding is not to be allowed, the administrator removes the ability for users to override the desired settings. For more information about the options available for this feature, see the Apache documentation [3].

Apache 1.2.0 also comes with suEXEC [16], which is a CGI wrapper. This feature is designed to change the UID of a CGI script to match that of the user who owns the script. But suEXEC is not part of the standard installation. (Installing suEXEC is not an easy process.)

Apache 1.2.0 also has features that allow the server administrator to set bounds on server resources, such as the CPU time and RAM, for CGI programs. The directives RLimitCPU, RLimitMEM, and RLimitPROC all have default values of whatever the underlying operating system defaults are. Together these directives should be able to prevent against attacks such as complete memory allocation. If used independently, however, the user could get around the limitation by exploiting the other unlimited methods. For example, if the server administrator merely sets the server so that the number of processes could not exceed five, the attacker could make four processes which all have high priority so that they would use up all or most of the CPU time. Since these features do not appear in versions of Apache prior to 1.2.0, it is highly recommended to upgrade to the latest version of Apache (version 1.3 is currently in its alpha testing phase).

3.2. Stronghold 2.0

Stronghold is an enhanced commercial version of Apache. The configuration on the version we tested was identical to that of Apache. The new release of Stronghold will have a GUI configuration. Stronghold is designed to act as a secure server. It has built-in capabilities for generating certificates and doing SSL encryption, and comes with a Server Certificate. Since it is a commercial product, the technical support is probably better than that of Apache. An NT version of Stronghold 2.0 is now in the beta stage.

3.3. Netscape Fast-Track v3.0

The Netscape Fast-Track Web server, by default, does not parse any SSI files. Once SSI parsing is enabled, Netscape servers would only parse files with the .shtml extension. The server can be configured to parse all files. The servers can also be configured to parse files according to directories such that they can either allow or deny execution from within an SSI line. If execution is not allowed, then the user cannot use the exec or include directives. The server administrator can set which file extensions and which directories the server will parse. However, by default, making changes to these settings will effect the entire Web server.

When setting up the server, the server administrator can specify the Web facilitator to be a user that does not physically exist. Root, or whoever originally starts the server, will execute the original process; and all other processes will be run by the Web facilitator. This prevents scripts (programs) from accidentally having access to files they are not supposed to, since scripts will have the same access to files as the Web facilitator. If the Web facilitator is a fictitious user, scripts will only be permitted to write or delete files that any user on the system can.

3.4. Zeus server

Zeus Server is a product of a British company. A fully functional evaluation copy can be obtained free of charge for a 30-day trial from their Web site[17]. By default, the server does not parse any SSI files. The administrator can turn on SSI parsing for the root directories and user directories separately. Once SSI parsing is turned on, Zeus server only parses files with extension .shtml. Turning on parsing does not allow CGI execution. CGI execution is turned on via another option, and once again it can be turned on for the root and user directories separately.

Once CGI execution is permitted, CGI programs must be executed either directly (specifically calling the .cgi file in the URL) or via the cgi parameter with the exec directive. If the user tries to use the cmd parameter, he will receive an error message in his HTML file. Another nice feature of Zeus Server is that it has something called Sandbox CGI. This allows the server administrator to set bounds on the CPU time and RAM that CGI programs have access to. This prevents users from purposely, or accidentally, interfering with the normal process of the server. Unfortunately, not all operating systems support this feature. Hence, the server administrator may want to test this feature on his server computer to determine whether he can safely rely on this feature.

One drawback of this server is that the Web facilitator must actually exist on the server. This means that the server administrator should generate a user with minimal rights to run the server. As before, if the Web server was run by the root, CGI programs would have full access to the server, which could lead to tragic results.

4. Web servers on windows platforms

The Web servers on the Windows platforms have slightly different features and options from the Web servers on the UNIX platforms. SSI is also handled differently in Windows 95 and in Windows NT.

Windows 95 and Windows NT are two different operating systems, but the Web servers on these platforms act in similar ways. We have tested the following three different Web servers: Netscape Fast-Track 2.0 (Windows 95 and NT versions), Netscape Enterprise 3.0 (NT only), and O'reilly WebSite Professional (NT only). Due to the extreme similarities in functionality of the different Web servers, this section is divided into functionality subsections instead of product subsections.

4.1. Capabilities of SSI

The Netscape Web servers for Windows 95 and NT all have default configurations that forbid users to run SSI. These servers can be configured to parse any file extensions that are desired. By default, once parsing is enabled, Netscape servers will only parse files with the .shtml extension. The servers can be configured to parse certain extensions in one directory and other extensions in another directory. WebSite Professional parses SSI files with the .html-ssi extension. Like the Netscape servers, extensions can be manually added or removed as desired.

SSI is divided into two different categories under all of these Web servers. The first category only allows SSI directives that do not execute user programs. This means that users are restricted to such SSI directives as echo and flastmod. The second category allows SSI directives that can execute user programs and CGI scripts.[1] Thus, this category is potentially more dangerous.

Users can write CGI scripts to do virtually anything they desire under the Windows 95 and Windows NT platforms. If a CGI script is made as a batch file, then it can do anything a person can normally do in a DOS window, including viewing and deleting files, even if they lie outside the normal scope of the Web server. With a series of SSI lines (or CGI scripts), users could scan the entire system on the Web server computer, and delete or view any file of others. They can do so without even knowing anything about how the system is configured (e.g. drives, directory structure). See Example 5 in Section 2 for an example of the steps an attacker could use to probe a system under the Windows platforms.

As shown in Example 1 in Section 2, a malicious user could also crash a Windows 95 Web server computer by running a simple C program: for(;;) malloc(1024). Executing this program or a similar one in DOS-CGI or Win-CGI will use up all available RAM of a Windows 95 Web server computer in a few seconds, yielding a system crash. No commands (such as soft reboot) can bring the Web server up and running, and so manual reboot is required to bring the server computer back to life.

If the same program is executed on a Windows NT Web server, however, the effect is much different. Windows NT employs a robust memory management scheme. It automatically utilizes unoccupied hard disk space as virtual memory. Thus, although running the C program described above will slow down the Web server computer, it does not bring it to a complete halt until it uses up all memory and available hard disk space. We have tested this program on a PC with 80MB RAM and a 90MHZ CPU running Windows NT, and we found that after about half an hour the program was still running and had allocated 184MB of virtual memory. Although the computer was noticeably slower, it was still able to respond to new commands and open new processes. In other words, the Web server, and more importantly the Web server computer, was still functional.

4.2. Directory access

Access rights of parent and children directories are another possible point of security holes. In all of the Windows Web servers we have mentioned, if the parent directory is set to have greater rights than a child directory, the child directory will inherit the parent's rights. This inheritance of rights holds true even if the child's rights are explicitly set to be lower than its parent's. Although this structure does not typically produce security problems if virtual directories are used, it may create a security problem if a virtual directory is accessible through its parent directory. If the URL uses the virtual name, then the user will be restricted to the rights assigned to that virtual directory. If a user gains access through the directory structure, he will inherit the greatest rights of the ancestor directories.

Now for the good part, Windows 95 and Windows NT servers can configure certain directories as CGI directories and allow users to execute CGI scripts only in these designated directories. Moreover, the server can be configured to only allow certain types of CGI. In fact, the administrator must manually list the directories they want to allow CGI access from within. Therefore, the Web server can prevent users from generating CGI scripts by forbidding users to gain write access to these directories. However, once users gain rights to create their own scripts, there is no way of stopping them from running harmful

[1] There are several different types of CGI: DOS (or shell), standard (Perl or other scripting languages), and Windows.

CGI scripts.

5. Security solutions

Garfinkel and Spafford [7] suggest that it might be more secure to run a Web server on a Macintosh computer. Macintosh computers have no command-line interpreter, so break-ins may be more difficult. We have not tested this concept, but it seems logical. However, it may be possible to execute commands if the Macintosh Web server has a PC board, which may be used to comprise the advantage of using a Macintosh computer as a Web server.

In this section, we will focus on Web servers running UNIX, Windows 95, and Windows NT operating systems. We form a number of security measures, based on our investigation and analysis of security holes in SSI, to protect Web servers from the attacks we described earlier in the paper. We first provide a list of general security measures that are independent of the operating system used by the Web server. Following these recommendations, we further provide a number of more specific solutions according to which operating system the Web server is running.

5.1. General security measures

1. Keep the server software up to date. New versions of server software and patches are routinely released to fix security holes or other bugs found in early versions.

2. The server administrator should carefully review the needs of his users and the security risks involved with those needs. Once the server administrator has decided what types of access are allowed and to whom, he will need to configure his server to allow only the access as specified. If the server administrator discovers that his Web server does not support the type of configuration he desires, he should consider using a different Web server.

3. Once the server configuration is determined, the system administrator should thoroughly test the Web server to confirm that restrictions have been properly set and his clients have been confined in an appropriate environment to work within. In other words, clients should be given access rights for doing the things they need do, but nothing more.

4. As suggested in [2], consider not allowing SSI at all. Most things that can be done via SSI, can also be done with the use of scripts and crontabs. For example, we can use utilities such as sed and awk to create headers and footers. For a good source on how to use these tools to automate the creation of headers and footers, the reader is referred to [6].

5. Run the Web server on a computer designated to running only the Web server. Running other daemons on the same server may compromise the Web server if one of these daemons are compromised.

6. Do not store critical Web files and user Web files on the same server [14]. By separating this type of information, we can restrict the average user from having access to certain critical Web files or capabilities, while allowing the official pages to have access to these features and files.

7. Keep any scripts that come with the Web server up-to-date. Software vendors often release new versions of these scripts to fix known bugs or security holes.

5.2. Solutions for UNIX web servers

The following are our suggestions for Web servers running in an UNIX environment. These recommendations are in addition to, and not in place of, those listed in Section 5.1.

1. Do not run the Web server as root. While the CERT advisory 95-04 [5] suggests to run the Web server as nobody, Ruben et al. [14] suggest to run it as a genuine and unique user with membership in a unique group. This way, there is no need to worry about the Web server sharing rights with other programs which are running as nobody.

2. If SSI is allowed, all users must be restricted to SSI directives that cannot execute programs. Users can still easily include dynamic features such as "date last modified" and where the viewer is coming from, but they would not be able to execute commands or scripts from within directives, and so they could not use the attacks we have described. We can restrict users from using executable SSI directives in NCSA-derived Web servers, such as Apache and Stronghold, by putting the following line in the server options:

   ```
   Options IncludesNOEXEC
   ```

   In Web servers with a Web-based configuration, such as those by Netscape and Zeus, make sure that the "Without exec tag" is chosen instead of "With exec tag".

3. If an NCSA-derived server is used, disable the ability of users to override the server settings with the use of their own .htaccess file. This may not allow users to create password protected directories, but it will be well worth it. This can be accomplished by putting the following line in the user's directory entry in the Web server configuration file:

   ```
   AllowOverride None
   ```

   This will prevent users from overriding any settings. If really necessary, we could replace None with a different directory directive, but do not put the Options directive on this line, as this would allow users to turn back on all SSIs and use them.

4. Disable any unnecessary services [7]. Commenting out their lines in inetd.conf will eliminate some of these services. Other services require that their "rc" files be eliminated.

5.3. solutions for windows 95/NT Web servers

The following are our suggestions for Web servers running in a Windows environment. These recommendations are in addition to, and not in place of, those listed in Section 5.1.

1. Allow CGI to be run from within only secure and well-monitored directories. These directories are the only ones in which execution of scripts should be allowed.

2. Only trusted users should be allowed to create or modify CGI scripts lying within executable directories. The Web administrator should review these scripts after any alterations are done. The focus of the review should be two-fold. First, make sure the script itself does not initially compromise security. Second, make sure that any Web viewer or Web user arguments are thoroughly checked for correctness. If this is not done, the scripts could be used to achieve undesired results and possibly execute one of the attacks discussed in this paper.

3. Make sure no interpreters or shells are in any of the Web server's cgi-bin directories [7].

4. In Windows NT, use the access list to deny access to all ports except desired ones; disabling IP services requires manual manipulation of the registery file, which can be dangerous in itself [7]. Not doing this could open a computer to attack such as the Windows OOB Bug [8].

Final Remarks. After seeing an early version of this paper, the Web server administrator of our university has taken certain necessary security measures we suggeseted in this paper, to improve the Web server security of our university. However, this should in no way be interpreted as an invitation to try some of the attacks we described in this paper on our Web servers; and we humbly beseech our gentle readers: Please Don't.

References

[1] ActiveX and Web Security Loopholes. E-mail received from *TipWorld*, 1997. (TipWorld is located at http://www.tipworld.com. This particular issue can also be found at URL http://www.uncg.edu/~jqkarro/Netscape/Security/ActiveX.html.)

[2] Anonymous. *Maximum Security*. Sams.net Publishing, 1997.

[3] Apache Core Features. URL http://www.apache.org/docs/mod/core.html, 1997.

[4] W. Cheswick and S. Bellovin. *Firewalls and Internet Security*, Addision-Wesley, 1994.

[5] CERT advisory 95-04: NCSA HTTP Daemon for UNIX
vulnerability. URL ftp://info.cert.org/pub/cert_advisories/CA-95:04.NCSA.http.daemon.for.unix.vulnerability, 1995.

[6] D. Dougherty. *SED and AWK*. O'Reilly & Associates Inc., 1992.

[7] S. Garfinkel, and G. Spafford. *Web Security and Commerce*. O'Reilly & Associates Inc., 1997.

[8] S. Jenkins. Windows OOB Bug. URL http://www.winfiles.com/bugs/oob.html, 1998.

[9] J. Karro. A C++ counter program. URL http://www.uncg.edu/~jqkarro/counterCode.C, 1997.

[10] B. McWilliams. Can Your Webmaster Watch You? URL http://www.pcworld.com/cgi-bin/database/body.pl?ID=970827180448, 1997.

[11] G. McGraw, and E. Felton. *Java Security: Hostile Applets, Holes, and Antidotes*. Wiley Computer Publishing, 1997.

[12] The Netcraft Web Server Survey. URL `http://www.netcraft.com/survey/`, 1997.

[13] N. Neulinger. CGIWrap. URL `http://wwwcgi.umr.edu/~cgiwrap/`, 1997.

[14] A. Rubin, D. Geer, and M. Ranum. *Web Security Sourcebook: A Complete Guide to Web Security Threats and Solutions*. John Wiley & Sons, Inc., 1997.

[15] B. Schneier. *Applied Cryptography—Protocols, Algorithms, and Source Code in C*, 2nd edition, John Wiley and Sons, 1996.

[16] Apache suEXEC Support. URL `http://www.apache.org/docs/suexec.html`, 1997.

[17] Zeus Technology. URL `http://www.zeus.co.uk/`, 1997.

Rule-Based Filtering for Java Applets

Pietro Iglio, Fausto Fraticelli, Luigi Giuri
Fondazione Ugo Bordoni
Roma, Italy
e-mail: {iglio, faustof, giuri}@fub.it

Abstract

Java has been designed with a sophisticated security model that prevents applets downloaded from an untrusted network to attack the local system. However, malicious applets could exploit bugs in the virtual machine in order to gain access to system resources to perform unauthorized operations.

This paper discusses the problem of intercepting such applets through a set of filtering rules that can be applied before a fixed version of the virtual machine is released. Moreover, we present an implementation of a filtering tool that can be used either as a firewall extension or as a virtual machine extension.

1 Introduction

Java is both a general purpose programming language and a platform introduced by Sun Microsystems. Since Java can be used to build distributed applications that can run unchanged on a large range of computer systems, it is going to become the primary choice for the development of Internet/Intranet applications.

The main reason for the popularity of Java is due to the fact that real world organizations demand software solutions that are multi-platform, compatible with Internet technologies, and secure.

Java's architecture involves two main features: a language that is both compiled and interpreted, and a virtual machine (JVM). The compilation of a Java source code prepares it to be interpreted by the virtual machine. This means that the result of the compilation is a binary code that can only be executed by the Java virtual machine, and not by a real processor. In other words, in order to execute Java binary code on any platform it is sufficient to provide a Java virtual machine for that platform. The binary code is a set of *bytecode* instructions, and the compiled file has the extension `.class`.

Java is a trademark of SUN Microsystems, Inc. Other company and product names reported in this paper may be claimed as trademarks.

An *applet* is a special kind of network-oriented Java application. A*ppl* stands for 'application' and *et* for 'net'. Applets can be loaded from a Web server into the Web browser, and are generally used to dynamically enhance browser functionalities. For instance, applets can be used to add active contents to static HTML pages, thus enhancing the possibility of interaction between the user and the Web server. The most popular Web browsers, such as Netscape Navigator and Microsoft Internet Explorer, already support Java applets.

Several implementations of Java are available. The Java Development Kit by Sun Microsystems, currently at version 1.1.6, is the reference implementation. It is freely available at [JDK]. Every implementation generally provides a compiler, and a virtual machine.

One of the major attractions of Java is its advanced security model. Since the first Java release, there has been a growing interest around Java security.

In Section 2 we shall describe the basic features of the Java security model. Later, we shall point out some potential security risks due to the download of applets from untrusted sources, solutions already available, and their limits. In Section 4 we shall introduce an extension of the Java security model that can be easily adapted to existing implementations to protect systems against applets that, in order to gain unauthorized privileges, might exploit bugs in the specific implementation. Finally, we shall provide some implementation details and we shall finish with our conclusions.

2 Java security model

The Java security model relies on four distinct layers. The first one is the programming language, that imposes several restrictions in order to disallow any kind of dangerous operation, such as direct memory reference, out-of-range array access, illegal type casts, and so on.

The next one is the virtual machine, that performs runtime checks on array bounds and type conversions. Furthermore, the virtual machine is responsible for verifying that a bytecode has really been produced by a valid Java compiler, otherwise an attacker could modify

0-8186-8789-4/98 $10.00 © 1998 IEEE

a compiled program to bypass the restrictions imposed by the programming language rules.

The third layer is represented by the runtime library, that includes classes to create windowed interfaces, access system resources such as the file system, and so on. Since the only way to access system resources from a Java program is through the runtime library, appropriate security checks in the corresponding functions ensure that untrusted programs cannot access them.

Finally, the runtime environment implements a security policy. This can be done writing a subclass of the `SecurityManager` class, and making it the system's security manager. The runtime environment, unlike the previous three layers, is the only layer that is implementation dependent.

3 The Problem

The Java security model provides a good level of protection against hostile applets coming from an untrusted network as long as the layers implementing the security model have no bugs. Unfortunately, past experiences have proved that software systems are likely to contain bugs that can be used to gain unauthorized privileges. Operating systems, such as UNIX-derivatives, have been subjected to such kind of attacks for years.

Java is not going to be an exception. In fact, some bugs in widely adopted implementations of the Java Virtual Machine have been recently discovered. For example, a serious bug has been discovered in the digital signing library of Java Development Kit (JDK) 1.1.1. A malicious applet could exploit this bug to forge its signing identity and gain unauthorized privileges. Another example of a security bug is the "IP Number Bug", discovered in JDK 1.0.2, and described in [IP]. This bug allows an applet to determine the IP address and local hostname of an host placed behind a firewall and then send this address to the server (normally the IP address of such host behind a firewall should be hidden to external entities).

Another reason to believe that Java will be subjected to attacks exploiting implementation bugs is that the Java platform is continuously growing with the addition of new system libraries, covering a large number of application domains, and being developed by different vendors. Past experiences have shown that adding new features to a software system increases the probability of introducing bugs.

Since bugs are a reality in the software industry and cannot be ignored when considering security issues, an organization should be ready to adopt appropriate countermeasures when a new bug in a Java Virtual Machine implementation is discovered.

Nowadays, when a bug is found users have to wait for the related patches to use their Java interpreter without risks. This can be a problem, since Java implementors can take weeks to provide patches. Moreover, many users are not aware of these kinds of problems, and they do not upgrade their Java interpreter often enough.

For these reasons, it could be very helpful to have a system that is able to temporarily protect a Java interpreter from applets trying to exploit bugs before a definitive solution is provided by Java vendors. Also, it would be useful for an organization to have some sort of central control against this kind of attacks.

Several solutions have been proposed to control or to filter applets loaded from the network. For example, there are applets controllers that allow users to monitor the set of applets currently running on the local host, to change the thread's priority, to stop or to kill applets, to set a personal security policy, to block applets coming from a suspicious URL and so on. This is a sort of active protection and requires a certain degree of expertise.

Passive protection against hostile applets can be obtained using an applet filter that accepts only applets incoming from a subset of trusted hosts. An example of a tool providing this kind of protection is described in [PRI]. Other tools, such as the one described in [SUR], provide both active and passive protection.

However, these solutions are still unsatisfactory as far as bugs are concerned. In fact, to the best of our knowledge there is no tool that can be effectively used against bugs.

With the solution proposed in this work, we try to address this problem. Our approach, integrated with classic approaches, could substantially improve site protection against malicious applets.

4 Rule-based Filtering

In this section we propose an extension of the Java security model based on applet analysis against a set of filtering rules that can be customized according to user needs. In the next sections we shall provide more details about the filtering algorithm and about an implementation of the filtering module.

The central idea is fairly simple and is based on the following points:

- before a class instance for an untrusted applet is created, the JVM receives the applet in the form of a class file, called applet bytecode;

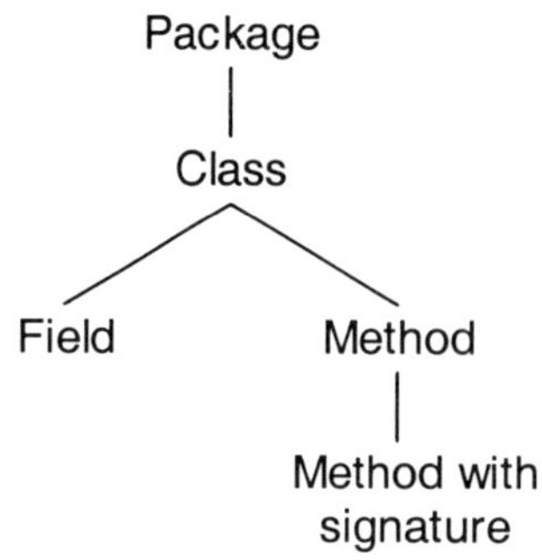

Figure 1. Hierarchy within a Java library.

- the applet bytecode structure contains information about every package, class, method or field the applet is going to use directly;
- an applet cannot perform any (dangerous) operation if it's stopped before a class instance is created;

Therefore, the traditional security model can be extended by adding an extra module. This module examines the applet bytecode to retrieve information about what the applet is going to use, compares this information with a set of user rules, and rejects every applet that does not satisfy any of these rules.

For example, a security policy might require that applets coming from an untrusted Web site cannot open network connections. The original sandbox model allows an applet to open a network connection with the originating server. According to our solution, network connection could be denied specifying a network-blocking rule.

Another example is the following: suppose that a security bug is discovered in a JVM implementation. In the bug report it is explained that applets can gain unauthorized access to system resources performing a particular call to a specified class method. Our filter, on the other hand, allows the user to stop any applet invoking that method. Ultimately, a user could disable the whole package.

This is an example of two filtering rules:

```
RULE test1
  STOP java.lang.reflect:Method.getModifiers

RULE test2
  STOP java.net:Socket.getInetAddress
```

Using these rules together we can block all applets that invoke the methods `getModifiers` of `java.lang.reflect.Method` class and the method `getInetAddress` of `java.net.Socket` class. This is a very restrictive mechanism because every applet that uses such methods is rejected. This can be relaxed by executing applets recognized to be trusted according to their origin and proprietary.

Rule-based filtering represents both a patching and preventing solution. It can be used to patch a bug, and also to prevent a potential security risk due to a specific use of a library. For instance, if a client wants to forbid the use of the Java networking library, even if no bugs are known on this package, he or she can refuse all applets that have references to the `java.net` package.

In the rest of this section we provide a formal description of syntax and semantics for filtering-rules.

A single rule is composed of a set of *conditions*. A condition can be used to either enable or disable applets matching the given criterion. One might think of several kinds of filtering criteria. In our work, a filtering criterion is represented by a reference to specific items among the following:

- package
- class
- method
- field
- method with a specified signature (i.e., the type of each parameter, to distinguish overloaded methods)

In the rest of this work we shall refer to these with the generic term *item*. Items can be organized in a hierarchy, as shown in figure 1. The syntax used to represent a rule has the following form:

```
RULE rulename
  [STOP | ALLOW] criterion
  ...
  [STOP | ALLOW] criterion
```

```
for each entry in method_table
      perm = ALLOW
      child = getMatchingChild(root, getPackage(entry))

      if child == NULL then continue
      if flag(child) != NULL then perm = flag(child)

      child = getMatchingChild(child, getClass(entry))

      if child == NULL then goto check_perm
      if flag(child) != NULL then perm = flag(child)

      child = getMatchingChild(child, getMethod(entry))

      if child == NULL then goto check_perm
      if flag(child) != NULL then perm = flag(child)

      child = getMatchingChild(child, getMethodWithSignature(entry))

      if child == NULL then goto check_perm
      if flag(child) != NULL then perm = flag(child)

check_perm:
      if perm == STOP then return Failure
done

return Success
```

Figure 2. Filtering algorithm: the main loop.

where `criterion` can be one of the following:

- *package*:* (matches any reference to *package*)
- *package*:*class*.* (matches any reference to *class* from *package*)
- *package*:*class.method* (matches any reference to *method* of *class* from *package*)
- *package*:*class.method*($type_1$,...,$type_n$) (matches any reference *method*($type_1$,...,$type_n$) of *class* from *package*)
- *package*:*class.field* (matches any reference to *field* of *class* from *package*)

A *filter* is a set of rules. A *class use* is a particular reference to a given field or method of a given class from a specific package in a Java program, and is represented as:

- *package*:*class.method*($type_1$,...,$type_n$)
- *package*:*class.field*

Note that a class use is a special case of criterion.

Given a rule *r* and a class use *cu*, we say that *r stops cu*, written $r \rightarrow$ **stop** *cu*, if and only if:

$$(\exists\, cond_1 \in r\colon cond_1 = \textbf{stop}\ c_1 \wedge (c_1 < cu)) \wedge$$
$$(\neg\exists\, cond_2 \in r\colon cond_2 = \textbf{allow}\ c_2 \wedge (c_1 < c_2 < cu))$$

where $c_1 < c_2$ if c_2 is an ancestor of c_1, according to the hierarchy in figure 1.

Analogously, given a rule *r* and a class use *cu*, we say that *r allows cu*, written $r \rightarrow$ **allow** *cu*, if and only if:

$$(\exists\, cond_1 \in r\colon cond_1 = \textbf{allow}\ c_1 \wedge (c_1 < cu)) \wedge$$
$$(\neg\exists\, cond_2 \in r\colon cond_2 = \textbf{stop}\ c_2 \wedge (c_1 < c_2 < cu))$$

Given a rule *r* and a class use *cu*, it is possible that *r* neither allows nor stops *cu*. In this case we say that *r ignore cu*.

Given a filter *f* and a class use *cu*, we say that *f stops cu*, written $f \rightarrow$ **stop** *cu*, if and only if:

$$\exists\, r \in f\colon r \rightarrow \textbf{stop}\ cu$$

That is, if a single rule stops a class use *cu*, then the whole filter stops *cu*, even if there are other rules that allow or ignore *cu*.

To allow access to a field or execution of a method, our system requires that there are no rules that stop the corresponding class use, meaning that **stop** is stronger than **allow**. Formally, given a filter *f* and a class use *cu*, we say that *f allows cu*, written $f \rightarrow$ **allow** *cu*, if and only if:

$$\neg\exists\, r \in f\colon r \rightarrow \textbf{stop}\ cu$$

that is equivalent to:

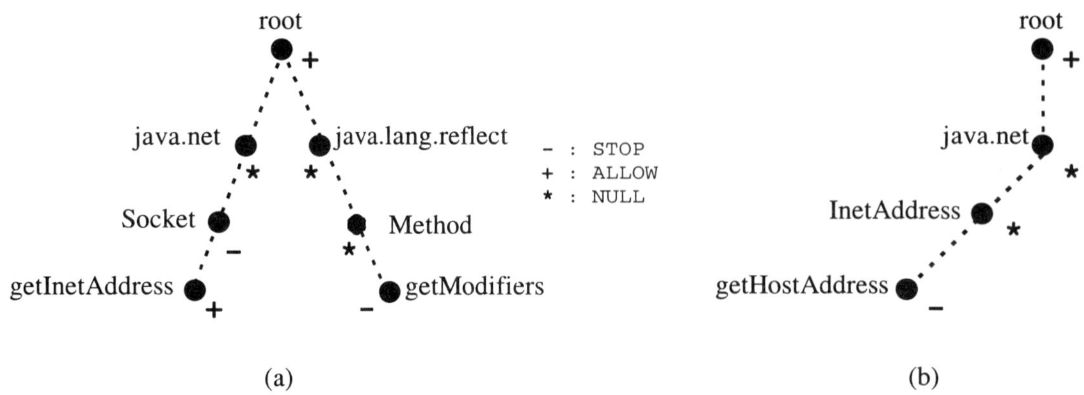

Figure 3. Examples of rule tree.

$\neg(f \rightarrow \textbf{stop}\ cu)$

More restrictive systems should require that a class use is allowed only if every rule in the filter allows it. Anyhow, this is not convenient as far as security administration is concerned, since in this case every class use should be considered, i.e. not ignored.

5 Filtering Algorithm

In order to minimize the performance overhead of our filtering module, we have developed an efficient algorithm to check every applet loaded from the network against the set of given rules. Furthermore, this algorithm has been implemented in ANSI C and packaged to be used as an extension of a JVM or a firewall. It takes an applet bytecode as input and returns `true` if the applet bytecode satisfies any rule, or `false` otherwise.

The filter analyzes the class file structure of applets. This structure contains all information needed by our filter to know which *items* (as defined in the previous section) are referred by the applet, plus the bytecode instructions for each local method.

At start up time, the filter loads the given rules and creates a corresponding tree structure, that we call *rule tree*. Each node in the rule tree is associated to an item and a flag that can assume three states: NULL, STOP or ALLOW, according to the semantics of rules explained in the previous section. The top node is the root, whereas nodes in the second, third, fourth and fifth level correspond respectively to packages, classes, methods (or attributes) and methods with signature, as shown in figure 2.

At this point the filter is ready to accept strings corresponding to applet bytecode and to compare such strings against the loaded rules.

The main steps of the algorithm are:

1) A `perm` variable is initialized to ALLOW. This variable indicates the checking status during the execution of the algorithm.
2) The set of fully qualified names of methods and fields referred by the input applet are extracted from its bytecode and stored into two structures, `methods_table` and `fields_table`.
3) For each entry in `methods_table`, the filter extracts the corresponding package, class and method name.
4) If the package name matches with a first level node in the rule tree, the filter checks if the matching node is set to STOP or ALLOW, and sets `perm` to this value. If the matching node is set to NULL, `perm` is left unchanged.
5) If the package name does not match any node at the first level, it goes to step (7).
6) Starting from the matching node, steps (4) and (5) are repeated for the class name, the method (or field) name and the "method with signature" name. If the end of the tree is reached, it goes to step (7).
7) If `perm` is STOP, then the applet is rejected. Otherwise the loop is continued. If the loop reaches the end (i.e. `perm` is ALLOW for every entry), the applet is accepted.

A more formal description of the above algorithm is shown in figure 2.

The main advantage of our algorithm is that the amount of rules does not have effect on the complexity of our filter. In fact, the rule tree reduces memory space, because each filtering item is reported just one time

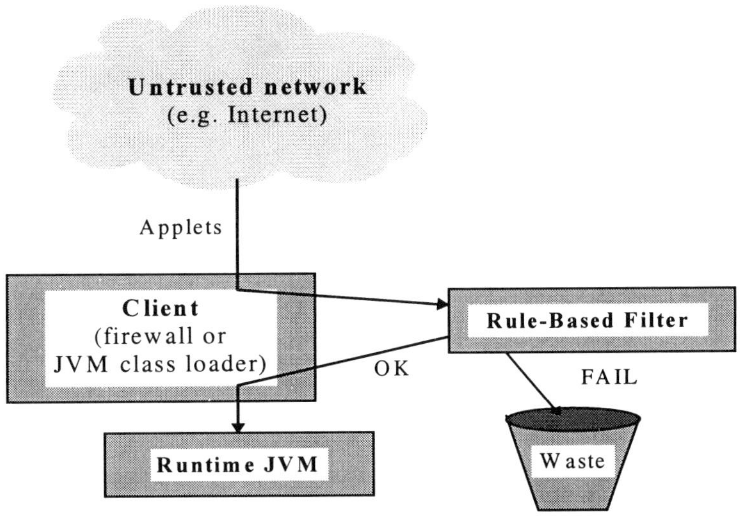

Figure 4. Using the filter with client applications.

inside the tree. The rule tree also reduces checking time because the depth of tree is fixed to three and the binary search is used to find matches. We can calculate the time complexity. Supposing m is the number of methods and fields used by the applet and n is the maximum number of children that could have a node on the tree, the complexity is $O(m*log(n))$ where the only variable depending on the number of all different rules is n.

Our filter is a static controller, so it does not reduce the performance of a Java code execution because classes are checked just once at load time. Moreover, only classes loaded from the network are checked by the filter. So the filter has a minimum impact on performances.

6 Examples

In this example we consider again the two rules:

```
RULE test1
  STOP java.lang.reflect:Method.getModifiers

RULE test2
  STOP java.net:Socket
  ALLOW java.net:Socket.getInetAddress
```

The corresponding rule tree is shown in figure 3a. Now, supposing we load an applet that contains an invocation to the `java.net.Socket.getPort()` method. In this case, the `methods_table` structure will contain an entry for this method. First, the package `java.net` is matched with the corresponding node in the rule tree. Since this node is marked `NULL`, `perm` is left unchanged and the children node (`Socket`) is considered. In this case, `perm` gets the value `STOP`. Since no children node matches with method `getPort()`, the `perm` value is returned, and the applet is therefore rejected. Analogously, an applet containing a reference to `Method.getName()` from the package `java.lang.reflect` is accepted, as when the `Method` node is reached no matching children is found, and the `perm` value corresponding to the `root` node is returned.

Let us suppose that another applet contains an invocation to the method `java.net:Socket. getInetAddress()`. In this case, the method `getInetAddress` is matched with the corresponding node in the rule tree. Since this node is marked `ALLOW`, perm takes this value and the test succeeds. Note that, in this case, the `STOP` flag of the `Socket` node is overridden by the `ALLOW` flag of the `getInetAddress` node.

Let's consider an example involving two conflicting rules:

```
RULE test3
 STOP java.net:InetAddress.getHostAddress

RULE test5
 ALLOW java.net:InetAddress.getHostAddress
```

The resulting rule tree is shown in figure 3b. In this case, the conflicting node `getHostAddress` gets the value `STOP`, as `STOP` is stronger than `ALLOW`, as explained in Section 4. Therefore, an applet containing a reference to the `getHostAddress` method will be rejected.

In the following example we provide some rules that could be used to prevent some reported bugs concerning popular JVM implementations:

```
RULE HotJava_Signing
  STOP java.lang:Class.getSigners
```

Such a rule is related to a bug found in the HotJava JVM implementation and reported by the Secure Internet Programming Group at Princeton University [PRI]. It stops any applet referring to the `getSigner` methods from class `Class` in the package `java.lang`.

```
RULE Netscape_IP_and_HostName
  STOP java.net:InetAddress.getLocalHost
  STOP java.applet:AppletContext.showDocument
```

Such a rule stops applets that could take advantage of the "IP Number Bug" described in Section 3.

The following rule:

```
RULE Disable_Network
  STOP java.net:*
```

stops any applet that wants to access the network. Such a rule could be useful, for instance, to prevent attacks such the one reported in [IP].

Note that, in case of conflict, more specialized conditions override more general ones. For example, consider the following rule:

```
RULE conflict_example
  STOP java.lang:*
  ALLOW java.lang:System.*
```

If this were the case, according to the first condition, any applet containing a reference to the package `java.lang` should be stopped. The second condition enables any applet containing a reference to the class `System` included in the package `java.lang`. Since the second condition is more specific than the first one, it will be stronger. Therefore, the rule `conflict_example` will stop any applet containing a reference to the `java.lang` package, unless it is a reference to the class `System`.

7 Implementation Details

A relevant feature of our implementation is that the filter can be plugged into a regular Java Virtual Machine or into a firewall that is able to intercept applets (we shall use the generic term *client* to refer to both). In this way, a new protection layer is added to the standard Java security layers. In both cases, the way our filter works is shown in figure 4.

Filter rules are stored in a configuration file that is loaded at start up time. Since this is a plain text file, the set of active rules could be updated very easily using Internet services such as e-mail or usenet. Also, a security-related organization could maintain a Web site containing rules that prevent known attacks.

To insert our filter, it is only required that the client passes the string corresponding to the applet bytecode to the filter before the applet is instantiated.

In the case of the JVM, the applet bytecode is retrieved by the `loadClass()` method of the `ClassLoader` class. In a real JVM implementation, this method generally looks like this:

```
public synchronized
Class loadClass(String name, boolean link) {
  Class c = cache.get(name);
  if (c == null) {
     byte stream[] = loadClassData(name);
     c = defineClass(stream,0, stream.length);
     cache.put(name, c);
  }
  return c;
}
```

The `loadClassData()` method returns the string corresponding to a class, that is passed to `defineClass()` to define a new class. Therefore, in our extended JVM, the `loadClass()` method can be modified as follows:

```
public synchronized
Class loadClass(String name, boolean link) {
  Class c = cache.get(name);
  if (c == null) {
     byte stream[] = loadClassData(name);
     if (checkClass(stream, String result)
         == CHECK_OK) {
        c= defineClass(stream,0,stream.length);
        cache.put(name, c);
     }
     else
        cache.put(name, null));
  }
  return c;
}
```

`checkClass()` is a call to a native method implemented in our filter. The filter is built as a dynamic library. In case an applet is rejected, an empty class is passed to the `defineClass()` method. In our real implementation, based on Netscape Navigator, we actually throw an exception that is reported in the Java console of the browser. Thus, if a Web page contains an applet that is not accepted by the filter, the browser displays an empty area, as if the applet was not available on the Web server. A more sophisticated implementation could return a special applet "Rejected" in place of rejected applets. The "Rejected" applet could show an error message with the rule that caused the non acceptance of the original applet.

Note that, since the filter is called before the applet is instantiated, malicious code in the applet cannot by-pass the filter itself. Also note that `loadClass()` is not involved for system classes, because they are loaded by the `findSystemClass()` method.

Similarly, the filter could be used by a network firewall that is able to intercept applets. The advantages of having the filter on the firewall rather than as an extension of the JVM are:

- **centralized management**: a system administrator could be responsible to keep the set of rules updated in order to protect a whole organization when new bugs are discovered in a JVM;
- **no installation required**: clients can use regular Web browsers without changing the JVM to use the filter;
- **efficiency**: even thin clients could be protected by the filter without performance overhead;

However, intercepting applets at firewall level is not an easy task for a firewall, as discussed in [MAR], mainly because applets can be encapsulated inside archive files (e.g. zip, jar).

8 Conclusions

In this paper we have shown how a rule-based applet filter can protect a system against malicious applets trying to exploit bugs in the Java Virtual Machine. We have also presented an implementation of such a filter that can be used either as a firewall extension or as a virtual machine extension.

The approach presented here could be improved by adding new functionalities to the filter. For example, new rules such as the following could be added:

- NoSubclass: to block those applets that subclass a specified class, e.g.:
  nosubclass java.lang:Class
- MatchByteCode: to check if the applet contains a string representing a malicious sequence of bytecode instructions (a similar technique is used by virus scanning tools), e.g:
  matchbytecode "<bytecode string>"

Another possible extension could be to integrate our module with a filter like the one described in [PRI]. This tool allows the user to specify a set of Internet addresses, each one marked allow or deny. Only applets coming from an address marked allow are accepted. Integrating this tool with the one presented here, applets could be classified, depending on their originating URL, into allow (the applet is accepted without checking, e.g. applets incoming from the local network), deny (the applet is rejected unconditionally), and filter (the applet is accepted only if it is approved by the rule-based filter).

References

[IP] Netscape JVM IP Number Bug, http://www.alcrypto.co.uk/java/

[JDK] Gosling J. et al., *The Java Language Specification*, Addison-Wesley, 1996. Available on-line at http://www.javasoft.com

[MAR] Martin D. M., Rajagopalan S., Rubin A. D., "Blocking Java Applets at the Firewall", in Proceedings of IEEE Symposium on Network and Distributed System Security, IEEE Computer Society Press, 1997.

[MCG] McGraw G., Felten W. F., *Java Security: Hostile Applets, Holes and Antidotes*, Jon Wiley & Sons, 1997.

[MET] Mehta N., "Expanding and Extending the Security Features of Java", 7th USENIX Security Symposium Proceedings, San Antonio (Texas), Jan 1998.

[PRI] Secure Internet Programming Group at Princeton University, http://www.cs.princeton.edu/sip.

[SIG] JDK 1.1.1 Signing Flaw, http://www.javasoft.com/security/getSigners.html

[STE] Sterbenz A., "An Evaluation of the Java Security Model", 12th Annual Computer Security Applications Conference, San Diego (CA), Dec 1996.

[SUR] Finjan SurfinShield, http://www.finjan.com

[TIS] Trusted Information Systems, Inc. http://www.tis.com

Controlling Applets' Behavior in a Browser

Vesna Hassler, Oliver Then
Information Systems Institute
Technical University of Vienna
Argentinierstrasse 8/3rd floor, 1040 Vienna, Austria
hassler@infosys.tuwien.ac.at

Abstract

In this paper we discuss methods of protecting Java-enabled Web browsers against malicious applets. Malicious applets involve denial of service, invasion of privacy and annoyance. Since system modification by applets is generally impossible because of the Java security concept, denial of service is of major concern. Invasion of privacy may be caused by applets staying resident in the browser and collecting information about a user. Annoyance may, for example, be caused by advertisment applets that constantly appear on a Web site frequently visited by the user. A general solution to confront such attacks is to have some mechanism within the browser to monitor applets' activities. This mechanism should enable manual or automatic stopping of malicious applets. To illustrate it we present a special applet, called AppletGuard, that allows the user to observe and control the applets in the browser and, based on an applet's properties, stop or suspend the applet, or just warn the user that something dangerous might be going on.

1. Introduction

In this paper we propose a method of protecting Java-enabled Web browsers against malicious applets. Malicious applets involve denial of service, invasion of privacy and annoyance [1]. A general solution to confront such attacks is to have some mechanism within the browser to monitor applets' activities. This mechanism should enable manual or automatic stopping of malicious applets, such as applets that start many threads or use more memory or other resources than allowed. At the time of this writing, we have not seen such a mechanism in any browser implementation yet, which effectively means that all Java-enabled browsers we know are prone to such kind of attacks.

Although the Java security model [3] has significantly improved so that system modification by applets is generally impossible, there are some potential attacks that Java doesn't currently attempt to prevent, such as the abuse of some not necessarily sensitive resources (e.g. CPU cycles, memory and windows) [7]. In other words, there are no resource quotas for untrusted classes. Recovering from denial of service attacks is in most cases not very difficult, e.g. you may have to reboot your machine. However, if the machine has to be available for some critical tasks, denial of service could be very serious. An applet can also perform a degradation of service attack, which means that it significantly reduces the performance of the browser without stopping it [11].

The same type of mechanism that would enable us to control denial of service applets would also give us the possibility to monitor many different kinds of applets' properties, such as the applet name or the time interval within which an applet is active in the browser. For example, some users might like to disable advertisement applets on a Web page they frequently download (annoyance). Or, measuring the time can help detect subtle attacks such as using a machine for an exhaustive encryption key search. The same mechanism could help detect invasion of privacy caused by applets staying resident in the browser and collecting information about the user.

To illustrate this protection mechanism we present a special applet, called AppletGuard, that allows the user to observe and control the applets in the browser. Based on an applet's properties, the browser can stop or suspend the applet, or just warn the user that something dangerous might be going on. The AppletGuard protects against denial of service attacks caused by applets that use excessive resources, or against applets with specific properties. The actual implementation uses some security bugs in the older versions of JDK (Java Development Kit [2]). However, our approach does not depend on JDK security holes, but is rather generic. In the last section we discuss the possibilities to implement the described mechanisms based on the customizable parts of the Java security, namely Class Loader and Security Manager.

2. Browser protection mechanisms

A set of protection mechanisms as part of the browser, with special privileges to access all threads running in the browser, would enable the user to

- monitor all applets' activities in the browser,
- manually or automatically stop applets based on specific properties, and
- stop all applets s/he does not want to run longer after leaving their Web page.

In the examples given later we measure the number of threads and stack frames used by an applet as well as check the names of applets, but it could equally be possible to use the mechanism to controls applets based on other properties, such as

- the time an applet is active in the browser, and/or automatically stop all applets hanging around for more than a predifined time interval, or
- the number of windows started by an applet, or
- the applet's memory consumption, or
- the applet's CPU time, or
- the applet's source (i.e. URL, see also [8]), or
- the applet's digital signature (i.e. certificate).

If based on any of the properties an applet appears "suspicious" to the browser, it should be possible to stop or suspend selected threads or the whole applet. In case of suspension, the browser should ask the user if s/he wishes to continue execution.

In the sequel we discuss the possibilities of implementing these mechanisms. Our discussion is based on the customizable parts of the Java security model, namely Class Loader and Security Manager.

2.1. Applet Class Loader

The `ClassLoader` class in the `java.lang`, package is an abstract class that provides the programming interface and partial implementation for all Java class loaders. There are usually several class loaders in operation; the applet class loader installs each applet in a separate name space (applets from the same page and source may share a class loader). Java's security rules prohibit applets from creating class loaders.

The applet class loader could be modified to prevent from loading all applets whose class name contains a predefined substring or comes from a predefined sources. The substrings to watch for would be specified by the user in the user's preferences, or, for example, by klicking on the applet's area in the browser and selecting "Always prevent from loading" from a pop-up menu. A similar approach is described in [8] where the authors actually replaced the applet class loader in the browser class library by their version.

2.2. Security Manager

The `SecurityManager` class in the `java.lang`, package is an abstract class that provides the programming interface and partial implementation for all Java security managers. It is meant to be defined by the browser through subclassing to perform run time checks on dangerous methods. In an application the security manager can be set only once. The security manager can determine which classes are involved in the current request and which class loader is responsible for that class. If the responsible class loader is the applet class loader, it knows that the request comes from the untrusted code.

If the browser wishes to control, for instance, the number of threads that can be created by an applet, the security manager's method `checkAccess(ThreadGroup)` which is invoked when a new child thread or child thread group is created, should check how many threads have already been started by the applet before allowing it to start a new one. The number of threads might be defined by the user's preferences, or by the browser's default values. The browser might also suspend the applet and ask the user whether to permit it to start a new thread. However, the problem with this method is that the security manager doesn't know whether a thread is being created or an entire thread group is being destroyed [6].

Another example is to limit the memory used by an applet. This could be achieved by counting the stack frames used by an applet or by a thread group. It could be partly implemented in such a way that the security manager's method `checkAccess(ThreadGroup)` computes the number of stack frames used by a thread group or by an applet and, if the number were higher than allowed (by either the user preferences or the browser default values), it would not permit starting a new thread. However, that could not prevent an existing thread from using more memory (stack frames) than allowed since the security manager does not have all the information it needs to do resource tracking (i.e. it is stateless).

To prevent such attacks, some monitoring mechanism should periodically check the number of threads started by an applet, and the threads' status. Such mechanism cannot be implemented by using the security manager approach only. According to the JavaSoft's security architects, it would be a very difficult task to provide a generic way of resource tracking without "slowing everyting down" [9]. Similarly, a monitoring mechanism would be necessary to periodically check for open threads belonging to presumably no longer active applets.

3. AppletGuard

In this section we illustrate some of the browser protection mechanisms. For this purpose we present a special applet, called AppletGuard, that allows the user to observe and control the applets in the browser and, based on an applet's properties, stop or suspend the applet, or just warn the user that something dangerous might be going on. The AppletGuard protects against denial of service attacks caused by applets that use excessive resources, or against applets with specific properties. The source code is available from [12].

The idea to write the AppletGuard is based on AssassinApplet from [1]. The actual implementation uses some security bugs in the older versions of JDK (Java Development Kit [2]). The bugs allow each applet to access, and even stop, the threads not belonging to its group. It can be efficiently misused with the older versions of the Netscape browser (2.x and 3.x), but we use it to protect the browser against misbehaving applets. Netscape 4.x does not allow an applet to access the thread groups other than its own. For the current status of the JDK security see [3].

3.1. Java threads

Java-enabled browsers can start multiple threads of execution (multithreading) which also means that several applets can run in parallel within a browser. An applet has at least one thread (the applet itself), but it can also start new threads to accomplish various tasks. The idea our AppletGuard is based on is to install a thread that monitors and controls all other threads in the browser.

Each Java thread in the browser is a member of a thread group [5]. Some threads are automatically produced by the browser when it is started, and some threads are user or applet threads. Most browsers allocate a thread group for each applet [4]. If a thread is started by an applet it is automatically assigned to the applet thread group called applet-CLASSNAME.class (Figure 2). In other words, all threads started by the applet will belong to this group. Each thread group has a parent group, which yields a tree-like structure. An example thread hierarchy in the browser is shown in Figure 1.

```
       System group
            |
        Main group
        /   |   \
Applet1 Applet2 Applet3
 group   group   group
```

Figure 1: An example thread hierarchy

In Sun Microsystems' security policy for JDK 1.0.*, and consequently in all browsers that are based on it (like Netscape 2.*), there is a thread access bug: each applet can access all threads from other thread groups, i.e. not only its own threads. This bug can be misused to write a malicious applet that can monitor and even stop all the threads in the browser (i.e. all System group threads) [1], as well as count the stack frames (memory) used up by a thread.

In Netscape 3.*-JDK 1.1.* the major thread bug was removed, but we discovered that there is still a possibility to gain control over all applet threads in the browser. To achieve this it is necessary to overwrite any applet function that has a thread in the Main thread group (e.g. `paint()`). With this bug it is possible to monitor and stop other applets' threads, but we could not find out how to count their stack frames.

3.2. AppletGuard's functionality

In our experimental implementation it is very important the AppletGuard to be the first applet loaded after starting the browser. In this way it cannot happen that the browser or even the machine freezes due to a denial of service attack already taking place. The AppletGuard's basic functionality can be described as follows:

1. Spawn a monitoring thread.
2. Go one level up in the thread hierarchy and save this thread group's reference.
3. From this thread group downwards, scan all threads.
4. For each scanned thread, display its status and check if it exhibits malicious behavior (i.e. starts to many

threads or uses up to many stack frames) or has specific properties.

5. Stop misbehaving threads.

The steps 2-5 can be repeated for all thread hierarchy levels. With this approach, most denial of service attacks coming from other applets can be timely discovered and stopped. Specifically, it is possible to

- *prevent an applet from starting too many threads*: the status of all threads is displayed in the AppletGuard window so that they can be stopped manually or automatically
- *prevent an applet from using to much memory*: the number of stack frames used by an applet is also shown in the AppletGuard window, so that based on this information the malicious applet can be stopped
- *prevent an applet to stay resident in the browser after the user has left the applet's Web page*: the status of all applets' threads is shown in AppletGuard window, so it can be easily noticed if there are some threads hanging around belonging to the supposedly stopped applets
- *stop all applets containing a predefined substring in the name*: in this way it is possible to disable e.g. advertisement applets that are a nuisance to the user

If the user prefers to stop selected applets or threads *manually*, only a warning is shown in the status display each time an applet's properties match the properties selected to be watched for (e.g. number of threads or name). If the user wants the applets to be stopped *automatically*, a status message informing him/her about an action is shown in the status display.

3.3. AppletGuard's options

In Figure 2 the main window of the AppletGuard is shown. We loaded the AppletGuard immediately after starting the browser (it can be e.g. on the home page). Figure 2 shows the intial status. We can see that the AppletGuard starts two threads, Thread-1 and AppletGuard2, both belonging to the AppletGuard2 applet.

If we push the Options button in Figure 2, the options window (Figure 3) pops up. We can select manual or automatic killing (i.e. stopping) of applets. If we select automatic killing, all applets starting more than 7 threads and using more than 7 stack frames will be stopped automatically. If we select manual killing, we can delete selected applets and threads in the main window by pushing the Stop button.

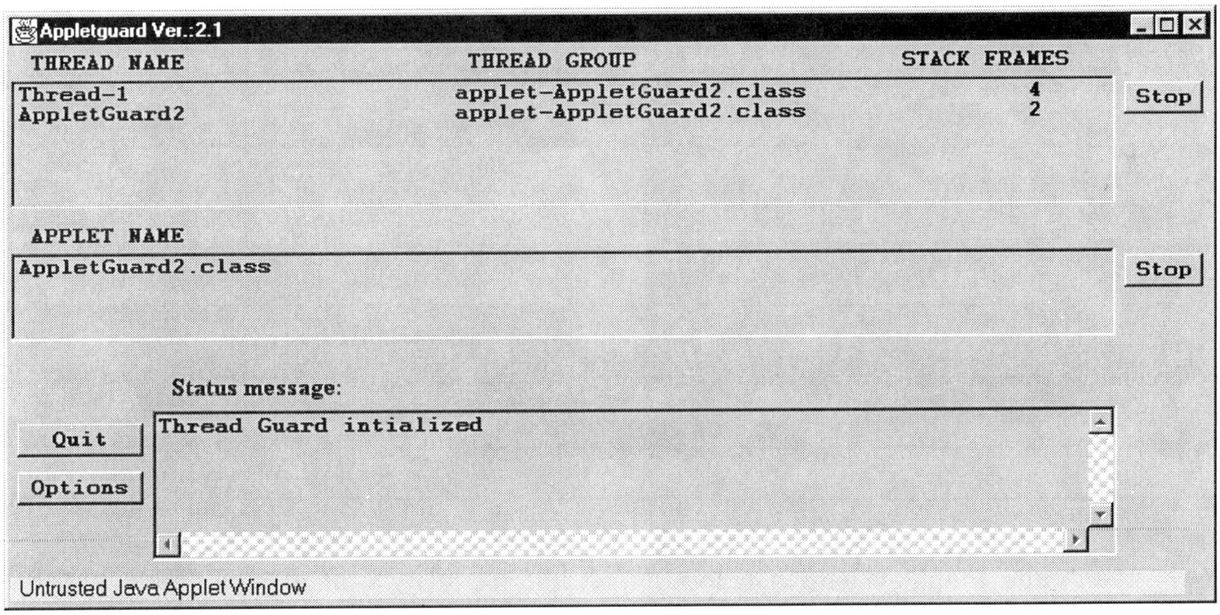

Figure 2 : AppletGuard main window

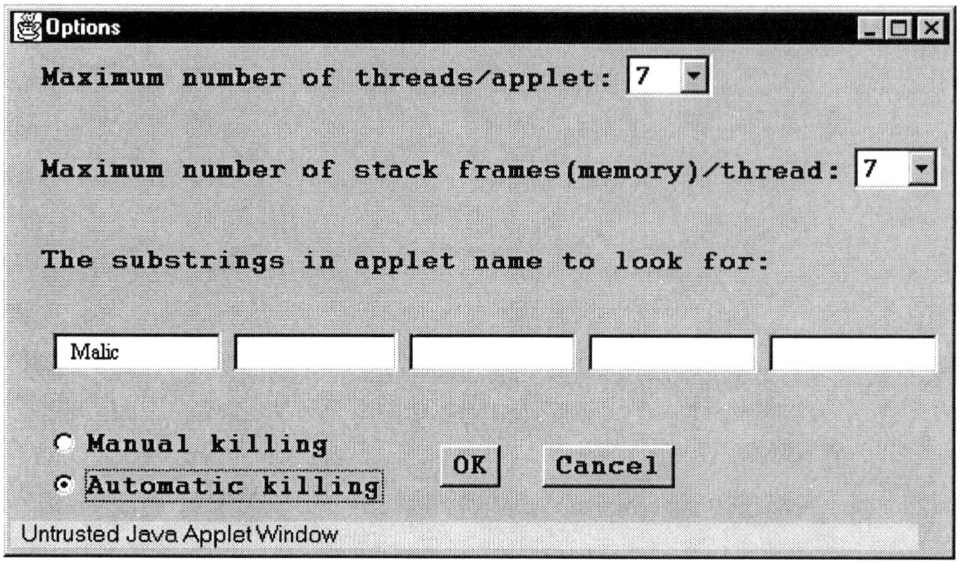

Figure 3: AppletGuard options window

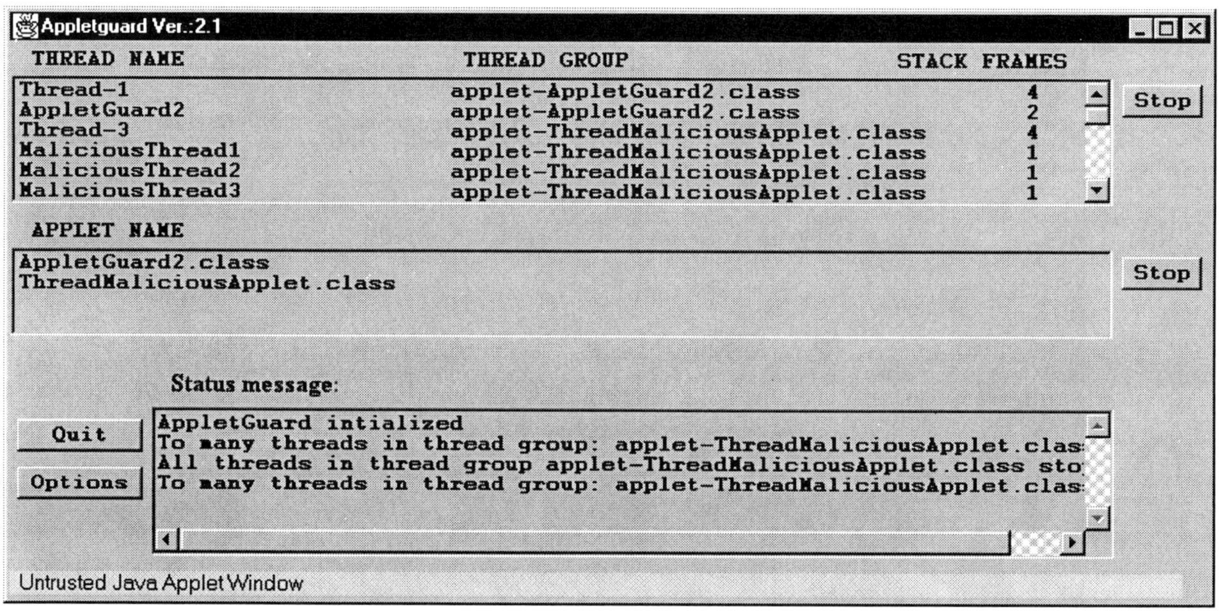

Figure 4: AppletGuard in action: Applet with too many threads is stopped

3.4. Example 1

In Figure 4 we can see how the AppletGuard works when the browser is attacked. We select the option for automatic killing in the options window (Figure 3) and load the ThreadMaliciousApplet that tries to start 20 idle threads. Since we don't allow more than 7 threads to be started by any applet, ThreadMaliciousApplet is automatically killed with the status message "*All threads in thread group applet - ThreadMaliciousApplet.class stopped*" (second status message in Figure 4).

3.5. Example 2

In the second example we select the option for manual deleting and load the same misbehaving applet again. The AppletGuard displays it in the topmost status frame: Thread-3 and many MaliciousThreads (Figure 4). Since this attack is not so serious, i.e. it does not freeze the browser, we are able to select (using the mouse) the applet *ThreadMaliciousApplet.class* in the middle status frame and stop it by pushing the Stop button. However, some more serious attacks could disable any kind of manual intervention, so it is recommendable to enable automatic killing.

3.6. AppletGuard should be a part of the browser

Unfortunately, this implementation of the AppletGuard cannot be used for serious protection. Suppose a malicious applet knows about the existence of the AppletGuard. The only thing the malicious applet has to do in order to disable the AppletGuard is to first stop all applets running in the browser using the same technique we are using to protect the browser. The newest version of the Netscape browser (4.x) does not allow any applet to access other groups' threads anyway.

4. Summary and conclusions

In this paper we discuss some mechanisms to protect a Java-enabled browser against malicious applets, such as the applets causing denial of service attacks, or applets that are annoying the user. The mechanisms are based on a method for monitoring and controlling Java applets and their threads running in the browser. Such mechanisms should be part of each Java-enabled browser, but we have not seen any implementation so far. To illustrate our ideas, we wrote a special applet called AppletGuard which enables the user to monitor and, if necessary, stop selected threads and applets. We tested the AppletGuard with older versions of the Netscape browser (2.x and 3.x). It does not offer perfect protection since the AppletGuard has only the privileges of a normal applet. We also discussed the possibilities to implement the mechanism based on the Java class loader and Java security manager, and realized that it would be difficult since they do not offer a straightforward way for resource tracking. We hope to see similar mechanisms as a part of Java-enabled browsers in the near future.

We started to implement the AppletGuard in September 1997. At the time of finalizing the camera-ready version of the paper (September 1998) we found out that the HotJava browser (version 1.1.4) from Sun Microsystems implements a mechanism to monitor and selectively kill applets. However, there is no possibility to configure the browser to watch for applets having specific properties, as with the mechanism described in the paper. Additionally, we unfortunately discovered a security flaw in the browser: with our AppletGuard we could kill all threads from the HotJava thread group, including the threads implementing the thread monitoring mechanism (ThreadCountApplet and ThreadListApplet). They couldn't even be loaded again, although it was generally impossible for the AppletGuard to access other applets' threads. We then tried to kill the AppletGuard from the HotJava browser. However, although the HotJava thread monitor showed that the AppletGuard had been killed, it wasn't quite true, since we then killed the HotJava monitoring threads by the same allegedly "dead" instance of AppletGuard.

References

[1] McGraw, G., E.W. Felten, *Java Security. Hostile Applets, Holes, and Antidotes*, John Wiley & Sons, Inc., 1997

[2] Java Development Kit, Sun Microsystems, http://www.javasoft.com/products/jdk/1.1/index.html

[3] Java Security, Javasoft, http://www.javasoft.com/security/

[4] The Java Tutorial, http://www.infosys.tuwien.ac.at/NEW/Services/Docu/Java/Tutorial/

[5] Oaks S., H. Wong, *Java Threads*, O'Reilly, 1997

[6] Glenn Vanderburg et al., *Maximum Java 1.1*, Sams.net Publishing, 1997

[7] Michael Morrison et al., *Unleashed Java 1.1*, Sams.net Publishing, 1997

[8] Dirk Balfanz, Ed Felten, "A Java Filter", Technical Report 567-97, Department of Computer Science, Princeton University, October 1997

[9] Java Security Archive, http://java.sun.com/security/hypermail/java-security-archive/index.html

[10] Vesna Hassler, Oliver Then, "Controlling applets' behavior in a browser", Technical Report TUV-1841-98-03, Distributed Systems Group, Technical University of Vienna, 1998

[11] Drew Dean, Edward W. Felten, Dan S. Wallach, and Dirk Balfanz, "Java Security: Web Browers and Beyond", *Internet Beseiged: Countering Cyberspace Scofflaws*, Dorothy E. Denning and Peter J. Denning, eds. ACM Press (New York, New York), October 1997

[12] Oliver Then, " Monitoring applet protecting against denial of service attacks", Informatikpraktikum II, Distributed Systems Group, Technical University of Vienna, February 1998, http://www.infosys.tuwien.ac.at/Courses/Results/Praktika/AppletGuard/

Plenary Panel Session

Computer Security and the Millenium

Moderator

F. C. Smith, Santa Fe Attorney

The risks of civil or criminal liability are increasing as information systems pervade new aspects of corporate and professional life. For computer security professionals this means that the risks of liability for the individual professional and their employers or agents will increase accordingly when a network intrusion or other computer security breach is alleged to have caused damage to an individual or company. These new risks can affect not only the status and bank account of the professional, but the bottom line of an enterprise. It is imperative to be able to identify and assess not only the security risks that must be dealt with, but also the very real legal risks that will be increasingly involved in providing network security in globally connected networks.

Two experienced litigators, Michael Pezzulli and Kip Byrne, together with two recognized technical experts, Linda MacCarthy and David Bailey, will discuss several recent decisions that have attempted to impose legal liability on service providers and sysadmins. The panel will be moderated by Fred Chris Smith, an attorney and computer security consultant. The panel will generalize from those cases about what can be expected as the contract and tort bars begin to smell the virtual blood and educate themselves during the YK2 legal feeding frenzy. The panelists will discuss some of the legal problems that security systems and management policies can create in the form of privacy violations for negligent disclosures, or breach of contract allegations by third parties for lost, altered, or unavailable information. Historical examples will be discussed to demonstrate how the development of better security software, hardware, and management policies and procedures will require even greater vigilance to insure that these technologies are properly implemented and do not afford easy targets for adverse litigation when something does go wrong or is alleged to have gone wrong.

The legal problems that arise in professional areas, without widely accepted standards, will be entertained, as will the traditional legal doctrines and concepts which have evolved to deal with accidents, negligence, and criminal acts in other high reliance technologies, industries, and institutions, and which by analogy can be expected to apply to network security failure litigation. The focus will be on identifying litigation risks, developing strategies to manage and reduce predictable legal risks, learning how to think about the unintended legal consequences of network security practices, and discussing how to avoid unnecessary, frivolous, or bogus legal liability claims.

Wachet auf! Computer Security and the Millennium

F. C. Smith
Santa Fe Attorney
fsmith@trail.com

D. J. Bailey
Bailey-Mayfield Associates
dbailey@acm.org

Abstract

Sleepers awake! The Y2K Problem may or may not be a technological disaster. But either way, the aftermath of the technological problems will be legal problems. Litigation over who should have done what will include damage claims for failures of software and liability for failure to prepare. The legal problems will be a disaster costing potentially trillions of dollars. Once the frenzy of litigation over Y2K has finished, the lawyers involved will look for other technological issues with similar characteristics and problems, and they will find computer security. This article brings these issues into focus and suggests how some businesses may respond, including methods to judgement proof the company. If such a strategy succeeds, computer security professionals could find themselves liable and stuck in a dwindling minority of asset rich targets in an increasingly dangerous cyber-space.

1 Year 2000 Disclosure and Its Effects

There are new signs that the great American tradition of legalizing the technological sublime is rapidly being applied to computer networks. Computer security professionals may soon find lawyers prescribing (and proscribing) rules that govern many aspects of their daily lives. New legal rules may cover the policies, procedures, and priorities for providing adequate security in computer networks.

Federal legislation has recently been introduced [1] which will encourage companies to share information about the Year 2000 (Y2K) problem. Disclosure statements will describe corporate status and the remediation process which they have put in place. The intended purpose of this legislation is to encourage companies to disclose information about their state of compliance and the problems that they foresee arising from Y2K failures. The incentive for inducing this cooperative behavior among competitive businesses is a set of considerations that would apply in future legal actions. Limits would be placed on the uses adversarial advocates might make of the disclosures in lawsuits taken against the disclosing party. That this is a nontrivial consideration can be seen from estimates of future litigation costs. Estimates of the litigation costs and potential damage awards which are expected from the complicated Y2K chain reaction failures currently run into the trillions of dollars.[1]

While various groups will continue to debate whether the plaintiffs' bar should be allowed to proceed in its traditional role, suits have already been filed attempting to compensate victims of damage caused by technological negligence. Meanwhile, Congress seems likely to accept a combined Administration/industry request for creation of some degree of immunity or safe harbors in an effort to avert the worst predictions of a Y2K melt-down.

The requirement for disclosure, and the corresponding fears of industry, are real. Certain federal regulatory agencies have begun to require disclosure in an attempt to protect consumers and investors. For example, the SEC has increased its disclosure requirements. The Commission became concerned that despite its earlier requirement, publicly traded companies have not sufficiently disclosed their Y2K readiness. The SEC now requires [2] all regulated companies to disclose clearly their state of readiness, including analysis of any problems which can be anticipated. Moreover, companies are now required to disclose their estimated costs of compliance, their "most reasonably likely worst case scenarios," and their contingency plans for what to do in the case of a Y2K failure in their own system or that of a "material" third party.

Lawyers are already having a field day explaining to corporate management the need to acquire legal expertise to assist them in planning how to avoid the coming onslaught of litigation.[2] Here is one but example among many found on law firm web sites and in magazine articles of the kind of advice corporate management is receiving.

[1] Legal views of the Y2K problem and cost estimates can be found in various places. For example, http://year2000.dci.com or http://www.2000legal.com The SEC's latest estimate is much lower, just hundreds of billions of dollars.

[2] To track the legal status of the Y2K Problem, see the excellent web site produced by Vito Peraino at http://www.2000law.com.

0-8186-8789-4/98 $10.00 © 1998 IEEE

> "More than ever, the SEC guidance also points to the retention of qualified, knowledgeable Y2K counsel. Counsel grounded in the technical as well as legal requirements is essential to translate the jargon of the Y2K project managers into the requirements of the SEC disclosure guidelines. Additionally, the SEC guidelines suggest that companies include an analysis of their legal exposures in the context of possible (or reasonably likely) failures. These are not simple exercises, and companies should take care that these analyses are performed comprehensively, accurately and with all things related to Y2K projects, promptly." [3]

2 Post-Millennial Network Security

Corporate managers already realize that there will be a high legal cost involved in dealing with the negative effects of their increasing dependence on computer technology. The new legal efforts underway to mitigate the anticipated downside from a Y2K failure should provide a warning to network security and risk management officers. The Y2K problem is just a warm-up for the legal profession. The first legal bite into the network apple is not going to come from actual lawsuits filed and litigated, but from the costs for obtaining competent legal advice about how to avoid litigation. Those lawyers who are now tooling up for Y2K litigation are also preparing themselves and their clients for future lawsuits related to liabilities stemming from inadequate security.

Certainly, lawyers can help prevent unnecessary liability. They can also make sure their corporate clients are in the best position to pursue legal remedies against those who damage their interests by negligent, reckless, or criminal acts. Given the technological uncertainties that face businesses, the old adage of paying for an ounce of prevention to avoid paying for a pound of cure rings true. Whatever happens over the next few years, one thing seems certain: the opportunity to get paid for becoming Y2K competent will encourage thousands of attorneys to educate themselves about computers and networks. They will soon grasp that there are more fundamental problems with the software revolution than the occasional programming shortcuts which led to Y2K. They will find a surprising number of long tolerated and serious security holes creating causes of action for enterprising attorneys and their clients.

These problems are different. They are more complex, harder to repair, and far more likely to breed litigation than the Y2K foibles we have considered so far. For one thing, disclosure of Y2K problems doesn't have any problem of completeness. What Y2K processing means is easy to define:

> " (c) YEAR 2000 PROCESSING- The term 'Year 2000 Processing' means the processing (including, without limitation, calculating, comparing, sequencing, displaying, or storing), transmitting, or receiving of date or date/time data from, into, and between the twentieth and twenty-first centuries, and during the years 1999 and 2000, and leap year calculations." [1]

A program either does this correctly everywhere, or there is somewhere, some situation where it doesn't do it right. Security is different. It is easy to detect that you don't have it, but impossible to assert (correctly) that you do. This means, at the very least, that there must be some standard of "good enough" to measure against since "absolutely secure" isn't possible, and there must be some standard of "good enough" to cover the completeness of your disclosure.

Completeness comes in two other forms, as well. First, there is a "hidden defects" issue in that almost all operating systems have hard to discover security holes. The software development and analytic techniques of the 1980's that were intended to make all vendor operating systems more secure turned out to be very expensive and slowed the development process intolerably. Additionally, the market for secure operating systems was very small and has not grown. As a result, the general state of operating system security has improved but little in the last 25 years.

There are two reasons for the hidden defects problem:

1. Operating systems are very complex and making them secure has always been and will continue to be a secondary consideration for most systems. Making them work at all is more important, as is adding new features to make them more attractive in the marketplace.

   It would be amusing to discuss the reasons that even sophisticated computer people are willing to accept "products" that don't work correctly, that never will work correctly, and that come with disclaimers instead of warranties. Why people think that "thousands of bugs fixed" is a positive statement to make in an advertisement is also an interesting anthropological study, but we live in an environment where this is commonly accepted as good news. Eventually, we forget about old bugs and learn to avoid them. If they happen to be security flaws that no one is exploiting at the moment, they fade in importance only to bite us years later.

2. Adding security is almost always an after thought in part because the few operating systems where security wasn't secondary have not been commercial suc-

cesses. When this is the situation, fixing a problem almost always creates others because something that wasn't "security relevant" suddenly becomes so.

Suppose you are trying to improve the security in your house. You have a strong lock on the front door but the burglars never notice because they know to go around the back where they can crawl in a window. When you get tired of that, you solve the problem by putting ornamental iron work on all the windows. Now they kick in the front door. The strength of the door was never relevant to security before, but may become so when other problems are fixed. This is a typical artifact of our traditional piecemeal approaches to security.

There is one more completeness issue that may, in the end, be the worst. That is disclosing, or worse, forgetting to disclose, things we have always known or have learned to work around. There might even be problems in the computer system that existed in the earlier paper system. If complete disclosure of security status becomes the law, as it might, failure to disclose problems that we have long since learned to tolerate could become expensive. Maybe we could get away with disclosing that protection isn't any worse than it was before. How about this disclosure?

> "This computer system is unable to protect patient records from misuse by the people that are authorized to use them. On the other hand, we were never able to provide that protection before and you never complained. This computerized system is every bit as good at protecting the records as the previous paper system, so don't complain now."

While the disclosure statement above is intended to be humorous, there is a serious point. Security problems in computer systems may turn out to be legacy problems from earlier ways of doing business, or they may be the result of inadequate analysis at the time of the transition to the computer system. Making an adequate computer security disclosure which does not generate a lawsuit may turn out to be far more vexing than complying with Y2K requirements.

3 Duties of the Networked Corporation

Other problems, arising from the actions of network managers, may create corporate liabilities. These could result in potentially devastating damage claims by network users or adversely affected third parties. Sometimes taking action during an incident can be as bad as not taking action.

Recently Peter Hall, an independent film maker, sued his ISP for terminating his service during a spamming incident allegedly based on a false report that Hall was the source of the spamming. Hall's suit alleges [4] that he was falsely accused of spamming and that he was terminated without the required notice or an opportunity to defend himself. He claims that his business was damaged due to a mistake and a failure to properly conduct a due diligence investigation before the ISP took drastic action. Termination of his account and subsequent failure to deliver his e-mail in a timely manner, he claims, entitles him to damages. (See Carl Kaplan's article in the New York Times [5] for further description of the incident.)

Cases like this, or action by the Congress in response to incidents of this kind will result in additional duties being imposed on businesses that provide networked services or just have network connections. If duties arise from suits like the Hall suit, they will consist of a collection of individual duties. For example, that suit could well result in a legally recognized duty for ISP's to deliver e-mail even if they have cut off service to some customer. The result could be a patchwork of things a company is expected to do or not do. The Congress could then perform an actual service by trying to fill in some of the holes in the quilt to make a uniform surface. Their history, however, is to get upset over particular services or technologies and try to legislate do's and don'ts that, at worst, will be obsolete before the ink dries, and, at best, begin to address a small part of a needed change.

So, if some miracle occurs and a generalized duty to be secure arises from some combination of legislative and judicial action, what will the results be? One strong possibility is that many businesses will be faced with mandates to implement security measures that they believe they don't need or that they can't afford.

New kinds of lawsuits, like Hall v. Earthlink, over the management of network resources, and the need for due diligence in investigating and responding to complex network situations will also require legal advice. Advice will be needed if litigation is to be avoided, when the business is forced into litigation, and when litigation is the best remedy for incidents directed against the network business.

4 Liability for Dangerous Premises and Other Unintended Consequences of Being in Business

A large, looming problem which can be seen to be headed for litigation, is the use of physical world analogies by enlightened attorneys to craft litigation claims for cyber-incidents. One obvious example of this likelihood is the expanding case law which supports claims of injury by invitees or innocent bystanders for the criminal acts of third parties that occur on company property. These claimed injuries occur on a premises, such as a parking structure or lot, which can be depicted and proved to be a "dangerous place."

The theory of dangerous places has been well developed through case law. The classic example is a poorly lit and poorly guarded parking structure which has a past history of criminal activity. The history of criminal activity at the place in question (or at similar nearby places) is important because it leads to a conclusion that future criminal activity is likely—something the proprietor can foresee and should take steps to prevent. In the network, an analogous situation might be a facility operated by an Internet Service Provider (ISP). ISP's have a history of being successfully taken over by outsiders, and, absent adequate disclosure of the dangers, a business customer might well expect that their particular ISP will have done something to prevent this from happening. If the ISP fails to adequately protect its users from foreseeable risks, they could find themselves accused of operating a dangerous place. They could be expected to pay for claims of damages in amounts that could threaten the business.

Operating a dangerous premises is just one possible analog of situations to be found in the physical world. The idea that operating an electronic business is somehow simpler than operating a physical business may be found to be untrue once enterprising lawyers begin to tease out the analogies between the physical and electronic worlds through the unpredictable process of litigation.

5 A Scorched Earth Response to "Jurismania"

Requirements for disclosure of Y2K status and problems will lead inexorably to discovery of both old and new security problems. An ineluctable effect of increased connectivity between businesses, constructed on poor network security is an enormous increase in legal actions. Paul Campos [6] refers to this effect as "jurismania." Corporate management will have to get beyond the hype about e-commerce and the endless array of software solutions, in order to face the potential for legal liabilities they didn't know they had.

Regardless of how the "worst case scenarios" of Y2K actually turn out, there will be no avoidance of tort and contract lawsuits predicated on analogies to physical situations. Suits will be based on a combination of legal theories such as failure to disclose risks, negligent management of known security risks, and poor management of the behavior of users, managers, and third parties who are connected to the network and dependent on its security.

Given these uncertainties and the likelihood of adverse litigation or the need to bring lawsuits on behalf of the company, sage legal advice on network liability issues may soon become essential. The fraction of networking costs due to legal expenses could turn out to be large.

The final bite by the lawyers may well come in the form of advice to make the corporation judgment proof by creating a virtual corporation. This is a legal strategy of scorched earth which may turn out to be perfectly legal. In a world and an economy that is becoming irreversibly legalized, it may make perfect sense.

In a series of articles, angry rejoinders and responses, [7, 8, 9] Professor Lynn LoPucki has set out the arguments as to why this strategy does make perfect legal sense in a world suffering from jurismania. The essence of this strategy is to place all of the corporate assets and cash flow in a separate entity which has nothing to do with the operating part of the corporation. The operating part of the corporation is structured so as to be devoid of my unencumbered assets which would invite the envy of potential adverse litigants and their attorneys.

Some have taken issue with Professor LoPucki's argument and have countered with arguments that no self-respecting, American, God-fearing company would ever structure itself in such a way. It would be anti-social to create such a structure simply to avoid having to pay damages to the customers or innocent victims of the company's negligence. Unfortunately, there are indications that this is already going on.

At the very least, businesses in an increasingly connected and interdependent network must consider that they may be the only deep pocket with assets worth going after when someone is damaged or alleges that their interests have been adversely affected. They will certainly need to examine the judgement proofing actions of their partners and other connected third parties. Lawyers who understand the inclusive logic behind the increase in network interdependence must point this out to their corporate clients as a potential liability. Corporate clients who fail to join a potential parade of judgement proofing, may find themselves part of a dwindling minority of asset rich targets. Computer security professionals in these companies may liable and stuck in an increasingly dangerous place.

6 Conclusion

The continuing hype of the Y2K crisis has made both companies and the bar acutely aware of the potential for liability for poorly designed computer software and embedded systems. The hype of positive network effects has all but concealed the negative side of the interdependence that comes with increasing connectivity and expanding electronic commerce. With the recent pronouncements by the Congress and the SEC, requiring clear and comprehensive disclosures of Y2K readiness, many companies and their lawyers are beginning to plan for large contingency funding for litigation.

Once the feeding frenzy over Y2K abates, many of their lawyers will come to recognize that the same analysis of liabilities will apply to other network failures. Network and computer system security is one such area which can be anticipated to cause injuries to customers and third parties. Potential claims arising out of well known network security vulnerabilities can be expected to exceed the wildest estimates of Y2K litigation costs and damage awards, which are already over the trillion dollar mark.

Given the combined uncertainties of Y2K and an unstable software foundation for an expanding electronic commerce, the need to limit liability will push corporations and legal counsel to try new and unorthodox methods. One of the most elegant methods of limiting liability known is to make the corporation judgment proof by eliminating assets from the operating segments of the corporate structure and encumbering assets needed to operate. Such a legal and business strategy, if successful, could spread and make it increasingly less likely that companies will seriously attempt to fix the problems which give rise to the potential legal liabilities which will result from the continued use of flawed software.

References

[1] "Year 2000 information and readiness disclosure act," September 1998. Draft legislation from the Model Legislation commission.

[2] Securities and Exchange Commission, "Interpretation: Disclosure of year 2000 issues and consequences by public companies, investment advisers, investment companies, and municipal securities issuers." Agency Interpretation, August 1998. Release Nos. 33-7558; 34-40277; IA-1738; IC-23366; International Series Release No. 1149. http://www.sec.gov/rules/concept/33-7558.htm.

[3] "Countdown 2000." Lexis Law Publishing, August 1998. Vol 1, Issue 7.

[4] US DISTRICT COURT SOUTHERN DISTRICT OF NEW YORK, "Peter Hall and Big Bad Productions, Inc. v. Earthlink Network, Inc.." See http://www.metaltiger.com/delinquent/litigation.html for Peter Hall's description of the case., July 1998.

[5] C. S. Kaplan, "Filmmaker sues ISP over termination of e-mail service," *New York Times*, August 14, 1998.

[6] P. F. Campos, *Jurismania: The Madness of American Law*. Oxford University Press, 1998.

[7] L. LoPucki, "The death of liability," *Yale Law Journal*, vol. 106, no. 1, p. 1, 1996.

[8] J. White, "Corporate judgment proofing: A response to Lynn LoPucki's "The death of liability"," *Yale Law Journal*, vol. 107, no. 5, p. 1363, 1998.

[9] L. LoPucki, "Virtual judgement proofing: A rejoinder," *Yale Law Journal*, vol. 107, no. 5, p. 1413, 1998.

Track A

Electronic Commerce

Chair

K. Keus, German Information Security Agency

A Scheme for Analyzing Electronic Payment Systems

Lucas de Carvalho Ferreira
IC/Unicamp and DEX/UFLA
DEX, Campus da UFLA
37200-000 Lavras MG
Brasil
lucasf@ufla.br

Ricardo Dahab
IC/Unicamp
Caixa Postal 6176
13083–970 Campinas SP
Brasil
rdahab@dcc.unicamp.br

Abstract

This paper presents a scheme for the design, analysis and comparison of electronic payment systems. Three systems are described in detail through this scheme.
Keywords: payment systems, analysis and design of payment systems.

1 Introduction

The field of electronic commerce and especially electronic payment systems has flourished in the past few years. The possibilities opened by the popularization of the Internet have forced many companies and research teams to turn their eyes to this new commercial universe. The first problem that has to be addressed before the Internet could become a huge marketplace is finding a way to securely transfer monetary value over the network.

In recent years, many systems have been proposed and implemented that allow two parties to transfer monetary value on a network of computers. Some of these protocols had significant implications on the way people do commerce on the Internet and new protocols are being deployed that may have much stronger implications in the development of the electronic marketplace.

With a number of payment systems available, people now need ways to analyze these systems and choose the one most suitable to their needs. Some work has been done in the direction of clarifying and classifying the way electronic payment systems work [2, 11, 7, 1, 3, 8]. Some of these works describe payment systems characteristics and their intrinsic requirements [2, 3, 7], while others classify payment systems by their functional behavior [8]. We believe a more integrated approach should be used to achieve a broader understanding of electronic payment systems.

We will here extend previous work on the classification of electronic payment systems and build a functionality model for those systems. This model was based on the analysis and understanding of several designs of electronic payment systems and seems to be comprehensive enough to be used with most existing systems.

We first present our proposed scheme for classifying and analyzing electronic payment systems; then we show how this scheme can be used to understand three important payment systems; a summary of the analysis of many known systems is shown in the tables of Appendix A.

2 Proposed Scheme

In this section we present the scheme we built to analyze payment systems characteristics. Figure 1 presents the scheme and its four subparts, each serving a single purpose: (i) describe payment systems typification through common characteristics; (ii) present desirable requisites of payment systems; (iii) describe system functioning from the user's perspective; (iv) present implementation aspects of the system. The next subsections present each of these subparts in detail.

2.1 System Typification

All electronic payment systems present characteristics that help us classify and understand the systems and their applications. We identified the following characteristics:

Exchange Model

- **Token-based.** Here transactions are made by the exchange of tokens of predefined value, much like coins or bank notes. In these systems, users must buy tokens from a central authority before being able to start a payment transaction. Token-based systems are also called *cash-like* systems.

0-8186-8789-4/98 $10.00

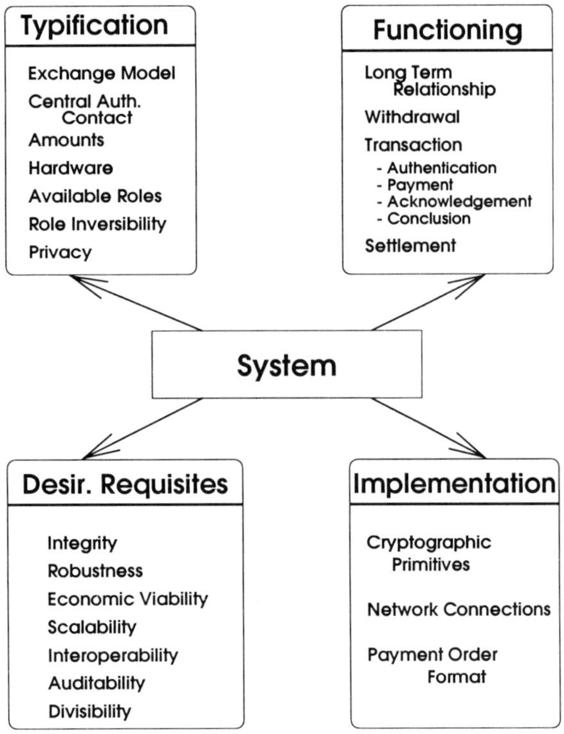

Figure 1. Four Aspects that Characterize Electronic Payment Systems

- **Notational.** Payment transactions in notational systems are done by the settlement of balances in accounts managed by the system's central authority. In this kind of system, users exchange documents which enable value transfers, such as payment orders, and define the value of each of these documents. Familiar examples of such systems are bank cheques. Notational systems are sometimes called *credit/debit systems.*
- **Hybrid.** Some systems make use of signed tokens that have their value specified by the user at the time of the transaction.

Central Authority Contact

- **On-line.** The central authority must be contacted during each transaction, in order to "bless" all value transfers. These systems are usually built over the Internet and must cope with the (possibly high) cost of on-line network connections needed for each transaction. Examples are Internet based systems (E-cash, First Virtual, SET) and debit card based systems (Visa Electron, Carte Bleue).
- **Off-line.** Systems of this type allow users to make transactions without contacting the system's central authority at the exact moment each transaction occurs. Some time in the near future, the payee must contact the central server to settle things up, but this contact may be delayed until the user believes it is appropriate. The payee must be able to verify payment validity without help. An example is project CAFE payment system.

Payment Values

- **Micro-payments.** Only very small values are involved, typically from US$ 0.001 to a few dollars.
- **Small to medium payments.** These values may be transferred on the Internet with a good level of security, usually US$ 1.00 to US$ 500.00.
- **Big payments.** Larger values (over US$ 500.00) require greater security than the Internet can provide today.

Hardware

- **Specific.** Systems need special hardware, like tamper-proof devices or smart cards.
- **General purpose.** Only common computers are needed. Systems may be implemented on any platform and do not require special hardware.

Possible Roles Each party in the transaction must take one of the roles specified in the system. Usual roles are payers, payees (users) or banks.

Role Inversibility

- **Unchangeable roles.** Each user has a predefined role such as buyer, seller or bank. To act in two different roles, users have to register at least twice, once for each role.
- **Interchangeable roles.** These systems allow users to assume different roles when convenient. Thus, they allow transferring values among users. However, in general, no system allows users to become the bank.

Privacy

- **Existent.** In this case, systems protect, to some extent, user's privacy, allowing anonymous purchases, secure transfer or protection of critical information. Some systems guarantee that critical information will be available only to those parties that need it.

- **Non-existent.** Systems do not use cryptographic techniques to protect information transfers. External means must be used if necessary.

Divisibility It must be possible to change a high valued token for smaller valued ones. Four divisibility levels are used to classify payment systems:

1. users are able to divide their own tokens, without necessarily engaging in a purchase/sale transaction.
2. the central authority may be contacted to make change online.
3. the payee may hand some change back.
4. there is no divisibility. It may be a notational system.

2.2 Desirable Requisites

There are requisites that would be desirable in a general model of electronic payment systems. However, attention should be payed to the fact that in some contexts, some of these requisites could be unnecessary or undesired. Usually, only a subset of them is considered for a specific application.

Integrity. The system must provide the means to detect or prevent unauthorized data modification.

Robustness. The system should behave as expected under unforeseen circumstances, not allowing the loss of information or of currency, or enter an inconsistent state, should a problem occur. Robustness may be achieved through the use of ACID transactions [2].

Economic Viability. Cost of transactions must be compatible with the values transferred through the system.

Scalability. A system must be able to cope with the addition of new users and with the increase of the quantity of money involved in its operation without a significant loss of performance.

Interoperability. A system must make possible the exchange of money with other systems. For example, it must be possible to exchange a cheque for cash.

Auditability. The system must provide auditing facilities so that errors or misuse may be detected.

2.3 System Functionality Description

Electronic payment transactions consist of the following steps:

Establishment of Long Term Relationship. Initially, a user makes contact with a financial institution responsible for managing the payment system and establishes a long term relationship with it. This financial institution is called a *bank* or *controlling entity*. The registration with the bank may involve opening an account, acquiring some piece of software or even initialization of authentication methods, such as public key generation and certification.

Withdrawal. In this stage, a user obtains from the bank the monetary means necessary to engage in payment transactions. This is accomplished by transferring electronic coins, charging a smart card or issuing a credit certificate.

Transaction. This is the main stage of any payment system, in which the transfer of values actually occurs. It typically involves four consecutive substeps:

1. **Authentication.** It may be necessary for the parties of a transaction to identify themselves, to ensure that each is an authorized user of the system.
2. **Payment.** The payer sends electronic money to the payee.
3. **Acknowledgment.** The payee may send the payer a receipt corresponding to the transaction.
4. **Conclusion.** If all parties agree on the outcome of the transaction, it can be ended without problems. If there is any disagreement, a dispute resolution protocol may be started.

Settlement. The payee sends the electronic money to the bank to be converted into *real* money, or deposited into an account, or in some cases, the payee may choose to receive the value in electronic currency of the same kind or ask for it to be converted to another kind of electronic currency.

2.4 Implementation Aspects

Some aspects of an electronic payment system are linked to its implementation, and are shown in the system specification. This section presents some important implementation aspects in the analysis of a payment system.

Cryptography. Describes all cryptographic algorithms that are used in the system, specially: symmetric ciphers, asymmetric ciphers, digital signatures, certificates and hashing.

Network connections. Quantity and type of network connections needed by the system.

Token or payment order format. Shows the contents and organization of the tokens or payment orders used in the system.

3 Three systems in detail

In this section, we use the scheme outlined above to get a better understanding of three popular electronic payment systems, that were chosen because they represent different kinds of payment systems and illustrate the benefits attained by the use of the scheme.

3.1 PayWord

PayWord is a micro-payment system designed by R. Rivest and A. Shamir [10]. It is efficient for repeated payments to the same vendor, and is designed to reduce the use of public-key algorithms through the use of hash functions and fast symmetric ciphers.

The system is based upon the use of hash chains to represent monetary value. A hash chain is a sequence $n_0, n_1, \ldots, n_k$, where

$$n_i = h(n_{i-1}), i \geq 1,$$

h is a strong cryptographic hash function and n_0 is a random number. The chain is used backwards, from n_k to n_0. Since h must be hard to invert, it is computationally infeasible to obtain n_i from n_{i+1}.

To make a payment, the user must first generate a hash chain, sign n_k, and send it to the vendor. Then, each monetary unit spent corresponds to the value x of the chain such that $h(x)$ is the previously spent value, currently held by the vendor.

3.1.1 System Typification

Exchange model: *token based.* Users have certificates that enable them to generate hash chains to be used as payment tokens. All chains are user-vendor specific.

Central Authority Contact: *off-line.* The broker gives each user a certificate which enables generation of tokens. Brokers may sign certificates and redeem tokens off-line.

Payment Values: *micro-payments.* The system avoids the use of asymmetric ciphers at the cost of lowering security, and is only adequate for payments under US$ 1.00.

Hardware: *general purpose.* The system is software based and makes no use of specialized hardware.

Available Roles: *buyer, vendor, broker.* Brokers manage buyer accounts and emit certificates. Vendors must register with the brokers to be able to settle received tokens.

Role Inversibility: *unchangeable roles.* The actions and relationships of a user are strongly dependent on the current role of that user. A user may register as vendor and buyer but only act as one of them at a particular transaction.

Privacy: *non-existent.* PayWord does not provide privacy and the user must be identified in each payment. Data in transit is not protected.

Divisibility: *level 4.* The system's design does not include divisibility but the designers suggest that chain values could be negotiated.

3.1.2 Desirable Requisites

Integrity: *partially guaranteed.* Digital signatures are used to maintain certificate integrity. Tokens are not protected by integrity mechanisms.

Robustness: *no particular mechanism specified.*

Economic Viability: *viable.* System designers tried to reduce the use of digital signatures and avoided the use of asymmetric ciphers, thereby lowering the overall cost of the system. We believe this system's cost is adequate to be used with micro-payments.

Scalability: *high.* This system is highly scalable, specially since all operations involving brokers may be done off-line.

Interoperability: *not specified.* The system's design does not account for interoperability.

Auditability: *guaranteed.* All players in the system are identified and certificates are needed to engage in a payment transaction.

3.1.3 System Functionality Description

Establishment of Long Term Relationship: Each buyer must choose a broker and ask for a certificate. This certificate enables the buyer to generate hash chains and to use those chains to make payments. The buyer agrees to pay for all chains signed using his private key.

Withdrawal: The buyer must generate a hash chain, sign the last value, and present it to the broker. This signature indicates that the buyer agrees to pay for each of the values in the chain. The values must be used from the last generated to the first and the commitments (signed values) are vendor specific.

Transaction:

1. **Authentication:** The buyer must be identified and must send the vendor the commitment for a hash chain and his certificate, so that the vendor can verify his signature on the commitment.
2. **Payment:** Each time a buyer makes a payment, he must send one of the values in the hash chain to the vendor. The number of monetary units paid in each payment may be calculated by

   $$j - k$$

   where n_k is the hash value transferred for this payment, and n_j is the last value the vendor knows of. The vendor must verify the validity of each payment by applying the hash function as many times as needed to get the last known value of this chain.
3. **Acknowledgement:** There is no receipt in this system.
4. **Conclusion:** This system does not have a conclusion stage.

Settlement: The vendor redeems the received hash chains by contacting a broker and sending him the buyer's commitment and the last known hash value of the corresponding chain. The broker will generate all hash values of the chain up to the one appended to the commitment in order to verify the chain. If the commitment signature is good and the broker could generate all values in the signed chain, the vendor will receive the corresponding value.

3.1.4 Implementation Aspects

Cryptography:

Digital signatures: are used but no specific algorithm is mentioned.

Certificates: all public keys must be certified. The algorithm is not specified.

Hashing: are used to generate chains. No algorithm specified.

Network connections: *One connection.* Only the buyer and the vendor need to be in contact during each transaction.

Token format: hash chains with signed root. Each of the values of the chain is a token.

3.2 E-cash

Digicash's E-cash [5] is one of the most popular electronic payment systems in use today. It is an Internet based system with full user anonymity by the use of *blind signatures*[4]. The central authority must apply a signature on a blinded user generated token.

This system is already in use by several banks from the United States, Germany and Finland. Of this date, Digicash has not yet made available full specifications of E-cash, so this analysis makes use of unofficial data available on the payment system (as in [9]).

3.2.1 System Typification

Exchange model: *token based.* E-cash tokens are called coins, which are numbered and have an expiry date. The bank must blindly sign all coins.

Central Authority Contact: *on-line.* The bank that signed a coin must be contacted to verify its validity during a transaction.

Payment Values: *small payments.* This system was designed to be used in the Internet, and the coins must be stored in users' computers. Although the system makes use of strong cryptographic algorithms and would probably be secure even for large payments, the general lack of security in coin storage precludes the use of E-cash for large values.

Hardware: *general purpose.* The system may be implemented on any kind of computer platform.

Available Roles: *user and bank.* Users may buy or redeem tokens from the bank.

Role Inversibility: *interchangeable roles.* All users of the system may act as payer or payee. Only the bank role cannot be played by any user.

Privacy: *existent.* E-cash is based on blind signatures and guarantees payer's anonymity. Only in case of dispute the payer must be identified; the bank and the payee are always identified. The order description is sent unencrypted and may be seen or tampered with by an external observer.

Divisibility *level 2.* Divisibility is attained by depositing coins and withdrawing smaller valued coins.

3.2.2 Desirable Requisites

Integrity: *guaranteed.* Coin integrity is guaranteed by the use of digital signatures.

Robustness: *Some mechanisms are provided.* The payer and payee must agree on the order contents and price. The transactions are independent if there is no double spending of coins and the system allows the user to recover lost coins.

Economic Viability: *viable.* The cost of operating the system is compatible with the values considered.

Scalability: *potentially low.* Users who want to participate in a payment transaction must have accounts in the same bank, so bank E-cash servers are possible bottlenecks of the system. Banks must also maintain a list of used coins and may be overwhelmed by the size of this list.

Interoperability: *not possible.* There is no interoperability as E-cash banks operate independently, working only with their own coins.

Auditability: *possible.* Users must sacrifice their anonymity to prove involvement in a transaction. Banks must maintain logs of all deposits to potentially identify the users involved in the transactions.

3.2.3 System Functionality Description

Establishment of Long Term Relationship: Each user must have an account with an E-cash bank and ask it to open a special E-cash account. From this account, users may withdraw and deposit E-cash coins. The user must also acquire and install E-cash's software.

Withdrawal: The user must generate electronic coins, blind them and send them encrypted to the bank together with a signed request indicating which kind of coins are needed. The bank blindly signs them, associating with each coin a user specified value. The bank withdraws the total value of those coins from the user's account and sends the coins back to the user. The user unblinds the coins and may start using them.

Transaction:

1. **Authentication:** The payee presents a payment request to the payer containing: amount, description and its ID.
2. **Payment:** The payer sends coins and a hash of the payment instructions to the payee, encrypted with the bank's public key. The payee then contacts the bank that signed these coins to check them against a spent coin list and to verify the payment instructions. The payee will then proceed to the settlement stage if the coins have not already been spent.
3. **Acknowledgement:** There is no receipt in this system.
4. **Conclusion:** There is no conclusion stage in this system.

Settlement: After receiving a positive acknowledgment of coin and payment instruction verification, the payee has two possibilities of action: deposit the coins or generate new coins of same total value of the verified coins and ask the bank to blindly sign them.

3.2.4 Implementation Aspects

Cryptography:

Symmetric cipher: Triple-DES: used together with the asymmetric cipher in the secure envelope model to protect data transfers.

Asymmetric cipher: RSA.

Digital Signature: RSA, used to sign message hashes.

Hashing: SHA.

Network connections: *2 connections.* One connection is needed for communication between payer and payee and another is needed so that the payee may present the coins to the bank for validation.

Token format: All coins have: serial number, keyversion and bank's signature. The serial number must have a special form so the bank may identify valid numbers and the keyversion is used to determine value, currency and expiry date. The system also makes use of payment instructions containing the bank ID, amount, currency, number of coins, timestamp, payee ID, product description hash and a payer secret hash. This information is used to prevent coin stealing and to enable users to prove payments.

3.3 Internet Keyed Protocol

Designed by IBM's research labs to be an adequate system for transactions using credit cards or account numbers on open networks, such as the Internet, iKP [6] is, in reality, a system that may be used to securely transmit account numbers on the Internet.

This system has three distinct levels: on the first one, only controlling authorities must have a certified public/private key pair; on the second level, all vendors must also have such a certificate; on the third and last level, all participants must have a certified key pair. This level hierarchy allows for a gradual deployment of the system, with an increasing level of security.

3.3.1 System Typification

Exchange model: *notational.* iKP is based on traditional payment processing systems for credit or debit card transactions and, as such, is a notational system.

Central Authority Contact: *on-line.* The entity that processes credit card transactions (acquirer) or the bank responsible for the debit account must be contacted during each transaction. This entity will interface the iKP system with the traditional banking or credit card system, where the actual accounts are managed.

Payment Values: *small to medium payments.* Credit card transaction cost makes the system too expensive to work with microtransactions and credit (debit) card transactions have an upper limit. So, the system should be used for small to medium transactions.

Hardware: *general purpose.* The system may be implemented on any kind of computer platform.

Available Roles: *payer, payee and controlling entity.* Payer and payee must be registered with one of the system controlling entities (issuers and acquirers).

Role Inversibility: *unchangeable roles.* As in traditional credit card systems, the roles are fixed. A party enrolled as a vendor (or payee) can not use this system to make payments to other parties.

Privacy: *existent.* The payer's identity (card number) is protected from the payee and the controlling authority has no access to the order contents. Message security and privacy is guaranteed by extensive use of cryptography, but the system does not allow anonymous transactions.

Divisibility *level 4.* This is a notational system.

3.3.2 Desirable Requisites

Integrity: *guaranteed.* This system makes use of digital signatures and certificates to protect message integrity and all implementations must take care of locally stored data integrity. The initial message is not encrypted so an intruder can intercept and modify thc initial invoice, causing denial of service. In levels 2 and 3, all vendors must have a certified key pair and could sign this invoice to prevent forgery.

Robustness: *guaranteed.* All ACID properties are guaranteed for each transaction.

Economic Viability: *viable.* This system is viable for values in the range of common credit card or cheque transactions. Those are the transactions this system aims at making possible over the Internet.

Scalability: *high.* iKP is as scalable as traditional credit card systems. Many banks and credit card associations may take part of the system and use the same certifying infrastructure.

Interoperability: *not planned.* The authors have not planned integration with other systems.

Auditability: *possible.* Logs and digital signatures allow accurate system auditing to detect fraud or malfunction. In level 3 (3KP), the system allows non-repudiation of all transactions.

3.3.3 System Functionality Description

Establishment of Long Term Relationship: Each user must choose one of the controlling authorities of the system and register with it. In a level 2 or 3 system, users may be asked to generate asymmetric encryption keys to be certified. All users get the master key from the certification hierarchy so they are able to verify certificates. Each user must get the system's software applications.

Withdrawal: none.

Transaction:

1. **Authentication:** In level 2 or 3 systems, each user must identify itself by sending its certificate to the other party. In level 1 systems, the parties only exchange data needed to initialize the transaction such as transaction ID and invoice. The vendor (payee) must tell the payer which acquirer was chosen to process this transaction by sending its certificate.
2. **Payment:** The payer gets the invoice, verifies it and composes a payment order with value, product description hash, account or credit card number and, optionally, a PIN. This payment order is encrypted with the acquirer's public key.
3. **Acknowledgement:** There is no receipt in this system.
4. **Conclusion:** On receipt of the payment order, the payee contacts the acquirer to verify the transaction validity. The acquirer will inform the outcome of the transaction and the payee must send this information to the payer.

Settlement: Settlement is done automatically when the transaction is verified, in the conclusion step.

3.3.4 Implementation Aspects

Cryptography:

Asymmetric cipher: RSA.

Digital Signature: RSA with the same keys.

Certificates: PKCS format.

hashing: MD5.

Network connections: *2 connections.* One connection is needed for communication between payer and payee and another is needed so that the payee may present the payment order to the acquirer.

Payment order format: Each payment order includes the payment value, a hash of identification information shared with the payer and payee, the payer's account number, a random number chosen by the payer and, optionally, a password or PIN. These data are encrypted with the acquirer's public key.

4 Conclusion

This paper presents a systematic way to analyze and compare electronic payment systems. The main points of the analysis scheme are typification, desirable requisites, functioning and implementation aspects.

Now and in the near future, many payment systems will be available to end users, vendors or financial institution and there will be a strong need for tools that enable people to choose which payment system is best suited to their needs. One of the main contributions of this work is to provide a systematic way to, after having enrolled all the requisites of an application, get an insight on the suitability of a system or to choose one from many systems. We strongly believe the analysis and comparison of payment systems should be done in light of the target application (i.e. information or hard goods sales, pay-per view etc.).

Another contribution of this work is in giving a systematic view of the way payment system's work. This result may be used to help when designing a new payment system, especially to identify overlooked aspects of the design.

We do not believe that there will ever be a universal payment system (i.e. a system suited to all needs) and so the comparison and analysis of payment systems must be done in the context of the intended application or future use.

Acknowledgements

The second author is partially suported by research grant PRONEX-FINEP 107/97

References

[1] N. Asokan, M. Steiner, and M. Waidner. The state of the art in electronic payment systems. *IEEE Computer*, pages 28–35, September 1997.

[2] L. J. Camp and M. Sirbu. Critical issues in internet commerce. *IEEE Communications Magazine*, pages 58–62, May 1997.

[3] L. J. Camp, M. Sirbu, and J. D. Tygar. Token and notational money in electronic commerce. In USENIX Association, editor, *Proceedings of the first USENIX Workshop of Electronic Commerce: July 11–12, 1995, New York, New York, USA*, pages 1–12, Berkeley, CA, USA, July 1995. USENIX.

[4] D. Chaum. Blind signatures for untraceable payments. In D. Chaum, R. L. Rivest, and A. T. Sherman, editors, *Advances in Cryptology - Proceedings of Crypto 82*, pages 199–203. Plenum, 1982.

[5] Digicash web site.
URL: http://www.digicash.com, 1997.

[6] P. Janson and M. Waidner. Electronic payment systems. Activity Paper 211ZR018, Semper/IBM Zurich Research Lab, May 1996.

[7] B. C. Neuman. Security, payment and privacy for network commerce. *IEEE Journal on Selected Areas in Communications*, 13(8):1523–1531, october 1995.

[8] T. Okamoto and K. Ohta. Universal electronic cash. In J. Feigenbaum, editor, *Proceedings of Crypto 91, LNCS 576*, pages 324–337. Springer-Verlag, 1992.

[9] D. O'Mahony, M. Peirce, and H. Tewari. *Electronic Payment Systems*. Artech House, 1997.

[10] R. L. Rivest and A. Shamir. Payword and micromint: Two simple micropayment schemes.
URL: http://theory.lcs.mit.edu/ rivest/RivestShamir-mpay.ps, 1995.

[11] A. Schoter and R. Willmer. Digital money online: A review of some existing technologies. Technical report, Intertrader Ltd., February 1997.

A Summary of other systems

A.1 Typification

	Exchange	Central Auth.	Amount	Hardware	Roles	Invers.	Privacy	divisib.
Fisrt Virtual	notational	online	micro	general	BVS	no	no	4
Globe ID	notational	online	small	general	BVS	no	yes	4
Payme	token	online	small	general	UE	yes	yes	2
SET	notational	online	small to medium	general	BVE	no	yes	4
PayWord	token	off-line	micro	general	BVE	no	no	4
MicroMint	token	off-line	micro	general	UE	yes	no	4
CAFE	hybrid	off-line	small	specific	PRE	yes	yes	1
E-cash	token	online	small	general	UB	yes	yes	2
iKP	notational	online	small to medium	general	PRE	no	yes	4
Millicent	token	off-line	micro	general	BVE	no	yes	3
NetBill	notational	online	micro	general	BVE	no	yes	4
NetCash	token	online	small	general	BVE	yes	yes	2
NetCheque	notational	online	small	general	BVBk	yes	no	4
CyberCash	notational	online	small	general	BVS	no	yes	4

Letters in the *Roles* column mean:

B	buyer	**V**	vendor
S	central server	**U**	user
E	controlling entity	**P**	payer
R	payee (receiver)	**Bk**	bank

A.2 Desirable Characteristics

	Integrity	Consistency	Viability	Escalab.	Interoper.	Audit.
Fist Virtual		√	√	√		√
Globe ID	√	√	√			√
Payme	√		√	√		
SET	√	√	√	√		√
PayWord			√	√		√
MicroMint			√	√		√
CAFE	√	√	√	√	√	√
E-cash	√	√	√			√
iKP	√	√	√	√		√
Millicent	√		√	√		√
NetBill	√	√	√			√
NetCash	√		√	√	√	
NetCheque	√		√		√	√
CyberCash	√	√	√			√

A.3 Implementation Aspects

	Cryptography	Net connections	Payment orders
Fist Virtual		3	account number
Globe ID	asymmetric cipher signature hash	2	not specified
Payme	symmetric cipher (IDEA) asymmetric cipher (RSA) digital signature (RSA)	2	token value serial number Bank's identity validity bank's signature
SET	symmetric cipher (DES) asymmetric cipher (RSA) digital signature (RSA) certificate (X.509) hash	2	credit card data transaction ID value product description hash
PayWord	digital signature certificate hash	1	hash chain value
MicroMint	*Hashing*	1	hash function collision
CAFE	digital signature (Schnorr)	1	public keys vendor ID date value
E-cash	symmetric cipher (Triple-DES) asymmetric cipher (RSA) digital signature hash (SHA)	2	serial number keyversion bank's signature
iKP	asymmetric cipher (RSA) digital signature (RSA) Certificate (PKCS) hash (MD5)	2	hash of general data account number random number
Millicent	hash (MD5)	1	vendor ID value serial number buyer ID validity authenticity certificate
NetBill	symmetric cipher (DES) asymmetric cipher (RSA) Certificate *Hashing* (SHA)	2	Kerberos ticket account number
NetCash	symmetric cipher asymmetric cipher digital signature certificate hash	2	issuer ID issuer address validity serial number value issuer's signature
NetCheque	symmetric cipher hash	1	value currency date buyer's account number vendor ID buyer's signature
CyberCash	symmetric cipher (DES) asymmetric cipher (RSA) digital signature (RSA) hash	2	credit card number value hash of item's description

Multifunctional Smartcards for Electronic Commerce - Application of the Role and Task Based Security Model

Kathrin Schier
University of Hamburg, Faculty of Informatics
D-22527 Hamburg, Germany

Abstract

Electronic commerce demands different security requirements for its many different applications. In the near future one smartcard may be used for many electronic commerce applications, such as payment systems, access to banking services and financial transactions over the Internet. A role and task based security model (R&T model) can ensure a secure access to many different services through an application based security framework. It can be used and implemented in a multifunctional smartcard in order to ensure both the users personal need for application based security and his right to informational self determination - as the fundamental right of privacy is defined in the German legal system. A successful application of the model can help the user navigate a secure way through the jungle of electronic commerce.

1 Electronic commerce

The ever increasing growth of the virtual business world will lead to more and more electronic based payment systems. The present day use of credit and debit card based payment is already widespread. It will become more commonplace, because of the increasing acceptance of such cards within the retail trade. The number of businesses accepting electronic payment is steadily growing. The introduction of the „electronic wallet" in Germany will increase the use of electronic money and therefore decrease the use of conventional currency. In the future one or more cards will be used for a wide variety of purposes, not only in electronic commerce. In general, the probability is high that one multifunctional card will achieve wider acceptance than a large number of single function cards.

Although the Internet was never designed for secure transactions, it has become the technical medium for network based financial transactions. The need for the development of secure payment systems has therefore become blatantly apparent. The multitude of payment media, including credit and debit cards, cheques and traditional currency, has spawned a corresponding number of technical systems which support them. Even though many of them are already in use, no single system has become accepted as the de facto standard. A review of different electronic payment systems and their security aspects can be found in [1], [2] and [3].

One special property of conventional currency should not be neglected: Anonymity. Transactions cannot be traced back to individual customers, the identity of which therefore remains unknown. The billing and accounting systems related to cheques and credit cards presuppose a direct link between customer and transaction. The anonymity property cannot therefore apply to these media. Electronic payment systems need to preserve the anonymity property of traditional currency while also offering a payment mode which links individuals and their transactions. Unfortunately, most electronic wallet systems do not support anonymous use. These systems protocol individual transaction data, which allow them to reidentify individual users. The transactions are protocoled by a separate clearing house, which allows the electronic wallet transactions to be treated as a different account. Financial institutions claim that this system, by which the bank and the clearing house both store transaction data, makes checks for misuse possible and therefore more secure. The loss of anonymity may, however, affect the behaviour of the consumer and infringe on personal rights. The right to informational self determination is endangered, unless an anonymous payment system is not available.

There is a trend within the financial community towards offering services, such as money transfer, checking the status of accounts, etc., as so-called „home banking". Home banking services can be accessed directly („online") from the users home computer via the Internet. As homebanking becomes more and more widespread, additional services, such as stock market trading or investment information, will also be made available. In addition to this, automatic teller machines (ATM) will eventually provide access to all banking services. Personal contact between the customer and the bank employee will be reduced and finally substituted by the networked based direct banking services. This shift in emphasis towards online banking services may not always be of advantage to the customer. These risks and other global digital commerce problems are discussed in [4].

Developments to date show that, in order to support the large number of existing electronic commerce applications, many different cards are required. A typical (physical) wallet contains a variety of cards, including bank and credit cards, social security cards, telephone cards, customer cards. This ever increasing multitude of „plastic", with its associated volume of personal identification numbers (PIN), already tends to confuse the user. Not only does the risk of forgetting PINs increase, but also the danger of associating a card with the wrong PIN. This causes added risks, such as the customer may be tempted to write down the PINs and keep them in the wallet.

Most of these applications, such as electronic payment systems, network based financial transactions and electronic banking services, will use a smartcard for their implementation. This paper presents an electronic commerce application of the role and task based security model (R&T model) for multifunctional smartcards [5]. One multifunctional card implementation of the R&T model model could support not only several different electronic commerce applications, but also non-financial functions. For each application the user will have an individual security level, which is already wellknown from single application cards. For a specific application the user can choose the required security level, which may e.g. offer an anonymous use. Before describing the R&T model in a semi-formal way, some requirements are mentioned.

2 Requirements

For every Information Technology (IT) system security requirements have to be defined, as well as any other requirements, including functional or technical aspects. The security requirements of an IT system will be gained through a security policy, describing the security properties. A security model realises a special security policy to support the security properties of an IT system. A security model can have formal or semi-formal character. It describes the rules for accessing data objects in an IT system, enforcing e.g. the security properties of confidentiality [6] or integrity [7]. Other models, such as role based access control [8], [9], [10] or a formal privacy model [11] are very interesting for multifunctional smartcard applications. Role based access control supports access to an object according to the role in which the user is acting. The „formal privacy model" supports access to an object depending on privacy principles associated with a users task. These two approaches can be combined to achieve individual security level for each application.

Based on role based access control model and formal privacy model, a combination of both, namely a role and task based model supports the user to perform different tasks and act in different roles. The role and task based model (R&T model) has two dimensions (roles and tasks) compared to the basic models (either roles or tasks). Therefore it supports more detailed granularity for individual security levels. The R&T Model will guarantee maximum security if it will be implemented in the security kernel of a smartcard operating system. Due to the technical conditions of a smartcard, its operating system protects the data stored in chip very efficiently.

Subjects represent user processes. A subject can choose **tasks** to perform and **roles** to act in. Tasks are hierarchically structured, so that tasks may be composed of tasks. Tasks describe what can be done, roles describe how it can be done. A subject can have one (or more) actual role-task combination. A subject can only perform more than one role-task combination, if these combinations are not mutually exclusive to each other (separation of duty). Every role-task combination provides a list of **procedures** and **objects**. The procedure-object list defines the access to objects. Objects are data objects, stored on the card.

A user chooses a task and a role in which he wants to perform the task. Within his actual role-task combination provided procedures will access defined objects. The access to objects depends on the actual role and task context. A chosen task and a chosen role are associated with a specific security. Each security level defines which data will be transmitted and what kind of information will be openly available.

The following requirements for a security policy are defined, which can be realised by the R&T model:

- The user is the **owner** of the data. While choosing individual roles and tasks he can enforce his right for informational self determination and decide himself who should access which data, stored on his smartcard. For the usage of this right it is important to have either an active user or to configure the card for the user.
- It is important to have a **configuration** for standard applications. Especially for technically inexperienced persons it should be easy to use the card without any security disadvantages. The use of the smartcard should only enable an active administration, but not enforce it.
- The **role and task based model** supports **different multifunctional applications**, not only in the area of

electronic commerce. For electronic commerce, the model should offer both an anonymous role and a non anonymous one. Another role can provide the card as an access medium for network based transaction and banking services.

- A **trustworthy institution** is necessary to support the user while administrating the card. This institution should have a consulting position for all technical, organisational and legal questions.

3 The R&T-Model

A multidimensional security model has been developed, that helps the user to use different applications with varying security requirements within the electronic commerce. The R&T model increases security and privacy. The model provides tasks for the user to perform and roles to act in. Tasks are authorised for users in a many to many relationship. Tasks can be performed in different roles. Roles are also authorised for subjects and describe a structure for action executing procedures on defined objects. Procedures accessing objects depend on the role and task context. The R&T model provides administrators with the capability to regulate who can perform what kind of actions, when and on which objects. New users can be authorised for roles very easily and can also be revoked without any effort. This concept allows a great capability of administrative support. The problem of interest conflicts between role-task combinations will be solved with the principle of static and dynamic separation of duty. This implies that a role-task combination can only be authorised for a user, if there is no other authorised combination for the user, which is mutually exclusive with the proposed combination (static separation of duty). Furthermore a user can only perform a new role-task combination, if this combination is not mutually exclusive with any other combination the user is currently performing (dynamic separation of duty).

A smartcard is suggested for implementation. It can be used as a data base and as an access medium. All personal data which is necessary for payment transactions and any other financial services is stored on the smartcard. All roles and tasks are stored on the card as well. Their definition depends on the application context. Within each role and task context, the minimum of data will only be released. The user can decide by himself which role he wants to act in and therefore which of his data is accessed. Each role and task combination defines an individual security level. To define the R&T model as a state machine model variables, rule and transition functions are needed. In this paper I concentrate on the variables and the rules. The detailed transition functions can be read in [12].

The following variables and rules describe the R&T model.

3.1 Variables

To describe the R&T model, variables are needed, such as subjects, roles, tasks, procedures and objects. A users process is represented by a subject. To perform a procedure on an object, a subject has to activate a task and be active in a role. To choose a task and a role, the task must be authorised for the subject and the role must be authorised for the task. Variables are sets of elements. To use the variables, functions are necessary to find out what elements are belonging to a special set under special conditions. The result of the function can be a single element as well as a set of elements.

Subjects: Subjects are active entities of the model. They represent the users.

$$\text{Subjects} = \{s_1,\ldots,s_n\} \tag{1}$$

Tasks: Subjects can perform different tasks. Subjects can activate in at least one task at one time, which they can choose from a set of authorised tasks.

$$\text{Tasks} = \{t_1,\ldots,t_m\} \tag{2}$$

Subjects can perform different tasks which are authorised for them. The function *Authorised_Tasks* shows the set of tasks, which are authorised for the subjects s_i.

$$\text{Authorised\_Tasks}(s_i) \subseteq \text{Tasks} \tag{3}$$

The function *Active_Tasks* shows the set of active tasks of the subject s_i at that time.

$$\text{Active\_Tasks}(s_i) \subseteq \text{Tasks} \tag{4}$$

Roles: A subject can act in different roles, to perform special tasks.

$$\text{Roles} = \{r_1,\ldots,r_o\} \tag{5}$$

The roles must be authorised for the subject. The set of roles is shown by the function *Authorised_Roles.*

$$\text{Authorised\_Roles}(s_i) \subseteq \text{Roles} \tag{6}$$

The chosen active roles of a subject are given by the function *Active_Roles*.

$$\text{Active\_Roles}(s_i) \subseteq \text{Roles} \quad (7)$$

A subject can have authorised role-task combinations as well as active role-task combinations:

$$\text{Authorised\_Roles\_and\_Tasks } (s_i) \subseteq \text{Roles} \times \text{Tasks} \quad (8)$$

$$\text{Active\_Roles\_and\_Tasks } (s_i) \subseteq \text{Roles} \times \text{Tasks} \quad (9)$$

Static separation of duty: A subject can only perform more than one task or role or role-task combination, if one task (role, combination) is not mutually exclusive with any other task (role, combination) which is authorised for the user. This property preserve the policy of static separation of duty. The following functions give the set of tasks (roles, combinations) which are mutually exclusive with the proposed task t_j, (roles r_i, combinations r_i, t_j).

$$\text{Mutually\_Exclusive\_Roles}(r_j) \subseteq \text{Roles} \quad (10)$$

$$\text{Mutually\_Exclusive\_Tasks}(t_j) \subseteq \text{Tasks} \quad (11)$$

$$\text{Mutually\_Exclusive\_Roles\_and\_Tasks}(r_i, t_j) \subseteq \text{Roles} \times \text{Tasks} \quad (12)$$

Dynamic separation of duty: In some organisations a subject can be allowed to perform more than one task (role, combination) without having any conflicts of interest when acting in independently, but may entail conflicts when acting in simultaneously. Dynamic separation of duty allows more flexibility in simultaneous performing of tasks (roles, combinations). The following functions show the list of mutually exclusive tasks (roles, combinations) for a proposed active task t_j, (role r_i, combination r_i, t_j).

$$\text{Mutually\_Exclusive\_Active\_Roles}(r_i) \subseteq \text{Roles} \quad (13)$$

$$\text{Mutually\_Exclusive\_Active\_Tasks}(t_j) \subseteq \text{Tasks} \quad (14)$$

$$\text{Mutually\_Exclusive\_Active\_Roles\_and\_Tasks}(ri, tj) \subseteq \text{Roles} \times \text{Tasks} \quad (15)$$

Procedures: Within each task and role combination procedures are provided to access objects in a controlled way. Procedures realise the controlled access to objects. There is a set of procedures which can be used in the model.

$$\text{Procedures} = \{p_1,\ldots,p_p\} \quad (16)$$

Objects: Objects are passive entities of the model, the data objects.

$$\text{Objects} = \{o_1,\ldots,o_r\} \quad (17)$$

Allowed Access: The controlled access to objects are realised with procedures depending on the role-task combination of a subject. In the beginning it has to be defined, which procedures should access which objects in which role-task-context. The set of allowed access is specified by a tupel with the elements subject, role, task and a list of several pairs, containing procedures and objects.

$$\text{Allowed\_Access} = \{(s_i, r_j, t_k, [(p_l, o_m)])\} \quad (18)$$

The function *Active_Access* shows the access to one or more objects, which is allowed at that time within the proposed framework of the subjects chosen role and task. The result of the function gives a list of pairs (procedure, object) with at least one element.

$$\text{Active\_Access}(s_i, r_j, t_k) = [(p_l, o_m)] \quad (19)$$

3.2 Rules

The following rules define conditions for the R&T model, which have to be fulfilled to meet the system requirements, mentioned above.

Rule 1: Role Authorisation

A task can never be performed in an active role if it this role not authorised for that task.

$$\forall \text{ r:Roles:}$$

$$\text{Active\_Roles (t)} \in \text{Authorised\_Roles (t)} \quad (20)$$

Rule 2: Task Authorisation

A subject can perform a task, only if the task belongs to the set of authorised tasks for the subject.

$$\forall \text{ s:Subjects:}$$

$$\text{Active\_Tasks (s)} \subseteq \text{Authorised\_Tasks (s)} \quad (21)$$

Rule 3: Role and Task Authorisation

A subject can perform a role-task combination, only if the role-task combination belongs to the set of authorised combinations for the subject.

$\forall$ s:Subjects:
Active_Roles_and_Tasks (s) $\subseteq$
Authorised_Roles_and_Tasks (s) (22)

Rule 3: Task Hierarchy

Tasks can be structured hierarchically. Tasks can be represented as a parent relationship, as an ordered pair $((t_{i+1}, t_i), >)$, where t_{i+1} is the parent and t_i is the child. The relation „>" means „contains". If a task t_j is authorised for a subject s and contains the task t_i, then the task t_i is also authorised for the subject s.

$$\forall \text{ s:Subjects}, t_{i,j}\text{:Tasks}, i \neq j:$$
$$t_j \in \text{Authorised\_Tasks (s)} \wedge t_j > t_i \Longrightarrow$$
$$t_i \in \text{Authorised\_Tasks (s)} \quad (23)$$

Rule 5: Static Separation of Duty

5.1: A role can be authorised for a subject, only if there is no other authorised role for the subject, that is mutually exclusive with the proposed role.

$$\forall \text{ s:Subjects}, r_{i,j}\text{:Roles}, i \neq j:$$
$$r_i \in \text{Authorised\_Roles (s)} \wedge$$
$$r_j \in \text{Authorised\_Roles (s)} \Longrightarrow$$
$$r_i \notin \text{Mutually\_Exclusive\_Roles } (r_j) \quad (24)$$

5.2: A task can be authorised for a subject, only if there is no other authorised task for the subject, that is mutually exclusive with the proposed task.

$$\forall \text{ s:Subjects}, t_{i,j}\text{:Tasks}, i \neq j:$$
$$t_i \in \text{Authorised\_Tasks (s)} \wedge$$
$$t_j \in \text{Authorised\_Tasks (s)} \Longrightarrow$$
$$t_i \notin \text{Mutually\_Exclusive\_Tasks } (t_j) \quad (25)$$

5.3: A role-task combination can be authorised for a subject, only if there is no other authorised role-task combination for the subject, that is mutually exclusive with the proposed combination.

$$\forall \text{ s:Subjects}, r_{i,j}\text{:Roles}, t_{k,l}\text{:Tasks}, (r_i, t_k) \neq (r_j, t_l):$$
$$(r_i, t_k) \in \text{Authorised\_Roles\_and\_Tasks (s)} \wedge$$
$$(r_j, t_l) \in \text{Authorised\_Roles\_and\_Tasks (s)} \Longrightarrow$$
$$(r_i, t_k) \notin \text{Mutually\_Exclusive\_Roles\_and\_Tasks } (r_j, t_l) \quad (26)$$

Rule 6: Dynamic Separation of Duty

6.1: A subject can perform a new role, only if this role is not mutually exclusive with any other roles the subject is currently acting in. Two or more active roles of one subject at the same time must not be mutually exclusive.

$$\forall \text{ s:Subjects}, r_{i,j}\text{:Roles}, i \neq j:$$
$$r_i \in \text{Active\_Roles (s)} \wedge r_j \in \text{Active\_Roles (s)} \Longrightarrow$$
$$r_i \notin \text{Mutually\_Exclusive\_Active\_Roles } (r_j) \quad (27)$$

6.2: A subject can perform a new task, only if this task is not mutually exclusive with any other tasks the subject is currently performing. Two or more active tasks of one subject at the same time must not be mutually exclusive.

$$\forall \text{ s:Subjects}, t_{i,j}\text{:Tasks}, i \neq j:$$
$$t_i \in \text{Active\_Tasks (s)} \wedge t_j \in \text{Active\_Tasks (s)} \Longrightarrow$$
$$t_i \notin \text{Mutually\_Exclusive\_Active\_Tasks } (t_j) \quad (28)$$

6.3: A subject can perform a new role-task combination, only if this role-task combination is not mutually exclusive with any other combination the subject is currently performing.

$$\forall \text{ s:Subjects}, r_{i,j}\text{:Roles}, t_{k,l}\text{:Tasks}, (r_i, t_k) \neq (r_j, t_l):$$
$$(r_i, t_k) \in \text{Active\_Roles\_and\_Tasks (s)} \wedge$$
$$(r_j, t_l) \in \text{Active\_Roles\_and\_Tasks (s)} \Longrightarrow$$
$$(r_i, t_k) \notin \text{Mutually\_Exclusive\_Active\_Roles\_and\_Tasks } (r_j, t_l) \quad (29)$$

Rule 7: Object Access

While planning an application it has to be specified, which procedures should have access to which objects depending on the role-task-context a subject has. A procedure can be executed only if there is a role and task context for the proposed subject, which allows the specified access to objects via procedures.

$$\forall s_i\text{: Subjects}, r_j\text{: Roles}, t_k\text{: Tasks}, p_l\text{: Procedures},$$
$$o_m\text{: Objects,:}$$
$$([(p_l, o_m)]) \in \text{Active\_Access} \Longrightarrow$$
$$(r_j, t_k) \in \text{Active\_Roles\_and\_Tasks(s)} \wedge$$
$$(s_i, r_j, t_k, [(p_l, o_m)]) \in \text{Allowed\_Access} \quad (30)$$

Beside variables and rules, transition functions are necessary to describe a state machine model. These are the following:

- Choose task
- Choose role
- Execute

It is possible for the user to change the order in choosing. There are two possibilities: Choosing first a task and then a role, or choosing first a role and then a task. It makes no difference for the execution, so that two ways are allowed, see figure 6.

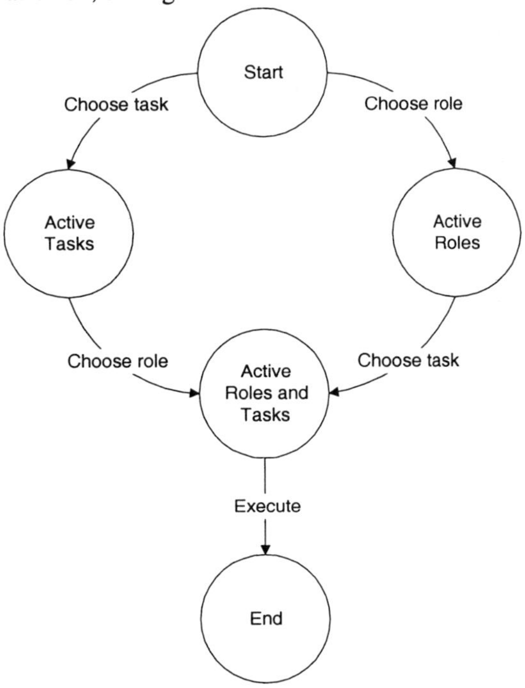

figure 1: Transition functions

4 Application

In order to show the applicability of the R&T model to the area of electronic commerce the following example with hypothetical users, tasks and roles has been chosen. It is a german application example, with regard to common german electronic commerce activities.

In this application example the card is used for different purposes within the electronic commerce. The first decision is WHAT should be used, this leads to the task. The second decision is HOW should the task be performed, now it comes to the role. The following symbols are used to specify a *card application*, with its *tasks* and *child task* as well as their *roles* a *user* can act in.

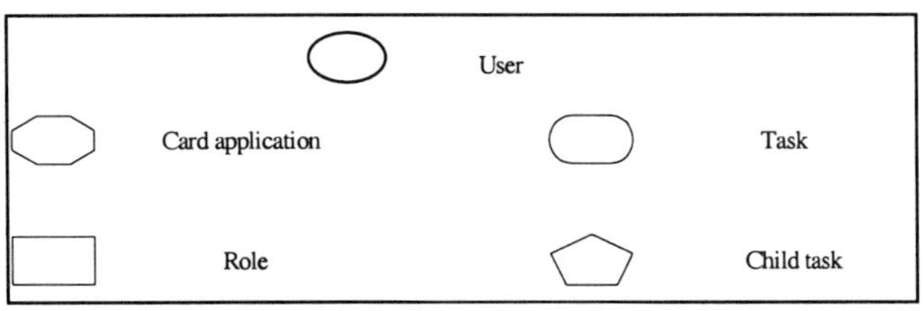

figure 2: Used symbols

The variables in this example are the following:

Subjects = {card holder, bank},
Tasks = {Money transfer, Banking, Administrating},
Roles = {Electr. wallet holder, EC-card holder, Credit card holder, Bank administrator},
Procedures = {Read, Write, Append, Delete, Create},
Objects = {Name, Account no, Bank information, Creditcard no, Limits}.

The application has a *money transfer* task, a *banking* task and an *administrating* task. Possible roles are Electronic wallet holder, EC-card holder, Credit card holder and Bank administrator. The use of a smartcard is assumed, whereby the *card holder* and a *bank* constitute the set of permissible card users, shown in figure 2.

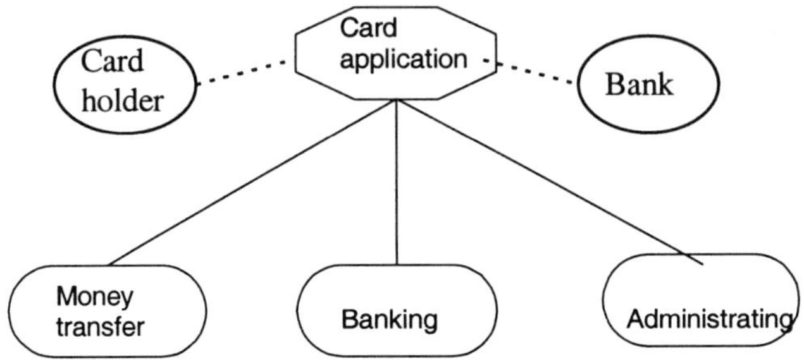

figure 3: Application and tasks

The application of the card is parted into an electronic commerce use, containing money transfer and banking and an administrating use. The three tasks of *money transfer*, *banking* and *administrating* are authorised tasks for the card holder. For the bank only the task of administrating is authorised.

Authorised_Tasks(Cardholder) = {Money transfer, Banking, Administrating}

Authorised_Tasks(Bank) = {Administrating}

The authorised roles for the subjects are the following:

Authorised_Roles(Cardholder) = { Electronic wallet holder, EC-card holder, Credit card holder}

Authorised_Roles(Bank) = {Bank administrator}

The tasks can be composed of tasks. In the following the three tasks are described in detail. The task of money transfer and its child tasks is shown in figure 3. The money transfer task contains two tasks within this hierarchy. The *money transfer* can be money *paying* or money *accepting*. These two tasks can be done in different roles describing HOW the tasks are performed. Both the paying and the accepting task can be performed in the role of an *electronic wallet holder*, in the role of an *EC-card holder* or in the role of a *credit card holder*. The requirements for the task hierarchy are mentioned in rule 4, chapter 3.

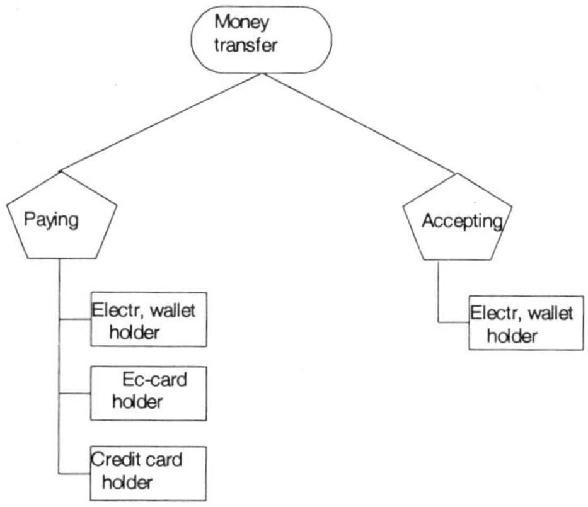

figure 4: Money transfer task and its roles

A task hierarchy is not necessary for each application. Task hierarchy supports a detailed composition of tasks and duties and therefore allows a high granularity. On the lowest task level (the child task) different roles are provided.

Figure 4 shows the task of *banking* providing all typical banking functions. This task contains child tasks as well as shown in the money transfer task. A user performing the banking task can *load* his *electronic wallet* (child task), can use *money transfer* (child task), can get *account statements* (child task) and other *accounting functions* (child task).

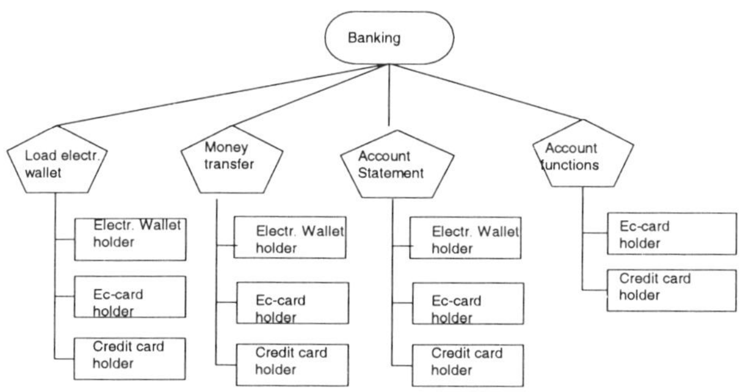

figure 5: Banking task and its roles

The task *load* money on the *electronic wallet* can be done in the role of the *electronic wallet holder*, which means loading cash money on the card. In the role of a *EC-card holder* the loaded money will be transferred from the EC-account of the user. If the role of the *credit card holder* is used the money loaded on the electronic wallet will be credited from the credit card account.

The user, who has chosen the task of *money transfer* can also choose the role in which he wants to perform the task of money transfer. In dependency of the chosen role, the money will be credited from the electronic wallet, from the EC-account or from the credit card account.

The task *account statement* is also possible in all roles. Dependent from the role the statement of the electronic wallet, of the EC-account or of the credit account will be listed. Only the task *account functions* is allowed for only two roles, the EC-card and the credit card holder.

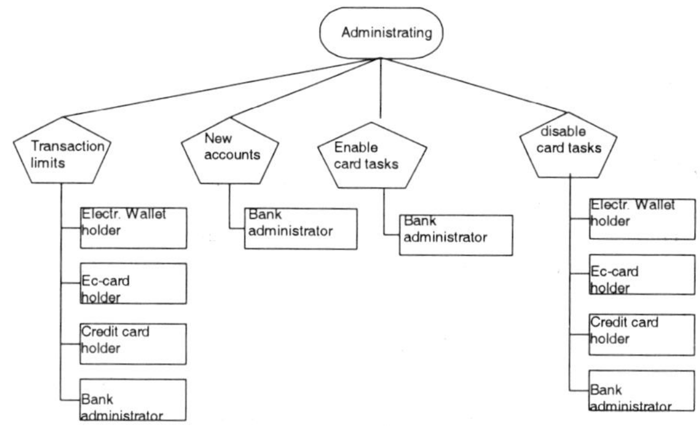

figure 6: Administrating task and its roles

The *administrating* task is parted into card configuration and management, see figure 5. In this example there are four administrating child tasks, *transaction limits*, *new accounts*, *enable card tasks* and *disable card tasks*. All of these four can be performed in the role of the *bank administrator*. He can set new transaction limits can create new accounts or can enable additional card tasks or disable old card tasks. In the roles of the *electronic wallet holder*, the *EC-card holder* and the *credit card holder* only two of the four tasks are allowed. The task of *transaction limits* can be performed in these three roles, because it makes sense if the special card holder wants to reduce his transaction limits in order to make sure not to spend too much money. These three roles are also allowed to *disable* some *card tasks*, if there are not wanted to be used.

For using the electronic wallet card, the user can choose a task to perform and a role to act in. After choosing a role and a task, the variables of the active roles and tasks are set. If the user wants to perform more than one role-task combination at the same time, the rule of dynamic separation of duty is checked. If the desired combinations are not mutually exclusive, they can be performed at the same time without any problems.

5 Conclusion

The role and task based security model is a framework which guarantees the individual security needs of its user. It provides many mechanisms which allow both secure and selective access to user data. The semi-formal model described above has been adapted to the special needs of electronic commerce. Roles and tasks have been defined, which provide maximum individual security, while allowing detailed access to electronic commerce services. An ordered list of procedures and objects must be specified for each role and task combination. This defines the permissible access to individual and public data. Procedures use and access different data objects, depending on the role and task combination.

The R&T model is not limited to applications within electronic commerce, but may also be applied to many other IT associated areas, where individual security requirements for different applications must be considered. The implementation of the R&T model on a smartcard, combined with biometric identification and enhanced authenticity, may facilitate both a secure and comfortable use of a wide variety of applications. The implementation is not limited to smartcards. It can also be realised complex computer systems without using smartcards, for example health care application systems.

The acceptance of R&T modelled electronic commerce systems is necessary and trust into these systems has to be build up. At the moment it is not clear if the shift away from traditional commerce and towards electronic commerce presents a chance or a risk to society in general.

References

[1] K. Schier: Vergleich und Bewertung aktueller Systeme im elektronischen Zahlungsverkehr, *Proceedings of the German UNIX User Group Conference (GUUG)*, September 1997.

[2] A. Engel, A. Lessig, K. Schier: Chipkartenbasierte Zahlungssysteme - Der Große Bruder im Portemonnaie, in: *Proceedings of the OmniCard '98*, Berlin, January 1998, p. 19-43

[3] K. Schier: Zahlungssysteme im Internet - Eine sicherheitstechnische Bewertung, *Proceedings of the Deutsche Internet Kongress (DIK)*, May 1998.

[4] K. Brunnstein, K. Schier: Global Digital Commerce: Impacts and Risks for Developments of Global Information Societies", in: J.Berleur and Diane Whitehouse, Ed., 'An ethical global information society: culture and democracy revisited', Proceedings of the IFIP WG 9.2 Corfu international conference, 8.-10. May 1997, Chapman & Hall

[5] K. Schier: A Role and Task Based Security Model for Multifunctional Smartcard Applications in the Area of Electronic Commerce, *Proceedings of the IFIP WCC '98, SEC'98 Conference*, Wien, Budapest, Kluwer, September 1998.

[6] D. E. Bell, L. J. LaPadula: Secure Computer Systems: Mathematical Foundations, *Technical Report, ESD-TR-73-278, Volume 1*, The MITRE Corporation, Bedford, MA, March 1973.

[7] D. Clark, D. R. Wilson: A Comparison of Commercial and Military Computer Security Policies, *Proceedings of the IEEE Symposium on Computer Security and Privacy*, April 1987.

[8] D. Ferraiolo, R. Kuhn: Role-Based Access Controls, *Proceedings of the 15th National Computer Security Conference*, Baltimore MD, October 1992.

[9] D. Ferraiolo, J. A. Cugini, R. Kuhn: Role-Based Access Control (RBAC): Features and Motivation, *Eleventh Annual Computer Security Applications Conference ACSAC '95*, New Orleans, Louisiana, 11-15 December 1995, *IEEE Computer Society Press*, Los Alamitos, December 1995.

[10] R. Sandhu, E.J. Coyne, H.L. Feinstein, C.E. Youman: Role Based Access Control Models, *IEEE Computer, 29(2)*, February 1996.

[11] S. Fischer-Hübner: Considering Privacy as a Security-Aspect: A Formal Privacy-Model, DASY Paper No 5/95, Institute of Computer and Systems Sciences, Copenhagen Business School, Copenhagen, May 1995.

[12] K. Schier: Vertrauenswürdige Kommunikation im elektronischen Zahlungsverkehr - Ein rollen- und aufgabenbasiertes Sicherheitsmodell für multifunktionale Chipkartenanwendungen, Dissertation am Fachbereich Informatik, 1999.

Modelling Secure and Fair Electronic Commerce

Alexander W. Röhm, Günther Pernul, Gaby Herrmann
Department of Information Systems
University of Essen, Germany

{roehm | pernul | herrmann}@wi-inf.uni-essen.de

Abstract

Security and fairness in business transactions are basic requirements demanded by any participant in electronic markets. In this paper we propose COPS as an infrastructure for building adaptable electronic markets with main focus on security and fairness and MOSS as a methodology for analysing and modelling the security semantics of business transactions. Both are necessary to control the risks involved in dealing (trading) with untrusted parties in an open electronic commerce environment. We address the phases information, negotiation and execution of a business transaction and discuss security requirements which in the past were recognised as being very important for electronic market participants but had only received limited or little attention in the electronic commerce research community.

1 Introduction

Some very fundamental requirements inhibit, or at least slow down the success and growth of Electronic Commerce (EC). The most important requirements, among others, are the lack of

1. a generic and user-friendly infrastructure supporting EC,
2. security and fairness as integral parts of the infrastructure,
3. methodologies for analysing and modelling the security semantics of business transactions.

The *generic and user friendly infrastructure* is mainly necessary for the demander in an electronic market. The demander usually is the driving force in a business transaction and thus the infrastructure must enable him easy access to an electronic market. Otherwise, many potential demanders will not participate in the electronic market which could endanger all the benefits of EC. *Security and fairness* is necessary for all market participants. A supplier will not offer his goods if, for example, secure payment is not guaranteed. The same is true for a demander. He will not participate if, for example, delivery is not guaranteed after payment. Both may not participate in the market if they are not treated by the market infrastructure in a fair way and if privacy and confidentiality is not guaranteed in a business transaction. For secure and fair EC it is essential to know about all security risks of a business transaction. This requires a careful analysis of all security relevant knowledge involved in processing the transaction. We call this knowledge the *security semantics* of the business transaction.

While the first two requirements are enabling services for EC the third requirement is necessary because EC forces rapid changes in the business behaviour of trading partners. The changes will lead to a reorganisation of well-established procedures and thus may make corrections of existing systems necessary and may also have effects on their security. In this paper we deal with all three issues. We develop an infrastructure for secure and fair EC, evaluate the infrastructure by means of an example in a direct search market and outline a technique used for modelling the security semantics of the involved business transactions.

The paper is structured as follows: In section 2 we discuss examples of security requirements in the different phases of a business transaction on an electronic market. Each of the phases has its own security requirements. In section 3 we introduce the COPS project. COPS has the goal to develop and implement a prototype of a generic market infrastructure for EC with its main focus on security and fairness for market participants. Each market participant in each phase of the business transaction is defined (1) by a set of services offered by the infrastructure, (2) by its communication relationships to other market participants, and (3) by a set of actions, conditions and events which are characteristic for this part of the business transaction. In section 4 we introduce MOSS, a methodology for carefully analysing the security semantics involved in (2) and (3). In section 5 the paper is concluded by giving a status report about the COPS and MOSS projects and by discussing our future planned work.

2 Security and Electronic Commerce

2.1 Basic Definitions

Some words on the term "security" are in order. There is no general agreement about the term and its semantics may also have changed over time. This paper uses a very broad definition of security in EC. In this paper we subsume under security

- the general definition: confidentiality, integrity, availability
- intellectual property involved in digital goods: authorship, ownership, copyright, right to use, originality,
- bindings: legal binding, mutual dependencies, non-repudiation
- privacy, anonymity, fairness, trust.

These are not exhaustive lists and may be extended by further relevant issues for EC. A well accepted definition of EC is that it "... is the sharing of business information, maintaining business relationships and conducting business transactions by the means of telecommunication networks." [12]. An important part of EC according to this definition are business transactions, that may take place in electronic hierarchies or electronic markets.

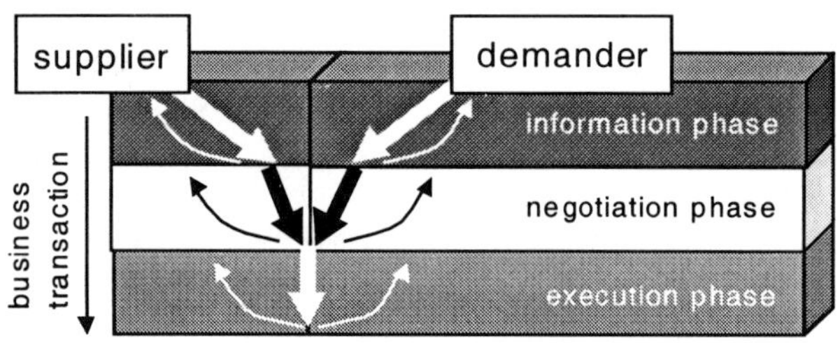

Figure 1: Business transaction phases

Any business transaction usually includes three phases (see fig. 1): the information phase, the negotiation phase and the execution phase (or settlement phase). In the *information phase* the demander (in few cases also the supplier) is searching for a matching business partner. For this purpose a demander asks potential suppliers for their offers. After he has collected these offers he chooses the one he prefers. After matching business partners are found the information phase terminates. During the *negotiation phase* the supplier and the demander have to find an agreement. Many details of the contract have to be fixed like the method of payment, the method of shipping and many others. All obligations for the supplier as well as the demander have to be mentioned in this contract. In the case all contract partners agree the negotiation phase terminates. During the *execution phase*, both the demander and the supplier have to meet the obligations described and fixed in the contract that they have made in the negotiation phase. The execution phase usually consists of two sub-phases: the payment and the delivery of goods phases. Both strongly depend on the type of the good and on the type of the market where the good is offered.

The different phases of a business transaction are processed in an interactive and iterative way. For example, if two matching partners cannot agree about signing a contract the negotiation phase terminates and the information process starts again. A market in which the three phases are supported by information and communication technology is called an *electronic market*. There also exists a broader definition which says that at least one of the three phases has to be supported by information and communication technology for a market to be an electronic market.

Each business transaction on an electronic market involves special risks that depend on the type of (electronic) media, the good and its value, the type of market and of course on the type of attacks that might occur. As a consequence for each phase of a market transaction certain security considerations are necessary. In an infrastructure for a secure electronic markets we have to cover a whole variety of security risks in all three phases by offering appropriate security services.

2.2 Examples of security requirements

During the *information phase* the market participants do have different security demands. When browsing through the Internet a demander has to be sure that an offer he is considering is still valid. Additionally, he must even be sure that the supplier is still in operation under the network address he found the offer. In the case both pre-conditions are valid and in order to reduce the trading risk the demander wants to accept only authenticated offers. But there are also security requirements for the supplier: For example, the supplier may want his offers to be confidential because otherwise the competitors may gain advantages.

The need for security services in the *negotiation phase* is obvious. Most important is the legal binding of contract partners. The contract and its security services must include enough information to find out who is in the right when demander and supplier later disagree. During this phase the probably most important security demands are integrity, authenticity and the legal binding of the contract partners on the content of the contract.

In the case that the *execution phase* is conducted electronically both the electronic payment and the transfer of goods have to be secure. For secure payments several proposals have been made by academics as well as industries. They offer different levels of security and privacy. Secure delivery of digital goods can have many different security demands depending on the type of good that has to be exchanged. For example digital represented shares have to be original but an additional (and often conflicting) requirement is that they have to be anonymous (they do not contain the name or even a pseudonym of their owner) for economic reasons. But there are also security demands in the execution phase that do neither depend on the good nor on the method of payment. For example the fairness problem is evident and not solved by simply making a contract. As an example consider a protocol which assumes delivery of the goods after payment. This is an unfair situation for the demander. The same is true for the supplier if delivery proceeds payment. Additionally the supplier needs a confirmation when he delivers the goods in order to prove that he has met his obligations. The same problem exists with the demander vice versa.

The security of EC is influenced by the different phases of a business transaction, the market participants, the type and value of the digital good, the type of the market (market structure). Because of the diversity of the different security requirements it is necessary to have a clear understanding about all these key factors influencing security and fairness in EC.

3 COPS - An Infrastructure for Secure and Fair EC

In figure 2 we give a graphical model of the underlying market infrastructure of the project COPS (Commercial Protocols and Services). The three levels (I,N,E) show the three phases of the business transactions, while the corner elements are representing the different participants of open markets in an open network. In the following we will discuss the role of each participant in the COPS market model and will show by means of an example how an open electronic market for free trade with original and anonymous emission permits may be realised in COPS.

Within each phase of the business transaction the required *services* for each participant to take part in the market and *protocols* to handle the co-operation between participants are supported.

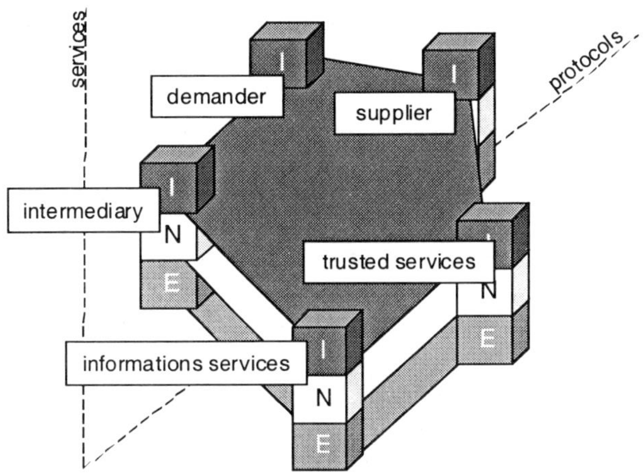

Figure 2: COPS Market Model

Market-based co-ordination can be classified into four categories: direct-search markets (where the future partners directly seek out one another), brokered markets (with the brokers assuming the search function), dealer markets (with the dealers holding inventories against which they buy and sell), and the auction markets [12, 3]. From this classification we derive four electronic market player roles: demander, supplier, electronic intermediary (cybermediary) and trusted third party. Together with the information services five roles of participants are considered in the COPS market model:

- The *demander* is the driving force of a transaction. Only in the information phase it is possible that a supplier offers products. All other phases are initiated by the demander. It is on the demander's side, where an infrastructure has to preserve the open character of an open market. In particular no or less technical or organisational preconditions for a demander to participate should exist. This openness generally includes, that there is no trust relationship between the business partners, which leads to additional security threads [1].
- The *supplier* has the choice to offer her/his goods either on a direct search market, through cybermediaries or on an electronic auction market. The choice will depend on the suppliers preferences, on the type of the good offered and on other strategic considerations.
- An electronic *intermediary* is trading information about products like their prices or quality. He offers product evaluation, quality assurance, or special combinations of products (e.g. travel agency). There are quite different

understandings of electronic intermediaries. All agree, that intermediaries will survive (despite the fact that direct producer buyer relationships are easier) in electronic markets, because they are able to produce an added value to electronic goods [2, 11].

- *Trusted third parties* play an important role in security infrastructures, because they are used for public-key certification. Public-key certification is a necessary requirement to support legal binding of contract partners to the contract. This is practically important for contracting but also for digital goods which often need authenticity, originality and similar properties. For future electronic markets we expect a lot of new tasks for trusted third parties. For example, we believe that the mass of communication can result in an increasing amount of lawsuits, so that traditional courts can not cope with it. Fortunately they don't need to, because in most cases an automatic court of arbitration will be able to judge. This „cyberjudge" is a new role of a trusted authority in the Internet and a legal system has to provide possibilities to appeal against decisions of the cyberjudge. We also propose the use of trusted third parties to realise fair electronic auction markets. In some cases the difference between cybermediary and trusted third party seems to disappear. In our understanding there is a distinguishing mark, that is based on the personal interests and the goals of the party. Consider as an example an anonymous mediated market: To simplify the example we take two parties, S who wants to sell a certain quantity of a good at the price of 100 Euro and D who ordered the same amount and is willing to pay 125 Euro. The intermediary would take the chance to earn 25 Euro. Intermediaries have own interests on the market but trusted third parties are supposed to do something transparent to A and B. For example, simply report the offers or in an exchange market meet all matching demands. Trusted third parties
- *Information services* provide technical information about the market infrastructure and the network. Examples are certificate directories or a special host which processes inquiries like: "What is the network address of a trusted third party issuing secure time stamps?".

Electronic markets reduce the trading immanent transaction costs, which can solve existing allocation problems for example in environmental policy. An example for this is the model of tradable emission permits which is supposed to efficiently and effectively reach given environmental goals. Each permit in this model allows its owner emission of a certain amount of toxins. Permits can be traded freely. When the permit is traded on an electronic market it has to be digitally represented, it must not be possible to forge or to copy it and finally the market should be anonymous.

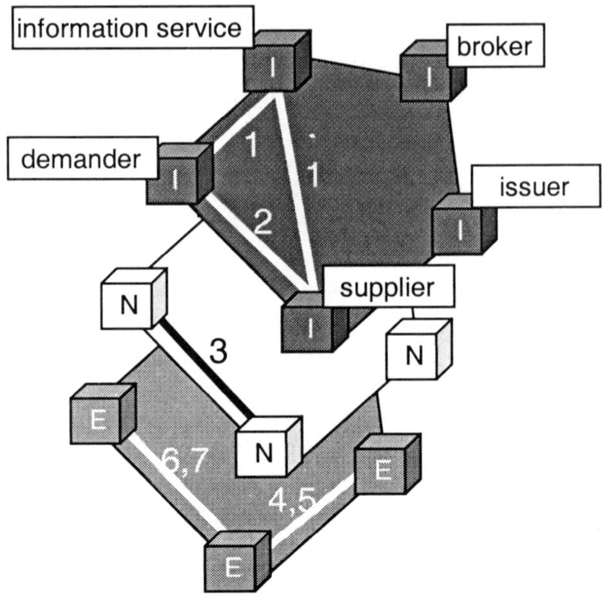

Figure 3: Business Transaction in COPS

In figure 3 we give an example of an open electronic market for free trade with original and anonymous emission permits. The example shows how the market may be realised in COPS and additionally how trusted authorities (in this example the issuer) can be used for guaranteeing originality and anonymity of digital goods. The example is from [9].

The business transaction is carried out in different steps. During the steps marked with 1 the demander and supplier search for each other. In step 2 the demander gets a binding offer from the supplier. This concludes the information phase of the transaction. In step 3, the contract terms are discussed, the contract is completed, and the demander sends a session key which is encrypted by using the public key of the issuer to the supplier. This is necessary for establishing the connection to the emission certificate and for preparing anonymity. The negotiation phase ends and the execution phase starts. During step 4 the supplier sends his original permit together with the encrypted session key to the issuer of the emission certificate. The issuer (trusted authority), deletes the old emission permit, generates a new original and encrypts it with the session key. Then the issuer sends it to the supplier in step 5, who gives it to the demander in step 6, who pays electronically in step 7.

It is important to note that it is only possible to guarantee a certain level of security if special care is given to the communication processes being part of the business transaction. In addition, it is necessary to carefully analyse all application dependent security semantics that are part of the business transaction. This is where the MOSS project comes into the picture.

4 MOSS: Modelling security semantics of business transactions

Business transactions usually are described by using business process models. A business process is modelled by an executive of the organisation and usually contains the following components: information about organisational units involved in processing the business process (e.g. departments, agents, roles, and machinery), tasks to be performed and their co-operation, informational units and their usage and structure, and behaviour of all the objects involved. The executive responsible for specifying the business process usually is not a security specialist. At a very high level only he has knowledge about requirements like "sensitivity", "legal binding", "high integrity", "copyright", and similar, and will assign the requirements to business process components.

In figure 4 we show by using the MOSS terminology the most important parts of the business transaction of the example introduced above from the viewpoint of the demander. We will not explain the details of the MOSS syntax and semantics because they are self explaining in the example. Additional information may be found in [6].

At the demander different departments and employees acting in different roles are involved in processing the business transaction. The business transaction is initiated in the purchase department and passes each of the three phases of a market transaction. In the graphic representation the following notation is used: The first row represents the departments which are responsible for execution of tasks and the left column represents the agents (roles responsible for) carrying out the tasks. In the information phase, companies are determined which could act as possible suppliers. They are invited to submit offers (task 2). Offers need to be

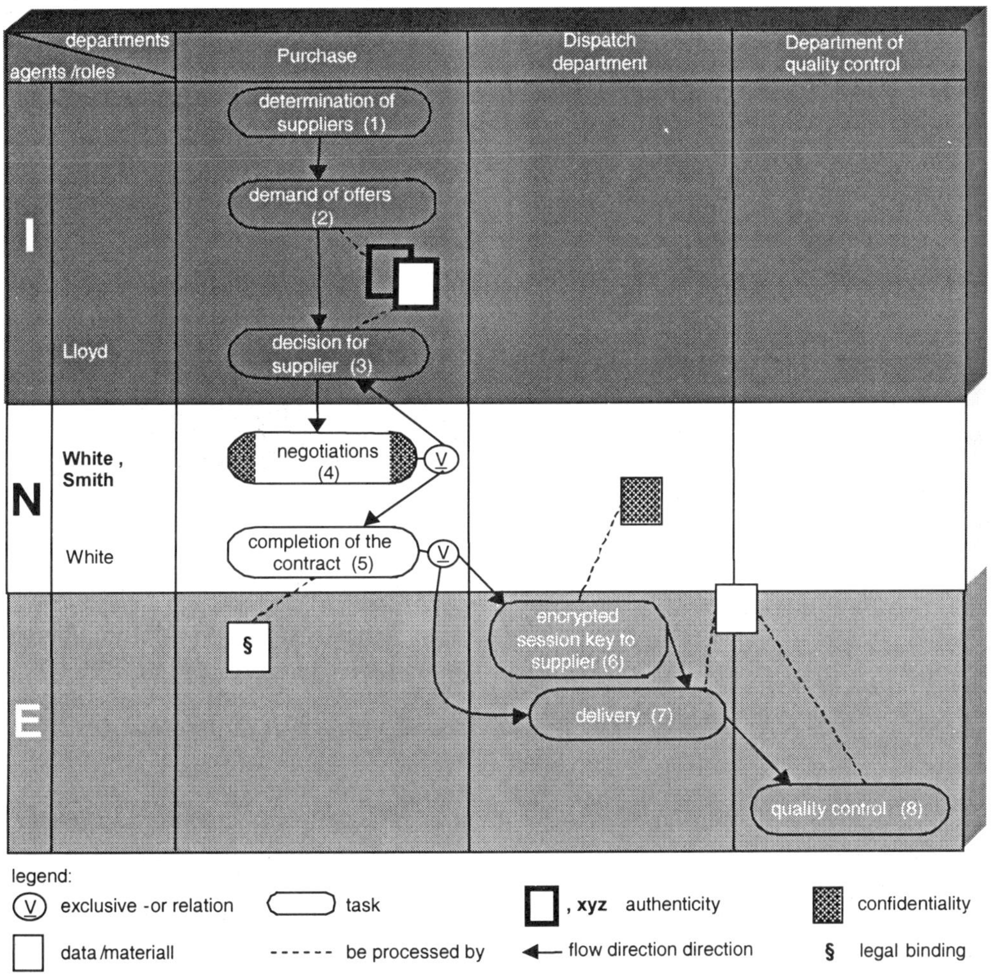

Figure 4: Business process extended by security semantics

valid for a specific period of time and must be *authentic*. Otherwise the decision about who will be chosen as supplier (task 3) is based on uncertain information. During the negotiation phase (task 4) negotiations with the chosen supplier take place which may lead to a completion of the contract (task 5) or to choosing another supplier (task 3). Negotiations may have several security requirements: First, the communication partners must be *authentic*. Second, negotiations are requested to be *confidential*. A completion of contract requires *legal binding* of both contract partners on the contract. During the execution phase the session key encrypted by using the public key of the issuer must be delivered to the supplier (task 6). To avoid competition disadvantages in the case of leaking out information, *secrecy* is demanded here. After the emission permits are delivered (task 7, waiting for delivery) a quality control (task 8) takes place. In this simple example of a market situation the demander at least has the following security requirements: authenticity, legal binding, and confidentiality (secrecy).

To realise a business transaction and its security requirements a more detailed analysis is recommended in MOSS. A detailed analysis is necessary because of two reasons: First, the executive responsible for specifying the business process usually is not a security expert. His understanding of the security semantics may be very vague and on an abstract level only. Second, a business process is not an isolated activity within an enterprise and there are interferences with databases, processing units, people involved, and others. Typically, for these components already models exist (i.e. data model). A security requirement in the business transaction must be supported by corresponding security constraints in related systems. Otherwise, these systems may be used by an attacker in order to gain information about the business transaction and a security hole exists.

5 Perspectives of business processes

In order to arrive at a complete understanding of the security requirements the MOSS business process model suggests to view a business transaction from at least five different perspectives (see figure 5).

- The *informational perspective* represents the information entities, their structuring and relationships between them. A common methodology for analysing and modelling the informational perspective is to use the Entity-Relationship approach [4].
- The *functional perspective* shows what activities (processes) are performed and which data flow occurs between activities. The functional perspective only represents the flow of data within the system. It may be modelled by using data flow diagrams [5].
- The *dynamical perspective* represents for each information entity all possible states and state transitions which may occur within the life cycle of the information entity. There are many different techniques available to model system dynamics. A common technique are state transition diagrams as used in OMT [8] and its successor UML.
- The *organisational perspective* shows where and by whom activities are performed. This perspective corresponds to the organigram of an organisation and to role models.
- The *business process perspective* represents the flow of work in terms of activities and information flow from the viewpoint of the whole business process. It consists of an integration of the functional and dynamic perspectives and references the informational and organisational perspectives. In MOSS it is modelled by using the method shown in the example given in figure 4.

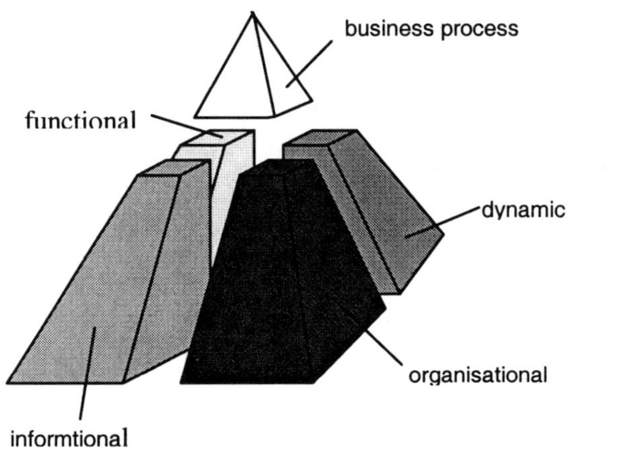

Figure 5: MOSS business process perspectives

In general, any requirement on business processes is represented in different perspectives with varying consequences. Consider a requirement "time dependency" of task execution (for example, task *a* should always be carried out before task *b*) which strongly influences functional and dynamic perspectives, does less influence the organisational perspective but does not influence the informational perspective of a business process at all. This is in contrast to requirements referring to security of business processes. They are more complicate to handle because they influence all perspectives of a business process at the same level of importance. In the case we have a security hole in one perspective the security of the whole business transaction is in danger.

In the following we focus on our example again and analyse the different perspectives of contract completion and the security requirement "legal binding" of the contract partners (task 4 in fig. 5). In the examples we use the following notation: Components of existing models or attributes which are not effected by security requirements are written using standard characters. The attributes with relevance to legal binding are given in bold face.

To guarantee legal binding of contract partners on a contract different regulations are required according to corresponding law. In many countries a document is legal binding if the agreement between the contract partners is provable. For provability a common method is the usage of signatures. If the contract is a traditional document (by paper) a way to realise legal binding of the contract is to have it signed by the contract partners. In business transactions on electronic markets a (electronic) document should be signed digitally. The following is based on the IuKDG [7], the German bill for digital signatures. This bill requests the following for legal binding of a digital signature: A digital signature is a seal based on the signed data. The seal is realised by asymmetric cryptography and is created by using the private key of the signatory. It is possible to ascertain the correctness of signed data and the identity of the signatory by using its public key which must be certified by a certification authority. Each certificate is assigned with a period of validity. Which cryptographic algorithms and which certification infrastructure should be used is not included in the bill because of possible future developments which could influence security of digital signatures.

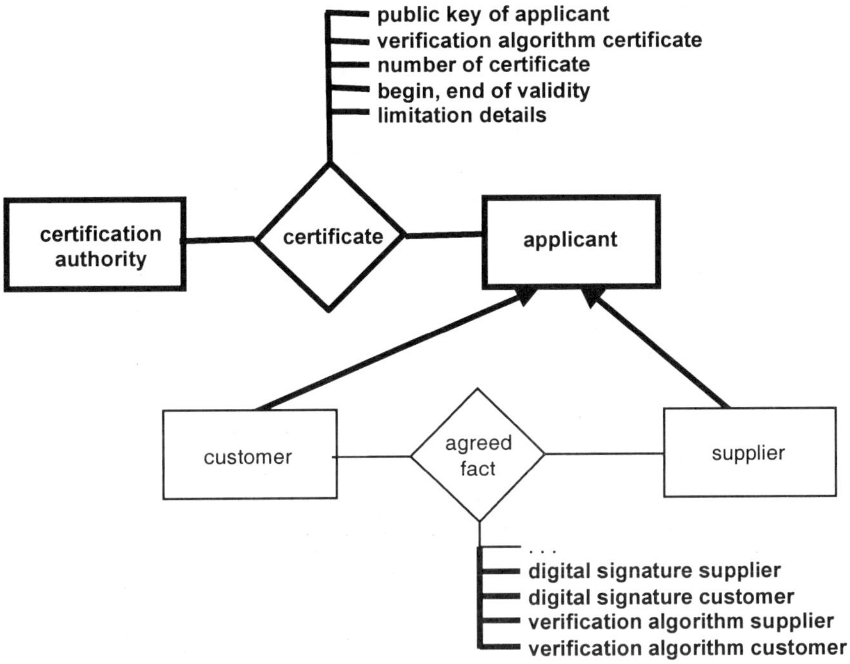

Figure 6: Informational perspective extended by security semantics.

5.1 Legal binding - informational perspective

In order to study what effects a digital signature has, we will first refer to the informational perspective of the business process of our example. As contracting information is usually stored in a database we assume the existence of a data model at the demander covering the demander-supplier relationship. According to IuKDG to sign an electronic document, the seal of each signatory and the corresponding certificates are necessary. In order to process the business transaction on an electronic market and to establish legal binding, the informational perspective of the business process must be extended by information about the signatories, the certificates used, and the (trusted) parties responsible for issuing the certificates. In figure 6 we have extended the customer-supplier-relationship of our example by appropriate data structures necessary for supporting legal binding. In particular these are: a new relationship type CERTIFICATE and modification of the existing relationship type representing the contract. The agreed fact is represented by a document which should be signed and the relationship type between customer and supplier must be extended by one field for the seal (digital signature) of each signatory and by information about what algorithm was used for signing. In addition, are necessary to guarantee the provability of digital signed contracts. These actions lead e. g. to extensions of the functional perspective of a process responsible for archiving. Again, in figure 7 necessary extensions due to

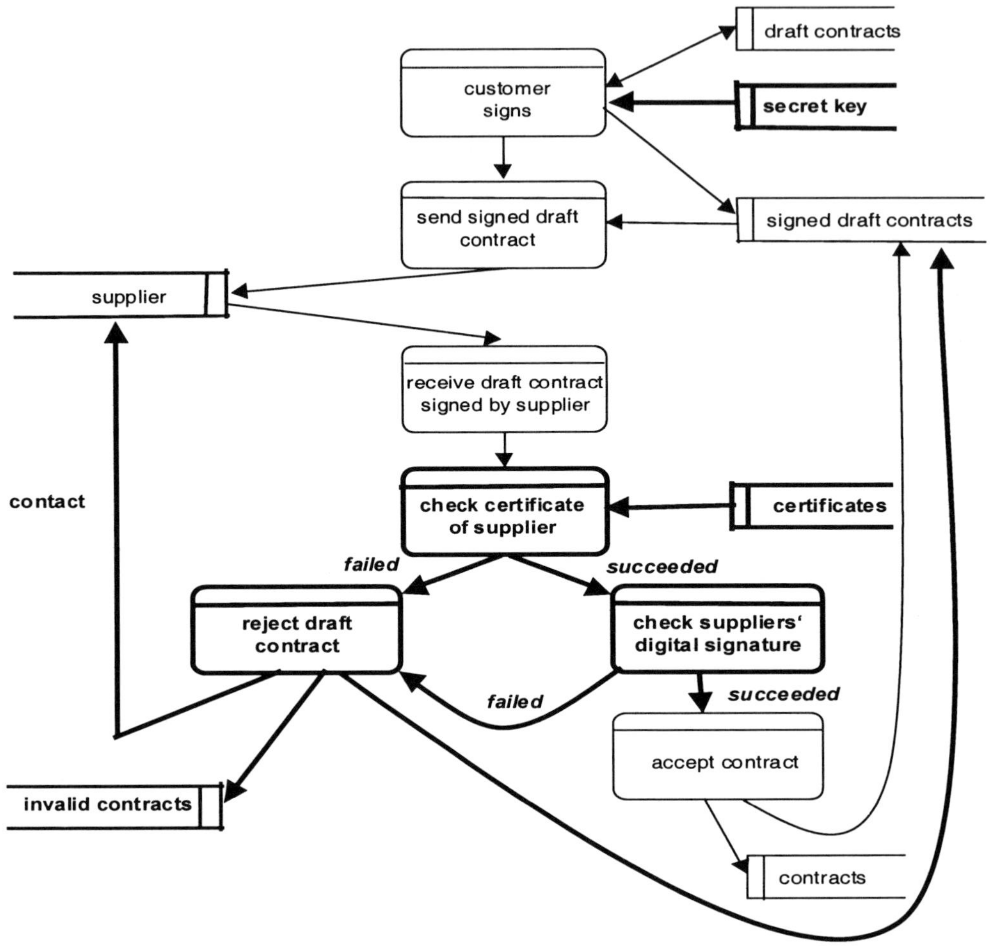

Figure 7: Functional perspective extended by security semantics

customer and supplier are specializations of a generic type applicant which must have a certificate relating the applicant to a certification authority.

5.2 Legal binding - functional perspective

During the process of completing a contract certain information flow takes place. The flow involved in the business transaction can be analysed in the functional perspective of the business process. To guarantee legal binding of the contract the functional perspective of the business process must be modified as follows (see figure 7): The document must be signed digitally by each contract partner and the signatures must be verified. Because a certificate of a public key may be expired (by time or by declaration of invalidity) additional actions security requirements in a functional model are given in bold face.

5.3 Legal binding - organizational perspective

Introducing legal binding to the business process has impacts to the organisational perspective, too. To check the validity of digital signatures and to initiate further actions, a new role in the organisation is necessary and leads to an extension of the organisational perspective. The additional role may be called SIG-MGR and is responsible for re-signing documents in case of certificates are no longer valid and for the verification of signatures. Additional roles may be necessary for key management. The role SIG-MGR may need the following authorisations: access to relevant certificates, right to re-sign contracts when the corresponding certificate of the own enterprise is expired or is declared invalid, right to ask a contract partner for re-signing a contract in the case contract partner's relevant certificate is expired or declared invalid. A role responsible for signing contracts may already exist in organisations having the authority of signing contracts in the traditional way. Such a role is necessary when introducing digital signatures too but needs to be extended by a new privileges to access relevant certificates.

One reason may be the following: If signatory party A signs and gives the document to contract partner B (which has no time restriction for the signing process) B will be able to look for a more favourable offer while delaying the signing process but A already feels bounded by his/her signature. These time restrictions may be one variation of the semantic meaning of a digital signature. To cover this aspect the business process model of our example must be extended.

Unfortunately, security requirements of a business

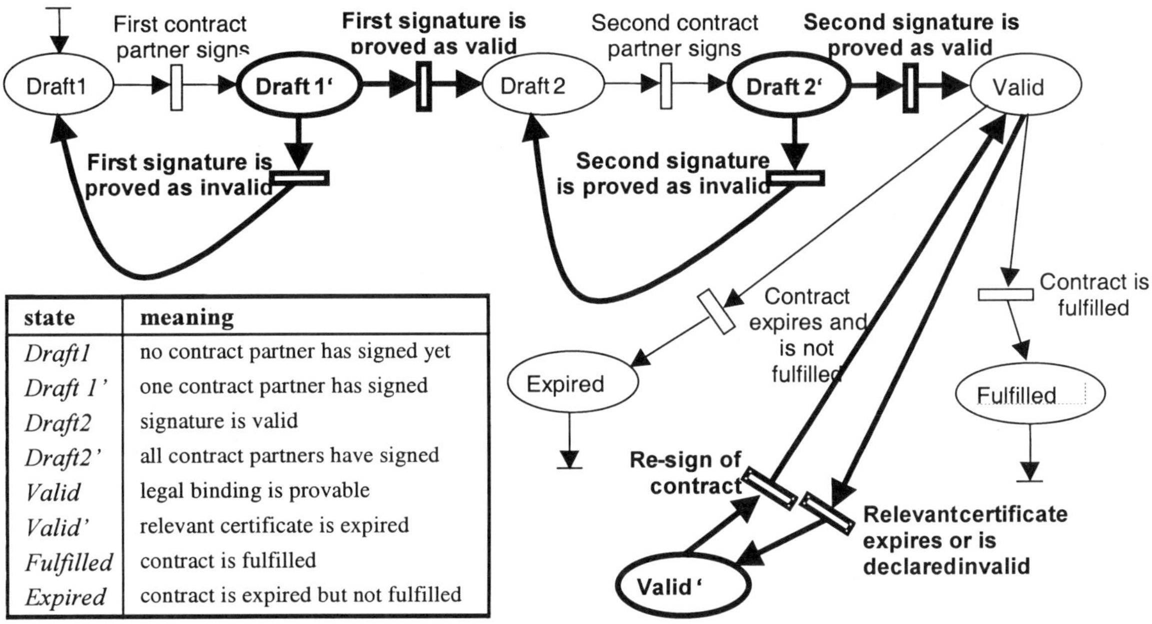

state	meaning
Draft1	no contract partner has signed yet
Draft 1'	one contract partner has signed
Draft2	signature is valid
Draft2'	all contract partners have signed
Valid	legal binding is provable
Valid'	relevant certificate is expired
Fulfilled	contract is fulfilled
Expired	contract is expired but not fulfilled

Figure 8: Dynamic perspective extended by security semantics

5.4 Legal binding - dynamic perspective

Similar to the other perspectives the legal binding on a contract has impacts on the dynamic perspective as well. In figure 8 we show the life cycle of entity type CONTRACT in terms of its different states. From a security point of view the state Valid' is important to note. It represents an object of type contract which is valid (i.e. signed) but the certificate of the signature is expired. This means we have the situation that a contract is valid but no longer provable. Each contract in this state must be re-signed.

It is important to note that the different semantics of digital signatures are not always clear and as discussed above the signing process is not always fair. In our example a signatory party (the demander) may demand the signing of the corresponding document by the contract partner (the supplier) within a specific period of time. For this requirement different reasons may exist.

transaction have effects on different perspectives of a business process. The example showed that legal binding as needed on electronic markets influences all perspectives of the business process. In MOSS we propose extensions to existing models which seem to be quite complex for the non security expert. However, the outlined extensions are identical for legal binding of a document in any business process requiring this functionality in identical legal environments. Therefore, these extensions may be reused.

6 Conclusion

Building secure and fair relationships in open electronic commerce requires the combination of several elements to address commercial, legal, and security concerns. In this paper we investigated this issue by firstly introducing COPS, an electronic commerce infrastructure, and secondly MOSS, a modelling environment for analyzing security semantics of business transactions.

COPS has its main focus on security and fairness, includes five different roles of market participants, supports all phases of a market transaction, and can be used to build markets with different structures. MOSS can be used to analyse the security semantics of business transactions. It supports different views on a business transaction in order to arrive at a comprehensive picture of the security requirement. Both projects are currently implemented as academic prototypes. COPS is based on a layered architecture [10]. So far we have extended a commercially available cryptographic library by a security abstraction layer, have implemented a public key directory for market participants, and are working on the implementation of a certification server. For MOSS we are currently building a graphical editor which supports the specification of the business process perspective and some syntactical and semantical parsing of the security constraints specified.

7 References

[1] Bons, R. W. H.: Designing Trustworthy Trade Procedures for Open Electronic Commerce. PhD-Series in General Management 27; Rotterdam School of Management; (1997).

[2] Buxmann, P; König, W.; Rose, F.: An Electronic Market for Java SoftwareElements. Proceedings of ECIS 97; (1997). http://java.wiwi.uni-frankfurt.de/papers/jr_ecis97.html (last accessed 8/1997

[3] Clemons, E.K.; Croson, D.C.; and Weber, B.W.: Reengineering money: the Mondex stored value card and beyond. International Journal of Electronic Commerce (1997). http://www.cba.bgsu.edu/ijec/ (last accessed 8/1997)

[4] Chen, P. P.: The Entity Relationship Model: Towards a Unified View of Data. ACM Trans. On Database Systems (TODS), Vol. 1, No. 1, 1976.

[5] Gane, C. P.; Sarson, T.: Structured System Analysis: Tools and Techniques. Prentice Hall, Englewood Cliffs, NJ, 1979.

[6] Herrmann, G.; Pernul, G.: Viewing business process security from different perspectives. Proceedings of 11th International Bled Electronic Commerce Conference, 1998.

[7] Informations- und Kommunikationsdienste-Gesetz - IuKDG (version from 7/13/1997).

[8] Rumbaugh, J.; Blaha, M.; Premerlani, W.; Eddy, F.; Lorensen, W.: Object-Oriented Modeling and Design. Prentice Hall, Englewood Cliffs, NJ, 1991.

[9] Röhm, A. W., Gerhard, M.: A Secure Electronic Market for Anonymous Transferable Emission Permits. In: Proceedings of Thirty-First Hawaii International Conference on System Sciences HICSS-31; (1998). http://www.wi-inf.uni-essen.de/~ifs/publ_97.html (last accessed 9/1997)

[10] Pernul, G., Röhm, A. W.: COPS: A Model and Infrastructure for Secure and Fair Electronic Markets. To appear: Proc. of Thirty-Second Hawaii International Conference on System Sciences HICSS-32; (1999).

[11] Sarkar, M.B.; Butler, B.; and Steinfield, C.: Intermediaries and cybermediaries: a continuing role for mediating players in the electronic marketplace. Journal of Computer-Mediated Communication, 1, 3, (1995). http://www.usc.edu/dept/annenberg/vol1 /issue3/vol1no3.html (last accessed 8/1997)

[12] Zwass, V.: Electronic Commerce: Structures and Issues. International Journal of Electronic Commerce; Vol. 1; No. 1; M.E. Sharp; 1996.

Track B

Architectures

Chair

J. Heaney, The MITRE Corporation

Security Architecture for a Virtual Heterogeneous Machine

Roger Wright
Computer Science Dept.
Naval Postgraduate School
Monterey, CA 93943
rewright@nps.navy.mil

David J. Shifflett
Rolands and Associates Corp.
500 Sloat Avenue
Monterey, CA 93940
dshifflett@gwdi.com

Cynthia E. Irvine
Computer Science Dept.
Naval Postgraduate School
Monterey, CA 93943
irvine@cs.nps.navy.mil

Abstract

We describe security for a virtual heterogeneous machine (VHM). Our security architecture is based upon separation of services into four distinct domains. It is designed to take advantage of operating system support for domains, where available. We have chosen to use emerging public key technology as an interim solution to provide domain separation. A prototype demonstration of our architecture has been developed.

1. Introduction

Science, engineering and defense are witnessing the emergence of a new approach to computation. It depends not on single isolated centers of excellence for high performance computing, but upon a network of computers bound together by an overlying framework that presents to users a powerful virtual heterogeneous machine (VHM) intended to support high throughput computing [19]. Applications may consist of a single thread of execution, a set of sequential jobs, or may be parallelized across several components of the underlying system. Some applications may require a variety of computational and storage resources ranging from desktop PCs for the submission of jobs to supercomputers for computationally intensive tasks.

Efforts are currently underway to define the VHMs which will manage user tasks. A major research area for these systems is the formulation of adaptive scheduling techniques based on task and network properties. Ultimately, the technologies emerging from the creation of an advanced computational infrastructure will be integrated into systems supporting finance, industry, and individual users. In all cases, security is a concern for these systems.

The diversity of the user population employing a VHM implies that one security solution may not be appropriate for all individuals or even for all tasks of one particular individual. We are collaborating in a research project to investigate the properties and services of a VHM and are examining security concerns and technologies in that context. This paper is a report on the progress of that effort.

We will describe how notions of privilege and system integrity can be incorporated into an architecture intended to execute in a heterogeneous computing environment. The remainder of the paper is organized as follows. Section 2. outlines the objectives and high level architecture of the VHM to which our protection architecture is being applied. Section 3. describes the security requirements for the system. Section 4. describes the security architecture we have developed for the VHM. Our prototype implementation and its use of the Intel Common Data Security Architecture, is discussed in section 5. Section 6. will contrast our work with that of several other VHM security efforts and will describe our future plans. Section 7. provides a summary.

2. Management System for Heterogeneous Networks

The intent of the Management System for Heterogeneous Networks (MSHN, pronounced "mission'") is to construct a virtual heterogeneous machine designed to run as an application on a variety of operating systems and hardware platforms [11]. It will provide end-to-end support for applications in distributed and heterogeneous, shared environments. In addition to supporting compute-intensive jobs, MSHN is intended to provide a responsive and flexible execution environment for real-time, interactive, and I/O-intensive tasks. When heterogeneous resources are simultaneously shared by several applications, each with its own unique quality of service (QoS) requirement, MSHN will be able to efficiently assign resources to the applications so that they will attain their requested QoS.

0-8186-8789-4/98 $10.00 © 1998 IEEE

Each *job* is characterized by code and a dataset. An instance of a job will be the code and a particular dataset and is associated with a particular user. For each job, MSHN will maintain historical data describing the job's *compute characteristics*. When a new request to execute the job with a particular dataset is issued, the scheduler will use the job's compute characteristics as well as dynamic information about network and resource loading. The scheduler will make decisions regarding resource allocation to maximize the QoS for a particular job. For example, suppose job A has historically run in 10 minutes on resource X and in 20 minutes on resource Y. When a request to execute the job is issued the scheduler may decide to wait five minutes so that the job can be run on system X rather than schedule it immediately on system Y. In an open environment, even when using the same resource, consistent QoS for jobs may not be guaranteed. Network congestion and load at the compute resource can impact job performance.

Use of MSHN is optional. In theory, users could attempt to decide where a job might best be executed, however, several projects [14][5] have demonstrated that a scheduling and job management service can provide significant benefits, just as traditional operating systems support applications through local resource management services.

These early resource management system demonstrations lacked the ability to address quality of service requirements in a highly distributed and dynamic heterogeneous environment. MSHN will address these issues. It will monitor the load on a large pool of resources and will advise jobs as to the best strategy for achieving QoS objectives for a particular run. It is anticipated that, despite the extra processing required for MSHN to provide monitoring and advisory services, the performance advantages will outweigh the slight computational tax imposed by the VHM. User involvement in the scheduling and execution of jobs might be streamlined through the use of a special MSHN shell that would hide MSHN processing.

2.1 MSHN VHM

The proposed MSHN VHM [15] consists of five major components, as depicted in Figure 1: a user client, three MSHN core services, and a client on each computational server. (The Audit Server will be discussed in a subsequent section.) An assumption of the MSHN architecture is that the physical machines running MSHN components are not necessarily dedicated to MSHN processing. Thus, jobs on a computational server may be divided into two categories: those taking advantage of the services provided by MSHN and those that do not.

Client libraries will "wrap" user jobs at the application origination points and at the compute resources. These libraries are intended to provide the services of the MSHN VHM transparently: legacy application code will require no modification to be executed in the MSHN environment. Adaptive applications will benefit from environmental information that may be signalled to them through the MSHN services.

The Resource Requirements Database is used to store initial estimates of per job requirements and to maintain a record of the resources that have historically been consumed by a particular job. This may include the level of service requested by the users as well as priorities for particular classes of applications. As experiential data are accumulated, the resource requirements for the execution of future instances of the job are adjusted.

The Resource Status Server is the most dynamic of those maintained by MSHN. Here information regarding the resource consumption by all currently executing jobs on the VHM is maintained. In addition, client library monitors associated with the network and computational resources provide up-to-date information regarding the availability of resources on the VHM.

The Scheduling Server maintains a set of algorithms used to produce advisory schedules for jobs. If the Resource Status Server flags a job as being bogged down, a request may be issued to the scheduler to seek a better scheduling strategy for the task. That strategy may include task checkpointing and relocation [16].

A MSHN project goal is to provide support not only for traditional static applications, but to enhance the performance characteristics of dynamic and adaptive applications. This is particularly the case in environments where the load on resources is not predictable, but perhaps best characterized probabilistically. Consider, for example, an adaptive application in which a user asks for time-critical processing that will return high precision and high fidelity results. As the application is executed, MSHN will use the client libraries associated with all jobs on the VHM to monitor the resources of the VHM, quantifying and accounting for uncertainty throughout the distributed processing mechanism. Intermediate reports on job status and resource usage are transmitted by the client libraries to the Resource Status Server. Should available resources be insufficient to achieve the original time, precision and fidelity objectives, the MSHN Scheduler will trigger a notification to the client library of the affected application. In the case of

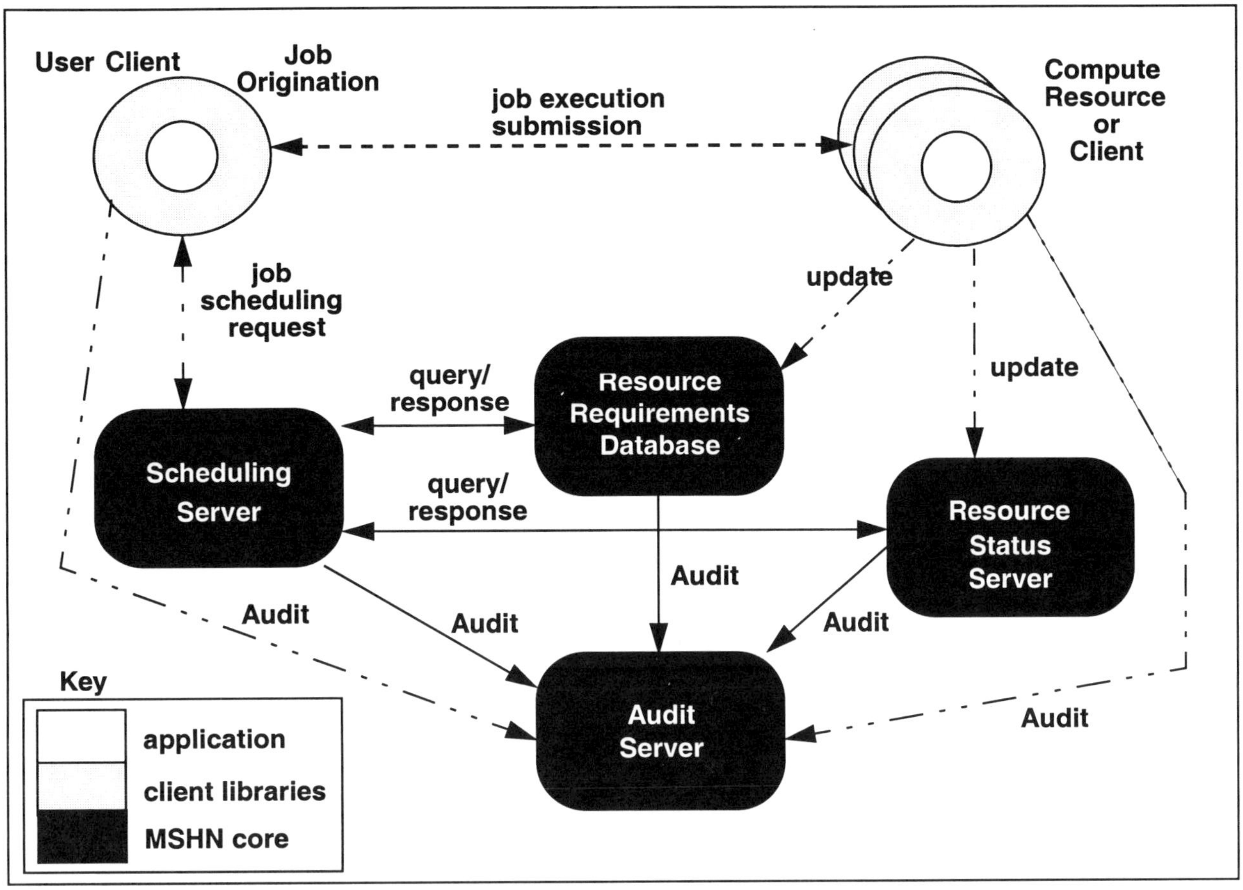

Figure 1. MSHN Architecture

an adaptive application, the application can adapt to the changed environment, thus satisfying modified, and realistically achievable QoS objectives. Special client libraries could provide adaptivity services to legacy applications. Upon completion of the task, results are returned to the user, while a summary of resource usage by the job is recorded in the Resource Requirements Database.

MSHN jobs consist of both code and the data set to be processed by that code. The need to define the job both in terms of its code and data set, or at least a characterization of the data set, arises from quality of service objectives for each job. Consider for example, code that will compute Fast Fourier Transforms (FFTs) on seismic data. Clearly the granularity and duration of the data will affect the amount of processing required. Hence, despite the fact that the code applied to both a short event and a long one is the same, the jobs differ in terms of the computational resources they will consume. As noted above, a variety of QoS requirements may also be associated with a job. Of course, a group of security requirements may also be bound to an instance of a job as a result of the particular code or data involved. A detailed discussion of application security requirements will be given in the next section.

3. Security Requirements

The MSHN security mechanisms are intended for an environment in which users elect to use MSHN services to enhance the quality of service they receive on their jobs. Users request advisory schedules from MSHN core services. When the schedule is returned, jobs are submitted to compute resources under user control and executed in the context of user accounts. Dynamic and summary job status information is reported to MSHN core services via client libraries which "wrap" the user's unaltered job. During job execution, the MSHN scheduler may send revised scheduling information to the client libraries. Under certain conditions, a job may be moved to a different compute resource. If the job is adaptive, information relayed by the MSHN scheduler permits the job to modify its runtime characteristics in order to achieve desired quality of service goals.

This sketch of MSHN activity shows that the VHM depends upon communication between distributed hosts: those providing MSHN core services and those executing client libraries on behalf of users. In the remainder of this section we will present our approach to providing for the integrity of MSHN core components and client services within the networked environment. In addition, we will describe how the MSHN core supports security requirements such as integrity and confidentiality for the jobs it manages.

3.1 General Constraints and Assumptions

Certain MSHN design goals affect several choices regarding the security architecture. These are:

- Use of MSHN is optional. An advisory schedule obtained from the MSHN Scheduler is optional. A user may still choose to execute a job using MSHN clients at compute resources, but the compute resources selected by the user may not correspond to those suggested by the MSHN Scheduler.
- MSHN will not require modification of existing applications.
- MSHN will not require modification to the underlying operating system of any system it uses. This includes MSHN user clients, servers hosting MSHN core components, and MSHN services on compute resources.
- No MSHN component will have arbitrary control over any host. By this we mean that execution of MSHN will not require supervisory or, in Unix terminology, "root" privilege.
- It is assumed that users do not wish to subvert their own jobs with bogus run-time parameters, which would also result in corruption of the Resource Requirements Database. (Users can, of course, always elect to execute their jobs without the benefit of MSHN services.)
- User jobs are not required to reside permanently at compute resources. Code and data can either be bundled and sent to compute resources with the request for execution. Eventually, the MSHN client libraries are envisioned to be capabile of fetching code and data for a job from appropriate repositories.

Assumptions applicable to the security architecture are:

- A user will not attempt to corrupt his own jobs. If a user is concerned that his jobs will be corrupted by other jobs he may be executing on a compute resource, then the best remedy is to establish a separate principle for the execution of jobs managed by MSHN. The underlying operating system, through its mechanisms for the separation of user processes is expected to support this objective.
- Users will be required to log in when accessing compute resources, thus execution on resources will be by a principle representing the user rather than the MSHN core.
- For each user, MSHN will maintain a list of compute resources for which the user is authorized.
- MSHN will rely upon the existence of a public key infrastructure (PKI). The security architecture depends upon the existence and integrity of standard directory services such as X.500 or LDAP and the provision of standardized certificates such as those defined by X.509 v3. All elements of the MSHN architecture must have facilities to support certificate-based public key technology. Support for symmetric key cryptography is also required in most applications of public key cryptography.
- It is assumed that the MSHN client libraries do not contain malicious code.
- Compute resources will be known to the MSHN core. The list of resources will be administratively updated.

3.2 Policy

The security policy we wish to enforce for the MSHN components is as follows.

- Only authorized elements of the MSHN core services, such as the MSHN Scheduler, can query the Resource Status Server and the Resource Requirements Database for job status information. (Authentication and Access Control)
- Communications between the elements of the MSHN core services should be protected from unauthorized modification and disclosure. (Communications Integrity and Confidentiality)
- Status and summary information provided by client libraries to the Resource Status Server and Resource Requirements Database should be identifiable to the granularity of a particular run of a user job. This will prevent bogus updates to MSHN databases by malicious jobs outside of MSHN's purview. It will also permit the identification of rogue jobs which may have been corrupted and are misbehaving. (Authentication, Access Control and Denial of Service)
- Status and summary information provided by client libraries to the MSHN core databases should be protected from unauthorized modification and disclosure while in transit. (Communications Integrity and Confidentiality)
- Dynamic scheduling advice provided by the MSHN

Scheduler to client libraries supporting jobs at compute resources should be identifiable on a per job basis. It is not sufficient for the client library to know that scheduling information has, in fact, come from the MSHN Scheduler. In addition, the client library must be able to ascertain that the scheduling information is intended for the particular job being supported by the client library. (Authentication)

- Dynamic scheduling advice provided by the MSHN Scheduler to client libraries supporting jobs at compute resources should be protected from unauthorized modification and disclosure while in transit. (Communications Integrity and Confidentiality)
- Information maintained in MSHN core databases should be available only to authorized users. Some earlier resource management systems [14] had no notion of access control. The emphasis in these efforts was on scheduling and performance, not security, so everyone was privileged and had access to all job status information.

  A mechanism must be implemented to limit access to job status information. It is expected that there may be tension between limiting access to this information and providing statistically significant accumulations of runs to improve scheduling decisions.
- For each job, historical data on that job can be restricted to a set of authorized users. At first glance, this does not appear to be very hospitable. Why should historical information be restricted when it will help everyone run the job better? Suppose there is a job used for battle planning and that its execution statistics are stored in the Resource Requirements Database. Also suppose that an enemy wants to find out about this job. He could pretend to be submitting a request to run the battle planning job and would obtain from the scheduler advice on where to position his run. Even though he might not have a copy of the code and data, the historical data could yield information regarding the best systems to use for executing the job, duration of the run, and other exploitable information.

  Thus, in the interest of encouraging use of MSHN, a user can always request that MSHN provide a schedule for his instance of the job. Whether that schedule reflects historical information would depend upon the user's access to the historical data associated with other users' runs.

3.3 Accountability

Individual accountability is essential in any system intended to securely process information on behalf of users. Accountability permits liability to be established in the case of violations of policy. If the objective is to establish liability such that the perpetrator of an illicit act can be punished, then accountability must be sufficient to provide proof that the accused perpetrator is at fault.

Since MSHN is running as an application on operating systems that may or may not provide an adequate foundation for our security objectives, we must temper our accountability requirements. Corruption of an underlying operating system lacking penetration resistance could result in corruption of MSHN accountability mechanisms. It would be difficult to send someone to prison for violating MSHN security policy and it would be difficult to successfully litigate contractual agreements based upon the chain of assurance and accountability evidence provided by a VHM dependent on intrinsically weak platforms. So accountability in MSHN can act as a deterrent to abuse by relatively law abiding users, but it will not stop the determined opponent.

Accountability in MSHN will depend upon the identification and authentication of users, first at their local clients and subsequently to the MSHN core service and compute servers. Authentication and audit will provide the mechanisms to tie the user's identification to the system activities he has invoked and create a record of those activities considered security relevant.

Non-repudiation is described as a mechanism such that the sender of a communication is unable to deny that the message was sent and the receiver is unable to deny its receipt. The audit mechanism can serve as a trusted third party providing non-repudiation services for MSHN users. Clearly, a third party beyond MSHN is needed if non-repudiation services are required for transactions between MSHN and its users.

3.4 Assurance

Security enforced for MSHN components does not depend upon enforcement mechanisms built into MSHN itself, but instead upon underlying policy enforcement mechanisms that may be provided by operating systems and perhaps high assurance platforms. This is in concert with the philosophy [12] that more privileged mechanisms are

- more likely to embody the fundamental notions of the reference monitor concept [4] and
- more likely to have undergone scrutiny by qualified and unbiased personnel able to assess the assurance claims made about the mechanism.

The security architecture for the VHM will be

designed to take advantage of mechanisms provided by more privileged underlying components. Our objective is to provide the intermediate interfaces necessary so that underlying medium to high assurance mechanisms can be used to protect communications associated with the VHM and user jobs as information is moved across unprotected networks.

We wish to prevent unauthorized updates to critical MSHN databases. Suppose that MSHN core components execute on dedicated servers. Then the likelihood of corruption of MSHN core databases by malicious applications is substantially reduced as is the possibility of exfiltraton of information by malicious software. In such an environment, the use of session keys provides a reliable mechanism to bind the components into a virtual domain.

How does the notion of privilege work in MSHN? Ideally, we would like to have each platform in the VHM provide a minimum of four protection domains: one for the user's application, one for MSHN client resource libraries and services, and one for MSHN protection services. Layered beneath these three domains would be more privileged domains associated with the underlying OS and its libraries. We envision certain essential public key technologies located in highly privileged domains. These include the key distribution centers and the certificate authorities.

4. MSHN Security Architecture

MSHN security is based upon the establishment of the following domains:

1. MSHN Core Domain
2. Client Library Domain
3. Application Domain

Each domain will authenticate itself to other domains using certificate-based technology. The basis for believing the certificates is the integrity provided at the certificate authorities, hence the certificate authorities are the most trusted components of our VHM security architecture. User tasks will be separated on a per-task basis using appropriate keys

Keys	Description	Key Type	Creator	User	Key Life	Purpose
K_m	MSHN Core Session Key	S	MSHN Core Master	MSHN Core Servers	per core instance	• high speed transmission of message traffic between core components
K_j	Job Session Key	S	MSHN Core	Client Library of job	per task	• identifies MSHN-relevant communications to MSHN Core • transmit audit records • authentication of per-job status information to MSHN Core
K_c	Client Library Session Key	S	MSHN Core	Client Library of Job	per task	• per-task intra-client domain management functions
K_a	Application Session Key	S	MSHN Core	Task Clients on behalf of application	per task	• application-level task communications • receive job execution results
$C_{pub/pri}$	MSHN Core Server Key	P	KDC or user	MSHN servers; one per server	KDC defined	• permits clients to authenticate communications to MSHN servers • core session key distribution • digital signatures
$R_{pub/pri}$	Computer Resource Client	P	KDC or server administrator	used by all MSHN compute resources	KDC defined	• receive job session key
$U_{pub/pri}$	User client key	P	KDC or user	Client Library	KDC defined	• receive job session key • user authentication

Table 1: Key Usage in the MSHN Security Architecture

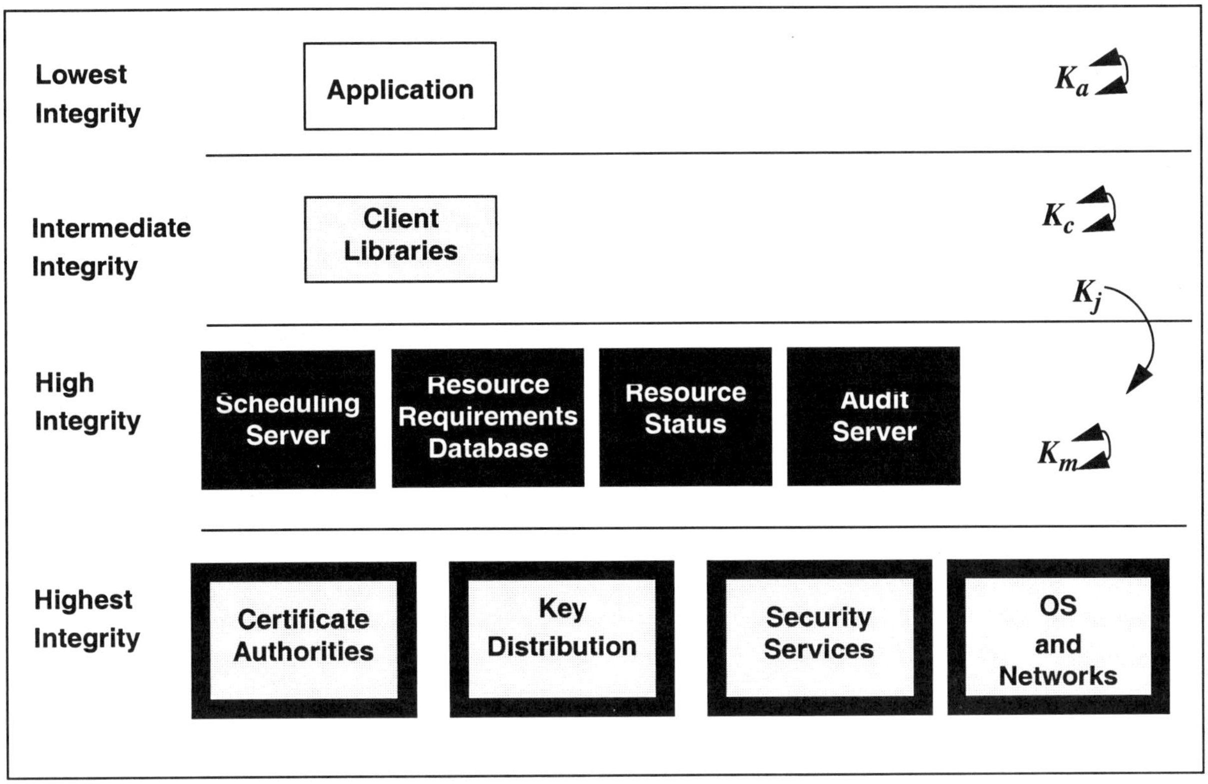

Figure 2. MSHN Security Domain Architecture

supplied to each domain. Within MSHN, the highest integrity domain, viz. the MSHN Core, will manage the creation and allocation of session keys used by lower integrity domains. Thus the client domains are issued per-task keys when a job is scheduled and these keys are used for dynamic task management and Core database updates. In addition to being isolated on a per-task basis, each domain is able to distinguish communications from members at its integrity from those of entities of greater or lesser integrity. The MSHN domains are illustrated in Figure 2. Policy is allocated to each of these domains and they are organized hierarchically. This is in keeping with notions of *balanced assurance* for distributed systems [13].

4.1 MSHN Core Domain

The MSHN core domain contains the basic MSHN core services: the Scheduling Server, the Resource Status Server, and the Resource Requirements Database. For the security architecture, we have added an Audit Server. The correct function of these servers is essential to insuring that jobs receive useful scheduling advice; the corruption of either their data or algorithms would render MSHN potentially useless or even detrimental to job performance and quality of service. Thus we assign to these system elements a high integrity level.

The MSHN Scheduling Server will make scheduling decisions based upon the conjunction of authorization information and other scheduling information. When a scheduling request is issued to MSHN, the Scheduling server will first determine the systems accessible by the user. This list of systems will be input to the scheduling algorithms and an advisory schedule will result. Thus for the same job and all other factors being equal, two users could have different schedules depending upon their access to compute resources.

4.2 Client Library Domain

The client libraries will occupy a domain of intermediate integrity. A copy of the client libraries will be available to each user's job. Although users might share the text of client libraries, viz, the client library code, when executing on the same machine, each instance will have separate data. Client libraries will also be able to securely communicate with client libraries on other compute servers. This will permit coordination of parallel processing or checkpointing and movement of an application to a different compute server.

4.3 Application Domain

This domain is intended for user jobs. Each application will be distinct. Distributed, security-aware applications may contain their own end-to-end mechanisms or may use underlying security services.

A legacy application need not become "security aware" in order to be protected. When users request scheduling and process management services of MSHN, they may include protection services as part of the QoS specification for their jobs. The scheduling advisor will determine the best way to meet those protection needs within the VHM accessible by the user. Along with the scheduling recommendations returned to the user, algorithms and keys held by the underlying layers will be available to protect communications for distributed applications. We note that exposure of keys to applications is not intended: either keys are cryptographically protected or completely hidden by the underlying mechanism.

4.4 Mechanisms

Cryptographic mechanisms will be used to isolate and protect the elements of the MSHN architecture in "lightweight" domains. Table 1 describes the major keys used in our design. Key types are for symmetric, S, and public/private, P, cryptography. We intend to support updates of session keys during job runs. The frequency of these updates will be defined as part of the quality of service for security. It is expected that, as the public key infrastructure matures, key distribution centers (KDCs) will issue public/private key pairs. In the interim, individual systems may be required to act as their own KDCs.

4.4.1 Core Keys. The MSHN core will be assigned its own set of keys. Each MSHN core server will have a public/private key pair, $C_{pub/pri}$. These key pairs will be issued by a key distribution center (KDC) and can be verified by a certificate authority (CA) for inter-component authentication.

We believe that symmetric key cryptography provides the most efficient technique for the frequent communications that will be required between MSHN core components. Core components associated with a particular instance of MSHN share a MSHN-wide session key, K_m. This key permits the use of fast symmetric algorithms for the efficient transmission of core-relevant data.

A question that arose in our analysis was how to handle replicas of MSHN core services. This might occur in situations where the system is highly distributed and replicas of one or more MSHN core services are placed at strategic points in the network. Since it is desirable that a client be able to send updates to any one of the replicated servers of a particular type, e.g., Resource Status Server, with a consistent result across the entire system, the session keys of clients could be available to all status servers. Alternatively, dynamic key exchange algorithms could provide protected communications between core components.

4.4.2 Client and Application Keys. The MSHN Core will be responsible for issuing session keys for each job. These keys will be protected enroute to the compute resource using public key algorithms with $R_{pub/pri}$. There will be three session keys associated with each job: a Job Session Key, K_j, a Client Library Session Key, K_c, and an Application Session Key, K_a.

The Job Session Key will be used by the compute client to transmit status information back to the MSHN Resource Status Server and to the Audit Server. It will be used by the MSHN Scheduler to transmit advisory information dynamically to the user client and the compute client. For example, information regarding dynamic job adaptation can be transmitted to the compute client. A database tying user IDs to job IDs and session keys will be distributed across relevant MSHN core servers such as the Scheduling Server and the Audit Server.

The Client Library Session Key will be used for intra-domain management of clients associated with a particular job both at the user's platform and at the compute resources.

The Application Session Key is provided for the benefit of the application. It represents the keys and algorithms proposed by the MSHN core to meet the protection requirements specified by the user for the particular instance of the job run.

4.4.3 User Authentication. Individual users will have public/private keys, $U_{pub/pri}$. User's public keys will be stored in certificates which are available to all elements of the system through a directory service. The MSHN Scheduler will be able to authenticate the user using public key technology. The user will digitally sign messages using his private key and the scheduler will validate the source of the signed message with the user's certified public key.

5. Prototype Demonstration

A prototype demonstration of the MSHN security

architecture has been implemented [20]. In keeping with the emphasis on commercial-off-the-shelf PCs embraced by the Navy's IT-21 initiative [7], our demonstration is implemented on three Windows NT Platforms. One platform served as the user interface from which jobs were submitted. A second platform hosted the MSHN Core database and scheduling services, each executing as a separate process. The last platform played the role of a compute resource. (Clearly, in a complete implementation compute resources might be high performance processors.)

For this demonstration we chose all certificates to be homogeneous and selected X.509 v3 certificates [6] for use throughout the VHM for authentication mechanisms.

5.1 Security Layer

One of our principle concerns has been the provision of security services within the context of a well engineered, modular architecture. Toward this end, we have defined a set of security services to be provided to MSHN core components and clients. This thin service layer allows us to achieve the support for heterogeneous platforms sought by the project. Also, it permits us to postpone API choices so that services presented by several APIs can be used, such as CDSA [3] and GSS-API [1]. Thus, a variety of security implementations can be used and these will be transparent to the VHM core, clients, and applications.

The security services layer consists of the following interfaces exported to MSHN core services and client libraries:

mshn_sl_init Initialize databases for MSHN security layer and create any necessary security contexts.

mshn_sl_create_cert Create a certificate with the specified parameters

mshn_sl_get_cert Obtain a certificate for the specified principle

mshn_sl_cert_verify Check that the specified certificate is valid

mshn_sl_cert_revoked Determine if the specified certificate has been revoked

mshn_sl_get_public_key Return the public key for the principle associated with the specified certificate

mshn_sl_get_private_key Return the private key for the specified subject. Note that, in the implementation, the private key is not actually returned, but a handle to the key is provided and this handle is used as a parameter to encryption or decryption functions. Thus the private key is never exposed.

mshn_sl_put_audit Write a record to the audit file or server

mshn_sl_encrypt Encrypt the specified data using the specified key and algorithm

mshn_sl_decrypt Decrypt the specified data using the specified key and algorithm

mshn_sl_sym_key_gen Create a key to be used with symmetric encryption and decryption.

mshn_sl_asym_key_gen Create a public/private key pair to be used with asymmetric encryption and decryption. Only information about the private key is exported, the key itself is not exposed.

mshn_sl_msg_digest Hash the specified buffers and generate a message digest.

mshn_sl_sign Produce a signature for the specified data in two steps: create a message digest and then encrypt the message digest.

mshn_sl_sig_verify Verify a digital signature for a specified data-signature pair.

5.2 Common Data Security Architecture

The Intel Common Data Security Architecture (CDSA) has been used as the basis for a proof of concept demonstration of the MSHN core services.

CDSA is intended to provide a basic security infrastructure for use with personal computers. It is a layered architecture and is intended to be modular, portable and adaptable. It has currently been implemented on Windows NT, a system of particular interest to the U.S. Navy as a result of its IT-21 initiative. An implementation of CDSA by RSA Security is underway and will provide the components on Unix platforms. In the interim, we have implemented a subset of the MSHN Security functions on a Unix platform using SSLeay encryption software[22] (a public implementation of SSL [9]).

CDSA consists of three primary layers:

- a set of system security services
- the Common Security Services Manager (CSSM)
- add-in security modules.

The add-in security modules are organized by the CSSM so that service provider interfaces (SPIs) can be defined for each module job manager.

Services are separated into four categories:

cryptographic services: An add-in cryptographic service module can provide the following functions

- bulk encryption and decryption
- creation and verification of digital signatures
- cryptographic hash creation
- key generation
- random number generation
- encrypted storage of private keys. We note here that ultimately the protection of keys, must depend upon a system-based protection mechanism.

trust policy services: The intent of the trust policy services is to provide access control over various system activities. Certificates are presented to the trust policy manager and access decisions are made according to information contained in the certificate.

certificate services: For a PC, the certificate services provide a self-contained certificate management mechanism. This module provides support to create new certificates, create certificate revocation lists (CRLs), sign and/or verify certificates and CRLs, import and export certificates created using other formats, extract information such as public keys from certificates, reinstate revoked certificates and search CRLs. The flexibility of these services with respect to certificate format makes them particularly attractive during the current period of evolving standards. For our current work, we have chosen the X.509 v3 format.

data store services: These modules are intended to provide secure and persistent storage for non-volatile information such as certificates and CRLs. Clearly in a system where assurance is of significant importance, data store services would be relegated to an underlying high assurance TCB and the access control mechanisms of the TCB would be used to ensure that only authorized users (or processes acting on behalf of those users) had modify access to security-critical databases.

6. Other Work and Future Plans

The Sigma project is addressing heterogeneity on the enclave level with its exploration of Internet Interoperability Protocol gateways to support Common Object Request Broker Architecture (CORBA) [2] interoperability [17]. This work is not directly integrated into a VHM management system and provides only a highly coarse level of access control and enclave protection. However, this effort could be viewed as complementary to ours as the MSHN security mechanisms could be used in an environment supporting Sigma controls.

Globus [8] is using a proxy-based system to permit computation on behalf of users on remote resources. The mechanism bears a remarkable similarity to Kerberos [18] and currently suffers from several scalability and trust domain drawbacks. Our approach provides a more straight forward path toward accountability.

Legion [21] claims to permit users to define policies at the granularity of objects. It is *ad hoc* with respect to privilege in that privilege is minimized everywhere -- no element of the system is responsible for any element other than itself. In addition, Legion does not provide for certificate authorities or key distribution centers. Instead, Legion-specific unique object identifiers are required globally to support key management. It appears that instead of supporting interoperability with respect to key management, Legion is dictating a homogeneous approach.

6.1 Future Work

Quality of service and security can sometimes be regarded as conflicting rather than complementary goals [10]. During crises, it is likely that demands upon a system may be significantly higher than during normal operations. This may mean that tasks may be required to adapt in order to provide a minimal level of service. We plan to explore the possibility of providing information to users and administrators regarding the performance costs incurred by using security measures commensurate with the sensitivity and reliability associated with the task. Hence the security requirements of different tasks can be met with measures of differing "strengths." At this juncture, we are not suggesting that security measures can be relaxed for a job with an assigned sensitivity and reliability.

Another area of future activity will be in the development of an audit mechanism for the VHM. As noted earlier, we plan to use a combination of audit and digital signatures as the cornerstone of non-repudiation services in our VHM.

Lacking a Unix implementation of CDSA, a Unix version of our prototype was created using SSLeay. In a fully layered architecture, SSL might depend upon CDSA for security support.

7. Summary

This paper has described a security architecture intended to support a virtual heterogeneous machine. A consistent set of choices must be made to construct data structures and mechanisms to use the underlying environment effectively. We build assurance into the system by relying on underlying mechanisms rather than constructing our own.

Our architecture for the MSHN VHM consists of four domains: the underlying operating sytsem, MSHN Core Services, Client Services, and Application. Domains start with their own identification and authentication evidence provided by key distribution centers and certificate authorities. When the VHM is started, the Core Services establish their own cryptologically defined domain. Client Services submit job requests to the Core and are provided with session keys which establish per-session domains that permit communication between Clients and Core Services.

Using underlying services, Clients create domains on behalf of Applications, to which they provide handles to keys for application-level communications security.

Future work will integrate quality of service mechanisms into this architecture and explore the creation of high assurance audit mechanisms.

Acknowledgements

We wish like to thank Timothy Levin for his critical reading of the manuscript and helpful comments.

References

[1] Global Security Services Application Programming Interface, RFC 2078.

[2] The Common Object Request Broker: Architecture Specification, December 1993.

[3] Common Data Security Architecture Specification, Intel Corporation, Santa Clara, CA release 1.2 edition February 1998. http://developer.intel.com/ial/security/.

[4] Anderson, J.P., Computer Security Technology Planning Study. Technical Report ESD-TR-73-51, Airforce Electronic Systems Division, Hanscom AFB, Bedford, MA, 1972. (Also available as Vol. I, DITCAD-758206, Vol. II DITCAD-772806).

[5] Bricker, A., Litzkow, M.,l and Livny, M., Condor Technical Summary, Technical Report CS-TR-92-1069, Computer Science Department, University of Wisconsin, Madison, WI, January 1992.

[6] CCITT. Recommendation X.509: The Directory - Authentication Framework, 1989. also ISO/IEC 9594-8.

[7] Clemmins, A., IT-21: The path to Information Superiority, CHIPS, July 1997.

[8] Foster, I., Karonis, N., Kellelman, C., Koenig, G., and Tuecke, S., A Secure Communications Infrastructure for High-Performance Distributed Computing, In *Proceedings 6th IEEE Symposium on Distributed Computing*, pages 125-136. IEEE Computer Society Press, 1997.

[9] Freier, A., Karlton, P., and Kocher, P., *The SSL Protocol, Version 3.0*, Netscape Communications, March 1996. URL: http://home.netscape.com/eng/ssl3/index.html6.

[10]Greenberg, I., Lunt, T., Clark, R., and Wells D., Secure Alpha: Security Policy and Policy Interpretation for a Class B3 Multilevel Secure Real-Time Distributed Operating System, Technical Report ELIN A003, SRI International, Menlo Park, CA, April 1993.

[11]Hensgen, D., and Kidd, T., MSHN design documents. note, February 1998.

[12]Irvine, C. E., Acheson, T.B., Thompson, M. F., Building Trust into a Multilevel File System, In *Proceedings 13th Nation Computer Security Conference*, pages 450-459, Washington, DC, October 1990.

[13]Irvine, C.E., Schell, R. R., and Thompson, M.F., Using TNI Concepts for the Near Term Use of High Assurance Database Management Systems. In *Proceedings Fourth RADC Database Security Workshop*, Little Compton, RI, April 1991.

[14]Kidd, T., Hensgen, D., Freund, R., Moore, L., SmartNet: A Scheduling Framework for Heterogeneous Computing, In *International Symposium On Parallel Architectures, Algorithms, and Networks*, Beijing, China, June 1996.

[15]Kresho, J.P., Quality Network Load Information Improves Performance of Adaptive Applications, M.S. thesis, Naval Postgraduate School, Monterey, CA September 1997.

[16]Litzkow, M., Tannenbaum, T., Basney, J. and Livny, M., Checkpoint and Migration of UNIX Processes in the Condor Distributed Processing System, Technical Report CS-TR-97-1346, Computer Science Department, University of Wisconsin, Madison, WI, April 1997.

[17]Sebes, J. and Benzel, T. C. V, SIGMA: Security for Distributed Object Interoperability Between Trusted and Untrusted Systems, Technical draft paper, Trusted Information Systems, Mountain View, CA 1996.

[18]Steiner, J., Neumann, B. and Schiller, J., Kerberos: An authentication System for Open Network Systems, Usenix Conference Proceedings, pages 191-202, 1998.

[19]Stevens, R., Woodward, P., DeFanti, T., and Catlett, C., From the I-Way to the National Technology Grid, Comm. A.C.M., 40(11):51-60, 1997.

[20]Wright, R., Integrity Architecture and Security Services Demonstration for Management System for Heterogeneous Networks, M.S. Thesis, Naval Postgraduate School., Monterey, CA, June 1998.

[21]Wulf, W., Wang, C., and Kienzle, D., A New Model of Security for Distributed Systems, UVa CS Technical Report CS-95-34, University of Virginia, Richmond, VA, August 1995.

[22]Young, E. A., SSLeay, June 1997. ftp://ftp.psy.uq.oz.au/pub/Crypto/SSL.

Authorization in Enterprise-wide Distributed System
A Practical Design and Application

Vijay Varadharajan
Univ. of W.Sydney, Australia

Chris Crall and Joe Pato
Hewlett-Packard, USA

Abstract

As companies migrate from a centralized to a distributed computing environment, the administration and management of security policies, in particular authorization policies, is becoming an increasingly difficult task. This paper considers the design of an authorization system that is suitable for distributed applications. It discusses the architectural design principles, describes the constructs of the authorization policy language and outlines the authorization service and components involved. The paper gives some examples policy specifications and illustrates how privileges are specified and evaluated as well as how privilege resolutions are achieved.

1. Introduction

In a distributed system, when a request for a certain service is received by one principal (agent) from another, the receiving principal essentially needs to address two questions. Firstly, is the requesting principal the one it claims to be? Secondly, does the requesting principal have appropriate privileges for the requested service? These two questions relate to the issues of authentication and authorization. There are also other security concerns such as auditing, secure communication, availability and accountability. There have been several efforts in recent years which have addressed distributed authentication. However distributed authorization has not been considered to the same extent, even though there have been a large body of work in access control for stand alone systems and relational databases. There has been some work on providing a general framework for expressing authorizations using default logic by Woo and Lam [1]. Recently there has been some further work on the use of logic for expressing authorizations by Jajodia, Samarati and Subrahmanian [2] and a logic based approach for modeling and reasoning about transformations in authorization policies by Bai and Varadharajan [3]. However several open problems remain in the design and the implementation of secure authorization service for distributed applications, especially in large scale commercial systems. This is the focus of this paper. Currently most applications make authorization decisions using application specific access control functions in conjunction with local files which are often inflexible and inadequate. In this paper, we consider the architecture, design and implementation of an authorization service that is suitable for distributed applications. We describe an Authorization Server which is a rule based authorization facility for applications. It provides application developers with facilities to perform simple access control checks to complex business logic authorization. Administration is provided with an easy to use graphical user interface or batch interface that enables administrators to manage relatively large numbers of users with consistent policies across applications. The work described in this paper has been designed and developed into a practical system [4]. A number of people have been involved in the design, development and implementation of this Authorization Server [5]. Throughout this paper, when "we" is used it refers to this team of people. The work on this project began in 1993 and the first version of the system was completed in 1995 which was subsequently released as a commercial product in 1996. The only other system that the authors are aware of is the Adage System proposed in 1996 by the Open Group[12], which is currently under development. We are in the process of preparing a separate technical report comparing the features of Adage with our system.

The paper is organized as follows. Section 2 presents an overview of the authorization framework for distributed systems. It discusses the different perspectives of the developers, administrators, end users and policy setters. Then it describes some of the key architectural design principles involved in the development of a distributed authorization service and outlines the authorization architecture and its components. Section 3 describes the language constructs used to specify the authorization policies. It then gives some examples of policy

0-8186-8789-4/98 $10.00 © 1998 IEEE

specifications using the language. Finally section 4 concludes the paper.

2. Authorization System

2.1 Authorization Perspectives and Needs

The authorization framework that we have developed is aimed at addressing the needs of several classes of users. The users within an enterprise who have to deal with security include the developer, the security administrator, the policy setter and the end user.

The Developer's View

Application security today is implemented as part of the programming effort. The security logic is written for each application. There are unique policies set per application based on developers knowledge and skill level. Our authorization framework removes security processing from the application logic. This is accomplished by defining appropriate authorization attributes (such as transaction attributes and privilege attributes) and by formulating rules that specify how the authorization decision is computed and processed during the evaluation outside of the application logic. There are several benefits that arise from this strict separation. An important practical consequence is that it results in a consistent application programming interface across all applications and platforms thereby allowing common policies across them. Furthermore, checking of access rights is abstracted away from a particular application. This enables the developers to concentrate on the business logic instead of reinventing the security portion of the application.

The Administrators View

Today, each application is often administered uniquely. A custom security process for administering the required security information, such as user names, passwords and privilege capabilities, is required. Enterprise wide security policies are difficult to implement consistently across all applications and these policies are even more difficult to verify. Certain security tasks require more than one administrator to check the correctness of the task. The aim of our authorization system is to help consolidate security administration. Rather than dealing with each application subsystem and its security component separately through a different tool, the authorization server offers a consistent view of principals, profiles and their privileges for a given application

The End User View

End users today suffer most from the fact that each system and each application implements its own security mechanisms. Authentication mechanisms are not consistent, which causes the user to obtain and remember many different user names and passwords. When each application provides its own authorization facilities, the user can be confused by the different policies in the application. For example, why is a bank manager's limit in one banking application is $1500 and in a related application it is $2000? Within this authorization system, security related attributes of a user are consistent throughout the range of similar applications.

The Policy Setter View

Policy setters require management tools to ensure that the policies are correctly implemented. The authorization system proposes the notion of a profile that provides a way of grouping privileges to establish common access rights for sets of users. The policy setters are therefore able to set and test authorization policies.

2.2 Authorization Architectural Design Principles

The design of any security service involves at least the following aspects: security information used in the provision of the security service, the security mechanisms that are required to support the service and the authorities involved in the management of the service. In the case of authorization service, the security information used ranges from user identities to group identities to role information to location information to actions and parameters associated with the actions. In fact, from an architecture point of view, it is important to understand the characteristics of the different types of the authorization security information [13]. Some security information is what we refer to as being generic and static in nature. For instance, typically we put identity based information into this category. Then there is security information that is specific but still somewhat static in nature. For instance, role based access information falls into this category. Roles are specific to organizations and they are reasonably static in the sense that they are unlikely to change on a day to day or even on a monthly (or even yearly) basis. In fact, one of the main benefits of an access control system based on role based information is to simplify the management of access privileges. Then we have security information that is specific and dynamic in nature. Specific in the sense that the information may relate to specific applications or parts of applications or files. Dynamic in the sense that the information is prone to state changes.

Such a classification of different types of authorization information in turn helps to understand better the requirements on their management. First, the authorities involved in the management of these different types of authorization information are likely to be different. Not only the strategies with respect to when the changes and updates to these information take place are likely to be different but also who are allowed to make these changes are likely to vary. For instance, the specification and changes to the role information in an organization will be the responsibility of a certain group of people who can be different to those responsible for setting the privileges for a specific file or application in a server.

From an architectural point of view, such a characterization also leads to some basic design principles. First, it is appropriate to store the static and generic authorization information in some form of a central server within a domain, which is responsible for a collection of clients and server principals. Second, the dynamic and specific authorization information can be stored near or in the target, enabling the target system authorities to be involved in their management. From a distribution point of view, static and generic authorization information (stored in a central server within a domain) can be "pushed" by the client principal to the target principal. In fact, static and specific information can also be pushed in a similar fashion. Finally, specific and dynamic authorization information needs to be "pulled" at the time of the decision process.

Based on these principles, conceptually one can have the following trusted components: a trusted authority dealing with generic and static security information, a trusted authority dealing with specific and static information and a trusted component dealing with specific and dynamic information. The first two authorities can be architected as centralized servers (one per domain) servicing a number of clients and targets within the domain. The third component resides at the target (or some entity attached to or close to the target) as it is often dependent on the state of the application or resource under consideration. These architectural design principles have been used in the design and implementation of a distributed authorization service considered in this paper.

2.3. Authorization Mechanisms

Access Control Lists (ACLs) have been one of the traditional mechanisms that have and are being used in many existing systems and applications. They associate lists of users to every type of access for a resource. The access types are typically actions such as read, write, execute, create, append, modify and delete. Any user on the list for a particular action is allowed to perform that action. The benefits and problems of ACLs are very well known. We will just illustrate one or two issues that are relevant for this paper. For instance, ACLs have limitations in expressing the types of controls necessary in many applications. For example, it is difficult to create numerical limits for transactions with ACLs. Moreover, ACLs are inherently resource based. Most ACL systems today store the lists at the resource (within the application). A common nightmare with ACL based systems is the difficulty of their maintenance especially if the administrative tools are not common across the ACLs in all applications. If the authorization information is distributed which is the case in distributed applications, it makes answering questions about a user's access rights very difficult. For example, to remove an employee who has left the company from all ACLs usually requires the administrator to edit the ACLs in each application to determine if the user has access rights, and if so, remove those rights. This can be a very time consuming process. Our authorization system focuses on the users and groups of users making it a more natural and intuitive approach for many business requirements.

The other well known mechanism that has been used in the provision of the authorization service is the capabilities. A capability is essentially a ticket that provides the holder with some type of access right. A capability system requires the user to acquire this ticket before performing the access; the ticket is presented at the time of access. If all the information necessary for computing the access rights is available outside the application, then a capability system can work well. However in applications where some of the information necessary to make the access determination is inside the application, the capability system does not have all the information it needs. For instance, in an Automated Teller Machine (ATM) system, a capability system might be able to determine that the ATM card looks valid, the check digit on the account is correct, the bank information looks valid and so on, but only the bank applications know if the request to withdraw money is valid since only the bank applications know whether the account has enough money in the account and if the user is over his/her daily withdrawal limit. The decision on whether or not to allow the request to take place must be made from within the application and is dependent on its state.

Based on the architectural design principles outlined earlier, let us now consider a variation on the access mechanism. This mechanism uses a separate object to define the access rights for a particular action. The access object, referred to as an entitlement, contains a rule that defines the access and operands (attributes) used in the rule evaluation. Once the entitlement has been defined, it can be assigned to individuals or groups of individuals. This assignment also includes providing values for some of the attributes in the rules. Separating the authorization control into a separate object provides flexibility in the way authorization is administered and the manner in which it is evaluated. The administration is controlled by the owner/administrator of the entitlement. Access to the application can be provided to any individual to whom the administrator assigns the entitlement. In addition, the evaluation can be outsourced to a separate module that is optimized to perform evaluations on entitlements. This frees the applications from performing the authorization evaluation and the developer from having to create this evaluation code. This access mechanism forms the basis of the authorization service proposed in this paper and the design of the Authorization Server.

2.4 Types of Authorization Checks

Another fundamental aspect that needs to be considered in the design of the distributed authorization service is the types of authorization checks and their location. In practice, there are different places at which authorization checks can be made. The closer the check is to the application, the more integrated the authorization system is into the business logic. In general, there are three basic approaches.

- Application check at start-up/connection time : In this approach, the check may be performed by the application or by some component that is a front end to the application. This check determines only whether or not a user has access rights to the applications. Once the application is started, this authorization system performs no further checks.

- Function Access : This check is made purely on the type of function/transaction being requested. This may or may not include parameters from the request in the authorization decision. As with "application check at start-up/connection time" above, this check can be embedded in the application or performed by some front-end component. However, in the case of a front-end component, more sophistication is required for the front-end to recognize one function/transaction request from another.

- Business Logic : This evaluation is performed not only on the function/transaction being requested, but it includes parameters sent by the user, information from the authorization database, and parameters from calculations from within the application program. This is the most complete check that can be performed and it must be embedded in the business logic of the application.

The Function Access checks provide the ability to verify that a principal is allowed to execute a specific function or transaction. The Business Logic checks can be as simple or as complex as needed for the specific application. All the information input by the user or available to the program in any way can be built into a rule and used to verify access. Both the Function Access and the Business Logic checks can be used to protect any code segment, transaction or action.

2.5 Authorization Service Stages

In the design of the distributed authorization service, we consider two stages namely the administration phase and the runtime or the evaluation phase. The administration phase involves facilities and services for the specification of authorization policies, updating and deleting of policies and their administration. The runtime phase is concerned with the use of the authorization policies in the evaluation of the access requests. The representation of the authorization policy information can be different in these phases. In fact, there are at least two arguments for maintaining distinct representations of authorization information in these two phases. First, there is the information captured by the language that can be compiled out before access decision time. For example, the meaning of inheritance and override depends only on the user and not on the server and transaction attributes. This enables the authorization system to make the access decision faster, by avoiding the search of the inheritance hierarchy. Secondly, it is possible to envisage different strategies for replication of the information needed for administration versus the information needed for access evaluation decisions at thc application servers. This in turn has implications in terms of interfaces and components required in the authorization service design. In terms of interfaces, there will be at least two interfaces namely the administration interface used by the administrators and the policy setters, and the runtime evaluation interface used by the clients and application servers during access decision time. There may also be another interface used for auditing purposes. For instance, the configuration and the management of the authorization server may require an independent auditor to monitor whether the access policy meets the required controls.

2.6 Authorization Service Components

In terms of components, the authorization service requires an administration component where the authorization policies are entered and stored in one representation, and an runtime evaluation component which stores the authorization rules at a different representation for runtime access (Figure 1). Additional subsystems in the overall security architecture include Authentication Server and their associated libraries. The Authorization Server depends on the authentication service for reliable identification of principals; currently authentication service provided by DCE [6] and Kerberos [8] are supported.

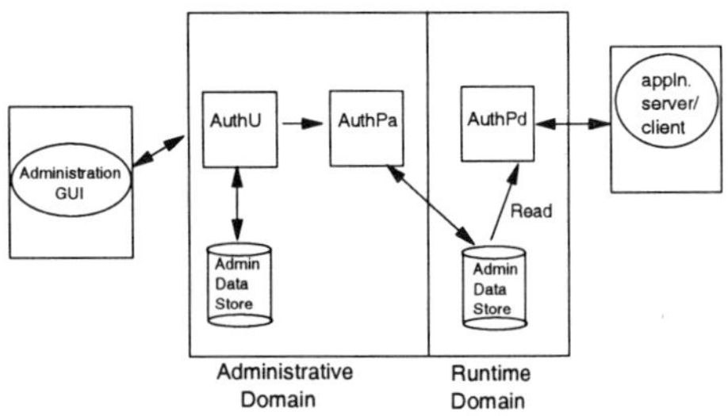

Figure 1: The Authorization Server

The authorization system supports three levels of checks. Level I and Level II authorization checks are concerned with the permission for a client to have interface and operation access to a server. Level I check is made at the client side. Level II check is made at the server side. Interface corresponds to an application server. For DCE [6] applications, this is equivalent to the name of the interface specified in the IDL file. For GSS-API [7] applications, this is application-defined, however typically it is the process name. Operation corresponds to an application subroutine or procedural call. For DCE applications, this is equivalent to the name of the procedure specified in the IDL file. For GSS-API applications, this is application-defined, however typically it corresponds to a single named client request. Level III checks are business authorization rule checks. Applications ask the Authorization Server for a Yes or No decision on a specific authorization rule. The application passes the parameters (transaction attributes and values) that are compared with the authorization information stored in the Authorization Server (privilege attributes and values) for a given authorization rule (entitlement).

The administrative domain is concerned with the setting up and management of privileges and profiles granted to principals. The AuthU server controls the administrative database which stores information describing principals, entitlements and profiles. The interface to this store is implemented by the administration store access library and is used by the administration client GUI or through a batch utility. AuthU information is the master set information and can be used to generate the runtime database. The runtime domain consists of an evaluation engine server called AuthPd and the runtime database. The runtime database is written to by AuthPa and read by AuthPd. When an entitlement is created, AuthU calls AuthPa to add an entry to the rule set and to create a table to contain the privileges for the new entitlement. When an entitlement is deleted, its entry in the rule set is removed and the table for the entitlement is deleted. Each time a change is made to the list of privileges, enable times or profiles of a principal or another profile, AuthU goes through a process of evaluating and resolving the privileges and profiles in order to keep the runtime database up to date. It is optimized for efficient processing of the authorization request. AuthPd uses the information stored in the runtime database to decide on authorization requests.

3. Authorization Policy Language

We believe that a language based approach to authorization is required not only for supporting a range of access control policies but also in separating out the policy representation from policy enforcement. The authorization policy language enables an administrator to specify authorization polices required in their system. The two fundamental characteristics of such a language are its expressive power and its analytical power. It should be simple thereby enabling the administrators and policy setters to use the language in specifying their polices while at the same time having sufficient expressive and analytical power to represent and evaluate a range of policies used in practical systems. This section describes the basic constructs of the language. We feel that our language is powerful enough to specify all the commonly used policies such as discretionary access control, role based access control, separation of duty, and delegation. In section 3.3, we consider some simple policy examples using the language. In terms of the ability to specify policies in practice, the authorization system has a graphical user interface allowing the security administrators and the policy setters to easily define their polices. We will not be describing this user interface in this paper. This can be found in [5].

3.1 Language Constructs

The basic constructs of the language include the following : Principal Records, Entitlements, Privileges, Attributes, Rules, Profiles, Time-related Parameters and Privilege Operators. Let us now briefly consider each of these elements in turn.

Principal Record

A principal in the system is any entity that can be authenticated and that wishes to access certain resources. It could be a user, a client or a server application. A principal record has several elements associated with it namely the principal name, the principal type, the principal identity value, profile membership list, privileges list, and enabled flag. The principal name identifies the name of the principal and the principal type is used to qualify both the name and the identity value. For instance, if the principal type is "DCE", then the identity value is the UUID value retrieved from the DCE Registry. The profile membership list contains a list of the names of the profiles of which this principal is a member. We give the definition of a profile below. A principal inherits all the privileges found in all the profiles in this list. The privileges list contains the privileges a principal has for entitlements. The enabled flag is a Boolean flag that indicates if the principal record is to be activated. The date and time specification information associated with this flag indicate the range of dates and times during which the principal is enabled. The earliest is called the enabled time and the latest is called the disable time.

Entitlements

An entitlement defines the authority granted to a principal to perform a certain task or to access some information. For example, in a financial application, an administrator can create an entitlement called Withdraw to allow authorized principals to withdraw cash from a system. A Withdraw entitlement could specify, for example, that a user Fred can withdraw $5000 between Monday to Friday from a Cash Management Account. Alternatively, a medical application might have entitlements such as Read-Patient-Record and Discharge-Patient. In general, an entitlement has the following components: entitlement name, transaction attributes, privilege attributes, the access rule, default privileges, enabled flag and information, and entitlement privileges. Let us look at each of these components in turn.

All entitlement names are unique across both the administrative and runtime components of the authorization system. We define two types of attributes : transaction attributes and privilege attributes. Each of these attributes have type information associated with them. Transaction attributes of the entitlement are passed from the application server to the authorization system which are used in the decision making. These correspond to parameters in the access decision rule. Such parameters include values such as the day of the week on which the transaction is being attempted. The other type of attributes is the privilege attributes. The privilege attributes are values defined by the security administrator when specifying a privilege for an entitlement. For example, consider again the entitlement Withdraw. This may have privilege attributes such as Valid-Currency (which has values such as dollar) and Amount-Limit (which can have values such as 5000). These attributes are parameters of an access rule and these have been determined at administration time when the access rule was specified.

There are two ways of adding a privilege. One way is to add it to a profile and principal records. We will consider these later when we define the profile. The other way is to add them as default values in the entitlement. This is useful when a specific privilege is required by many principals.

A subset of the privilege attributes are designated as key attributes. Key attributes are used when multiple sets of privileges must be assigned to the principals for a particular entitlement. For instance, if a set of users are performing transactions on a variety of different currencies, then they can be assigned different limits for each type of currency. Here the currency type can be designated as a key attribute. Note that values of the key attribute must be unique though the values for other privilege attributes may not be.

In general, the transaction attributes are compared with the privilege attributes in determining whether an access request is to be granted or not. This is achieved by the rule in the entitlement. The rule is used by the authorization system to determine if a particular transaction should be authorized for a given principal. It is a logical expression that specifies how transaction attributes are compared with the privilege attributes. Rule elements are composed of the following : a transaction attribute, a comparator (such as =,>,<,>=,<= and <>) and a privilege attribute. Rule elements in an entitlement rule can be combined using AND and OR logical operators and nested parenthesised expressions. The AND operator has higher precedence than the OR operator when no parentheses are used. This leads to the specification of general logical expressions in the entitlement rule. Let us consider a simple example of entitlement.

Example Entitlement

Entitlement Name : Withdrawal

Transaction Attributes :

Account-Type : string

Check-Amount : bignum (type large integer)

New-Balance : bignum

Key Privilege Attributes :

Valid-Account : string

Non-Key Privilege Attributes :

Check-Limit : bignum

Credit-Limit : bignum

Max-Amount : bignum

Rule :

Valid-Account := Account-Type & (Check-Amount <= Check-Limit | New-Balance <= Credit-Limit)

The intention of this rule is to grant authority to withdraw money from a given account type according to one of the limiting factors: either a specific withdraw amount limit (Credit-Limit) or the sum of the withdrawal amount together with the customer's outstanding balance is less than or equal to the Credit-Limit.

The entitlement specification also has a Boolean enable flag which indicates whether the entitlement is activated or not. If the flag is true, then the date and time specifications in the rule can be used in the decision making. If an entitlement is not enabled when a request for authorization is made (that is, the flag is false or the date and time of the transaction are outside the range of the enable time and disable time), then the request is denied, regardless of any privileges held by the principal attempting the transaction.

Finally, an administrator can also define a principal independent entitlement. This entitlement is not associated with any particular principal (that is, it does not have a principal identity value associated with it) and is automatically applied to all principals. This is useful in many commercial situations in policy definition. An example of such a situation is given in section 3.3 where we consider some example policy specifications.

Profiles

The profile construct allows to group entitlements for a class of principals. It helps to simplify the process of assigning privileges to principals. It is clear that roles can be easily defined using the profile construct. First a set of privileges are grouped together in terms of profiles and these are then associated with one or more principals. For instance, profiles can be used to provide the same privileges to a class of principals say all senior bank managers. If groups of principals require the same privileges, it is easier to create a profile and add it to their profile membership list rather than specify the individual privileges for each principal. Profiles can also be used to group privileges for related sets of responsibilities; for example, the privileges required to perform transactions in Japanese Yen.

A profile has the following components: Profile Name, Profile Membership List and Privileges List. The name of the profile is unique within the authorization system. The profile membership list contains the names of the profiles that this profile inherits. A principal that is a member of a given profile (that is, a principal that lists this profile in its list of profile memberships) is granted all the privileges in all the profiles inherited by that profile, and all the privileges listed in the profile. The privileges list contains the list of privileges that this profile has for entitlements. The order the profiles are listed is significant as well as the order the privileges are listed in the privileges list are significant. We will see this aspect when we consider conflict resolution of privileges and profiles.

A key concept in the formulation of profiles and assignment of privileges is the notion of inheritance. Inheritance makes it easier to build and manage sets of privileges so that the same privileges need not be defined repeatedly. For example, consider the following: an administrator creates a profile called Teller that defines all the privileges granted to bank tellers. A principal that becomes a member of the Teller profile automatically has all the privileges defined in it. Let us now create another profile called Senior-Teller which defines all the privileges granted to say senior tellers. Let the Senior-Teller profile include the Teller profile within its specification. Then the senior tellers who are members of the Senior-Teller profile gain all the privileges defined in Teller and Senior-Teller. Inheritance can be supported to varying levels of depth and in our authorisation system, it is supported to a depth of 10. In general, such a inheritance process can create conflicts in privileges. We resolve these conflicts using overrides which are described below.

Time related Parameters

The authorization language allows administrators to specify the times the entitlements, privileges and principals are active. Each privilege has two associated date and time pairs, "effective from" and "effective to" times. Each pair consists of a starting date and time and ending date and time. Each principal and entitlement has two associated date and time pairs, "enabled from" and enabled to". Each pair consists of a starting date and an ending date and time. Each principal and each entitlement has an associated enabled/disabled flag. These time related parameters provide the administrator the flexibility to specify a range of policies. For instance, the administrator can specify a valid time range when a basic element is active. So a branch manager's privileges can be granted to an assistant manager only for the time period the branch manager is away on vacation. This is an example of delegation with a time-out. Administrators can also specify the time a group of related changes becomes active. For example, consider the situation when bringing a new application on-line, an administrator wishes to create the entitlement (s) for the application, modify the existing profile(s) to grant privileges for the application, and modify the principal records to add user-specific privileges. All these changes to the authorisation system are to become effective at the same specific time in the future.

Privilege Operators

The language has a set of privilege operators to specify, modify and override privileges assigned to principals in the authorization system. These operators include addition or replacement (AR), replacement (RE) and deletion (DE). AR is the most commonly used operator. If no matching is found, then the specified privilege is added to the privilege list. If a matching is found, this privilege overrides the matching privilege. A privilege marked with a RE operator can only override another privilege. If no matching privilege is found, in this case, it is not added to the privilege list. If the matching privilege is deleted at a later time, then the corresponding privilege marked with RE is also deleted. The DE operator is used to remove a specific privilege. A specific form of the DE operator DE:all is used to delete all privileges that a principal has for a particular entitlement. Let us consider an example to illustrate the use of these privilege operators in policy specifications.

Consider again the entitlement Withdraw.

Entitlement Name : Withdraw

Key Privilege Attributes :

Valid-Currency : fstr (string of up to 256 chars)

Valid-Start-Day : wkday : (1 : Sun to 7: Sat)

Valid-End-Day : wkday

Privilege Attributes :

Amount-Limit : sint (32-bit signed integer)

The AR privilege operator is used to grant a particular privilege to a principal or profile.

For example, consider

AR :Withdraw:

Start-Time: End-Time: Valid-Currency="USD", Valid-Start-Day="2", Valid-End-Day="6", Amount-Limit="10000"

This is a privilege for the Withdraw entitlement that grants the principal the ability to withdraw up to 10000 US dollars from Monday through Friday. The AR operator means that this privilege overrides any matching privilege encountered in the authorization administration and is added to the list if no matching privilege is found.

The RE privilege operator is similar to the AR operator except that the privilege can only override another privilege. This feature of the RE operator makes it most useful when the override is to limit the authority of the principal rather than to extend it. For instance, let the profile Teller contain the above privilege and a principal Jeff was granted the Teller profile. Jeff was then given the following privilege in his principal record privilege list :

RE:Withdraw:

Start-Time: End-Time: Valid-Currency="USD", Valid-Start-Day="2", Valid-End-Day="6", Amount-Limit="5000"

In this case, the RE privilege will override the AR privilege; Hence Jeff will only be able to withdraw $5000 and any attempt to withdraw a higher amount will be denied. If the AR privilege in the Teller profile is later deleted, since the RE privilege does not add any privilege, the effect is that Jeff will have no withdraw privilege. If the AR operator had been used instead, then the privilege to withdraw $5000 would be added to the list and Jeff would still have that privilege even if the privilege to withdraw up to $10000 was deleted from the Teller profile.

The DE privilege operator is used to remove a specific privilege. Any privilege that matches the effective times and key privilege attribute values of this privilege will be deleted from the list of privileges. For example, let the Teller profile contain the following privilege :

AR :Withdraw:

Start-Time: End-Time: Valid-Currency="USD", Valid-Start-Day="2", Valid-End-Day="6", Amount-Limit="10000"

Assume that the principal Jeff was granted the Teller profile and then given the following privilege in his principal record privilege list. :

DE :Withdraw:

Start-Time: End-Time: Valid-Currency="USD", Valid-Start-Day="2", Valid-End-Day="6"

Note that only the values for key privilege attributes are necessary for privileges using the DE operator. Hence it is not necessary to specify a value for the Amount-Limit. The DE operator causes the AR privilege to be deleted. Thus Jeff will no longer have a privilege for Withdraw and any attempt to withdraw funds will be denied.

3.2 Resolving Privileges and Profiles

When entitlements, privileges and profiles are changed, the privileges and profiles must be evaluated and resolution is required for the changes that may affect the privileges in other places. The administration component of the authorisation system determines how each new privilege or profile affects the privileges that are already in other lists and determines the changes that must be made to the runtime database. This is done by following the inheritance tree of each profile and determining which privileges to add or delete. The resulting privilege lists are then used to update the authorization runtime information. Principal privilege lists must be evaluated whenever any one of a principal's privileges is changed and whenever there is a change to a profile where the principal is a member. Privilege resolution is the process of evaluating and determining which privileges apply to a principal or profile and therefore should be applied at authorization runtime.

The authorization administration component comprises principal, profile and entitlement tables. During resolution, these are changed into the runtime schema that consists of a rule table and a number (n) of different entitlement tables. Each row of an entitlement table corresponds to a privilege for a particular principal (indexed by principal identity value). Each privilege consists of zero or more privilege attributes. During the resolution process, privilege overrides may occur if two privileges match. Privileges match if they have the same entitlement name, values for all the key privilege attributes, and beginning and ending effective date and times.

The order of evaluation is specified as follows:

- Privileges found later in a privilege list override matching privileges found earlier in the privilege list.
- Privileges from profiles that are evaluated later in a profile list override matching privileges from profiles found earlier in a profile list.
- Profile lists are evaluated before a principal's privilege list. Therefore, privileges for principals take precedence over privileges for profiles.

The steps used in the evaluation are as follows:

First the principal record to be resolved is extracted.

- The hierarchy of any profiles a principal has in its profile list and principal list is then traversed and resolved each in order, from the first in the list to the last. The result is a list of privileges for all the profiles.
- Then the privilege operators are applied. For each privilege in the list, the operators are applied for each privilege. The result is a cumulative list of privileges.
- The enable flags on principals and entitlements, and effective times of privileges are then applied to see which privileges are not relevant because of time. This results in an update list.
- The changes are then consolidated. The list of current privileges is compared with the list of privileges on the update list. Any duplicates and privileges that are not operative because of current privileges are deleted. This results in the list of privileges to enter into the runtime database.
- Finally, the runtime information is updated.

3.3 Some Simple Examples

The basic constructs of the proposed authorization policy language can be used to specify a range of access control policies. This section gives some common examples of access control. In the interest of space, the examples do not include all the necessary preliminary declarations and intializations. Nonetheless we hope they convey the required information.

3.3.1 Privileges using Logical Rules

Consider the entitlement Withdraw below.

Entitlement Name : Withdraw

Transaction Attributes :

Account-Type

Amount

Key Privilege Attributes :

Valid-Account

Non-Key Privilege Attributes

Max-Amount

Rule :

Account-Type := Valid-Account

Amount <= Max-Amount

Assume that the policy requires the administrator to grant principal John multiple privileges for this entitlement in order to authorize him to withdraw up to $5000 from his savings account and up to $1000 from his cheque account. This can be achieved by granting to John the following :

Withdrawal : From-Time : To-Time : Valid-Account= Savings, Max-Amount = '5000'

Withdrawal : From-Time : To-Time : Valid-Account = Cheque, Max-Amount = '1000'

3.3.2 Delegation : Time Related Parameters

The (dates and times of privileges) and (dates, times and flags of principal and entitlement) interact to determine whether or not a given privilege is in effect for a given entitlement and a given principal. This interaction is a three-step process: (1) The effective times of the privilege define a range specific to that privilege. (2) The enabled to and from times of the principal are reconciled with the effective times of the privilege. The resulting times are: (a) the later of principal's enabled from time and the privilege's effective from time and (b) the earlier of the principal's enabled to time and the privilege's effective to time. The goal is grant the principal the least amount of authorization time. (3) Finally, regardless of the effective range for this privilege, the overriding factors are the enable flag and the time range of the entitlement. If the entitlement is disabled (either because the enabled flag is turned off or because the enabled flag is turned on and the enabled to time has passed), the privileges are not evaluated. If the entitlement is enabled, the effective times in the privileges are used.

Temporary Time Limited Delegation

These effective times can be used to temporarily grant authority to a principal for whom no privileges exist. When the effective times are enabled for the principal and entitlement, the principal will be authorized from the beginning effective time to the ending effective time. For example, Wayne needs authority to perform withdrawals for a week while his superior is on vacation. We can give Wayne a temporary privilege, with an effective start time of May 18, 1997 at 8:00 AM and an effective ending time of May 22,1997 at 5:00 PM. As of the effective start time, Wayne will be authorized to perform withdrawals. Of course, all the other parameters of the transaction must be valid for the authorization request to be granted. As of the effective ending time, Wayne will not be authorized to make withdrawals, and any requests he makes for withdrawals will be denied.

One can provide a variety of other features such as using times for overriding privileges, using overlapping privileges to grant temporary authority and using multiple privileges to temporarily remove authority. Let us consider another example.

Temporary Removal or Reduction of Privileges

To temporarily remove or reduce an authority of a principal, one may need to create multiple privileges for the same authority but with coinciding effective times and the correct limits. Consider a user Tom having a privilege to withdraw up to $5000. To reduce his ability to withdraw to $100 for one week from May 18 to May 22, the following can be done:

- Change the existing privilege so that its ending effective time is May 18 at 8:00 AM.
- Create a new privilege for withdrawal with a limit of $100 and effective times of May 18 at 8:01 AM through May 22 at 5:00 PM.
- Create another privilege for withdrawal with the original limit of $5000 and effective times of May 22 at 5:00 PM through "No end date".

Using the same example, one can completely remove Tom's authority to withdraw dollars for the same period, instead of simply reducing his limit. This can be accomplished by not creating the second privilege. This will result in Tom not having any effective privilege for withdrawal during the same period specified.

3.3.3 Simple Role Hierarchy

One of the important advantages claimed for the role based approach is that it can model better the structures of real world organizations [9]. A typical part of such structures is a hierarchical ordering of responsibilities with more senior positions encompassing all the privileges of the more junior positions plus some extra privileges. For example, consider a hypothetical structure for a bank branch where there are Branch Managers, Accounts Managers, Loans Managers and Tellers. Let the profile Teller have all the entitlements that are needed for a teller principal to carry out his/her functions. Let E1 and E2 be the extra entitlements required for the accounts manager profile. Let E3 and E4 be the extra entitlements required for the loans manager profile. Let E5 and E6 be the extra entitlements required for the branch manager. The profiles for accounts manager, loans manager and branch manager can be created as follows:

Profile Name : Accounts Manager

Profile Membership : Teller

Privileges:

1. E1;
2. E2;

Profile Name : Loans Manager

Profile Membership : Teller

Privileges:

1. E3;
2. E4;

Profile Name : Branch Manager

Profile Membership : Accounts Manager, Loans Manager

Privileges:

1. E5;
2. E6;

3.3.4 Principal Independent Entitlements

A principal independent entitlement is not associated with any particular principal and is automatically applied to all principals. This is useful in many commercial situations. For example, to globally enable/disable the ATM Server and the Bank Server applications for all principals, a principal independent entitlement such as Server-Hours with key attribute Valid-Server can be implemented.

Server-Hours : Start-Time : End-Time : Valid-Server = "ATM-Server"

Server-Hours : Start-Time : End-Time : Valid-Server = "Bank-Server"

The authorization system automatically assigns these two privileges to all the principals. The Start-Time and End-Time are now controlled for the ATM-Server and the Bank-Server for all principals.

3.3.5 Simple Separation of Duty

Finally, let us consider a simple example of separation of duty. This is where one or a group of principals is not allowed to perform two classes of actions [10]. For instance, a principal which has the privilege to create a document should not have the privilege to certify the same document say for external release. This can be specified as follows:

Let Create-Doc and Certify-Doc be the respective entitlements and let Creator and Certifier be the respective profiles and let Memo be the document.

Profile Name : Creator

Profile Membership : None

Privileges : AR : Create-Doc: Start-Time : End-Time: Valid-Doc = “Memo”

Profile Name : Certifier

Profile Membership : None

Privileges : AR : Certify-Doc: Start-Time : End-Time : Valid-Doc = “Memo”

Here the separation of duty can be achieved in two ways, either at the profile level or at the principal record level. For instance, consider the specification of separation of duty using the principal record privilege list. If a principal say Jane was granted the Creator profile then she can be restricted from doing the certification by adding the following in her principal record privilege list:

DE : Certify-Doc: Start-Time : End-Time: Valid-Doc = “Memo”

Similarly, a principal having the Certifier profile can be restricted from creating the same document using

DE : Create-Doc: Start-Time : End-Time: Valid-Doc = “Memo”.

4. Discussion

As companies migrate from a centralized to a distributed computing environment, the administration and management of security policies in particular authorization policies is becoming an increasingly difficult task. The authorization system described in this paper provides a way of modeling a range of enterprise security policies. It contains a logical repository of authorization rules that capture the access policies in an organization. Rules indicate what entitlements a user requires to invoke a particular operation on specific information. Application developers can use the rule based entitlements to make complex decisions without having to develop the code themselves. It allows the developer to concentrate on the business logic leaving the complex authorization logic to the Authorization Server. Following on from this, the work has been extended for use with web based applications.

Our authorization system provides a *user view* of the entitlement. The security administrator is able to focus on *what* a user or group of users is entitled to do based on their assigned business responsibilities. As a business process typically consists of multiple transactions, each of which consists of multiple operations, it is easier to see exactly what business capabilities are being granted to whom. In contrast, in a *resource based view* provided by the ACLs, it is necessary to specify entitlements and restrictions on a per-interface basis, indicating which users or groups are permitted to access to particular operations and/or information objects.

The policy language constructs presented in this paper in terms of profiles, entitlements and rules are powerful enough to specify a variety of commonly used access policies. In this paper, we have given some examples showing how access policies based on identities, roles and delegation and time based restrictions can be achieved. Profiles can inherit entitlements from other profiles making it possible to build a hierarchy of privileges. Currently, we are in the process of using this language to specify policies in a large scale system that has identity-based, role-based, separation of duty, delegation and joint action based access [11] requirements.

References

1. T.Y.C. Woo and S.S.Lam, Authorizations in Distributed Systems : A Formal Approach, Proceedings of the IEEE Symposium on Research in Security and Privacy, 1992, pp 33-50.
2. S.Jajodia, P.Samarati and V.S.Subrahmanian, A Logical Language for Expressing Authorizations, Proceedings of the IEEE Symposium on Security and Privacy, May 1997.
3. Y.Bai and V.Varadharajan, A Logic for State Transformations in Authorization Policies, Proceedings of the IEEE Computer Security Foundations Workshop, June 1997.
4. Hewlett-Packard, "HP Adds Value to DCE Security Framework with Praesidium Authorization Server, DCE Application Development Trends Magazine, August 1996.
5. Hewlett-Packard, Authorization Server : Administration and Programming Reference Guide 1997.
6. Open Software Foundation (OSF), Distributed Computing Environment : Administration Guide, Security Services 1995, Practical DCE Programming and DCE User Documentation, Prentice Hall.
7. IETF (IAB), RFC 1508 and 1509, Generic Security Service API, 1993.
8. IETF (IAB), RFC 1510, The Kerberos Network Authentication Service, V5, 1993.
9. R.Sandhu, E.Coyne, H.L.Feinstein and C.E.Youman, Role Based Access Control Models, IEEE Computer, Feb.1996, pp 38-47.
10. M.J.Nash and K.Poland, "Some Conundrums concerning Separation of Duty", Proceedings of the 1990 IEEE Symposium on Security and Privacy, May 1990.
11. V.Varadharajan and P.Allen, "Supporting Joint Actions Based Security Schemes in an Object Model" Lecture Notes in Computer Science, LNCS Vol.1172, pp 207-219.
12. M.E.Zurko and R,Simon, "User-Centered Security", Proceedings of the New Security Paradigms Workshop, 1996.
13. V.Varadharajan, "Secure Authorization for Distributed Applications", Short (5 Minute) Paper Presentation, IEEE Symposium on Security and Privacy, May 1995.

Private Desktops and Shared Store

Bryony Pomeroy and Simon Wiseman

Defence Evaluation and Research Agency (DERA)
Malvern, England

Email: s.wiseman@eris.dera.gov.uk

Abstract

Modern interconnected computer systems handling classified information can be built using mainstream COTS software platforms. The technique provides each user with a private desktop in which to work, along with services for sharing data. Within a desktop, the user is helped to label their data. When data is shared, labelling prevents accidental compromise, but other measures defend against other forms of compromise.

Purple Penelope is a prototype that extends Windows NT security to support this approach. It adds discretionary labelling, easy to use role based access controls and effective Accounting and Audit measures to shared files.

1. Introduction

In recent times there have been two important changes in the way computer systems are used and procured, but traditional approaches to providing computer systems that handle classified information have not been adapted to account for them. Increasingly, systems need to be highly interconnected to maximise business efficiency, and they need to be built from mainstream off-the-shelf components to reduce the risks inherent in system integration with niche market products and bespoke developments. Security demands, however, have traditionally either forced systems to work in isolation or to use software with specialised security functionality that only serves the niche market of government systems.

In the UK Ministry of Defence, these problems were recognised and work was put in hand to devise an alternative strategy. The result is called the domain approach, and it affects both the way security requirements are expressed and the way in which they are implemented.

With the new approach, the security aspects of the business requirement are expressed in terms of domains. A domain is a logical place where people carry out their work using software. Domains relate to the way a computer system is used, rather than its design or implementation.

The concept of information domains, which is found in the DoD Goal Security Architecture [1], differs from that of security domains. Information domains are a way of describing high level policy with regard to how a class of information can be used, whereas security domains are about how information is used and exchanged. This places security domains at a lower level of abstraction and therefore easier to relate to the level below - that of implementation.

The new implementation strategy is to divide a system into a number of separate communities, which themselves contain a number of private desktops and a number of shared services. Each user in a community has their own private desktop, and while classified information remains within a user's private desktop the system places no constraints on them. It is only when information is moved between the private desktop and some shared service, such as a shared filestore or email, that constraints are imposed.

Communities are formed so that the people who work within a community are all cleared for all the data handled by that community – in other words each community is either Compartmented or System High. This means the security mechanisms needed within a community can be relatively lightweight.

Additional shared services are used to connect communities together. Here, the connections may be Multi Level, meaning some people in one community may lack clearance for information handled in the connected community, as a result the required security controls will need to be more stringent than those internal to a community.

The approach is practical because the lightweight security controls needed within a community can be built by configuring the assured C class functionality found in mainstream operating system products, in particular Unix and Windows NT. More specialised security functionality is needed in the firewalls and guards which support the services shared between communities, but these products are much more self contained and so the integration risks are minimised.

This paper focuses on the implementation strategy of the domain approach, rather than the new way of specifying security requirements. The paper aims to show how separating private desktops from shared services permits the security mechanisms that control sharing to be made more effective. The paper describes a prototype implementation, called Purple Penelope, implemented as an add-on to Windows NT. The prototype was built by DERA, but the software has been licensed to Argus Systems who have developed it into a product called Deep Purple[2]. In addition, TRW have been investigating, under a collaboration agreement, the possibility of providing a product in the future[3].

In section 2, the paper provides a justification for adopting mainstream COTS software and identifies the different ways in which information may be compromised. The rationale for separating private desktops and shared services is then given and the kind of security functionality required to defend against the different causes of compromise is outlined.

A detailed description of the security functionality provided in a Purple Penelope private desktop is given in section 3, while sections 4, 5 and 6 describe the labelling, role based access controls and Accounting and Audit functionality in the Purple Penelope shared filestore. Space does not permit the techniques used in implementing Purple Penelope to be described in detail, but the reasons for the more unusual design choices in the functionality are discussed.

[2] http://www.argus-systems.com/

[3] edwin.d.patton@trw.com

2. A Justification for the Approach

2.1 Adopting Mainstream COTS

The implication of having highly interconnected systems is that not all users will be cleared for all the information handled by all the systems. That is, overall the system of systems will operate in Multi Level Mode.

Conventional approaches to providing Multi Level Mode systems call for the provision of Mandatory Labelling[4]. This is a property of a system whereby all data is labelled, but the originator of some information is able to mandate the minimum label that data conveying the information can have. For example, if a user enters some data and labels it Confidential, then no information extracted from that data can appear in the computer system labelled Unclassified, regardless of the activities of other users or software.

Operating systems providing B class functionality [2] were designed to support the mandatory labelling property. Unfortunately, providing the functionality serves no purpose unless some assurance is given that it does indeed support the property. This assurance is expensive and time consuming to provide, which prolongs time-to-market, so as the mass market appears not to require B class functionality, there is no incentive for it to be included in products. Hence it is available in only a few niche market products, such as the Compartmented Mode Workstation [3].

The use of B class operating systems brings considerable risk to a project, because there are an increased number of integration problems when applications are ported into the highly constraining security environment. In addition, since support for products is generally given in proportion to the size of the market, development of these niche products often trail behind their mainstream equivalents, leading to user dissatisfaction.

For these reasons, the use of mainstream off-the-shelf products is to be preferred. This is despite the disadvantages of needing more frequent software and hardware updates. It may even be that the approach is more costly overall, because of the continual upgrading of hardware and software required, but the real compelling advantage is the reduced risk of failing to provide an effective system.

[4] We use the term "mandatory labelling" although others may be tempted to use "mandatory access control" here. However the latter term is defined and used ambiguously, referring at different times to either requirements or mechanisms, which causes great confusion, and so its use is avoided here.

The use of mainstream products means a new implementation strategy is required, and so it is important to show that it provides adequate protection to the classified information. To do this, two questions must be answered:

- what must the security functionality defend against?
- what assurance is needed that the defences are designed and implemented properly?

The answer to the first question is that information must be protected against the following five causes of compromise:

a. accidents caused by the legitimate users of the system;

b. the actions of a traitor, i.e. a legitimate user betraying the trust placed in them;

c. Trojan Horse software unwittingly invoked by a legitimate user, which enables others to use the legitimate business processes within the system that are available to that user;

d. someone exploiting an implementation flaw to gain access that they should not have;

e. legitimate users failing to follow operating procedures.

The first three causes of compromise are the primary reasons for implementing technical security measures. The latter two, however, are secondary in that they are concerned with compromises arising because of some flaw introduced by the implementation of the primary measures, either through technical or procedural failings.

The answer to the second question is not addressed in this paper, since that is a policy issue, but the drive to use mainstream products means systems must be designed so no more assurance is needed than is available in these products. In practice this means system designs requiring more than Common Criteria [4] EAL4 assurance should be avoided, because higher assurance is only found in a few specialised products.

2.2 Private Desktops and Sharing

Modern office software is designed to allow people to work in isolation, punctuated with short bursts of sharing. That is, a workstation is designed to be used by one person at a time, but connectivity allows information to be shared when necessary.

Thus a workstation provides a user with a private desktop environment, which includes processing power, disc storage and a human-computer interface (screen with windows, keyboard etc.). Different users, working in their own desktop environment, can communicate through a variety of shared resources, most notably email and shared file storage of some sort. They cannot, however, access the desktop resources of another user directly (the operating system's security mechanisms will be configured to prevent this).

Applications which allow users to work closely together in real time, such as whiteboarding and video conferencing, do require desktop-to-desktop communication. The approach being taken is to find ways of compartmenting a desktop, so that such applications can be run in isolation. This has proved possible to some extent, though assurance is difficult to achieve, but the details are beyond the scope of this paper.

The key to finding a successful strategy for using mainstream software to handle classified information, is to recognise that modern software works in this way. Rather than attempt to alter the desktop environment by adding security mechanisms which control the way information is shared, it is better to control sharing as information crosses the boundary between private desktop and shared services. This mimics the way classified information is handled in the paper world, where documents being drafted are locked away by the user, but once they have been completed and filed more stringent controls are applied to the way they are shared.

The most important consequence of this approach is that a system then contains two kinds of filestore: that which belongs to a private desktop and that which provides a means of sharing data between desktops. The security requirements for these two kinds of filestore turn out to be vastly different, and it is recognising this distinction that permits mainstream products to be used in practical implementations.

2.3 Defending Against Compromise

In this sub-section, each of the five causes of compromise is considered in turn, and suggestions are made as to the kinds of security mechanism that would provide some defence.

Accidental release. The most obvious form of accident is where either the wrong data is released or it is released to the wrong user. The real concern is that someone may observe data for which they lack clearance (in this paper, clearance is used loosely to cover nationality caveats and codewords as well), so a reasonable defence is to label all the data in a private desktop and compare this against the clearance of the recipient when data is shared.

In the case of shared storage, the label of data is preserved when it is made shared. Subsequently, the label is used to mediate observation of the data – that is data can only be observed if the user's clearance dominates the file's classification. In the case of email, the label of data in a message can be compared against the clearance of the recipients and delivery prevented if necessary.

Labelling does not prevent all accidents, because it is possible for a user to accidentally mislabel some data. This may be because an application does not show them all the data, for example Word does not show deleted data when a document is fast-saved, or because they have simply overlooked some sensitive data in a large document. Such mistakes can be countered by automatically removing redundant content from released data, for example by forcing a slow-save of Word documents, and by scanning the content and alerting the user if it appears to be at odds with the label, for example by "dirty word" searching. Such measures cannot be 100% effective, but they are not the prime defence against mistakes so this is not seen to be a problem.

The labelling mechanism is required to defend against mistakes when sharing data, so it is important that users give reasonably accurate labels to their data. Thus users must be able to freely and easily change labels on their private data as they see fit. Without any constraint on relabelling private data, the originator of some information cannot mandate its label when they release it, but must rely on those people who observe the released data to use their discretion when further distributing the information. Hence this kind of labelling is called discretionary labelling, and is akin to what happens in practice in the paper world.

Deliberate release. Information may be compromised if a traitor deliberately releases data to an inappropriate recipient. As data is to be labelled, this means that the traitor must deliberately mislabel the data before releasing it. Mandatory labelling would provide some defence against this, but for reasons already discussed it should be avoided. Instead, the approach is to allow traitors to proceed but to deploy effective Accounting and Audit measures so that they can be traced should a compromise come to light or be suspected.

A traitor can only compromise the data that they can access, so an important measure against traitors is to ensure that users can only access the data they need to carry out their job. In terms of email, this comes quite naturally, because people tend to send messages to only those who need them, unless global distribution lists are used routinely. With file sharing, controls applied to files and directories can be used to limit what people can access.

Access to data should be controlled on the basis of a user's role in the organisation. In addition, the ability to set these controls should itself be governed on the same basis. The provision of such controls is not, however, enough. It is often the case that a system provides sophisticated C class controls, but they are so difficult to set that users do not bother with them. Thus the required Role Based Access Controls must be such that they can be used in an effective way, and Accounting and Audit should be deployed to ensure that users do indeed utilise them appropriately.

Trojan Horse release. Someone may use Trojan Horse software to compromise information that is not directly accessible to them. The first line of defence against Trojan Horse attack is to try and keep the Trojan Horse code out of the system, which can be done by scanning incoming data. The second line of defence is to prevent the code executing, which is possible for genuine executables through configuration control, although this does not help with interpreted code such as macros. The third line of defence attempts to stop the Trojan Horse from releasing data unnoticed by the user. This can be achieved by ensuring that whenever an application makes a request to release data, a User Sanctioned Release mechanism gains the user's approval. This last barrier is important because it is the only one that can be assured in practice.

To be effective, the user must be trained to reject any request to release data which is unexpected, which means the confirmation request must come only once and at the time the user expects it. A trusted path interface must also be used to ensure that the Trojan Horse cannot fake the user's approval.

Faced with the User Sanctioned Release mechanism, a Trojan Horse may attempt to effect a release by modifying data that the user is intending to release. However, this kind of attack can be complex to coordinate and risks discovery, which will usually reveal the identity of the attacker, making it an unattractive technique to the attacker. In addition, the content checking measures discussed above, taken to defend against accidental mislabelling of data, will provide a good defence.

Implementation flaws. The possibility of an implementation flaw being exploited to compromise information is tackled through penetration testing and evaluation, which includes component testing. With a complex system, these techniques are practical only if the system is structured so that only a few components are critical to overall security.

The overall system of systems is structured into communities which interact through shared services. The inner workings of a community are hidden from other communities at the IP level through the actions of firewalls, and at the application level by guards. Within a community, the inner workings of one desktop are hidden from other desktops through use of C class functionality, notably in the filestore, and by the operating system encapsulating the lower level networking services, which is a side-effect of C class functionality in a networked environment. Such mechanisms are beyond the scope of this paper

Failing to follow procedures. Some security is invariably provided by procedural rather than technical means. For example, while passwords might be used as part of a technical User Identification mechanism, it is the responsibility of the users to follow proper password management procedures. Thus if users routinely shared passwords amongst themselves, because this makes it easier for them to carry out their work, the User Identification mechanism ceases to be an effective means of identifying individual users, so Accounting and Audit no longer provides individual accountability, which can be thought of as a compromise. In effect, the human part of the implementation now contains a security flaw.

To counter this secondary cause of compromise, Accounting and Audit measures can be used to check that operating procedures are followed. For example, if a user is found to logon to a workstation at a time when physical security logs indicate they are not present, the user is clearly an impostor. When the real user logs in subsequently, they should notice that the time of last login is incorrect and raise an alarm. If they fail to do so, it might be that they are sharing their password with a colleague, or that they are not paying attention to the last login time. In either case, they are not following procedures and a security inspection should take remedial action.

3. Purple Penelope Private Desktops

Within a community, each user has a private desktop. Working within their desktop environment, the user can run applications and use a clipboard to transfer data between applications. The running applications (processes) can interact with the user through windows and store data in a private filestore, which is structured into directories.

Every private file and directory has a security label associated with it, as does the data in the clipboard. Simple processes, such as commercial applications running without any special customisation, are associated with a range of labels (though it is usually a closed range and thus equivalent to one label). In order that the user is aware of these security labels, Purple Penelope uses a screen stripe to display the range of labels of the process which owns the window that has focus. In addition, the label associated with any data held in the clipboard is displayed in the screen stripe.

A process is associated with a label range, rather than one simple label, because this allows applications to show meaningful label information in the screen stripe when the user selects a number of individually labelled data items. For example, if an application displays a number of targets which potentially have different labels, the process can set its label range according to the labels of those targets which the user has selected, and this is then visible to the user in the screen stripe.

A process may change its associated label range by using an explicit call to the Purple Penelope API, or it may be changed implicitly as a side effect of some call to the standard Windows API (Win32). Similarly, the label of the clipboard may be changed explicitly or implicitly. The API routines involved are described below.

More sophisticated processes are not themselves labelled, but instead they associate label ranges with some of their windows. The labelling functionality then behaves as if the process is associated with the label range of the last labelled window to have focus. This kind of functionality is useful for applications that have windows showing data with different labels. For example, in a word processor that allows several documents to be opened at once, windows displaying documents would each be labelled. As focus switches between these windows, the effective label of the process changes. Many windows are not associated with documents, for example each menu and button bar is a window, and these are left unlabelled so when they receive focus the process' effective label remains unchanged.

Such sophisticated window labelling can be added to existing customisable applications, such as Microsoft Word and Outlook. It can also be built into business applications created using "toolkit" applications such as Microsoft Access or Visual Basic.

When data is copied or moved from one labelled container and merged with the existing data in another, the label of the destination container floats to reflect the change. It so happens that there are no

circumstances where the source will be labelled by a range, but the destination can be, in which case both the lower and upper bounds of the destination range are made equal, i.e.
dest.lower := dest.upper := (dest.upper LUB source)

files are used to control their observation. That is, a shared file cannot be copied or opened for read unless the clearance of the user dominates the label of the file. Similarly, the label of a shared directory controls whether a user is able to list the files in that directory. To access a file in any way, the user's clearance must dominate the labels of all directories on the path.

Win32 Function	Purpose	Labelling Behaviour
handle := CreateFile(*name*,*mode*)	Open file, creating new file if necessary	New files labelled Unclassified; Existing files opened regardless of label
ReadFile(*handle*,*buffer*)	Read data from file	Process/window floats by file label
WriteFile(*handle*,*buffer*)	Write data to file	File floats by process/window label
CopyFile(*source*,*dest*) dest is in desktop filestore	Copy file	The label of the new file is set to the label of the original file
MoveFile(*source*,*dest*)	Rename file or directory	Label of file or directory is preserved
CreateDirectory(*name*)	Create directory	New directories are labelled Unclassified
data := GetClipboardData()	Get data from clipboard	Process/window label floats by clipboard label
SetClipboardData(*data*)	Put data into clipboard	Clipboard label set to upper limit of current process/window range

Figure 1: Win32 routines and desktop labelling

Figure 1 lists the routines in the Windows API that have additional behaviour relating to labelling in the Purple Penelope desktop.

To support new applications and the enhancement of existing applications which can be customised, Purple Penelope also provides its own API. The routines related to labelling on the desktop are listed in figure 2.

When files are copied into the shared filestore, the user is prompted with a dialog box to sanction the release. This sanction is obtained in order to prevent Trojan Horse code in an application from modifying the shared filestore without the knowledge of the user. To be effective in revealing Trojan Horse activity, it is vital to ensure a Trojan Horse cannot simulate a user's input to the dialog box. That is, the dialog box must be on a trusted path.

Purple Penelope API Function	Labelling Behaviour
setFileLabel(*name*,*label*)	The label of the file or directory is changed (raised or lowered)
label := getFileLabel(*name*)	Returns the label of the file
setCurrentLabelRange(*labelRange*)	Process/window label is changed (raised or lowered)
labelRange := getCurrentLabelRange()	Returns the label range of process/window
selectLabelledWindow(*window*,*labelRange*)	Window becomes labelled with label range specified and if the process is labelled it ceases to be so
setClipboardLabel(*label*)	Sets the label of the data in the clipboard
label := getClipboardLabel()	Returns the label of the data in the clipboard

Figure 2: PP API routines and desktop labelling

4. Labelling in the Shared Filestore

Files and directories in the shared filestore are labelled, as they are in the private filestore within a user's desktop. Unlike private files, shared files cannot be written, though files can be copied into the shared filestore (writing and copying are different operations in Windows NT). Also, labels on shared

Although Trojan Horses are normally thought of in terms of attacks against confidentiality, they may also attack integrity or availability of data. Thus all modifications of the shared filestore are subjected to a trusted path sanction.

The trusted path dialog that is presented to the user by Purple Penelope gives a description of the requested operation and permits 3 responses. The user can click "ok" to allow the requested action to continue, or "cancel" if they caused the request to be made in error. If, however, the dialog box appears unexpectedly or the described operation is not what was expected, this is an indication that a Trojan Horse attack is underway, and the user is expected to click "alert". This first sends a message to the security officer prompting them to mount an investigation and then fails the request.

Win32 Function	Purpose	Labelling Behaviour
handle := CreateFile(*name*,*mode*)	Open file	Fails if access mode is write, file does not exist, or user's clearance does not dominate label of file
ReadFile(*handle*)	Read data from open file	Process/window label floats by the file label
CopyFile(*source*,*dest*) dest is in shared filestore	Create dest as a copy of source	Label of dest set to label of source, release confirmed using trusted path
source is in shared filestore	Create dest as a copy of source	Fails if user's clearance does not dominate label of file
MoveFile(*source*,*dest*) within shared filestore	Change the name of source to dest	Label of file is preserved
DeleteFile(*name*)	Delete file	Confirmed using trusted path
CreateDirectory(*name*)	Create new directory	Label of new directory set to Unclassified; Confirmed using trusted path
RemoveDirectory(*name*)	Delete existing directory	Confirmed using trusted path

Figure 3: Win32 routines and shared filestore labelling

Confidentiality is not compromised if a user deletes data that they are not cleared to observe. Deletion is, however, an issue of integrity and availability, but for this clearance is not an adequate control. After all, a secret clearance does not permit someone to delete all secret data. Thus, Purple Penelope controls deletion by role based access controls, which are described later, rather than labels. That is, users can delete shared files that they are not cleared to see.

In the private desktop, a user can label data higher than their clearance permits and yet still be able to observe it. This feature is useful on those rare occasions when a user must prepare a report which they ultimately will not be able to observe. Once the report is finished and copied to the shared filestore, however, the labelling prevents the user observing the shared copy (though they can still see the original in their private filestore).

The label of a shared file can be raised or lowered only if the user is cleared to observe the file. In the current implementation, users are allowed to raise the label above their clearance which allows the possibility of a user selecting too high a label by mistake. Although such a mistake ought to be caught when the user is asked to sanction the request, if they fail to notice the error it is difficult to recover from it. So, it is planned to ask for additional confirmation when the new label is higher than the user's clearance.

Figures 3 lists the Win32 routines that have additional behaviour relating to labelling in the Purple Penelope shared filestore, while figure 4 lists the relevant functions in the Purple Penelope API.

5. RBAC in the Shared Filestore

Purple Penelope allows access to data to be controlled on a need-to-know or need-to-do basis in terms of the role a user plays in the organisation. A role is essentially a set of users, but to allow them to be managed more easily, they can form a graph

PP API Function	Labelling Behaviour
setFileLabel(*name,label*)	Fails if user's clearance does not dominate label of file and all directories on the path; Confirmed using trusted path

Figure 4: PP API routines and shared filestore labelling

structure (unlike the flat structure of NT's groups which are used to implement them).

Each role contains a set of users and a set of roles. A user is a member of any role that contains them, and of any role that contains a role which contains them. Structuring roles in this way makes it easier to change an organisational structure, for example when military systems are deployed.

Figure 5 shows an example, in which Al and Joe are members of the Ops role. By placing the Ops role in the Purple Palace role, Al and Joe would instantly become members of Purple Palace. Conversely, if the Intel role is removed from Purple Palace, Wendy would cease to be in Purple Palace but Fred would remain, because he is in the role directly as well as by virtue of his membership of Intel.

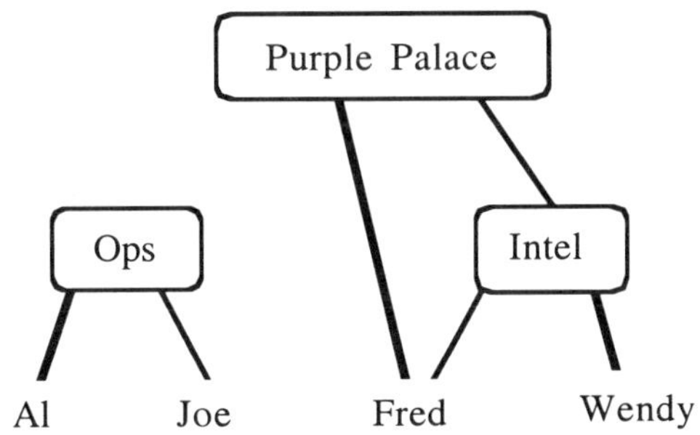

Figure 5: Example role structures

In traditional filestores role based controls are applied to files, but this can be confusing to users because different applications have a different effect on the controls when files are edited. Some applications create a new file and then replace the old file with it, thus the controls on the new file are set to some default and the controls appear to change. Other applications modify the existing file, so the controls remains unaltered.

In Purple Penelope, applications are not permitted to write to shared files, so this problem does not arise. Unlike labels, however, the role based controls applied to a file are potentially too complex to show the user in the screen stripe. Thus it is likely that users will make mistakes, or simply not bother to set the controls accurately when they share new files.

Thus in Purple Penelope, role based controls are focused on directories rather than on individual files. This has the advantage that the structure of directories changes infrequently and the names can be chosen to reflect their use and hence imply their access control characteristics. For example, users in the Intel role may create a directory called *product* which they allow users in the Ops role to observe. Subsequently, the Intel users know that any files placed in the *product* directory will be accessible to Ops users.

At any one time in Purple Penelope, each user is a member of one or more roles. When a user logs in, they are able to perform any actions permitted by any of their roles. That is, unlike many other systems, there is no notion of a current role to be selected when the user logs on. The idea here is that more flexible working practices can be accommodated, with users conducting multiple tasks within one logon session.

Sometimes roles rather than labels are used to separate different kinds of information, for example live and exercise data. If a user is in both such roles there is an increased chance of accidental contamination of one kind of information with the other. Giving users the option of "switching off" some roles would help avoid problems, but Purple Penelope does not support this as it cannot be implemented with NT groups.

Purple Penelope's role based access controls in the shared filestore associate a role, called the custodian, with each shared directory. Any users belonging to this role are able to govern access to the files in the directory (in NT, each file and directory has an owner that can control how the file is accessed, so to avoid confusion with a very similar concept, the term custodian was coined). That is, the custodian of a directory is able to relabel, rename or delete it, or change its role based controls.

Shared directories also have a set of exporter roles and a set of observer roles associated with them. To place a file in a directory, a user must be a custodian or an exporter of the directory, and a custodian or observer of all parent directories. To observe a file in a directory, a user must be a custodian, exporter or observer of the directory and all its ancestors. The observers, exporters and custodian of a directory can only be altered by a custodian of the directory.

Although the focus for role based controls is on directories, files too have a custodian role. This is used primarily to control relabelling of the file, but in addition the custodian of a file may delete it even if they are not a custodian of the directory containing it.

When a file is exported into the shared filestore using the Purple Penelope API, the application chooses one of its roles to be the file's custodian. To support use of the standard Win32 API, which does not expect such a parameter, each user has a default role that is used to set the custodian. A user can change this default role at any time and this does not affect what they can observe or do, just what role becomes custodian of files they create through standard interfaces (the default role should not be confused with the current role found in some other systems). Regardless of how the application chooses the role, the user confirms it as part of the Trusted Path release sanction.

A directory can be set so that the custodian of any file placed in it is set to the directory's custodian. This behaviour is useful, for example, in workflow systems where control over a document is passed from one group of users to another as it travels along the workflow. When files are copied into directories that inherit files in this way, the user has the opportunity to cancel the release, should they wish to retain control of the file, when the trusted path sanction appears. In NT, file ownership cannot be given away (except through the use of privilege and non-standard interfaces), but Purple Penelope's inheritance feature amounts to giving ownership away in a controlled fashion.

Win32 Function	Purpose	RBAC Behaviour
handle := CreateFile(*name*,*access*)	Open file	Fails if user is neither a custodian nor an observer of directories on the path
CopyFile(*source*,*dest*) dest is shared filestore	Copy file	Fails if the user is neither a custodian nor an exporter of the parent directory; The new file's custodian is set to the user's default role, unless directory inherits custodianship; Custodian selection confirmed on trusted path
MoveFile(*source*,*dest*)	Rename source as dest	Fails if the user is neither a custodian nor an exporter for the source and destination parent directories; Confirmed on trusted path
DeleteFile(*name*)	Delete file	Fails if the user is neither a custodian of the file nor of the directory; Confirmed on trusted path
CreateDirectory(*name*)	Create directory	Fails if the user is neither a custodian nor exporter of the parent directory; The new directory's custodian is set to the user's default role, and its observer and exporter lists are set to empty; Confirmed on trusted path
RemoveDirectory(*name*)	Delete directory	Fails if the user is neither a custodian nor an exporter of the parent directory; Confirmed on trusted path

Figure 6: Win32 routines and shared filestore RBAC

Figure 6 lists the Win32 functions which have additional behaviour pertaining to role based controls.

Figure 7 lists the functions in the Purple Penelope API which support role based access controls.

6. A&A in the Shared Filestore

Accounting and audit functionality is provided in all secure systems, but invariably the information in the accounting logs is impenetrable and accessible only to the administrator. By focusing attention on sharing, Purple Penelope is able to make logs more informative and more generally accessible. The intention here is to give the custodians of information the opportunity to notice if it is being used inappropriately, and to draw the attention of any potential traitors to the fact that their misdemeanours are liable to be discovered.

In the Purple Penelope shared filestore, each file has a log associated with it that contains information about just that one file. Similar logs for directories are planned but are not yet implemented. Further logs are associated with each user, recording logon/logoff times etc. and details of any failed attempts to read shared files. Some accounting information is collected directly by Purple Penelope system software, but other information is collected by NT's accounting mechanisms and then transferred by Purple Penelope from the NT logs to the Purple Penelope logs.

Accounting and Audit in the shared filestore is needed to trace the cause and extent of any compromise involving shared files. To do this, it is important to be

PP API Function	RBAC Behaviour
setLabelOfFile(*name*,*label*)	The user must be a custodian of the file or directory; Confirmed on trusted path
copyFilePP(*source*,*dest*,*role*)	As CopyFile but explicitly sets new file's custodian
setDirectoryObservers(*name*,*list*)	Sets the observers of the directory to the given list of roles; Fails if the user is not a custodian of the directory; Confirmed on trusted path
setDirectoryExporters(*name*,*list*)	As for setDirectoryObservers, but changes the exporters
setDirectoryCustodian(*name*,*role*)	Sets the custodian of a directory to the given role; Fails if the user is not a custodian of the directory; Confirmed on the trusted path
list := getDirectoryObservers(*name*)	Returns the list of observers for the directory; Fails if the user is neither a custodian, observer nor exporter
list := getDirectoryExporters(*name*)	As for getDirectoryObservers, but returns the exporters
role := getDirectoryCustodian(*name*)	Returns the directory's custodian; Fails if the user is neither a custodian, observer nor exporter
setDirectoryInheritance(*name*,*bool*)	Starts or stops a directory inheriting files placed in it; Confirmed on the trusted path
setDefaultRole(*role*)	Sets the user's default role
role := getDefaultRole()	Returns the user's default role

Figure 7: PP API routines and shared filestore RBAC

able to trace what information has been released by whom, and which users subsequently observed it. This cannot be established by examining the names of files that have been released and observed, as it is not possible to track the flow of information through modern applications.

For Accounting and Audit to be effective, it must be possible to examine the content of shared files, but this cannot be done once files are deleted. So in Purple Penelope, when shared files are deleted, they are actually moved into a special directory of deleted files. This directory is only accessible to the administrator, but files still retain their label and accounting log. Should some information be found to have been leaked, it is now possible (though potentially expensive) to search through the shared filestore looking for files that contain it. Note that replacing a shared file with another of the same name is treated like a delete followed by a copy, so the original version of the file is preserved along with its log.

A file log contains a list of entries, starting with one which identifies how the file first became shared. Information is then recorded if the file is observed, relabelled, renamed or deleted. Note that, when a file is renamed the file log remains associated with the file under its new name, and when a file is deleted the event is recorded before the file is moved, along with its log, to the directory of deleted files.

With regard to observation, only the first time a particular user observes a file is recorded. This is because it is the time of first observation that is required when a compromise is investigated - if a user first observed a file after its data was compromised, they need not be investigated further. This stance helps to minimise the amount of accounting information that must be analysed.

The way accounting information is stored favours establishing which users have seen a file, but does not help find which files a user has seen. This latter question need only be answered when a traitor has been discovered and the extent of the damage is being established. At this point, scanning the logs for the required information is not an unreasonable overhead.

A user can observe a file's accounting log if they are a custodian of the file, except if the file has been deleted. An administrator can observe the logs of any file for which they are cleared. The information in the logs is clear and concise, and relates directly to the business that was conducted. The reason this is possible is that shared files cannot be modified (only replaced). Files in the private desktop can be modified, but accounting is not attempted here as the focus is on sharing. Thus the move to private desktops and shared services has been key in providing effective Accounting and Audit.

Win32 Function	Purpose	Logged information
handle := CreateFile(*name,access*)	Open file	if successfully opened: read event type; user's identity; date and time
CopyFile(*source,dest*) source is shared filestore	Copy file	file copied event type; destination file name; user's identity; date and time
dest is shared filestore	Copy file	file created event type; file's label; source file name; user's identity; date and time
MoveFile(*source,dest*)	Rename	rename event type; destination file name; user's identity; date and time
DeleteFile(*name*)	Delete file	delete event type; user's identity; date and time (note: the file is not actually deleted, but is moved to the log of deleted files)

Figure 8: Win32 routines and Shared filestore A&A

Figure 8 shows what information is logged regarding shared files by extensions to existing Win32 functions, while figure 9 describes the logging for relevant functions in the Purple Penelope API.

7. Summary

The separation of a system into private desktops and shared storage has been key in the formulation of the domain approach and to implementing Purple Penelope. It allows mainstream off-the-shelf applications to work in the kind of environment for which they were designed by shifting the focus of attention for stringent security away from the desktop and onto the sharing of data.

This paper has concentrated on sharing in a filestore, but a similar approach to labelling and Accounting and Audit can be taken for email. Less clear is what kind of role based access controls need to be provided for email, and how is it best to provide them. For example, distribution lists are key to controlling need-to-know for email traffic, but how should updating them be controlled? This is a topic for further research.

8. References

[1] "Department of Defense Technical Architecture Framework for Information Management. Volume 6: DoD Goal Security Architecture", version 3.0, April 1996. (http://www-library.itsi.disa.mil:8018/tafim/)

[2] "Trusted Computer Security Evaluation Criteria", US Dept. of Defense Standard 5200.28-STD, December 1985.

[2] "Compartmented Mode Workstation: Results through Prototyping", P.T.Cummings et. al., Procs. IEEE Symp. on Security and Privacy, Oakland CA, April 1997, pp2-12.

[3] "Common Criteria for Information Technology Security Evaluation", Final Committee Draft International Standard 15408.

PP API Function	Logged information
setLabelOfFile(*name,label*)	relabel event type; user's identity; date and time; the new label
log := openFileLog(*name*)	returns a copy of the file's log, but this is not logged

Figure 9: PP API routines and shared filestore A&A

Track A: Panel Session

Opening the Doors, Selectively, to the Big Ten Virtual Library

Moderator

D. Brink, Gradient Technologies

The panel members will include representatives from some or all of the following schools:

- Pennsylvania State University
- Ohio State University
- University of Minnesota
- University of Wisconsin

The Committee on Institutional Cooperation (CIC)—a consortium of leading research universities that includes the eleven members of the Big Ten conference—are working together to open the combined contents of their libraries to more than 600,000 students and faculty throughout the alliance. This landmark virtual electronic library will ultimately provide authorized CIC patrons with uniform, secure Web-based access to all CIC library collections. Although techniques such as IP screening and firewalls are being used in the short term as the libraries come together, screening IP addresses is not enough to meet the long-term requirements of identifying specific patrons and ensuring that they are authorized to request books, journals, periodicals, research reports, etc. The CIC universities are collaborating to build simpler, stronger security solutions that will accommodate the reality of different authentication technologies at each school, yet still provide a common authorization model for secure, Web-based access across institutions.

This panel session will describe how four members of the CIC—Penn State, Ohio State, Minnesota, and Wisconsin—are jointly working on the implementation of such a solution in a collaborative project referred to as TRICAAP (ThRee Institutions of the CIC Authentication and Authorization Project). Participants will describe:

- The security technologies used for authentication at each campus, which include both public-key (X.509v3 certificates) and secret key (Kerberos/DCE) solutions
- The approach being used to establish a common authorization mechanism for securely sharing Web-based resources across campuses
- The objectives, organization, and status of the TRICAPP project
- Future work related to TRICAAP.

Track B

High-Speed Networks

Chair

A. Friedman, National Security Agency

A Hardware Independent Encryption Model for ATM Devices

Herbert Leitold
Institute for Applied Information Processing and Communications, Graz University of Technology
Herbert.Leitold@iaik.tu-graz.ac.at

Udo Payer
Institute for Applied Information Processing and Communications, Graz University of Technology
Udo.Payer@iaik.tu-graz.ac.at

Reinhard Posch
Institute for Applied Information Processing and Communications, Graz University of Technology
Reinhard.Posch@iaik.tu-graz.ac.at

Abstract

Faced the migration towards broadband networking technologies, formerly visionary applications, as divers as teleworking, telemedicine, or electronic commerce are expected to emerge to broad usage. This makes confidential communication in broadband networks a challenging basic condition.

In this paper, we present an ATM encryption model that is focused towards independence of both the hardware of the end user device, and the application utilizing ATM as transport media. Therefore, the ATM cell stream is intercepted by high-speed data encryption standard (DES), TripleDES encryption hardware using well defined, standardized interfaces. Considering the various access rates ATM is defined for, the encryption unit being developed is designed independent of the physical media, capable of supporting transmission rates up to 155 Mbps. Thus, the solution is applicable to broadband-integrated services digital network (B-ISDN) end user devices, ranging from narrowband to multi-Mbps access rates.

1. Introduction

Multimedia telecommunication increasingly influences the everyday life. Especially the impressive advances in broadband networking technologies are assumed to cause sweeping changes in the way we work, live, and socialize. Faced the potential sensitivity level of multimedia applications carried via broadband networks, such as teleworking, telemedicine, or commercial applications, it is obvious that confidential communication is of paramount importance.

There is a common recognition that ATM will play an important role in the field of broadband telecommunications. This is mainly caused by the fact that ATM promises to support the communication demands of the variety of communication profiles, such as voice, video, and digital data transmission. In addition to service independence, ATM is a promising approach for residential broadband accesses and wide area network (WAN) communication via public infrastructures, as expressed in [1]. This is caused by the fact that ATM is defined basically independent from the physical media. Consequently, ATM is used with a variety of physical media, ranging from narrowband n*64 kbps to multi-Mbps and even Gbps links. This makes ATM suitable for promising residential access technologies, like cable television (CATV) network modems [2], or asymmetric digital subscriber line [3]. However, as expressed in a talk “ATM: Dangerous at any Speed” by Schulzrinne [4], respectively addressed in [5], ATM is vulnerable to eavesdropping and unauthorized access.

Combining the statements made in the previous paragraphs, applications carrying sensitive information via ATM deliberately demand for confidentiality. Considering the variety of different applications demanding security arouses interest in migrating ATM to a network technology offering security services on demand. This is expressed by the efforts made by the ATM Forum, the leading alliance of telecommunication service providers, manufacturers, and researchers in the ATM arena, to standardize ATM security, covering data confidentiality, data integrity, access control and authentication [6]. In this paper, we present an encryption model compliant to this foreseeable standard and, simultaneously, independent of the ATM hardware. Thus, the encryption hardware being developed as the core piece of the model is applicable to the variety of ATM end user devices.

The remainder of the paper is structured as follows: Section 2 outlines the ATM basics by describing the ATM protocol architecture and security interaction model. Section 3 surveys recent research in the area of confidential communication in ATM networks by discussing different proposals and outlining the ATM Forum standard. Basing on these approaches, section 4 presents the hardware independent DES/TripleDES ATM encryption module capable of handling up to 155 Mbps. Section 5 addresses the important topic of key-agile encryption by giving a closer look at the implementation of the hardware and, finally, conclusions are given.

0-8186-8789-4/98 $10.00

2. ATM interaction and protocol model

ATM is a switching technique based on the statistical multiplexing of fixed size packets, called ATM cells. Similar to other packet switching techniques, such as X.25 or Frame Relay, ATM is connection oriented by the means of virtual connections (VCs). An ATM network consists of a set of ATM switches interconnected by point-to-point ATM links. Two different types of interfaces are defined:

- UNI: Between an end system and an ATM switch the user network interface (UNI) [7] is defined.
- NNI: The network network interface (NNI) [8] is defining the routing of signaling information in larger clouds of ATM switches.

Within an ATM network the security relevant interactions can be divided into user-to-user interactions between the end systems, user-to-network interactions between the user and ATM switches, and network-to-network interactions between ATM switches. In this paper we focus on user data confidentiality. Thus, the user-to-user interactions are discussed.

An example of such an ATM interaction scenario consisting of three ATM end devices A, B, and C, and two ATM switches is shown in figure 1. In addition to the components and network interfaces involved, two VCs, $VC_{1(B \leftrightarrow C)}$ and $VC_{2(A \leftrightarrow C)}$ are outlined as a dashed line, a dotted line respectively.

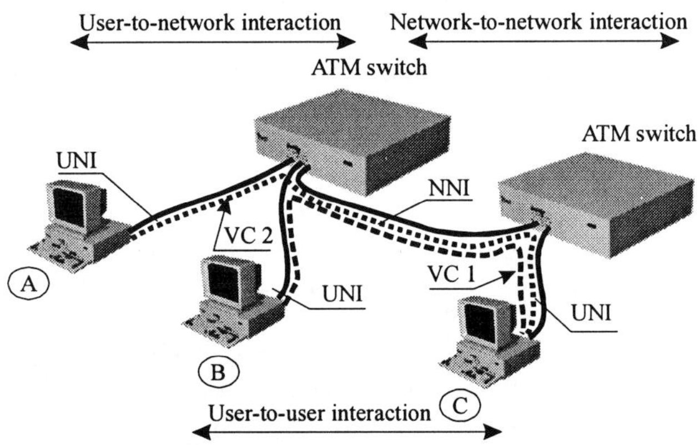

Figure 1. ATM interaction model

The ATM protocol architecture, the B-ISDN protocol architecture respectively, has been standardized by the International Telecommunication Union – Telecommunication Standardization Sector (ITU-T) as recommendation I.321 [9]. Closely related to the ISDN protocol model, it consists of several planes: Firstly, the management plane to maintain the network operational. Secondly, the control plane defines the signaling functions needed for establishing and controlling the communication channels (VCs) that can be either a virtual path connection (VPC), or a virtual channel connection (VCC). Finally, the user plane is responsible for exchanging the user data via the communication channels (VCs).

Within the user plane and the control plane, several protocol layers are defined:

- AAL: At the top of the protocol model, the ATM adaptation layer (AAL) transforms the native user data into ATM cells, consisting of five octets header information and 48 octets payload. Therefore, AAL is subdivided into the two sublayers convergence sublayer (CS) defining general procedures and functions that convert between ATM and non-ATM formats, and the segmentation and reassembly (SAR) sublayer dividing the native user data into ATM cells.
- ATM layer: The ATM layer performs cell switching, virtual path identifier (VPI) virtual connection identifier (VCI) translation, and cell multiplexing and de-multiplexing.
- PHY: Finally, the physical layer (PHY) transforms the ATM cell into a bit stream. Therefore, the transmission convergence (TC) sublayer of PHY adapts the ATM cells to the transmission frame by performing cell header error checksum (HEC) processing, cell delineation, and cell rate decoupling. The physical media dependent (PMD) sublayer finally transforms the ATM cells to a bit-stream that is transmitted over the physical infrastructure, such as synchronous optical network (SONET) or synchronous digital hierarchy (SDH).

In figure 2 the ATM protocol reference model [9] is shown, sketching the layers described above, as well as the different planes: control plane, user plane, and management plane.

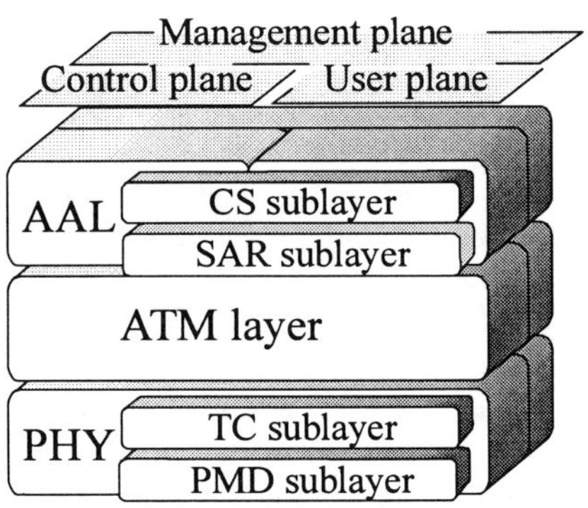

Figure 2. ATM (B-ISDN) protocol reference model

Having briefly described the basics of ATM, we follow up in discussing different approaches to provide confidential communication in ATM networks and in outlining the ATM Forum standardization efforts. This is done in the following section 3.

3. ATM confidentiality approaches

Generally spoken, any encryption mechanism operates on the protocol payload, leaving the protocol headers unchanged, as the header information is needed for transmitting the data and maintaining the communication. With reference to figure 1 note, that for confidential user-to-user communication the encrypted information traversing the network needs to transparently pass the intermediate nodes. As ATM switching is done at the ATM layer in the user plane, the encryption process must be embedded into the ATM protocol model in a way that no changes to the ATM cell header are made.

Considering the protocol architecture shown in figure 2, ATM encryption can take place on several layers, each solution having its specific advantage and disadvantage. This is described in the following subsections 3.1 to 3.4.

3.1. Application layer encryption

The first class of approaches proposed in the literature is applying encryption to the application layers, such as the internet protocol (IP), the file transfer protocol (FTP), etc. These protocols located above ATM make the solution independent of the transport system. However, application layer encryption requires adaptation of a multitude of applications and services and, thus, overrules the benefit of service independence offered by ATM.

3.2. AAL layer encryption

Using the AAL service data unit (AAL-SDU) as the payload to encrypt is advantageous for LAN-based traffic, as one certain AAL (AAL-5) is mainly used for computer-based communication [10]. Thus, this class of providing confidentiality in ATM networks was proposed several times. Generally spoken, AAL-layer encryption can be further divided into two approaches:

- On the one hand, the AAL-SDU can be accessed at the interface between the AAL sublayers CS and SAR. E.g., this has been proposed in [11] by introducing a "Data Protection Layer" (DPL) between the AAL sublayers. The scenario of intercepting the information between the AAL sublayers is schematically depicted as interception (a) in figure 3.
- On the other hand, the data stream can be intercepted at the AAL to application program interface (API). This scenario is shown as interlayer (b) in figure 3. In [12] this approach is proposed as a "CryptoNode" intercepting the data at the direct memory access (DMA) interface between the ATM hardware and the host. Similar architectures have been published in [13] as a secure AAL (SEC-AAL) layered above AAL, or in [14] as a "Solution for Frequent Communications" (SFFC) which is closely related to the IEEE 802.10A model for LAN-based traffic.

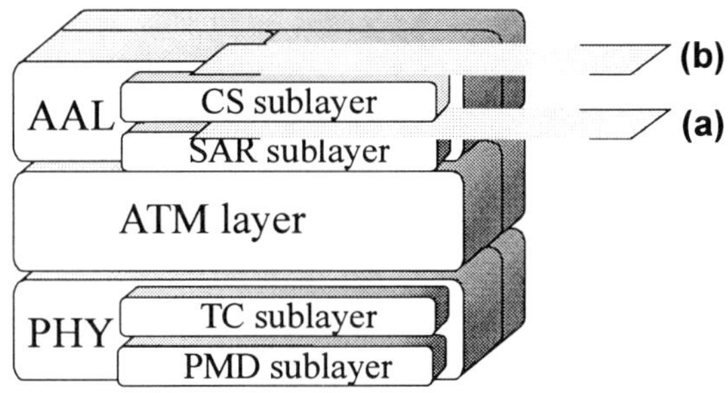

Figure 3. AAL layer encryption

However, although the AAL layer encryption approaches are applicable to the various standards existing to embed ATM into computer based LANs, the main drawback is that the approach is limited to this one service class.

3.3. ATM cell level encryption

Encryption can take place at the ATM cell level, such as described in [5]. This approach has its main advantage in being independent of the service applied on top of the ATM layer. Thus, ATM cell level encryption using DES [15] as default ciphering method, and TripleDES or FEAL as optional methods was chosen by the ATM Forum Security Working Group standardizing ATM security [16]. The compliance classes of the ATM Forum Security Specification 1.0 specify cipher block chaining (CBC) and a counter mode as operational modes [17].

Two interfaces exist where ATM cells can be accessed: On the one hand, the interface between the ATM layer and the AAL can be intercepted, shown as (a) in figure 4. On the other hand, ATM cells pass the interface between the ATM and the physical layer. The scenario of intercepting this interface is sketched as (b) in the following figure 4.

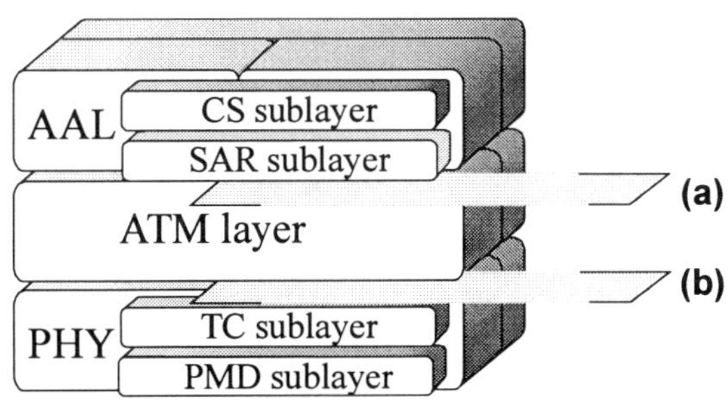

Figure 4. ATM cell level encryption

3.4. PHY layer encryption

Applying the encryption process to the physical layer leads to the PHY layer approach, such as encrypting the whole SONET synchronous payload envelope (SPE). Located below the ATM layer this results in encrypting and, thus, modifying the ATM cell header. Violating the requirement of encrypted information transparently passing the intermediate nodes, this approach requires decryption at the ATM switches. Thus, for the user-to-user interaction model this hop-to-hop confidentiality approach is not further discussed.

With the precondition of an ATM cell level-based approach as standardized by the ATM Forum (see previous section 3.3), we follow up discussing the application of the encryption unit to ATM hardware. This is done in the following section 4.

4. Hardware independent architecture

The transmission rates ATM is defined for, ranging to multi-Mbps and Gbps, deliberately demand for hardware implementation of the encryption unit. This makes the hardware architecture of ATM end devices worth considering. With reference to the protocol model shown in figure 2, ATM devices usually consist of a PMD device extracting the transmission frame out of the bitstream received. This frame is passed to a TC controller extracting the ATM cells from the transmission frame. Finally, the ATM cells are passed to a SAR processor integrating both the ATM, and the AAL layer. Thus, the only interface allowing to access ATM cells is the one between the SAR processor and the TC controller. This interface has been standardized by the ATM Forum as the Universal Test & Operations Physical Interface for ATM (UTOPIA) [18]. The whole scenario is shown in figure 5 on the example of a typical ATM network interface card.

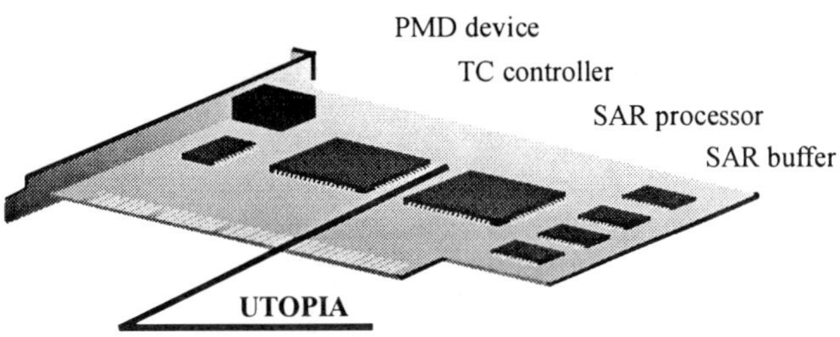

Figure 5. Typical ATM device architecture

Basing on this architecture, the DES/TripleDES encryption unit intercepts the UTOPIA by offering a TC device interface to the SAR processor and, vice versa, substituting a SAR interface to the TC controller. The main advantage of this concept is, that the encryption unit can be applied to any ATM device supporting UTOPIA. In fact, this is the majority of ATM access solutions established in the market, ranging from ATM network interface cards to wide area network (WAN) multiplexers and ATM backbone network routers.

In addition to the platform and hardware independence, by supporting UTOPIA at the interface to the TC controller the approach allows to apply the encryption hardware to a variety of different physical media, provided that the SAR processor and the DES/TripleDES unit are capable of handling the top level rate. For instance, the 155 Mbps SONET optical carrier 3 concatenated (OC3c) mainly used in ATM LAN environments, and the 2 Mbps E1 signal used in ATM WAN environments can be supported alternatively. This scenario is shown in figure 6.

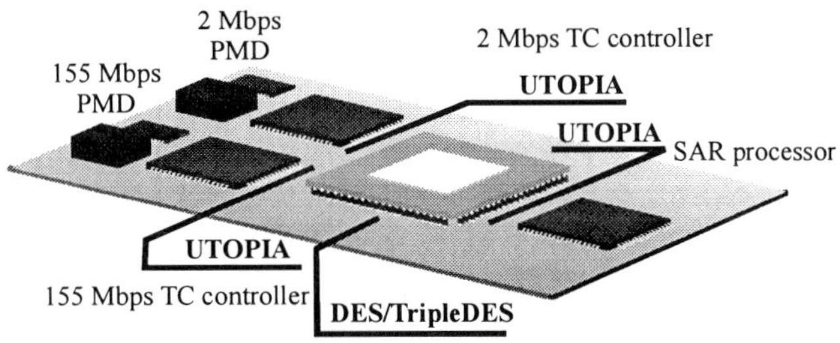

Figure 6. Hardware and media independent UTOPIA intercepting encryption

Note, that several information flows have to pass the encryption unit unmodified. These are mainly signaling, management, or maintenance flows. As these flows are bound to certain VPI/VCI pairs or payload type identifier (PTI) value, the decision of passing an ATM cell in plain text is made upon the ATM cell header information.

This completes the description of the basic architecture of applying the hardware independent encryption unit to ATM devices. The discussion has not revealed handling encryption keys, so far. This is described in the following section 5, discussing the implementation of the encryption hardware in more detail.

5. Key agility at UTOPIA rates

It has been acquired in the statements made in the previous section 4 that for concerns of hardware independence the ATM encryption unit interfaces to the outside world using UTOPIA. UTOPIA is an hardware interface operating, in the usual case, at a clock rate of 25 MHz. Two eight bit width data busses are provided, one receive direction (Rx) from the TC controller to the SAR processor, and one transmit direction (Tx) from the SAR processor to the TC controller. Thus, in each direction Rx and Tx a maximum bandwidth of $BW_{UTOPIA} = 200$ Mbps is offered.

Considering SONET OC3c as the top level signal to be supported, reducing the rate of 155.52 Mbps by the overhead caused by SONET calculates to $BW_{OC3c} = 149.76$ Mbps. However, for concerns of simplicity the following considerations neglect the fact that the maximum throughput to be supported is the one the physical media is capable transmitting. Thus, ATM cells are considered as transmitted tightly packed via UTOPIA. As stated previously, an ATM cell consists of five octet header information followed by a 48 octet payload which neatly fits to the eight octet block length of DES and TripleDES. This results in a ATM cell size of $l_{CELL} = 53$ octets. Thus, the minimum cell arrival period t_{CELL} calculates to:

$$t_{CELL} = \frac{l_{CELL}}{BW_{UTOPIA}} = \frac{53 \times 8}{200} = 2.12\ \mu\text{s}. \qquad (1)$$

Considering the statistical multiplexing ATM is based on, each consecutive cell might belong to a different VC. Both the user expectancy, and the ATM Forum security specification take unique session keys for each VPC or VCC for granted, which is referred to as ATM per-VC encryption. This results in reloading the session key to the DES/TripleDES key unit for each consecutive cell in the worst case. With reference to formula (1), this can result in reloading two session keys each 2.12 µs, if both the Rx, and the Tx direction transfer cells at the rate BW_{UTOPIA}. This is known as key agile encryption. At this point it is worth mentioning, that the VPI/VCI pair in the ATM cell header identifying a key is of length 28 bit at the NNI, 24 bit at the UNI respectively. This results in a huge key address space of 2^{24} at the UNI.

The problem of key agile encryption has been addressed in [19] by trading off silicon against computational power for performing key reloads. It was shown that alternately invoking multiple encryption cores for each direction results in a solution to the key agility problem, as due to introducing an artificial additional delay of one cell period t_{CELL} a sufficient period is given to fetch a session key whilst the previous ATM cell payload is being encrypted. However, further research has shown that the distribution of ATM cells to multiple cores requires complex control and key access logic, forming a tough stipulation at the clock rates required. Thus, an alternative was followed integrating a content addressable memory (CAM) into the encryption hardware. The CAM stores the session keys on very large scaled integrated (VLSI) encryption hardware. The basic architecture of the encryption hardware is shown in figure 7.

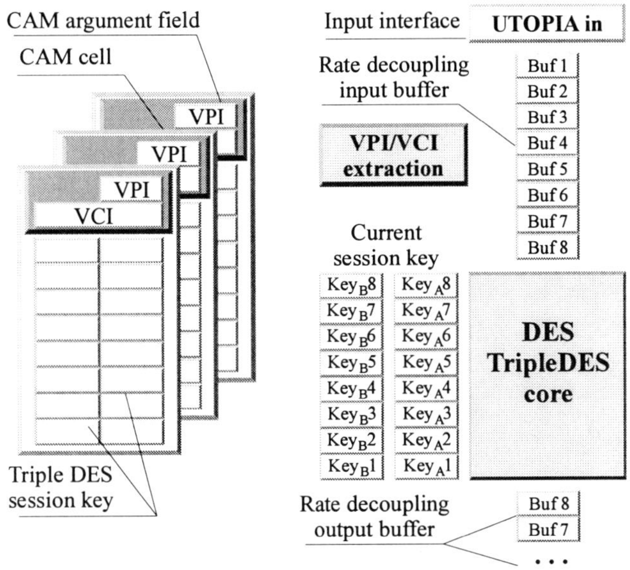

Figure 7. Architecture of the ATM encryption unit

One encryption core is needed in that approach for each direction Rx and Tx. The basic components of the encryption hardware shown in figure 7 are, as follows:

- Encryption core: The DES/TripleDES encryption unit consists of a core supporting electronic code book (ECB) and CBC operational mode, and a key unit holding the session key of the data currently processed. Obviously, the encryption core forms the throughput bottleneck when operating in TripleDES CBC mode. Cycle based simulation of the overall system has shown that an internal clock rate of almost 250 MHz is required. The performance critical components of the DES/TripleDES core unit have been designed in a full custom design methodology and have been simulated. For 0.6 µ and 0.8 µ complementary metal oxide semiconductor (CMOS) processes this has shown that the required performance can be achieved.
- Input, output interface: These are the UTOPIA interface modules to physically connect the encryption unit to the TC controller, respectively the SAR processor.
- Clock rate decoupling buffer: Buffers of at least eight octets decouple the UTOPIA clock from the internal clock of the encryption hardware in a way that the encryption core can request a subsequent block on demand, respectively forward an encrypted block to the output interface at its full internal clock rate. As stated above, the computational power of the encryption core is the throughput bottleneck of the system. Consequently, it is deliberately required that the encryption core suffers no congestion during handing over from one data block to the subsequent one. Furthermore, enhancing the buffer sizes shown as

eight octets in figure 4 by further five octets is required to optimize the performance during the ATM cell header to ATM cell payload transition phase.

- VPI/VCI extraction unit: VPI/VCI values are extracted from the cell header to address the session key needed to encrypt the ATM cell payload.
- CAM: Finally, a number of CAM cells consist of the VPI/VCI values associated with a negotiated session key as the CAM argument, respectively the session key itself. Note, that even if the encryption core unit supports CBC as operational mode, this feature is limited to a continuous data stream associated to one certain session key. Thus, for using the core in the statistically multiplexed ATM environment, the last encrypted block of an ATM cell is to be stored in the CAM as well, respectively has to be loaded to the DES unit with the first payload block of the subsequent ATM cell. In addition, information indicating the encryption algorithm and the operational mode is stored in the CAM. Depending on the sensitivity level of a certain communication, this allows to negotiate plain text transfer, DES, or TripleDES, as well as ECB and CBC separately for each VC.

Considering that one of main advantages of ATM is that a variety of communication profiles is supported, it is worth considering how the encryption scheme presented influences Quality of Services (QoS) parameters of services demanding in its delay requirements. With reference to figure 7, the additional delay caused by encryption is mainly caused by the period needed to encrypt one eight octet block, as traversing the buffers can be neglected. In fact this is the minimal delay to expect, if confidential communication is needed. As state-of-the-art ATM switches introduce delays of at least two to five cell periods, even if the ATM switch buffers are unloaded, the additional delay caused by the encryption unit can be neglected.

What has not been described within this key agility section so far is, how negotiated session keys are loaded to the encryption unit. The ATM Forum defines three methods to establish transparent end-to-end communication channels for negotiating session keys:

- Initial key exchange: Additional UNI signaling security information elements (IEs) are defined, supporting two way and three way key exchange methods to negotiate session keys during the VC establishment phase.
- User plane blocking: An alternative to the security IEs is to block the user plane immediately after a VC has been established and grant the key exchange protocol exclusive access to that VC. After the session keys have been established, the VC is handed over to the application. This approach is used as a workaround, if security IEs are not supported by the ATM switches.
- Key re-negotiation: To limit the lifetime of a certain key, re-negotiation of the session keys is performed using organization and maintenance (OAM) cell flows as an in-band security state maintenance channel.

To follow the approach of being independent of the hardware the encryption unit can be applied to, the session keys are transmitted to the encryption unit using OAM flows. As the OAM cells are transmitted to the encryption hardware via the UTOPIA, this results in a model that does not require hardware interfaces additional to that standardized one. It is worth mentioning at this place, that performing the key exchange protocol is done by a security entity within the signaling software. To cover both key exchange methods described above, namely the initial key exchange using security IEs, and the key re-negotiation using OAM flows, the local signaling security entity extracts the session keys negotiated with the remote security entity, and embeds these session keys to OAM cells. Finally, the local security entity transmits these OAM cells to the local encryption hardware, which extracts the session key and loads the session key to the CAM. The same procedure is invoked to update or release a key.

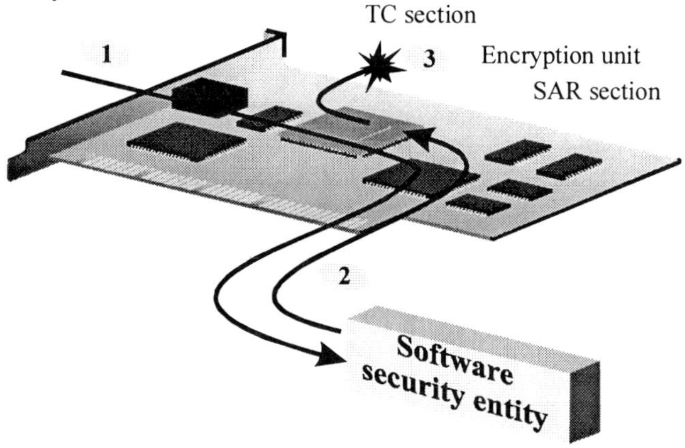

Figure 8. Key download sequence

The scenario of downloading session keys to the key agile encryption unit is shown in figure 8: Phase (1) represents the key negotiation taking place between the end-systems by the means of asymmetrical key exchange mechanisms. In phase (2) the session key is downloaded to the key agile encryption unit as a specific OAM cell. Finally, the encryption unit removes the session key download cell from the cell stream by dropping the cell in phase (3).

6. Conclusions

The paper has discussed a project targeting confidential communication in ATM networks. By comparing different approaches to ATM encryption, intercepting the ATM cell stream at a well-defined, standardized interface, namely the UTOPIA, has been identified as an approach fitting best to existing state-of-the-art ATM hardware components. Beside being compliant to the ATM Forum security specification, the main advantage of the resulting encryption hardware is the independence from the hardware used. Consequently, the DES/TripleDES hardware capable of handling the SONET OC3c rate can be integrated into existing ATM end user devices. In addition, by supporting UTOPIA the different physical media ATM is defined for are supported using the same encryption unit.

Per-VC encryption has been identified as a challenging task, as the statistical multiplexing of ATM cells requires a key agile encryption module. By integrating a CAM unit into the VLSI encryption hardware, key agility has been addressed, keeping the additional delay caused by encryption to a minimum, which is important to not affect the QoS of service classes sensitive to additional delays.

Acknowledgements

The development of the encryption hardware presented in this paper is funded by the European Commission, DG XIII, within the ACTS Programme, project Secure Communication in ATM Networks (SCAN), project number AC330.

References

[1] B. Khasnabish, "Broadband to the Home (BTTH): Architectures, Access Methods, and the Appetite for it", *IEEE Network,* January/February 1997, vol. 11, no. 1, pp. 58-69.

[2] E.J. Hernandez-Valencia, "Architectures for Broadband Residential IP Services Over CATV Networks", *IEEE Network,* January/February 1997, vol. 11, no. 1, pp. 36-43.

[3] K. Maxwell, "Asymmetric Digital Subscriber Line: Interim Technology for the Next Forty Years", *IEEE Communications Magazine,* October 1996, vol. 34, no. 10, pp. 100-106.

[4] Schulzrinne, H., *ATM: Dangerous at any Speed?*, Proceedings of IEEE Gigabit Networking Workshop GBN'95, Boston, Massachusetts, USA, 1995.

[5] D. Stevenson, N. Hillery, and G. Byrd, "Secure Communications in ATM Networks", *Communications of the ACM*, February 1995, vol. 38, no. 2, pp. 45-52.

[6] M. Peyravian, T. Tarman, "Asynchronous Transfer Mode Security", *IEEE Network,* May/June 1997, vol. 11, no. 3, pp. 34-40.

[7] Dobrowsky, G., (Ed.) *ATM User-Network Interface Version 3.1 Specification*, The ATM Forum, Technical Committee, 1994.

[8] Goguen, M. (Ed.), *Private Network-Network Interface Specification Version 1.0*, The ATM Forum, Technical Committee, 1996.

[9] ITU-T, *B-ISDN Protocol Reference Model and its Application*, Recommendation I.321, International Telecommunication Union, Telecommunication Standardisation Sector, 1991.

[10] I.F. Akyildiz, K.L. Bernhardt, "ATM Local Area Networks, A Survey of Requirements, Architectures, and Standards", *IEEE Communications Magazine*, July 1997, vol. 35, no. 7, pp. 72-80.

[11] Deng, R.H., L. Gong, and A.A. Lazar, *Securing Data Transfer in Asynchronous Transfer Mode Networks*, Proceedings of GLOBECOM'95, Singapore, 1995.

[12] Chuang, S.C., *Securing ATM Networks*, Proceedings of the ACM Conference on Computer and Communications Security, New Dehli, India, 1996.

[13] Forné, J., J.L. Melús, *An integrated solution for secure communications over B-ISDN*, Proceedings of 2nd Joint IFIP T6/TC11 Working Conference on Communications and Multimedia Security, Essen, Germany, 1996.

[14] Laurent, M., O. Paul, and P. Rolin, *Securing communications over ATM Networks*, Proceedings of 12th IFIP TC11 Conference SEC'97, Kopenhagen, Denmark, 1997.

[15] ANSI, *American National Standard for Data Encryption Algorithm (DEA)*, ANSI 3.92, American National Standards Institute, 1981.

[16] Tarman, T.D (Ed.), *ATM Security Specification Version 1.0 (Straw Ballot, February 1998)*, STR-SEC-01.01, The ATM Forum, Security Working Group, 1998.

[17] ANSI, *American National Standard for Information Systems-Data Encryption Algorithm-Modes of Operation*, ANSI 3.106, American National Standards Institute, 1983.

[18] ATM Forum, *Utopia Level 2, Version 1,* af-phy-039.000, The ATM Forum, Technical Committee, 1995.

[19] Leitold, H., R. Posch, *B-ISDN user-plane confidentiality by ATM cell stream intercepting encryption*, Proceedings of 3rd Joint IFIP T6/TC11 Working Conference on Communications and Multimedia Security, Athens, Greece, 1997.

Secure Signaling and Access Control for ATM Networks

Rajan Shankaran and Vijay Varadharajan
School of Computing and IT, University of Western Sydney, Nepean
PO Box 10, Kingswood, N.S.W 2747, Australia
Email: {rshankar,vijay}@cit.nepean.uws.edu.au

Abstract

Asynchronous Transfer Mode (ATM) is seen to be a technology that allows flexibility, efficiency and manageable bandwidth on demand to be achieved in high- speed networks. ATM is able to support a variety of applications including voice, video, image and data with different quality of service requirements. This paper addresses the design of security services in ATM networks. It considers the placement of a security layer between the AAL and the ATM layer that provides confidentiality, integrity and data origin authentication in the user plane. The paper then considers secure signaling and describes a public key based authentication and key management protocol that can be integrated as part of secure call setup. This protocol is part of an overall public key infrastructure framework for ATM networks. Finally the paper discusses the issues involved in the provision of access control service at the connection setup phase and the user data transfer phase.

1 Introduction

Computer networks are having a dramatic effect on the way we interact and communicate with one another. Although today's computer networks are capable of supporting many useful applications, they often inadequately address the needs of emerging multimedia applications with high bandwidth and real-time traffic requirements. Asynchronous Transfer Node (ATM) is often described as the technology that will allow flexibility and efficiency to be achieved in high-speed, multimedia networks. A basic attraction of ATM networks is their ability to carry different types of information, namely voice, data and video from one user to another over a local or a wide area. Therefore, it is clear that securing these different types of information over high speed ATM networks is critical. This paper addresses the issues involved in the design and implementation of security services in ATM networks.

The paper is organised as follows. Section 2 briefly introduces the ATM Protocol Reference Model (PRM) and section 3 considers the security services required to counteract security threats in ATM networks. Section 4 considers the option of placing the security layer between the AAL and the ATM layer in the user plane. It describes the design of confidentiality, integrity and data origin authentication services in the user plane. Section 5 addresses secure signaling in ATM networks. A peer entity authentication scheme and a key establishment protocol is considered and its integration with the existing signaling messages as part of ATM call setup is described. Section 6 discusses a public key infrastructure for ATM networks. Finally, section 7 considers the issues involved in the design of access control service in the user plane and the control plane.

2. ATM Protocol Reference Model

A diagrammatic representation of the ATM protocol reference model is shown in Figure 1. It is based on the standards developed by the ITU [1]. The model includes three planes, namely the user plane to exchange user information, the control plane to monitor signaling information and the management plane to maintain the network operations. The protocol reference model is divided into three layers: physical layer, the ATM layer and the ATM Adaptation Layer (AAL). The physical layer defines a transport method for ATM cells between two entities. It has a medium dependent sublayer (responsible for the correct transmission and reception of bits on the physical medium) and a transmission convergence sublayer (responsible for mapping the ATM cells to the transmission system used). The ATM layer is where transparent transfer

0-8186-8789-4/98 $10.00

of the fixed-size 53-byte cells or ATM service data units between communicating upper-layer entities is defined. The AAL defines a set of service classes to fit the needs of different user requests and converts incoming user requests for services into ATM cells for transport.

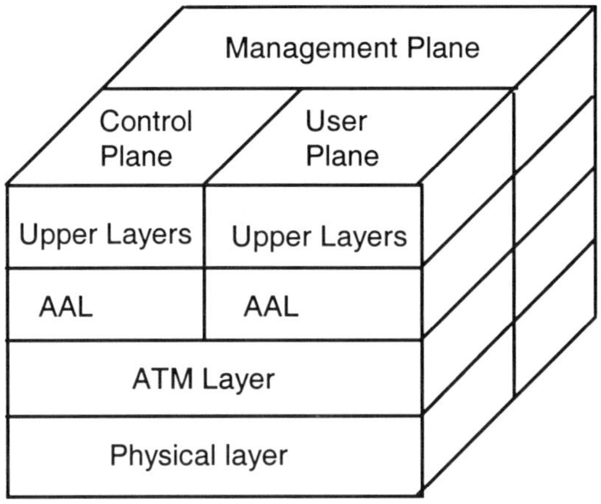

Figure 1 : The ATM Protocol Reference Model

3 Security Concerns

The fundamental issues that we need to consider when addressing security in networks are:

- Security services and mechanisms that are required
- Placement of security services in the protocol stack
- Management of security services and mechanisms

ATM networks are able to carry different types of information - voice, video and data - which can be of private and sensitive nature. Therefore, like any other network, ATM networks are susceptible to a variety of security threats and attacks. These include the following attacks : (a) violating the secrecy of the communications via eavesdropping, (b) confounding the receiver with corrupted messages via unauthorized modification of information, (c) deceiving either the sender or the receiver or both about the identity of the other party via masquerading, (d) denying a message has been received or sent via repudiation and (e) causing denial of service by either blocking access to the network or by continuous deletion or generation of messages so that the target is either depleted or saturated with meaningless messages. To counteract these threats we need security services such as information confidentiality, integrity, authentication, access control and non-repudiation. In general, to counteract the denial of service attack additional mechanisms over and above security mechanisms are required. We will not be considering this service separately in this paper, though other security services and mechanisms can help to detect some such attacks thereby reducing the degree of severity of this threat.

The high speed nature of ATM networks implies that potentially high volume of data can be transferred over ATM networks; this in turn may increase the necessity to change the keys more often than in other networks. This implies that some traditional full key distribution and management protocols may not be applicable in this situation. Furthermore, the separate out-of-band signaling path offers the opportunity for integrating the security management protocols such as key management as part of the signaling phase in the control plane.

4 Security Layer for User Data Transfer

In this section, we consider the provision of confidentiality, integrity and data origin authentication in the user plane. While the mechanisms which provide these services could be placed at different points in the ATM PRM, it is preferable to place them together. Placing them together will help to simplify the implementation of cryptographic mechanisms. Theoretically, it is possible to place the security mechanisms within or between any of the three main layers of the ATM PRM.

- Security functions in the Physical Layer, between the Physical and the ATM Layers and in the ATM Layer.
- Security functions in the AAL.
- Security functions between AAL and the ATM Layer.
- Security functions above the AAL.

The advantages and disadvantages of each of these options have been discussed in detail in [2]. We will only briefly summarize some of the major points.

If the security mechanisms are placed within the Physical Layer, then the entire 53 bytes of each ATM cell can be encrypted providing complete confidentiality. Such a placement also makes the security mechanism fully transparent to all higher layers. However, some major drawbacks are that the switches have to decrypt and re-encrypt the entirety of each cell, as the switches need to read the cell header to be able to route the cell itself involving high overheads. Furthermore, such a scheme will require a complex key management system in order to establish and manage keys in the switches as well as at the endpoints. Also, the payload in each cell would be vulnerable at the switch, as it will be in plain form since the entire cell needs to be decrypted. In addition, if integrity checking is done at this level then it will require additional segmentation functions, as the integrity operations necessarily add extra data thereby making the overheads unacceptable.

If the security layer is to be placed within the AAL, then the obvious site is between the segmentation and reassembly (SAR) and the convergence sublayers [3]. This allows the confidentiality and integrity services to operate on the CS-PDUs before they are broken into SAR-PDUs. The integrity check is performed on a CS-PDU block. The major issue associated with this option is in its practical implementation. Logically, it is possible to insert such a secure layer between the sublayers of the AAL. In practice, this approach may not be feasible as the AAL is usually implemented as a single unit, without a separate accessible interface between the sublayers. This is an important issue to take into account in any realistic proposal for ATM security.

The placement of security mechanisms *between* the ATM and the AAL makes them transparent to the adjacent layers. This also avoids the practical implementation problem noted above. In this case, the security mechanisms operate on the fixed size SAR-PDUs. The entire cell payload can be encrypted, as the header is added by the ATM layer below. However, cryptographic mechanisms may introduce data expansion. This is not a major problem, as there are mechanisms such as feedback chaining techniques and stream ciphers that can be used which do not cause data expansion. Providing integrity checking at this level does result in additional cell segmentation requirements. There is insufficient space available at the final SAR-PDU to add integrity checking. We suggest that an additional SAR-PDU is to be generated to support integrity service. In fact, this additional PDU can be used for cryptographic synchronization.

If the security layer is placed above the AAL (as in [4]), then the security functions operate on CS Service Data Units (SDUs). However, in general, there could be several different higher layers that may operate on top of the AAL Layer. Hence the interface of the security layer needs to be adapted to these different higher layers. With this approach, the responsibility for security is effectively passed onto to the upper layers and user applications. Furthermore, note that in this case all the ATM network header information (including those added by the AAL) will be in the clear.

4.1 Security Services Design

In our design, we have selected the option of placing the security layer is between the AAL and the ATM layer.

The confidentiality service is provided by encrypting the contents of the cell (without the header which is added by the ATM layer below) using a non-expanding encryption algorithm. Possible choices include the use of a block cipher algorithm such as the Data Encryption Standard (DES) in Stream Cipher Feedback mode (CFB) or in the Cipher Block Chaining mode (CBC) with the CFB mode for the end part of the message. The establishment of the key to be used in the encryption and decryption of messages is addressed later when we consider secure signaling and key management. At this stage, let us assume that a symmetric key for use in confidentiality service has been negotiated between the communicating entities and the key has been stored in some secure management information base (MIB) at their respective ends. We refer to this key as the confidentiality dialogue key (cdk). Both the cipher modes mentioned above require an Initialization Vector (IV). In fact, we refer to this IV as the confidentiality Initialization Vector (cIV). For a given cell stream, a cIV is chosen. The cIV will either be transmitted in-band or if this is the first transmission then it is transferred as part of the initial setup negotiation process.

The integrity service is provided using a cryptographic integrity checksum ICV. The ICV can be calculated in a number of ways; for instance, this may be done by producing a message digest using an encryption algorithm or using a strong one-way function (such as a strong hash function) and then encrypting or signing the message digest using appropriate symmetric key or private key (of a public key system). Our design uses the another symmetric dialogue key, called the integrity dialogue key (idk)[1] used in the calculation of the

[1] Though we present a general scheme with separate keys and IVs for confidentiality and integrity, in some circumstances, it

ICV, negotiated at the time of virtual channel establishment phase. The security layer calculates a single ICV for a given stream of SAR-PDUs. When the receiving entity calculates the ICV on the received data, any mismatch will cause the entity to discard that data and retransmission of this stream of SAR PDUs (cells) will be necessary. This makes the error recovery process easy to implement. While it may appear that the retransmission of a stream of cells poses an unnecessary performance degradation, selective retransmission would be harder to implement and would pose greater performance problems.

Assuming that the dialogue keys are securely established as explained below, the calculation of the ICV provides a limited form of data origin authentication. This is because only the two entities which have established the secure channel as part of the secure call setup procedures have access to the dialogue keys. Assume that the entities A and B have established the dialogue keys and that a message (a stream of cells) is received by B from A, together with the appropriate ICV. Given the correct ICV, B knows that the message could have only been generated by A or itself. If it did not generate the message, then it knows that the message can only come from A.

5 Secure Signaling in the Control Plane

In this section, we consider the design of peer authentication and key management service using the signalling protocol in the control plane. In the ATM signaling sequence, during the call setup phase, only the messages SETUP and CONNECT occur on an end-to-end basis; that is, these messages are carried transparently through the network to the endpoints. Therefore, given existing standards, the only option that we have is to design a two-way mutual authentication protocol and integrate it within this existing signaling framework. The integration is achieved by embedding the authentication messages in the end-to-end SETUP and CONNECT User to Network Interface (UNI) signaling messages. Using the terminology of Q.2931 [5], these authentication messages are referred to as Security Information Elements (SIEs). The secure signaling ATM architecture is shown in Fig.2.

may be sufficient to use a single dialogue key and IV to provide both confidentiality and integrity.

There are a number of existing protocols that can be used to provide mutual peer authentication and key distribution between the calling and the called parties. We propose a combined nonce and timestamp based peer entity authentication protocol based on X.509 [6]. The advantage of a combined nonce and timestamp scheme is that it helps to reduce the stringent requirements on the storage of the nonces. The window associated with the timestamps acts as the period for which the nonces need to be maintained to determine freshness. This in turn reduces the number of nonces that need to be stored at a given time. Our authentication protocol is an end to end protocol which implies that switches can be involved in the signaling process without having to deal with security related data.

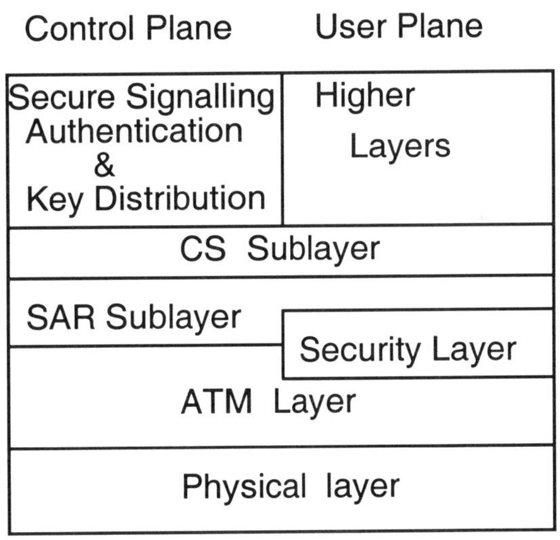

Figure 2 : Secure Signaling ATM Architecture

The secure call setup protocol requires security-related information to be transported between end systems. In the ATM signaling procedure, each message comprises several Information Elements, which carry connection specific information such as Called/Calling Party Identifiers and VCC address. The ATM UNI specification provides a large number of such Information Elements [1]. It also allows specification of additional IEs and furthermore these can be of variable sizes. We propose the following two new Security Information Elements (SIEs) that are required in our authentication and key distribution protocol described below.

Certificate IE: This IE specifies the identity of the communicating party and its certificate.

Authentication Token IE: This IE includes several sub-fields given below.

- SIE ID: This identifies the security information element. It contains a unique ID that has end to end significance. A version number is also associated with the IE.
- Security QoS Parameters (SQoS): This denotes Security related Quality of Service related Parameters such as the level and type of authentication (such as one-way, mutual), and the levels of confidentiality and integrity. The SQoS parameters in the SETUP message reflect the levels offered by the calling party and the ones returned in the CONNECT message denote the parameters chosen by the called party.
- Confidentiality Parameters (C-Pars): This denotes Confidentiality service related Parameters such as the list of algorithms, the size of IVs, block size, confidentiality keying information and information related to padding. Using this field, the sender provides a list of algorithms for confidentiality with the necessary parameters ordered according to its preferences. The receiver uses the corresponding SIE in the CONNECT message to identify the selected algorithm and its preferences.
- Integrity Parameters (I-Pars): This denotes Integrity service related Parameters such as the list of algorithms, the size of IVs, block size, integrity keying information and padding related information. Using this field, the sender provides a list of algorithms for integrity with the necessary parameters ordered according to its preferences. The receiver uses the corresponding SIE in the CONNECT message to specify the chosen algorithm and its preferences.
- Signature: The signature is computed over the SIE and optionally over a part of the signaling message.

Alternatively, we can split the Authentication Token IE and specify SIEs for SQoS, C-Pars and I-Pars. This would be helpful if different authentication protocols are to use the same SIEs.

5.1 Secure Call Setup Protocol

Notations used in the description of the protocol are as follows:

A, B: Identities of the two communicating parties.

SK_A, SK_B: Private keys of A and B respectively.

PK_A, PK_B: Public keys of A and B respectively.

C-Pars: Confidentiality operation parameters

I-Pars: Integrity operation parameters

Cert_A, Cert_B: Certificates of A and B respectively.

Kc_AB, Ki_AB: A's contribution to confidentiality (c) and integrity (i) dialogue keys.

Kc_BA, Ki_BA: B's contribution to confidentiality (c) and integrity (i) dialogue keys.

N_A: Nonce generated by A.

T_A: Timestamp generated by A.

{Message}SK_X: This notation implies <(H(Message))S_X>. That is, the hashed value of the message is signed using the private key of X. H is assumed to be a strong one way hash function such as the Secure Hash Standard (SHA) [7].

[Message]PK_Y : Message is encrypted using key PK_Y.

When A wishes to be authenticated by B, it sends its certificate and a new authentication token. These two security information elements (SIEs) form part of the SETUP message. Note that the SETUP message already includes other information elements such as Called Party Number, Calling Party Number and Connection Identifier. Hence these are not repeated here. It should be noted that a separate Security Association Identifier parameter is not included in the attribute list as we use the VPCI and VCI addresses to uniquely identify the security association. This is used to store and retrieve the keys and other parameters in the Secure Management Information Base.

Let us consider the following protocol steps.

A -> B: A, Cert_A, T_A, N_A, B, {T_A, N_A, B, C-Pars, I-Pars, SQoS, Kc_AB, Ki_AB}SK_A, [Kc_AB, Ki_AB, C-Pars, I-Pars, SQoS]PK_B.

This message contains a timestamp T_A and a nonce N_A to prove its freshness and to protect against replay attacks. A's contributions to both confidentiality and integrity dialogue keys are encrypted using the public key of the called party B. The security related parameters such as the SQoS, C-Pars and I-Pars are also protected using the public key of B. Furthermore, nonce, timestamp and other security related parameters are hashed and signed using the private key of A. The certificate of A is also sent.

Upon reception of the SETUP message, B verifies the certificate, and then uses the public key of A recovered from the certificate to verify the authentication token. It checks the integrity of the message and whether B itself is the intended recipient. It checks the timestamp and the nonce to establish whether the message is fresh. It also extracts the security association parameters from the message. If the checks fail or if the security related QoS is not acceptable to B, then it sends a RELEASE COMPLETE message. Otherwise, it sends a CONNECT message which contains the following:

B -> A: B, Cert_B, T_B, N_A, A, {T_B, N_A, A, C-Pars, I-Pars, SQoS, Kc_BA, Ki_BA}SK_B, [Kc_BA, Ki_BA, C-Pars, I-Pars, SQoS]PK_A.

B sends to A its certificate along with its authentication token. The token includes A's random number N_A proving to A that the message is fresh and is a reply to A's request. The token also contains B's contribution to the dialogue keys encrypted under the public key of A. The security related parameters SQoS, C-Pars and I-Pars indicate the choices selected by B from the ranges proposed by A in the SETUP message. A upon receiving the message verifies B's signature to check if the message originated at B. It checks whether the timestamp is current and the received random number N_A is identical to the one it sent earlier. It then extracts the key K_BA as well as the security association parameters accepted by B. If the checks fail or if the security related QoS is not acceptable to A, then a RELEASE message is sent terminating the connection; otherwise CONNECT ACKNOWLEDGE message is sent to B.

Now A and B can use Kc_AB and Kc_BA to form the confidentiality dialogue key. This could be done using any publicly known agreed function. Similarly, Ki_AB and Ki_BA can be combined to form the integrity dialogue key. We have used contributions from each of the communicating parties in the calculation of the dialogue keys. Other options include either A or B generating the dialogue keys and sending it to the other.

This procedure completes the establishment of security association related attributes and the authentication process in conjunction with the VCC setup. Furthermore, the negotiation of security related quality of service parameters during the call setup phase enables the two communicating entities to establish a common set of security capabilities between them for their communications.

7. Secure Signaling and PKI

The authentication and key management protocol proposed above assumes that a public key infrastructure (PKI) is in place within the ATM environment. In this section, we outline a PKI model for ATM networks and consider the protocols necessary to facilitate secure communication between the ATM nodes and the PKI authorities.

Logically, a large ATM network can be divided into different certification domains each of which has a CA which fits in the overall hierarchy of CAs. A node in a given domain registers its public key with the CA of that domain. That is, the domain CA vouches for the public key of a node that resides within its domain. Every node residing within a domain has access to the public key of the CA of that domain. In the case where the two nodes wishing to communicate with each other reside within the same certification domain, they can validate each other's public key certificate using their CA's public key.

When the two nodes reside in two different domains, there are two common ways of achieving inter-domain certification:

1. Hierarchical Certifications: The first approach uses the hierarchical certification model. For instance, we can have a root CA similar to the IETF's [8] Internet Policy Registration Authority. This root CA certifies the public key of every CA that is immediately beneath it and this process is followed recursively. At the bottom most level, the leaf CA certifies the public keys of nodes below it. In order for the nodes to communicate, the source node sends to the destination node a full certification path, that is, its own certificate along with every superior CA's certificate up to the root CA. The assumption here is that every node knows the root CA's public key.
2. Cross Certification: Alternatively, if there exists cross-certification between CAs, then

this helps to shorten the certification path. Cross-certification involves two CAs certifying each other directly without going through their higher level CAs. Therefore, greater the number of such cross certification links, in general, shorter the certification paths. However cross-certification between two CAs involve prior communication between them, which can be part of inter-CA registration process.

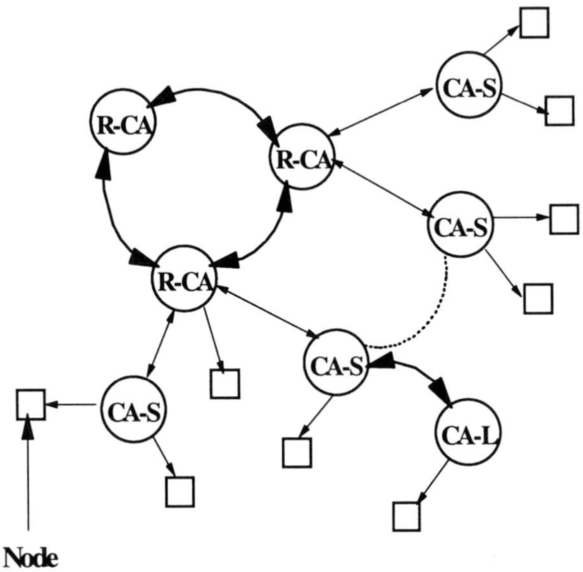

R-CA : Root CA(R-CA)

S-CA : Subordinate CA

L-CA : Leaf CA(L-CA)

Figure 3 : PKI Model for ATM Networks

Let us consider a hybrid structure which forms the building block of ATM PKI. This is similar to the one proposed in [9]. The ATM environment is split into domains each of which is governed by a root CA. There could be several hierarchical tree paths existing under this root CA (Figure 3). Every subordinate CA in the hierarchical tree must have a defined path leading to the root CA. The root CAs of these domains cross certify each other. This mechanism is more practical as it does not insist on the presence of a single root CA. Subordinate CAs of one domain may also cross certify other subordinate CAs in other domains. However, if a root CA as well as the subordinate CA are part of the same organisation, then certain organisational constraints are likely to be imposed based on the overall security policy of the organisation. Each node maintains the public key of the root CA and the public key of the parent CA (which issued its certificate) along with the certification path all the way up to the root. The node also maintains all the cross certificates issued by a CA in its certification path. Each CA maintains the public key of the root CA, public key of parent CA, certification path up to the root along with cross certificate and other access control information.

The ATM PKI protocols allow the end nodes and CAs to transfer PKI messages between them using the existing ATM signaling procedures. In this paper, we only consider the initial registration and certification phase. The full report [10] describes message structures and protocols in detail for subordinate CA registration and certification, cross-certification and certificate revocation.

7.1 Registration and Certification

There are several schemes that can be used to achieve initial registration and certification of end nodes. No one method is suitable for all situations due to a range of policies which a CA may support. Initial registration and certification refers to the situation where the end node has not had any previous contact with the PKI. Where the end node already has certified keys then some simplifications are possible.

One scheme would be to assume that the registration of the public key occurs in some out-of-band manner. Another possibility could involve the use of some out-of-band information to establish an initial session key between the end node and its CA. This session key is then used to protect the registration and certification messages between the CA and the end node. The end node sends a certification request along with its public key. We assume that the end node has the capability to generate a public key - private key pair. The certification request is protected using the initial session key which is only known to the CA and the end node. Furthermore the end node needs to prove to the CA that it has the private key corresponding to the public key for which the certificate is being requested. Alternatively, the CA can be trusted to generate the public key - private key pair; in this case, the CA must be trusted to destroy the private key once it has been sent to the end node. From a security point of view, it is advisable to avoid the latter alternative.

The certification request from the end node is sent as part of the overall call SETUP message of the signaling procedure. The security information element (SIE) included in the message is signed using the private key of the end node and then encrypted using the session key shared between the

CA and the end node. Let us now briefly outline some of the relevant fields in this SIE.

- Message Reference Number: This number enables the CA to correlate the message with a previously issued reference number (obtained by out-of-band means).
- Source ID: Identity of the end node making the certification request.
- Destination ID: Identity of the issuing CA.
- Timestamp: Time at which this message was generated.
- Certificate Version: This field is intended to facilitate orderly changes in the certificate format over time. By specifying this field, the end node is able to request a particular version of the certificate.
- Serial Number: Serial number uniquely identifies a certificate generated by an issuing CA. No two certificates issued by the same CA can contain the same serial number.
- PKInfo: This contains the public key of the node to be incorporated into the certificate.
- Signing Alg: The algorithm used by the node to sign this information element.
- Signature: This contains the signature of the information element.

CA can verify the request using the shared session key, retrieve the public key from the SIE and validate the signature. If the checks are successful, then the CA responds by generating the node certificate and sending it to the node as part of the CONNECT message. The SIE generated by the CA is then encrypted using the session key and is included in the response message. The fields in this SIE are as follows:

- Message Reference Number: Same as that was used in the certificate request SETUP message.
- Status: This field specifies the status of the response by the CA: Granted, Granted with Modification, Rejected. In the case of rejection, the rest of the fields in the SIE are left blank.
- PK-CA: The public key of the issuing CA. (Immediate parent of the node).
- PK-RootCA: The public key of the root CA in the domain.
- PrivK: Private key of the end entity in case CA generates the key pair.
- Certificate: The certificate of the requesting node.
- CertPath: This contains the certification path from the node to the root. This also includes all the cross certificates issued by a CA in that certification path.
- CRLPath: Certification Revocation List (CRL) path from the node to the root. This also includes the current copy of the CRL issued by the parent CA.
- Digital Signature: The entire IE is signed by the CA using its private key.

8. Access Control

Access control is concerned with preventing unauthorised use of network resources. For instance, within a computer system, the threat corresponds to users and processes accessing files, memory or processor without authorisation. Over a network, the threat may be in the form of access to a network resource. This may be a simple component such as a printer or a terminal, or a more complex one such as a database or some applications within a database. In the case of ATM networks, access control is primarily concerned with whether a connection is authorised to proceed. An access control mechanism specifies and enforces an authorisation policy, which is a set of rules defining the conditions under which one entity can access another. Typical access control mechanisms by means of which such policies can be implemented include access control lists, capabilities and security labels. While the mechanism may be product specific, the format of the access control information needs to be in a standardised form if interoperability is to be achieved. We now consider what types of access control mechanisms that are required at both the call setup phase as well as the user data transfer phase.

8.1 Access Control in the Call Setup Phase

Access control rules during the call setup phase are to be associated on a per connection basis rather than on a per packet basis. This implies that for every host to host communication, a security association is created on a per virtual channel basis during the call setup. Such access control rules can be implemented in a firewall placed at the boundary between a trusted and an untrusted network. In the case of an ATM network environment such a firewall can be placed between the wide area public WAN and the local area networks. In practice, such a firewall and access control rules can be realised within an ATM switch. For instance, consider a host A in LAN1 sending a SETUP message over a WAN to establish a call with another host B in LAN2. Firewall F1 resides at the boundary between LAN1 and WAN and the firewall F2 resides between WAN and LAN2. This SETUP message is intercepted by the firewall F1 and it ensures that the access control policies at the source end are satisfied in terms of whether the requested connection is allowed or not. It may optionally add appropriate security information to the original SETUP message to indicate that this request has been verified by the firewall. Such information can include security parameters such as A's and F1's identities and other information such as sensitivity level indicators and types of algorithms supported by the network. These are included as security related information as part of the authentication token SIE. These additional information are signed using the private key of the firewall F1. Any sensitive parameters are also encrypted using the public key of F2. F2 ensures that the request is conformance with the access policies of its local site LAN2. F2 now forwards the setup message to host B. If the access rules are not satisfied, F2 sends a RELEASE message. After receiving the SETUP message, B responds by sending a CONNECT message. Now, F2 sends a CONNECT1 message with appropriate return SIEs. When F1 receives the CONNECT1 message, it forwards the appropriate CONNECT message to host A. The flow of messages in this modified call setup protocol is shown in Figure 4

Once the call setup phase is complete, a virtual circuit is established between the calling and the called host via the firewalls. Since the firewalls intercept the call setup messages, they have the ability to deny access from the network for any call that does not confirm to the security policies of their local sites.

8.2 Access Control : Data Transfer Phase

The firewalls should be capable of validating and filtering ATM cells without slowing down the high-speed traffic which flows through it. Therefore, a cell by cell filtering technique is not acceptable as it might hamper the throughput considerably. Our approach recommends the insertion of an access control label (which is negotiated as part of the call setup messages) within each CS PDU. At the receiving firewall, if the label happens to be within the allowed range, then the corresponding C S PDU is transferred; if not, the entire CS PDU is discarded. As with any other label based access control schemes, it is necessary to have a trusted process that associates security labels with the information.

8.3 Secure Management Information Base

Conceptually, a Security Management Information Base (SMIB) stores the security information that is required for configuring and managing secure associations in ATM networks. These information are stored in the form of managed objects. Each managed object is defined by its attributes, a set of management operations, and internal actions and notifications which the managed object translates into management messages. In practice, such a SMIB is implemented in a distributed manner. In general, the objects in the SMIB fall into two categories system objects and secure connection objects. The system objects apply to the entire system regardless of any individual connection whereas secure connection objects are tied to specific virtual channel connections.

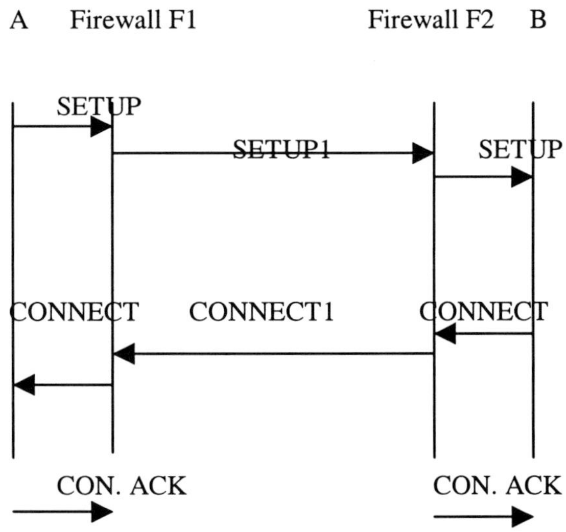

Figure 4: Secure Call Setup with Firewall

System objects declare properties and resources supported by a particular system implementing the ATM security layer. These objects are divided into several categories such as Conf-Alg, Integ-Alg, Sec-Labels, Sec-Context, Trust-Auth and Domain. Each of these is represented as an object type. For instance, Conf-Alg specifies the characteristics of an encryption algorithm supported by the local network system such as DES and RSA. It identifies the modes of operation, block size, key lengths, the synchronisation information required and Initialisation Vector characteristics. Similarly, the Integ-Alg object specifies the characteristics of the algorithm used to produce the integrity checksum value. For instance, this can be defined using a message digest algorithm followed by a signature algorithm. Sec-Labels object declares a single security label or a range of security labels accepted by the local network system. It defines the value of the label as well as the authority issuing the labels. The Sec-Context specifies the types of security services supported and their characteristics. The Trust-Auth object specifies the parties that are trusted by the network system such as the Certification Authority. The Domain object includes all the necessary information which permits the identification of the local system within its domain.

The Secure Connection type object specifies the characteristics of the connection. These include the security context in use, the encryption algorithm in use, the keys used for encryption and decryption, the initialisation vectors used in the confidentiality and integrity algorithms, the signature key used, the security label attached to the CS PDUs, and VCI/VPI of the secure association.

9 Conclusions

In this paper, we have considered the provision of security services in ATM networks. Security services for the protection of user data such as confidentiality, integrity and data origin authentication have been incorporated within a layer placed between the AAL and the ATM layer. By placing the security layer at the ATM-AAL layer interface, we have transparently integrated the security mechanisms within the PRM thereby avoiding the possibility of impinging upon the functionality of any of the layers within the PRM. Then the paper considered the provision of additional security services such as peer entity authentication, key establishment and secure call setup. We considered a peer entity authentication and key establishment protocol and its integration within the existing ATM signaling procedures as part of the overall call setup messages. Our approach is based on the use of public keys and enables the two communicating parties to establish dialogue keys as well as the exchange of cryptographic related parameters such as the IV and other security attributes. We have also outlined how such a public key based authentication protocol can fit into an overall public key infrastructure for ATM networks. Finally the paper discussed the issues involved in the provision of access control mechanisms both at connection setup phase and user data transfer phase. Access control mechanisms at the connection phase can be realised using firewalls which separate the untrusted and trusted domains of the network. ATM firewalls can administer access control by intercepting ordinary connection calls from the hosts and by verifying whether they conform to the security policies of the local sites. Firewalls can perform mutual authentication and negotiate security contexts during the virtual channel connection setup. Access control in the user plane can be achieved by associating security labels with the CS PDUs. The full report [10] compares our approach to security in ATM networks with other related work [4, 11,12,13,14].

10 References

[1] D.Ginsburg. ATM: Solutions for Enterprise Internetworking, Addison-Wesley Longman 1996.

[2] V.Varadharajan, R.Shankaran and M.Hitchens "A Practical Approach to the Design and Management of Secure ATM Networks", Proc. of the 20th National Information Systems Security Conference 1997.

[3] R.H. Deng et al, *"Securing data transfer in asynchronous transfer mode networks"*. Proceedings of Globecom' 95, Singapore, 1995.

[4] M. Laurent et al, *"Securing communications over ATM networks"*. In Proceedings of IFIP SEC'97 Security Conference, Copenhagen, Denmark, 1997.

[5] ITU-T, Q.2931, B ISDN Application Protocols for Access Signaling, 1995.

[6] ITU-T, X.509 The Directory Authentication Framework. Revised 1992.

[7] NIST Federal Information Processing Standards (FIPS), Secure Hash Algorithm Standard, Revised 1995.

[8] IETF, Internet Public Key Infrastructure, http://www.ietf.org/security/

[9] W.Burr, Federal Public Key Infrastructure Technical Specifications, 1995.

[10] R.Shankaran, Security in ATM Networks, Thesis, University of W.Sydney, 1998, In Prepartion.

[11] S.C.Chuang, *"Securing ATM networks"*, Proc. of the Third ACM Conf. On Computer and Communication Security, 1996.

[12] ATM Forum, Phase 1 ATM Security specification, ATM Forum 95-1473R5, 1996.

[13] M.Peyravian and T.Tarman, "Asynchronous Transfer Mode Security", IEEE Network, Vol.11, No.3, May/June 1997.

[14] D.Stevenson et.al, "Secure Communication in ATM Networks", Communications of ACM, Vol.38, No.2, Feb.1995.

Security Services in an Open Service Environment

Reiner Sailer
Institute of Communication Networks and Computer Engineering
University of Stuttgart, Pfaffenwaldring 47, D-70569 Stuttgart, Germany
sailer@ind.uni-stuttgart.de

Abstract

Emerging telecommunication services use, store, or transmit sensitive personal data to form individual network services. We suggest an add-on approach to realize secure telecommunication services which saves the huge investments into existing network infrastructure of the ISDN. This is done by adding trusted runtime environments that contain security functions to existing service infrastructure. This approach aims at separating sensitive service functions from highly complex functions of public telecommunication networks. We propose an enhancement of existing network service interfaces by standardized security service interfaces to enable the provision of open security services. Separated security control functions of independent service providers, however, might not be trusted by network operators. Therefore, this contribution particularly considers gateway functions implementing access control and ancillary conditions concerning network integrity.

1 Introduction

The term t*elecommunication service* (also called *service)* denotes a set of related functions of telecommunication systems that support a certain communication between remote terminal equipment or between terminal equipment and central servers located within networks. Telecommunication services are classified in terms of bearer services and teleservices. This classification bases on the location of those functions that are involved in a service.

Bearer services only include functions of the network. Consequently, bearer services support switched connections between terminals or between terminals and centralized network infrastructure (e. g. servers). *Teleservices* base on bearer services and additionally include functions within terminal equipment or shared network servers.

We discuss telecommunication services as applications, because they evolve to be used independently of data channels in the future. Furthermore, teleservices process more and more personal data and are no longer restricted to a single telecommunication network.

This work has been funded by the Gottlieb Daimler- and Karl Benz-Foundation (Ladenburg, Germany) as part of its Kolleg *Security in Communication Technology*.

Generally, requirements on telecommunication services concerning security are described in terms of *confidentiality, integrity* and *availability.* These terms are broadly known and understood. Security requirements must be related to objects (data or functions that are to be protected) to form *security goals*.

Def.: Services that offer a verifiable "degree of security" by use of security functions are called *security services*. Thereby, a security function directly contributes to the implementation of security goals.

Consequently, security services satisfy certain security requirements in a comprehensible way. They comprise both security enhanced conventional services and new services.

Def.: A *service is called secure* concerning one party, if and only if all security goals of this party with respect to this service are fulfilled in a comprehensible way.

Fig. 1 illustrates the classification of telecommunication services depending on the location of the respective service functions. The proposed "add-on" approach shows: conventional teleservices plus additional security functions enable (i) security enhanced telecommunication services (e. g. anonymous calls, encrypted data transfer) and (ii) new autonomous security services (e. g. public key certificate retrieval services). In doing so, added security functions are executed on security enhancements of terminal equipment (e. g. security modules, [18]) or on trusted servers reachable over telecommunication networks (Fig. 1).

Signalling systems are used by distributed service functions to exchange synchronization data in order to interactively realize complete telecommunication services. In ISDN, we distinguish signalling protocols applied at user network interfaces (UNI, e. g. DSS1, [7]) and at network node interfaces (NNI, e. g. SS7, [12]). There are additional protocols that enhance the signalling interface between network nodes and centralized service nodes of the Intelligent

0-8186-8789-4/98 $10.00 © 1998 IEEE

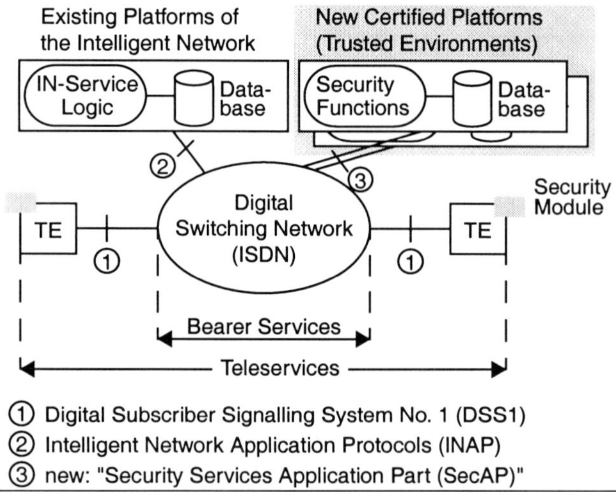

Figure 1: Services and interfaces of the ISDN / IN

Network (INAP, [13]). The ISDN user part (ISUP, [12]) bases on the SS7 and includes functions to setup and clear connections in ISDN (not explicitly shown in Fig. 1).

We focus on teleservices that span functions within terminal equipment, network nodes and certified service platforms. Today's value-added services are realized by use of the so called Intelligent Network (IN). The IN has mainly been introduced to accelerate service creation and service provision. In its current peculiarity, the respective IN application protocols are not flexible enough to serve as a basis for open and network independent security services.

Therefore, enhancements of the user network signalling system (DSS1, see Fig. 1) are proposed that support the synchronization of security services. These protocols are summarized as Security Supplementary Services (SSS).

Furthermore, there is need for additional signalling protocols between core network functions and specialized security service functions (interface 3 in Fig. 1). Following the naming convention of existing users of the SS7, these new application level protocols altogether are referred to as the Security Services Application Part (SecAP).

This contribution introduces open service interfaces that enable trusted service functions to be included into existing telecommunication services. In addition, standardized protocols are added (SecAP basing on SS7, SSS basing on DSS1) that support the synchronization of distributed security functions. The proposed interfaces promote an evolution of existing telecommunications infrastructure to satisfy currently ignored and evolving security goals.

Arising obstacles – resulting of requirements like robustness and autonomy of existing telecommunication services of the ISDN – introduced by enhancements of open interfaces form an interesting research area and are particularly addressed within this contribution.

Challenges concerning the addition of security functions to existing service infrastructure are discussed in section 2. In section 3, a domain concept is introduced that leads to efficient and effective location strategies for security functions in heterogeneous service environments. The application of the domain concept to single communication systems and communication networks is described in section 4. Proposals for more efficient gateway functions (firewall functions, etc.) that secure signalling interfaces against outsider attacks complete section 4. Finally, section 5 illustrates the use of open security signalling interfaces by an exemplary anonymity service.

2 Challenges and related work

There are several possibilities to allocate security functions. Security functions serving users should be located as close to the user as possible, e. g. within security modules, user terminals, or additional black boxes controlled by users. The allocation of security functions serving users within telecommunication networks is justified if and only if they contribute to or profit from the following attributes:

- availability of security functions or security control data (e. g. certificates)
- centralized operation, administration, and maintenance
- economy of scales (e. g. shared use of very expensive highly secure runtime environments)

As the public ISDN was not planned to fulfil developing security requirements, we must search for possibilities to integrate new security infrastructure into existing networks. This infrastructure must satisfy existing and emerging security requirements. One way to reach this goal is to provide interfaces over which remote security service functions may interact with core network functions.

Based on these interfaces, it is possible to cope with changing requirements of users, service providers and network operators. Security goals stated for telecommunication services may differ, depending on the parties involved. The next definition extends the definition of secure services related to a single party to a definition taking into account security needs of all parties, affected by a service:

Def.: A telecommunication service is called *multilaterally secure*, if and only if security goals of all parties, that are affected by this service, are taken into account in a balanced way.

Affected parties include subscribers, users, network operators, service providers, and manufacturers. Concerning multilateral security, it is not necessary that all security goals are guaranteed because they may be inconsistent with one another.

The definition of multilaterally secure services is not as strong as the definition of secure services concerning one party. But it is the strongest definition addressing the security needs of all parties that are affected by a service.

2.1 Requirements of security services

We discuss security services that base on the signalling systems SS7 and DSS1. These services should be independent of a specific network infrastructure and therefore must base on open and standardized interfaces. Security functions must be located wherever sensitive data appears. Therefore, they must be distributed over different networks to realize global security services. For this reason, synchronization of respective service functions – i. e. the exchange of control data – extends across network boundaries.

Fig. 2 shows *distributed security functions* that cooperatively form security services. Addressing and access to services supported by existing signalling networks is done over service access points (SAP^{Sec}). Supplementary functions included in Fig. 2 provide means for the exchange of security control data between communication systems that host distributed security functions (addressing, routing, link functions, security message and parameter types).

Services of the signalling network (SS7) and the user network signalling (DSS1) must be enhanced to offer this kind of supplementary services. An adaptation sublayer enhances DSS1 to provide SAP^{Sec} (see section 4.1); the enhancement of SS7 is included within SecAP. The SAP^{Sec} must be an open and standardized interface in order to enable flexible use of such interfaces by different implementations of security functions or plug-in security modules.

Protocols describe the messages, their interpretation by receiving entities (here: security functions), and the synchronization of associated distributed security functions. These protocols between security functions will differ at the UNI and NNI. At the UNI these protocols are summarized as Security Supplementary Services Protocols (SSS).

These protocols are mostly used to support end-to-end security services or access to shared security servers reachable over the network. They base on SAP^{Sec} service interfaces. At the NNI these protocols are called Security Services Application Part (SecAP). The SecAP not only enables access to central security services, but also provides means to link security functions and existing services (e. g. services basing on the ISUP). Interworking between SSS and SecAP protocols can be done within local exchanges. This enables network operators, to control the services accessed by use of their network infrastructure (see also section 4) over the UNI. Requirements on environments for distributed security functions form a first challenge:

Challenge 1 – Environmental Requirements: Security functions need *secure runtime environments*. They must share *means for synchronization*, i. e. means for the exchange of security control information. Security functions need open service access points to interact with core network services (SAP^{Sec} in Fig. 2). Standardized protocols (SSS, SecAP) are needed for the interaction of different implementations of security functions forming security services. There must be mechanisms *to link security functions with existing services* in order to achieve secure telecommunication services.

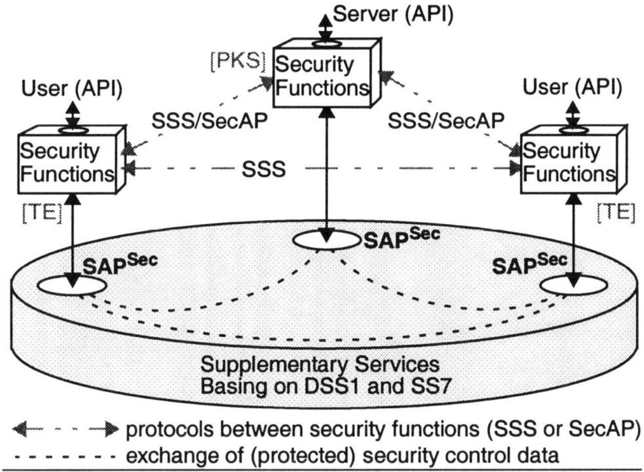

Figure 2: Protocols and SAPs for security services

Authentication services and public key certificate retrieval services are examples of autonomous security services. Authentication processes within the users' terminal equipment (TE, see Fig. 2) exchange authentication tokens within signalling messages (e. g. by use of SAP^{Sec} basing on services of the underlying SS7 or DSS1).

In this example, the terminals retrieve the required public key certificates from a public key certificate server (PKS) reachable over the network. An interaction of the related security functions with existing network services is not necessary. This kind of security services is called autonomous. Autonomous services only depend on the underlying signalling network in order to exchange security control information (authentication tokens, public key certificates, valid certificate revocation lists).

Within user terminals, of course, also autonomous security services may be linked with conventional telecommunication services to achieve secure telecommunication services. This means for example, that a connection setup may be admitted if and only if an accompanying authentication has been completed successfully. From a network service view, end-to-end authentication and connection setup are independent from each other. However, they can be linked within user terminals on demand. Which conventional services are combined with which security services is a matter of the security policy applied.

Assume a security service that satisfies security goals concerning one party. Consequently, respective service functions that form this security service must run on a runtime environment that is trusted by this party. Otherwise the security functions may be compromised and no matter what security goals are demanded by a party, the resulting service will not satisfy them in a comprehensible way. Concerning different parties that are affected by telecommunication services, areas of tension include:

- access control to network, service, or terminal resources
- access control to sensitive user data processed by core network services or value-added services
- call accounting and billing

Some areas of tension are negligible, if network operator and service provider are identical. More conflicting security goals appear, if several network operators or service providers are involved in a single service (see example in section 5).

Challenge 2 – Inclusion of Trusted Third Parties: There is need for trusted runtime environments and trusted service functions within service processing. In order to enable multilaterally secure services, there is need for the interaction of core network service functions with security service functions hosted in remote runtime environments. Accordingly, we need *interfaces to include functions of TTPs* into existing telecommunication services.

It is quite unlikely that there will be a single TTP that is trusted by all participating parties. Therefore, a logical "Common Trusted Third Party" will comprise of several TTPs that interact to solve conflicting security goals.

2.2 Requirements concerning network integrity

Especially, requirements of users and network operators concerning the robustness and autonomy as prerequisites of *network integrity* must be explicitly addressed by solutions that shall enhance network and service security. We quote from some other literature to backup the outstanding relevance of these aspects of network security:

Recent public network outages have shown that robustness and autonomy are really threatened even by existing signalling and service interfaces and by network functions that are mainly controlled by experienced operating personal. J. C. McDonald concluded in [4] – with respect to SS7 outages in 1988 – that the most serious mistake was to rely on an assumption that major failures could not happen. Another mistake was to ignore the serious consequences of large computer network failures in terms of economic disruption and the loss of industry credibility.

An assumption made by K. Ward [5], that "the integrity problems are fundamentally concerned with network control; that is, the transmission and processing of control information" has proven to be valid.

Concerning the telecommunication infrastructure, new threats arise by processing control data that originates from external security service infrastructure. Falsified control data may cause huge damage within telecommunication networks. The most severe consequences include:

- network nodes crash because of software failures
- network functions are manipulated (e. g. accounting)
- unauthorized and unrecognized access to network functions (e. g. administration accounts, service profiles)

Because software and hardware are very complex and are subject to permanent changes, it cannot be excluded that forged or incorrectly composed signalling messages also harm network infrastructure that only routes and forwards these messages. Even signalling network functions of the Message Transfer Part of the signalling system (layers 1 to 3) are subject to attacks concerning the availability and integrity of network nodes. As a consequence, also the availability and integrity of services depending on such network nodes are threatened. In addition, the network load introduced by the exchange of security control data is subject to accounting, at least if the related security service is not correlated with the network provider offering the exchange capabilities.

Consequently, there is need for access control concerning (security) control data before it is processed within the network. Concerning security services, the related access control functions have to be included in the path between security functions that are not (or not equally) trusted.

Open security signalling interfaces (protocols for the exchange of security control data between distributed security functions) support *security gateway functions* by offering standardized identifiers that enable protection by screening and filtering. Thus, open interfaces enable network operators to switch dedicated security functions on and off and to react quickly to misuse of service features or to software errors that might be exploited by attackers.

Challenge 3 – Network Integrity: Interconnecting separated service infrastructure with core network infrastructure implies *the need for strong security gateways to screen and filter on control data* that originates from separated security infrastructure or other networks (not equally trusted infrastructure) before this data is processed within or transported by the respective telecommunication network.

Finally, there must be fall-back mechanisms to ensure network operation even without the availability of additional security service functions to maintain the autonomy and robustness of today's ISDN services.

2.3 Related work

Concerning environmental requirements (challenge 1), there is a lot of ongoing work. Security modules as a runtime environment for security functions are discussed in [18]. End-to-end security functions are discussed in [1], [8], [9], and many other contributions. Solutions to anonymity services are discussed in [6] and [19], but their implementation within existing service environments is not straightforward. Compatibility of security functions is promoted by the ATM Forum [20]. It agrees on broadly applicable encoding and algorithms that are used in ATM user network signalling and network node signalling protocols.

Regarding the inclusion of TTPs into network services (challenge 2), there is a long way to go. Secure runtime environments for TTPs are already in use, but neither are they connected to networks for on-line access via signalling nor are there any standardized protocols to include such TTPs into network service provision.

Referring to network integrity connected with control data originating from external network infrastructure (challenge 3), a lot of firewall-like solutions have been proposed for public networks (e. g. Q.705, [12]). Gateway functions are established at network boundaries that block all except basic and verified signalling messages. By this, unauthorized manipulative or accidental control of internal network functions caused by processing foreign control data is restricted. Mostly, these gateway functions have a very bad granularity and a lot of services do not work over network boundaries. There is some work on firewalls for IP networks (dynamic filtering, etc.) that might improve existing solutions if applied to SS7 and DSS1. Today, mainly screening and filtering is applied at these gateways. No cryptographic functions are currently applied. Therefore, the authenticity of control messages arriving over transit networks can't be verified. The worth of screening and filtering such messages is therefore restricted.

3 Domain concept – separation & mediation

The domain concept introduced here bases on an early article by Rushby and Randell [14]. Their idea is developed to a method whose application promotes assessable and scalable security in heterogeneous service environments.

A domain is characterized by *uniform* threats, assumptions about attackers, security goals, and ancillary conditions concerning security. The domain boundaries are supervised by gateways. Consequently, a domain is a part of a service environment that can be secured independently from other parts of the service environment. In order to enable interaction of associated parts of the service environment over domain boundaries, data can enter or leave a domain by means of so called mediation functions. Mediation functions implement access control functionality.

Fig. 3 shows a telecommunication network that is divided into five different domains. For example, functions within domains A, B and TTP may interact to realize security services (exchange of control data: type 1, 2 in Fig. 3). The figure illustrates also remote access to TTPs (type 3 in Fig. 3), whereby the supporting operator of the signalling network may account the exchange of control data by flat

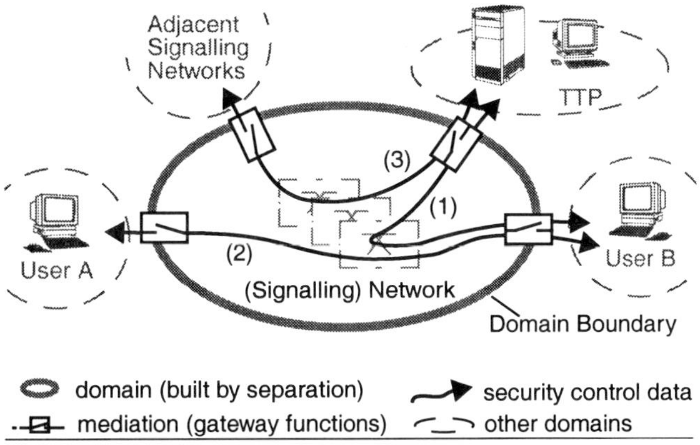

Figure 3: Security domains regarding signalling

rates or based on the amount of control data exchanged. Concerning network integrity, we focus on scalable protection measures that can be applied by network operators to control remotely produced control data that is transmitted over their signalling network or processed within their service nodes. Such control data includes security control data exchanged between domains A, B and TTP to realize security services.

Separation aspects of signalling network domains: Separation mechanisms (mostly access control mechanisms) ensure that control data enters a domain only through a few well defined gateways. By this, separation ensures that all data is inspected by mediation functions before it leaves or enters the network domain.

This contribution focuses on a network operator's signalling network and on respective control data that is processed within this signalling network. Control data created within the network operator's domain is trusted by default, i. e. the network domain consists of equally trusted infrastructure and administration staff.

Mediation aspects of signalling network domains: Control data enters and leaves a network operator's domain to synchronize distributed functions forming teleservices and network services spanning multiple networks. Mediators inspect control data before it leaves or enters the network operator's domain (Fig. 3). The kind of security function applied on control data that is leaving a domain depends on the security goals related with the respective control data and the domains that will be crossed. Efficient access control functions are applied on control data that enters the network operator's domain. For example, well known firewall functions can act as mediators for incoming control data at the domain boundary.

If there are areas within a domain which are less secure – and therefore need stronger security mechanism – than other parts of the respective domain, this domain should be refined into subdomains. Consequently, additional gateways must be installed and administrated to secure these emerging subdomain boundaries. Resulting subdomains can be secured in an efficient and effective way. Finally, the impact of security breaches within one domain on other domains is limited. The number of separate domains and belonging gateways must be weighted up against advantages resulting of more efficient security mechanism and achieved autonomy and robustness.

Outsourcing sensitive service functions like access control and call accounting to TTPs would lastly reduce security requirements on core network switches. This would contribute to more independence between network operators and switch manufacturers.

Today, call accounting and access control are partly included in local exchanges. The security of these sensitive functions depends on the security of the underlying hardware and software. Both hardware and software modules are very complex and hardly verifiable by network operators.

4 Applying the domain concept to security services in ISDN/IN

This section proposes enhancements of service environments by additional functions and physical network infrastructure to show possible approaches regarding the challenges in section 2. The domain concept introduced in section 3 is applied to achieve efficient and effective security gateway functions.

Respective gateways must secure the signalling network of a network operator against outsiders that might try to misuse open security service interfaces of this signalling network. In addition, they restrict the impact of failures of adjacent signalling networks. The main ideas are summarized briefly:

- Sensitive functions located within the public network are separated from less sensitive network functions by introducing new network infrastructure (hardware and software) that is operated by Trusted Third Parties and adapted to evolving needs of network users. Security functions within user terminals may run on plug-in security modules.
- The proposed security services are included into the public ISDN over security service interfaces. Service functions supporting these interfaces are implemented in application level signalling protocols (application parts of the SS7), protocols of the user network interface (basing on DSS1), service control functions, or management functions of the public ISDN.

The goal is an overlay security service network that has designated links to existing service infrastructure in order to profit from the huge investments into existing network infrastructure. These links are used to access security services, to exchange security control data, and to combine separated security functions with conventional services.

4.1 Communication system level approach

This section depicts the application of the domain concept to single communication systems. It is suited for security enhancements of user terminals, security servers reachable over the network, and for single network nodes that need an independent security environment (e. g. management centers). As an example, Fig. 4 shows different ways for enhancing service interfaces of communication systems by an interface to access or include additional security service functions.

We consider communication systems basing on DSS1 for this approach (e. g. conventional user terminals, small security servers using DSS1 signalling, user side of local exchanges). Communication systems basing on SS7 are handled in the next section.

Fig. 4a shows an approach, where new security functions are integrated into existing service control functions. This approach is not scalable, needs changes of existing service functions, and has low capabilities to build domains. This approach is not considered because it does not contribute to open security service interfaces and because it is not flexible.

Fig. 4b shows the approach followed within this contribution. Clearly separated security functions may run in specialized security modules. Open interfaces (SAP^{Sec}) promote compatibility and availability of implementations satisfying changing needs of users in different environments (ISDN, GSM, B-ISDN, etc.). This results in independent security functions that may be employed as plug-in security enhancements for various telecommunication services. The separated address space (by use of separated service access points) enables independent filtering and screening. The Security Adaptation Layer (SAL) includes

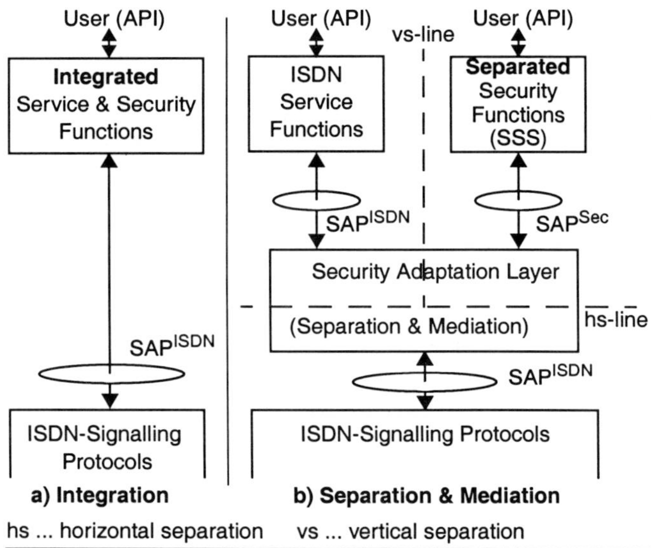

Figure 4: Security enhancements of ISDN services

gateway functions to separate the internal services from the signalling network (horizontal separation). At the same time, the SAL separates security functions from conventional ISDN service functions by use of isolated service access points (vertical separation in Fig. 4b).

Consequently, there are three domains, that are controlled by a single adaptation layer: the external network domain (no security assessment possible for users), the highly secure domain hosting security functions (building signatures, authentication functions), and the moderately secure domain of conventional services (connection control, applications). Mediation is done within the SAL by invoking security functions (e. g. authentication) that enhance conventional services. The SAL is called an adaptation layer because it translates requests at the SAP^{Sec} to requests of the SAP^{ISDN} and vice versa. The SAL is implemented as a transparent sublayer in between layer 2 and layer 3 or above layer 3 of the D-Channel protocols.

The separated security functions (SSS) may be implemented in specialized security modules [18] that are plugged into a terminal on demand. The SSS can be implemented similar to the ISDN supplementary services. Security service functions thereby are triggered either on demand by the user (via an application programming interface, API) or automatically by the SAL (via SAP^{Sec}).

Encapsulating separation, mediation, and adaptation into a single transparent sublayer saves the investments in existing network and terminal infrastructure and represents a flexible approach to security services on demand.

4.2 Communication network level approach

The proposed approach to enhance communication network services by security functions particularly takes into account the economy of scales reached by shared security functions. Therefore, the building blocks of the domain concept (*separation*, *mediation*) and the building blocks for security enhancements (*adaptation* to existing infrastructure, *linking* security functions and conventional services, *secure runtime environments*) are not implemented within a single adaptation layer in every network node as for single communication systems.

The network domain consists of many network nodes that are equally trusted. To build a domain boundary, every network node that is connected to external infrastructure (gateway exchanges, local exchanges) must implement *separation* functions. *Adaptation* functions are responsible for the inclusion of separated security functions. They are supported and implemented where needed: (i) at local exchanges, the SSS security protocols of the UNI must be translated to SecAP security protocols of the NNI and vice versa (similar to ISDN supplementary services); (ii) at shared security servers and security enhanced network nodes, adaptation functions are needed to include security functions into service provision.

The SAP^{Sec} for the network internal access of security functions and the adaptation of separated security functions is implemented by a new application part of the SS7, namely the Security Services Application Part (SecAP). This application part is addressed by use of a new subsystem number that is to be configured into the MTP-routing (as an equivalent to a new identifier for the SAP^{Sec} at the UNI). The synchronization of security functions and conventional service functions is done at the application service level (e. g. by service control functions).

If the set of security functions that can be accessed over network boundaries shall be restricted, there is need for further interworking at network boundaries. The network internal SecAP may be restricted for internetworking (similar to restrictions according to the international ISUP [10]). This results in restricted services spanning multiple networks. In this case, the SecAP and the restricted SecAP must be implemented in every gateway exchange over which security services are enabled.

M*ediation* functions are responsible for inspecting service control data leaving or entering the network domain (access control functions). These are to be integrated between level 2 and 3 of the MTP or within the SecAP in order to inspect incoming and outgoing signalling messages. There are two basic approaches to implement mediation functions for network domains:

- Mediation functions are integrated in every gateway exchange and local exchange (integrated with separation functions). This approach is currently implemented for ISDN internetworking. One reason for this is, that at the gateway exchange there is some context information available that is used for access control (distinguishing network operators by information about the incoming link or link set, screening calling party numbers by use of their association with subscriber lines, etc.).
- The other extreme denotes separation functions at network boundaries that redirect all messages (that shall leave or enter the network domain) via central network nodes implementing mediation functions.
- Making profit from both extremes, mediation functions are located both at the gateways and within shared network nodes. Most of the signalling traffic should be handled directly at the gateways and only traffic that needs particular inspection (security control data concerning accounting, electronic coins for on-line payment, etc.) is relayed over specialized security nodes.

The lower part of Fig. 5 shows an exemplary configuration of terminals and TTPs interconnected by a communication network. The upper part of Fig. 5 depicts the signalling protocols that are included in the terminals, TTPs, and ISDN-exchanges to synchronize security functions. To

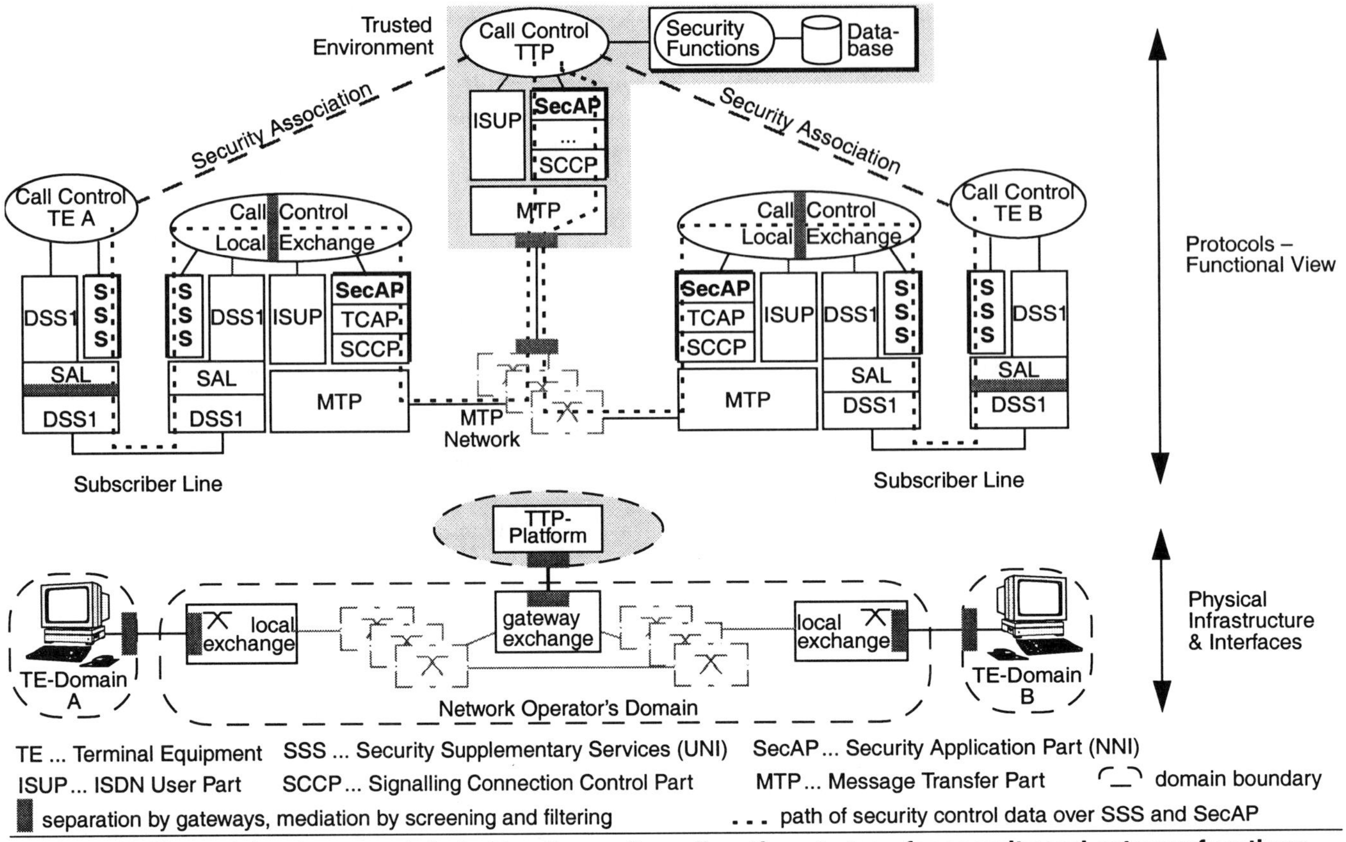

Figure 5: Network level approach to "add-on" security – allocation strategy for security and gateway functions

reduce complexity, only a single network operator and a single service provider are participating in the service.

In the exemplary configuration of Fig. 5, the network operator may not be affected by the service (except from transporting control data between the security functions). Classical examples of such services are end-to-end authentication services that are supported by TTPs (e.g. public key servers, see [17]). Security services that protect user data that affects network functions need synchronization with service functions of the core network. Section 5 presents an anonymity service by inserting multiple TTPs in the connection establishment.

Fig. 5 depicts the enhancements at the UNI and at the NNI to support the synchronization of security service functions. The *SSS* enhancement of the UNI serves as a basis for negotiating and realizing security services over the user network interface. The SSS base on the SAP^{Sec} that is provided by the security adaptation layer (SAL, see also Fig. 4b).

The NNI is enhanced by the SecAP. It bases on the Message Transfer Part (MTP) and the Signalling Connection Control Part (SCCP) of the SS7. The MTP offers services to transport signalling messages to a given destination signalling node. The SCCP uses services of the MTP and offers connectionless and connection-oriented network services. The SCCP is used by the TCAP to exchange security control data between distributed security service functions. The SecAP uses the Transaction Capabilities Application Part (TCAP) of the SS7 to realize powerful security protocols. Synchronization of security services with core network services over SecAP and ISUP is shown in more detail in section 5 and in [17].

4.3 Access control at network boundaries

Providing open interfaces, we should not forget to study the consequences. Kuhn et al state in [2] that "when switching from proprietary to standardized open interfaces, intruders can more easily attack a system whose behaviour is standardized and well known, or which shares common flaws with other systems built on the same standards".

This effect must be compensated by specialized strong security gateway functions supervising these interfaces. On the other hand, open interfaces enable quick response to known threats and promote high quality products by competition among manufacturers and service providers.

In the following, we will focus on access control mechanisms to protect the robustness and autonomy of the core network against outsider attacks over the SecAP and SSS interfaces. Thereby, we focus on the SecAP, over which service providers or adjacent network operators insert control data that is processed or merely transported by control functions of the core network. However, the SSS interface also bears some potential misuse (that can be treated similar to the approach proposed for the SecAP below):

- By supporting the exchange of security control data between terminal equipment (end-to-end), covered channels may be established by users. These channels can be used for fraudulent exchange of data.
- The synchronization of security services and core network services may lead to dependencies between both. Therefore, fraudulent use of SSS may trigger security service functions of TTPs or functions within the network that decrease the robustness of network services.

The SecAP bears more serious potential for misuse of network resources, because the SecAP directly binds separated security service functions into network services. Concerning network resources, the level of control over the SecAP is much higher than control achievable by security functions triggered over the SSS interface. Therefore, there is need for strong *mediation* functions.

Control data is exchanged within the signalling system by means of so called message signalling units (MSU). MSUs include standardized field identifiers depicting the included type of control data. These identifiers depend on the protocols used by the service functions to exchange control data (ISUP, TCAP, SCCP, SecAP, SSS in Fig. 5).

At first, access control is implemented by the common channel signalling system (SS7) itself: the outband signalling system prevents control or management processes within the network from being directly manipulated by user data (natural separation). In addition, parameters of signalling messages are inspected by interworking functions within local exchanges before they are translated from DSS1 to ISUP.

Accordingly, access control concerns signalling messages and parameters that originate from adjacent signalling networks. Two protection mechanisms are employed at the respective external signalling interfaces:

- *Filtering* decides, whether a signalling message may pass into (or leave) the network based on access control lists (ACLs). These ACLs specify for each identifier and respective contents and for each direction (in / out), whether a message may pass or whether the respective message or parameter should be discarded. Today, filtering is mainly done on address information.
- *Screening* is stronger than filtering. The address information contents of a signalling message that serves as a basis for filtering is verified, using context information. Such context information may be the signalling link, on which the message has been received and related addresses that are accessible over this link. At the network node interface, claimed address information includes the network indicator and the originating signalling point code. If the contents of a message field have proven to be invalid, the screening function either discards the message, inserts screening information and default contents, or corrects the contents if possible.

No attackers are assumed inside the network domain. For that reason, mediation (by screening and filtering on control data) at the network boundary is effective against attacks. This facilitates the management of access control lists, screening functions, and filtering functions applied in the respective gateways and minimizes the number of gateways to be installed. Basing on open signalling interfaces, these gateway functions protect core network infrastructure against misuse due to forged or incorrectly composed signalling messages inserted at network boundaries.

Message Signalling Units include several identifiers that may serve as a basis for screening or filtering [15],[16]:

- network indicators (bind the validity of a message to a network domain, e. g. national network or international network)
- originating/destination point codes (network addresses)
- subsystem numbers and service indicators (denoting the protocols used to exchange control data within a signalling message)

The quality of access control depends on the authenticity of the identifiers that are screened and filtered. Fig. 6 illustrates the screening of signalling messages and the filtering on various parts of addresses used in the common channel signalling system in ISDN.

Introducing powerful service interfaces like SecAP, over which sensitive network functions may be controlled, demands for stronger access control functions at network boundaries. Today, control data that applies to sensitive network functions (billing, management etc.) is not sent over network boundaries. Respective parameters or messages are dependent of the respective network provider. These so called national parameters or national messages are usually discarded when crossing gateways of the signalling network. The adjective "national" is to be superseded by "operator dependent" considering a rising number of emerging network operators. Therefore, keeping to this strong strategy would disable or limit a significant part of value-added services also within a single country.

More powerful screening functions are enabled by introducing message fields that identify services or service providers that are responsible for their contents. Based on such message fields, screening and filtering functions can switch services on and off depending on the respective provider or security service. This is done by discarding or forwarding respective parameters or messages. Consequently, messages exchanged by the SecAP shall additionally include (standardized) identifiers denoting security service providers and classes of security service functions (SecSI, Fig. 6).

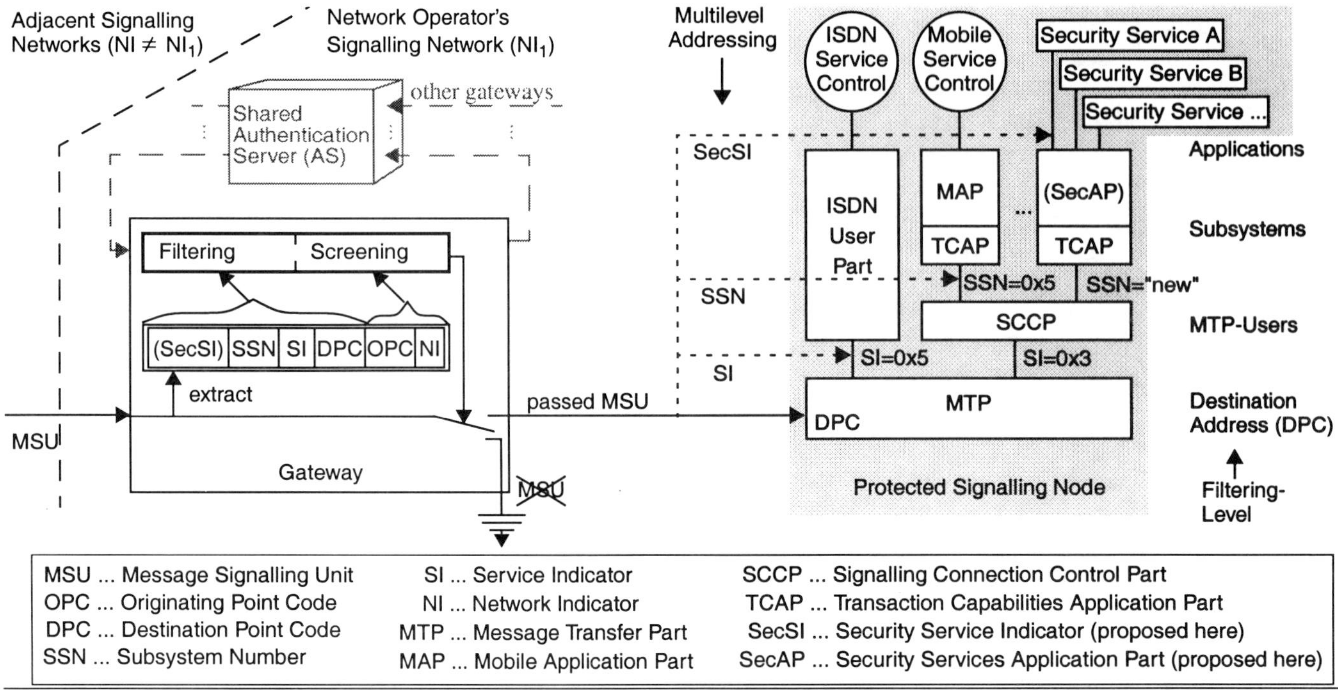

Figure 6: Access control at network boundaries by screening and filtering on address information

However, to achieve effective access control, there is need for *more effective authentication* of the contents of signalling messages. New parameters are to be introduced into signalling messages. These parameters may denote digital signatures or message authentication codes of service providers and serve as a basis for decisions whether a message is discarded or passed through the screening function. Such cryptographic authentication data can be used in cases where given context information is not sufficient to verify screening data (e. g. address information).

Taking into account a composition of the extreme approaches mentioned in section 4.2, more time consuming and costly authentication, screening, and filtering can be done in a shared authentication server that is unique to a signalling network whereas less complicated checks (screening, filtering) are done within the gateways. As outlined in Fig. 6, signalling messages that need authentication are transferred to the authentication server (AS). The AS discards signalling messages or parameters that fail to pass the integrity and authentication checks. Authenticated messages are sent back to the gateway. The gateway recognizes the authenticated messages by the incoming link. If the whole signalling message is transferred to the AS (not shown in Fig. 6), there is no need for keeping state information within the gateways. The ATM-Forum's approach to signatures computed over selected fields of signalling messages [20] and new approaches to signing variable parameters (e. g. addresses as a result of global title translations) should be taken into consideration.

Altogether, an enhancement of "context information" by cryptographic information improves screening by offering authentic information for access control. Network operators are enabled to switch dedicated services on and off by screening on the respective identifiers. Cryptographic context information (e. g. message authentication codes, signatures) promote the independence of logical information for screening from physical context information. This is particularly important for roaming services increasing strongly along with Open Network Provisioning. With roaming services, only few physical context information can be utilized because related control data is received over intermediate signalling systems. The respective international standards dealing with network interconnection in ISDN and in general ([10], [11]) can be enhanced by procedures to handle such cryptographic context information.

5 Exemplary service – anonymous calls

A short example illustrates the use of external services to realize anonymity services. This example also includes the control of data channels (ISUP) and the synchronization of additional security functions and core network functions. Fig. 7 depicts the signalling and switching events needed to hide the routing of a call. Usually MIX-functions are used to hide the association of communicating parties in a call [6]. For this purpose, MIXes mediate the connection. Instead of connecting users A and B directly, the connection is routed from user A to MIX_1, from MIX_1 to MIX_2

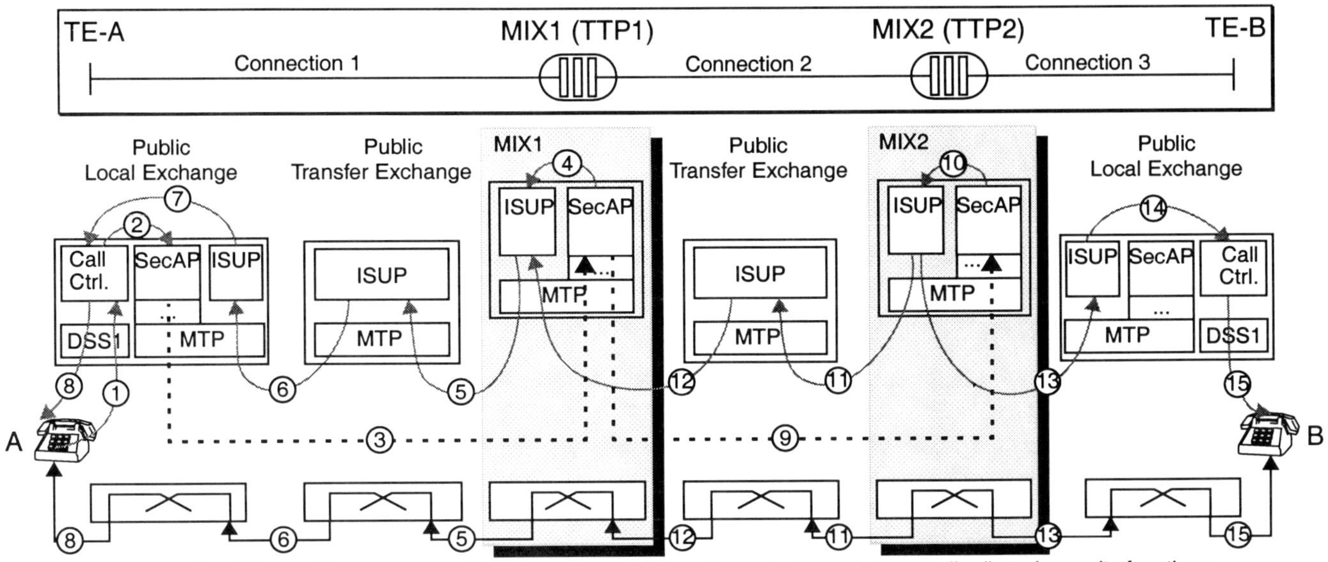

Figure 7: Exemplary use of signalling protocols as a basis for anonymity services

and from MIX_2 to user B. We do not describe the MIX functions in detail, but we assume the following:

- User A wants to call user B using ISDN services. He wants to be sure that the network operator is not capable to deduce with whom he communicates.
- Anonymity service providers MIX_1 and MIX_2 are trusted by user A and user B and do not work together to break the anonymity. A addresses MIX_1, including the encrypted address of MIX_2 to be used by MIX_1. The final address of user B is encrypted by A in a way that only MIX_2 will be able to decrypt the endpoint of the call.
- There is a lot of traffic that ensures that it is not possible for an outsider or the network provider to follow a call setup or shutdown through the MIXes because there are many connections being put up and shut down at the same time between the MIXes. In this case an outsider is not able to establish which incoming call belongs to which outgoing call at a MIX without the help of the MIX itself.

Fig. 7 shows the flow of signalling messages for the establishment of an anonymous call. An outsider following the call will lose the call at MIX_1 if starting at user A. He will lose the call at MIX_2 if starting at user B. Usually, anonymity demands for stronger mechanisms, i. e. more MIXes due to stronger requirements and weaker assumptions. We focus mainly on signalling requirements of security services; not on the implementation of the security services itself. This exemplary realization ensures that the connected parties are not deducible by using signalling or state information of the public switches. They are not intended to be absolutely secure against timing attacks.

At first, user A will book an anonymous call at the local exchange (1 in Fig. 7) by using SSS and SecAP (SSS is not shown in Fig. 7). This will be indicated over the user network interface and translated into signalling requests (2) delivered to the first MIX configured for user A (3). A will on-hook and wait for a call-back initiated by MIX_1. This callback solution is flexible concerning the billing of the call and tolerant against timing requirements. Translating request 3 to a connection request for the ISUP within MIX_1 may be done by using a common control that has access to both ISUP and SecAP (4). This part of the connection is established backwards using conventional ISUP-signalling (5,6,7). The lower part of Fig. 7 illustrates the sequence in which the switched data channel is established between adjacent ISDN exchanges. The identifiers are related to the respective call setup signalling using the ISDN User Part.

The establishment of the second part of the call is done in the same way. MIX_1 decrypts the address of the next MIX (MIX_2) and sends a request to MIX_2 (9). MIX_2 translates the request to an ISUP request (10) and establishes an ISDN connection with MIX_1 (11,12). The two parts of the connection are combined within MIX_1, and cannot be associated by outsiders. MIX_2 recognizes that he is the last MIX and decrypts the final address B. Afterwards MIX_2 establishes a conventional ISDN connection via an ISUP request (also covered by action 10 in Fig. 7) to user B (13,14). This incoming anonymous call may be indicated at the user's terminal equipment like a call originating from MIX_2 (15). It is also possible to send additional security control information to the call control of local exchange B in order to indicate user B that there is additional information available. Such information may be the identity of A encrypted in a way that only B is capable to decrypt it.

The three segments of the connection (upper part of Fig. 7) cannot be associated by outsiders or by MIX_1 or MIX_2. MIX_1 doesn't know to whom MIX_2 forwards the connection. MIX_2 does not know by whom the connection was initiated because he only knows that the connection originates from MIX_1. It is not possible to associate the call initiated by user A and the call indicated at user B, if MIX_1 and MIX_2 do not co-operate and the different parts of the connection cannot be concatenated by supervising incoming and outgoing calls at the MIXes. Of course the communicating parties might be deduced by eavesdropping the data exchanged over the established ISDN connection. But this kind of attack must be handled by security mechanisms within the users' terminal equipment and the MIXes. They have to recode user data to hinder the association of incoming user data with outgoing user data.

The described solution bases on open interfaces within the SS7. Whether there will be open interfaces and which services may be offered by the network operators to third parties will greatly dependent on the development of efficient security mechanisms to protect the core network infrastructure against misuse or integrity attacks over these interfaces (see also section 4).

6 Conclusion and outlook

In fact, the proposed approach applies the framework of Open Network Provisioning (ONP) to security service providers and to providers of sensitive network functions (accounting, etc.). This leads to new requirements on service interfaces over which these – from a network operator's view – outsourced service features may be integrated into network services [3]. Consequently, such interfaces must (i) be internationally standardized, (ii) provide compatibility mechanisms, and (iii) provide or support powerful means to protect interconnected network infrastructure. This ensures the presumed overall service behaviour and limits the risk of network disruption, degradation of the quality of services, and the risk of outages resulting from misuse or incorrect operation of network functions.

Introducing cryptographically protected context information enables the verification of parameters that are used as a basis for access control. It preserves the autonomy of network operators and the robustness of services and represents a prerequisite for efficient fall-back mechanisms.

There is need for efficient implementations of screening and filtering in order to prevent security functions from getting the bottleneck of interworking. The proposed interfaces are valuable in an environment of competing network operators, service providers, and manufacturers and promote *tailor-made* (fitting individual needs), *efficient* (scalable, easy to integrate, compatible), *multilaterally secure* (balancing security goals), and *trustworthy* services.

7 References

[1] W. Burr: Security in ISDN. NIST Special Publication No. 500-189, September 1991.

[2] R. Kuhn, P. Edfors, V. Howard, C. Caputo, T. S. Phillips, A. Booz, H. Booz: Improving Public Switched Network Security in an Open Environment. IEEE Computer, August, 1993.

[3] R. Kickartz, H. Gottschalk: Concepts of Telekom for Open Network Provision (ONP) - Considerations on Network Integrity and Network Operators Autonomy. XV ISS, April 1995, Vol. 2.

[4] J. C. McDonald: Public Network Integrity - Avoiding a Crisis in Trust. IEEE JSAC, Vol. 12, No. 1, January, 1994.

[5] K. Ward: The Impact of Network Interconnection on Network Integrity. British Telec. Engineering, Vol. 13, January, 1995.

[6] A. Pfitzmann, B. Pfitzmann, M. Waidner: ISDN-MIXes: Untraceable Communication with Very Small Bandwidth Overhead. Proceedings KiVS, Mannheim, Februar 1991.

[7] ITU-T: Digital Subscriber Signalling System No. 1, Network Layer. ITU-T Recommendations Q.930-Q.940, Geneva, 1993.

[8] E. D. Myers: STU-III – Multilevel Secure Computer Interface. Proceedings of the 10th Annual Computer Security Applications Conference, Orlando, Florida, December, 1994.

[9] R. Sailer: Integrating Authentication into Existing Protocols. 5th Open Workshop on High Speed Networks, Paris, 1996.

[10] CCITT Recommendation Q.767: Application Of The ISDN User Part Of CCITT Signalling System No. 7 For International ISDN Interconnections. Geneva 1991.

[11] CCITT Recommendations Q.601-Q.699: Interworking Of Signalling Systems. Melbourne, November 1988.

[12] CCITT Recommendations Q.700-Q.766: Specifications Of Signalling System No. 7. Melbourne, November 1988.

[13] ITU-T Q.1211: Introduction To Intelligent Network Capability Set 1. International Telecommunication Union, March 1993.

[14] J. Rushby, B. Randell: A Distributed Secure System. IEEE Computer, July, 1983.

[15] H. Gottschalk, B. Gotthart: Zeichengabesystem Nr. 7 – Stabilität und Sicherheit, Einsatz eines Monitoringsystems. Der Fernmelde-Ingenieur, 49. Jahrgang, Heft 11/12 1995.

[16] B. Kowalski: Security Management System SMS. Der Fernmelde-Ingenieur, 49. Jahrgang, Heft 4/5 1995.

[17] R. Sailer: An Evolutionary Approach to Multilaterally Secure Services in ISDN / IN. Proc. of the 7th International Conference on Computer Communications and Networks. Lafayette, LA, October 1998.

[18] A. Pfitzmann, B. Pfitzmann, M. Schunter, M. Waidner: Trusting Mobile User Devices and Security Modules. IEEE Computer, February 1997.

[19] A. Jerichow, J. Müller, A. Pfitzmann, B. Pfitzmann, M. Waidner: Real-Time Mixes: A Bandwidth-Efficient Anonymity Protocol. IEEE JSAC, Vol. 16, No. 4, May 1998.

[20] ATM Security Specification – Version 1.0 (Draft). ATM Forum BTD-SECURITY-01.04, September 1997.

Track A

Cryptography

Chair

E. Siarkiewicz, Rome Labs

ID-Based Cryptographic Schemes Using a Non-Interactive Public-key Distribution System

Yuh-Min Tseng, Jinn-Ke Jan
Institute of Applied Mathematics
National Chung Hsing University
Taichung, Taiwan, ROC
E-Mail:jkjan@amath.nchu.edu.tw

Abstract

In 1984, Shamir proposed the idea of a cryptographic system based on identification information and presented an identity-based signature scheme. He also presented as an open problem to find an ID-based public-key cryptosystem or public-key distribution system. In the past, many previously ID-based public-key distribution systems have been proposed. However, none of these is an ID-based system in Shamir's sense because each user's public key is not only the identity of the entity but also some additional random numbers. Maurer and Yacobi developed a non-interactive ID-based public-key distribution system. In their scheme, except for the identity of the entity, there were no public keys, certificates for public keys or other information required to be exchanged. However, they do not construct an ID-based signature scheme, user identification scheme or conference key distribution system. In this paper, we provide a slight improvement of the Maurer and Yacobi's scheme in that the trusted authority only adds one public value over the original scheme. Based on this, we provide not only a non-interactive public-key distribution system, but also a directed signature scheme, a user identification scheme and a conference key distribution system. Thus, a non-interactive public-key system will be more practical and complete for various kinds of applications. The security for the proposed schemes is based on the one-way hash function assumption and the difficulty of computing the discrete logarithm for a composite modulus.
Keywords: Cryptography, Public-key distribution system, Discrete logarithms, Signature, Identification , Non-interactive, ID-based cryptosystem

1. Introduction

In an open telecommunication network, it is required that each entity be able to secure communication with another entity over an insecure channel. In 1976, Diffie and Hellman [5] proposed a secure key distribution system for distributing a common session key between two entities. In this system, every entity needs to select a secret key and compute a corresponding public key. Conventionally, the public keys of entities are kept in a public directory. The common session key between two entities can be computed by either entity, based on his own secret key and another entity's public key. However, the authentication of the public keys is a serious problem.

Since the public keys are exposed to the public, an adversary can successfully enter a corresponding fake public key without being detected if there is no effective authentication method [19]. In order to prevent an adversary from fraudulently impersonating another entity, the public keys should be verified before using them. A commonly used solution is that the public key be accompanied with a certificate [11] generated by a trusted authority using a digital signature scheme, such as the RSA [22] or the ElGamal [6] signature schemes. However, this approach has a potential problem. It wastes both storage in the system and valuable computing time performed by verifiers.

In 1984, Shamir [23] introduced the idea of a cryptographic system based on identification information (e.g., name, address, and physical description). In this system, the public key of each entity is nothing but an identity, which can be defined as that part of the identification information. The public key is explicitly verified if that entity's identity is known, without running an interactive public-key authentication. Therefore, an ID-based system can be used in a completely non-interactive manner. There is no public-key file required in this system. However, Shamir did not succeed in constructing an ID-based public-key cryptosystem and public-key distribution system, but only succeeded in constructing an ID-based signature scheme.

Under Shamir's concept, much research has been devoted to various kinds of ID-based cryptographic schemes. Several ID-based public-key cryprosystems [8,25] and ID-based public-key distribution systems [2,3,10,13,20,21] have been proposed. Although these schemes have been called ID-based public-key systems, none of these is an ID-based system in Shamir's sense because the public key of each entity is not only an identity, but also some random number selected either by the entity or by the trusted authority.

The notion of self-certified public keys was introduced by Girault [7]. The public key is derived from the signature of the entity's secret key with his identity, signed by the system authority using the system's secret key. That is, the self-certified public key is determined by both the system authority and the entity. The public key of each entity need not be accompanied with a separate certificate to be authenticated by other users. Therefore, the self-certified public keys contribute to reducing the amount of storage in certificate-based public-key schemes.

From the above discussions, even though the certificate-based system, the self-certified system and many previously so called ID-based public-key systems which are intended to function in a non-interactive manner, some additional integers must be inserted by the entity or the trusted authority. The number of additional integers is at least equal to or greater than the number of all of the entities in the system.

In 1991, Maurer and Yacobi [15] developed a non-interactive ID-based public-key distribution system which was based on a novel trapdoor one-way function of exponentiation modulo a composite number. However, the failure of the scheme was found and modified against this failure in literature [14,16] and the final version was presented in literature [17]. This trapdoor one-way function allows a trusted authority to compute the discrete logarithm of a given number modulo a public known composite number, but this is infeasible for an adversary without knowing the factorization of the composite number [4,22]. Because not every identity possesses a discrete logarithm modulo composite number, they are presented with two methods, the squaring method and the Jacobi symbol method. Both methods guarantee the ability to compute the discrete logarithm of a given identity number modulo composite number.

In the Maurer and Yacobi's scheme, except for the identity of each entity, there are no public keys, certificates for public keys or other information required to be exchanged. Lim and Lee [14] modified the Maurer-Yacobi scheme using a modified trapdoor one-way function and presented a lot of applications. Their modified scheme used the Jacobi symbol to determine a user's identity number. That is, the user's ID is not really his (or her) identification information.

For the above reason, in this paper, we provide a slight improvement of the squaring method in the scheme proposed by Maurer and Yacobi. Based on the modified scheme, we propose several cryptographic schemes, such as a directed signature scheme, a user identification scheme and a conference key distribution system. Thus, the non-interactive public-key system will be more practical and complete for various kinds of applications.

This paper is organized into six sections. In the next section, we introduce the non-interactive public-key distribution system proposed by Maurer and Yacobi. In Section 3, we first modify the scheme proposed by Maurer and Yacobi. Then, based on this modified scheme, we propose three cryptographic schemes that include a directed signature scheme, a user identification scheme and a conference key distribution system. In Section 4, we analyze the security of our schemes. In Section 5, the performance of the proposed schemes is discussed. Finally, a summary is given in Section 6.

2. Review of a non-interactive public-key system

The non-interactive public-key system proposed by Maurer and Yacobi, is briefly described in this section. The reader can see the original paper [17] for more details.

Because not every identity number that corresponds to some identification information is guaranteed to have a discrete logarithm modulo composite number, Maurer and Yacobi presented two methods which enable the identity number's discrete logarithm modulo composite number to be produced. The first method is the squaring method and the other is the Jacobi symbol method. Because our improvement is based on the squaring method, we only review the squaring method in the Maurer-Yacobi scheme. It consists of two phases, the system initialization phase and the user registration phase. The procedures of both phases are described as follows.

System Initialization Phase: For the system setup, a trusted authority chooses three or four primes p_j such that the numbers $(p_j - 1)/2$ are odd and pairwise relatively prime [18]. The length of each prime p_j is chosen small enough such that in computing the discrete logarithms modulo each prime is feasible but factoring the product is completely infeasible. Therefore, let $N = p_1 \cdot p_2 \cdot p_3 \cdot p_4$, where each p_j are the selected primes satisfying the above conditions and their length is chosen to be between 60 and 70 decimal digits.

User Registration Phase: When a user U_i with the identity ID_i wants to join the system. The trusted authority chooses, once and for all, a secret random multiplier t from $Z^*_{\phi(N)}$, where ϕ is the Euler's totient function. Then, the trusted authority computes

$$s_i = t \cdot \log_g(ID_i^2)(mod\phi(N))$$

, where g is a primitive element in $GF(p_j)$, for $1 \leq j \leq 4$.

From the above descriptions, the system parameters are summarized as follows:
(1) the secret values of the trusted authority: p_1, p_2, p_3, p_4 and t.
(2) the public values of the trusted authority: N, g.
(3) the secret key of U_i: s_i.
(4) the public key of U_i: ID_i.

The public key of every entity consists entirely of public identity information, but is not dependent on additional information. This is the reason why the Maurer and Yacobi's scheme can be used in a truly non-interactive manner. Moreover, how to achieve the non-interactive public-key distribution is presented. Once the system is set up, any two users U_i and U_j in the system can compute the common key between them using

$$K_{ij} \equiv (ID_j)^{2s_i} \equiv g^{vs_is_j} \equiv (ID_i)^{2s_j} \equiv K_{ji}(modN)$$

, where $v \equiv t^{-1}(mod\phi(N))$. The non-interactive public-key distribution system is based on a variant of the Diffie-Hellman system with composite modulus N. Each user can generate the common secure key from his own secret key and the other user's public key.

3. Our schemes

Generally, an ID-based cryptosystem consists of three phases: the initiation phase, the user registration phase and the application phase. First, we modified the first two phases of Maurer- Yacobi's scheme[17]. Only one public value for the authority were increased. Thus, several applications can be constructed based on this modified scheme. In this section, we present three ID-based cryptographic schemes using the modified non-interactive public-key system. Our schemes can provide digital signature, user identification and conference key distribution. The initiation phases and the user registration phases of the three schemes are the same respectively.

3.1. System setup scheme

In this subsection, first we present the improvement for the Maurer and Yacobi's scheme and then give a comparison.

System Initialization Phase: For the system setup, the trusted authority chooses four primes p_j between 60 and 70 decimal digits where for each p_j such that the numbers $(p_j - 1)/2$ are odd and pairwise relatively prime [18]. Thus, let

$$N = p_1 \cdot p_2 \cdot p_3 \cdot p_4.$$

The trusted authority also selects an integer e in $Z^*_{\phi(N)}$ and computes the secret value d which is like the parameters in the RSA scheme [22] which satisfies

$$e \cdot d \equiv 1(mod\phi(N)).$$

User Registration Phase: When a user U_i with the identity ID_i wants to join the system. The trusted authority chooses, once and for all, a secret multiplier t at random from $Z^*_{\phi(N)}$ The trusted authority computes

$$s_i \equiv e \cdot t \cdot \log_g(ID_i^2)(mod\phi(N))$$

, where g is a primitive element in $GF(p_j)$, for $1 \leq j \leq 4$ and $v \equiv t^{-1}(mod\phi(N))$. Finally, the trusted authority also publishes a one-way function $h()$ [1].

The system parameters of the modified scheme are summarized as follows:
(1) the secret values of the trusted authority: p_1, p_2, p_3, p_4, t, v and d.
(2) the public values of the trusted authority: N, g, e, and $h()$.
(3) the secret key of U_i: s_i.
(4) the public key of U_i: ID_i.

Compared to Maurer and Yacobi's scheme, there are only one additional public value e. The one-way function $h()$ is used to compress the signing message for the ID-based signature scheme and protect the conference key distribution system from the replay attack. Since the modulus N is chosen to be infeasible to factor, specialized attacks applicable to the RSA scheme are ineffective in our scheme, e.g., it is infeasible to find d with the known e. Thus the additional public values in our scheme do not reduce the security of the system.

3.2. Directed digital signature scheme

This signature is different from an ordinary signature in its directedness to a specific receiver. Suppose that a user U_i wants to sign a message M and sends it to U_j. The signature generating procedure is as follows.

U_i first chooses a random integer r in Z_N^* and computes the signature for message M, i.e., (A, B), where

$$\begin{aligned} A &= g^{e \cdot r}(modN) \\ B &= (ID_j^2)^{s_i \cdot h(M,A)} \cdot g^r(modN). \end{aligned}$$

Afterwards, U_i sends M, A, B to the U_j.

Upon receiving the set M, A, B, U_j can verify the signature of message M as

$$B^e \equiv (ID_i^2)^{e \cdot s_j \cdot h(M,A)} \cdot A(modN).$$

If the above equation holds, then the signature for message M by U_i is verified. The correctness of this equation can be easily seen as follows:

$$\begin{aligned} B^e &\equiv (ID_j^2)^{s_i \cdot h(M,A) \cdot e} \cdot g^{e \cdot r}(modN) \\ &\equiv g^{v \cdot d \cdot e \cdot s_i \cdot s_j \cdot h(M,A)} \cdot A(modN) \\ &\equiv (ID_i^2)^{e \cdot s_j \cdot h(M,A)} \cdot A(modN) \end{aligned}$$

It can be seen that the verifier only uses the identity of the signer to verify the signature verification equation. There is neither interaction with nor access to the public files of the system.

3.3. User identification

Let us see how a user U_i proves his identity to a verifier without revealing his secret key s_i. The user identification scheme uses a challenge-response-type interactive protocol. The detailed procedure is described as follows:

Step 1: U_i sends his ID_i to the verifier U_j.

Step 2: The verifier randomly selects an integer r in Z_N^* and computes

$$Y = (ID_j^2)^r(modN).$$

Then U_j sends Y to U_i.

Step 3: U_i computes and sends U_j the integer Z as

$$Z = Y^{s_i}(modN).$$

Step 4: Upon receiving Z, U_j verifies the following equation

$$Z \equiv (ID_i^2)^{r \cdot s_j}(modN)$$

If the above equation holds, U_i is identified. The correctness of this equation can be easily seen as follows:

$$\begin{aligned} Z &\equiv Y^{s_i}(modN) \\ &\equiv (ID_j^2)^{r \cdot s_i}(modN) \\ &\equiv (g^{v \cdot s_i \cdot d})^{r \cdot s_j}(modN) \\ &\equiv (ID_i^2)^{r \cdot s_j}(modN) \end{aligned}$$

3.4. Conference key distribution

A secure conference key distribution system must guarantee that all and only the participants share a common conference key. In this subsection, we propose a conference key distribution system which distributes the conference key in a broadcast format. The proposed conference key broadcast system consists of four phases: the initiation phase, the user registration phase, the conference key distribution phase and the key recovery phase. The first two phases are the same as that for the scheme proposed in the previous subsection. We will only describe the remaining phases in detail as follows:

Conference key distribution phase: Without loss of generality, let U_0 be the chairperson of a conference and U_i, $(i = 1 \ldots m)$ be the attending participants. U_0 performs the following tasks:

Step 1: Randomly choose an integer r in Z_N^* and get a time-sequence T from the system and compute

$$\begin{aligned} C &= g^r(modN) \\ V &= h(C \| ID_0 \| T \| CK) \\ K_{0i} &= (ID_i^2)^{s_0 \cdot V} \cdot g^{r \cdot e}(modN) \end{aligned}$$

, where $i = 1 \ldots m$.

Step 2: Randomly choose a conference key CK in Z_N^* and construct a Lagrange interpolating polynomial [9,12] with degree $m-1$ using m points $(K_{0i}, CK + ID_i)$ as

$$\begin{aligned} P(x) &= \sum_{k=1}^{m} (CK + ID_k) \prod_{j=1,,j \neq k}^{m} \frac{(x - K_{0j})}{(K_{0k} - K_{0j})}(modN) \\ &= c_{m-1}x^{m-1} + \cdots + c_1 x + c_0(modN) \end{aligned}$$

Step 3: Broadcast $(ID_0, C, V, T, c_0, c_1, \cdots c_{m-1})$.

Conference key recovery phase: Upon receiving $(ID_0, C, V, T, c_0, c_1, \cdots c_{m-1})$, each U_i, $(i = 1 \cdots m)$ can perform the following steps to recover CK:

Step 1: Check the validation of the time sequence T. If it is not a valid time sequence, then terminate the recovery phase.

Step 2: Compute the shared common key with ID_0 as

$$\begin{aligned} K_{i0} &= (ID_0^2)^{s_i \cdot V} \cdot C^e(modN) \\ &= (ID_i^2)^{V \cdot s_0} \cdot g^{e \cdot r}(modN) \\ &= K_{0i} \end{aligned}$$

Step 3: Recover the conference key CK by evaluating $P(K_{0i})$ as

$$P(K_{0i}) = c_{m-1}(K_{0i})^{m-1} + \cdots + c_1 K_{0i} + c_0(modN)$$

$$\begin{aligned} &= CK + ID_i(modN) \\ CK &\equiv CK + ID_i - ID_i(modN) \end{aligned}$$

Step 4: Check whether the following equation holds:

$$V = h(C\|ID_0\|T\|CK).$$

From the above descriptions, it can be seen that the participants can verify the chairperson's ID from the received ciphertext and recover the valid conference key CK.

4. Security analysis

In the Maurer-Yacobi scheme, by choosing the prime factors for N appropriately so that the trusted authority can feasibly compute discrete logarithm modulos for each prime factor. But computing a discrete logarithm modulo N without knowing the prime factors of N is nevertheless infeasible. It can be shown that computing a discrete logarithm modulo for the composite number N is at least as difficult as factoring the modulus. Because the system setup phase of our scheme is the same as one for the Maurer-Yacobi scheme expect for an increase of one value, we omit the discussion here. The detailed description can be found in the literature [17].

In the following, some possible attacks against the three proposed schemes are presented under the above discussion. Attacks 1 and 2 are plotted against the directed digital signature scheme, and Attacks 3 and 4 are plotted against the identification scheme, while Attacks 5 to 7 are plotted against the conference key broadcast scheme. As we can see, none of them can break our schemes.

Attack 1: An adversary tries to reveal the signer U_i's secret key s_i from the signature (A, B) of the message M. It is equivalent to the difficulty of computing the discrete logarithm modulo the composite number N. Thus, U_i's secret key s_i will never be revealed to the public.

Attack 2: An adversary tries to impersonate U_i and forge his signature (A, B) for a message M. The impersonator may calculate B satisfying the following verification equation

$$B^e \equiv (ID_i^2)^{e \cdot s_j \cdot h(M,A)} \cdot A(modN).$$

However, the calculation of B for the above equation implies the computation of the discrete logarithm modulo the composite number N. Thus, the impersonation attack can not be successful.

Attack 3: An intruder knows Y, Z and $Z = Y^{s_i}(modN)$ which are the transmitted messages between U_i and U_j. Trying to solve s_i from this information is equivalent to computing the discrete logarithm modulo the composite number N.

Attack 4: An intruder tries to impersonate the user U_i by forging the Z' from two challenged questions r and r' provided by a verifier. Obviously, it is still computationally infeasible to derive r.

Attack 5: An intruder wants to impersonate the chairperson U_0 by replaying the previous broadcast messages of a conference or forging the messages. If the impersonator broadcasts the previous messages sent by U_0, it will not be successful because of the invalid time sequence. Moreover, the expiration of T and the authentication of U_0 will be effectively verified in step 4 of the conference key recovery phase. As for an impersonation attack by forging the broadcast messages at a valid time sequence T', the impersonator must forge the valid K_{0i}s, $(i = 1 \cdots m)$ shared with all participants. However, the calculation of s_0 is equivalent to the computation of the discrete logarithm modulo the composite number N.

Attack 6: A nonattending user of the conference wishes to derive the same CK from the transmitted messages of a conference. The nonattending user can obtain $(ID_0, C, V, T, c_0, c_1, \cdots c_{m-1})$. The nonattending user U_j can recover the correct CK after reconstructing the polynomial $P(X)$from the transmitted messages only if he computes the correct K_{0i} of some participant U_i. For obtaining the correct K_{0i}, he must know U_i's secret key s_i. However, this imply the computation of discrete logarithms modulo the composite number N. Hence, a nonattending user cannot obtain the same CK from the transmitted messages.

Attack 7: Conspiratorial participants in the conference who wish to derive the chairperson's secret information. This attack for conference key distribution systems was developed by Simbo and Kawamura [24] and is denoted the SK attack. With our scheme, the chairperson's secret key is only contained in K_{i0}s, the participants must compute s_0 from K_{i0}. This is equivalent to the computation of the discrete logarithm modulo the composite number N. Therefore, the proposed schemes can withstand the conspiracy attack.

5. Performance

We first present the computational complexity of the system setup phase for the proposed schemes. It is like as the computational complexity of the Muarer-Yacobi's scheme. Note that an important feature of the Muarer-Yacobi's scheme is that most of the running time is spent in the system set up phase. The four primes between 60 and 70 decimal digits are chosen such that in computing discrete logarithms modulo for each prime is feasible for the algorithm in literature [17], but not trivial. Fortunately, computing the discrete logarithms modulo for each prime factor are independent so that this process suited for parallel implementation. Therefore, it is necessary that the trusted authority have a powerful computer.

Let us consider the performance of our proposed schemes. The performance evaluation of the proposed schemes concerns the total bit-string length of transmitted messages and the time complexity. For convenience, the following notations are used to analyze the computational complexity and the transmission cost for the three proposed scheme: $|X|$ is the bit-string length of the message X; T_h is the time for executing the adopted one-way function h; T_{mul} is the time for modular multiplication; T_{exp} is the time for modular exponentiation; T_p is the time for constructing a Lagrange interpolating polynomial with degree $m-1$ using m points. T_{pe} is the time for evaluating a polynomial with degree $m-1$ for given a input value. Note that the time for computing modular addition and subtraction is ignored, because they are much smaller than T_h, T_{mul}, T_p, T_{pe} and T_{exp}.

For the digital signature scheme, the performance evaluation is analyzed in two parts. First, a user generates the digital signature (A, B) for a message M. Thus, the size of the digital signature is $|A| + |B|$, which is bounded to $2\log|N|$. The time complexity of generating a digital signature is the time for computing (A, B) which includes the time to compress the signing message into a digest with shorter length using the one hash function $h()$. Therefore, it requires $4T_{exp} + T_h + T_{mul}$ in total. Second, upon receiving the set (M, A, B), a verifier computes $h(M, A)$ and then verifies the digital signature. It requires $4T_{exp} + T_h + T_{mul}$.

When any user U_i wants to prove his identity to a verifier, Step 1 and Step 3 in the identification scheme are performed by U_i which requires T_{exp}. The verifier performs the other steps in this scheme. It requires $3T_{exp}$. The transmitted messages between U_i and the verifier are ID_i, Y and Z. The size of the transmitted messages is $|ID_i|+|Y|+|Z|$ which is bounded to $|ID_i| + 2\log N$ bits.

As for the conference key distribution scheme, the chairperson U_0 performs the conference key distribution phase and generates the broadcast messages $(ID_0, C, V, T, c_0, c_1, \cdots c_{m-1})$. Therefore, the size of the transmitted messages is $|ID_0| + |V| + |T| + (m + 1)\log N$.

In the following, let us consider the time complexity of the conference key distribution scheme. U_0 first computes C and V which requires $4T_{exp} + T_h + T_{mul}$. Then, U_0 computes the common secret key K_{0i} shared with each participant U_i, $1 \le i \le m$, which requires $(2m+1)T_{exp}$. Thus, $(2m+5)T_{exp} + T_h + T_{mul}$ is required in this step. Next, U_0 constructs the polynomial $P(X)$ with degree $m-1$ using m points, T_p is required. So the time complexity of the conference key distribution phase computed by the chairperson requires $(2m+5)T_{exp} + T_h + T_{mul} + T_p$ in total.

Upon receiving $(ID_0, C, V, T, c_0, c_1, \cdots c_{m-1})$, each user U_i, $(1 \le i \le m)$ authenticates the chairperson U_0 after checking the validity of T and then computes the common secret key K_{0i} shared with the chairperson. $3T_{exp} + T_h + T_{mul}$ is required. Then, U_i obtains the conference key CK using Horner's rule [9,12] to evaluate $P(K_{0i}) mod N$, which requires T_{pe}. So each participant performs the conference key recovery phase which requires $3T_{exp} + T_h + T_{pe}$ in total.

6. Conclusions

In this paper, we modified the Maurer and Yacobi's non-interactive public-key system. Three cryptographic schemes based on the modified scheme have also been successfully generated. These schemes enable a non-interactive public-key system that is more practical and complete for various kinds of applications. Meanwhile, the proposed schemes also have the advantage that the public key for every entity is only his identity with no additional information. We have demonstrated some possible attacks against the proposed schemes. Under the one-way hash function assumption and the difficulty of computing discrete logarithms modulo the composite number N, we have shown that the proposed schemes are secure against these attacks.

References

[1] C. Boyd and A. Mathuria, Systematic design of key establishment protocols based on one-way functions, IEE Proc. Comput. Digit. Tech., 144(2):93-99 (1997).

[2] T. Chikazawa and T. Inoue, A new sharing system for global communication, in: Proc. GLOBECOM'90, 1990, pp. 1069-1072.

[3] T. Chikazawa and A. Yamagishi, Improved identity-based key sharing system for multiaddress communication, Electr. Lett., 28(11):1015-1017 (1992).

[4] D. Coppersmith, A. M. Odlyzko, and R. Schroeppel, Discrete Logarithms in EMBED Equation —, Algorithmica, 1:1-15 (1986).

[5] W. Diffie and M. E. Hellman, New directions in cryptography, IEEE Trans. on Info. Theory, 22(6):644-654 (1976).

[6] T. ElGamal, A public key cryptosystem and a signature scheme based on discrete logarithms, IEEE Trans. Info. Theor., 31(4):469-472 (1985).

[7] M. Girault, Self-certified public keys, in: Proc. EUROCRYPT'91, 1991, pp. 491-497.

[8] L. Harn and S. Yang, ID-based cryptographic schemes for user identification, digital signature, and key distribution, IEEE J. on sele. areas in comm., 11(5):757-760 (1993).

[9] E. Horowitz and S. Sahni, Fundamentals of Computer Algorithms, Computer Science Press, INC., 1978.

[10] T. Hwang and J. L. Chen, Identity-based conference key broadcast systems, IEE Proc. Comput. Digit. Tech., 141(1):57-60 (1994).

[11] ISO/IEC 9798-3, Information technology - Security technique - Entity authentication mechanism - Part 3: Entity authentication using a public key algorithm, ISO, 1993.

[12] D. E. Knuth, The art of computer programming: Volume 2, 3nd edition, Addison-Wesley, MA, 1997.

[13] K. Koyama, Secure conference key distribution schemes for conspiracy attack, in: Proc. EUROCRYPT'92, 1992, pp. 449-453.

[14] C. H. Lim and P. J. Lee, Modified Maurer-Yacobi's scheme and its application, in: Proc. Auscrypt'92, 1992, pp. 308-323.

[15] U. M. Maurer and Y. Yacobi, Non-interactive public-key Cryptography, in: Proc. EUROCRYPT'91, 1992, pp. 498-507.

[16] U. M. Maurer and Y. Yacobi, A remark on a non-interactive public-key distribution system, in: Proc. EUROCRYPT'92, 1993, pp. 458-460.

[17] U. M. Maurer and Y. Yacobi, A non-interactive public-key distribution system, Designs, Codes and Cryptography, 9:305-316 (1996).

[18] U. M. Maurer, Fast generation of prime numbers and secure public-key distribution system, Journal of Cryptology, 8(3):123-155 (1995).

[19] M. Michels and P. Horster, On the risk of disruption in several multiparty signature schemes, in: Proc. ASIACRYPT'96, 1996, pp. 334-345.

[20] E. Okamoto and K. Ohta, How to utilize the randomness of zero-knowledge proofs, in: Proc. CRYPTO'90, 1991, pp. 456-475.

[21] E. Okamoto and K. Tanaka, Key distribution system based on identification information, IEEE Journal on Selected areas in comm., 7(4):481-485 (1989).

[22] R. L. Rivest, A. Shamir, and L. Adelman, A method for Obtaining Digital Signature and Public Key Cryptosystem, Comm. ACM, 21(2):120-126 (1978).

[23] A. Shamir, Identity-based cryptosystem based on the discrete logarithm problem, in: Proc. CRTPTO'84, 1985, pp. 47-53.

[24] A. Simbo and S. Kawamura, Cryptanalysis of several conference key distribution systems, in: Proc. AISACRYPT'91, 1991, pp. 265-276.

[25] S. Tsujii and T. Itoh, An ID-based cryptosystem based on the discrete logarithm problem, IEEE J., SAC-7(4):467-473 (1989).

Two Improved Algorithms and Hardware Implementations for Key Distribution Using Extended Programmable Cellular Automata

C. N. Zhang and M. Deng
Department of Computer Science
University of Regina, TRLabs
Regina, SK. Canada S4S 0A2
zhang@cs.uregina.ca

R. Mason
Department of Electronics
Carleton University
Ottawa, ON. Canada K1S 5B6

Abstract

In this paper, we present two efficient algorithms and a simple hardware structure for the implementation of Diffie-Hellman key distribution in $GF(2^n)$. Two algorithms investigated are improved table look-up algorithm and binary algorithm. The hardware structure is an extended programmable cellular automata (PCA), which is much more flexible and can be used for key distribution and conventional cryptography. Based on our improved methods and PCA structure, we implement two hardware systems for Diffie-Hellman key distribution. With very high speed and simple logic circuit features, these hardware systems are ideally suited for VLSI implementation.

1. Introduction

The Diffie-Hellman key exchange (DHKE) algorithm is the first implementation of public-key cryptographic system[8], and it has been used for key distribution via an insecure network. In this algorithm, each communication side needs to distribute a public key to the other side and then generates a common secret key for the subsequent use in a conventional symmetric-key cryptographic system. Originally, it involved integer operations (modular exponentiation), and later it has been modified to be applied in the GF(2^n) [1, 2].

The modified DHKE works as follows: users A and B share a common irreducible polynomial $P(x)$ over $GF(2)$ with degree n, and a polynomial $E(x)$ over $GF(2)$ with degree less than n. Firstly, the user A selects a random integer $C \leq 2^n - 2$, computes his public key $E_a(x) = E^C(x) \bmod P(x)$, and then sends it to user B. Meanwhile user B selects a random integer $D \leq 2^n - 2$, and then computes and sends his public key $E_b(x) = E^D(x) \bmod P(x)$ to user A. Now user A can compute $(E_b^C(x)) \bmod P(x) = E^{CD}(x) \bmod P(x)$, and user B can compute $(E_a^D(x)) \bmod P(x) = E^{CD}(x) \bmod P(x)$. It is obvious that both user A and user B have a common secret key that is $K(x) = E^{CD}(x) \bmod P(x)$.

Computing exponent C (D) is a discrete logarithm problem. Analysis has shown that the modified DHKE will be secure in practice if the degree of $P(x)$, n, is 127-bit or longer [1, 2].

The essential operation of the modified DHKE algorithm is a polynomial modular exponentiation, which can be performed by a series of polynomial modular multiplications. Due to the computational simplicity of arithmetic operations in $GF(2)$, the hardware implementation of the modified DHKE algorithm is much simpler and faster than hardware implementations of the original DHKE algorithm.

The major objective of this research is to investigate new techniques to further speed up the modified DHKEA implementation such that a low cost real-time key distribution system can be built. To achieve this, the following two aspects and corresponding techniques are proposed:

1. Improved algorithms for reducing the total number of the polynomial modular multiplications.

   Two improved algorithms: improved exponent table lookup algorithm and improved binary algorithm are presented. The first one is used if the given polynomial E(x) is fixed or will not be changed in a short time, otherwise the second one can be used. Both improved algorithms take advantage of the normal form of the binary redundant representation of the exponent, and it has been proven that an average of 33% of the num-

0-8186-8789-4/98 $10.00

ber of polynomial modular multiplications can be saved compared with conventional methods.

2. Simple and fast hardware implementation of the polynomial modular multiplication.

   An extended programmable cellular automata (PCA) structure is proposed. It is simple, regular and well suited for VLSI implementation. An n-cell extended PCA is used to compute $A(x) * B(x)\ mod\ P(x)$ in $n+14$ clock cycles where n is the degree of the $P(x)$. The time duration of each cycle is the time delay of a few logic gates plus the time for state change of the D flip-flop. Thus, very high throughput can be achieved. In addition, the extended PCA also can be used for one-key encryption and decryption.

This paper is organized as follows: In Section 2, two improved DHKE algorithms are presented. In section 3, after a brief introduction of the programmable CA, an extended programmable CA is proposed. PCA-based hardware implementations of the two improved DHKE algorithms are given in section 4. Section 5 is a conclusion.

2. Two Improved DHKE Algorithms

2.1. The Improved Binary DHKE Algorithm

Consider the computation of $E^D(x)\ mod\ P(x)$ where the degree of $P(x)$ is n. It can be proven that $E^D(x)\ mod\ P(x)$ can be done by the following algorithm (i.e. square-multiply algorithm) [3], where D is represented by a binary form: $D = \Sigma_{i=0}^{n-1} d_i 2^i$.

ALGORITHM 1. (the binary DHKE algorithm in GF(2^n))
Step1: $C := 1$;
Step2: Repeat Step2a and Step2b for $i := n-1$ *downto* 0;
Step2a: $C := C^2$ mod $P(x)$;
Step2b: if $d_i = 1$ then $C := CE(x)$ mod $P(x)$;
Step3: Halt. C is the result.

The total number of the basic operations (polynomial modular multiplications) is $n + l$ where l is the total number of non-zero bits of D. In order to reduce the total number of non-zero bits of D, we have proposed the normal form of the binary redundant representation which guarantees the total number of non-zero bits is minimum in respect to the following binary redundant representation [9].

DEFINITION 1. *A binary redundant representation (BRR) of an integer D ($D \leq 2^n$) is a binary radix polynomial $D = d_n 2^n + d_{n-1}2^{n-1} + ... + d_1 2^1 + d_0$(or written as $D = (d_n d_{n-1} ... d_0)$ where d_i in {0,1,-1}, i=0, 1, ..., n.)*

The following procedure can be used to convert the binary representation into the normal form of the binary redundant representation.

Procedure 1.(converting integer D from binary form into the normal form)
begin
R:=false; (R is a binary variable)
for $i := 0$ *to* $n-1$ step 2 do case ($d_{i+2}d_{i+1}d_i$ and R) of
000 $\overline{R}$: begin d_{i+1}:=0; d_i:=0; R:=false end;
000 R: begin d_{i+1}:=0; d_i:=1; R:=false end;
001 $\overline{R}$: begin d_{i+1}:=0; d_i:=1; R:=false end;
001 R: begin d_{i+1}:=$\overline{1}$; d_i:=0; R:=false end;
010 $\overline{R}$: begin d_{i+1}:=1; d_i:=0; R:=false end;
010 R: begin d_{i+1}:=0; d_i:=$\overline{1}$; R:=true end;
011 $\overline{R}$: begin d_{i+1}:=0; d_i:=$\overline{1}$; R:=true end;
011 R: begin d_{i+1}:=0; d_i:=0; R:=true end;
100 $\overline{R}$: begin d_{i+1}:=0; d_i:=0; R:=false end;
100 R: begin d_{i+1}:=0; d_i:=1; R:=false end;
101 $\overline{R}$: begin d_{i+1}:=0; d_i:=1; R:=false end;
101 R: begin d_{i+1}:=$\overline{1}$; d_i:=0; R:=true end;
110 $\overline{R}$: begin d_{i+1}:=$\overline{1}$; d_i:=0; R:=true end;
110 R: begin d_{i+1}:=0; d_i:=$\overline{1}$; R:=true end;
111 $\overline{R}$: begin d_{i+1}:=0; d_i:=$\overline{1}$; R:=true end;
111 R: begin d_{i+1}:=0; d_i:=0; R:=true end;
end;
end.

For example, let $D = 101111$, the normal form the binary redundant representation is $D = 110000\overline{1}$.

Using the normal form of the binary redundant representation of D, the binary algorithm can be modified as follows:

Algorithm 2. (the improved binary DHKE algorithm)
Step 1: $C := 1$;
Step 2: Repeat Step 2a and Step 2b for $i := n$ *downto* 0;
Step2a: $C := C^2$ mod $P(x)$;
Step2b: if $d_i = 1$ then $C := CE(x)$ mod $P(x)$
else if $d_i = \overline{1}$ $C := CE^{-1}(x)$ mod $P(x)$;
Step3: Halt. C is the result.

Using the same example $D = 1011111$, because of $D = 110000\overline{1}$, the improved binary algorithm computes

10 times basic operations compared with 13 times in the binary algorithm.

In general, we have proven that if $n = 25$ then total number of the basic operations saving on average is 30.8%, and up to 33% saving can be achieved when $n \geq 50$ [9]. Note that $E^{-1}(x)$ mod $P(x)$ is defined by $(E^{-1}(x)\ mod\ P(x)) * (E(x)\ mod\ P(x)) = 1$ and can be calculated by the extended Euclid algorithm [3]. Note that as $P(x)$ is irreducible, $E^{-1}(x)$ mod $P(x)$ exists and is unique.

2.2. The Improved Table Look-up DHKE Algorithm

In the case that the polynomial $E(x)$ is fixed or will not be changed for a period of time, the following table look-up method can be used for the DHKE computation ($E^D(x)$ mod $P(x)$.

Algorithm 3. (the table look-up DHKE algorithm)

Precomputing $C_i(x) = E^{2^i}(x)$ mod P(x), $i = 0, 1, ..., n-1$.

Step 1: $C := 1$;

Step 2: for $i := n-1$ *downto* 0 do
  if d_i=1 then $C = C * C_i$ mod $P(x)$

Step 3: Halt, the result is in C.

The total number of the basic operations is equal to the number of non-zero bits in the binary representation of D.

Again, the normal form of the binary redundant representations can be used to reduce the total number of the basic operations in the above table look-up algorithm. The modified table look-up DHKE algorithm is as follows:

Algorithm 4. (the improved table look-up DHKE algorithm)

Let $D = d_n d_{n-1} ... d_0$ is the normal form of the binary redundant representations of D, and all $C_i(x) = E^{2^i}(x)$ mod P(x), $(i = 0, 1, ..., n)$, $C_i^{-1}(x) = E^{-2^i}(x)$ mod $P(x)$, $(i = 0, 1, ..., n-1)$, are precomputed.

Step 1: $C := 1$;

Step 2: for $i := n$ *downto* 0 do
  if d_i=1 then $C = C * C_i$ mod $P(x)$
  else if $d_i = \bar{1}$ then $C = C * C_i^{-1}$ mod $P(x)$

Step 3: Halt, the result is in C.

Note that all negative powers of $E(x)$ in modular $P(x)$, $E^{-2^i}(x)$ mod $P(x)$, (i=0, 1, ..., n-1), can be precomputed by the extended Euclid algorithm. For example, $C_1^{-1}(x) = E^{-2}(x)$ mod $P(x)$ can be solved by $C_1^{-1}(x) * E^{-2}(x)$ mod $P(x)$=1.

For the same integer $D = 1011111$, the binary redundant representation of D is $110000\bar{1}$, so the improved look-up table method needs to compute $(E^{64}(x) * E^{32}(x) * E^{-1}(x))$ mod $P(x)$ to get $E^D(x)$ compared with $(E^{64}(x) * E^{16}(x) * E^8(x) * E^4(x) * E^2(x) * E(x))$ mod $P(x)$ required by the original algorithm.

In general, it requires l times of the basic operations compared with $n + l$ required by the improved binary algorithm where l is the number of non-zero bits in the normal form of the binary redundant representations of D. Since $l \leq n/2$ (guaranteed by procedure 1), the improved table look-up DHKE algorithm is at least 3 times faster than the improved binary algorithm. The overheads of the improved table look-up DHKE algorithm are a $2(n+1)$ elements table and the time delay for table accesses.

3. An Extended Programmable Cellular Automata

A Cellular Automata (CA) is an array of cells where each cell is in any of the permissible states. At each discrete time step (clock cycle) the evolution of a cell value depends on some rule which is a function of the present states of its neighbors and its own. For instance, in a 2-state 3-neighbourhood CA, the evolution of the ith cell can be represented as a logic function of the present states of (i-1)th, (i)th, and (i+1)th cells: $X_i(t+1) = f\{X_{i-1}(t), X_i(t), X_{i+1}(t)\}$, where f represents the combinational logical function as a CA rule implemented by a combinational logic circuit (CL). Figure 1 is a 4-cell 3-neighborhood CA.

The additive CA limits the logic operations of the logic function to XOR or XNOR, which is particularly useful for some applications, including CA-based encryption and decryption [6]. In the rest of the paper, the CA is referred to the additive 3-neighborhood CA.

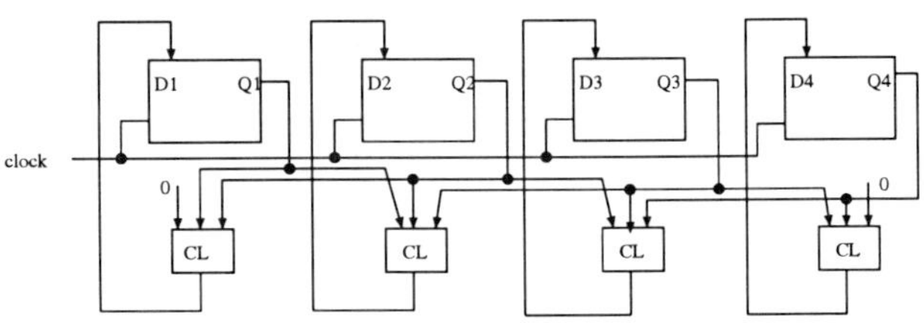

Figure 1. A 4-cell 3-neighborhood CA structure

A Programmable CA (PCA) is a CA whose CL is not fixed for each cell, but controlled by a number of control signals such that different functions (rules) can

C_l	C_m	C_r	Rules
0	0	1	X_r
0	1	0	X_s
0	1	1	$X_s \overline{\oplus} X_r$
1	0	0	X_l
1	0	1	$X_l \overline{\oplus} X_r$
1	1	0	$X_l \overline{\oplus} X_s$
1	1	1	$X_l \overline{\oplus} X_s \overline{\oplus} X_r$

Table 1. PCA Rules

be generated. Figure 2 is a 3-neighborhood additive PCA cell structure.

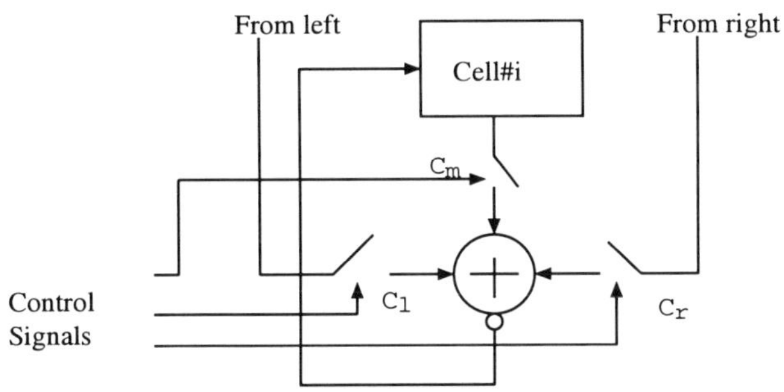

Figure 2. A 3-neighborhood additive PCA cell structure

The values of the control signals C_l, C_m, C_r and corresponding functions (rules) of the PCA are listed in table 1 where X_s represents the value of a cell itself. X_r is its right neighbor and X_l is its left neighbor.

This 3-neighborhood additive PCA has been used for conventional block and stream ciphers [6]. A 2-D (two-dimensional) pipelined/parallel PCA block cipher has been built to interface with a PCI bus and provide an encryption rate of 256 Mbps [5, 4].

The polynomial multiplication, $A(x) * B(x)$ mod $P(x)$ in $GF(2^n)$ is the basic operation of both the improved binary and the table look-up DHKE algorithms. In [7], a linear feedback shift register (LFSR) was presented to compute $A(x) * B(x)\ mod\ P(x)$. The LFSR configures the non-zero coefficients of $B(x)$ as the positive feedback, and the non-zero coefficients of $P(x)$ as the negative feedback to the corresponding D flip-flops. Then the $A(x) * B(x)$ mod P(x) can be obtained by shifting the coefficients of $A(x)$ to the LFSR. Figure 3 shows a 6-cell LFSR for $A(x) * B(x)\ mod\ P(x)$ where $B(x) = x^5 + x + 1$ and $P(x) = x^6 + x^5 + x^4 + x^3 + 1$.

Note that $P(x)$ must be primitive and the computation can be done by $m+1$ clocks where $m \leq n$ is the polynomial degree of $A(x)$.

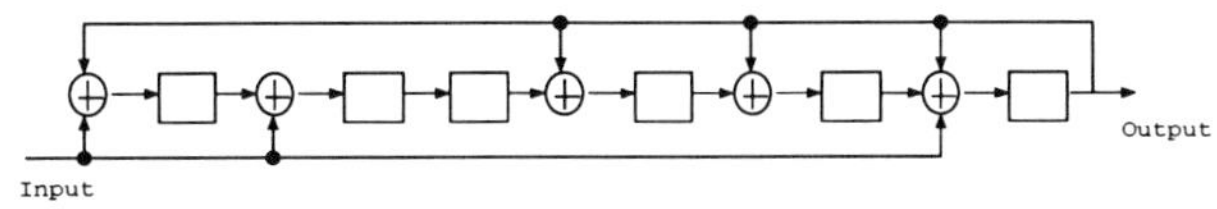

Figure 3. A LFSR for simultaneously multiplying by $X^5 + X + 1$ and dividing by $X^6 + X^5 + X^4 + X^3 + 1$

It is clear that the LFSR can not be directly used for the improved binary and table look-up DHKE algorithms since neither $A(x)$ or $B(x)$ is fixed. In the following, we propose an extended PCA structure which maintains all functions of the original PCA and can be used to implement $A(x) * B(x)$ mod $P(x)$ efficiently without any constraints.

The logic structure of the extended PCA cell is shown in figure 4. Each cell in the extended PCA has two control signals C and K. C is used to choose a cell's neighbors, and K is used to choose XOR or XNOR operation for a cell. If C is '1', then the cell chooses itself as middle input and right neighbor as right input. If C is '0', the cell chooses the boundary of its leftmost neighbor as middle input and rightmost neighbor as right input. If K is '1', then the operation is XOR. If K is '0', then the operation is XNOR. The rules of the extended PCA are also based on combinations of control signals C_l, C_m, C_r and are same as those defined in table 1.

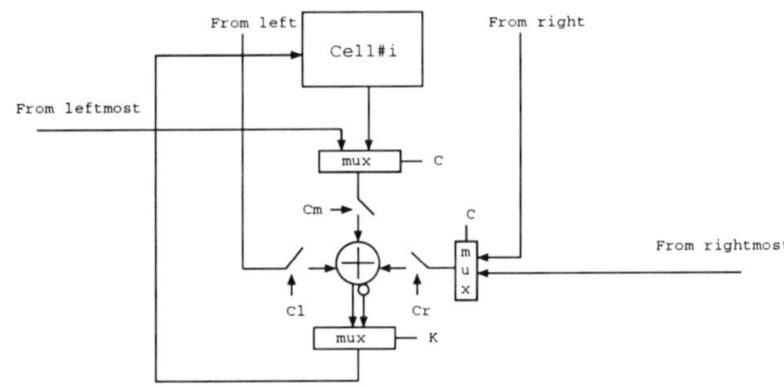

Figure 4. logic structure of extended PCA cell

Note that the proposed extended PCA is a flexible structure which can be used as a conventional 3-neighborhood additive PCA as well as a programmable LFSR by choosing the proper control signal values. If C is '1' and K is '0', then the extended PCA is a conventional PCA. If C is '0' and K is '1', as the rightmost neighbor and boundary of leftmost neighbor can be regarded as positive feedback and negative feedback values, the extended PCA becomes a programmable LFSR.

For example, in order to implement the LFSR in figure 3, we set $C = 0$ and $K = 1$. Then set $C_l = 1$, the coefficients of $B(x)$ as the control signal C_m, and coefficients of $P(x)$ as the control signal C_r. The PCA implementation is shown in figure 5.

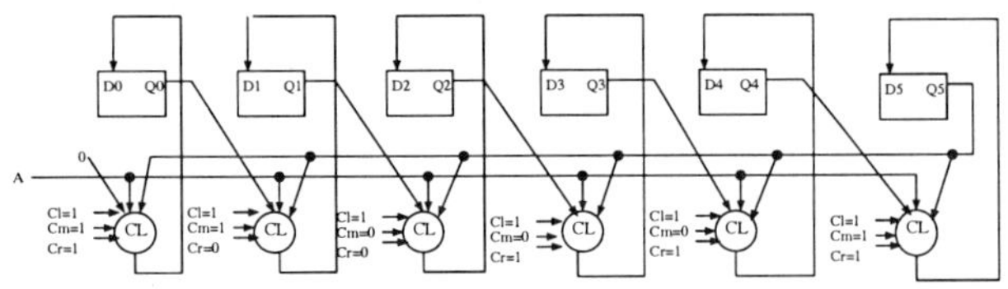

Figure 5. The extended PCA structure for simultaneously multiplying by $X^5 + X + 1$ and dividing by $X^6 + X^5 + X^4 + X^3 + 1$

4. PCA Implementations of Improved DHKE Algorithms

The computation of $A(x) * B(x)$ mod $P(x)$ can be done by two extended PCAs as shown in figure 6. PCA1 is configured as a shift register by setting $C = 1$, $K = 1$, C_l=1 and $C_m = C_r = 0$ for storing and shifting coefficients of one polynomial $A(x)$ to PCA2, and PCA2 is configured as a programmable LFSR by setting $C = 0$, $K = 1$, C_l=1 and C_m, C_r according to the coefficients of the other polynomial $B(x)$ and divisor polynomial $P(x)$. After n cycles, the polynomial modular multiplication result $A(X) * B(x)$ mod $P(x)$ is in PCA2.

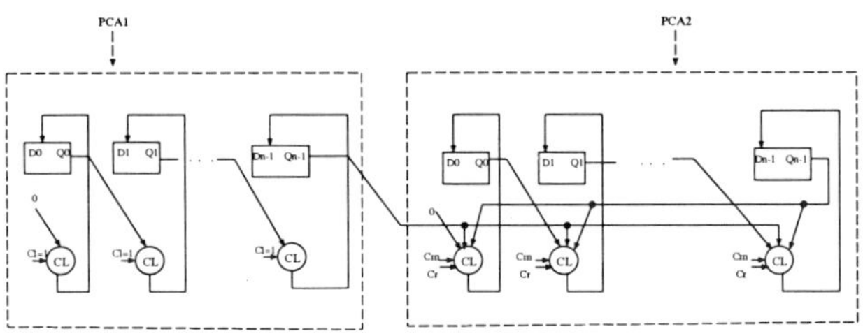

Figure 6. Two PCA circuit for computing A(x)*B(x) mod P(x)

4.1. PCA Implementation of the Improved Table Look-up DHKE Algorithm

Based on the improved table look-up algorithm, we have designed a hardware system for key distribution by using above two PCA structures. Figure 7 shows the logic circuit design of the system.

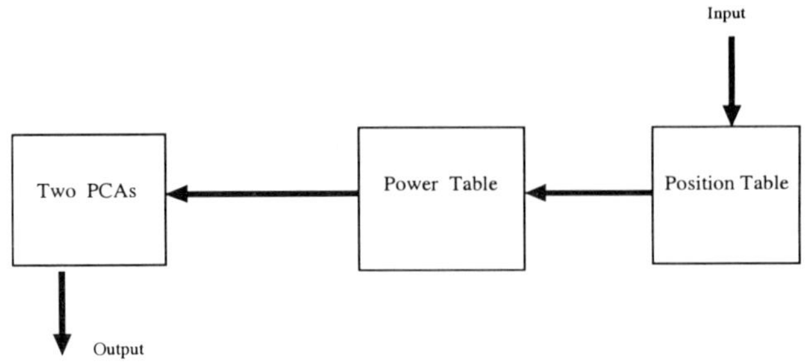

Figure 7. Hardware design for the improved DHKE table look-up algorithm

In figure 7, the *Power* table stores all positive and negative binary powers of $E(x)$ *mod* $P(x)$, and the *Position* table stores the bit positions of all non-zero bits in D. The contents of the *Position* table provides an index (address) to access corresponding powers of $E(x)$ in the *Power* table. The *Power* table is precomputed according to the given $E(x)$ and $P(x)$, and the *Position* table is loaded according to input D. The elements in *Position* table will be examined one by one to choose proper binary powers to configure the C_m in PCA2. Once a binary power of E(x) is chosen, the two PCAs will compute a basic operation. This process will be repeated until all elements in the *Position* table have been examined.

4.2. PCA Implementation of the Improved Binary DHKE Algorithm

In the case that $E(x)$ needs to be changed often, the improved binary DHKE algorithm can be used. A hardware design for this algorithm is shown in figure 8.

Initially, the $E(x)$ and $E^{-1}(x)$ *mod* $P(x)$ are computed and stored in the *Computation* table. The D is in the normal form of the binary redundant representation and stored in a shift register. Each digit of D is represented by two binary bits in the register (00 for 0, 10 for 1 and 11 for $\overline{1}$). Each cycle two most significant bits shifted out are used as an index to access the *Computation* table (if the two bits are 1x) or do nothing (if the two bits are 0x). If the *Computation* table is accessed, C_m in PCA2 will be set according to $E(x)$ or $E^{-1}(x)$ mod $P(x)$. The process will be repeated $(n + 1)$ times until all bits of D have been examined.

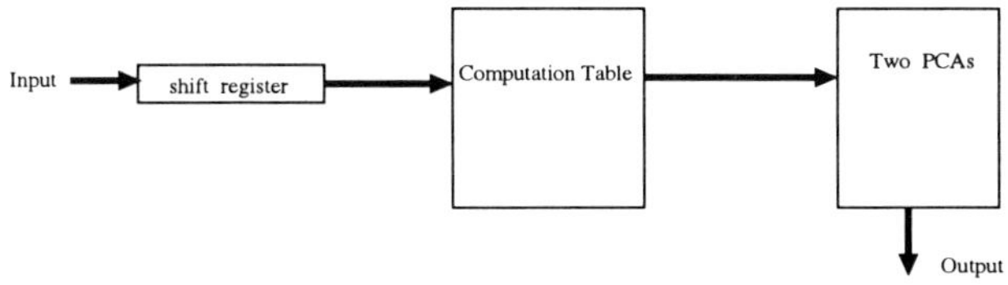

Figure 8. Hardware design for the improved DHKE binary algorithm

5. Conclusion

In this paper, we have presented two improved algorithms for the Diffie-Hellman public key exchange method by introducing the binary redundant representation and its normal form. The speed-up of both proposed algorithms are significant. Up to 33% of the basic operations can be saved compared with the conventional algorithms. The extended PCA structure allows us to use the same VLSI architecture for both conventional symmetric-key and public-key cryptographic systems. Two PCA-based hardware implementations for both improved DHKE algorithm are presented. They are simple, programmable and cascadable, and ideal for VLSI implementation.

References

[1] D. Coppersmith. Fast evaluation of logarithms in fields of characteristic two. *IEEE transactions on information theory*, IT-30(4):587–594, July 1984.

[2] D. M. Gordon and K. McCurley. Massively parallel computation of discrete logarithms. In *Proceedings of Crypto'92, Lecture Notes in Computer Science*, Berlin: Springer-Verlag, 1992.

[3] D. E. Knuth. *The Art of Computer Programming.* Addison-Wesley, Reading, MA, 1981.

[4] R. Mason, T. Peng, and C. N. Zhang. 264 mbps encryption using 2-d pipeline/parallel fpga cellular automa. In *FPA-98*, Ottawa, Canada, 1998.

[5] R. Mason, C. N. Zhang, S. Lee, and M. Deng. High speed encryption using a 2-d cellular automata implemented in a single fpga. In *The 10th International Conference On Wireless Communications*, pages 325–331, Calgary, Canada, 1998.

[6] S. Nandi, B. K. Kar, and P. P. Chaudhuri. Theory and applications of cellular automata in cryptography. *IEEE Transactions On Computers*, 43(4):1346–1356, December 1994.

[7] W. W. Peterson. *Error-Correcting Codes.* MIT Press Cambridge Massachusetts, London, 1972.

[8] D. W. and H. M. New directions in cryptography. *IEEE transactions on information theory*, IT-22(6):644–654, Nov 1976.

[9] C. N. Zhang. An improved binary algorithm for rsa. *Computer Math. Applic.*, 25(6):15–24, January 1993.

Complexity Measure of Encryption Keys Used for Securing Computer Networks

Mostafa A. Bahie-Eldin
Egyptian Armed Forces

Alaa A. Omar
Tech. Res. Dep., Cairo, EGYPT

Abstract

The best way to secure and to get safe electronic payment systems through computer networks is with encryption. The strength of the encryption technique is mainly depending upon the encryption key. One of the basic criteria to evaluate the strength of the key is the complexity measure. In this paper, the Ziv-Lempel complexity for binary random sequences, as well as for finite sequences employed to generate the encryption keys is examined. The complexity versus the sequence length is investigated, and the comparison with the lower bound is done. The obtained results show many interesting points. Among of them: first the random sequence satisfies the lower-bound in all different lengths. Second, Ziv-Lempel complexity for the linear feedback shift registers (LFSR) sequences depends on both the initial condition and on the characteristic polynomial of the LFSR. Third, the complexity depends on the length of the sequence.

1. Introduction

Computers and telecommunication systems are increasingly being used to process information that is sensitive to an individual, a company, or society. The rapid growth in the number of networks with geographically dispersed nodes which are handling such information is resulting in commercial security assuming much greater importance than in the past [9]. Among the most important uses of this technology is ***electronic commerce***: performing financial transactions via electronic information exchanged over telecommunications lines. The **Internet** is important as a facilitator of electronic commerce. Its use to conduct business between organisations is growing and it is now seen by many as an important means to reach the consumer [7]. With such commercial use, the potential loss from unauthorized access and inappropriate disclosure, modification, and retention of information make the implementation of security and privacy measures critical. A key requirement for electronic commerce is the development of secure and efficient electronic payment systems.

The best way to protect the confidentiality of data accessed through computer networks is with encryption. Strong encryption is the kind of encryption that can be used to protect information of real value against organised criminals, multinational corporations, and major governments. Strong encryption used to be only military business; however, in the information society it has become one of the central tools for maintaining privacy and confidentiality.

Encryption is a transformation of data that varies based on a secret parameter called an ***encryption key***. Encryption falls into two main classes: symmetrical (conventional) encryption and asymmetrical (public-key) encryption [2]. Using symmetric (or conventional) cryptosystem like the Data Encryption Standard (DES), triple-DES, and IDEA, data transformed (or encrypted) using an encryption key is scrambled in such a way that it can only be unscrambled (or decrypted) by a similar transformation using the same encryption key. The scrambled data is called ciphertext, and the original or subsequently unscrambled data is called plaintext. When the sender and receiver share an encryption key known only to them, data can be encrypted before transmission, and decrypted after transmission, protecting the data from disclosure to eavesdroppers. In symmetrical encryption, the encryption and decryption keys are identical, and the security depends on the security of the key.

2. Cryptography Design Consideration

To design a cryptosystem, the ***algorithm*** and the ***used key*** are the two main components. A designer should be very wary of published algorithms. Generally, no algorithm that depends on its secrecy is secure. In software, disassembly and reverse-engineering of the algorithm can be done. Experience has shown that a vast majority of algorithms which are dependent on their secrecy, have been proven weak in reality. The security of the system mainly depends upon the used key. Note, keys have limited lifetimes for a number of reasons. The most important reason is protection against cryptanalysis. Each time the key is used, it generates a number of ciphertexts. Using a key repetitively allows an attacker to build up a store of ciphertexts (and possibly plaintexts) which may prove sufficient for a successful cryptanalysis of the key value. If you suspect that an attacker may have obtained your key, then your key is considered compromised.

In selecting a good key, one should consider the following:

1. Keys should not have many repeating characters.

0-8186-8789-4/98 $10.00 © 1998 IEEE

2. If they have any pattern to the eye they should not be used.
3. Keys must be kept secure.
4. Keys should be as long as practical.

Research in cryptanalysis can lead to possible attacks against either the key or the algorithm. Another reason for limiting the lifetime of a key is to minimise the damage from a compromised key. It is unlikely that a user will discover that this key has been compromised by an attacker if the attacker remains "passive". Relatively frequent key changes will limit any potential damage from compromised keys. Ford [4] describes the life cycle of a key as follows:

- key generation and possibly registration for a public key.
- key distribution.
- key activation deactivation.
- key replacement or key update
- key revocation
- key termination, involving destruction and possibly archival.

Good cryptographic systems should always be designed so that they are as difficult to break as possible. It is possible to build systems that cannot be broken in practice (though this cannot usually be proved). This does not significantly increase system implementation effort; however, some care and expertise is required. There is no excuse for a system designer to leave the system breakable. Any mechanisms that can be used to circumvent security must be made explicit, documented, and brought into attention of the users.

In theory, any cryptographic method with a key can be broken by trying all possible keys in sequence. If using ***brute force*** to try all keys is the only option, the required computing power increases exponentially with the length of the key. However, Key length is not the only relevant issue. Many ciphers can be broken without trying all possible keys. In general, it is very difficult to design ciphers that could not be broken more effectively using other methods. Designing your own ciphers may be fun, but it is not recommended in real applications unless you are a true expert and know exactly what you are doing. There are evaluation criteria for key-strength. Among of them are: Randomness properties, complexity, periodicity and correlation immunity of the key outputs, and nonlinear function of the employed algorithm.

3. Ziv-Lempel Complexity for Finite Sequences

There are several different complexity measures: linear complexity [5], quadratic complexity [6], and maximum order complexity, used to examine pseudo-random sequences in cryptography. Another complexity measure for finite sequences is defined by Ziv and Lempel [11]. ***Ziv-Lempel complexity*** measure is a measure of the rate at which new patterns emerge as we move along the sequence.

Let A^* denote the set of all finite sequences over a finite alphabet A. Let $l(\sigma)$ denote the length of $\sigma \quad A^*$ and let

$$A^n = \{\sigma \quad A^* \& l(\sigma) = n\}$$

The null-sequence Λ, i.e., the sequence of length zero, is assumed to be an element of A^*.

A sequence $\sigma \quad A^n$ is fully specified by writing $\sigma = s_1 s_2 \ldots s_n$. The sequence $\sigma(i, j)$ indicates a substring of σ that starts at position i and ends at position j. That is, $\sigma(i, j) = s_i s_{i+1} \ldots s_j$, for $i \leq j$ and $\sigma(i, j) = \Lambda$, for $i > j$.

Q is called a *prefix* of σ, and σ is called the *extension* of Q if there exists an integer i such that $Q = \sigma(1, i)$. It is convenient to identify prefixes of σ by means of π according to $\sigma\pi^i = \sigma(1, l(\sigma) - i)$, $i = 0, 1, \ldots$.
The *vocabulary* of a sequence σ, denoted by $v(\sigma)$, is the subset of A^* formed by all the substrings, $\sigma(i, j)$, of σ.

Example 1: $v(0100) = \{\Lambda, 0, 1, 01, 10, 00, 010, 100, 0100\}$

When a sequence σ is extended by concatenation with one of its substrings, say $W = \sigma(i, j)$, the resulting sequence $R = \sigma W$ can be viewed as being obtained from σ through a simple copying procedure whereby $r_{m+l(\sigma)} = w_m$ is copied from r_{i+m-1}, $m = 1, 2, \ldots, j - i + 1$. The same recursive copying procedure could be applied to generate an extension $R = \sigma Q$ of σ, which is much longer than warranted by any substring in $v(\sigma)$.

Definition 1:

i. An extension $R = \sigma Q$ of σ is *reproducible* from σ, and write $\sigma \varnothing R$, if $Q \quad v(R\pi)$.

ii. A position p of σ such that $Q = R(p, l(Q) + p - 1)$ (i.e., a starting position of σ that enables the copying procedure described above) is called a *pointer* for the reproduction $\sigma \varnothing R$.

Example 2: $001 \varnothing 00101010$ with $p = 2$.

Definition 2: A nonnull sequence σ is said to be *producible* from its prefix $\sigma(1, j)$, if $\sigma(1, j) \varnothing \sigma\pi$ and $j < l(\sigma)$. Producibility of σ from $\sigma(1, j)$ will be denoted by $\sigma(1, j) \quad \sigma$, and $\sigma(1, j)$ will be referred to as a *base* of σ.

Example 3: $01 \quad 0100$ with $p = 1$, but $01 \not\varnothing 0100$.

Definition 3: Consider an m-step production process of a sequence σ and let $\sigma(1, h_i)$, $i = 1, 2, \ldots, m$, be the m states of the process. Note that $h_1 = 1$ and $h_m = l(\sigma)$. The parsing of σ into

$$H(\sigma) = \sigma(1, h_1)\sigma(h_1 + 1, h_2) \ldots \sigma(h_{m-1} + 1, h_m)$$

is called the *production history* of σ and the m substrings $H_i(\sigma) = \sigma(h_{i-1} + 1, h_i)$, $i = 1, 2, \ldots, m$, where $h_0 + 0$, are called the *components* of $H(\sigma)$.

Definition 4: A component $H_i(\sigma)$ and the corresponding production step $\sigma(1, h_{i-1})$ $\sigma(1, h_i)$ are called *exhaustive* if $\sigma(1, h_{i-1}) \varnothing \sigma(1, h_i)$. A history (or, production process) is called *exhaustive* if each of its component is such.

Definition 5: The Ziv-Lempel complexity of a sequence σ, $c(\sigma)$, is defined to be

$$c(\sigma) = c_E(\sigma)$$

where $c_E(\sigma)$ is the number of components in the exhaustive history of σ.

In [11] it is shown that almost all sequences of length n have complexity exceeding $\frac{n}{\log n}$. This value will be used as a threshold of complexity for random sequences. Mund [8], considered minimal and maximal values of the Ziv-Lempel complexity in the following example.

Example 4: Let σ be a sequence, then

i. If σ = 111...110, then Z-L complexity = 2

Note that the linear complexity for σ has a maximum value.

ii. If σ = 111...100...0, then Z-L complexity = 3

iii. If σ = 000...011...10, then Z-L complexity = 2.

4. RESULTS

Case I: *Complexity of Random Sequences*

In Table 1, we compute the Ziv-Lempel complexity for a binary random sequence. The complexity is computed at different lengths of the random sequence. In Fig. 1, we draw the complexity versus the sequence length and we also compare the complexity with the lower-bound condition, i.e. $n / (\log n)$. We can show that the random sequence satisfies the lower-bound in all different lengths.

Table 1 Ziv-Lempel Complexity for different random sequences

Seq. Length	Complexity	Seq. Length	Complexity
100	18	1000	108
200	29	1500	150
300	41	2000	193
400	50	2500	231
500	61	3000	269
600	70	4000	347
700	80	5000	423
800	88	7500	600
900	97	10000	775

We can use the Z-L complexity as a parameter to differentiate between different available sequences. There are two approaches:

First, we demonstrate the complexity value versus the sequence length, n. From this demonstration we can calculate two values:

1. The complexity at different sequence lengths n.

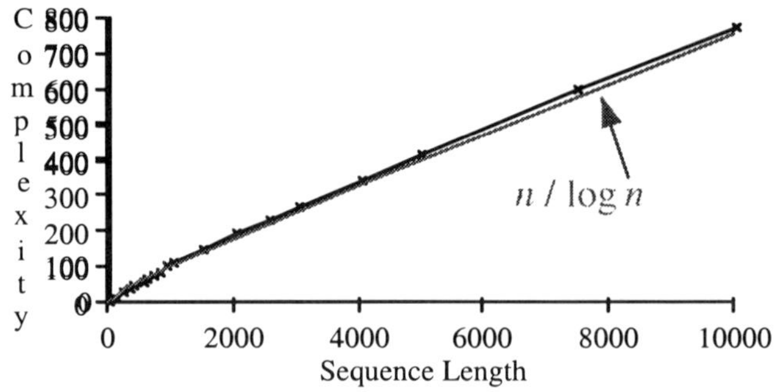

Fig. 1 Complexity against sequence length

2. The rate of complexity increase (α).

The significance of these two values is illustrated as follows:

1. As complexity increases the sequence is better.
2. The rate of changing in α indicates the sequence period.

It is clear that the rate of change of the complexity value can be used to calculate the sequence period too some accuracy value.

The second approach, we manipulate the Z-L complexity value as a random variable. To clarify this point we made different runs, e.g. n = 100, 200, 300, and 400. The procedure is explained before. The significance of this approach is that the mean value and the variance of this random variable is used for judgement between different sequences. As the mean value increases and the variance decreases, the sequence is better, see Table 2.

Table 2 Distribution of Z-L Complexity for different sequence of lengths

Sequence Length = 100		Sequence Length = 200	
Complexity	Events	Complexity	Events
15	0.01	27	0.025
16	0.07	28	0.085
17	0.14	29	0..2
18	0.34	30	0.255
19	0.28	31	0.305
20	0.16	32	0.12
		33	0.01

Sequence Length = 300		Sequence Length = 400	
Complexity	Events	Complexity	Events
38	0.063	47	0.0275
39	0.267	48	0.0725
40	0.343	49	0..265
41	0.20	50	0.2725
42	0.097	51	0.22
43	0.03	52	0.1025
		53	0.0325
		54	0.0075

Case II: ***Complexity of a Periodic Sequence***

Let $s_0, s_1, \ldots, s_{p-1}$ be a periodic sequence where p is its period. Mund [8] computed the Z-L complexity of the periodic sequence.

Theorem: *In a periodic sequence with period p the Z-L complexity has a constant value after maximal* $2p - 1$ *positions of the sequence have been considered.*

Ziv-Lempel complexity for the LFSR sequences depends on both the initial condition and the characteristic polynomial of the LFSR. Also the complexity depends on the length of the sequence. In the case of periodic sequences, Z-L complexity becomes fixed after the first period of the sequence. This means that we can determine the periodicity of a periodic sequence by using Z-L complexity algorithm, see Table 3.

In Table 4, we compute the average complexity for each LFSR and we draw a curve between the average complexity viruses the sequence lengths, see Fig. 2.

Table 4 Ziv-Lempel complexity for different LFSR Sequences

Seq. Length	Complexity	Seq. Length	Complexity
9	18	133	108
18	29	262	150
35	41	510	193
68	50	1032	231

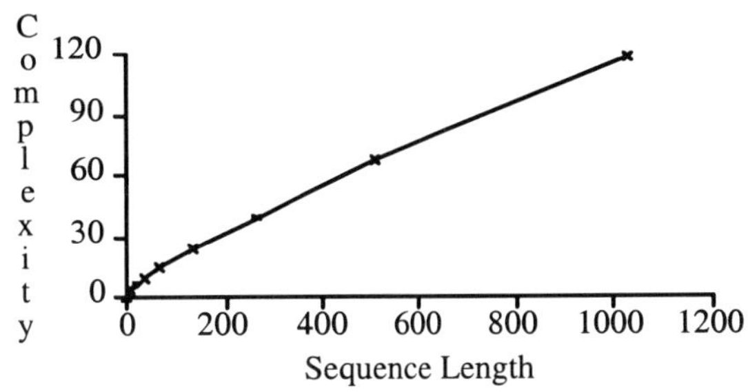

Fig. 2 The curve of Table 4

Table 3 A Complexity of an LFSR sequence depends on both its initial condition and its characteristic polynomial

l	Ch. polynomial.	n	Complexity	m	Complexity	$n/\log n$
3	$1 + x + x^3$	9	4 ∅ 3 times 5 ∅ 4 times	$> n$	4 ∅ 1 times 5 ∅ 5 times 6 ∅ 1 times	2.84
	$1 + x^2 + x^3$		4 ∅ 2 times 5 ∅ 5 times		5 ∅ 7 times	
4	$1 + x + x^4$	18	6 ∅ 4 times 7 ∅ 9 times 8 ∅ 2 times	$> n$	6 ∅ 3 times 7 ∅ 7 times 8 ∅ 5 times	4.32
	$1 + x^3 + x^4$		6 ∅ 6 times 7 ∅ 9 times		6 ∅ 5 times 7 ∅ 8 times 8 ∅ 2 times	
5	$1 + x^2 + x^5$	35	9 ∅ 8 times 10 ∅ 19 times 11 ∅ 4 times	$> n$	9 ∅ 5 times 10 ∅ 18 times 11 ∅ 8 times	6.82
	$1 + x + x^2 + x^3 + x^5$		9 ∅ 6 times 10 ∅ 21 times 11 ∅ 4 times		9 ∅ 4 times 10 ∅ 18 times 11 ∅ 9 times	
6	$1 + x + x^6$	68	13 ∅ 1 times 14 ∅ 8 times 15 ∅ 33 times 16 ∅ 21 times	$> n$	14 ∅ 7 times 15 ∅ 26 times 16 ∅ 30 times	11.17
	$1 + x + x^4 + x^5 + x^6$		14 ∅ 8 times 15 ∅ 38 times 16 ∅ 16 times 17 ∅ 1 times		14 ∅ 6 times 15 ∅ 33 times 16 ∅ 23 times 17 ∅ 1 times	

Cont. **Table 3**

7	$1 + x + x^7$	133	22 ∅ 10 times 23 ∅ 15 times 24 ∅ 62 times 25 ∅ 37 times 26 ∅ 3 times	$> n$	2 ∅ 9 times 23 ∅ 11 times 24 ∅ 56 times 25 ∅ 46 times 26 ∅ 5 times	18.85
	$1 + x^2 + x^3 + x^4 + x^5 + x^6 + x^7$		23 ∅ 11 times 24 ∅ 63 times 25 ∅ 49 times 26 ∅ 9 times		23 ∅ 7 times 24 ∅ 53 times 25 ∅ 57 times 26 ∅ 10 times	
8	$1 + x + x^3 + x^5 + x^8$	262	39 ∅ 42 times 40 ∅ 117 times 41 ∅ 79 times 42 ∅ 15 times 43 ∅ 2 times	$> n$	39 ∅ 33 times 40 ∅ 113 times 41 ∅ 81 times 42 ∅ 26 times 43 ∅ 2 times	32.6
	$1 + x^2 + x^3 + x^4 + x^8$		38 ∅ 3 times 39 ∅ 68 times 40 ∅ 115 times 41 ∅ 58 times 42 ∅ 11 times		38 ∅ 2 times 39 ∅ 51 times 40 ∅ 122 times 41 ∅ 66 times 42 ∅ 14 times	
9	$1 + x^4 + x^9$	519	65 ∅ 7 times 66 ∅ 32 times 67 ∅ 125 times 68 ∅ 174 times 69 ∅ 134 times 70 ∅ 37 times 71 ∅ 2 times	$> n$	65 ∅ 6 times 66 ∅ 26 times 67 ∅ 116 times 68 ∅ 167 times 69 ∅ 148 times 70 ∅ 43 times 71 ∅ 5 times	57.5
	$1 + x^3 + x^4 + x^6 + x^9$		66 ∅ 33 times 67 ∅ 131 times 68 ∅ 193 times 69 ∅ 120 times 70 ∅ 32 times 71 ∅ 2 times		66 ∅ 25 times 67 ∅ 121 times 68 ∅ 188 times 69 ∅ 134 times 70 ∅ 40 times 71 ∅ 3 times	
10	$1 + x^3 + x^{10}$	1032	116 ∅ 42 times 117 ∅ 82 times 118 ∅ 224 times 119 ∅ 347 times 120 ∅ 249 times 121 ∅ 64 times 122 ∅ 15 times	$> n$	116 ∅ 36 times 117 ∅ 75 times 118 ∅ 207 times 119 ∅ 340 times 120 ∅ 276 times 121 ∅ 68 times 122 ∅ 21 times	103.1
	$1 + x^2 + x^3 + x^8 + x^{10}$		115 ∅ 2 times 116 ∅ 23 times 117 ∅ 138 times 118 ∅ 317 times 119 ∅ 360 times 120 ∅ 153 times 121 ∅ 27 times 122 ∅ 3 times		115 ∅ 2 times 116 ∅ 18 times 117 ∅ 116 times 118 ∅ 311 times 119 ∅ 363 times 120 ∅ 173 times 121 ∅ 37 times 122 ∅ 3 times	

5. Conclusions

For random sequences, The rate of changing in complexity value indicates the sequence period. Ziv-Lempel complexity for the LFSR sequences depends on both the initial condition and on the characteristic polynomial of the LFSR. Also, the complexity depends on the length of the sequence. In the case of periodic sequences, Ziv-Lempel complexity becomes fixed after the first period of the sequence. This means that we can determine the periodicity of a periodic sequence by using Ziv-Lempel complexity algorithm. Also, we can say that the sequence length of any bit stream can be calculated approximately by means of Ziv-Lempel complexity.

References

[1] G. Brassard, Modern Cryptology, Volume 325 of lecture notes in computer science, Springer-Verlag, 1988.

[2] W. Diffie, and M. Helman, "New directions in cryptography", IEEE Trans. on Inform. Theory, Vol.22, No.6, Nov.. 1976.

[3]W. Diffie, and M. Helman, "Privacy and authentication: An introduction to cryptography", IEEE Trans. on Inform. Theory, Vol.25, No.3, Mar.1979.

[4] W. Ford, computer communication security-principles, standard protocols and techniques, Prentice-Hall, New Jersey, 1994.

[5] J. D. Golic, "On the linear complexity of functions of periodic GF(q) sequences", IEEE Trans. Inform. Theory, Vol. IT-35, No.1, 1989, pp.69-75.

[6] E. L. Key," An analysis of the structure and complexity of nonlinear binary sequence generators", WEE Trans. Inform. Theory, Vol. IT-22, No.6, 1976, pp.732-736.

[7] B. C. Neuman, "Security, payment, and privacy for network commerce,'" IEEE Journal on selected area in communication SAC, Vol.13, No.8, October 1995.

[8] Mund, S., "Ziv-Lempel complexity for periodic sequences and its cryptographic applications", in Lecture Notes in Computer Science 547; Advanced in Cryptology: Proc. Eurocrypto'91, Davis, Ed., pp. 114-126. Berlin: Springer-Verlag, 1991.

[9] K. Preston, "Security measures in communication networks," Electrical Communication-Vol. 60, No.1, 1986.

[10] Summers, Rita C. (1997), Secure computing: threats and safeguards, McGraw Hill, 1997.

[11] J. Ziv, and A. Lempel, "Universal algorithm for sequential data compression", IEEE Trans. Inform. Theory, Vol. IT-22, No. 1, 1976, pp.75-81.

Track B

Intrusion Detection

Chair

C. Schuba, Sun Microsystems Laboratories

Detecting Anomalous and Unknown Intrusions Against Programs*

Anup K. Ghosh, James Wanken, & Frank Charron
Reliable Software Technologies
21515 Ridgetop Circle, Suite 250
Sterling, VA 20166
poc:aghosh@rstcorp.com
www.rstcorp.com

Abstract

The ubiquity of the Internet connection to desktops has been both boon to business as well as cause for concern for the security of digital assets that may be unknowingly exposed. Firewalls have been the most commonly deployed solution to secure corporate assets against intrusions, but firewalls are vulnerable to errors in configuration, ambiguous security policies, data-driven attacks through allowed services, and insider attacks. The failure of firewalls to adequately protect digital assets from computer-based attacks has been boon to commercial intrusion detection tools. Two general approaches to detecting computer security intrusions in real-time are misuse detection and anomaly detection. Misuse detection attempts to detect known attacks against computer systems. Anomaly detection uses knowledge of users' normal behavior to detect attempted attacks. The primary advantage of anomaly detection over misuse detection methods is the ability to detect novel and unknown intrusions. This paper presents a study in employing neural networks to detect the existence of anomalous and unknown intrusions against a software system using the anomaly detection approach.

1 Introduction

The connectivity of the Internet to corporate, academic, and home users' desktop machines has become ubiquitous. The Internet has enabled nearly seamless connectivity of users via email and World Wide Web pages among other services. While the Internet has enabled the boon of electronic commerce, it has also been an enabling medium for computer-based attacks against corporate and university assets exposed to the Internet.

Firewalls were initially touted as the panacea to computer security problems. By restricting access to computer systems through known ports, firewalls served to eliminate computer exploitation attacks through network services that run often unbeknownst to the host site. Now, it is commonly understood that firewalls merely reduce exposure rather than eliminate vulnerabilities in computer systems. Computer-based attacks can compromise digital assets in spite of firewalls by exploiting errors in firewall configuration, exploiting ambiguities in security policies, obtaining access around firewalls through backdoors and computer modems, attacking network services allowed through the firewall, and using insider privilege to gain unauthorized access to sensitive assets. Furthermore, firewalls often engender a false sense of security that results in relaxed security at the individual host machines. As a result, once a penetration through or around a firewall is successful, internal webs of trust between computers can be exploited to obtain increasing levels of access to sensitive assets.

The failure of firewalls to adequately secure computer systems has led to the growth of the intrusion detection software industry. Intrusion detection software attempts to detect possible attacks against software systems in real time before critical assets are compromised. While no one purports intrusion detection software to be a silver bullet to computer security problems, combining intrusion detection with other security mechanisms such as firewalls, strong access controls, one-time passwords for remote authentication, secure shells, and regular auditing can provide defense in depth that can stymie the majority of computer-based attacks. Without the assistance of intrusion detection systems, most organizations are not aware

*This work was funded by the Defense Advanced Research Projects Agency (DARPA) under Contract DAAH01-97-C-R095. THE VIEWS AND CONCLUSIONS CONTAINED IN THIS DOCUMENT ARE THOSE OF THE AUTHORS AND SHOULD NOT BE INTERPRETED AS REPRESENTING THE OFFICIAL POLICIES, EITHER EXPRESSED OR IMPLIED, OF THE DEFENSE ADVANCED RESEARCH PROJECTS AGENCY OR THE U.S. GOVERNMENT.

0-8186-8789-4/98 $10.00 © 1998 IEEE

of the number of attacks they experience on a daily basis against their intrusion detection systems. Intrusion detection systems often have two components: (1) detection of possible attacks, and (2) response to attacks. This paper addresses the first component, *i.e.* how to effectively detect attacks against computer systems. The second component involves implementing an organization's policy for either blocking an attack in progress or entrapping the attacker in a snare.

Intrusion detection techniques can be partitioned into two main approaches: misuse detection and anomaly detection. Misuse detection methods attempt to model attacks on a system as specific patterns, then systematically scan the system for occurrences of these patterns [Kumar and Spafford, 1996, Lunt, 1993,
Garvey and Lunt, 1991, Porras and Kemmerer, 1992, Ilgun, 1992, Monrose and Rubin, 1997]. This process involves a specific encoding of previous behaviors and actions that were deemed intrusive or malicious. Anomaly detection assumes that intrusions are highly correlated to abnormal behavior exhibited by either a user or an application. The basic idea is to baseline normal behavior of the object being monitored and then flag behaviors that are significantly different from this baseline as abnormalities, or possible intrusions. See [Lunt, 1993, Lunt and Jagannathan, 1988, Lunt, 1990, Lunt et al., 1992, D'haeseleer et al., 1996, Porras and Neumann, 1997] for sources on anomaly detection approaches.

The most significant disadvantage of misuse detection approaches is that they will only detect the attacks for which they are trained to detect. Novel attacks or even variants of common attacks often go undetected. In a time when new security vulnerabilities in software are discovered and exploited every day, the reactive approach embodied by misuse detection methods is not feasible for defeating malicious attacks.

The main advantage of anomaly detection approaches is the ability to detect novel attacks against software systems, variants of known attacks, and deviations from normal usage of programs regardless of whether the source is a privileged internal user or an unauthorized external user. One drawback of anomaly detection approaches is that well-known attacks may not be detected, particularly if they fit the established profile of the user. Once detected, it is often difficult to characterize the nature of the attack for forensic purposes. Another drawback of many anomaly detection approaches is that a malicious user who knows he or she is being profiled can change his or her profile slowly over time to essentially train the anomaly detection method to learn his or her malicious behavior as normal. Finally, a high false positive rate may result for a narrowly trained detection algorithm, or conversely, a high false negative rate may result for a broadly trained anomaly detection approach.

In this paper, a novel anomaly detection approach to intrusion detection is described. Because new vulnerabilities in software are reported on a daily basis in forums such as Bugtraq[1], the challenge of intrusion detection research is to create techniques that can detect novel attacks against computer systems. The status quo in commercial intrusion detection software is represented by misuse detection approaches that scan for known attacks. These techniques cannot detect novel attacks against computer systems, and often times they do not detect simple variations on known attacks.

A key distinction of the work presented here is that intrusion detection is performed on software programs. Most intrusion detection systems analyze either network traffic or host system logs. This work focuses on system processes because attacks against computer systems are in fact attacks against specific software programs. By analyzing the usage or mis-usage of specific software programs, computer-based intrusions can be tracked at a finer grain of resolution. The work of Forrest et al. also examines system processes for anomalous behavior, however, their approach captures system calls from programs and uses a table look-up algorithm for detecting potential intrusions [Forrest et al., 1997, D'haeseleer et al., 1996]. An application of machine learning to intrusion detection has been developed elsewhere as well [Lane and Brodley, 1997]. Lane and Brodley's work is similar in that machine learning is used to distinguish between normal and anomalous behavior. However, their work is different in that they build *user* profiles based on sequences of each individual's normal user commands and attempt to detect intruders based on deviations from the established user profile. Rather than building profiles on a per-user basis, our work builds profiles of *software behavior* and attempts to distinguish between normal software behavior and malicious software behavior. The advantages of our approach are that vagaries of individual behavior are abstracted because program behavior rather than individual usage is studied.

The approach described here applies machine learning techniques to learn the normal behavior of a particular program in order to detect aberrations. By providing detection at the software process level, mul-

[1] `Bugtraq` can be viewed on-line at http://www.netspace.org/lsv-archive/bugtraq.html

tiple, diverse, and overlapping detectors can be embedded within the software infrastructure to provide system-wide coverage.

2 Employing Anomaly Detection Using Neural Networks

Desiring the ability to detect novel or unknown intrusions, the anomaly detection approach was employed in this research. Neural networks are used to learn the normal behavior of the monitored process and to detect potential intrusions against the software. The defining aspect of this approach is that anomaly detection is performed at the software process level using machine learning techniques.

Monitoring at the process level adds a layer of abstraction such that abnormal process behavior can be detected irrespective of individual users' behavior. This layer abstracts out users' individual behavior and allows anomaly detection against the set of all users' behavior. The approach taken in this research enables both observable external states such as program input/output as well as internal states that can be captured via instrumentation to be employed in training a neural network for detection of misuse. Thus, if the source code of the monitored program is not readily available, it does not preclude the use of neural networks for intrusion detection. The advantage of the black-box approach is that it can be used to detect malicious attacks against commercial software where the source code is unavailable. The added advantage of using a white-box–capable approach is that it allows access to internal states of a program which provides additional information in detecting anomalous program behavior. Differentiation between anomalous and normal behavior will occur by creating expectations about a program's usage and behavior and then attempting to detect deviations from the normal behavior.

Expectations of normal program behavior are created by dynamic analysis of the process under normal operational conditions. This approach differs from model-based approaches that specify either correct usage or, conversely, misusage of programs [Kumar and Spafford, 1996].

An architecture of the system for analyzing programs for malicious behavior is shown in Figure 1. The system was designed to enable different applications, neural networks, and test vectors to be used interchangeably. Thus, the architecture was constructed such that any of these components can be extracted and replaced with a different version without affecting the other components.

The approach begins with training neural networks with supervision; *i.e.*, feedback is applied to the network during training to indicate whether the input is normal or anomalous. Training with supervision requires labeled input, so it is not feasible for on-line detection of intrusions. However, in cases where historical or archival data exists, it can be useful for training a network to learn normal behavior and in some cases for recognizing non-normal behavior. This approach to anomaly detection permits programmatic detection of intrusions based on deviations of normal behavior without the need for a detailed specification model of correct behavior.

During recall, or during the on-line operation mode of the tool, the neural network classifies inputs and internal states as either anomalous or normal. Anomalous inputs and anomalous internal states are assume to be indicators of potentially dangerous behavior. The approach has proven to be easily modifiable to monitor other processes than those already tested.

One drawback of this approach is that the training period of the neural network may take on the order of hours or days to complete. However, other approaches that build up user profiles suffer from this same problem. Another pitfall to be aware of is that the network is only as good as the data on which it has been trained. It not known what effect different training sets would have on the results presented in this paper. The final drawback of our implementation is that if new data is added to the training set, the neural network has to be re-trained over the entire training set, instead of just the data that was added to the training set.

2.1 Backpropagation network

The backpropagation network, or backprop, is probably the most commonly used neural network. The standard architecture consists of an input layer, at least one hidden layer (neurons that are not directly connected to the input or output nodes), and an output layer. Typically, there are no connections between neurons in the same layer or to a previous layer.

Backprops have generalized capability. As such, they can produce nearly correct outputs for inputs that were not used in the training set. In theory, no more than two hidden layers are needed in a neural network since the network can generate arbitrarily complex regions in the state space [Lippmann, 1991]. One of the backprop's main drawbacks, though, is that it tends to be very computationally complex and is time consuming to train. Backprops are well-suited for applications in classification, function approximation, and prediction [Jain et al., 1996]. For the purposes of intrusion detection, the backprop is well-suited for

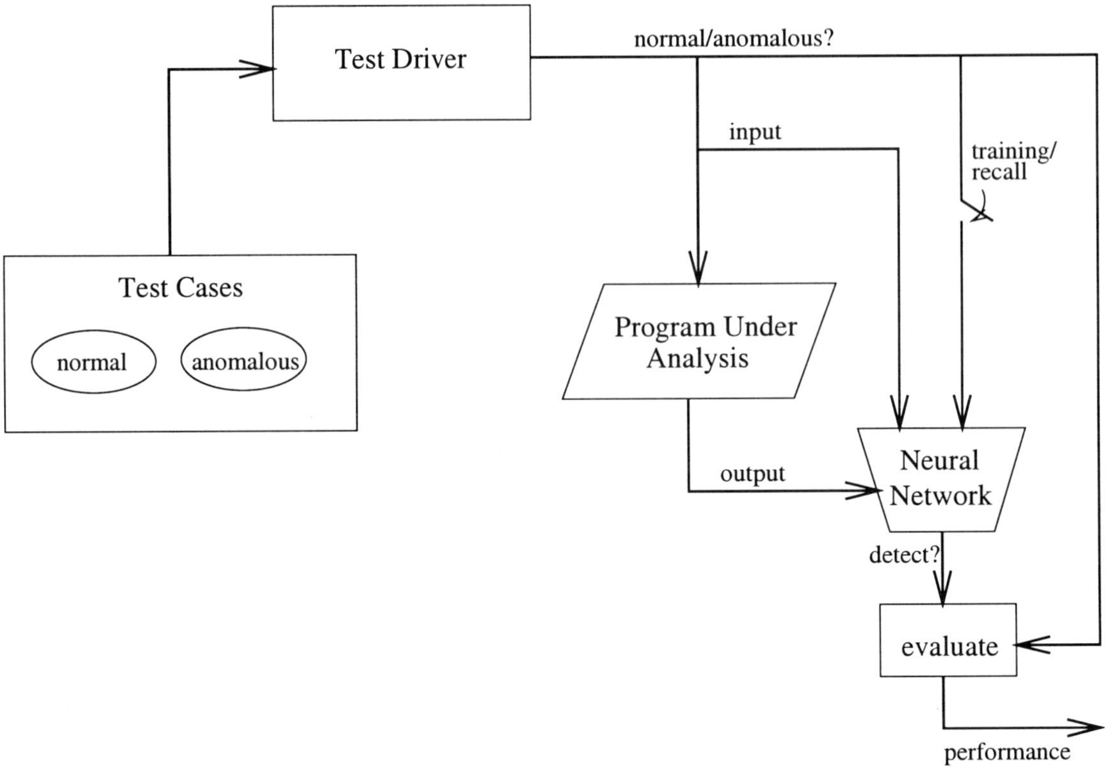

Figure 1: An architecture for analyzing programs for anomalous or malicious behavior using neural networks.

classifying normal behavior and flagging anomalous behavior.

The training cycle of a backprop proceeds in two distinct phases. First, the input is submitted to the network and the activations for each level of neurons are cascaded forward. In the training phase, the desired output is compared with the network's output. For instance, in training with supervision, the desired output for anomalous data is an intrusion detection. If the vectors do not agree, the network updates the weights starting at the output neurons. Then, the change in weights is calculated for the previous layer. This process continues to cascade through the layers of neurons toward the input neurons, hence the name backpropagation.

3 Neural Network Implementation

The backprop implementation provided many advantages in this work. Backprop networks are very good at classifying complex relationships, which in the case of anomaly detection, is useful for classifying normal and anomalous states.

The generalized backprop neural network is shown in Figure 2. The input layer of the network governs the number of inputs and internal states that the network uses in classification. Likewise, the output nodes govern the total number of classes the network is classifying. The backprop is trained with supervision; thus, the desired outputs for each input pattern is supplied to the network during the training phase.

4 Experimental Analysis

The objective of the experimentation described in this section is to determine how effective the implemented neural network is at detecting misuse of programs. The approach examines program inputs as well as internal states to determine if the program is being mis-used.

The experiment was designed to detect potential misuse of system programs, such as `lpr`. The Linux `lpr` program can be subverted on certain platforms using a buffer overflow attack. It should also be noted that this experiment was performed using both black-box as well as white-box analysis because access to the source code for the `lpr` program was freely available. This experiment was run repeatedly using different initial weightings of the neural network in order to account for potential statistical out-liers in the results.

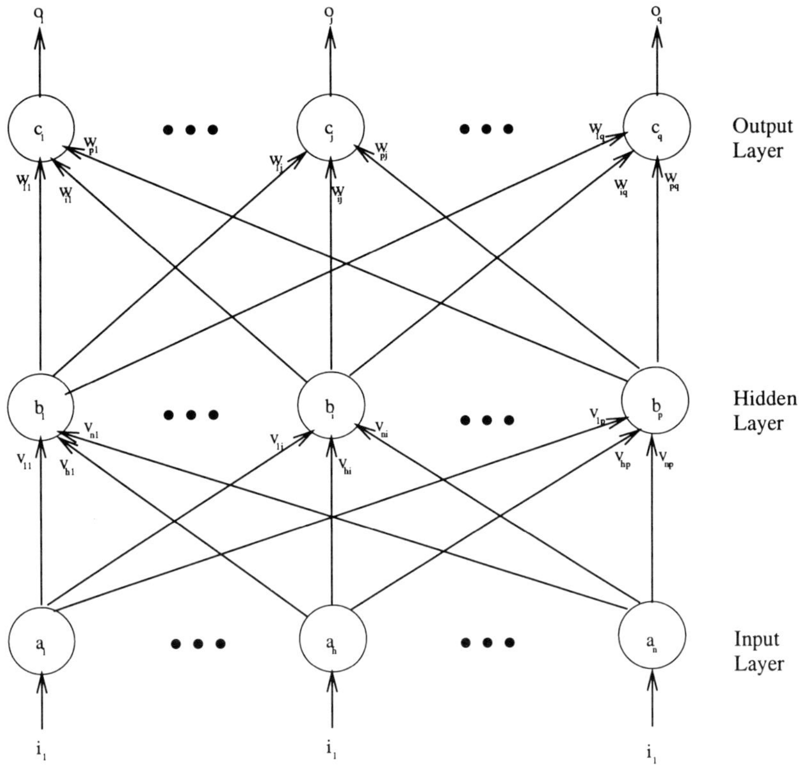

Figure 2: Topology of the elementary backpropagation network architecture with one hidden layer, **n** input nodes, and **q** output nodes.

5 Linux `lpr` Exploitation Experimental Results

5.1 Introduction

This set of experiments explores the use of a neural network to detect anomalous use of the standard Linux `lpr` program. The linux `lpr` program is known to have a buffer overflow vulnerability which can be exploited through input. This exploit uses a buffer overflow attack on specific `lpr` flags to enable the user to execute a root shell or perform other root-privileged commands. The goal of this experimentation is to determine how effective the neural network is in detecting anomalous use of system programs. To this end, the neural network was trained with malicious, normal, and in some cases, random input. This set of experiments also examines the use of internal states in the process of anomaly detection.

5.2 General description

The `lpr` program is exploited in the following manner. An auxiliary program was written which filled a large character buffer. At the end of this buffer, specific character strings were added to overwrite the return address of the stack frame with the address of a new instruction to be executed, which was placed elsewhere in the buffer (this instruction was usually a /bin/sh). The program would then `exec` an `lpr` child process with this buffer as one of the flag arguments. During the experimentation, both this auxiliary program and the `lpr` program were modified to write specific inputs and internal states to a file to be used as inputs to the neural network.

The neural network's input patterns consisted of a combination of inputs from two distinct sources. The first source was the character buffer passed to the `lpr` program as a flag argument. To encode the character buffer, only the last 75 positions were used. This was done in an attempt to reduce the difference between a normal flag input, typically on the order of 10-30 characters, and an overflow buffer of approximately 4,000 characters. Thus, for the overflow attempts, only the last 75 of the 4,096 characters were used as inputs, and for non-overflow attempts, the entire string was used (unless of course it exceeded 75 characters). To encode these 75 input characters, they were given the value: (integer value of character) / 128.0, and 0.0 was used to pad any of the unused inputs.

The second source of input was the internal `len`

variable in the `lpr card()` function. The `card()` function was chosen because most of the `lpr` flag inputs are funneled through this particular procedure. The `len` variable is interesting because it represents the length of the input parameter. The `len` variable from `card()` constituted an additional 8 inputs (since the procedure could be executed multiple times), and was encoded by: (`len` value)/1032, where 0.0 was used to pad any of the unused inputs.

5.3 Training sets

The input patterns for the neural networks' training sets were constructed from the following sets: malicious inputs, normal `lpr` inputs, and random inputs. Malicious inputs were generated using the exploit program mentioned above. The malicious inputs did not necessarily generate `/bin/sh`, but were generated to look very similar. The normal `lpr` inputs were generated by printing valid files, with various flag options. The random inputs were generated using the `fuzz` program [Miller et al., 1995] and were limited to a length of 80 (only 75 characters could be used).

5.4 Recall set

To test the performance of each of the neural networks trained below, one recall set was created for all `lpr` experiments. The recall set consisted of 150 normal `lpr` inputs, 50 malicious inputs, and 50 random inputs. *All of these input patterns were unique from those used in the training sets.* The recall sets for the different networks were only modified in the experiments to include the specific subset of input patterns that were necessary for a particular network. Hence, if the internal state was not used to train the network, then the inputs corresponding to the `len` variable would also not be clamped to the network during the recall phase.

5.5 Experiments

The neural network used in the `lpr` exploit experiments was a 3 layer backpropagation network whose architecture consisted of a hidden layer, an input layer, and an output layer. There were 125 nodes in the hidden layer, 1 output node, and a variable number of input nodes.

Table 1 summarizes the experimental setup for the six experiments. The inputs to the neural network (NN) are distinguished between the experiments by whether the inputs were external `lpr` inputs or internal `lpr` states. External inputs represent standard input to the `lpr` program. If the `len` variable was used as an input to the neural network, then the *internal* column is checked in the table. The number of input nodes, hidden nodes, and output nodes for each of the neural network experiments is also given in the table. The other distinguishing parameter between the experiments is whether random input was used to train the network. If random data was used in training the network, then this column is checked in the table. The neural network was trained to classify random data as anomalous, since the network attempts to distinguish between normal use and anomalous use of a program. The goal of the experimentation is to determine which of these parameters are most useful (or conversely least useful) for detection of misuse of a program.

5.5.1 Discussion of results

Table 2 shows the results from all six experiments. All experiments were run 30 times using 30 different initial weights of the network. The performance of the network is evaluated based on the percentage of the inputs it classified correctly, the percentage of false positives, and the percentage of false negatives. A false positive is defined as a normal input that was classified as anomalous by the network. A false negative is defined as an anomalous input that was classified as a normal by the network. Either of these two distinctions would constitute an error in classification by the network. The results are presented as averages, minima, and maxima over these runs in these categories.

To summarize the results, the best results were obtained in Experiments 3 and 4 when the neural network was trained with random data generation. Recall, that the neural network was trained to classify random data as anomalous. Including the internal state variable `len` in addition to the external `lpr` inputs did not impact the results significantly. In fact, in Experiments 5 and 6, where the neural network was trained and tested on the internal `len` variable exclusively, the results were the weakest. Arguably, training with the internal `len` variable exclusively was too narrow for detection of a range of anomalous and malicious usage.

The neural network in Experiment 6 did not converge to an acceptable mean squared error, so its results were omitted. In Experiment 5, the error rate was approximately 20%—exclusively false negatives. In none of the experiments were false positives detected. Since the training was heavily biased with normal inputs, in no cases did the neural network incorrectly classify a normal input as an anomalous input (the false positive case).

As a simple benchmark for comparison, consider a monkey instead of a neural network that is choosing whether a given input is normal or anomalous. The monkey uses a simple algorithm for determining

	NN Inputs		NN Layers			
Num	external	internal	Inputs	Hidden	Outputs	Random Data Included
1	x		75	125	1	
2	x	x	83	125	1	
3	x		75	125	1	x
4	x	x	83	125	1	x
5		x	8	125	1	
6		x	8	125	1	x

Table 1: Experimental setup for detection of anomalous use of `lpr` program.

whether the input is normal or anomalous—he flips a coin. The likelihood that the monkey will classify an input as normal is 50% as is the likelihood that an input will be classified as anomalous. The actual inputs sent to the program have the following prior probabilities: 40% were anomalous while 60% were normal. The probability that the monkey commits a false negative is the probability that an anomalous input was sent to the program and that the monkey said it was normal. Since these are independent events, the false negative probability is 20%. The probability that the monkey commits a false positive is the probability that a normal input is sent and that the monkey said it was anomalous. The false positive probability is calculated similarly and is 30%. The results from using a neural network on the whole do better than the monkey. No false positives were detected (compared to 30% for the monkey), while false negatives for the neural network ranged from 0.4% to 19.9% (compared to 20% for the monkey). For some experiments (*e.g.*, Experiments 1, 2, and 5), the neural network did as bad as the monkey for false negatives (these are explained in the discussion below), while in others it did extremely well compared to the monkey (*e.g.*, Experiments 3 and 4).

In intrusion detection systems, reducing the false positive rate is perceived as a greater responsibility than reducing the false negative rate. The reasoning is that an excessive false positive rate can lead to a "cry wolf" syndrome where nobody pays attention to the intrusion detection software after awhile. On the other hand, provided multiple, overlapping detectors, a small false negative rate is tolerable as missed attempts by one detection unit may be correctly classified by another. A discussion of the results from each of the experiments is presented next.

Experiment 1 This experiment can be considered the baseline for the `lpr` exploit experiments (see Table 1). It demonstrates how well the neural network performed when training only on the accessible `lpr` inputs, a reasonably sized test set, and without training randomly generated input. From Table 2 we see that the baseline error rate was 20%, exclusively composed of false negatives.

Experiment 2 This experiment extends the baseline experiment, (Experiment 1), by not only using the accessible inputs to the `lpr` program, but also the internal state (represented by the `len` variable in the `card()` function). This experiment attempts to determine if by using an internal program state whether the performance of detection can be improved. The results do not indicate any significant impact, let alone improvement. The results are too similar to Experiment 1 to be statistically significant.

Experiment 3 The network was trained with random inputs to further diversify its notion of anomalous inputs. The idea is to expose the network to a number of different types of anomalous input, rather then strictly well-known intrusion attempts. Training with randomly generated inputs may be one way of detecting novel intrusion attempts. The performance of the network was excellent in this experiment. The average error rate for this experiment was only 0.9%. We can conclude that including randomly generated patterns in the training set vastly increased the performance of the network allowing the network to correctly classify a wide range of input patterns with a very high degree of accuracy. The results indicates that an anomaly detection approach may be useful over misuse detection in detecting novel, unknown intrusion attempts—especially when trained with random data classified as anomalous.

Experiment 4 This experiment extends Experiment 3, by including the internal state variable `len`. Once again, the goal is to determine if by adding in internal state information, whether the performance of the neural network will be improved. As seen from the Table 2, adding the internal variable once again did not statistically impact the results.

Num	Classified Correct Avg	Classified Correct Min	Classified Correct Max	False Positive Avg	False Positive Min	False Positive Max	False Negative Avg	False Negative Min	False Negative Max
1	82.5%	80.1%	88.4%	0.0%	0.0%	0.0%	17.5%	11.6%	19.9%
2	81.9%	80.1%	85.7%	0.0%	0.0%	0.0%	18.1%	14.3%	19.9%
3	99.1%	98.0%	99.6%	0.0%	0.0%	0.0%	0.9%	0.4%	2.0%
4	98.8%	97.6%	99.6%	0.0%	0.0%	0.0%	1.2%	0.4%	2.4%
5	80.2%	80.2%	80.2%	0.0%	0.0%	0.0%	19.8%	19.8%	19.8%
6									

Table 2: Results of detection from anomalous use of `lpr` program.

Experiment 5 This experiment uses the internal state exclusively as the input to the neural network during training and recall. The results were the worst of all the experiments, but not significantly worse than experiments 1 and 2. A closer look at the data revealed that on recall, all the anomalous data randomly generated were classified as normal by the network (the false negative case). This contributed to the large false negative rate for this experiment. The reason is that the randomly generated data had a length approximately close to that of the normal training set. On the other hand, the network did very well in correctly classifying all anomalous input that were buffer overflows. Using strictly the `len` variable is effective at detecting buffer overflows, but not in detecting other potential misuses of a program.

The problem stems from the fact that the single internal variable chosen does not provide sufficient information to classify the input patterns. Inspecting the training set reveals that all of the anomalous input patterns are exactly the same, when one is only looking at the internal variable `len`. Thus, it is no surprise that the network converged to a state in which only this input vector was classified as anomalous. To alleviate this problem, a few steps can be taken. The first is that additional internal variables could be used. A second is to pair this internal state with inputs, as was done in the earlier experiments. This experiment reveals one of the problematic areas encountered in this research, namely, identifying which information provides maximum utility for detection of anomalous behavior.

Experiment 6 The neural network in Experiment 6 did not converge to an acceptable mean squared error, so its results were omitted.

6 Conclusions

This paper describes novel work in using neural networks for detecting misuse of programs. Two important observations result from this work. First, the results demonstrate how misuse of programs can be detected using neural networks. The results indicate that training with randomly generated data lead to the best performance in detection of possible novel misuse attempts—an area in which most misuse detection approaches are weak. Furthermore, the results show the benefit of applying anomaly detection at the process level such that abnormal process behavior can be detected irrespective of individual users' behavior. This approach abstracts out users' individual behavior and allows anomaly detection against the set of all users' behavior.

The experiments also raise an interesting discussion about using internal program states in training the neural networks. Choosing useful internal states is in general a very difficult process. How a particular state is identified as being important is a time consuming task, usually relying heavily upon code inspection. The final experiment also provides a warning for not placing too much emphasis on a particular internal state, or a single input for that matter. The best approach seems to be to take a broad, yet representative sample of inputs and internal states. Further research will attempt to identify important internal states for anomalous use of programs. These results may be important in not only detecting attempted misuse of programs, but also erroneous program behavior.

References

[D'haeseleer et al., 1996] D'haeseleer, P., Forrest, S., and Helman, P. (1996). An immunological approach to change detection: Algorithms, analysis and implications. In *IEEE Symposium on Security and Privacy*.

[Forrest et al., 1997] Forrest, S., Hofmeyr, S., and Somayaji, A. (1997). Computer immunology. *Communications of the ACM*, 40(10):88–96.

[Garvey and Lunt, 1991] Garvey, T. and Lunt, T. (1991). Model-based intrusion detection. In *Proceedings of the 14th National Computer Security Conference*.

[Ilgun, 1992] Ilgun, K. (1992). Ustat: A real-time intrusion detection system for unix. Master's thesis, Computer Science Dept, UCSB.

[Jain et al., 1996] Jain, A., Mao, J., and Mohiuddin, K. M. (1996). Artificial neural networks: A tutorial. *IEEE Computer*, 29(3):31–33.

[Kumar and Spafford, 1996] Kumar, S. and Spafford, E. (1996). A pattern matching model for misuse intrusion detection. The COAST Project, Purdue University.

[Lane and Brodley, 1997] Lane, T. and Brodley, C. (1997). An application of machine learning to anomaly detection. In *Proceedings of the 20th National Information Systems Security Conference*, pages 366–377.

[Lippmann, 1991] Lippmann, R. (1991). *An Introduction to Computing with Neural Nets*, chapter Part 1, pages 5–23. IEEE Press, Piscataway, NJ. in Neural Networks Theoretical Foundations and Analysis.

[Lunt, 1990] Lunt, T. (1990). Ides: an intelligent system for detecting intruders. In *Proceedings of the Symposium: Computer Security, Threat and Countermeasures*. Rome, Italy.

[Lunt, 1993] Lunt, T. (1993). A survey of intrusion detection techniques. *Computers and Security*, 12:405–418.

[Lunt and Jagannathan, 1988] Lunt, T. and Jagannathan, R. (1988). A prototype real-time intrusion-detection system. In *Proceedings of the 1988 IEEE Symposium on Security and Privacy*.

[Lunt et al., 1992] Lunt, T., Tamaru, A., Gilham, F., Jagannthan, R., Jalali, C., Javitz, H., Valdos, A., Neumann, P., and Garvey, T. (1992). A real-time intrusion-detection expert system (ides). Technical Report, Computer Science Laboratory, SRI Internationnal.

[Miller et al., 1995] Miller, B., Koski, D., Lee, C., Maganty, V., Murthy, R., Natarajan, A., and Steidl, J. (1995). Fuzz revisted: A re-examination of the reliability of UNIX utilities and services. Technical report, University of Wisconsin, Computer Sciences Dept.

[Monrose and Rubin, 1997] Monrose, F. and Rubin, A. (1997). Authentication via keystroke dynamics. In *4th ACM Conference on Computer and Communications Security*.

[Porras and Kemmerer, 1992] Porras, P. and Kemmerer, R. (1992). Penetration state transition analysis - a rule-based intrusion detection approach. In *Eighth Annual Computer Security Applications Conference*, pages 220–229. IEEE Computer Society Press.

[Porras and Neumann, 1997] Porras, P. and Neumann, P. (1997). Emerald: Event monitoring enabling responses to anomalous live disturbances. In *Proceedings of the 20th National Information Systems Security Conference*, pages 353–365.

Intrusion Detection
Applying Machine Learning to Solaris Audit Data

David Endler
Department of Electrical Engineering and Computer Science
Tulane University
New Orleans, LA 70118
endler@eecs.tulane.edu

Abstract

An Intrusion Detection System (IDS) seeks to identify unauthorized access to computer systems' resources and data. The most common analysis tool that these modern systems apply is the operating system audit trail that provides a fingerprint of system events over time. In this research, the Basic Security Module auditing tool of Sun's Solaris operating environment was used in both an anomoly and misuse detection approach. The anomoly detector consisted of the statistical likelihood analysis of system calls, while the misuse detector was built with a neural network trained on groupings of system calls. This research demonstrates the potential benefits of combining both aspects of detection in future IDS's to decrease false positive and false negative errors.

1 Introduction

Over the past several years, computer attacks and break-ins have become commonplace. Numerous attacks have been successfully launched on government installations, company systems, and personal user accounts resulting in loss of privacy, research, or proprietary information. Almost all existing computer systems safeguard information through access controls such as passwords or file protections. However, from following high-profile stories in the popular press about computer and information theft, it is clear that these mechanisms are insufficient.

Today's Internet community has a significant level of access to and awareness of security holes and system vulnerabilities, propagated through mailing lists, web sites, and newsgroups. Intruders can often easily exploit and gain unauthorized access simply by executing a downloaded C program or UNIX shell script. Other intruders are somewhat more insidious and indirect, hiding their activities and rarely taking part in extended periods of strange or unusual behavior [21]. Simple network probing experiments [4] suggest that there are many more intrusions taking place than are being reported or noticed by administrators on the Internet.

1.1 Intrusion Detection

It is therefore imperative to detect these unseen system attacks in an automated monitoring environment. Intrusion detection quite simply seeks to detect violations in an organization's security policy. Sometimes only through careful analysis of a system's audit data can intrusive activity be detected. *Audit trails*, the chronological record of system activities logged to files, are usually generated in huge amounts each day. For humans to manually comb through these files is unfeasible and a waste of manpower. Thus, it is desirable to have a computerized intrusion detection system to effectively and efficiently

- expose intrusions in real-time to circumvent possible damage or theft resulting from the intruder while
- cut down on the tediousness of human analysis

Research and applications of intrusion detection techniques has resulted in its classification into two main categories, *anomaly detection* and *misuse detection*.

Anomaly detection is based on the assumption that misuse or intrusive behavior deviates from normal system use [7]. In general, most anomaly detection systems *learn* a normal system activity profile, and then flag all system events that statistically deviate from this established profile. One of the strengths of anomaly detection is the ability to abstract information about the normal behavior of a system and detect attacks regardless of whether or not the system

0-8186-8789-4/98 $10.00

has seen them before. Most behavior models are built using metrics that are derived from system measures such as CPU usage, memory usage, number and time of logins, network activity, etc. The main weakness of anomaly detection systems is their vulnerability to an intruder who breaches the system during their learning phase. A savvy intruder can gradually train the anomaly detector to interpret intrusive events as normal system behavior.

Misuse detection seeks to discover intrusions by precisely defining them ahead of time and watching for their occurrence [13]. For example, many well known attacks can be discovered by searching for distinguishing patterns or events in the audit trails. The main shortcoming of misuse detection is that future attacks cannot be predicted or detected without hard-coding them into the IDS attack database.

1.2 The Solaris Basic Security Module

The Solaris SHIELD Basic Security Module (BSM) provides security features defined as C2 in the Trusted System Evaluation Criteria (TCSEC) [22]. The audit trails produced by the BSM include detailed information about the specific system events attributable to a user. BSM data has been successfully put to use in past intrusion detection systems [1][12]. BSM recognizes 243 built-in system signals that are individually recorded and timestamped in a main audit logfile. Two more signals were added to this system which were setuid `EXEC_VE` and setuid `EXEC`. Another alteration was that failed signals were given a signal number of 245 added to the original number for a total of 488 possible signals. For example, depending on a user's UNIX shell, typing `ls` may generate some 30 to 100 signals that are recorded and attributed to that user as a result of the command's execution. The Solaris operating system can record different types of signals that fall under the categories of audit options available [22]. All possible system events (signals) for each user were recorded for use in this research.

2 Machine Learning and Intrusion Detection

Intrusion detection systems that are trained on system usage metrics use inductive learning algorithms. To simulate this learning process using a computer model is otherwise known as machine learning. Machine learning can be viewed as the attempt to build computer programs that improve performance of some task through learning and experience.

Our goal of designing machine learning applications with regard to computer security is to reduce the tediousness and time consuming task of human audit analysis.

The most commonly applied theory in many machine learning models is *Pattern Classification.* If we conceive of a pattern as a pair of variables: Pattern = [v, w], then the goal of Pattern Classification is to infer w from v, in other words, giving names w to observations v [19]. These observations v are most commonly represented using vectors of measurements or *features.*

$$v = [v_1 \ v_2 \ ... \ v_n]^T$$

While it would seem beneficial to have as many descriptive features as possible, it has frequently been observed in practice [3] that beyond a certain point, the inclusion of additional features leads to worse, rather than better performance.

2.1 Representing the BSM Signals as Features

Recent work [14] has involved learning the normal UNIX commands of four students over the course of a semester. By converting audit data into overlapping sequences of tokens, the researchers were able to apply a similarity measure to compare with the normal training data. Using this method it was possible to capture the "casual nature" of users' actions and create normal usage profiles for each user.

Another approach to learning from sequence data involves developing feature vectors based on a sequence of events [8]. Such aggregate features that can drastically improve detection include the derived characteristics of the number of arguments to a program, the number of times a user logs in per day, or the type of permissions on files accessed and created by the user. Choosing the best features based on raw audit data is challenging, and involves an expert's knowledge of the domain being studied.

In each of the two methods that were developed in this research, the signals from BSM were extracted and then converted to vector pattern representations. This enabled the learning simulator to process the input, allowing for simple interpretations of the results.

3 Approach and Learning Algorithms

Misuse and anomaly detection each have their own drawbacks. The limitation of the known attacks database in misuse detectors makes it necessary to predict all manners of intrusion before they occur. Anomaly detectors are vulnerable to knowledgeable hackers who tamper with an account during the learning phase of normal behavior patters. This research implements working models of both misuse and anomaly detection, with the eventual goal of combating the drawbacks of each method by combining them into one real-time system. Both models use the same BSM audit data to predict intrusive behavior in the form of UNIX buffer overrun attacks to attain root access. By melding the end results of each detection method with each other, it is possible to improve false negative and positive rates.

3.1 Statistical Anomaly Detection

With a statistical approach to anomaly detection, a system learns the behavior of users, applying the type of metrics previously mentioned. As the system is running, the anomaly detector is constantly measuring the deviance of the present behavior profile from the original. *Only* normal training data is learned by the system, which then attempts to extrapolate anomalous behavior through low probabilistic outputs of the testing data (running phase) outputs. However, false positives and negatives can be generated due to the inadequacy or insensitivity of the statistical measures chosen. Whether enough normal training data was collected is usually a concern as well.

3.2 Neural Networks in Misuse Detection

Neural networks have the ability to learn from an environment by applying an iterative process of adjustments to their internal structure. A neural network is a mathematical mechanism modeled from human brain behavior, able to be applied to a wide range of purposes. A misuse detection approach consists of training the neural network on a sequence of information units (or commands), which are represented on a more abstract level than an audit record [6]. Input to the neural network consists of a group of features that describe one command. This input data can be easily represented using pattern classification techniques, whereby each pattern of features is classified as normal or abnormal system behavior. The neural network uses non-linear regression to abstract information from the abnormal training cases to predict future attacks. For this experiment, the specific type of neural net that was used was a Multi-Layer Perceptron(MLP). The MLP was chosen for its ease of simulation and its past success in pattern classification.

3.3 Simulated UNIX Users

The BSM data used in this experiment originated from a Sparc ELC with 32 megabytes of memory installed with the core Solaris 2.5 operating system. The system was completely unpatched to allow for the exploitation of vulnerabilities of the operating system. Four simulated users were used to generate BSM audit data on this system over the period of about six weeks. Each user over this period had his own profile of system usage which can best be generalized below.

USER1 logs in during regular intervals and uses a wide variety of computing intensive applications. Once this user logs in, she starts an X session, and may launch xterms, `netscape`, `ghostview`, or various other programs. USER1 uses the tcsh shell.

USER2 regularly logs in, checks his email, and telnets to other machines. USER2 uses the csh shell.

USER3 infrequently logs in, and often runs many setuid programs like `ps`, `w` and `passwd`. She also runs many administrative commands such as `df` and `mount`. USER3 uses the sh shell.

USER4 logs in intermittently only to check email, fingers for friends on the network, and sometimes initiates a talk session if a friend is logged in. USER4 uses the tcsh shell.

All of these users' actions were recorded using BSM and later extracted using `praudit` and piped through Perl preprocessing scripts.

4 Anomaly Detection Approach

The underlying idea behind computer security anomaly detection is the ability to extrapolate strange user behavior based just on the normal patterns that the detector learns. *Behavior* is an imprecise term and often difficult to define in terms of a computer user. A method was needed to encode the actions of a user from the BSM audit data format to a mathematical representation that can be statistically analyzed. We wanted to develop a normal profile for each user, and then try to detect anomalous actions (buffer overrun attacks) based on a statistical classifier.

4.1 Feature Extraction of the BSM Logs for the Anomoly Detector

BSM audit data is stored in a binary file which requires processing with the `praudit` program to translate into a readable format. Once the audit file was in a format that could be easily parsed, expert knowledge was used to determine how to extract meaningful features from this format. Drawing from both past sequence data [5] [17] [8] and user profile [17] [14] research, the following preprocessing technique was developed.

Given the original `praudit` translated file of BSM audit data (with *all* users' information), a Perl program separated each of the four users' audit signals into four respective BSM audit files. For each user file, the entire sequence of audit events was converted into a a file of correlated numbers that represent those signal events. For instance, when an `EXEC_VE` signal is received, this is represented as the number 24. If the signal received a failed return value, then 245 is added to the base signal value. Therefore, if a user tries to execute a program, the `EXEC_VE` call would be converted to a 24, or a 269 if permission is denied. Here is an example of how the conversion would look like for the following snippet of audit data for a user called endler. In the original data, each entry represents a token which begins with a `header` and ends with a `return`.

```
header,88,2,AUE_ACCESS,,Thu Apr 02 16:47:36 1998, + 479993000 msec
path,/home/endler/.hushlogin
subject,endler,endler,user,endler,user,295,294,24 0 h42.s92.tulane.edu
return,failure: No such file or directory,-1
header,126,2,AUE_OPEN_R,,Thu Apr 02 16:47:36 1998, + 490003000 msec
path,/usr/share/lib/zoneinfo/US/Central
attribute,100644,bin,bin,8388616,267714,0
subject,endler,endler,user,endler,user,295,294,24 0 h42.s92.tulane.edu
return,success,4
header,137,2,AUE_CLOSE,,Thu Apr 02 16:47:36 1998, + 490003000 msec
argument,1,0x4,fd
path,/usr/share/lib/zoneinfo/US/Central
attribute,100644,bin,bin,8388616,267714,0
subject,endler,endler,user,endler,user,295,294,24 0 h42.s92.tulane.edu
return,success,0
header,115,2,AUE_CLOSE,,Thu Apr 02 16:47:36 1998, + 630005000 msec
path,/etc/.name_service_door
attribute,150444,root,root,42467328,2,41680896
subject,endler,endler,user,endler,user,295,294,24 0 h42.s92.tulane.edu
return,success,0
header,106,2,AUE_EXECVE,,Thu Apr 02 16:47:36 1998, + 630005000 msec
path,/usr/bin/tcsh
attribute,100777,endler,user,8388616,120375,0
subject,endler,endler,user,endler,user,295,294,24 0 h42.s92.tulane.edu
return,success,0
header,125,2,AUE_OPEN_R,,Thu Apr 02 16:47:36 1998, + 630005000 msec
path,/devices/pseudo/mm@0:zero
attribute,20666,root,sys,8388616,15061,3407884
subject,endler,endler,user,endler,user,295,294,24 0 h42.s92.tulane.edu
return,success,3
header,110,2,AUE_OPEN_R,,Thu Apr 02 16:47:36 1998, + 650002000 msec
path,/usr/lib/libc.so.1
attribute,100755,bin,bin,8388616,72240,0
subject,endler,endler,user,endler,user,295,294,24 0 h42.s92.tulane.edu
return,success,4
```

This snippet would be converted into entries with timestamps and signal numbers.

```
16:47:36 260
16:47:36 73
16:47:36 113
16:47:36 113
16:47:36 24
16:47:36 73
```

When processing the `EXEC_VE` and `EXEC` system calls, and either invokes a setuid program (which can be detected in the audit data), the derived feature number is converted to 244 and 245 instead of 24 and 8 respectively. For purposes of the buffer overrun exploits that we were searching for, this made the most sense to further describe the `EXEC_VE` call since most of these attacks use setuid root programs. Deciding which aggregate feature(s) to select (e.g., setuid `EXEC_VE`, return code) is entirely dependent on the creators of the detection system, making experimentation sometimes the most practical solution for feature selection.

Once the timestamped signal files have been created for each of the users, the actual training data is produced. The training data is in the form of feature vectors with 488 members (for the 488 possible signals). Here is how the training data feature vectors are created from the first set of files.

The entire sequence of signals is stored in an array fashion. Given the entire sequence of signal numbers for a user, we create a sliding window which will determine how many signals to consider in one pattern. Following is an example of window length five ($w = 5$) incremented by a step of 1 to generate the follow patterns of signals. Using the audit trail snippet we generated above, the sequence 73 113 113 24 73 is converted with this sliding window concept to:

```
260 73 113 113 24
73 113 113 24 73
113 113 24 73 11
113 24 73 11 28
...
```

Then the final training data file is converted to an accumulation of feature vectors with 488 members that count the total number of signals appearing in each sequence. So the first vector pattern of the training data file will look this with the 113th element equal to 2, and the 260th, 73rd, and 24th elements equal to 1.

```
0 0 0 0 0 0 0 0 0 0 0 0 0 0 0 0 0 0 0 0 0 0 0 0 1 0 0 0 0 0 0 0 0 0 0 0 0
0 0 0 0 0 0 0 0 0 0 0 0 0 0 0 0 0 0 0 0 0 0 0 0 0 0 0 0 0 0 0 0 0 0 0 0 1
0 0 0 0 0 0 0 0 0 0 0 0 0 0 0 0 0 0 0 0 0 0 0 0 0 0 0 0 0 0 0 0 0 0 0 0 0
0 0 2 0 0 0 0 0 0 0 0 0 0 0 0 0 0 0 0 0 0 0 0 0 0 0 0 0 0 0 0 0 0 0 0 0 0
0 0 0 0 0 0 0 0 0 0 0 0 0 0 0 0 0 0 0 0 0 0 0 0 0 0 0 0 0 0 0 0 0 0 0 0 0
0 0 0 0 0 0 0 0 0 0 0 0 0 0 0 0 0 0 0 0 0 0 0 0 0 0 0 0 0 0 0 0 0 0 0 0 0
0 0 0 0 0 0 0 0 0 0 0 0 0 0 0 0 0 0 0 0 0 0 0 0 0 0 0 0 0 0 0 0 0 0 0 0 0
0 1 0 0 0 0 0 0 0 0 0 0 0 0 0 0 0 0 0 0 0 0 0 0 0 0 0 0 0 0 0 0 0 0 0 0 0
0 0 0 0 0 0 0 0 0 0 0 0 0 0 0 0 0 0 0 0 0 0 0 0 0 0 0 0 0 0 0 0 0 0 0 0 0
0 0 0 0 0 0 0 0 0 0 0 0 0 0 0 0 0 0 0 0 0 0 0 0 0 0 0 0 0 0 0 0 0 0 0 0 0
0 0 0 0 0 0 0 0 0 0 0 0 0 0 0 0 0 0 0 0 0 0 0 0 0 0 0 0 0 0 0 0 0 0 0 0 0
0 0 0 0 0 0 0 0 0 0 0 0 0 0 0 0 0 0 0 0 0 0 0 0 0 0 0 0 0 0 0 0 0 0 0 0 0
0 0 0 0 0 0 0 0 0 0 0 0 0 0 0 0 0 0 0 0 0 0 0 0 0 0 0 0 0 0 0 0 0 0 0 0 0
0 0 0 0 0 0 0 0
```

Thus for each window of w tokens, a feature vector of 488 elements is created. Each line was then prepended by a 0 to classify the pattern as a normal system event since all of our training data is of normal usage.

Dependent on the histogram function (discussed in the next section) being applied to our data, the best value for w must be determined that will optimize our detection of abnormal system events. Three values for w were tested to get a sense for the best length, 6, 10, and 15. For all four users, the lowest sequence length of 6 the was most successful in identifying anomalous behavior. Different data sizes were used for each user's normal profile, which must be taken into consideration before making any generalizations about optimal sequence length. It has been shown that optimal sequence window lengths vary per user and the respective normal profile size being used [14].

The testing data consisted of the users' normal sessions, interspersed with several simulated break-ins to the account. During each break-in, the intruder uploads a buffer-overun exploit binary, and executes it, obtaining root access. The audit data was collected from all of these sessions and converted in the same manner described above for the training file, with a 1 prepended to window vectors that represent the actual attack taking place.

Once the training data was assembled in the desired format, a statistical classifier was applied to the normal patterns. After the classifier had generalized the normal usage for each user, the testing patterns were evaluated and an output value was given to each, representing the likelihood of normal pattern usage. We then marked areas as anomalous by looking at output likelihood values below a certain threshold value.

4.2 The Histogram Classifier

There are many methods to handle pattern classification using statistical analysis. For the purposes of this research, the histogram classifier [3] was used to estimate the likelihood of normal and abnormal classes by creating a set of histograms for each input feature. The histogram classifier belongs to a larger group called likelihood classifiers. Using the data collected above as the training set, all of the patterns were classified as normal. The test data consisted of the same format as the training set, except actual UNIX buffer overrun exploits were executed by simulated intrusions into the accounts. The test data included both normal and abnormal classified examples, signified respectively by a 0 or 1 as the first number in the pattern.

Maximum likelihood classifiers estimate the scaled probability density function, or *likelihood*, for each class, $p(X|A)P(A)$ where A represents a class label, X is the input feature vector for a pattern, $p(X|A)$ is the likelihood of the input data for class A, and $P(A)$ is the prior probability for class A [18]. Using the histogram classifier, the range of possible output values was divided into *bins*. The likelihood value assigned to each bin is proportional to how many training patterns occur in that bin's region. During the testing phase of our system, the likelihood values for each pattern are determined with $p(v|A)$. It is important to have a large representative set of normal data since low likelihood values will occur only when the user exhibits behavior outside of his profile. So by training on normal profile patterns, we can detect abnormal behavior by looking at very low likelihood values for our testing patterns.

The problem with the histogram classifier, and with pattern classification in general, is the curse of dimensionality. The difficulty with using the histogram function is that the number of histogram bins grows exponentially with the dimension N of the measurement space [19]. Thus, the more features we have, the more impractical it becomes to apply the histogram classifier. The solution was to reduce the number of features used in each pattern vector. The initial attempts at feature reduction were attempted using the LNKnet simulator's built-in algorithms. More successful results were achieved using human handpicked features which were selected using experience with the buffer overrun attack domain.

4.3 LNKnet Simulator

The LNKnet software package was developed to simplify the application of the most important statistical, neural network, and machine learning pattern classifiers [18]. For the purposes of this research, all training, testing, and feature selection/reduction was performed using this tool. The LNKnet software has a graphical user interface which allows the user to apply the statistical histogram approach mentioned earlier. The software is also capable of UNIX shell scripting which executes the same algorithms in a batch mode. The LNKnet package was compiled and used on a Sun Sparc Ultra Server 3000, single CPU, with 256 Megabytes of RAM, running Solaris 2.5.1.

Once the Perl scripts generated the normal classified training file mentioned above, LNKnet was then used to build a histogram model which was representative of a user's normal behavior. The testing data was then evaluated using this learned classifier model and the outputs for each pattern were then extracted from the log file. Scatter plots were then graphed with respect to time, and anomalous behavior patterns could then be inferred from a very low output value for the normal classifier.

All input features in the testing and training data were normalized to maintain stable and low output ranges for analysis.

5 Misuse Detection Approach

The underlying idea behind the misuse detection approach is to train our detector on both normal *and* abnormal (intrusive) patterns. Instead of learning the behavior of users over time, this method learns an entire event and creates a feature vector from this. For example, instead of the sliding window used in the anomaly detection approach, a sequence of signals was grouped into an event. In describing how this method works, the *event* is used to mean the collection of signals associated with a particular command or action. For instance, if a user types `ls` and generates 45 associated signals in the audit data, all 45 signals are understood to be included in that event.

5.1 Feature Extraction of the BSM Logs for the Misuse Detector

Using the collected signals of both user and system level events from the same audit source as the training data, feature vectors were generated as before using all 488 measures. A separate file contained the time stamps for each pattern so that we can correlate the data for graphing purposes. An event is extracted from the BSM audit logs by combining all signals within several microseconds that have the same audit session id. Each event pattern is then classified as normal or abnormal system behavior with a 0 or 1 respectively prepended to the pattern. For instance, this is the pattern that records a user typing `ls`.

```
0 0 0 1 0 0 0 0 0 0 0 0 0 0 0 1 0 0 0 0 0 0 0 0 1 0 0 0 4 0 0 0 0 0 0 0 0
0 0 0 0 0 0 0 0 0 0 0 0 0 0 0 0 0 0 0 0 0 0 0 0 0 0 0 0 0 0 0 0 0 0 0 0 6
0 0 0 0 0 0 0 0 0 0 0 0 0 0 0 0 0 0 0 0 0 0 0 0 0 0 0 0 0 0 0 0 0 0 0 0 0
0 0 10 0 0 0 0 0 0 0 0 0 0 0 0 0 0 0 0 0 0 0 0 0 0 0 0 0 0 0 11 0 0 0 0 0 0
0 0 0 0 0 0 0 0 0 0 0 0 0 0 0 0 0 0 0 0 0 0 0 0 0 0 0 0 0 0 3 0 0 0 0 0 0
0 0 0 0 0 0 0 0 0 0 0 0 0 0 0 0 0 0 0 0 0 0 0 0 0 0 0 0 0 0 0 0 0 0 0 0 0
0 0 0 0 0 0 0 0 0 0 0 0 0 0 0 0 0 0 0 0 0 0 0 0 0 0 0 0 0 0 0 0 0 0 0 0 0
0 0 0 0 0 0 0 0 0 2 0 0 0 0 0 0 0 0 0 0 0 0 0 0 0 0 0 0 0 0 0 0 0 0 0 0 0
0 0 0 0 0 0 0 0 0 0 0 0 0 0 0 0 0 0 0 0 0 6 0 0 0 0 0 0 0 0 0 0 0 0 0 0 0
0 0 0 0 0 0 0 0 0 0 0 0 0 0 0 0 0 0 0 0 0 0 0 0 3 0 0 0 0 0 0 0 0 0 0 0 0
0 0 0 0 0 0 0 0 0 0 0 0 0 0 0 0 0 0 0 0 0 0 0 0 0 0 0 0 0 0 0 0 0 0 0 0 0
0 0 0 0 0 0 0 0 0 0 0 0 0 0 0 0 0 0 0 0 0 0 0 0 0 0 0 0 0 0 0 0 0 0 0 0 0
0 0 0 0 0 0 0 0 0 0 0 0 0 0 0 0 0 0 0 0 0 0 0 0 0 0 0 0 0 0 0 0 0 0 0 0 0
0 0 0 0 0 0 0 0
```

The prepended 0 signifies a normal system event. The test data was generated in the same format and from the same audit source as the anomaly detection test records. Each pattern's timestamp was stored for both training and testing to allow for future correlation with the anomaly detection results.

5.2 Neural Networks

Neural networks are powerful mathematical structures that lend themselves well to pattern classification problems. One goal of this research was to determine whether it was possible to generalize enough information about malicious activity by extracting BSM features, and learn by example using a neural network, to predict future malicious actions. Using the training data that was collected from the main file of all system-wide events mentioned in the previous section, buffer overrun exploits were recorded and added as patterns to the training data, classified as abnormal. The curse of dimensionality also affected our neural network model, which required either fewer features in our patterns or significantly more samples to be sucessful. Feature reduction was performed, and as with the anomaly detection approach, hand-picking the features based on knowledge of the problem domain provided the most successful results.

5.3 LNKnet Simulator

LNKnet was also used for the Multi-Layer perceptron neural network simulations. The only variables adjusted during each simulation were the number of epochs, the number of hidden-layer nodes, and the learning rate parameter. The types of abnormal training patterns were varied to observe the performance rate of the detector.

6 Experiment Results

The main goal of this research was to illustrate the benefits of combining the results of the two methods of intrusion detection. Another goal was to show that intrusion detection was indeed feasible using the BSM audit data converted into feature vectors using the aforementioned techniques.

The training audit data consisted of 6 weeks worth of the users' normal user audit data. The testing phase of this experiment consisted of auditing the four simulated users for 50 minutes, while they performed various buffer-overrun attacks on the system. The total number of signals collected for the training and testing phases respectively was 22444 and 25457.

6.1 The Anomaly Detector

The procedure behind the anomaly detection phase of this experiment involved

1. Initial training on normal user profiles of different sequence samples using a histogram function to develop a classifier.

2. Analysis of testing samples using the histogram classifier against the respective sequence lengths to produce output.

3. Visual analysis of the output and selection of the proper output threshold to determine anomalies.

4. Selection of the best sequence length w for each USER's anomalous detections. Plotting of this sequence length versus time, so that we could correlate the data with our misuse detection method which is sampled over time.

The total amount of audit signals that were collected in the training data was 22444 which was divided up for USER1, USER2, USER3, and USER4 respectively: 6535, 2369, 3311, and 4310. The signals not accounted for belonged to system accounts such as root and lp which performed crontab and administrative commands. The testing data consisted of 25457 audit signals generated over the 50 minute interval. The test audit data was split up into user files again respectively for USER1, USER2, USER3, and USER4 with the following number of signals each: 9844, 4765, 4606, and 5683.

The training and testing files were first parsed with Perl scripts to separate each into four files for the respective users. The next step was to transform the files into feature vectors using another Perl script. The main variable that existed in creating the vector patterns for each file was the sliding window w. Each user then had three sets of training and testing files that utilized a window size of 6, 10, and 15 when creating the feature vector patterns.

Once the files were created, LNKnet was loaded and the vector values were normalized for use in the histogram plotting. Initially, all 488 features were used in the training and testing data. The resulting likelihood output values were too large to make any conclusions about the testing data at all. This was to be expected based on the previous discussion on the curse of dimensionality and large feature space. Because all of our input patterns were classified as normal, and the test pattern classifications were unknown, normal feature selection algorithms did not suffice.

It has been generally accepted that in pattern classification tasks, features must be first selected and reduced initially using experience and prior domain knowledge [19]. A set of 13 features was eventually selected by applying expert knowledge of buffer overruns and the audit signals generated by their occurrence. The signal features that were eventually chosen were 17, 24, 28, 40, 73, 77, 81, 113, 142, 178, 245, 318, and 386 from the signal list. Note that the numbers chosen to represent each system call was an arbitrary choice, and based on the order they are listed in the filesystem.

Once the feature size had been reduced from 488 to 13, substantial improvements in the results were then achieved. Using the histogram modeling function in LNKnet, each user's training files were learned and then applied to the respective data patterns. The output from each of these experiments consisted of two columns of histogram likelihood values, one for each of the classifiers used, *normal* and *abnormal*. The outputs for the abnormal classifier were all equal to 0 since there were no abnormal pattern examples in the training data as per the concept behind anomaly detection. The outputs for the normal classifier were extracted and examined from the log files with more Perl scripting.

To detect anomalous patterns from the histogram simulation runs, a value was selected for each output to represent the anomaly threshold. This threshold value was visually selected based on the graph of the scatter plots. Any outputs less than this value represented anomalous activity according to our model. For example, Figure 1 illustrates the threshold value of $6 * 10^{-}28$, in which the buffer overrun instances (shown by the arrows) were isolated by the histogram outputs below this value. The detector was quite successful in this instance, having only two false positives near pattern 4100.

For all four users, the signal sequence window length of 6 seemed to be the most successful in terms of the best false negative rate. Increasing the sequence window length for each user did not improve the anomalous discovery rate, although in the case of USER2, USER3, and USER4 the false positive rate was reduced. For the remainder of the experiments, the sequence window samples of length 6 were used since the highest percentage of anomalies was detected using this data.

Figures 1-4 show the selected anomaly outputs graphed over seconds, allowing us to overlap the results with the misuse detector later. The entire 50 minute testing period can be viewed on these figures, which consolidates the output values and enables our future correlation with the misuse detector. The different types of buffer overrun attacks executed by each user for the testing phase included `passwd`, `rlogin`, `eject`, and `ping` for USER1; `fdformat`, `ping`, and `rlogin` for USER2; `ping`, `eject`, and `rlogin` for USER3; `fdformat` for USER4. The arrows mark the exact patterns at which the exploits occurred so we easily see how many false positives and negatives exist.

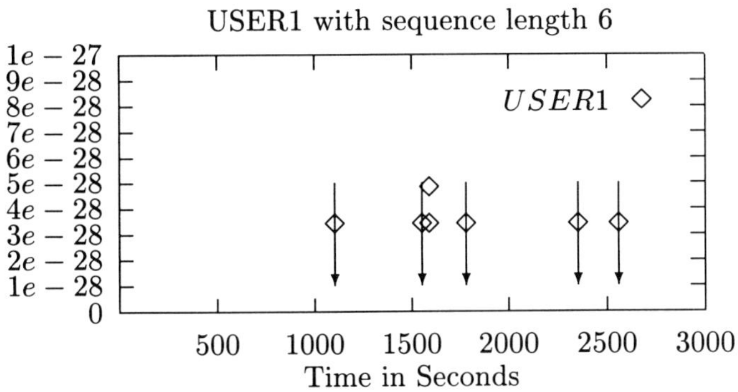

Figure 1: This is the Histogram plot for **USER1's** test data results with sequence size w equal to 6. The arrows represent when actual buffer overrun attacks were launched. The diamonds represent anomalous activity identified by the detector.

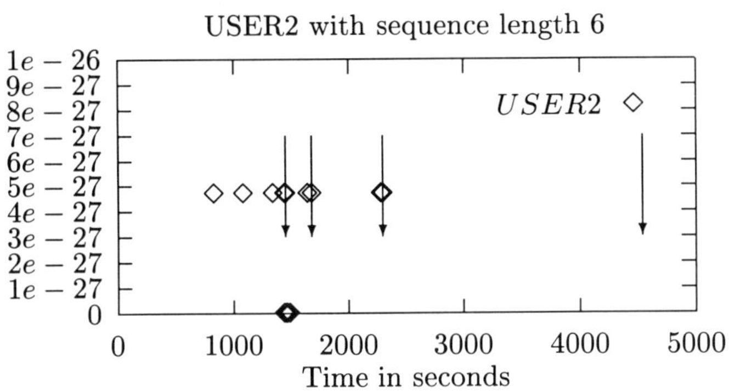

Figure 2: This is the Histogram plot for **USER2's** test data results with sequence size w equal to 6.

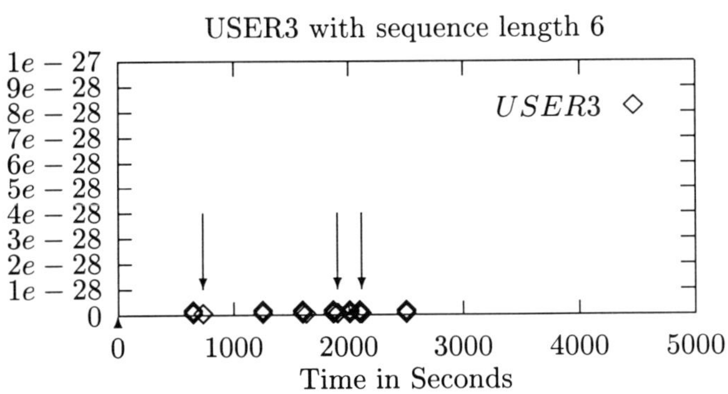

Figure 3: This is the Histogram plot for **USER3's** test data results with sequence size w equal to 6.

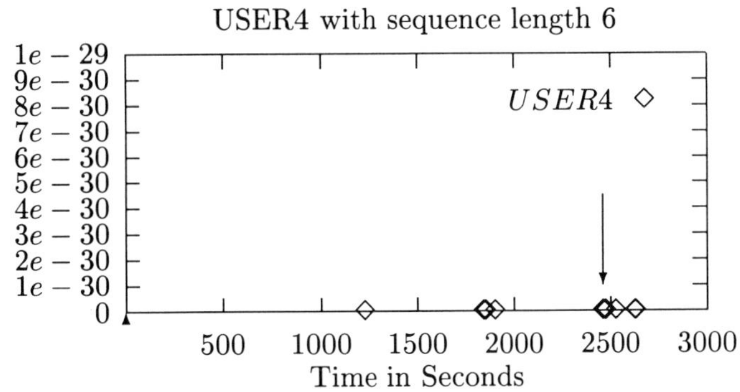

Figure 4: This is the Histogram plot for **USER4's** test data results with sequence size w equal to 6.

6.2 The Misuse Detector

For misuse detection, signals were consolidated into events so that each pattern represented a command and all the accompanying signals it generated. There were a total number of 362 and 569 events in the training and testing files respectively. The misuse detection procedure consisted of the following steps:

1. Initial learning on the *entire* normal training set with a Multi-Layer perceptron neural network simulator (LNKnet).
2. In addition to the normal data, buffer overrun attacks were recorded and specific patterns were individually added to the training set to see which other attacks could be extrapolated.
3. The entire testing data consisting of all users actions and system events was tested using each neural network and the results are shown in the extrapolation tables below.
4. Three combinations of two attacks in the training data were then used as the abnormal cases in the training data, creating three neural networks.
5. The entire testing data, consisting of all users actions and system events, was tested using these three neural networks and the results shown in the table below.
6. The best combination of two attacks was used to combine with the output of the anomaly detection methods discussed in the next section.

The central strategy behind misuse detection involves *training by example.* The main training file for the misuse detector initially contained all of the same normal usage data as the anomaly detection model. Pattern examples of buffer overrun attacks were then added to this training data in order to learn and extrapolate future attacks. Of the five buffer overrun attacks that were used in the testing phase, different combinations of attack patterns were added to the training data to see if the neural network could identify the other attacks in the test data.

The five different types of buffer overrun attacks that were executed in the test data include `passwd`, `rlogin`, `eject`, `fdformat`, and `ping`. Many combinations of the five attacks were included in the training set to see how successful the neural network was in generalizing and classifying future attack signatures.

The first approach was to use one buffer overun attack in the training data to see how many other attacks it could recognize. First, all of the attacks in the testing set were given a number to simplify identifying them. The numbers represent the order they are shown in the graphs with the arrows.

1. `ping` buffer overrun taking place at time 740 seconds by USER3.
2. `passwd` buffer overrun taking place at time 1110 seconds by USER1.
3. `fdformat` buffer overrun taking place at time 1460 seconds by USER2.
4. `rlogin` buffer overrun taking place at time 1556 seconds by USER1.
5. `ping` buffer overrun taking place at time 1685 seconds by USER2.
6. `rlogin` buffer overrun taking place at time 1785 seconds by USER1.
7. `eject` buffer overrun taking place at time 1910 seconds by USER3.
8. `rlogin` buffer overrun taking place at time 2119 seconds by USER3.
9. `rlogin` buffer overrun taking place at time 2305 seconds by USER2.
10. `eject` buffer overrun taking place at time 2353 seconds by USER1.
11. `fdformat` buffer overrun taking place at time 2461 seconds by USER4.
12. `ping` buffer overrun taking place at time 2564 seconds by USER1.

The best performing neural network variables were discovered after much testing and changing of parameters. For each of the simulations performed using the mulitlayer perceptron model, a hidden layer of 25 neurons, a learning parameter of .3 and an epoch length, of 2000 iterations were used.

With the following buffer overrun attacks, the Multi-Layer perceptron was able to extrapolate other attacks. The results of adding and trying each buffer overrun attack in the training data are shown in the table. The neural network was obviously able to extrapolate at least the one attack used in the training set for each instance shown below. The list of extrapolated attacks are the patterns that were classified as abnormal:

Attack Signature	Extrapolated Attacks
1	1, 3, 9
2	2, 10, 11, 12
3	1, 3, 9
4	2, 4, 5, 6, 8
5	2, 4, 5, 6, 8
6	4, 5, 6, 8
7	7, 11
8	2, 4, 5, 6, 8
9	1, 3, 9
10	3, 10, 12
11	7, 11
12	2, 10, 12

Using the information from these individual training instances fed into the neural network, groups of two attacks were then used in the training data. The following three sets of two attacks were used to train the neural network into better extraploation of more attacks.

Attack Combination	Extrapolated Attacks	Figure
2 and 7	2, 7, 10, 11, 12	5
1 and 5	1, 3, 4, 5, 7, 8, 9, 11	6
2 and 5	2, 4, 5, 6, 7, 8, 10, 11, 12	7

The combination of 2 and 5 seemed to be the most effective in extrapolating different types of attacks. This combination was used to combine with the anomoly detection results discussed in the next section. Notice that with both of the above neural net misuse detection runs, no false positives occured.

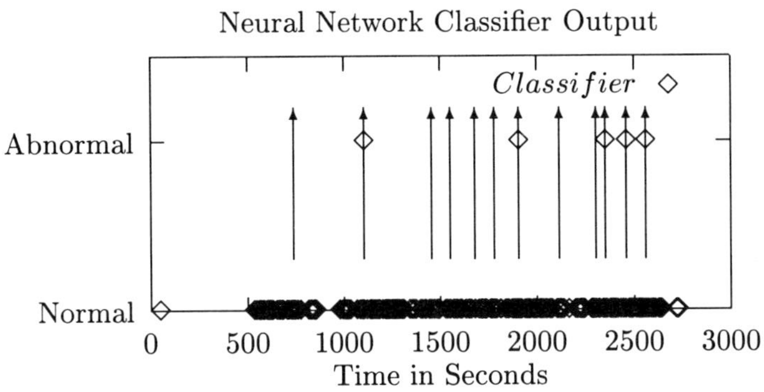

Figure 5: This is the classifier output for the two attacks 2 and 7 used in the training data. The arrows signify when attacks took place, and the diamonds show where the detector flagged an event as abnormal.

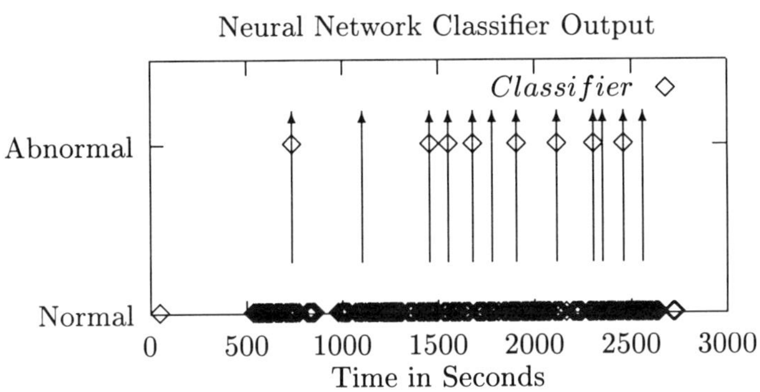

Figure 6: This is the classifier output for the two attacks 1 and 5 used in the training data.

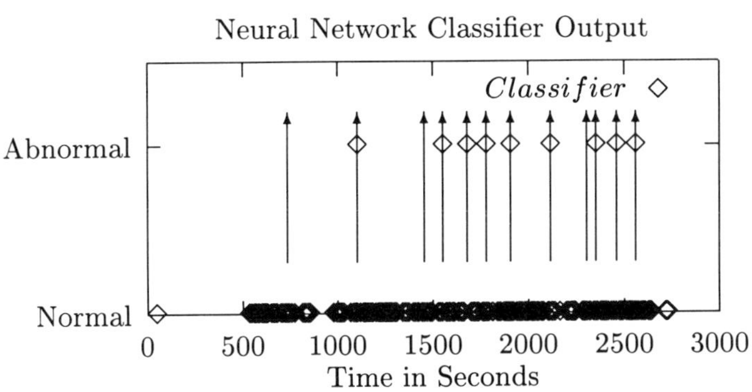

Figure 7: This is the classifier output for the two attacks 2 and 5 used in the training data.

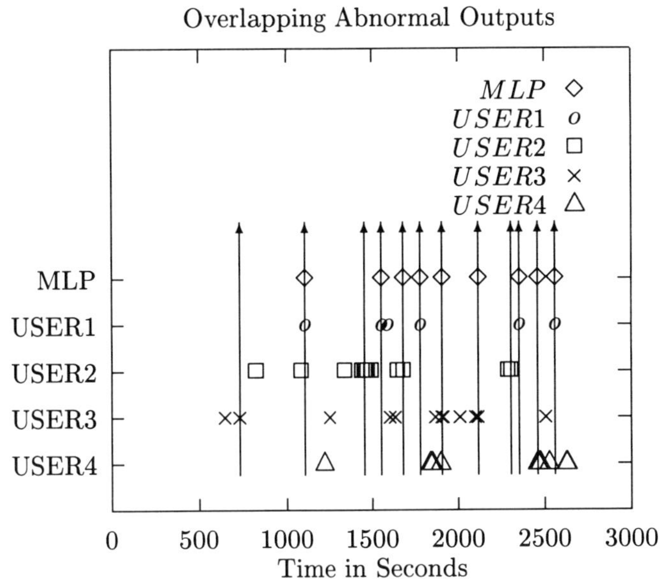

Figure 8: This is the combination of all anomalous output from the four users with the neural network Multi-Layer Perceptron results.

7 Putting it all Together

One of the major goals of this research was to combine both aspects of intrusion detection to improve the overall rate of detection. By combining the results of the anomaly and misuse detection models, it was possible to drastically reduce the false negative errors in detecting buffer overrun attacks. Looking at the output of all users' anomalies and the neural network output in figure 8 shows some overlapping in the outputs of both methods. If we look at just the overlapping features and consider all outputs equally abnormal, then figure 9 offers another perspective. By merging all output points, one can better see areas that require human audit analysis to determine if a real attack has taken place. In the way the abnormal data is presented in figure 9, it is possible to reduce the amount of false positive errors. By only considering regions of 30 or 60 seconds at a time, one such filtering process could consist of eliminating all regions with less than 2 or 3 abnormal outputs thereby cutting down on the false positive rate of detection.

8 Conclusions and Future Work

There were two main goals accomplished in this research. It was successfully shown that Solaris BSM audit data could be applied to both a misuse and

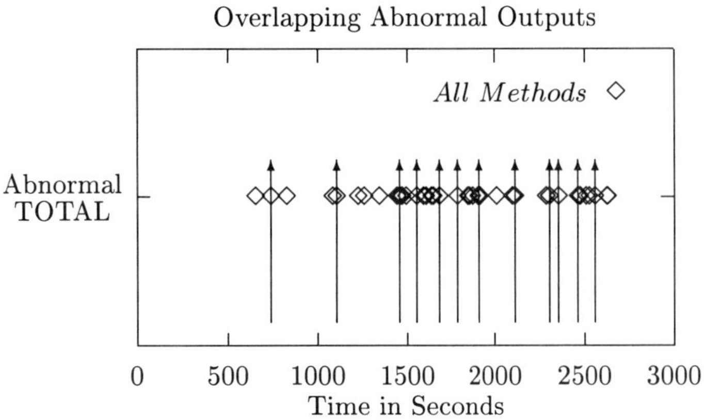

Figure 9: This is the overlapping of data points in figure 8. The graph illustrates an improved detection rate if both anomoly and misuse detection methods are combined.

anomaly detection model. While the NIDES system [1] has demonstrated this theory in practice drawing upon many data sources, this experiment was able to draw upon one source of data and utilize it differently for both types of detection. The two methods by which the BSM data was used to generate feature vectors proved to be fairly successful. The other goal of combining both detection models for more accurate detection results was also successful. By analyzing the final overlapping data points, it is possible to cull the output and consider only the time intervals that contain a certain amount of abnormally classified activity.

These preliminary experiments provide evidence that there is great promise in developing more advanced detection systems through BSM audit analysis and conversion. There is much room for the advancement of many aspects of this research. The signal profile size for each user's training data should be expanded and sampled randomly. The optimal window size w should also be more thoroughly analyzed, since it was shown [14] that optimal sequence lengths are user dependent. The feature selection done on both the anomaly and misuse detection models could be greatly improved from the hand-picked methods applied. More varied and real life user data samples would be desirable, in addition to more types of recorded attacks rather than just buffer overrun exploits.

Now that buffer overrun attacks have been shown to be capable of audit detection, other types of attacks and anomalous behavior should be further classified into the systems. One of the most important improvements that could be made to both models is the development of more detailed features such as arguments to `EXEC_VE` calls, host where the user originated from, and perhaps time between past x commands. Prior Probabilities were left untouched for these experiments, but adjusting the actual probability values of anomalies may have potential benefits.

The neural network aspect of the misuse detection model has vast room for exploration. The technique of clustering should be investigated with respect to the input space. While the Multi-Layer Perceptron is useful in many learning problems, other types of neural networks may be more successful when dealing with this type of pattern prediction and completion. The use of recurrent networks with BSM audit signals is an area that deserves more research, spurred on by experiments showing that predictive pattern matching could be achieved by using a neural network with feedback layers. The application of recurrent networks, as well as other neural networks such as Kohonen, Hoppfield, and RBF, has the potential of providing useful tools for audit sequence analysis.

The next logical step for this research will be to implement this model in real-time using actual user data instead of simulations. Audit reduction should be investigated to make this a performance feasible project. The sliding window of audit signals in the anomaly detector could "slide over" more than 1 signal at a time, reducing the number of patterns to be processed at once. Concept drift must be addressed by constantly retraining both detectors to keep up with the changing uses of a system. Also the neural network audit aspect could be reduced by filtering out audit signals that have little bearing on the detection process, thereby decreasing the preprocessing strain on the system.

9 Acknowledgements

I am very thankful to my advisor Dr. Mark Benard of Tulane University for his constant advice and encouragement. I am also grateful to Dr. Linda Lankewicz of Sewanee University for her useful comments and direction. I would especially like to thank Dr. Richard Lippmann of MIT Lincoln Laboratory for providing the LNKnet simulator software, offering helpful suggestions on how to handle audit data, and for his ongoing support.

References

[1] Debra Anderson, Thane Frivold, and Alfonso Valdes. "Next-generation Intrusion Detection Ex-

pert System (NIDES), A Summary." SRI Computer Science Laboratory, May 1995.

[2] Thomas G. Dietterich and Ryszard S. Michalski. "Learning to predict sequences." 1986. In Michalski, Carbonell, and Mitchell (Eds.). Machine Learning: An artificial intelligence approach. San Mateo, CA: Morgan Kaufman.

[3] Richard Duda and Peter Hart. *Pattern Classification and Scene Analysis.* New York: John Wiley and Sons, 1973.

[4] Dan Farmer. "Shall We Dust Moscow?" *http://www.trouble.org/survey.* December 18th, 1996.

[5] S. Forrest, S. A. Hofmeyr, A. Somayaji, and T. A. Longstaff. "A sense of self for unix processes." *Proceedings of the 1996 Symposium on Security and Privacy,* pages 120-128, Los Alamitos, CA, 1996. IEEE Computer Society Press.

[6] Kevin Fox, Ronda Henning, Jonathan Reed, Richard Simonian. "A Neural Network Approach Towards Intrusion Detection." *Proceedings of the 13th National Computer Security Conference,* pages 125-134, Washington, DC, October 1990.

[7] Jeremy Frank. "Artificial Intelligence and Intrusion Detection: Current and Future Directions." June 9, 1994.

[8] Haym Hirsh and Nathalie Japkowicz. "Bootstrapping Training-Data Representations for Inductive Learning: A Case Study in Molecular Biology." *Proceedings of the Twelfth National Conference on Artificial Intelligence.* (pp. 639-644). Seattle, WA.

[9] Todd Heberlien. "Haystack's Analysis: A brief Description." Internal Document, University of California, Davis 1991.

[10] K. Jackson, D. DuBoid, and C. Stallings. "An Expert System Application for Network Intrusion Detection." 1991

[11] H. Javitz and A. Valdes. "The SRI IDES Statistical Anomaly Detector." In *Proceedings, IEEE Symposium on Research in computer Security and Privacy,* 1991.

[12] Sandeep Kumar. *Classification and Detection of Computer Intrusions.* PhD thesis, Purdue University, August 1995.

[13] Sandeep Kumar and Eugene Spafford. "An Application of Pattern Matching in Intrusion Detection." Technical Report. June 17, 1994.

[14] Terran Lane and Carla Brodley. *An Application of Machine Learning to Anomaly Detection.* Purdue University, West Lafayette, IN, February 1997.

[15] Linda Lankewicz and Mark Benard. "Real Time Anomaly Detection Using a Nonparametric Pattern Recognition Approach." *Proceedings, IEEE Symposium on Research in Computer Security and Privacy,* 1990.

[16] Linda Lankewicz. *A Non-Parametric Pattern Recognition Approach to Anomaly Detection.* PhD. Thesis, Department of Computer Science, Tulane University, 1992.

[17] Wenke Lee and Salvator Stolfo, "Data Mining Approaches for Intrusion Detection." In, *Proceedings of the 7th USENIX Security Symposium,* San Antonio, Texas, January 26-29, 1998

[18] Richard Lippmann and Linda Kukolich. *LNKnet User's Guide.* MIT Lincoln Laboratory. 1993.

[19] Jürgen Schürmann. *Pattern Classification, A Unified View of Statistical and Neural Approaches.* John Wiley and Sons, Inc. New York: 1996.

[20] Michael Sebring, Eric Shellhouse, Mary Hanna, and R. Alan Whitehurst. "Expert Systems in intrusion detection: A case study." *Proceedings of the 11th National Computer Security Conference,* pages 74-81, October 1988

[21] Clifford Stoll. *Stalking the Wily Hacker. Communications of the ACM,* 31(5):484-497, May 1988

[22] Sun Microsystems. *SunShield Basic Security Module Guide.*

A SELECTION CRITERIA FOR INTRUSION DETECTION SYSTEMS

Edward Amoroso and Richard Kwapniewski, AT&T Laboratories
{eamoroso|rkwapniewski}@att.com

Abstract

A set of criteria is introduced for comparing and assessing intrusion detection systems. The theory, requirements classes, metrics, and practical application of the criteria are discussed. Fifteen specific requirements are described and broken into Class C, Class B, and Class A compliance. A questionnaire for obtaining vendor information is shown; advice and experiences from test evaluations are given based on our use of the criteria with several commercially available systems.

Introduction

In the course of our R&D work at AT&T Laboratories, we've developed an intrusion detection selection criteria that has helped us make management decisions about the comparison, selection, assessment, purchase, integration, modification, and use of intrusion detection system for our customers. In this paper, we outline the compliance requirements of the criteria to assist others in this increasingly important task for security managers and engineers. We also offer a questionnaire that has been helpful to us in obtaining information from vendors.

The purpose of our criteria is to provide a means for measuring the degree to which an intrusion detection system is likely to meet a set of local security requirements at AT&T. Since our company represents such a diverse R&D computing and networking environment, we felt that the resulting criteria may have some applicability to others in the community—hence, our decision to share the work here. As one might expect, an obvious challenge in the development of such a set of criteria is to include requirements that apply across these different local R&D environments. The Trusted Computer System Evaluation Criteria (TCSEC) [1] is an example criteria that has been used in this manner (with reasonable success) for operating system security. Our set of criteria includes three types of requirements for intrusion detection system technology (driven by discussions summarized in [2]).

- *Detection.* These requirements address functional and security issues related to the detection of intrusions in a target environment.
- *Response.* These requirements address functional and process-based activity initiated as a result of intrusion-related information.
- *Deployment.* These requirements address practical issues of installation, platform, integration, interoperability, and other areas. (This aspect of intrusion detection has been sadly neglected in the research community.)

Requirements in each of these categories are associated in our criteria with three degrees of compliance. Class A denotes full compliance with the requirement, Class B denotes a different compliance, and Class C denotes yet another compliance.

As we present the respective classes for a given requirement, it is assumed that Class A includes all requirements from Class B, which in turn includes all requirements from Class C (unless there is an obvious change from one class to the next that prevents such an inclusion relation). It is important to note here that during our use of the criteria in AT&T, systems meeting lesser compliance classes were *not* interpreted as being inferior to systems meeting greater compliance classes. In fact, in many of the applications we considered, lesser compliance ratings were considered more appropriate to the needs and budget of the organization. Off-line audit trail processing, for example, begs the use of systems that generally meet lesser requirements classes in the detection category of requirements.

As a final introductory note, we should make clear that procedural issues related to the use of

0-8186-8789-4/98 $10.00

intrusion detection system-generated information in an operational setting are neither addressed in the criteria nor discussed in this paper. This is important because we unequivocally prefer a bad intrusion detection tool in an excellent operational and correlation environment over a good intrusion detection tool in an operationally-impaired environment.

Criteria Requirements

As suggested above, the set of criteria is broken into detection, response, and deployment categories. In this section, we outline the key elements of these requirements classes.

Detection Requirements

Detection requirements focus on the degree to which an intrusion detection system can functionally detect real intrusions in computing and networking systems. We include four types of detection requirements in this category:

- *D1: Time to Detect Intrusions*
- *D2: Stored Knowledge About Intrusions*
- *D3: User and System Activity Profiling*
- *D4: Multi-Source Information Correlation*

The diagram in Figure 1 depicts the functional relationship between these detection requirements in a typical intrusion detection environment. The important aspects of these detection requirements are discussed below.

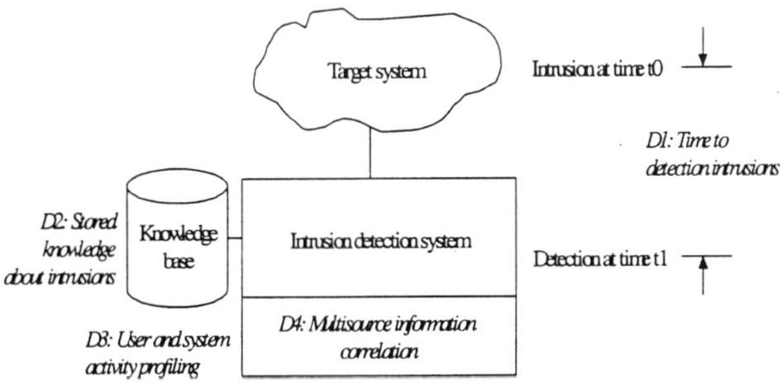

Figure 1. Relationship Between Detection Requirements

D1: Time to Detect Intrusions. This requirement focuses on the elapsed time between an intrusive event and its automated detection. We are aware of the caveats associated with this requirement and we know that this duration can vary depending on the environment. Furthermore, we acknowledge that detection of an event might require considerable operational activity by analysts using a variety of tools, methods, and procedures. Nevertheless, we believe that certain definitive statements can be made with respect to detection time. For example, a system that performs off-line analysis on audit data cannot provide real-time alarms, regardless of the processing environment.

In our criteria, Class C-compliant systems provide a functional capability for analysts to *eventually* detect intrusions, but perhaps well after the attack has completed. This may be on the order of days, weeks, months, or perhaps *never*. Many products such as off-line audit trail analysis tools operate at this class and in a great many environments, this is a suitable approach. In Class B systems, the intrusion detection system provides for more timely on-the-fly network information capture for prompt reporting of intrusions. Real-time reporting is expected to be on the order of minutes or hours. Typical techniques for this type of detection include software-based string matching of on-the-fly traffic, attack signature-based analysis of traffic, intelligent network packet sniffers, or SNMP-based capture and real-time analysis with respect to certain profiles. Class A systems include specially designed functionality to minimize time of detection. Hardware-based packet capture and processing solutions typically characterize this class of product. Real-time detection should be on the order of seconds or less. It has been our experience that most intrusion detection systems are considering hardware enhancements in their packet capture functionality to reduce the time to detection; in these cases, we've considered Class A compliance if evidence of success is apparent.

D2: Stored Knowledge About Intrusions. This requirement addresses the richness and extensibility of the intrusion knowledge base used in the product. Such knowledge bases should contain up-to-date, accurate, and complete sets of information about intrusions. This requirement attempts to measure the completeness and appropriateness of the attacks detected by the intrusion detection system. Obviously, no system will ever have the capability to detect 100% of attacks since new ones are created all the time. Furthermore, the amount of work required to encode a new detection approach, implement it in a product, and integrate the new product feature into an embedded base implies a significant time lag between discovery of an attack and its prevention in the community through intrusion detection. This implies that competent attackers will always be miles ahead of the attack detection tools.

In Class C systems, some set of intrusion profiles and content patterns is provided by the vendor and updated periodically. *Almost* every commercial intrusion detection system we are aware of meets this criterion. This does not imply that the vendors not supporting this class are inferior; in fact, these vendors typically point to the inherent weaknesses in using known attacks and usually target different Class B or Class A approaches instead. Class B systems allow the content patterns to be customized by the administrator. This may include the specification of string patterns with meaning in the target environment (for example, the string '/etc/shadow' is often used in Unix/Linux environments). These systems also include in-house experts actively and demonstrably engaged in attack-related research. Class A systems provide an API or language for users to specify customized intrusion profiles for non-trivial attack patterns. The problem here is that while some vendors do provide such a language, the tractability of actually encoding non-trivial attacks has not been easily demonstrated.

D3: User and System Activity Profiling. The ability to develop custom profiles of users and systems as the basis for detecting anomalous behavior is an attractive feature. A profile is some means for representing *expected* behavior. These profiles may result in statistical processing to determine the degree to which *observed* behavior deviates from stored profiles. This is a mature technology in most toll fraud and credit card fraud systems. It is not a mature technology in LAN/WAN environments carrying TCP/IP traffic. The reason for this—we believe—is not related to technology, but is rather a symptom of the lack of financial incentives for LAN/WAN profiling technology development (unlike the case in toll fraud).

We include no requirement for profiling in Class C systems. In a Class B-compliant system a profiling engine exists for specifying and capturing broad statistical information about system operation. The granularity of this information may be great. In Class C-compliant systems, this profiling granularity is increased considerably so that individual users profiles can be used with administrator-tunable thresholds. As one might expect, systems with extremely flexible user interfaces and configurations for specifying functionality will inevitably evaluate higher than ones without such flexibility. This is because in theory, profiling can be developed and used within the bounds of the intrusion detection system. We expect system and user profiling components to be the "next wave" of commercial intrusion detection features from system vendors.

D4: Multi-source Information Correlation. This requirement addresses the ability of an intrusion detection system to relate monitored traffic or alarms from different sources and at different times. This can be easily met if the essence of the requirement is simply to accept and display information. If, on the other hand, the requirement exists to process this multi-source information looking for patterns, then compliance becomes more difficult. A common question we ask with respect to this requirement is this: "If I detect an intrusion on a system running a proprietary protocol that no one has ever heard of (except me), then can I notify your intrusion detection system and have it integrate the event with ones from networks it *does* know about?"

In Class C-compliant systems, the requirement is that functionality must exist for multiple feeds of information to be collected in a common processing location for display and minimal response (e.g., paging, email). Nearly all vendors support this requirement. Class B-compliant systems must include tools to define and search for patterns of activity in the monitored traffic feeds. These tools should allow for searching on factors such as source and destination IP address, service port, protocol, and time. Class A-compliant systems must include an automated mechanism for incorporating out-of-band sources such as detected events from other networks, information pulled from news feeds, or real time operator generated input into the correlation processing. If, for example, a news feed is received that war has begun with country X, then a Class A system might automatically designate country X-originated packets as being potentially hostile. A Class A system must also provide some sort of API for accepting alarm messages from out-of-band sources. We feel that this functionality is absolutely critical in today's multi-platform, multi-protocol environments.

Response Requirements

The response requirements address the degree to which an intrusion detection system can respond to intrusion-related information. We include four intrusion detection response requirements in this category that correspond to the following:

- *R1: Types of Response Directives*
- *R2: Logging of Information*
- *R3: Identity Trace Back Analysis*
- *R4: Intruder Trap Support*

The diagram in Figure 2 depicts the relationship between these response requirements in a typical intrusion detection environment. The details of these response requirements are discussed below.

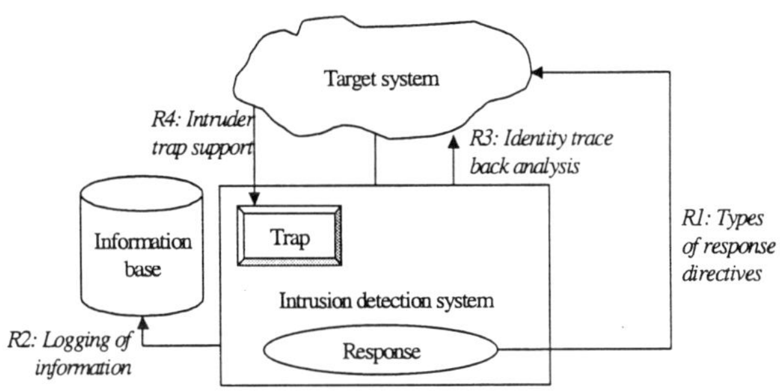

Figure 2. Relationship Between Response Requirements

R1: Types of Response Directives. Most current network security mechanisms, not to mention *all* intrusion detection systems, include some sort of alarm. We generalize alarms in our criteria to a notion of client/server response directives. On one end of our response directive spectrum, we envision client generated static alarms that provide an individual with information that requires human decision and management. On the other end of the spectrum are automatic feedback mechanisms that set up response functionality that may include sensor-initiated fine-tuning of sensors, laying of traps, or initiation of trace-back methods.

We define a Class C-compliant system as providing a static alarm display without any automated response capability. Messages on a console are typical examples in this class. The displayed alarm must indicate relevant information such as the type of suspected intrusion, the time and place at which it occurred, and any information on the intruder. We have not found an intrusion detection system that does not meet this class. Class B systems extend this mechanism to include some minimal and dynamic response capability such as message sent to an administrator (e.g., voice mail, paging, and email). Mechanisms such as transmitting an update to a router's access control list are considered desirable features in this class. Finally, Class A systems include a customizable auto-initiated response mechanism available through a well-defined application programming interface (API). The purpose here is integration of an intrusion detection system into an existing, mature disaster recovery and incident response environment. Without an API, this integration cannot be done effectively. The API must allow programmers to understand the detailed output and format of the intrusion detection system response directives.

R2: Logging of Information. This requirement addresses the means by which information is logged and protected by an intrusion detection system. It is vital for security events to be logged properly for various reasons. Studying the logs after an intrusion may help pinpoint security holes to be repaired. Logs may help clarify what is required for system recovery following a successful attack. Lastly, a detailed log can provide a step-by-step account of the attack, which can be used as evidence in a court of law.

No requirement exists for Class C-compliant systems in the area of auditing. Some environments exist in which audit trails are not needed for intrusion detection (e.g., an Intranet in which the firewall already performs auditing and the intrusion detection system is used for real time detection of certain patterns of activity). In Class B-compliant systems, a detailed audit record of user-selected actions is generated. Information in the audit records may include user name, system names, source/destination addresses, times, and commands issued. Class A-systems would include tools for processing audit trails. These tools would allow for background checking of archived data looking for patterns. They also would include a means for correlating information in a trail with currently active monitored data. Vendors are encouraged to focus on the integration of audit trail data from existing sources such as routers, servers, and firewalls.

R3: Identity Trace Back Analysis. This requirement describes the level of support for tracing and estimating the identity of an intruder. Following intrusions, a great deal of effort is usually consumed to identify the culprit. Often this endeavor also involves law enforcement officials and requires cooperation of other organizations or service providers. Unfortunately, this effort is usually performed in vain, partly because it is done too long after the fact. Trace-back describes the ability to automatically begin tracking down an intruder immediately upon detection of an attack. Anonymity-preserving walls such as service anonymizers and certain cryptographic protocols will almost always foil such attempts unless other, more clever techniques are used (see discussion below on traps).

Both Class C and Class B-compliant systems have no requirement for trace back. This follows our observation that this sort of functionality has not been fully developed to the point of easy commercial implementation. Class A-compliant systems utilize the appropriate tools (possible examples include *traceroute*, *finger*, and Internet cookies) to initiate trace back. These systems should also have the ability to correlate information from other systems to identify intruder identity. By the way, the trivial notion of spitting out the source IP address of an offending intruder is not considered trace-back. This issue of trace-back may be the most critical functional requirement for future intrusion detection systems. A vendor that captures this requirement in an effective product feature or tool kit will almost certainly dominate the market.

R4: Intruder Trap Support. This requirement indicates the level to which the system supports trapping of intruders using a deceptive honey-pot. Such a trap typically creates a virtual network environment which appears identical or better than the real environment to the intruder, but which contains no resources that cannot be compromised. Instead, it provides a climate similar to a law-enforcement sting operation into which attackers are lured and within which they may implicate themselves by their actions. Traps also furnish additional time for the intrusion

O1: Test and Verification: This requirement addresses the degree to which the intrusion detection system has been tested and verified. We included this requirement because intrusion detection is such a new technology and for deployment in our customer's

detection system and its administrators to track and identify the intruder.

Both Class C and Class B-compliant systems have no requirement in this area. This reflects our observation that this technology is not seen in any currently available systems; traps remain primarily in the research domain. In Class A-compliant systems, the system is able to divert a session to some external trap system. In Class A-compliant systems, intruders are seamlessly switched to a trap that is set-up and maintained as part of the system response process. To our knowledge, no currently available commercial system even comes close to meeting this requirement.

Operational Requirements

These requirements address practical product concerns related to the installation, use, and support of the intrusion detection system in an operational environment. The four requirements in this category are as follows:

- *O1: Test and Verification*
- *O2: System Security*
- *O3: Supported Network Media*
- *O4: User Interface*

The diagram in Figure 3 depicts the relationship between these operational requirements in a typical intrusion detection environment. The details of these operational requirements are described below.

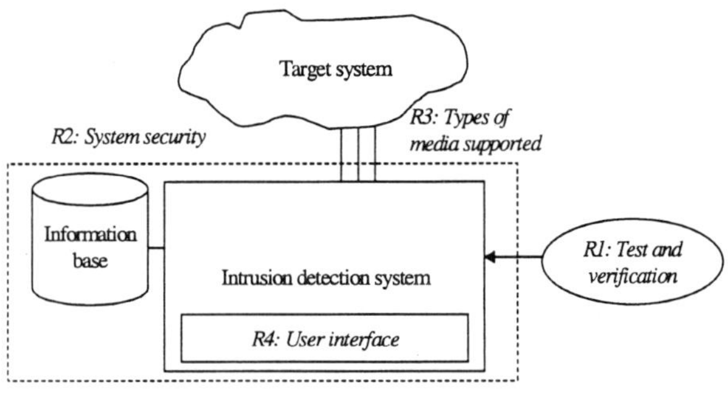

Figure 3. Relationship on Operational Requirements

environments, we deemed maturity as a critical issue. Ideally, test and verification of a product would be done in a realistic environment by the target end-user. However, since most organizations are not set up for such activity, we rely on the vendors to supply this information. Product use by a customer base should only be considered valid information if the product architecture has been relatively stable.

For Class C-compliant systems, no requirement is specified. In fact, the vast majority of systems are in this class due to the rapid time-to-market requirement for commercial systems, as well as the huge flux in design changes that we've seen in the past couple of years. This is depressing, but it is what we've observed. In Class B systems, the vendor supplies evidence that the system has been appropriately tested and verified using a well-defined test suite. These tests should be extensive and as exhaustive as possible. We are sympathetic to the use of formal methods, but we are skeptical of their practical usefulness in a non-trivial, feature-loaded product. Finally, in Class A systems, the vendor provides evidence of third-party testing by an independent organization that will supply documentation of test plans and results. It is our belief that market opportunities exist for appropriately-positioned companies to get into this intrusion detection system testing business.

O2: System Security. This requirement focuses on the degree to which the intrusion detection system protects its resources from malicious security attack. Techniques such as encryption and access control are typical controls used to ensure system security. Intrusion detection systems are important elements of any network and are thus likely targets for attack. This also implies, however, that the target environment will be relevant in determining an appropriate compliance class for intrusion detection system security.

Class C-compliant systems provide basic system security for its platforms including access control, some level of audit, and user authentication. Every vendor we examined appeared to meet these requirements. Systems meeting Class B requirements must include an encryption-based virtual private networking (VPN) capability for protecting communications. Many of the vendors we spoke with suggested that we provide our own VPN environment. Class B compliance was specified in these cases if specific functionality were included to support this VPN integration. It should not be made easy by vendors (we believe) for users to send clear text alarms across networks. Class A-compliant systems must include a security hardened base for servers (i.e., mandatory controls) and should include special functionality and networking configurations that are designed to enhance the stealth nature of the system. Our legacy at AT&T in developing hardened operating system bases may have influenced this requirement, but we strongly believe that crackers have a tougher time with such systems.

O3: Supported Network Media. This requirement indicates the types of network media on which the system can be connected. Network-based systems rely on their ability to capture data packets at the line rate of the network. This requirement rates the interfaces types offered. Note that the intrusion detection system must do more than simply provide the proper interface type. It must also have the ability to process data at the full interface line rate without dropping so many packets that the monitoring function becomes inoperable.

Class C-compliant systems must support low-speed speed LAN and WAN interfaces (up to 16 Mb/s) such as Ethernet, Token Ring, NxDS0, and DS1. Every system we examined was in this class. Class B-compliant systems must support high-speed LAN and WAN interfaces (up to 100 Mb/s) such as fast Ethernet, FDDI, and DS3. Class A-compliant systems must support very high-speed media (over 100 Mb/s) such as Gigabit Ethernet, ATM OC-3, and ATM OC-12. We hesitate to comment on vendor compliance here because product packet sniffers are changing as fast as we can type these words.

O4: User Interface. This addresses the type of interface provided to the intrusion detection system administrator for configuration and monitoring components. The user interface is a key feature of any intrusion detection system, as it provides the administrator with a window into the system for configuration, operation, and maintenance. It's worth noting that researchers, developers, and marketers tend toward flashy interfaces with lots of features; once these are embedded into operational settings, users tend to gravitate to that subset of these features most relevant and useful in their day-to-day activities.

Class C-compliant systems possess no formal user interface, but instead rely on resources available from the native operating system on which it resides. For example, to configure the system, the administrator may need to edit a certain configuration file. To view the list of detected events, the administrator may need to view a certain log file. Class

B systems extend this to provide a dedicated, command-line or GUI application as the user interface. All necessary operation can be performed from within that user interface. Class A systems provide a centralized GUI application, from which an administrator can remotely control and operate any component of the intrusion detection system.

Criteria Assessment Metrics

In order to use the criteria to compare different intrusion detection systems, the security engineer must establish some objective set of metrics. Some assessment approaches we've considered at AT&T include the following:

Flat Summation. Compliance for the three categories of four requirements (twelve total) can be associated with numeric values (e.g., C=1, B=2, A=3). Assessment of a given intrusion detection system would then result in a compliance vector with twelve entries, each of which would map to one of the numeric estimates. A simple summation could be used to compare systems. The advantage is simplicity; the disadvantage is that it overly simplifies the comparison and imposes an implicit equivalence among all of the requirements. It also ignores the fact that each requirement may be associated with an optimal score for the target environment's budget and security needs. As a result, flat summation was not used and is not recommended.

Partitioned Score. This technique uses the flat summation, but maintains the distinction between the three categories of compliance requirements. Thus, three summations would result, allowing environments to better compare relevant aspects of compliance. For instance, a system with poor operational scores might be acceptable in a research environment. This also inherits many of the drawbacks noted for flat summation and is not an approach we used.

Weighted Score. If certain criteria are considered more crucial for an intrusion detection system in a given environment, then a weight can be assigned to each requirement. Assigning meaningful weights to the already arbitrary numeric estimates for requirements is extremely challenging. In addition, this technique results in an intrusion detection system receiving different scores for different environments. While this is certainly appropriate, it complicates the process considerably.

Requirements Vector. The approach we did use involved system security engineering analysis of the various requirements classes to determine the optimal target for the local environment. A couple of example considerations here include the following:

- If the local media is a slow Ethernet with no plans to upgrade in the near future, then expensive support for higher capacity systems is not needed.
- If no existing response environment exists and the local administrators want simple alarm display, then expensive response APIs are not needed.

Alert readers might notice that we are specifically trying to avoid the Orange Book trap of rating systems in an order manner so that vendors can claim higher ratings than their competitors. We hope instead that system compliance criteria ratings have evolved to the more mature notion of matching appropriate requirements to those systems providing required features.

Concluding Remarks

Requirements for intrusion detection systems are beginning to emerge, both in the literature (see [3], for example), and in products. The criteria presented here provides an early attempt at trying to organize these emerging requirements into useful classes for assessment and comparison at AT&T. Some closing issues worth mentioning are the following:

- We recognize that the set of criteria as described in this paper introduces the potential for subjective interpretation of the intent of each requirement. This is the inevitable consequence of any requirements description presented in limited space.
- We created a questionnaire to assist in the obtaining of information from vendors about their intrusion detection products. In most cases, this was how we tried to determine compliance with a given class for each requirement. This questionnaire is included as an appendix.
- The vendors contacted in the course of our R&D work were cordial and receptive to our inquiries. *We have chosen to not list their names here in the interest of not spurring any marketing wars between those contacted and those not contacted by AT&T.* Answers to our questions were returned promptly and we set out to interpret their answers. One

problem is that most vendor systems are evolving so rapidly, that the validity of their answers was often incorrect by the time we documented our findings. This further explains our obvious reluctance to publish the results of our assessments here. Certain vendors would inevitably claim that we were not properly characterizing their most recent release.

- Performing the assessment was easy in some aspects of the criteria that included less subjective analysis. Certain operational requirements, for example, tend to be easier to determine compliance. Other aspects of the criteria, however, required more subjective analysis and were therefore more difficult to use.
- Additional work is needed to fine-tune these requirements for general use outside AT&T. For instance, their completeness and consistency have not been thoroughly investigated.

References

[1] Department of Defense, *Trusted Computer System Evaluation Criteria* (TCSEC), DoD 5200.28-STD, 1983.

[2] E. Amoroso, *Intrusion Detection: An Introduction to Internet Surveillance, Correlation, Trace Back, Traps, and Response*, Intrusion.Net Books, 1999.

[3] Mario Ibanez, "A Comparison of Firewalls and Intrusion Detection Systems," *SysAdmin*, Volume 6, Number 12, December, 1997.

Appendix A: Questionnaire

The art of developing a questionnaire involves including questions that supports the following goals:

- Obtaining the information you need (this is the most important criterion)
- Not divulging the detailed intent of the questionnaire (this helps avoid those interviewed from telling you what they think you want to hear)
- Promoting open, honest, appropriate, and reasonable answers (avoiding interpretation differences in questions is important)

The list of questions is presented below for your tailored use.

1. Do you know the average time the system takes to detect an attack, i.e. the time interval between the start of an attack and some alarm/response taking place?
2. Is a basic set of attack profiles included with the system?
2.1. Do you issue periodic updates to these? How are they transmitted to the user?
2.2. Is it possible for the user to customize these? If so, how (e.g. via an API)?
3. Does the system employ detection via data pattern matching?
3.1. Is a basic set of content patterns included with the system?
3.2. Do you issue periodic updates to these? How are they transmitted to the user?
3.3. Is it possible for the user to customize these? If so, how?
4. Does the system employ statistical profiling/anomaly detection?
4.1. Are the alarm thresholds user-configurable?
5. No system will be able to detect 100% of all attacks. Do you claim a percentage of detectable attacks or attack classes for the system, either from calculation or measurement?
6. How does the system protect itself from attack?
6.1. What type of authentication is required for the various system components?
6.2. Can the data transmitted between system components be encrypted? Which encryption schemes are used?
6.3. On what type of OS do the system components run? A commercial OS? A hardened OS?
6.4. What type of physical security, if any, is provided for the hardware components?
7. Can the system correlate various events occurring in different regions of a network?
7.1. Is there a mechanism to input a feed from a third-party device which could place the system in a higher/lower state of alert for certain attack types?
8. What type of alarms does the system provide?
8.1. Passive (e.g. console display message)?
8.2. Active (e.g. email, fax, pager)?
9. Can the system perform auto-initiated responses to attacks?
9.1. Can the user customize these responses?
10. What level of monitoring is available to the administrator?

10.1. Session information (e.g. source/destination addresses, usernames)?
10.2. Keystroke monitoring?
11. How does the system log intrusions?
11.1. Is there a playback capability for simulation/replay of attacks?
11.2. Does the system include a tool to archive logs?
12. To what level can the system attempt to trace an intruder?
13. As part of its response mechanism, can the system divert an intruder to a trap system, or "honeypot"?
13.1. Can the system be configured to act as a trap?
14. What types of network media are supported (e.g. 10 Base-T, FDDI, ATM)?
14.1. Can the system process data packets at the full line rate of the highest-speed interface supported?
15. What type of user interface is provided for system management?
15.1. Is it a GUI?
15.2. Is it centralized or distributed?
15.3. Which components, if any, are SNMP-manageable?
16. What negative impact, if any, does the system induce on a network?
16.1. Is there a network utilization impact, measured as an average/peak percentage?
16.2. Is there a similar percentage for any impacts to individual hosts (e.g. >CPU utilization)?
17. To what level can the system be scaled, in terms of networks and hosts?
18. What level of customer support is available during day-today system operation?
19. Is there reliability data on the hardware components, measured in mean time-between-failures (MTBF)?
20. Has the system been tested/verified by any outside organization?
20.1. Can a detailed test plan be provided to a potential customer who may want to verify system effectiveness against various attacks.

Plenary Panel Session

Protection of Critical Infrastructure

Moderator

S. J. League, IPTF-DISA

This session will provide an overview of Department of Defense (DoD) efforts that are under way in the area of critical infrastructure protection to meet one of today's great challenges to military readiness—the protection of the nation's critical infrastructure.

Presidential Decision Directive 63 (PDD 63)—Critical Infrastructure Protection—was signed on May 22, 1998. It establishes a national goal for the United States to achieve and maintain the ability to protect our nation's critical infrastructures (telecommunications, energy, banking and finance, transportation, water systems, and emergency services) within five years, with an initial operational capability by the year 2000. It proposes a public–private partnership to realize this goal and designates lead agencies responsible for coordinating with the private sector. It also recognizes that there are certain functions that are chiefly performed by the federal government and designates lead agencies responsible for coordinating all of the activities of the U.S. government for those functions. DoD is the lead agency for national defense. The PDD also charges each department and agency with the responsibility for the protection of its own critical infrastructures and requires a plan for the protection of those infrastructures to be developed within 180 days. DoD's critical infrastructures are the Defense Information Infrastructure, Public Works, Financial Services, Logistics & Transportation, C4ISR, Personnel, Health Affairs, Space and Emergency Preparedness. Their protection requires a concerted effort by all of the military departments and the defense agencies.

The threat is real; there are vulnerabilities and action must be taken! The need for action is emphasized by Presidential Decision Directive 63—Critical Infrastructure Protection.

DoD is required to:

- Serve as lead agency for national defense "special functions"
- Assign a chief infrastructure assurance officer (CIAO)—Art Money
- Cooperate and support the national coordinator for security infrastructure protection and counter-terrorism
- Develop a critical infrastructure protection (CIP) plan by November 1998 (well under way)
- Implement the CIP plan within two years (much more planning and coordination needed).

DepSecDef assigned ASD/C3I to direct DoD CIP efforts, lead the national defense "special functions," and serve as the DoD CIAO. Each federal agency must have a plan to implement PDD63 within two years. The DoD critical infrastructure protection plan:

- Lays out the department-wide management structure, mechanisms, and strategy to protect infrastructures critical to the DoD mission
- Describes our participation in the national program
- Describes a CIP life cycle: analysis and assessment, remediation, indications and warning, mitigation, response, and reconstitution
- Identifies program resources to accomplish our goals.

We face these issues and challenges:

- Public–private sector information sharing
- Working with their respective commercial sector counterparts to map the national infrastructures and their vulnerabilities in the various sectors
- Developing and implementing defense infrastructure sector assurance plans
- Enormous intergovernmental coordination task
- Comprehensive, fully integrated, and sustainable process for providing protection to essential elements of infrastructure
- Linking military operations/planning to the critical infrastructures/critical assets
- Reallocating appropriate level of resources to make a difference
- Coordinate infrastructure protection R&D efforts while taking into account private sector research
- Working to actually begin assuring our critical infrastructure systems.

Where are we going?

Bringing order to Mission Essential Infrastructures
to support Military Planning, Operations, and Readiness
during Peace, Operations, and War

Track A

Digital Signatures

Chair

V. Reed, The MITRE Corporation

Anonymous Secure E-Voting over a Network

Yi Mu and Vijay Varadharajan
School of Computing & IT, University of Western Sydney, Nepean,
PO Box 10, Kingswood, NSW 2747, Australia
Email: {yimu,vijay}@st.nepean.uws.edu.au

Abstract

In this paper, we propose two new anonymous secure electronic voting schemes that protect the privacy of the voters and prevent double voting. These schemes do not require any special voting channel and the communications can occur entirely over existing networks such as the Internet. The proposed schemes are based on ElGamal digital signature algorithm and can be applied to elections in a variety of situations ranging from an election in a small organization to a country.

Key Words: Secure Voting, Applied Cryptography.

1 Introduction

Electronic balloting and voting can make the election process more convenient and efficient if it can be achieved securely. Electronic voting raises several security issues such as privacy, fairness, verifiability and double voting. Some of these issues become further complicated if voter anonymity is required. As an open networked environment (e.g. Internet) is vulnerable to security attacks such as eavesdropping, masquerading, and illegal modification and access, design of secure electronic balloting and voting systems over such networks is not an easy task. There have been a number of research publications that have addressed this problem proposing secure electronic voting systems that satisfy the above requirements at various levels [1, 2, 3, 4, 5].

The protection of privacy of voters in an electronic balloting and voting system is viewed as one of the most important security requirements. In general, electronic voting systems can be classified into two types namely the non-anonymous and the anonymous. The first type strictly hides the content of votes in order to preserve the privacy of the voters [3, 4]. The theory behind this type of system uses secret sharing schemes [6, 7] and zero knowledge proofs [8]. The main drawback of these schemes is the computational complexity in vote counting procedures, which becomes prohibitive in large scale voting systems [4]. The second type of schemes protects the privacy of voters by hiding the identity of voters and leaves the content of votes in the clear, visible to the voting authority. Hence the complexity problem in counting votes in large scale systems is overcome in these systems. However, this type of schemes have to deal with the problem of double voting. From the best of our knowledge, the second kind of voting schemes has not been investigated so far. In this paper, we propose two new anonymous voting schemes based on a modified ElGamal digital signature scheme. The proposed systems ensure that the anonymity of voters is preserved while at the same time detecting double voting.

The rest of this paper is organised as follows. Section 2 introduces the modified ElGamal digital signature scheme and describes the cryptographic primitives required for our schemes. Section 3 describes the voting environment and the security requirements. Section 4 describes our Voting Scheme 1 which involves the use of a trusted authentication server. Section 5 discusses our Voting Scheme 2 in which the level of trust on the authentication server is reduced compared to the first scheme.

2 Cryptographic Primitives

This section presents the modified ElGamal's digital signature scheme and discusses its properties.

The security of ElGamal's digital signature [9] scheme is based on the difficulty of computing discrete logarithms in a finite field. In this scheme, users in the system share a public key, while the signer has a secret key which he or she uses to sign messages. We assume that the signer is A and one of other users is B. The digital signature scheme is as follows:

1. To generate a key pair, A first chooses a large prime $p \in \mathcal{Z}_p$, and two random numbers, $g \in \mathcal{Z}_p^*$ and $k \in \mathcal{Z}_{p-1}$. Then A calculates
$$y = g^k \bmod p, \qquad (1)$$
where k is the secret key of A and $\{y, g, p\}$ is the corresponding public key. Both g and p are public.

2. To sign a message m, A first chooses a random number r, such that r is relatively prime to $p-1$ and then computes
$$a = g^r \bmod p \qquad (2)$$
and
$$s = k^{-1}(ma - r) \bmod (p-1) \qquad (3)$$
to form the digital signature $\{a, s\} \in \mathcal{Z}_p^*$, where k^{-1} is the inverse of k. Note that we have made a small change in s. In the original ElGamal scheme, $s = r^{-1}(m - ka) \bmod (p-1)$. The security of the modified scheme is equivalent to the original scheme. (See Ref. [10], where some 13000 ElGamal based signature schemes have been summarized)

3. To verify the signed message, B checks
$$y^s a \bmod p \stackrel{?}{=} g^{ma} \bmod p. \qquad (4)$$
If the equality holds, the signature is valid.

The security of ElGamal's digital signature scheme is based on the difficulty of computing discrete logarithms in a finite field. That is, it is computationally infeasible to calculate the secret key given the public key; similarly, knowing the one-time number a, it is computationally infeasible to compute r. Without the secret key k and random number r, it is computationally infeasible to produce a digital signature (a, s). Each ElGamal signature computation requires a new value of r that must be chosen at random and the value of r cannot be used more than once.

Theorem 1 *For a given $k \in \mathcal{Z}_{p-1}$, if a and r are used more then once for ElGamal signatures, k can be computed without prior knowledge of k.*

Proof: Assume that a and r have been used to generate ElGamal signatures s and s' with respect to the messages m and m' respectively. k can be computed by
$$k = \frac{m'a - ma}{s' - s} \bmod (p-1). \qquad (5)$$
□

Therefore, the value of a or r must have never been used before. We can employ this property to prevent an individual from using a certain data more than once, if the data is related to either r or a. For instance, in an electronic balloting process, a voter is not allowed to vote for a certain candidate more than once. If a voting ticket contains the information of r or a, multiple use of the ticket will reveal the secret key of the voter. In fact, this scheme can be used in any system which requires to protect against multiple use of a certain data item.

3 Voting Environment

Our on-line electronic voting environment involves at least the following parties : Voters (Vs), an Authentication Server (AS) which is responsible for authenticating the Voters and granting Voting Tickets, Voting Servers (S's) that collect voting tickets from voters, and a Ticket Counting Server (TCS), and Trusted Certificate Authority/Authorities (CA). Authentic and secret communications between voters and servers in the proposed scheme are based on asymmetric key cryptosystems. Therefore, voters and servers do not share any secret.

The following requirements are to be met by the voting scheme.

- Anonymity of Voters: Identities of voters must not be revealed to other voters and Voting Server S. The authentication server

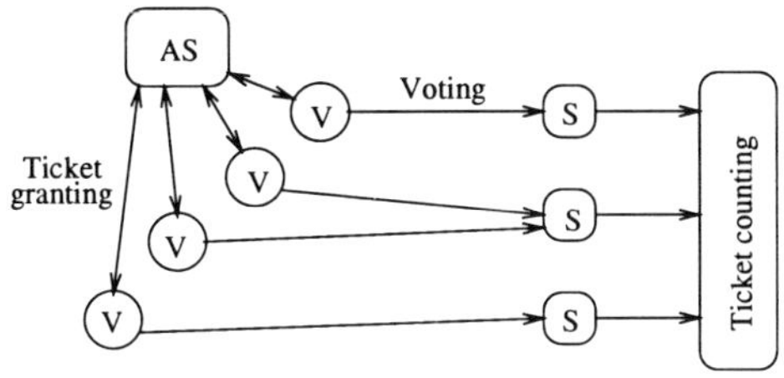

Figure 1: Illustration of the Voting Scheme.

cannot map any voting ticket to the corresponding voter's identity, unless the voter has double voted.

- Secrecy of Voting Tickets: The contents of a voting ticket should be secret and must be protected from unauthorized disclosure; while the contents are in the clear to Voting Servers.
- Authentication between Voters and *AS*: *AS* should know that the voters are legitimate for the given election and voters should know that *AS* is the authority which is issuing the voting tickets.
- Validation of Voting Tickets: Voting Server *S* is able to check the validity of voting tickets.
- Double Voting: It should not be possible for a voter to vote more than once[1]; if this occurs, then this can be detected and the identity of the voter revealed.

Our voting scheme involves four phases : voting preparation, voting, voting ticket collection, and ballot counting. Each phase involves a sequence of steps and is described using a suitable protocol and algorithm.

4 Voting Scheme 1

The Voting Scheme 1 described in this section assumes a trusted Authentication Server *AS*. It is trusted to authenticate the users correctly as well as not to vote on behalf of any other voters.

[1] In our case, double voting means to use a parameter for different messages or votes. It is OK for a voter to send the same message or vote twice or more – treated as one vote.

4.1 Voting Preparation

The voting preparation phase involves obtaining a voting certificate from a trusted Certification Authority and a valid voting ticket from *AS*. This phase is not anonymous; when requesting a voting ticket, the voter should prove his or her identity to the *AS*. The proof is based on a valid public key certificate and the voter's RSA digital signature on the request. All parameters in the voting ticket for a particular voter must be protected against unauthorized disclosure.

4.1.1 Voting Certificate

Assume that all parties hold a long term voting certificate which can be used for a number of elections. In fact, this could be the usual public key certificate that can be used for a variety of purposes such as electronic payment, email as well as voting. Obtaining such certificates can be done via either a secure online channel or an off-line method such as physical access to a *CA* that could act as a local election server. Let $Cert_X$ be the certificate of X and let the RSA secret key – public key pair for X be denoted as (d_x, e_x).

When requesting a certificate from a *CA*, a voter needs to generate a pair of RSA secret-public key $\{d_v, e_v\}$ and two large prime numbers; the product of the prime numbers forms a public modulo n, where $d_v e_v = 1 \bmod \phi(n)$. A voting certificate, containing parameters such as the voter's identity, serial number, RSA public key, lifetime, timestamp and *CA*'s identity, is signed by the *CA* using its secret key. The public key of the *CA* is assumed to be "really public" and widely accessible. For example, *CA*'s public key can be accessible and broadcast via the Web.

4.1.2 Obtaining a Voting Ticket

The preparation of an ElGamal secret key – public key pair has been given in section 2. Here, we selectively use certain parameters in the ElGamal algorithm to construct a voting ticket. It is reasonable to assume that *AS* is completely trusted by voters not to use voting tickets illegally. In order to ensure the anonymity of the voters, *AS* should not have any information on tickets and other parameters to be used in future voting processes. This is achieved using blind signature schemes [11, 12]. We assume that all public key encryption and digital signatures are based on the RSA algorithm.

The protocol for granting a voting ticket is as follows:

1. Before sending a request for a voting ticket to AS, V needs to prepare the following parameters: $x_1 \equiv gb^{e_a} \bmod n$ and $x_2 \equiv ab^{e_a} \bmod n$, where b is a blind factor and e_a is the public key of AS. The voter sends the following request message to AS.

   $V \rightarrow AS$: $V, AS, Cert_V, (x_1||x_2||t)^{d_v} \bmod n$, where t denotes a timestamp and $||$ denotes concatenation of bits.

2. Upon receipt of the request, AS validates the signature $(x_1||x_2||t)^{d_v} \bmod n$, chooses k at random ($k \in Z_{p-1}$), encrypts $x_3 = (k||t)^{e_v} \bmod n$, and computes the following digital signature.

$$x_4 \equiv (x_1^k x_2)^{d_a} = (ya)^{d_a} b^{k+1} \bmod n,$$

   where $y = g^k$ and d_a is the private key of AS. Then AS sends these blindly signed parameters to V:

   $AS \rightarrow V$: $AS, A, x_3, (x_4||t)^{e_v} \bmod n$.

   x_3 and x_4 have been encrypted with the public key of the corresponding V. Note that k no longer servers as the secret key of the voter, but the unique alias of the voter. k must be known to both AS and the corresponding voter. In the AS database, k is the unique index pointed to the real identity of the voter. We have assumed that k is chosen by AS; however it can be also chosen by the voter and is then sent to AS.

3. V decrypts x_3 to obtain k and removes the blind factor b^{k+1} to obtain the following:

$$x_4' \equiv (ya)^{d_a} \bmod n,$$

To construct a voting ticket, V needs to specify the candidate to whom he or she wishes to vote for. This information is included in m in a standard format that is assumed to be followed by all the voters.

$$m = \{\text{Candidate 1}||Yes||\text{Candidate 2}||No||...\}$$

The Voting Ticket is now constructed as $T \equiv \{a||g||y||x_4'||s||m\}$, where $s = k^{-1}(ma - r)$. AS stores k along with the identity of the voter, voter's public key certificate, and $(x_1||x_2||t)^{d_v} \bmod n$.

The number g should be different for each voter. This condition is important as shown by Theorem 2 below.

Theorem 2 *Consider two voters V_1 and V_2. If both of them use the same value of g and different values of r then V_1 and V_2 can double vote by exchanging the signed value of a.*

Proof: Let V_1 have r and V_2 have r' ($r \neq r'$). Then V_1 has $a = g^r \bmod p$ and V_2 has $a' = g^{r'} \bmod p$. After exchanging a and a' along with the associated r and r', V_1 can compute:

$$s' = k^{-1}(ma' - r') \bmod (p-1),$$

which is different from $s = k^{-1}(ma - r) \bmod (p - 1)$. Using Equation (5), we find

$$k \neq \frac{m'a' - ma}{s' - s} \bmod (p-1).$$

The case for V_2 is similar.

In order to overcome this attack using common g, we have introduced the digital signature, x_4' where

$$x_4' \equiv (ay)^{d_a} \bmod n,$$

x_4' provides a link between $k, g, a,$ and r which ensures that these values have to be used at the same time and hence the common g attack is overcome. AS must also ensure that there are no voters who share the same value of k. □

4.2 Voting and Collecting Tickets

Once a voter obtains a valid voting ticket from the AS, voting can immediately start. The voter votes by sending the Voting Ticket over a network to a Voting Server S.

1. The voter needs to fill out the message part of the voting ticket, m, to create a valid ticket. The voter then sends the ticket to S:

   $V \rightarrow S$: $S, (T||t)^{e_s} \bmod n$.

2. Upon receipt of T, S decrypts the ticket with its secret key and validates a, g, and y by verifying AS's signatures on x'_4. Then S validates s using $y^s a \bmod p = g^{ma} \bmod p$.

The voting process is anonymous in that the voter never sent his or her identity to the Voting Server. The main task of a Voting Server is to ensure the authenticity of voting tickets. This is done by checking AS's signatures on x'_4 and checking whether or not the parameters g, a and y have been used before by checking its own database. However these checks are not sufficient to provide the assurance that the voting ticket has not been used with other Voting Server(s); hence, a further check needs to be done by the Ticket Counting Server.

Note that voting tickets are untraceable and do not reveal any information about the voters; while the Voting Server can still ensure the authenticity of the received voting tickets. This is because all important data used in the construction of the ticket were blindly signed by the AS.

4.3 Counting Tickets

Voting Servers store voting tickets in voting boxes; for instance, each voting box might contain 100 such tickets. Once a box is full, it is sent to the Ticket Counting Server (TCS) over the network. The counting of tickets is done by TCS.

TCS checks for double voting where a voter may vote more than once with different Voting Servers. Double voting can be detected by checking whether the parameters (a, g, y) have been used more than once. Following this check, the balloted ticket is included in the ticket counting process where votes for each of the candidates are accumulated. This is done by examining the balloting information in m. Furthermore, if double voting occurs, then using Theorem 1, the TCS can compute k using the information from the two Voting Tickets and sends k to AS. AS can then find the identity of the voter.

5 Voting Scheme 2

In Scheme 1, AS is trusted not to generate any voting ticket without voter's consent and not to give k to others including S and TCS. The main difference between this scheme and the first one is that in this scheme the level of trust on the AS is reduced so that the above mentioned requirements for AS are no longer needed; while the anonymity of the voters is still preserved. We will not repeat the parts which are same as those in Voting Scheme 1.

5.1 Obtaining a Voting Ticket

In this scheme, the AS does not have complete information on the ElGamal secret key which has been used as the voter's alias mapping the voter's identity in the Voting Scheme 1; the AS shares only a portion of the secret key. In other words, AS cannot generate a voting ticket for any voter without the voter's consent.

The protocol for granting tickets is as follows:

1. Before sending a request to AS for a Voting Ticket, V prepares the following parameters: $x_1 \equiv g b^{e_a} \bmod n$, $x'_1 \equiv g^{k_1} b^{e_a} \bmod n$, and $x_2 \equiv a b^{e_a} \bmod n$, where b is a blind factor and $k_1 \in \mathcal{Z}_{p-1}$ is a secret parameter known only to the voter. The voter sends the following request to AS.

$V \rightarrow AS$:

$$V, AS, Cert_V, (x_1 \| x'_1 \| x_2 \| t)^{d_v} \bmod n.$$

2. Upon receipt of the request, AS validates V's signature, chooses k_2 at random ($k_2 \in Z_{p-1}$), computes $x_3 = (k_2 \| t)^{e_v} \bmod n$. and computes the following digital signatures.

$$\begin{aligned} x_4 &\equiv (x_1^{k_2} x'_1 x_1^{2k_2} x'_1 x_2)^{d_a} \\ &= (y_1 y_2 a)^{d_a} b^{3(k_2+1)} \bmod n, \end{aligned}$$

where we have assumed that $k = k_1 + k_2$, $k' = k_1 + 2k_2$, $y_1 = g^k$, and $y_2 = g^{k'}$. AS then stores k_2 along with V's identity in its database and sends the blindly signed x_4 to V:

$AS \rightarrow V$: $AS, V, x_3, (x_4 \| t)^{e_v} \bmod n$.

Note that x_4 is also important for eliminating the common g attack, since it provides a link amongst r, a, g, k, and k'.

3. V decrypts x_3 to obtain k_2, computes $k = k_1 + k_2$ and $k' = k_1 + 2k_2$, computes y_1 and

y_2, and removes the blind factor $b^{3(k_2+1)}$ to obtain:

$$x'_4 \equiv (y_1 y_2 a)^{d_a} \bmod n.$$

The voting ticket is now constructed as

$$T \equiv \{a\|g\|y_1\|y_2\|x'_6\|s_1\|s_2\|m\},$$

where $s_1 = k^{-1}(ma - r)$ and $s_2 = k'^{-1}(ma - r)$.

5.2 Voting and Collecting Tickets

The voting process is similar to that given in Voting Scheme 1. Here, we omit the details. Please note that this time it is not possible for the AS to learn the the identity of the voter, even if AS, S's, and TCS collude. This is because the AS does not have complete information on k and does not know the mapping between the voter and k_2. However, when a double-voting occurs, the AS can immediately compute k and k' in terms of Equation (5). With k and k', AS can solve

$$\begin{aligned} k &= k_1 + k_2, \\ k' &= k_1 + 2k_2, \end{aligned}$$

to obtain k_1 and k_2, which then leads to the identity of the voter.

6 Concluding Remarks

In this paper, we have proposed two secure anonymous electronic voting schemes which use a modified ElGamal digital signature algorithm. With these schemes, if a voter votes only once, then his or her identity will never be discovered by the Voting Servers and Ticket Counting Server. The Voting Scheme 1 assumes the existence of a trusted AS. In Voting Scheme 2, the level of trust in the AS is reduced so that voter anonymity holds even if Voting Servers, Ticket Counting Server and Authentication Server collude, since the AS has access to only part of the information on the unique alias of a voter. In fact, the security of our voting schemes is equivalent to that of the ElGamal digital signature. That is, if a voter only votes once, then discovering the voter's identity is equivalent to discovering the signer's ElGamal secret key.

References

[1] P. G. Neumann, "Security criteria for electronic voting," in *Proceedings of the 16th national computer security conference*, (Naltimore MD), pp. 478–482, 1993.

[2] J. Borrell and J. Rifà, "An implementatable secure voting scheme," *computer & security*, vol. 15, no. 4, pp. 327–338, 1996.

[3] R. Cramer, M. Franklin, B. Schoenmakers, and M. Yung, "Multi-authority secret-bollat elections with linear work," in *Lecture Notes in Computer Science 1070*, (EUROCRYPT'96), pp. 72–83, Springer, Berlin, 1996.

[4] R. Cramer, R. Gennaro, and J. Borrell, "A secure and optimally efficient multi-authority election scheme," in *Lecture Notes in Computer Science 1233*, (EUROCRYPT'97), pp. 103–117, Springer, Berlin, 1997.

[5] A. Fujioka, T. Okamoto, and K. Ohta, "A practical secret voting scheme for large scale elections," in *Lecture Notes in Computer Science 718*, (EUROCRYPT'94), pp. 244–251, Springer, Berlin, 1992.

[6] A. Shamir, "How to share a secret," *Communications of the ACM*, vol. 22, pp. 612–613, 1979.

[7] T. P. Perdersen, "Non-interactive and information-theoretic secure verifiable secret sharing," in *Lecture Notes in Computer Secience 576*, pp. 129–140, Advances in cryptology - CRYPTO'91, Springer-Verlag, Berlin, 1992.

[8] M. O. Rabin, *Digital Signatures.* Academic Press, New York, 1978.

[9] T. ElGamal, "A public-key cryptosystem and a signature scheme based on discrete logarithms," in *Adances in cryptology - CRYPTO'84, Lecture Notes in Computer Secience*, pp. 10–18, Springer-Verlag, Berlin, 1985.

[10] P. Horster, M. Michels, and H. Peterson, "Meta-Elgamal signature schemes," in

Proceedings of the second ACM Conference on Computer and Communications Security, (New York), November 1994.

[11] D. L. Chaum, "Untraceable electronic mail, return addresses, and digital pseudonyms," *Communications of the ACM*, vol. 24, no. 2, pp. 84–88, 1981.

[12] D. Chaum, A. Fait, and M. Naor, "Untraceable electronic cash," in *Advances in Cryptology – CRYPTO '88 Proceedings*, pp. 319–327, 1990.

The Solar Trust Model: Authentication without Limitation

Michael Clifford
Dept. of Computer Science
University of California, Davis
Davis, CA 95616
macliffo@engr.ucdavis.edu[1]

Charles Lavine
The Aerospace Corporation
2350 East El Segundo Blvd.
El Segundo, CA 90245
lavine@aero.org

Matt Bishop
Dept. of Computer Science
University of California, Davis
Davis, CA 95616
bishop@cs.ucdavis.edu

Abstract

The PEM and PGP/X.509 authentication models and the Biba Integrity Model have limitations inherent in their design that diminish their practicality in real world applications. The ICE-TEL trust model addresses some of these difficulties, and introduces a few new limitations. The Common Security Services Manager's Trust Policy Interface Specification provides the guidelines with which new trust policies may be encoded, but does not implement an actual policy. This paper describes a new model that permits both the identity of the sender of a message, and the trustworthiness of the sender of the message to be determined. The model works regardless of whether or not the message was signed by a certificate authority with which the recipient has a relationship. The model can be implemented without changing the format of certificates that are currently in use, and could be used as a module in a broader security framework, such as the Common Security Services Manager.

Introduction

This paper presents an alternative model for verifying the identity of the sender of a message that has been signed using a digital certificate [7,8]. The PGP/X.509 model [1] assumes an implicit transitivity of trust between participating parties. The PEM certification model [2] assumes that everyone in the world trusts one ultimate authority to verify the identities of other certificate senders. The PEM model also does not allow for multiple levels of trust within its certification hierarchy. Neither of these models provides a practical, universally applicable method of verifying the identity of the sender of a message. In the real world, trust is rarely transitive, and the concept of a single hierarchy has already given way to multiple corporate and governmental certifying authorities, each of which issues their certificates without being required to meet the standards of some ultimate certifying authority [5].

The Biba Integrity Model [3] provides for multiple levels of trust within an organization or system, but not between two autonomous systems. The Common Security Services Manager's Trust Policy Interface Specification [4] provides an API in which an open set of authentication policies may be implemented, and permits multiple certificate authorities (CAs) to sign the same message, but provides no method for verifying the trustworthiness of any of the CAs. The ICE-TEL trust model [9] eliminates the need for transitivity of trust, and permits certification along paths rather than in global CA hierarchies, but it does not provide for multiple levels of trust .

The model described in this paper enhances verification capabilities beyond other models by providing a method for designating many levels of trust, for permitting unlimited numbers of independent CAs with no requirement for a central authority, and for determining the trustworthiness of a message that has been signed by a CA with whom the receiver of the message has no direct relationship [5, 9, 10].

Background

The PEM certification model is described in RFC1422 [2]. It describes a certification hierarchy in which one root level authority, called the Internet Policy Registration Authority (IPRA), certifies a small number of lower level authorities. Each of these lower level authorities, known as Policy Certification Authorities or PCAs, can certify even lower level authorities known as Certification Authorities or CAs. CAs can then certify individuals. Certification requirements are passed down to lower level authorities, and can become increasingly restrictive as each authority

[1] Portions of this work were performed while the author was at The Aerospace Corporation.

0-8186-8789-4/98 $10.00 © 1998 IEEE

adds new restrictions onto those imposed upon it from higher level authorities. In this model, the transitive application of trust from higher level authorities to lower level authorities, and the dependence upon one root level authority, imply that all users of the model must implicitly place their trust and confidence in the certification policies of the IPRA. If a user either can not, or chooses not to accept the ultimate authority of the IPRA then, because of the transitivity of trust inherent in the PEM model, the user can not accept as valid any certificate signed by a CA under the IPRA.

The PGP/X.509 Web of Trust model derives from the ITU X.509 Authentication Framework's strong authentication procedure [1]. Messages are digitally signed using public key encryption. If a user does not know the sender of a message, they can find someone who does know the sender, either directly, or though one or more other people. Each person in the chain verifies the identity of the next person in the chain. Because there is no higher level certification authority, users are forced to trust the identity of the sender at position n in a chain, simply because the next closest person to them (at position *n-1*) says that person *n* can be trusted. The "web of trust" can verify the identity of a sender only if the recipient and the sender can be connected to each other through a chain of people who know each other. This requirement greatly limits its functionality.

In addition, the PGP/X.509 model does not offer any way to compute more than one level of trust. Users are forced to make a judgment as to how much they trust messages signed by the people that they know, and have no guidance in determining how much they can trust messages signed by someone elsewhere on the web of trust.

The Biba Integrity Model uses the concept of integrity labels to provide an ordering of data objects, and the subjects that may try to read from or write to the data objects [3]. Two properties, the Simple Integrity Property, and the Integrity *-Property, are used to determine the subjects that are permitted to read from, or write to, each object. The Simple Integrity Property permits a subject to write to an object only if the subject has an equal or higher integrity label than the object. The Integrity *-Property prevents a subject with read access to an object from modifying an object with a higher integrity label than the object that it can read from. While the Biba Integrity Model does provide a form of trust ordering if all of the subjects and objects involved have been assigned integrity labels within the same organization or system, it fails to create orderings of trust for subjects and objects that exist within completely autonomous systems. Subjects that have been labeled with an integrity level in one system have no basis for being labeled with any particular integrity label in another system. If subjects in one system were to be labeled at the lowest integrity label in another system by default, then subjects would be denied the ability to even read data in other systems. This prevents people in two independent organizations from being able to share data easily.

If, on the other hand, subjects were labeled with an integrity label in another system based on the integrity level that they have been assigned within their own system, then the two organizations must have some method of implicitly ensuring that they label subjects with integrity labels in exactly the same way within both of their organizations (or provide a mapping between labels). If the two organizations do this, then they would also have to agree that subjects at the same integrity label within one organization would have the same read and write privileges within the other organization. If these requirements are not met, then the notion of levels of integrity is rendered meaningless between separate systems or organizations.

The Common Security Services Manager's Trust Policy Interface Specification is an API released by the Intel corporation, that provides a wide variety of functions and services that support applications that require security features in their implementation [4]. Security policy modules can be plugged into a program using the API, and then used to calculate the level of trust that can be assigned to a message. Signatures by multiple certificate authorities can be handled by the API. However, the API does not specify a method of determining whether or not a CA with which the user has no relationship can be trusted. In addition, even though it provides functions with which trust policies can be built, it does not specify any specific procedure for implementing a trust policy.

The European Union's ICE-TEL project addresses many of the shortcomings in the other security models by combining some of the best features of some of the other models [4]. In the ICE-TEL model, users determine if they can trust a message that is signed by a particular CA. A message sent to a user from certificate authorities other than their own is signed first by the sender's CA, then by a chain of intermediate CAs until the message reaches the user's CA. The user's CA signs the message, and delivers it to the user. A user can verify the identity of the sender of a message by walking through the chain of signatures on the message, and verifying that each signature is valid. Cross certification is used to promote efficiency in the implementation of the model. Users are grouped into security domains, that are designed to aid the users in determining how the model should be applied to a particular message.

The ICE-TEL model provides a solution to some of the most significant problems with the other security models. Users are given the ability to trust messages that have not been signed by their own CA. The ICE-TEL model eliminates the transitivity of trust problem found in the PEM model. Additionally, a single CA hierarchy is not required for the ICE-TEL model to function, although hierarchies are present in the model.

The major drawback in the design of the ICE-TEL model is that it provides users with a flat model of trust.

When a certification path is considered trusted, it is trusted to the same degree as any other certification path. ICE-TEL provides users with no method of determining whether one certification path might be worthy of a higher degree of trust than another path. Although ICE-TEL does provide the ability to limit the length of a certification path, this only addresses the issue of how many CAs are permitted to sign a particular message, and not how differences among the CAs themselves might affect the trustworthiness of the message.

This presence of multiple levels of trust is an extremely important property, because it permits the computation of a most trusted or secure path for a message to take, and because it permits comparisons of the authenticity of data from multiple sources, or from the same source along multiple paths.. Without this ability, the ICE-TEL model can not determine whether or not a message should be trusted in a truly flexible manner. Instead, it must resort to a somewhat inflexible and complex array of cross certifying hierarchies and complicated algorithms that have limited efficiency and versatility.

A New Approach: The Solar Trust Model

The Solar Trust Model overcomes many of the limitations inherent in the designs of the other trust models. It does this by providing a simple and efficient method by which many levels of trust can be implemented, by permitting an unlimited number of independent CAs with no requirement for a central PCA, and by defining a procedure for determining the trustworthiness of a message that has been signed by a CA with whom the receiver of the message has no direct relationship.

To demonstrate how the Solar Trust Model works, let a CA be defined as any entity which issues digital certificates. If CA_1 and CA_2 are two certificate authorities, then CA_2 can establish a set of rules to determine how much it trusts messages signed by CA_1. This set of rules is called a trust relationship.

For example, suppose that Bob wants to read a document sent by Alice and signed by CA_1, which uses a fixed procedure to ensure Alice's identity. Now, if CA_1 can prove to CA_2 that the procedure used to verify Alice's identity meets CA_2's criteria, then CA_2 can be certain (i.e., to an adequate level of certainty) that Alice's document (which has been signed by CA_1) is indeed Alice's. On the other hand, if CA_3 is another certificate authority, and its policy for verifying the identity of a second person, say Ted, is unknown to CA_2, and Ted is sending a message to Bob, then CA_2 will not have adequate assurance to believe any claims about the identity of Ted made by CA_3.

If CA_2 has a set of rules that say that any certificate authority that uses the same procedures as itself for verifying the identity of the sender of a message can be trusted more than a certificate authority that does not use those procedures, and if CA_2 can verify that CA_1 uses these procedures, then CA_2 can say that it has a stronger trust relationship with CA_1 than with CA_3.

Let a solar system be defined as the representation of an ordering of trust relationships with respect to a specific certificate authority. It is helpful to think of a solar system as a series of objects that exist within concentric orbits around a central body, much as the planets in a solar system orbit around the sun. For any set of certificate authorities CA_1 through CA_n, CA_i is the central body or primary in its own solar system, and all of the other certificate authorities with which CA_i has established a trust relationship are objects or planets in orbit around the primary.

An ordering of trust can now be established for all certificate authorities which are planets in a solar system, with distance from the solar system's primary indicating the level of the trust relationship between the primary and a planet. A certificate authority places itself in the 0'th orbit of itself, because it trusts itself completely. Orbits 1 through n are occupied by all other certificate authorities in the solar system, where a certificate authority in orbit m is more trusted than a certificate authority in orbit m+1. It is possible for two or more certificate authorities to share the same orbit, or for orbits to be empty. If certificate authority CA_i does not have a trust relationship with certificate authority CA_x, then CA_x is not a planet in CA_i's solar system.

Note that since every certificate authority has its own solar system, the primary certificate authority in one solar system can (and often will) be a planet in another solar system, and that a certificate authority can be a planet in many different solar systems. It is also important to recognize that two certificate authorities do not necessarily have the same trust relationship with each other. Since a trust relationship is derived from a set of rules which each certificate authority independently establishes (although common rule sets can be established), there is no guarantee that two certificate authorities will ever have the same trust relationship with each other. Furthermore, if one certificate authority has a trust relationship with a second certificate authority, then it is not guaranteed nor is it necessary that the second certificate authority has a trust relationship with the first.

Although a certificate authority can establish direct trust relationships with many other certificate authorities, it is infeasible that it will establish such relationships with **all** other certificate authorities. The solar trust model solves this problem by establishing *indirect trust relationships*. For example, if CA_2 is a planet in the solar system of CA_1, and CA_3 is a planet in the solar system of CA_2, then CA_3 is a "*moon*" of CA_2 in the solar system of CA_1. This can be extended through any number of iterations. Since a certificate authority can be a planet in many different solar systems, that certificate authority can be a moon of many different certificate authorities in the same solar system. Although the moon of a planet is regarded as being in the same orbit as the planet, the moon is not considered to be the same entity as the planet.

It is important to understand that an indirect trust relationship does not imply a transitivity of trust. When trust is transitive, then if CA_1 trusts CA_2, and CA_2 trusts CA_3, then CA_1 must trust CA_3 in the same way that CA_2 trusts CA_3. In an indirect trust relationship, if CA_1 trusts CA_2, and CA_2 trusts CA_3, then CA_1 may or may not trust CA_3. Furthermore, since CA_1 relates to CA_3 indirectly, CA_1 is unlikely to trust CA_3 as much as it does CA_2.

At this point, it should be noted that if a message comes from a moon, it may appear to come from many different orbits. To resolve this issue, we define the *path of trust* taken by a message as the set of certificate authorities that sign the message in the order in which they are signed. For example, if a message is signed first by CA_3, then by CA_2, then by CA_1, the path taken by the message is CA_3, CA_2, CA_1. Given any two certificate authorities with an indirect trust relationship, it is likely that there is more than one path that a message could take between the two certificate authorities. However, the only path that counts is the one that the message actually takes. If a CA appears more than once on the same path of trust, it is regarded as a different CA each time that it appears.

In order to improve efficiency, it may be desirable for paths of trust between CAs to be computed in advance. There are several methods by which this may be implemented. In the first method, a three way handshake is used to send a trusted path to a CA that sends a message. For example, if CA_2 wished to send a message to CA_1, CA_2 would send a request for a trusted path to CA_1. CA_1 would then send an acceptable path of trust back to CA_2. CA_2 would then send its message to CA_1 along the path of trust. Note that CA_1 does not have to believe the origin of the path request from CA_2, since CA_1 can determine whether or not the final message came from CA_2, and can determine whether or not it trusts messages from CA_2. Another method would involve the computation of trust tables, which would be similar in form to the routing tables used in IP protocol routers. Finally the ICE-TEL trust model proposes publishing paths using public forums. [9]

In addition to establishing the orbit from which a message derives, the concept of a path of trust also allows the determination of the levels of trust for messages that are sent between certificate authorities that do not have direct relationships. When a message is first signed by a certificate authority, that certificate authority can attach a copy of its rule set to the message. As the message is passed from certificate authority to certificate authority, each certificate authority concatenates its rule set to the rule set that is passed to it, forming a *composite rule set*. The certificate authority that ultimately receives the message applies all of the rules in the composite rule set, until the message is either rejected as untrustworthy, or is accepted after meeting the requirements of all of the rules. The rule set for each individual certificate authority is represented using the Solar Trust Model Rule Set Header shown below.

Field A: Local Direct Range
Field B: Local Indirect Range *(m)*
Field C: Maximum Path Length *(p)*
Field D: Permitted Local Range for Next CA *(q)*
DATA

Figure 1. The Solar Trust Model Rule Set Header.

The following fields are represented in the Solar Trust Model Rule Set Header:

- *Field A*: Local Direct Range: Trust all messages that have been directly signed by a CA in an orbit with a number (k) no greater than this value.
- *Field B*: Local Indirect Range: Trust messages that have been indirectly signed by a CA in an orbit with a number that is less than or equal to this value. Do not trust any messages that have been signed by a CA in an orbit with a number that is greater than this value.
- *Field C*: Maximum Path Length: A message can be trusted only if the total number of CAs that have signed the message is no greater than this value *(p)*.
- *Field D*: Permitted Local Range for Next CA: A message that has been indirectly signed by a CA inside the local indirect range can be trusted only if it came from an orbit in that CA's system with a number no
- greater than this value *(q)*.

The examples that follow demonstrate the major classes of rules from which certificate authorities can derive their own rule sets. The figures beneath each new case show the order and rules whereby each new certificate authority adds its own signature to the data that it receives.

Case 1: Direct transmission through one certificate authority

In this case, a message is sent between two individuals who use the same certificate authority, and the certificate

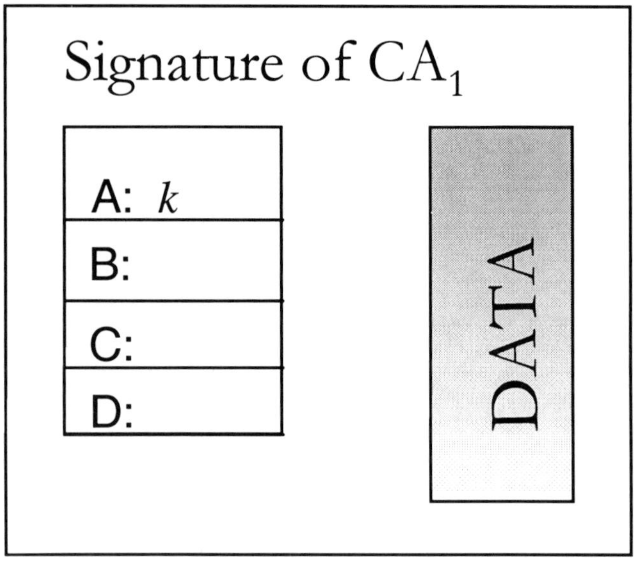

Figure 2. Format of a message sent between two users with the same certificate authority. CA_1 guarantees the identity of the sender of the message.

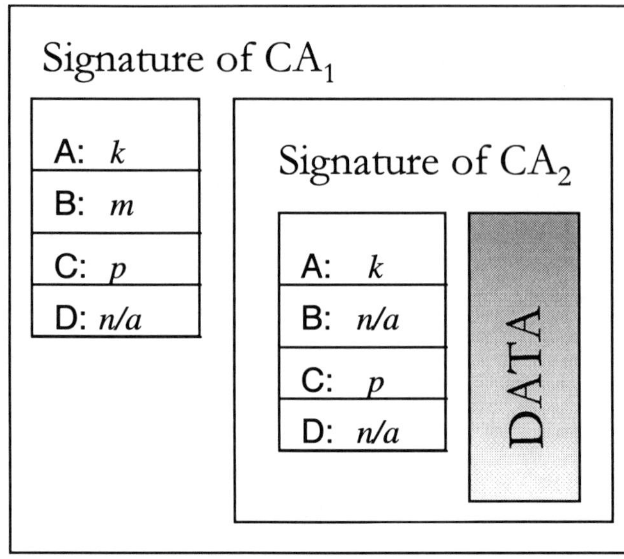

Figure 3. Format of a message sent between two users with different certificate authorities who maintain a direct trust relationship..

authority guarantees the identity of the message sender. (see Figure 2).

Case 2: Direct transmission within a solar system

In this case, a message is first directly signed by a certificate authority CA_2 which is a planet in the solar system of CA_1, and is then signed by CA_1. CA_2 might be located in any orbit in CA_1's solar system. In this case, the policy of CA_1 is directly applied. (see Figure 4). The possible policies are:

a) Trust only transmissions that are directly signed by CA_1 (Case 1).

b) Trust transmissions that are directly signed by any CA in the solar system, but only if they originate within some range of orbits between orbit 0 and some orbit m. Trust transmissions that are directly signed by any CA in the solar system. As long as CA_2 is within one of the orbits permitted by CA_1's policy, the receiver can trust the message. Otherwise, the receiver can not trust the message.

Case 3: Indirect transmission through multiple certificate authorities

Cases 1 and 2 assume that a message was directly signed by some certificate authority with a direct relationship to another certificate authority. In this case, an indirect relationship between certificate authorities is demonstrated. Additional policies are needed to handle messages that are signed by a certificate authority that CA_i, orbiting in the solar system of CA_2, does not have a direct relationship. These policies are designed to interpret the composite policies of other certificate authorities in order to achieve an appropriate composite rule set (see Figure 6). Examples of possible policies for this case include:

a) Trust only transmissions which were trusted under Case 2.

b) Trust transmissions which are trusted under Case 2, or which come from another CA's solar system, so long as that CA is trusted by CA_i under the rules in Case 2.

c) Trust transmissions that are trusted under Case 2, or that come from another CA's solar system, but only if they originate within some orbit, say orbit 3, in the other solar system.

d) Trust transmissions that are trusted under Case 2, or that have been signed by not more than four other certificate authorities.

e) Trust transmissions which pass through a CA in CA_i's solar system, so long as that CA falls within orbit 4 of CA_i's solar system.

f) Trust transmissions which pass through some certificate authority CA_j which lies within orbit 4 of CA_i's solar system, so long as the transmissions are trusted according to the policy of CA_j.

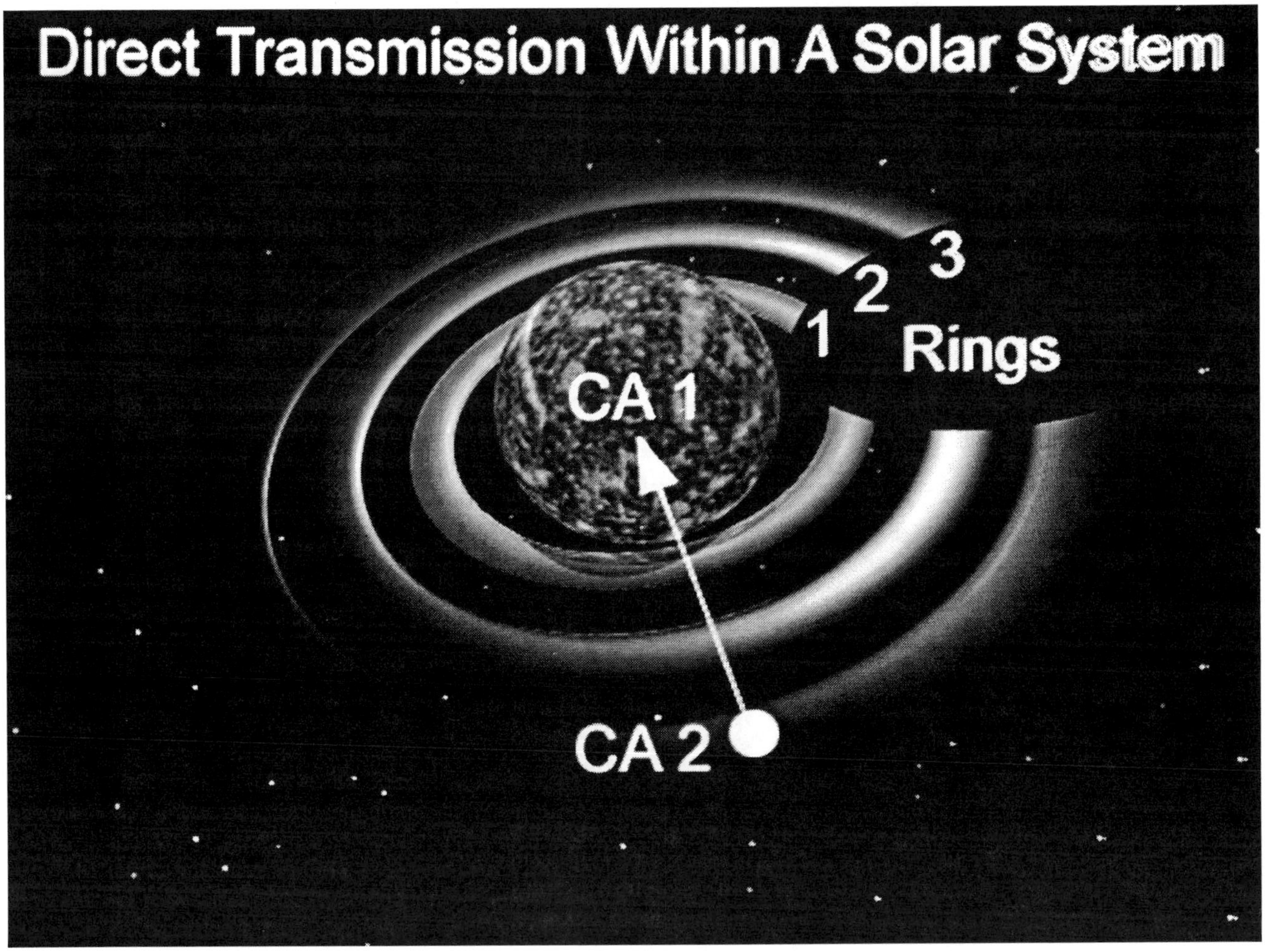

Figure 4. The solar system of CA_1. Ring 0 (CA_1 itself), plus the three next innermost rings are shown. CA_2 is located in ring 3 of CA_1's solar system. The arrow indicates that a direct path is taken by messages sent from CA_2 to CA_1.

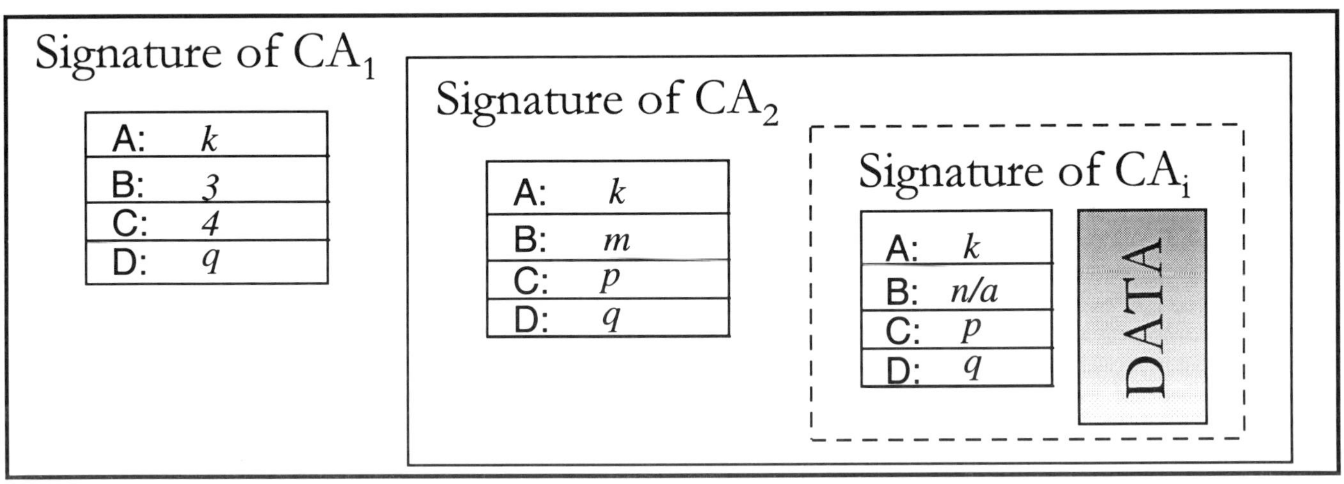

Figure 5. Format of a message sent between two users with different certificate authorities that have an indirect trust relationship. CA_1's rule set header requires that the message be signed by a CA in an orbit less than or equal to 3, and that the length of the path taken by the message be no greater than 4.

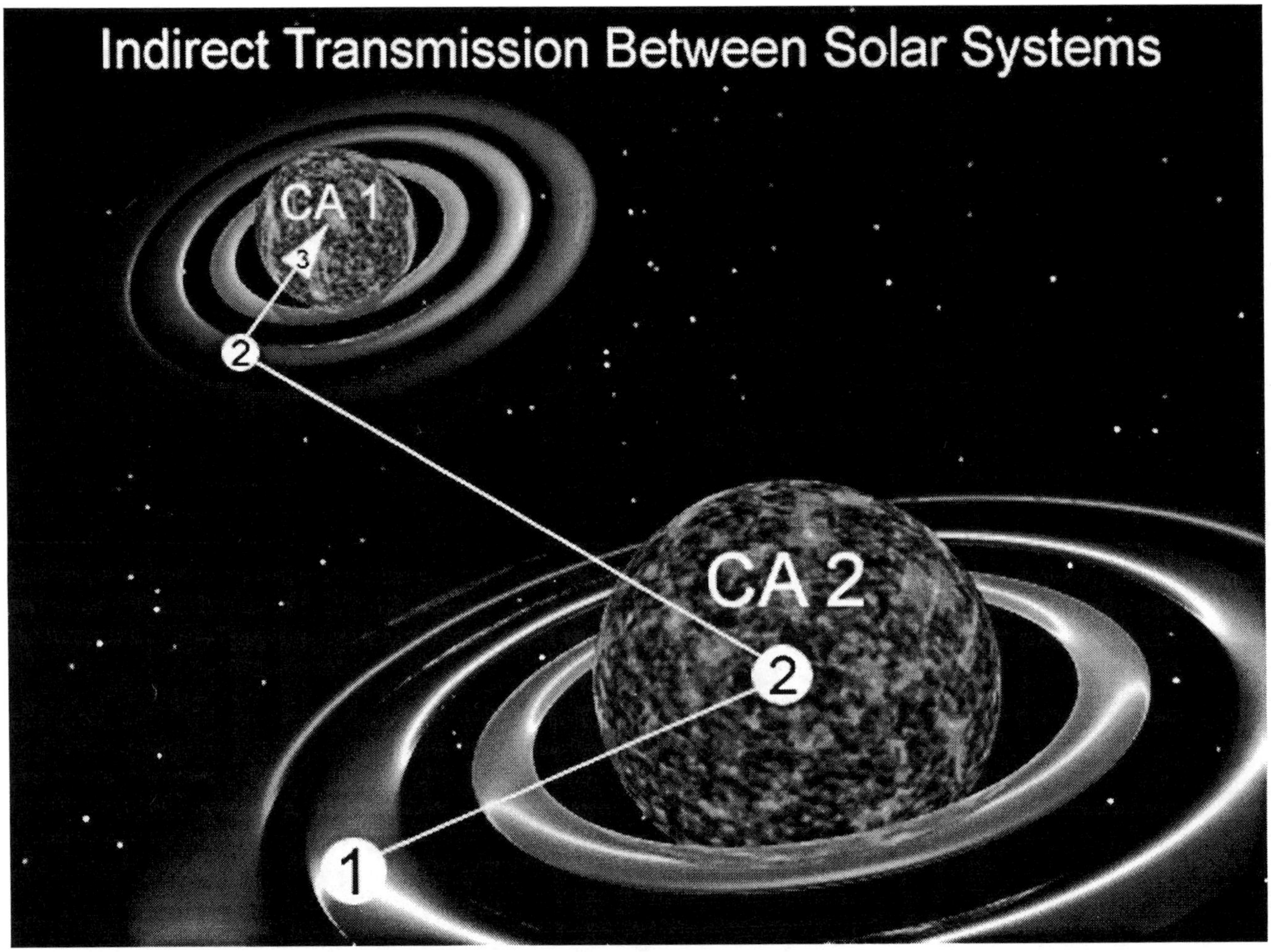

Figure 6. Path taken by a message signed by a certificate authority (1), in ring 2 of CA_2 (2), with an indirect trust relationship with CA_1 (3). CA_2 is in ring 2 of CA_1.

Conclusion

The Solar Trust Model addresses the shortcomings of the PEM, PGP/X.509 and ICE_TEL authentication models. It eliminates the need for a hierarchy of certificate authorities, while removing the limitations inherent in the design of the web of trust, and integrating dynamically computed levels and orderings of trust.

Rule set data can be added to a message just before the message is signed by a certificate authority, and can be stripped off and processed by the final recipient certificate authority. This ensures that a certificate authority signs its own rule sets, and provides for an easy method for the transmission of rule sets to the final certificate authority. In addition, it should be reasonably simple to implement software to process rule set data as a module inside of an API such as the Common Security Services Manager's Trust Policy Interface. Digital signatures and rule set data can be wrapped around any message, including other certificates, thus permitting the Solar Trust Model to be implemented on top of existing authentication services. Therefore, the Solar Trust Model can be implemented with no changes to existing hardware, and very minimal additions to existing software. Furthermore, it can be shown that the orbital structure of the Solar Trust Model can be reduced to a directed graph structure, with nodes on the graph representing certificate authorities, and lines on the graph representing trust relationships.

Both the Solar Trust model and Biba's model provide a partial ordering of a set of trust levels. The critical difference is that Biba does not specify any partial ordering of trust levels among different autonomous domains. The Solar Model allows such an ordering and, indeed, represents the ordering as a path among components of a solar system. Hence the Solar Trust Model is a generalization of Biba's model and can be used in contexts other than certification.

Future research directions include the implementation of the Solar Trust Model as a module in an API, and as an independent software application. Additionally, a detailed comparison between the Solar Trust Model and other security models will be performed using formal methodology to verify the correctness of the model. An analysis to determine the most efficient method for distributing trusted paths in advance of message transmissions will also be carried out.

References

[1] International Telecommunication Union. "Information Technology – Open Systems Interconnection – The Directory: Authentication Framework," *ITU-T Recommendation X.509*, pages 7-17. 1995.

[2] Kent, S. "Privacy Enhancement for Internet Electronic Mail: Part II: Certificate-Based Key Management." *Internet Report*, RFC 1422, February 1993.

[3] Biba, K. "Integrity Considerations for Secure Computer Systems." *U.S. Air Force Electronic Systems Division Technical Report* 760372, 1977.

[4] Intel Corporation. "Common Security Services Manager Trust Policy Interface (TPI) Specification Draft for Release 1.2", page 7, March 1997.

[5] L. Lpez, J. Carracedo. "Hierarchical Organization of Certification Authorities for Secure Environments." Proceedings of the Symposium on Network and Distributed System Security, Februrary, 1997, San Diego, CA.

[6] American National Standard Institute. "American National Standard X9.57. Public Key Cryptography for the Financial Services Industry: Certificate Management". 1996.

[7] R. Rivest, A. Shamir, and L. Adleman. "A Method for Obtaining Digital Signatures and Public-Key Cryptosystems". Comm. of the ACM, Vol. 21, No. 2 (pp. 120-126), Feb. 1978.

[8] Birrell, A., Lampson, B., Needham, R. and Schroeder, M. "A Global Authentication Service without Global Trust". Proceedings of the 1986 IEEE Symposium on Security and Privacy, April 1986.

[9] Young, A. Cicovic, N.K. and Chadwick, D. "Trust models in ICE-TEL". Proceedings. 1997 Symposium on Network and Distributed System Security. (pp. 122-133), Feb. 1997.

[10] Mendes, S. and Huitema, C. "A New Approach to the X.509 Framework: Allowing a Global Authentication Infrastructure without a Global Trust Model". Symposium on Network and Distributed System Security, Feb. 1995.

Mutual Authentication, Confidentiality, and Key MANagement (MACKMAN) System for Mobile Computing and Wireless Communication

Tasneem G. Brutch
Department of Computer Science
Texas A&M University
College Station, Texas 77843-3112, U.S.A.
tasneem@cs.tamu.edu

Paul C. Brutch
Department of Computer Science
Texas A&M University
College Station, Texas 77843-3112, U.S.A.
paulb@cs.tamu.edu

Abstract

In any distributed networked environment, security systems for network access and communication are necessary to allow legitimate hosts on the network to access the network services while denying non-registered hosts. Ideally, such systems should ensure both confidentiality and integrity of messages exchanged over the network. In this paper, we will discuss the deficiencies with the registration and authentication services provided by Global System for Mobile Communication (GSM), Cellular Digital Packet Data (CDPD), and IS-41. Next, we will present the design of the Mutual Authentication, Confidentiality, and Key MANagement (MACKMAN) system to provide a more secure registration and authentication service for mobile computing and wireless communication. The capabilities provided by MACKMAN include registration of legitimate hosts with the network, mutual authentication, and data confidentiality and integrity in a mobile and wireless environment. Data confidentiality and integrity are provided by using the public key Elliptic Curve RSA (ECRSA) cryptosystem in conjunction with a hierarchy of certification authorities for key distribution and management.

1. Introduction

In this section, we will define some of the terms which will be used in this paper. These terms are applicable to communication security and mobile computing. This will be followed by a discussion of some of the security considerations for mobile computing and wireless communication.

1.1. Terminology

Unilateral Authentication involves the verification of the claimed identity of the principal. *Mutual Authentication* involves the verification of the claimed identity of each of the communicating entities, to each other. Mutual authentication protects against billing fraud [1].

Cryptographic authentication gives the maximum security as compared to password-based and address-based authentication schemes [2]. In this method, a claimant *A* proves it's identity to *B* by performing a cryptographic operation based on a cryptographic key. The cryptographic key may be either a secret key from a symmetric cryptosystem, a public key from a public key cryptosystem [3], [4], [5] or a key from a shared secret data cryptosystem [5], [6].

The use of a cryptographic mechanism for authentication requires a *key management scheme,* which generally depends upon the structure of the exchanged messages [4], [7]. ISO defines key management as "the generation, storage, distribution, deletion, archiving and application of keys in accordance with a security policy" (ISO/IEC, 1989).

Certification Authorities (CA) are trusted third parties which bind the public key of a host with its identity (name or address). Individual users of the network do not have to verify the accuracy of a public key which is acquired from a certification authority [2].

Data *confidentiality*, *integrity*, and *location confidentiality* services are very important in the mobile and wireless environment which is globally scaleable over heterogeneous administrative domains. Data confidentiality prevents the unauthorized disclosure of data, while data integrity prevents against unauthorized modification of communicated data [2]. Location privacy prevents unauthorized entities from obtaining information regarding the location of communicating entities.

Mobility is generally a feature of networks such as infrared and radio networks, and value-added services provided by some wired networks such as Universal Personal Telecommunication. In systems supporting *mobile hosts (MHs)*, network users have the freedom of accessing the network with different geographic and administrative boundaries from different access points.

1.2. Security Considerations for Mobile Computing and Wireless Communication

The communication mechanism in mobile and wireless networks is broadcast, which raises security issues above and beyond those encountered in a wired network. In the absence of a fixed topology, mobile networks do not have physical protection against illegal access and eavesdropping. In such a dynamically changing system, mobile hosts entering remote domains need to have the ability to inherit permissions from their home agents while maintaining information and location security.

In general, security schemes for mobile computing should be designed such that the provision of security does not add significant delays during call setup and communication [8]. Wireless link bandwidth and the battery power available to mobile devices are both scarce commodities. Proposed security schemes should be efficient in the number and size of messages exchanged [6]. The provided security should not cause the channel bandwidth to increase [1], [8], or cause propagation of errors, nor should it result in increased error rates. In addition, security schemes for mobile computing and wireless communication should consider the following issues:

1) ***Trustworthiness of Intermediate Network*** is not a reasonable assumption in a large scale, administratively heterogeneous environment, and the architecture of a security scheme in a mobile and wireless environment should make minimal assumptions regarding the security of the underlying network(s). GSM assumes the trustworthiness of all intermediate networks [9].
2) ***Mutual Authentication*** between a network entity and a mobile host (MH) gives an MH the ability to authenticate the network entity, ensuring that it is not a malicious intruder [1]. GSM provides unilateral authentication, where only the host is authenticated. No provision is provided to authenticate the network.
3) ***Data Confidentiality*** [1] and ***Integrity*** provides protection against both active and passive intrusion by malicious agents. GSM does not provide data integrity during message exchange.
4) ***Untracibility*** requires protecting the *identity* [10], *location* [1], and *mobility information* of registered users from unauthorized entities [9]. A mobile host should be able to request network services without divulging any access control information to eavesdroppers. *Access control* defines relationships between a mobile host and the underlying network [10]. The *degree of untraceability* available to a mobile host depends upon the policies enforced by the underlying system, and the tradeoffs between cost and benefits. Complete untraceability is not provided in IS-41 and GSM based systems.
5) ***Time Synchronization:*** Mobile hosts may travel across various time zones and administrative authorities, therefore the use of strict time synchronization in security systems for mobile environments is not recommended [1]. All currently used standards use time synchronization.
6) ***Optional Security** and **Modes of Security:*** Authentication consumes bandwidth and power, which are both limited in wireless and mobile devices, therefore various modes of security should be made optional. Neither GSM, nor IS-41 based systems provide optional security for users [1].
7) ***Flexibility:*** The security system design should provide enough flexibility to incorporate future advances in shared-key cryptographic techniques. The mobile and wireless communication standards currently used do not provide this flexibility.
8) ***Interoperability*:** A security system for mobile environments should provide for interoperability between numerous variations and versions of cryptographic products. This is not provided by any of the currently used mobile and wireless standards for communication.

2. Protocols for Mobile and Wireless Communication

In this section, we will briefly introduce three protocols for mobile and wireless communication (GSM, CDPD, and IS-41). We will discuss deficiencies which exist in the registration and authentication service in each of these protocols. Next, we will present our motivation for developing a new security system to provide registration and authentication for mobile computing and wireless communication.

2.1. GSM Standard

Global System for Mobile Communication (GSM), is a standard for digital mobile personal communications. GSM was originally designed for use within Europe, however, since its introduction it has been adopted in numerous countries outside Europe [11], [8], [10], [12]. GSM was the first system to make provisions for security services such as authentication, confidentiality, and key distribution, and it was the first among cellular digital networks to provide anonymity to mobile hosts. Work is also underway in Europe in defining the security mechanisms for a third generation system called the Universal Mobile Telecommunication System (UMTS) for mobile and wireless communication [13].

2.1.1. Deficiencies of GSM Registration and Authentication.

1) GSM assumes the security of all intermediate networks traversed by messages between the Visitor Location Register (VLR) and Home Location Register (HLR), and all location information is transmitted unencrypted [9].
2) The provision of digital signatures, and hence data integrity is not available in GSM based systems.
3) GSM provides unilateral authentication, as opposed to mutual authentication [3].
4) GSM uses three proprietary and confidential algorithms, A_3, A_5 and A_8 for unilateral authentication and symmetric encryption. In a good cryptosystem, the security of the algorithm is inherent in the secrecy of the encryption/decryption key(s) and not in the secrecy of the encryption algorithm [14].
5) In addition to being classified, A_8 is a *symmetric* encryption algorithm [8]. It uses the same key for encryption and decryption. A compromise of key security would jeopardize the secrecy of every message exchanged in the system. If the key is compromised, an unauthorized person can pretend to be one of the communicating parties [14].
6) GSM centrally maintains three secure databases which contain key and host information. If the integrity of any of these databases is compromised, then so is that of every mobile host registered with the network.

2.2. Cellular Digital Packet Data (CDPD)

CDPD was developed by a consortium of several US based companies. It was specifically designed for data traffic instead of voice [15]. It is a complete architecture which includes a MAC layer. CDPD transmits data using the free slots from cellular voice communication. It allows network access from both fixed and mobile hosts. Security services provided in CDPD are mobile host authentication, key distribution, and data privacy.

2.2.1. Deficiencies of CDPD Registration and Authentication.

1) The authentication procedure is unilateral instead of mutual authentication. The foreign Mobile Data Intermediate System (MD-IS) is not authenticated, which opens it to the possibility of an intruder obtaining the Mobile-End System (M-ES) credentials by pretending to be the foreign MD-IS [15].
2) Since the wired network is assumed secure, messages exchanged between the home MD-IS and the foreign MD-IS are unencrypted, leaving communication open to eavesdroppers. These messages include the triplet containing the M-ES information. In CDPD, if eavesdroppers obtain the properties triplet, they can impersonate an M-ES indefinitely. This is because the authentication random numbers (ARNs) are generated by the home Authentication Server (AS). Since the M-ES does not compute ARNs, one intercepted triplet is sufficient to allow the intruder to infinitely generate more triplets and impersonate the mobile host (M-ES) [15].
3) CDPD uses a proprietary RC4 algorithm for encrypting all data. Similar to GSM, this leaves the system open to hackers who are willing to spend the time and resources to retrieve the algorithm by reverse engineering [15].
4) The Diffie-Hellman key exchange used by CDPD has the disadvantage that an intruder can obtain the real identity of the mobile host by launching a *man in the middle* attack [14]. Another disadvantage of this procedure is that the real identity of the mobile host is revealed to the foreign authority during the authentication process.

2.3. IS-41 Standard

The commonly used standard in North America is the *EIA/TIA Interim Standard 41,* and it pertains to the network signaling protocol, which evolved from the AMPS analog cellular system [16]. It uses a two-level hierarchical strategy using two databases: one in the home domain (HRL), and the other in the foreign domain (VRL) [17]. The algorithms used by the IS-41 standard for authentication, voice privacy mask, and signaling use private key cryptography. Its counter part standards for cellular devices are IS-54 (TDMA), and IS-95 (CDMA).

2.3.1. Deficiencies of IS-41 Registration and Authentication.

1) The Shared Secret Data (SSD) for user authentication is transmitted in clear text, making it susceptible to unauthorized interception by an eavesdropper. Although the synchronized call counter is used to detect an illegal clone terminal, it is more desirable for security to prevent the unauthorized disclosure of the authentication key [18].
2) IS-41 has system access flaws that allows the false registration of a handset impersonator in a different

location and false page response allowing phone calls to be received in an assumed identity [19].

3) Flaws in the unique challenge/response protocol can allow a handset impersonator to perform call origination [19].
4) IS-41 only provides one way authentication for system access, such as page response and unique challenges. Instead, IS-41 should provide two way authentication [19].

2.4. Motivation for the Development of a New Security System

Current security systems for mobile and wireless communication do not comprehensively meet all security requirements for the registration of hosts, mutual authentication, and key management. Due to the deficiencies in the existing protocols, we propose to develop a new security system to provide a more secure registration and authentication service for mobile computing and wireless communication. Some of the capabilities that this proposed system will provide are mutual authentication, digital signatures, and the use of non-proprietary public key cryptography.

In the next section, we will present our design of this new security system. We believe that this design will overcome many of the deficiencies found in the existing protocols.

3. Proposed Mobile Registration and Mutual Authentication System

The proposed Mutual Authentication, Confidentiality, and Key MANagement (MACKMAN) system is designed for mobile computing and wireless communication. This system will provide registration of hosts with the underlying network and mutual authentication between the hosts and the underlying network. For additional communication security, encryption and digital signatures will be provided.

3.1. Private Key vs. Public Key Cryptosystems

In our design, we chose to use the *Elliptic Curve RSA* public key cryptosystem for providing digital signatures, authentication, and encryption. The use of a private key cryptosystem was found unsuitable for providing digital signatures and authentication in a wireless and mobile environment based on the following disadvantages:

1) ***Key Distribution:*** In a private key cryptosystem, prior to communicating over an inherently insecure channel, each pair of users needs to select and exchange a secret key. Such an exchange would require a dedicated secure channel, which may be unavailable [20].
2) ***Key Management:*** In a private key cryptosystem, with an increase in the number of users the number of secret keys quickly becomes intractable. In a network of n users, with each pair of users requiring a separate key, the management of a total of $n(n-1)/2$ keys can quickly get out of hand [20].
3) ***Unavailability of Digital Signatures:*** In a private key cryptosystem, since both communicating parties use the same key for encryption, it is not possible for either one of them to prove to a third party the actual identity of the message originator [20].

3.2. RSA vs. Elliptic Curve Cryptosystems

In RSA, which is the most widely used public key cryptosystem today, the security of the cryptosystem depends upon the difficulty of factoring large integers. The implementation of RSA requires computationally expensive multiplication of integers modulo n, and exponentiation which requires repeated multiplication. Since battery/computing power and bandwidth are scarce commodities in mobile and wireless systems, the use of a computationally intensive cryptosystem, such as RSA, is not a feasible choice in such environments.

The use of Elliptic Curves in public key cryptography was published independently in 1985 by Neal Koblitz [21], and Victor Miller [22]. It was based on the discrete logarithm problem. The points considered form an abelian group, and are taken from an elliptic curve defined over a finite field K. The addition operation in the abelian group is easy to implement in hardware/firmware and software. Koyama et. al. [23] and N. Demytko [24] published two elliptic curve analogues of RSA in 1992 and 1994. In elliptic curve RSA (ECRSA), the discrete logarithm problem in abelian group is much harder to solve than the discrete logarithm problem in finite fields [20]. These systems are perceived to be as secure as the existing public key algorithms [20]. Some of the advantages of the elliptic curve algorithms based on discrete logarithms are:

1) ***Shorter key lengths*** [25].
2) ***Shorter signature size*** [25].
3) ***Faster implementation*** in hardware, firmware, and software [20].
4) ***The availability of a variety of elliptic curves for groups,*** allowing the same field K to be used by all users. This allows the use of the same hardware by everyone, with periodic curve E modification for additional security [20].
5) ***Non-existence of sub-exponential time algorithms*** [20].
6) ***Less implementation complexity,*** such as code size, gate count, and power consumption as compared to

RSA. This makes it ideal for implementations on smart cards with limited memory and processing power.

We propose the use of the ECRSA algorithm for both digital signatures and encryption in MACKMAN. This requires the use of two pairs of public/private keys for each mobile host; one pair will be used for digital signatures, and one for encryption. Messages will be first signed and then encrypted. The sender will sign the message with its private key for digital signature, and then encrypt the message using the intended recipient's public key for encryption. Upon receiving the message, the recipient will first decrypt it by using its own private key for decryption. The receiving host will then use the sender's public key for digital signature to retrieve the actual message.

3.3. MACKMAN System Confidentiality

Data confidentiality is provided by encrypting and digitally signing messages exchanged during the credibility establishment phase. Digital signatures help establish the authenticity of both sender and data. In addition, the proposed system will provide location confidentiality in mobile and wireless environments. Samfat and Molva present five different modes of host identity confidentiality [26]. The Mutual Authentication, Confidentiality, and Key MANagement (MACKMAN) system will provide for the *C1* mode of identity confidentiality. This mode is defined as follows:

C1: ***Concealing User Identity from Eavesdroppers:*** This mode of security is more commonly provided by mobile networks. According to this mode, the following of various aliases of a mobile host by an unauthorized eavesdropper should not reveal true identity of the mobile host.

The MACKMAN system will provide for *C1* mode by using temporary aliases [26]. These are used for domain separation so that the real identity of hosts is not revealed. The use of aliases is also useful in providing location confidentiality [27] and in dissociating source and destination addresses.

3.4. Key Distribution and Management Infrastructure

A key distribution and management infrastructure is proposed which can be used for authentication of management and data packets. This system will provide *performance transparency* and *operational transparency* to users. The use of a *Center-Based Key Distribution* approach [28] is proposed which would use trusted third parties, also known as *Certification Authorities (CAs).* The various certification authorities will be set up in a hierarchical structure, similar to that proposed in [29]. These will be employed both for key distribution during authentication, and for key distribution for encrypting and digitally signing the messages. The proposed certification authorities will form a tree structure with numerous levels. Upon receiving a request during the authentication and registration processes from a host, the certification authority receiving the request will provide keys and certificates to the host if it has the requested information. If it cannot provide the requested information, then the request will traverse the CA tree until a CA is reached which can provide the requested keys. The keys would then be sent back to the original leaf CA, which would communicate them to the requesting host. Figure 1 shows the proposed hierarchical structure of CAs.

Using a hierarchy of certification authorities along with public key cryptography will provide an added level of key security. Even if an intruder could get read access to one or more databases containing the public keys of all hosts, the only information that could be revealed would be the *public* encryption and signature keys. The secret keys would be kept at their originating sources, which would be much more difficult to compromise. A hierarchical structure also helps alleviate performance bottlenecks when storing, updating, and retrieving keys, since public keys are spread over multiple CAs.

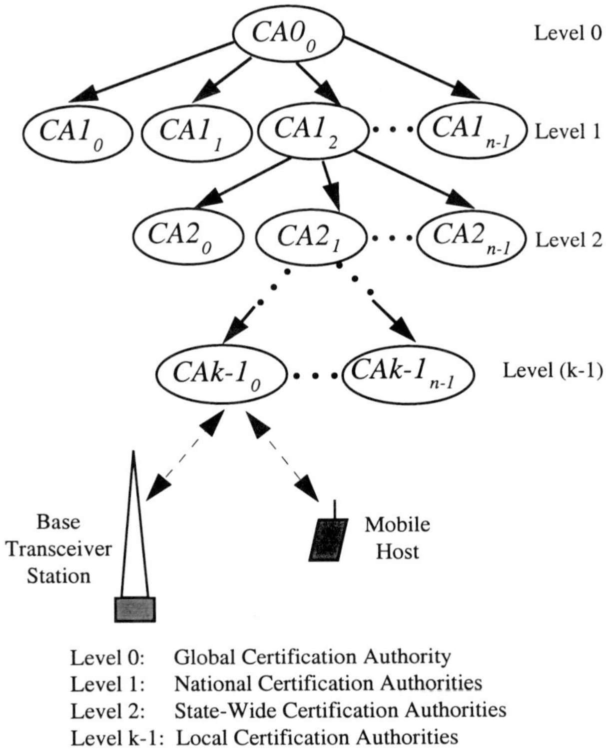

Figure 1. Hierarchy of Proposed Certification Authorities for Key Exchange.

3.5. Sequence Numbers

Similar to IS-41, we propose the use of *Sequence Numbers* to prevents against impersonation of mobile hosts and the cloning of mobile units. The sequence number is incremented in the mobile unit upon receiving a command from the network. The network would maintain a separate sequence number value for each mobile unit using network resources and services. During any network access attempt, the mobile host will send its sequence number to the servicing network, which would compare it to its own local copy of the sequence number variable. If multiple mobile hosts are using the same mobile host ID, then the value of the sequence number at the network will be greater than that at each of the mobile hosts sharing the common ID.

In case of a suspected cloning, the servicing network would contact the CA and a new key would be issued to the legitimate mobile unit. The mobile unit would then be required to go through the registration process again. This would preclude the clone from further accessing network services.

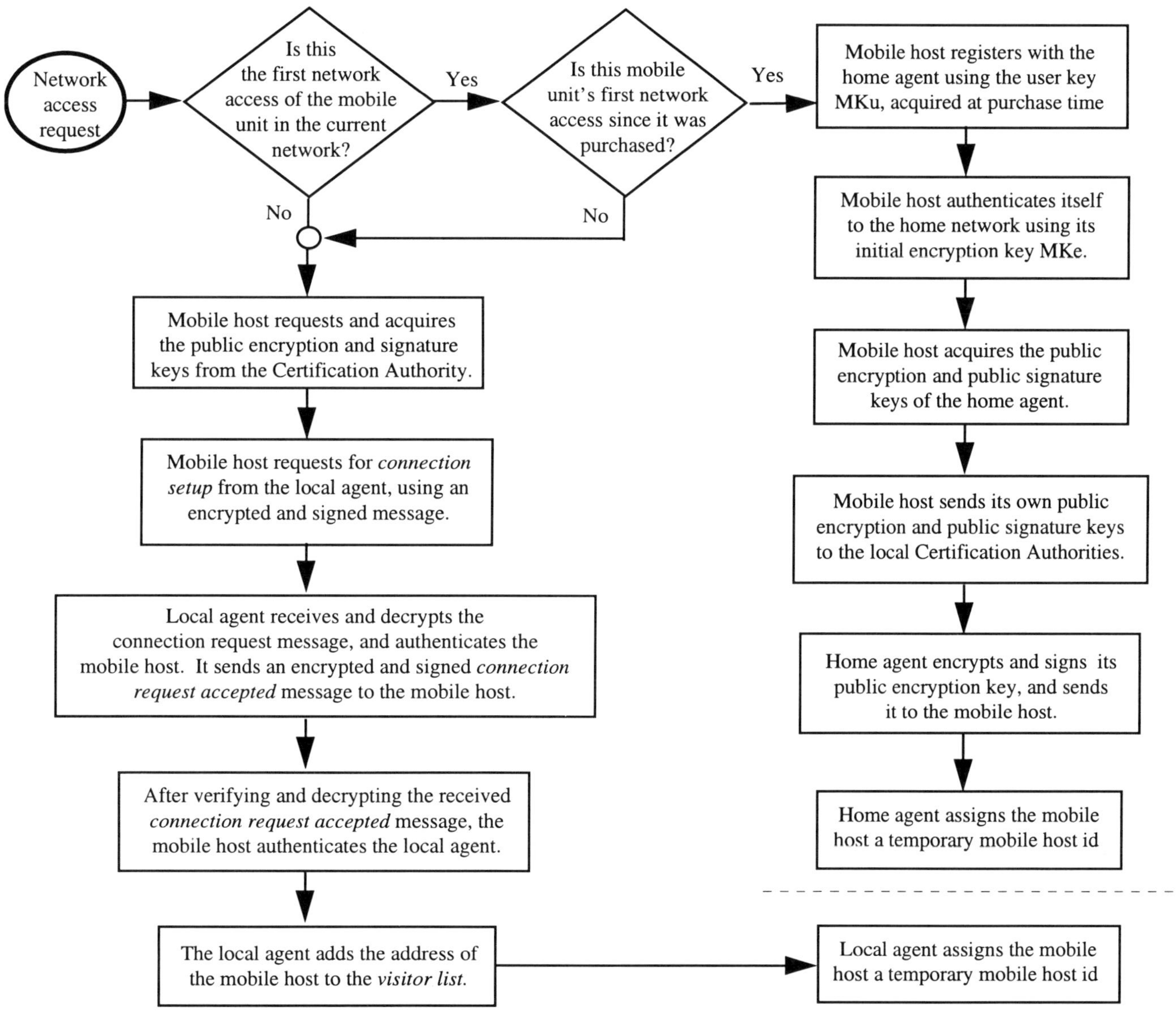

Figure 2. Overview of Registration and Mutual Authentication in MACKMAN System.

3.6. General Model for Registration and Authentication

The overall design of the MACKMAN system can be divided into the following three sections:

I. *Information Access:*
  - The user is provided with a key which is used to access the host.

II. *Credibility Establishment:*
  - The user enters the key in the host, which contacts the network for registration.
  - Upon verification of its identity by the network, the host is granted access to the network.
  - The information of the host is submitted to the associated network entity.

III. *Network Access:*
  - A host H_A wishing to establish communication with another host H_B initiates the authentication process.
  - Hosts H_A and H_B mutually authenticate each other using the public keys acquired from certification authority for encryption and digital signature.
  - Once authentication is complete, all further communication between hosts H_A and H_B is encrypted and digitally signed.

3.7. Initial Mobile Unit Registration and Authentication

Figure 2 provides an overview of the steps involved in registration and mutual authentication. We propose the use of *Subscriber Identity Modules (SIMs)* with mobile hosts [11]. SIM modules (or chips) contain information regarding the services authorized by the subscriber, and a unique key K_s, called the *Subscription Key (SK).* SK is used by the SIM card during authentication of the mobile host to the local network [16]. As currently practiced in the GSM based systems, the subscriber specific information may be downloaded electronically to the mobile host by a service shop authorized by the subscriber. The steps involved during registration of the mobile unit after its purchase are as follows:

I. *Information Access:*
  - Following the purchase of a mobile unit, the user is provided with a *User Key* (MK_u) using any secure mechanism of choice.

II. *Credibility Establishment:*
  - The user enters the previously acquired user key (MK_u) in the mobile unit.
  - The mobile host verifies the user key (MK_u) entered by the user against the value stored in the mobile unit during the manufacturing process.
  - The mobile host derives an encryption key (MK_e), using the user key MK_u, and the hardware address (MH_a) of its network interface device. The algorithm used by the mobile unit to compute the encryption key is mutually known to the home network and the mobile unit. In the proposed system, we will use the equation $MK_e = 2^{MK_u * MH_a * HHa} \bmod p$ to generate the encryption key for registration. Here p is a large prime number known to both the mobile host and the home network, and HH_a is the address of the home agent.
  - The mobile host encrypts the user key (MK_u) with the encryption key (MK_e), and using the cryptographically strong ECRSA encryption algorithm. The packet containing the encrypted user key is sent to the home network with its *Initial Registration (IR)* flag set. Each mobile host is associated with a home agent, which is associated with the home network of the mobile host.
  - Upon receiving the IR packet, the home network retrieves the address of mobile host from the packet, and queries its *User Key Database (UKDB)* for the corresponding user key (MK_u) and the hardware address (MH_a) of the mobile host.
  - The home network computes the encryption key (MK_e) using the same method as that employed by the mobile host $(MK_e = 2^{MK_u * MH_a * HHa} \bmod p)$. Using this encryption key, the home agent decrypts the IR packet sent by the mobile host and retrieves the user key (MK_u) from the IR packet.
  - If the MK_u stored at the home network is identical to that received from the mobile host in the IR packet, then the home network registers the mobile host as a legitimate subscriber. In response, the home network signs a copy of its *public encryption key* using its private signature key (HK_{sg}), and encrypts it with its previously generated encryption key (MK_e). The ECRSA public key cryptosystem will be used for signing messages. The home agent sets the *Registration Accepted (RA)* flag on the packet and sends it to

the mobile host. This completes the authentication of the mobile host to the network.

- Upon receiving the RA packet, the mobile host contacts the local CA, and requests for home agent's public keys acquired from certification authority for encryption and digital signature. The mobile host decrypts the message using MK_e, and verifies home agent's signature on the RA packet. It retrieves the public encryption key of the home agent, and compares it to the copy obtained from the certification authority.

III. ***Network Access:***

- The mobile host generates a pair of private/public keys for signing, and another key pair for encryption. A copy of mobile host's public signature key and public encryption key are encrypted using the initially generated MK_e. The mobile unit sends these to the certification authority. In all future communications with home network, the mobile unit will use the home agent's public encryption key for encrypting messages.
- For purposes of billing and accounting, the home agent sets the *billing status* flag to *1* in the home list, and sends an encrypted message to the local certification authority containing the mobile host's id and the value of its associated *billing status* flag. A value of *1* for the *billing status* flag indicates that the mobile host is in good standing with the home network, and it can be appropriately charged for using and accessing network resources. A *billing status* flag of *0* associated with the mobile host IP address would indicate that even though the mobile host has previously registered, it is not in good standing with the home network. Such a mobile host may not use a foreign network's resources on behalf of the home network.
- The home agent generates a pre-defined number of temporary mobile host aliases (TMHA), signs them with its private signature key, encrypts them with its private encryption key, and sends the message to the mobile host. One TMHA will be utilized per communication session by the mobile host, until all of them have been used. Prior to the depletion of TMHAs, the mobile host will request for a new set of TMHAs. Each home agent, in its home list, maintains a list of the last set of TMHAs issued to the mobile unit.
- Each home agent maintains a home list, identifying all mobile hosts that it is configured to serve and their associated TMHAs. The home agent in the home network generates the TMHAs by encrypting the host id of the requesting mobile host using different randomly generated encryption keys *e*. These encryption keys are kept by the home agent in an encrypted form. An encrypted copy of the TMHAs is sent to the mobile host by the home agent.

This completes the registration and mutual authentication process between the mobile host and the home network.

3.7.1. Key Generation. The algorithms used for key generation in MACKMAN system have the following desirable properties:

1) *Registration key* can be generated by all mobile hosts, without any scaleability problems.
2) *Public* and *private keys* for *encryption* and *digital signature* can be generated locally by all mobile hosts, home agents, and foreign agents without additional communication between parties and without any scaleability problems.

3.8. Mutual Authentication in Foreign Networks

When a mobile host enters a foreign network, it needs to go through mutual authentication with the foreign network before it is allowed access to the resources of the network. The mobile hosts, however, do not need to register with this network. If another illegal clone mobile unit is detected by the network, then the legitimate mobile unit would be required to register again with new keys. Here we provide an overview of the steps involved in mutual authentication between the mobile host and a foreign network.

I. ***Information Access:***

- The mobile host requests the public encryption and signature keys of the local network agent from the local certification authority. The mobile host starts a *sequence number* for communication with the local agent, which is a count of the number of messages received from the local agent. This is done to prevent cloning and message replay.
- Upon receiving the request, the local CA sends the public keys of the local agent to the mobile host.
- Immediately after sending the keys, the local certification authority also sends a request through its hierarchy for the public encryption and digital signature keys of the mobile host. If the mobile host's home network is not serviced by the current CA, then upon receiving the public keys of the mobile host the local CA caches the acquired keys and starts a timer.

- The cached public keys are purged from CA's cache when this mobile host relocates and sends a relocation message to this CA, or if the previously agreed timer expires.

II. ***Credibility Establishment:***

- The mobile host makes a request for connection setup between itself and the local agent. The entire request packet is signed by the mobile host using its private signature key and encrypted with the public encryption key of the local agent. This packet includes the address of the sending mobile host.
- Upon receiving the request, the local agent requests the public signature and encryption keys of the mobile host from the local certification authority. The certification authority sends the solicited keys to the local agent, which it had cached in step 3 of phase I above.
- The local agent decrypts the message and verifies the mobile host's signature with the public signature key acquired in the previous step.
- Following decryption and verification of the message from mobile host, the local agent authenticates the mobile host as a legitimate user. In order to authenticate itself to the mobile host, the local host sends a signed and encrypted *connection request accepted* message to the mobile host.

III. ***Network Access:***

- Upon receiving the *connection request accepted* message, the mobile host decrypts and verifies the message using the local agent's public keys acquired from CA for encryption and digital signature. If the mobile host succeeds in decrypting and verifying the message, then the local agent is authenticated to the mobile host. This completes mutual authentication between mobile host and the local network.
- The local agent adds the address of the mobile host to its *visitor list,* which includes all mobile hosts currently serviced by the local agent.
- The local agent in the visited network generates the TMHAs by encrypting the host id of the requesting mobile host using different randomly generated encryption keys *e.* These encryption keys are kept by the local agent in an encrypted form. An encrypted copy of the TMHAs is sent to the mobile host by the local agent.

This concludes the establishment of a strongly authenticated secure connection between the local agent and the mobile host, which is used for future communication between them.

4. Conclusion

In this paper, we presented the proposed Mutual Authentication, Confidentiality, and Key MANagement (MACKMAN) system for mobile computing and wireless communication. The MACKMAN design was motivated by the deficiencies found in the registration and authentication service of the existing protocols such as GSM, CDPD, and IS-41. MACKMAN employs mutual authentication and digital signatures to provide a more secure registration and authentication service for mobile computing. MACKMAN uses the public key Elliptic Curve RSA (ECRSA) cryptosystem for encryption and digital signatures. Elliptic Curve RSA was chosen over RSA, because ECRSA has shorter key lengths, shorter signature size, and a faster and less complex implementation. In addition, Elliptic Curve RSA is perceived to be as secure as RSA. The goal of the proposed MACKMAN system is to make mobile and wireless communication more secure by using public key cryptography in conjunction with a hierarchy of certification authorities.

5. References

[1] V. Bharghavan, and C. V. Ramamoorthy, "Security Issues in Mobile Communications," *Proceedings, Second International Symposium on Autonomous Decentralized Systems,* Phoenix, AZ., USA, Apr. 1995, pp. 19-24.

[2] R. Oppliger, *Authentication Systems for Secure Networks,* Artech House, Inc., Boston, 1996.

[3] Liu Jianwei, and Wang Yumin, "A User Authentication Protocol for Digital Mobile Communication Network User," *Proceedings, Sixth International Symposium on Personal, Indoor and Mobile Radio Communications,* Toronto, Ontario, Canada, Sept. 27-29, 1995, vol. 2, pp. 608-612.

[4] Ganesh Coomaraswamy, and Srikanta P. R. Kumar, "A Novel Method for Key Exchange and Authentication with Cellular Network Applications," *Proceedings, Second IEEE International Conference on Universal Personal Communications,* Ottawa, Ontario, Canada, Oct. 12-15, 1993, vol. 1, 186-190.

[5] S. Mohan, "Privacy and Authentication Protocols for PCS," *IEEE Personal Communications,* Oct. 1996, vol. 3, issue 5, pp. 34-38.

[6] S. Mohan, ,"Network Impacts of Privacy and Authentication Protocols for PCS," *Proceedings, IEEE Conference on Communications ICC '95,* Seattle, WA. USA, June 18-22, 1995, vol. 3, pp. 1557-1561.

[7] John Zao, Stephen Kent, Joshua Gahm, et al., "A Public-Key Based Secure Mobile IP," *The Third Annual ACM/IEEE International Conference on Mobile Computing and Networking, MobiCom '97,* Budapest, Hungary, Sept. 26-30, 1997, pp. 173-184.

[8] Charles Brookson, "GSM Security: A Description of the reasons for Security and the Techniques," *IEE Colloquium,*

Security and Cryptography Applications to Radio Systems, London, UK., 1994, pp. 2/1-2/4.
[9] Rafik Molva, Didier Samfat, and Gene Tsudik, "Authentication of Mobile Users," *IEEE Network,* vol. 8, issue 2, Mar/Apr. 1994, pp. 26-34.
[10] D. G. W. Birch, and I. J. Shaw, "Mobile Communications Security - Private or Public,", *IEE Colloquium, Security and Cryptography Applications to Radio Systems,* London, UK., 1994, pp. 5/1-5/6.
[11] Michael Walker, "Security in Mobile and Cordless Telecommunications", *Proceedings, Computer Systems and Software Engineering, CompEuro 1992,* The Hague, Netherlands, May 4-8, 1992, pp. 493-496.
[12] Y. Lin, "No Wires Attached," *IEEE Potentials,* vol. 14, issue 4, Oct./Nov. 1995, pp. 28-33.
[13] John Charles Francis, Holger Herbrig, and Nigel Jefferies, "Secure Provision of UMTS Services over Diverse Access Networks," *IEEE Communications,* vol. 36, no. 2, Feb. 1998, pp. 128-136.
[14] Bruce Schneier, *Applied Cryptography: Protocols, Algorithms, and Source Code in C,* John Wiley & Sons, Inc., New York, 1996.
[15] Yair Frandel, Amir Herzberg, Paul A. Karger, et al., "Security Issues in a CDPD Wireless Network," *IEEE Personal Communications,* Vol. 2, Issue 4, Aug. 1995, pp. 16-27.
[16] D. Brown, "Techniques for privacy and Authentication in Personal Communication Systems," *IEEE Personal Communications,* vol. 2, issue 4, Aug. 1995, pp. 6-10.
[17] Vijay K. Garg, E. Lee Sneed, and Waverly E. Gooding, "Subscriber Data Management in Personal Communications Services Networks," *IEEE Personal Communications,* June 1997, pp. 33-39.
[18] Shigefusa Suzuki, and Kazuhiko Nakada, "An Authentication Technique Based on Distributed Security Management for the Global Mobility Network", *IEEE Journal on Selected Areas in Communications,* vol. 15, no. 8, October 1997.
[19] Sarvar Patel, "Weaknesses of North American Wireless Authentication Protocol," *IEEE Personal Communications,* vol. 4, issue 3, June 1997, pp. 40-44.
[20] Alfred Menezes, *Elliptic Curve Public Key Cryptosystems,* Kluwer Academic Publishers, 1993.
[21] N. Koblitz, "Elliptic Curve Cryptosystem," *Mathematics of Computation,* vol. 48, 1987, pp. 203-209.
[22] V. Miller, "Uses of Elliptic Curves in Cryptography," *Advances in Cryptology -- CRYTO '85,* Lecture Notes in Computer Science, vol. 218, Springer-Verlag, 1986, pp. 417-426.
[23] K. Koyama, U. M. Maurer, T. Okamoto, and S. A. Vanstone, "New Public-Key Schemes Based on Elliptic Curves over the Ring Z_n," *Advances in Cryptology -- CRYPTO '91 Proceedings,* Springer-Verlag, 1992, pp. 252-266.
[24] N. Demytko, "A New Elliptic Curve Based Analogue of RSA," *Advances in Cryptology -- EUROCRYPT '93 Proceedings,* Springer-Verlag, 1994, pp. 40-49.
[25] Don B. Johnson, and Alfred J. Menezes, "Elliptic Curve DSA (ECDSA): An Enhanced DSA," *Seventh USENIX Security Symposium, USENIX 1998,* San Antonio, Texas, USA, Jan. 26-29, 1998, pp. 33-43.
[26] D. Samfat, and R. Molva, "A Method for Providing Identity Privacy to Mobile Users During Authentication," *Workshop, Mobile Computing Systems and Applications,* Santa Cruz, CA., USA, Dec. 1994, pp. 196-199.
[27] Dogan Kesdogan, and Xavier Fouletier, "Secure Location Information Management in Cellular Radio Systems," *Proceedings, Wireless Communication System Symposium,* Long Island, NY, USA, Nov. 27-28, 1995, pp. 35-40.
[28] J. D. Solomon, *Mobile IP - The Internet Unplugged,* PTR Prentice Hall, Upper Saddle River, New Jersey, 1998.
[29] L. Jianwei, W. Yumin, "Authentication of Mobile Users in Personal Communication System," *Seventh Symposium on Personal, Indoor and Mobile Radio Communications, PIMRC 1996,* Taipei, Taiwan, Oct. 15-18, 1996, pp. 1239-1242.

Track B

Assurance

Chair

R. Ross, National Institute of Standards and Technology

An Environment for the Specification and Analysis of Cryptoprotocols*

M. Debbabi Y. Legaré M. Mejri

Computer Science Department,
Laval University, Quebec, G1K 7P4,
Canada.
{debabi,legare,mejri}@ift.ulaval.ca

Abstract

In this paper, we present the environment CPV *(Cryptographic Protocol Verifier), a tool-set for the specification and analysis of cryptographic protocols. The* CPV *environment is based on the* LSFM *method that has been recently advanced as a formal, automatic and implicit verification method for security protocols. We recall briefly the essence of this method and present the architecture of the* CPV *environment. We discuss its main software components and details the key issues in its implementation. Finally, we illustrate the* LSFM *method and the* CPV *environment on two case studies.*

1 Motivations and Background

During the last years, a major interest has been expressed in the security of computer systems. This is mainly due to the dazzling expansion of Internet, distributed and parallel applications like electronic commerce, world wide web, databases, etc. In such contexts, information must be protected against mystification, destruction and disclosure. Accordingly, a great deal of interest has been expressed in the development and use of security protocols. Such protocols are based on cryptography.

A protocol is an orderly defined sequence of communication and computation steps. A communication step transfers messages from one principal (sender) to another (receiver), while a computation step updates a principal's internal state. A protocol with a security objective is called a cryptographic protocol. Cryptographic functions are used to achieve such an objective. In the literature, two major classes of cryptographic protocols have been advanced: authentication protocols and key distribution protocols. The primary objective of authentication protocols is to allow principals to identify themselves to each other. Key distribution protocols aim to distribute cryptographic keys between principals.

Nowadays, it is well known that the design of cryptographic protocols is error prone. Actually, several protocols have been shown flawed in computer security literature many years after their publication and use. Consequently, there is a desideratum that consists in elaborating formal frameworks together with the underlying tools for the specification and analysis of these protocols.

The main intent of this paper is to present the CPV (Cryptographic Protocol Verifier) environment, a tool-set for the specification and analysis of cryptographic protocols. The CPV environment is based on the LSFM method that has been recently advanced as a formal, automatic and implicit verification method for security protocols. The CPV environment has been implemented in Prolog. The GUI part of the environment has been implemented in C++.

Here is the way the rest of the paper is organized. Section two is devoted to the state of the art in terms of the formal specification and verification of cryptoprotocols. In Section 3, we recall briefly the LSFM verification method on which is based the CPV environment. As an illustration of the use of CPV, we present two case-studies in Section 4. The first case-study addresses the verification of the Woo and Lam protocol, while the second addresses the verification of the Needham Schroeder protocol. The architecture of CPV is detailed in Section 5. Finally, some concluding

*This research action has been supported by grants from the NSERC (Natural Sciences and Engineering Research Council) and FCAR (Fonds pour la Formation de Chercheurs et l'Aide à la Recherche).

0-8186-8789-4/98 $10.00 © 1998 IEEE

remarks together with a discussion of future work are ultimately sketched in Section 6.

2 Related Work

A great deal of interest has been expressed in the formal specification and verification of cryptoprotocols. Accordingly, this gave rise to plenty of specification languages, verification methods and dedicated environments. Good surveys together with detailed bibliographies could be found in [13, 17, 30, 37, 38, 42, 44, 48, 49].

The specification languages could be classified into three main categories: logical, model-based and operational. Logical methods consist in modeling the protocol as a set of formulas over some logic that is generally modal (epistemic, temporal and/or doxatic). The translation of a protocol into a set of formulas is referred to as idealization. It is error prone and not systematic. The most prominent security logic is BAN, advanced by Burrows, Abadi and Needham in [11, 12]. BAN is a modal logic that manipulates belief. Since then, plenty of derived logics have been advanced [1, 22, 26, 27, 36]. As an example of these derived logics, one can cite CKT5 [5, 13, 14, 15, 16, 47]. Logical methods are quite expressive and firmly established as a powerful formal method for the specification of cryptographic protocols. However, as we previously mentioned, the idealization step is error prone and not systematic. Model-based approaches are based on the idea of describing a model or a class of models that reflects the behavior of a given system. These models usually rests on set theory and are written using usual mathematical notation (sequences, maps, sets, etc). Axioms are formulas over the first order logic or written in a pre/post conditions style. Generally, the semantics is presented in a denotational form. Among the model-based specification languages that have been used in security, we can cite B and VDM [6, 7, 50], Ina Jo [28, 29] and Z [9, 46]. Although these formal methods are now firmly established and known to be of great use in specification and verification, it remains that these methods are not dedicated to cryptographic protocols. In addition, these methods need much of expert assistance during the verification process. Actually, they rely on manual or interactive theorem proving techniques.

Operational methods rest on the use of process algebra for cryptographic protocol specification. Representative languages of these category are LOTOS [10, 51, 52, 53], CSP [23, 24, 32, 33, 34, 35, 43, 45], SPI [2, 3], etc. The process algebra-based methods have been successfully used in the detection of several flaws in well known cryptographic protocols. The approach seems to be very promising and useful. However, it is well known that the underlying verification techniques, mainly those based on model-checking are problematic in the presence of processes that exhibit infinite behaviors. Accordingly, the infinite aspects of cryptographic protocols are usually not supported in the verification process. Notice also that the specification of security properties in terms of process agents or modal formulae is neither straightforward nor systematic.

Verification methods could be classified into two categories: syntactic and semantic. Syntactic methods are those that rest on the use of theorem proving. These methods establish protocol properties as theorems in some logic. Among the theorem provers that have been used in security protocol analysis, we can cite HOL [47], Isabelle [40, 41] and Coq [8].

Semantic methods are those that use model-checking techniques to establish protocol properties. These properties could be expressed logically (as a formula over some modal logic) or behaviorally (as an agent over a process algebra).

Concerning the tools and environments for the specification and analysis of cryptoprotocols, we can cite: CASPER [31], Murphi [18, 39] and Astral [25] as representatives of the tools that use an operational method for the specification together with model-checking for the verification; Coq and Isabelle as representatives for the tools that use a logical method for the specification together with theorem proving for the verification.

3 The LSFM Method

In this section, we briefly recall the main principles of the LSFM method. The latter has been reported in [19, 20, 21].

Actually, this method outperforms all the known methods for the analysis of cryptoprotocols. The method rests on simple, natural and elegant principles. It is formal, fully automatic and implicit. By implicit, we mean that it does not necessitate any specification of any protocol property or invariant. The method has been successfully used to detect many new flaws in known published cryptoprotocols. In this method, the analysis of a given cryptographic protocol is structured in three main steps:

- First, starting from a classical protocol description, we extract what we call protocol roles. Actually, a role is a protocol abstraction where the emphasis is put on only one principal. Such an abstraction allows us to point out, for each principal, his interpretation of the exchanged protocol messages.

- Second, the intruder abilities are automatically extracted. Apart from the well known abilities such as the complete control of the network, encryption and decryption, we consider all the computational abilities provided by the protocol itself. Generally, the intruder can initiate one or more sessions of the protocol so as to get or reconstruct a particular information to be used in an attack. In our approach, such computation abilities are captured as a finite proof system in which the inference is based on rewriting modulo syntactic unification.

- Third, the roles together with the proof system are combined to perform the protocol verification. The latter consists in checking whether one can instrument a particular role by answering all the challenges uttered by this role. The answers are merely theorems established in the deductive proof system.

For a complete and detailed presentation of this method, we refer the reader to [19].

4 Case Studies

In this section, we illustrate the LSFM method on two protocols, namely, the corrected version of the Woo and Lam protocol, and the Needham Schroeder protocol.

4.1 The Woo and Lam Protocol

The Woo and Lam authentication protocol [54, 55] has been shown flawed by many authors. In particular, Abadi and Needham presented an attack on this protocol in [4] and they suggested a new corrected version that we recall in Table 1. In spite of Abadi and Needham's correction, we have found, thanks to CPV, many other new flaws in this protocol. Some of these flaws have been reported in [19].

Basically, CPV follows the steps given hereafter. First, from the protocol specification, CPV extracts a set of roles. A role is a finite sequence of actions. An action is a triple of the form $\langle dir, m, P\rangle$ where dir is a direction symbol (either ? meaning input or ! meaning output), m is a message and P is a principal identifier. In the corrected version of Woo and Lam authentication protocol, this step yields the following:

$$Role(A) = \langle !, A, B\rangle\langle ?, N_b, B\rangle\langle !, \{N_b\}_{k_{as}}, B\rangle$$

$$\begin{array}{rcl} Role(B) & = & \langle ?, A, A\rangle \\ & & \langle !, N_b, A\rangle \\ & & \langle ?, \{N_b\}_{k_{as}}, A\rangle \\ & & \langle !, (A, B, \{N_b\}_{k_{as}}), S\rangle \\ & & \langle ?, \{A, N_b\}_{k_{bs}}, S\rangle \end{array}$$

$$Role(S) = \langle ?, (A, B, \{N_b\}_{k_{as}}), B\rangle\langle !, \{A, N_b\}_{k_{bs}}, B\rangle$$

Second, we perform on each role the so-called generalization operation. The latter aims to substitute in the roles, some messages by message variables. The rationale underlying such substitutions is that the replaced messages could not be checked from the structure, value and/or freshness standpoints. To make it clear, let us give an example. The third action in the role of B is $\langle ?, \{N_b\}_{k_{as}}, A\rangle$. Notice, that the principal B does not know the key k_{as}. Hence, he can check neither the value of the message $\{N_b\}_{k_{as}}$ nor its freshness. Consequently, this message will be replaced by a variable meaning that B can accept any message at that step. This pinpoints a vulnerability in the protocol. By applying this generalization operation on the three roles A, B and S, CPV yields the following generalized roles:

$$GRole(A) = \langle !, A, B\rangle\langle ?, X, B\rangle\langle !, \{X\}_{k_{as}}, B\rangle$$

$$\begin{array}{rcl} GRole(B) & = & \langle ?, A, A\rangle \\ & & \langle !, N_b, A\rangle \\ & & \langle ?, X, A\rangle \\ & & \langle !, (A, B, X), S\rangle \\ & & \langle ?, \{A, N_b\}_{k_{bs}}, S\rangle \end{array}$$

$$GRole(S) = \langle ?, (A, B, \{X\}_{k_{as}}), B\rangle\langle !, \{A, X\}_{k_{bs}}, B\rangle$$

Third, from the generalized roles, we extract a set of rules. Each rule corresponds to an output in a role. The rule premises contains all the received messages by the role until the concerned output, whereas the conclusion contains the output message. To each rule, we associate an attack scenario showing the rule feasibility using the protocol. The attack scenario contains all the steps in the role coming before the rule output. This step yields the rules shown in Table 2.

Message 1.	A	$\longrightarrow$	B :	A
Message 2.	B	$\longrightarrow$	A :	N_b
Message 3.	A	$\longrightarrow$	B :	$\{N_b\}_{k_{as}}$
Message 4.	B	$\longrightarrow$	S :	$A, B, \{N_b\}_{k_{as}}$
Message 5.	S	$\longrightarrow$	B :	$\{A, N_b\}_{k_{bs}}$

Table 1: The Corrected Version of the Woo and Lam Authentication Protocol

Finally, we extract a constraint set reflecting all messages that the intruder has to find to be able to attack a given role.

Since the protocol is a one-way authentication protocol, the intruder tries only to convince a principal playing the role B that he is the principal A. Then, the role to be attacked is B.

Let IS be the inference system containing the protocol generated rules within the intruder usual abilities and let K_I be the intruder initial knowledge. According to the B's generalized role, the constraint set associated to the corrected version of Woo and Lam protocol is:

$$\begin{cases} K_I & \models_{IS} \; A \\ K_I \cup \{N_b\} & \models_{IS} \; X \\ K_I \cup \{N_b\} & \models_{IS} \; \{A, N_b\}_{k_{bs}} \end{cases}$$

Once, the constraint set is generated, CPV uses a backward chaining on the inference system to simultaneously resolve this set of constraints. The resolution step yields many attacks among them the attack hereafter:

1.1	$I(A)$	$\longrightarrow$	B :	A
1.2	B	$\longrightarrow$	$I(A)$:	N_b
2.1	B	$\longrightarrow$	$I(C)$:	B
2.2	$I(C)$	$\longrightarrow$	A :	A, N_b
2.3	B	$\longrightarrow$	$I(C)$:	$\{A, N_b\}_{k_{bs}}$
1.3	$I(A)$	$\longrightarrow$	B :	X
1.4	B	$\longrightarrow$	$I(S)$:	A, B, X
1.5	$I(S)$	$\longrightarrow$	B :	$\{A, N_b\}_{k_{bs}}$

4.2 The Needham Schroeder Protocol

Following the same principles sketched in the above example, the role extraction step in the Needham Schroeder protocol 3 yields the following:

$$\begin{aligned} Role(A) = \; & \langle !, \{N_a, A\}_{K_b}, B\rangle \\ & \langle ?, \{N_a, N_b\}_{K_a}, B\rangle \\ & \langle !, \{N_b\}_{K_b}, B\rangle \end{aligned}$$

$$\begin{aligned} Role(B) = \; & \langle ?, \{N_a, A\}_{K_b}, B\rangle \\ & \langle !, \{N_a, N_b\}_{K_a}, B\rangle \\ & \langle ?, \{N_b\}_{K_b}, B\rangle \end{aligned}$$

Their associated generalized roles are respectively:

$$\begin{aligned} GRole(A) = \; & \langle !, \{N_a, A\}_{K_b}, B\rangle \\ & \langle ?, \{N_a, X\}_{K_a}, B\rangle \\ & \langle !, \{X\}_{K_b}, B\rangle \end{aligned}$$

$$\begin{aligned} GRole(B) = \; & \langle ?, \{X, A\}_{K_b}, B\rangle \\ & \langle !, \{X, N_b\}_{K_a}, B\rangle \\ & \langle ?, \{N_b\}_{K_b}, B\rangle \end{aligned}$$

The generation of the deductive system yields the rules shown in Table 4.

Finally, the constraint step yields the following:

$$\begin{cases} K_I & \models_{IS} \; \{X, A\}_{K_b} \\ K_I \cup \{\{X, N_b\}_{K_a}\} & \models_{IS} \; \{N_b\}_{K_b} \end{cases}$$

5 Architecture

In this section, we describe the architecture of CPV as illustrated by the figure 1. The environment CPV takes as input a specification of a protocol written in the standard notation and yields a sequence of flaws (attack scenarios) if any.

There are six major steps accomplished by CPV during the analysis of the protocol. Starting from a protocol specification, CPV parses the specification file to ensure the correctness of the syntax of the protocol. Then, it generates the generalized roles associated to the protocol. Afterwards, starting from these generalized roles, it generates the set of rules together with the intruder rules (initial knowledge of the intruder). Next, we generate the set of constraints that represent the security property that we would like to verify. Whatever is this security property, either authentication or secrecy, it can be reduced to finding a

	Inference Rules	Scenarios
R_1	$\frac{}{A}$	1. $A \longrightarrow I(B) : A$
R_2	$\frac{A}{N_b}$ $Fresh(N_b)$	1. $I(A) \longrightarrow B : A$ 2. $B \longrightarrow I(A) : N_b$
R_3	$\frac{X}{\{X\}_{k_{as}}}$	1. $A \longrightarrow I(B) : A$ 2. $I(B) \longrightarrow A : X$ 3. $A \longrightarrow I(B) : \{X\}_{k_{as}}$
R_4	$\frac{A, X}{A, B, X}$	1. $I(A) \longrightarrow B : A$ 2. $B \longrightarrow I(A) : N_b$ 3. $I(A) \longrightarrow B : X$ 4. $B \longrightarrow I(S) : A, B, X$
R_5	$\frac{A, B, \{X\}_{k_{as}}}{\{A, X\}_{k_{bs}}}$	4. $I(B) \longrightarrow S : A, B, \{X\}_{k_{as}}$ 5. $S \longrightarrow I(B) : \{A, X\}_{k_{bs}}$

Table 2: The Deductive Proof System Associated with the Corrected Version of Woo and Lam Protocol

1. $A \rightarrow B: \{N_a, A\}_{K_b}$
2. $B \rightarrow A: \{N_a, N_b\}_{K_a}$
3. $A \rightarrow B: \{N_b\}_{K_b}$

Table 3: The Needham Schroeder Protocol

	Inference Rules	Scenarios
R_1	$\frac{}{\{N_a, A\}_{K_b}}$ $Fresh(N_a)$	1. $A \longrightarrow I(B) : \{N_a, A\}_{K_b}$
R_2	$\frac{\{N_a, X\}_{K_a}}{\{X\}_{K_b}}$	1. $A \longrightarrow I(B) : \{N_a, A\}_{K_b}$ 2. $I(B) \longrightarrow A : \{N_a, X\}_{K_a}$ 3. $A \longrightarrow I(B) : \{X\}_{K_b}$
R_3	$\frac{\{X, A\}_{K_b}}{\{X, N_b\}_{K_a}}$ $Fresh(N_b)$	1. $I(A) \longrightarrow B : \{X, A\}_{K_b}$ 2. $B \longrightarrow I(A) : \{X, N_b\}_{K_a}$

Table 4: The Deductive Proof System Associated with the Needham Schroeder Protocol

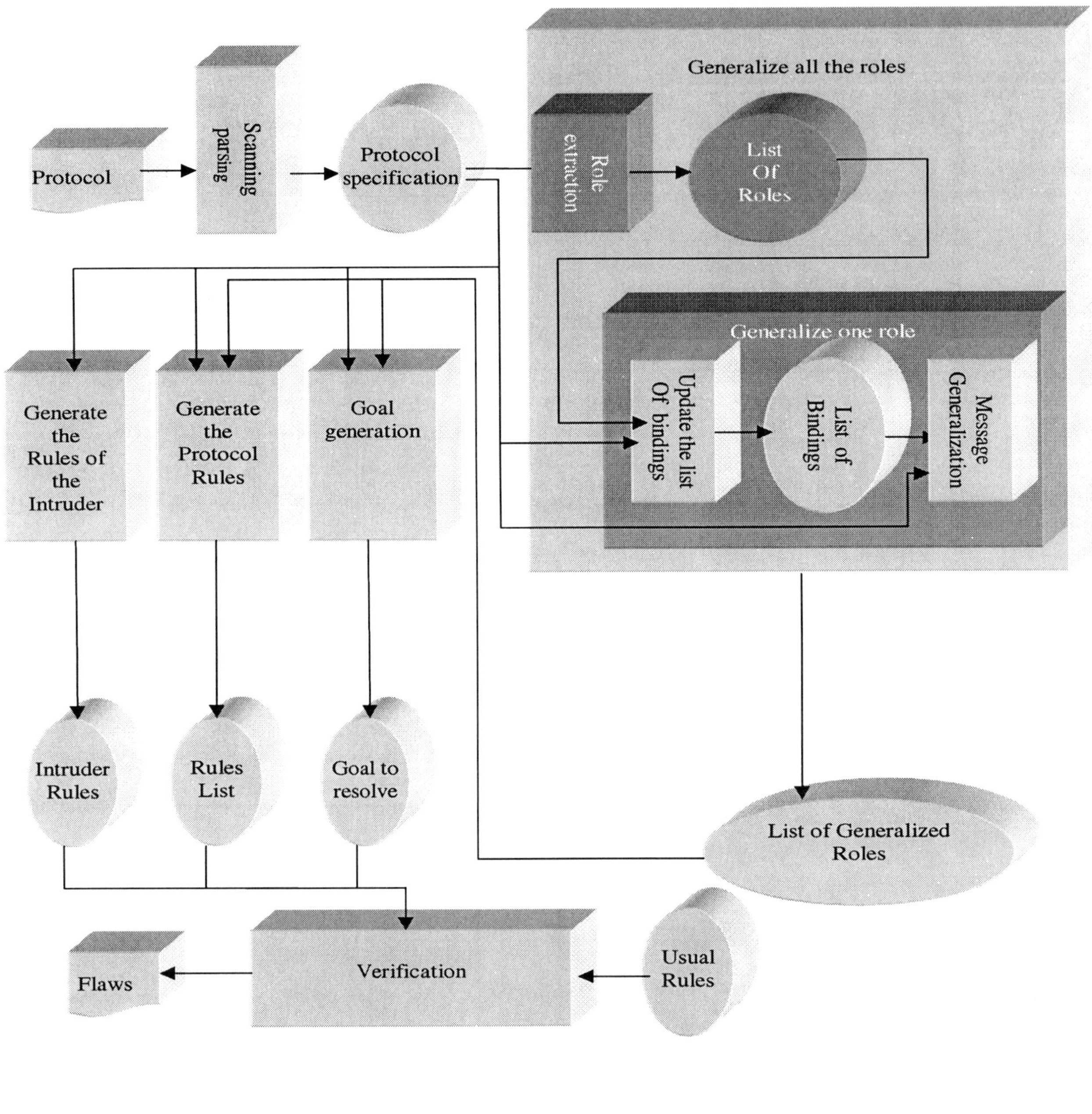

Figure 1: The Architecture of CPV

set of messages. In other words, if the security property is secrecy, then the verification amounts to figure out whether the intruder could get or not the secret messages. If the security property is authentication, then the verification is reduced to figure out whether the intruder could get or not those messages that are needed to impersonate some principal.

Using the previously generated rules and the usual rules, CPV resolves the constraints that constitute the goal and produces attack scenarios, if any. The usual rules represent the capabilities of the intruder like the capability to encrypt and decrypt a message with a known key.

The module `Scanning Parsing` takes as input a protocol that it parses to verify the correctness of the syntax and produces a structure `Protocol Specification`. This structure represents the specification of a protocol which means that it includes all the information about the initial knowledge of the principals and the intruder, the protocol communication steps and the limit of sessions that can be executed during an attack. This structure will be used to generate the generalized roles, the set of rules and the goals. Next, the program must produce the list of all generalized roles of the protocol.

The module `Generalize all the roles` creates a list of all the generalized roles of the protocol starting from the structure `Protocol Specification` produced by the module `Scanning parsing`. This module is made of three "sub-modules" that interact in a sequential manner. The first one is named the `Role extraction`. This "submodule" takes as input a specification of a protocol and produces as output the `List of roles`. A role is a list of steps a principal must accomplish to realize a protocol. The roles previously generated must be generalized before producing the rules of the protocol. The mechanism of generalization is implemented by the `Update the list of bindings` and `Message generalization` sub-modules. The first one produces the `List of bindings`. It needs the list of roles as well as the list of knowledge of the principals. The binding operation is done by binding a variable to each received message of a role that is unknown to it. In details, the sub-module extracts all the messages received by a role, opens all these messages using the knowledge of the role and retrieves all the messages that are part of the knowledge and the fresh messages of the role. The resulting list of messages is the list of messages that must be bound to a variable. The list of all messages bound to a variable constitutes the list of bindings. The last operation the program does is to generalize the role by replacing the received messages by the generalized version of each message. To produce a generalized version of a message, the program gives to the `Message generalization` submodule the list of bindings as well as the message to be generalized. It produces the generalized message by replacing each component of the message, that is part of the list of bindings, by its bound variable.

Using the list of generalized roles and some information contained in the structure `Protocol Specification`, the module `Generate the protocol rules` extracts the rules specific to the protocol under analysis. These rules are going to be used by the module `Verification` to resolve the goal produced by the module `Goal Generation`. Next, CPV generates the rules related to the knowledge of the intruder.

The module `Generate the rules of the intruder` takes as input the knowledge of the intruder contained in the structure `Protocol Specification`. These rules are going to be used to capture a part of the intruder behaviors. The remaining behaviors of the intruder are captured by the usual rules that are already built in CPV and that will also be used by the `Verification` module.

The `Goal generation` module extracts the list of constraints (or goals) that are essential to violate the security properties specified by the user at the beginning of the process. The list of goals is generated from the structure `Protocol Specification` as well as the list of generalized roles. Each different resolution of one of these goals by the module `Verification` will produce an attack scenario on the protocol.

Finally, the `Verification` module receives a goal to be resolved. The resolution of this goal will be done by using the list of protocol rules (`Generate the protocol rules module`), the list of usual rules that are already built in the system, and the list of rules of the intruder (`Generate the rules of the intruder module`). Using these inputs, the verification module tries to resolve the goal. Any solution that resolves the goal will be used to create attack scenarios. These attack scenarios will be shown to the user via the graphical user interface in the standard notation.

Tables 5 and 6 are snapshots that illustrate the GUI and the functionalities of the environment CPV.

6 Conclusion

In this paper, we presented the environment CPV, a tool-set for the specification and analysis of crypto-

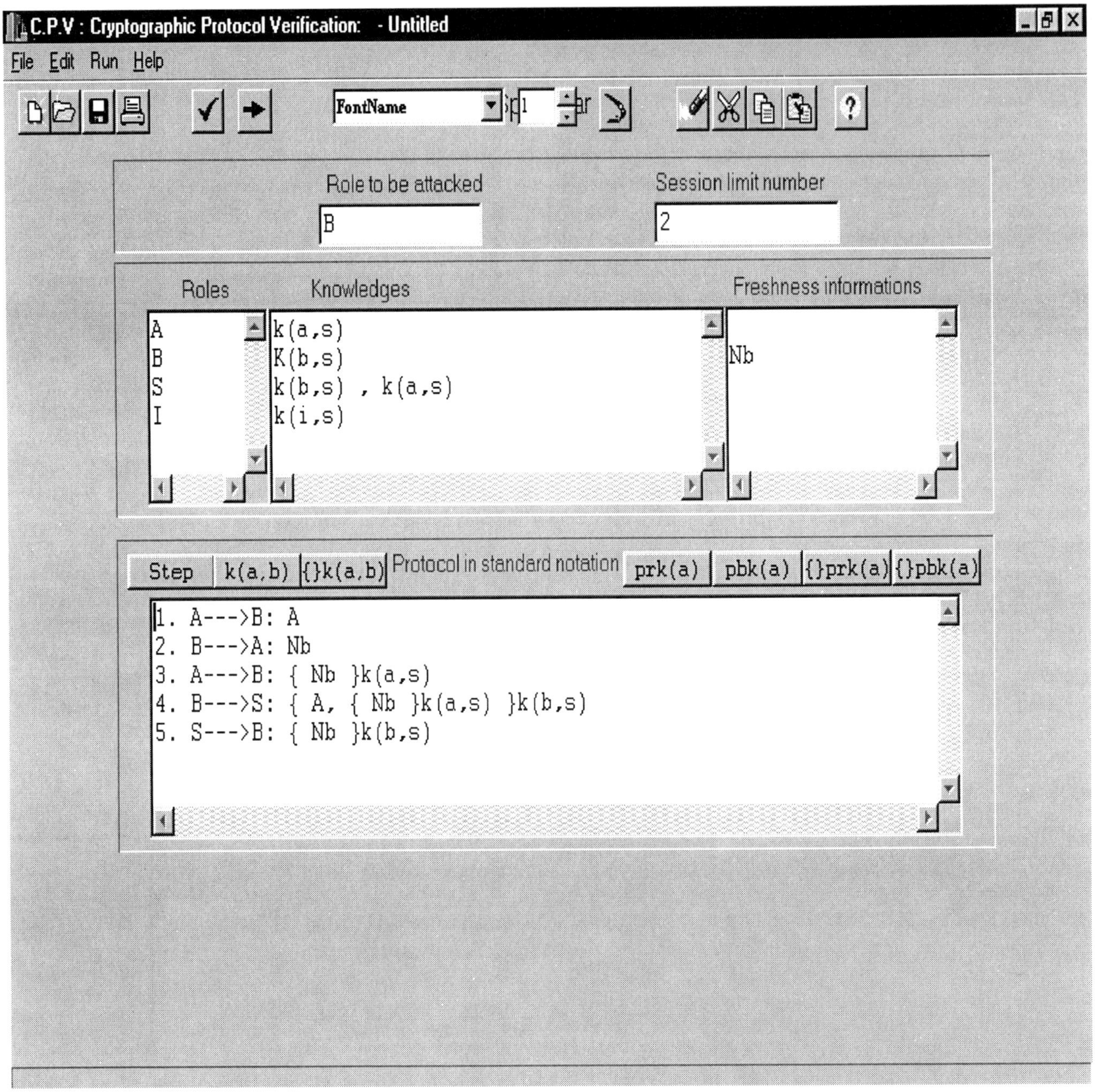

Table 5: The Specification of the Woo and Lam Protocol

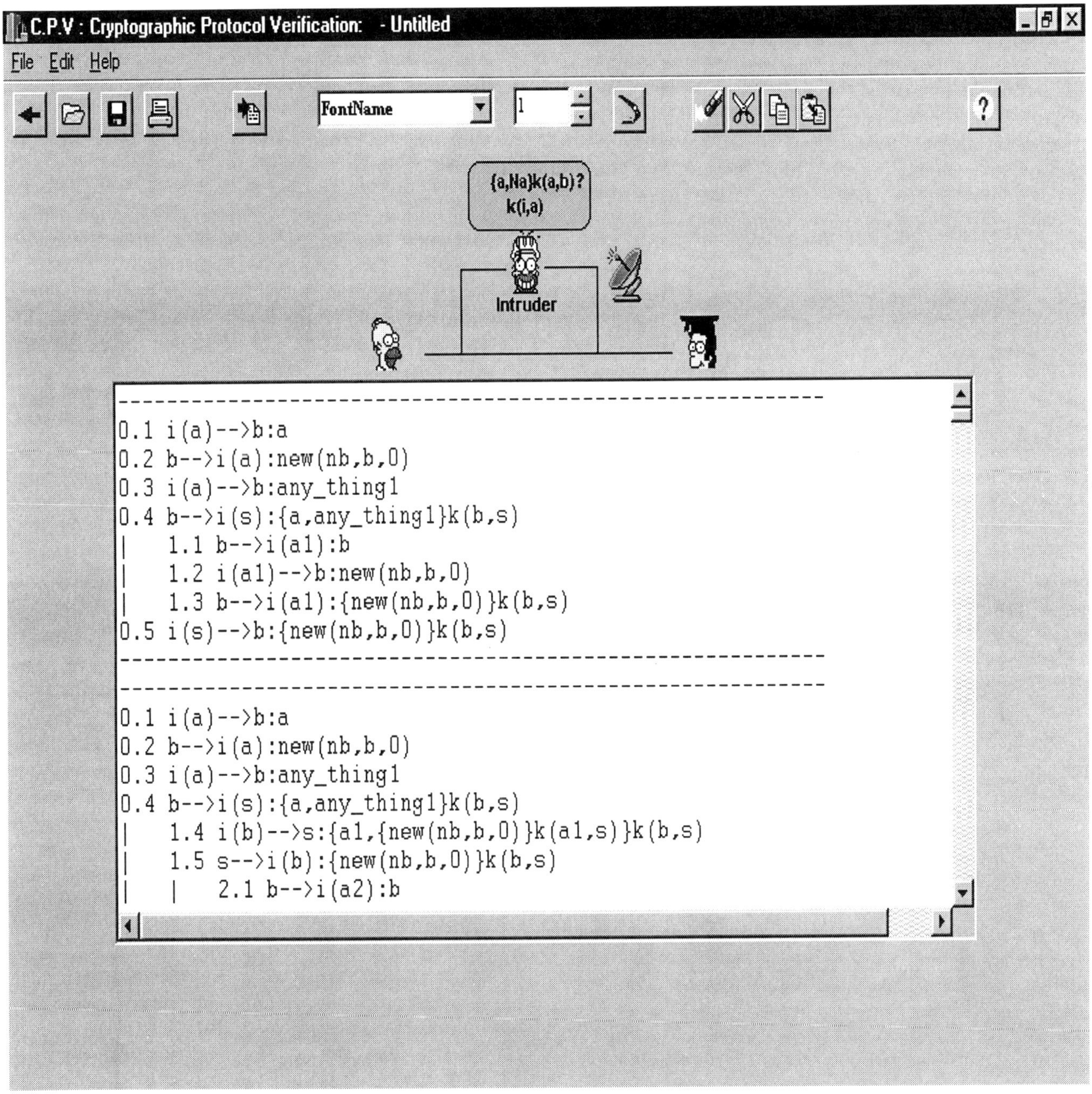

Table 6: Some Flaws in the Woo and Lam Protocol

graphic protocols. The CPV environment is based on the LSFM method that has been recently advanced as a formal, automatic and implicit verification method for security protocols. The LSFM method may be viewed as a new paradigm for the analysis of security protocols. Actually, it is formal and entirely automatic. Moreover, it is an implicit method i.e. it does not necessitate any specification of security property or invariant. We presented the architecture of the CPV environment. We discussed its main software components and detailed the key notions in its Prolog implementation. We illustrated the LSFM method and the CPV environment on two case studies. We presented also some snapshots that reflect some sessions under the CPV environment.

As future work, we envision to extensively use CPV in the automatic analysis of the cryptoprotocols that are available in the literature. The intention is to find unknown flaws in some of these known protocols.

References

[1] M. Abadi and Marc. R. Tuttle. A Semantics for a Logic of Authentication. In *Proceedings of the 10th Annual ACM Symposium On Principles of Distributed Computing*, pages 201–216, August 1991.

[2] Martin Abadi and Andrew D. Gordon. A Calculus for Cryptographic Protocols: The Spi Calculus. Technical report, DEC/SRC, December 1996.

[3] Martin Abadi and Andrew D. Gordon. A Calculus for Cryptographic Protocols: The Spi Calculus. In *Proceedings of the Fourth ACM Conference on Computer and Communications Security*. ACM Press, April 1997.

[4] Martin Abadi and Roger Needham. Prudent Engineering Practice for Cryptographic Protocols. Technical report, SRC DIGITAL, June 1994.

[5] P. Bieber. A Logic of Communication in a Hostile Environment. In *Proceedings of the Computer Security Foundations Workshop III*, pages 14–22. IEEE Computer Society Press, 1990.

[6] Pierre Bieber and Nora Boulahia Cuppens. Formal Development of Authentication Protocols. In *Proceedings of the BCS-FACS 6th Refinemment Workshop on Software Engineering and its Applications*, January 1994.

[7] Pierre Bieber, Nora Boulahia Cuppens, Thomas Lehman, and Erich van Wickeren. Abstract Machines for Communication Security. In *Proceedings of the IEEE Computer Security Foundation Workshop VI*, June 1993.

[8] Dominique Bolignano. An Approach to the Formal Verification of Cryptographic Protocols. In *Proceedings of the Third ACM Conference on Computer and Communications Security, CCS'96, New Delhi, India*, pages 106–118. ACM Press, 1996.

[9] Colin Boyd. Security Archituctures Using Formal Methods. *Journal on Selected Areas in Communications*, 11(5):694–701, June 1990.

[10] Colin Boyd. A Framework for Authentication. In *Proceedings of the European Symposium on Research in Computer Security, ESORICS 92*, volume 648 of *Lecture Notes in Computer Science*, pages 273–292. Springer Verlag, November 1992.

[11] M. Burrows, M. Abadi, and R. Needham. A Logic of Authentication. In *Proceedings of the Royal Society of London*, volume 426, pages 233–271, 1989.

[12] Michael Burrows, Martin Abadi, and Roger M. Needham. Rejoinder to Nessett. *ACM Operating Systems Review*, 24(2):39–40, April 1990.

[13] U. Carlsen. *Formal Specification and Analysis of Cryptographic Protocols.* PhD thesis, Université PARIS XI, October 1994.

[14] Ulf Carlsen. Cryptographic Protocol Flaws. In *Proceedings 7th IEEE Computer Security Foundations Workshop*, pages 192–200. IEEE Computer Society, 1994.

[15] Ulf Carlsen. Generating Formal Cryptographic Protocol Specifications. In *Proceedings 7th IEEE Computer Security Foundations Workshop.* IEEE Computer Society Press, 1994.

[16] Ulf Carlsen. Optimal Privacy and Authentication on a Portable Communications System. *Operating Systems Review*, 28(3):16–23, 1994.

[17] John Clark and Jeremy Jacob. A Survey of Authentication Protocol Literature. Unpublished article available at `http://dcpu1.cs.york.ac.uk/~jeremy`.

[18] D. L. Dill. The murphi verification system. In Rajeev Alur and Thomas A. Henzinger, editors, *Proceedings of the Eighth International Conference on Computer Aided Verification CAV*, volume 1102 of *Lecture Notes in Computer Science*, pages 390–393, New Brunswick, NJ, USA, July/August 1996. Springer Verlag.

[19] M. Debbabi, M. Mejri, N. Tawbi, and I. Yahmadi. A New Algorithm for the Automatic Verification of Authentication Protocols. In *Proceedings of the DIMACS Workshop on Design and Formal Verification of Security Protocols, September 3-5, 1997, DIMACS Center, CoRE Building, Rutgers University, New Jersey, USA*, pages 1–20, September 1997.

[20] M. Debbabi, M. Mejri, N. Tawbi, and I. Yahmadi. Formal Automatic Verification of Authentication Cryptographic Protocols. In *Proceedings of the First IEEE International Conference on Formal Engineering Methods, ICFEM'97, 12-14 November 1997, Hiroshima International Convention Center, Japan*, pages 1–10. IEEE Press, November 1997.

[21] M. Debbabi, M. Mejri, N. Tawbi, and I. Yahmadi. From Protocol Specifications to Flaws and Attack Scenarios: An Automatic and Formal Algorithm. In *Proceedings of the Second International Workshop on Enterprise Security, June 18-20, 1997 Massachusetts Institute of Technology (MIT), Cambridge, Massachusetts, USA*, pages 256–261. IEEE Press, June 1997.

[22] K. Gaarder and E. Snekkenes. Applying a Formal Analysis Technique to the CCITT X.509 Strong Two-Way Authentication Protocol. *Journal of Cryptology, 3(2)*, pages 81–98, 1991.

[23] Paul Gardiner, Dave Jackson, Jason Hulance, and Bill Roscoe. Security Modelling in CSP and FDR: Deliverable Bundle 2. Technical report, Formal Systems (Europe) Ltd, April 1996.

[24] Paul Gardiner, Dave Jackson, and Bill Roscoe. Security Modelling in CSP and FDR: Deliverable Bundle 3. Technical report, Formal Systems (Europe) Ltd, July 1996.

[25] C. Ghezzi and R. Kemmerer. ASTRAL: An Assertion Language for Specifying Realtime Systems. In *Proc. European Conf. on Software Engineering*, volume 550 of *Lecture Notes in Computer Science*, pages 122–146. Springer-Verlag, Berlin, 1991.

[26] V.D. Gligor and R. Kailar. On Belief Evolution in Authentication Protocols. In *Proceedings of the IEEE Computer Security Foundations Workshop IV, Franconia*, pages 103–116, June 1991.

[27] Li Gong, Roger Needham, and Raphael Yahalom. Reasoning About Belief in Cryptographic Protocols. In Deborah Cooper and Teresa Lunt, editors, *Proceedings 1990 IEEE Symposium on Research in Security and Privacy*, pages 234–248. IEEE Computer Society, May 1990.

[28] R. A. Kemmerer. Using Formal Verification Techniques to Analyse Encryption Protocols. In *Proceedings of the IEEE Symposium on Research in Security and Privacy*, pages 134–139. IEEE Computer Society Press, 1987.

[29] R. A. Kemmerer. Analysing Encryption Protocols Using Formal Verification Techniques. *IEEE Journal on Selected Areas in Communications*, 7(4):448–457, 1989.

[30] Armin Liebl. Authentication in Distributed Systems: A Bibliography. *Operating Systems Review*, 27(4):122–136, October 1993.

[31] Lowe. Casper: A compiler for the analysis of security protocols. In *PCSFW: Proceedings of The 10th Computer Security Foundations Workshop*. IEEE Computer Society Press, 1997.

[32] Gavin Lowe. An Attack on the Needham-Schroeder Public Key Authentication Protocol. *Information Processing Letters*, 56(3):131–136, November 1995.

[33] Gavin Lowe. Breaking and Fixing the Needham Schroeder Public-Key Protocol using FDR. In *Proceedings of TACAS*, volume 1055, pages 147–166. Springer Verlag, 1996.

[34] Gavin Lowe. Some New Attacks upon Security Protocols. In *Proceedings of the Computer Security Foundations Workshop VIII*. IEEE Computer Society Press, 1996.

[35] Gavin Lowe. SPLICE-AS: A Case Study in Using CSP to Detect Errors in Security Protocols. Technical report, Programming Research Group, Oxford, 1996.

[36] Wenbo Mao and Colin Boyd. Towards the Formal Analysis of Security Protocols. In *Proceedings of the Computer Security Foundations Workshop VI*, pages 147–158. IEEE Computer Society Press, 1993.

[37] Catherine Meadows. The NRL Protocol Analyser: An Overview. *Journal of Logic Programming*, 1994.

[38] Catherine Meadows. Formal Verification of Cryptographic Protocols: A Survey. In *Proceedings of Asiacrypt 96*, 1996.

[39] John C. Mitchell, Vitaly Shmatikov, and Ulrich Stern. Finite-state analysis of SSL 3.0. In *Proceedings of the 7th USENIX Security Symposium (SECURITY-98)*, pages 201–216, Berkeley, January26–29 1998. Usenix Association.

[40] Paulson. Proving properties of security protocols by induction. In *PCSFW: Proceedings of The 10th Computer Security Foundations Workshop*. IEEE Computer Society Press, 1997.

[41] Lawrence C. Paulson. Introduction to Isabelle. Technical Report 280, University of Cambridge, Computer Laboratory, 1993.

[42] C. Meadows R. Kemmerer and Jonathan Millen. Three Systems for Cryptographic Protocol Analysis. *Journal of Cryptology*, 7(2):79–130, 1994.

[43] Bill Roscoe and Paul Gardiner. Security Modelling in CSP and FDR: Final Report. Technical report, Formal Systems Europe, October 1995.

[44] A.D. Rubin and P. Honeyman. Formal Methods for the Analysis of Authentication Protocols. Technical Report Technical report 93–7, Technical Report, Center for Information Technology Integration, 1993. University of Michigan. Internal Draft.

[45] Steve Schneider. Security Properties and CSP. In *Proceedings of the 1996 IEEE Symposium on Security and Privacy*, pages 174–187. IEEE Computer Society Press, May 1996.

[46] Einar Snekkenes. Authentication in Open Systems. *In 10th IFIP WG 6.1 Symposium on Protocol Specification, Testing and Verification*, pages 313-324, June 1990.

[47] Einar Snekkenes. *Formal Specification and Analysis of Cryptographic Protocols.* PhD thesis, Faculty of Mathematics and Natural Sciences, University of Oslo, Norwegian Defence Research Establishment, P.O. Box 25, N-2007, Kjeller, Norway, January 1995.

[48] Paul Syverson. The Use of Logic in the Analysis of Cryptographic Protocols. In Teresa F. Lunt and John McLean, editors, *Proceedings of the 1991 IEEE Symposium on Security and Privacy*, pages 156–170. IEEE Computer Society, May 1991.

[49] Paul Syverson. Knowledge, Belief, and Semantics in the Analysis of Cryptographic Protocols. *Journal of Computer Security*, 1(3):317–334, 92.

[50] The commission of the European Communities CEC DG-XIII. Security Investigation Final Report. Technical Report S2011/7000/D010 7000 1000, CEC, September 1993.

[51] Vijay Varadharajan. Formal Specification of a Secure Distributed System. In *Proceedings of the 12th National Computer Security Conference*, pages 146–171, October 1989.

[52] Vijay Varadharajan. Verification of Network Security Protocols. *Computers and Security*, 8, December 1989.

[53] Vijay Varadharajan. Use of Formal Technique in the Specification of Authentication Protocols. *Computer Standards and Interfaces*, 9:203–215, 1990.

[54] T. Y. C. Woo and S. S. Lam. Authentication for Distributed Systems. *Computer*, 25(1):39–52, January 1992.

[55] T. Y. C. Woo and S. S. Lam. A Lesson on Authentication Protocol Design. *Operating Systems Review*, pages 24–37, 1994.

A Practical Approach to Measuring Assurance

George F. Jelen
G-J Consulting
gjelen@acm.org

Jeffrey R. Williams
Arca Systems, Inc.
williams@arca.com

Abstract[1]

*Assurance has been defined as "the degree of confidence that security needs are satisfied"[2]. The problem with this definition is that, unless one has a way to specify security needs in some measurable way, assurance can not be expressed in a measurable way either. The definition leaves the practitioner with the challenge of determining what "security needs" are, whether or not they have been "satisfied," and how to determine "confidence." In this paper, we define assurance as **"a measure of confidence in the accuracy of a risk or security measurement."** A critical feature of the view of assurance presented here is that it is orthogonal to the measurement of risk and security. High assurance ratings have traditionally been associated with high security and low risk. Our definition permits high assurance to be associated with low security and high risk as well. It also provides a way of deciding whether or not the assurance one has is sufficient.*

1. Introduction

1.1 Purpose of the paper

Informed decisions about security depend upon a complex set of factors related to both assurance and risk. This paper is intended to cast light on the relationships among these factors to enable informed decisions about security risks. The motivation for this work comes from the wide diversity of opinion about what assurance is, how it might be measured and communicated, and how one might combine and compare the assurance gained from various sources.

Although one might wish to be able to develop an absolute measurement of assurance (as well as of security and risk), this would imply, in the case of assurance, both a unit of measurement and at least a reasonably consistent means of measuring it. In our view, neither of these now exist nor are they likely to. What this paper offers instead is a way to take advantage of quantitative risk measurement methodologies and to employ them in such a way as to yield a rough measure of assurance that permits one to trade off the relative merits of seeking more evidence, and thus gaining greater assurance, against employing more safeguards, thus reducing risk. Although the method does not tell one exactly how much assurance she has, it does tell her whether or not she has enough.

Today's systems, and the enterprises in which they reside, are so complex that even the most capable risk measurement tools are unlikely to yield risk values that are much better than rough indications of *relative* risk—which, we should quickly add, is often quite good enough in many situations. The problem is that the value of risk, whatever it turns out to be, is likely to be surrounded by a fairly large but unknown amount of uncertainty. This can create a dilemma for the decision-maker who must then decide whether to invest in further safeguards, which will undoubtedly reduce the overall risk but could be both expensive and unnecessary, or to collect more evidence to reduce the amount of uncertainty surrounding the risk calculation—that which this paper calls *assurance*.[2]

1.2 Overview

Assurance has been defined as "the degree of confidence that security needs are satisfied" [2]. The problem with this definition is that, unless one has a way to specify security needs in some measurable way, assurance can not be expressed in a measurable way either. The definition leaves the practitioner with the challenge of determining what "security needs" are, whether or not they have been "satisfied," and how to determine "confidence." In this paper we propose specific ways to interpret these

[1] This research was partially supported by the National Security Agency under Contract Number MDA904-97-C-0223. It borrows heavily upon an earlier study by the authors and published as an ARCA report [1].

[2] For a thorough treatment of the relationship between evidence and assurance, see [1].

0-8186-8789-4/98 $10.00 © 1998 IEEE

terms in such a way as to make determining assurance more tractable.

In order to render the definition useable, we believe it is necessary to associate the terms in the definition with a measurement scale. For our purposes, the exact nature of the scale is not particularly important: the scale could employ numeric or "fuzzy" values, and it could be absolute or relative. For example, one might define "security need" as limiting annual loss expectancy from some cause to less than $100,000, or as restricting the extent of data corrupted by a virus to an amount no greater than that from user error. However, whether our statement of need is expressed in absolute (as in the first example) or in relative terms (as in the second), it ultimately requires a means and a scale of measurement. Determining whether or not virus-caused data corruption exceeds that from user error presumes some way of measuring both.

Once a measurement scale has been selected, "security need" can be expressed as a threshold value on that scale and a measurement of the actual level can be made. Simply comparing this measurement to the threshold value determines whether the need has been satisfied. However, the degree of confidence in this determination depends on the accuracy of the measurement. A large uncertainty in the measurement will impose a corresponding lack of confidence that the need has been satisfied.

In order to accommodate these factors, we offer the following definition of assurance:

"Assurance is a measure of confidence in the accuracy of a risk or security measurement."

This definition allows the concept of assurance to be associated with anything that can reasonably be considered a security or risk measurement method, and is not restricted to measures of specific properties like correctness or robustness.

In this paper, we argue that assurance is an integral part of the risk and security management processes. Our formulation is intended to be universal enough to embrace any assurance method. Within the security community, the heavy reliance on various criteria and evaluation processes to generate assurance has sometimes led practitioners to lose sight of their purpose, and therefore alternate methods for obtaining assurance have often been neglected. Because the method presented in this paper permits at least a rough measure of assurance, it is easier to understand and compare the costs and benefits of alternate sources of assurance evidence.

The paper will show how such a measure of assurance can be made by structuring the risk inquiry to yield information about uncertainty. We show how risks, along with their uncertainty, can be compared and evaluated. We then suggest ways of determining a course of action if the risks are found to be unacceptable.

2. Discussion

The view of assurance advocated in this paper assumes some means of measuring risk or security in which there exists uncertainty in the measurement. Since there will never be a way to measure either risk or security without introducing uncertainty, this approach to assurance should be universally applicable. In defining assurance in this way, we intend to imply nothing regarding the quality or the accuracy of any current risk measurement methods or tools. We merely note that such methods and tools exist and are in use. Our method will not and can not improve their accuracy, but it may raise the level of awareness in the uncertainty that surrounds their use.

2.1 A note on the examples

In the examples in this paper, since risk tends to be a more easily measurable quantity than is security, we have generally assumed that the measurements upon which the determination of assurance are based will be of risk rather than of security. Certainly, techniques for measuring, or at least estimating, the extent of risk are more prevalent than methods for measuring or estimating the amount of security. However, this is not meant to imply that a risk-based technique is required. As effective ways are found to "measure" security, the same approach to the calculation of assurance can be applied.[3]

2.2 Distinguishing assurance from security and risk measurements

In the paper, "What Color is Your Assurance," assurance is said to be "something said or done to inspire confidence" [3]. But one can inspire confidence in some given *thing* or in a *statement* about the thing. The notion of assurance advanced in this paper deals with the confidence we have in the statement, not the thing itself. In the security-assurance realm, there are really two questions:

1. How secure am I?
2. How confident am I of my answer to Question 1?

[3] There is a least one current effort, of which the authors are aware, aimed at defining measures or metrics for security. The Security Metrics Action Committee of the Process, Assurance and Metrics Working Group, part of the System Security Engineering Capability Maturity Model (SSE-CMM) initiative, is currently engaged in such an effort.

The first question deals with the notion of security, while the second deals with the notion of assurance as we define it. If a risk assessment is used to answer the security question, assurance addresses the confidence that one has in the risk value produced by that assessment.

A critical feature of the view of assurance presented here is that it is orthogonal to the concepts of risk and security. Keeping these dimensions separate helps to establish a clear distinction between them and thus reduces the confusion caused by any overlapping of their meanings. High assurance ratings have traditionally been associated with high security and low risk. Our definition permits high assurance to be associated with low security and high risk as well.

Confusing the assurance dimension with the security and risk dimension makes it very easy to miss the interesting cases where the two dimensions lead to seemingly conflicting conclusions. For example, consider a network component with a large number of security mechanisms, but no information to indicate whether or not they are correctly configured. Here, it is unclear whether the many mechanisms add or reduce the amount of assurance. By making the two orthogonal and independent, sources of added security can be considered separately from sources of added assurance. It is thus easier to recognize that it would probably be more useful to gather more specific information about the configuration than to add another security mechanism.

Figure 1 graphically presents the two separate dimensions and indicates where some common statements about security might fall. Although the figure depicts a risk-based measurement, a security-based measurement would work equally well.

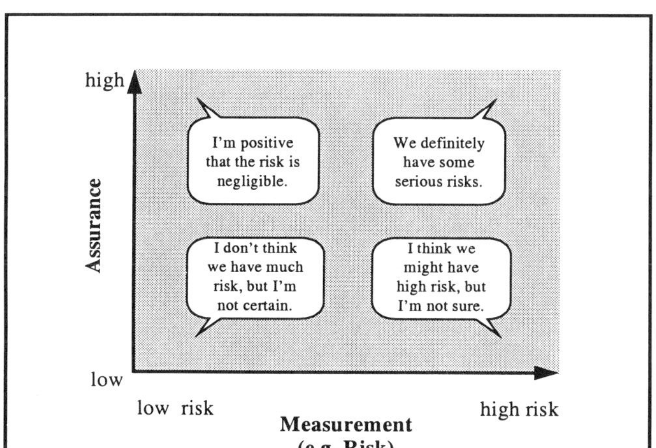

Figure 1: Assurance and Measurement Dimensions Are Orthogonal

2.3 Negative evidence

Our definition of assurance deliberately accommodates the concept of "negative" evidence. Negative evidence is information that tends to establish the existence and magnitude of specific insecurities of and risks to the system. Examples include such items as successful penetrations, criminal records, or OSHA violations.

All evidence tends to reduce the uncertainty (increase the confidence) in a risk estimate by providing more accurate information to assessors. Unlike positive evidence, however, negative evidence generally results in higher risk estimates.

3. A Measure of Assurance

In this paper we do not advocate a particular method for measuring security or risk, but simply note that methodologies and tools exist for such a purpose. We also recognize that these methods are not perfect; indeed, if they were, there would be no reason to explore uncertainty. This approach is intended to be general enough that it could be used with any risk measurement method as the basis for determining assurance.

3.1 Risk definition

As defined in this paper, the amount of assurance ultimately depends upon the confidence in the accuracy of the measurement of the risk or security associated with some enterprise. Therefore, in order to understand the concept of assurance, one first needs to understand risk. Since the concept of risk embodies threat, vulnerability and consequence, the paper discusses these first.

Threat has been defined as "any circumstance or event with the potential to cause harm to a system in the form of destruction, disclosure, modification of data, and/or denial of service" [4]. Expressed mathematically, *threat* can be defined as the probability that there exists an adversary or circumstance that, given an exploitable vulnerability, possesses the capability, and in the case of the adversary, the motivation and opportunity, to exploit that vulnerability.

Vulnerability is defined as a weakness in the physical layout, organization, procedures, personnel, management, administration, hardware or software that could be exploited to cause harm to an ADP system or to the enterprise in which it resides. Mathematically, vulnerability is the probability, given a threat as defined above, that the threat will succeed.

Events are threat-vulnerability pairs that lead to unwanted outcomes. They include successful malicious attacks on the part of adversaries, natural occurrences such as hurricanes or floods, and unintentional errors.

Likelihood is the probability that an unwanted event will occur. It is a function of both threat and vulnerability. It is the name we attach to the joint probability that not only does a vulnerability exist that can lead to harm, but also that the specific threat that will exploit that vulnerability is present. Applying the rule for calculating joint probabilities, likelihood can be expressed as:

$$Likelihood = Threat \bullet Vulnerability$$

Consequence expresses the impact, either harm or loss, associated with an exploited vulnerability. The impact could be economic, political, military, social, psychological, or any combination of them. The most common, and usually the easiest, method of expressing consequence is in monetary form, even if the impact is other than economic.

The concept of risk combines that of consequence with that of likelihood. *Risk* is a measure of the expected negative effect of a particular unwanted event. It can be expressed as a product of the likelihood of the event and the consequence or impact should that event occur.

$$Risk = Likelihood \bullet Consequence$$

One common method of expressing risk is as expected loss. Here, consequence is expressed in monetary form, such as the value in dollars that could potentially be lost, and likelihood is expressed as the probability that this consequence or monetary loss will actually occur.

3.2 Risk measurement uncertainty

Risk measurements have a great deal of uncertainty associated with them because someone must select values to insert in various elements of the risk equation or tool, such as the likelihood of a certain event's happening within the next year, or the frequency of use of a particular component. The risk assessor cannot know *exactly* what numbers to select, and must instead make an estimate based upon his best judgment. Some assessors may tend to be overly pessimistic, resulting in calculated risk values that are too high, while others may tend to be overly optimistic and yield risk values that are too low.

Rather than arbitrarily simplifying the risk picture by accepting a single value for risk, it is possible to manage the uncertainty associated with it in a way that enables a better understanding of the security issues involved.

Since the estimates are presumably based on the best information available at the time of the analysis, the numbers supplied may be more or less accurate, depending on the quality and completeness of that information. Therefore, the uncertainty associated with the calculated risk value has a great deal to do with the amount and quality of information available to those supplying the input data. Given a greater amount of high quality information, the risk analysis can produce a result with a narrower uncertainty, indicating higher assurance.

3.3 A mathematical model

The underlying mathematical model that describes the relationship between risk and assurance is taken directly from probability theory. Let R denote the "real" value of risk, and let R^* denote the estimated value of R resulting from a risk analysis. In order to obtain a measure of the precision of our estimate, R^*, one might attempt to find two positive numbers, δ and ε, such that the probability that the true value, R, is included between the limits $R^* \pm \delta$, is equal to $1 - \varepsilon$.

$$P(R^* - \delta < R < R^* + \delta) = 1 - \varepsilon$$

For a given probability, $1 - \varepsilon$, high precision of the estimate would obviously be associated with small values of δ. The interval $R^* \pm \delta$ is called the *"confidence interval"* or *"uncertainty"* of R, and the probability, $1 - \varepsilon$, is denoted as the *"confidence coefficient"* of the interval [5]. For example, one could say that there is a 95% probability that the overall risk associated with a particular enterprise, expressed as expected loss, is between \$4 M and \$7 M, or in other words, $1 - \varepsilon = 0.95$, $R^* = \$5.5$ M, and $\delta = \$1.5$ M.

Theoretically, assurance could be expressed as a (δ, ε) pair, as a confidence interval given a particular desired value of ε, or as a confidence coefficient given a desired value of δ. However, as a practical matter, we have found that expressing it as a confidence interval is the easiest and the most intuitive, where a small confidence interval is representative of high assurance.

Although this model combines the uncertainty from threat, vulnerability, and consequence, it is possible to consider them separately. For example, it may prove useful to distinguish between the uncertainty associated with likelihood and that associated with consequence. This idea is discussed later in the paper.

3.4 Investigating the uncertainty

The model described above is useless if there is no way to determine what the uncertainty actually is for a particular risk. Fortunately, there are several techniques that can help us gain an approximation of the interval, if not precisely measure it. We can employ existing risk assessment tools themselves to assist in developing a value for the uncertainty associated with their own measurements.

For each independent source of risk, available risk analysis tools allow a risk value to be computed. Additionally, for each source of risk, evidence can be amassed to generate estimates of the degree of confidence or assurance one has regarding the calculated risk value. For example, if one were interested in the risk from a data-mangling virus, he could develop estimates for the impact or adverse consequence of such a virus, the probability that the system would encounter such a virus, and the probability that, if encountered, the virus would result in the adverse consequence. He could also accumulate evidence to demonstrate that the above estimates were sound.

The following methods are examples of ways to determine a *confidence interval* and *confidence coefficient* for a particular risk. Most organizations applying these techniques are likely to discover that there is quite a large uncertainty associated with their risk measurements.

3.4.1 Best-case worst-case comparison method. One way to quantify the range of uncertainty is to perform a "best case" and "worst case" risk analysis. The "best case" analysis produces a lower bound figure for risk. This involves assuming minimum estimates for consequence, for the probability of attack (threat), and for likelihood of success (vulnerability). In this paper, we refer to this value as R_{min}. Similarly, a "worst case" analysis produces an upper bound value for risk, or R_{max}, by using high consequence and likelihood estimates. Best case assumptions might include, for example, that all the mechanisms work as advertised, that the number of threat agents is low, that the consequence is low, and that the probability of success is low. Worst case assumptions would assume the opposite.

Given a risk assessment tool or method, this approach is quite easy to perform since the tool or method can be used to obtain the necessary best and worst case measurements. One needs only to compute a value for risk twice, once with best case assumptions and once with worst case assumptions.

Figure 2 shows the best case and worst case estimates of R as a normalized value plotted on a scale from 0 to 1, where "1" represents the maximum possible consequence. The uncertainty is depicted as the distance between R_{min} and R_{max}.

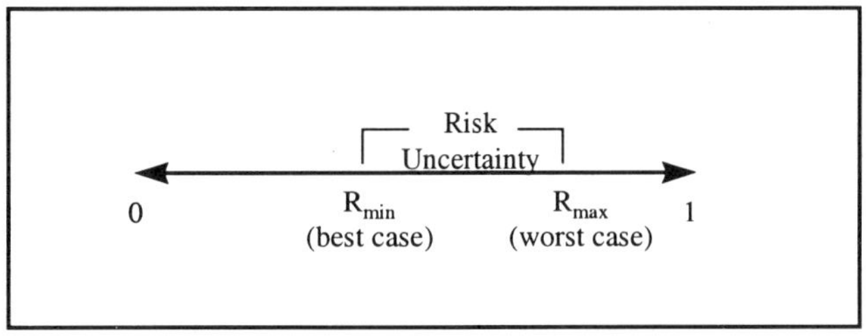

Figure 2: Determining Uncertainty Using Best Case-Worst Case Approach

3.4.2 Repeated measurements method. Another way to quantify the uncertainty is to take repeated measurements and calculate the standard deviation. This approach is more suitable when measurements of risk components (i.e., threats, vulnerabilities or consequences) can be repeated frequently on targets that are similar. For example, in products that are being built on an assembly line, an organization has the opportunity to make repeated quality measurements, gathering a large quantity of data. By calculating the standard deviation of these measurements, it can generate a value for the uncertainty associated with the defect rate of the product. The practical effect of employing the standard deviation is to fix the confidence coefficient, $1-\varepsilon$, at a particular value, i.e., 95 percent.

This method might be used, for example, in the process of selecting a firewall. By gathering information about vulnerabilities or flaws found in various firewalls, the likelihood of encountering these vulnerabilities in each product can be estimated. But the confidence interval can also be determined by exploring the standard deviation of those measurements. If the confidence interval is too large, the measurement is not of much use. But if enough information can be gathered to reduce the confidence interval to a reasonable range, the risk measurement can become quite meaningful.

In general, the repeated measurement method is more easily applied to the uncertainty associated with vulnerability than with other of the risk components. Fortunately, it is not necessary that the same method be used for all components: the two methods can be used together as part of the same risk assessment. Specifically, the best case-worst case method could be used to derive the uncertainty associated with threat, and the repeated measurement method could be used to derive the uncertainty associated with vulnerability. Both methods yield a lower bound value and an upper bound value for their respective components. The two lower bound figures and the two upper bound figures can be multiplied to produce lower bound and upper bound values for likelihood—the difference between them representing the uncertainty associated with likelihood.

3.5 Relationship between confidence coefficient and uncertainty

In applying the best case-worst case method described above, the resulting values for assurance can vary greatly depending upon who decides the input values for the two extreme cases. Each person will tend to apply a certain level of confidence in his or her risk estimates, albeit perhaps unconsciously. This level of confidence, expressed as the confidence coefficient, $1-\varepsilon$, represents the probability that the "real" value of R actually falls within the confidence interval defined by 2δ, the zone of uncertainty. One person, trying to be absolutely certain that R falls within this zone (equivalent to a value for $1-\varepsilon$ close to 100 percent), will choose to make the confidence interval very large, accepting a very large amount of uncertainty. Another person might be willing to accept only a very small amount of uncertainty and a smaller confidence interval, effectively applying a much smaller value for $1-\varepsilon$.

This means that uncertainty (or confidence interval, 2δ) and the confidence coefficient, $1-\varepsilon$, are interdependent. To be absolutely certain that R falls within the confidence interval, the interval must include the entire possible range. Similarly, reducing the uncertainty by shortening the interval causes the confidence coefficient to decrease. At the limit, this means that zero uncertainty can only be obtained with zero confidence.

An example should make the relationship clear. First, suppose a company has determined that they are 95% sure that their expected loss to the enterprise will be between \$4M and \$7M. Management decides that they need to do something about security and decrees that they must have a more exact estimate of expected loss. So the risk assessors return with a value of \$5.26M, but express zero confidence in their answer. Dissatisfied with this uncertainty, management revises its direction and tells them to produce an answer with 100% confidence. In this case, the assessors find that they are absolutely sure that the expected loss will fall somewhere between \$0 and \$100M—the latter figure being the point at which the company's catastrophic insurance kicks in.

Obviously, the company must find an acceptable compromise. To make results comparable, the same confidence coefficient must be used across risk estimates. The advantage of explicitly specifying this confidence coefficient is that people performing the risk analysis are much more likely to produce comparable numbers regardless of whether they are, by nature, conservative or optimistic.

The approaches described above have involved fixing the confidence coefficient, $1-\varepsilon$, at a particular level in order to enable comparisons among risks. Since the level of certainty can be described as a percentage, a natural choice might be the standard statistical significance level of 95%, which would be the value if the "repeated measurements" method were used.

Another possible approach for fixing the confidence coefficient is to give all the participants a qualitative verbal standard intended to represent a given level of certainty. The legal field has produced a number of such standards for evaluating arguments [6]. These include:

- Substantial evidence (a considerable amount)
- Preponderance of the evidence (more than the evidence against)
- Clear and convincing evidence (what a reasonable person would believe)
- Evidence beyond a reasonable doubt (no reasonable person can doubt)

Such verbal standards may have more meaning to the people performing the risk assessment than a "percentage" of certainty. Since the particular standard chosen matters much less than the fact that everyone use the same one, the substitution of legal standards for quantitative ones should not affect the utility of the results.

3.6 Consequence uncertainty

When attempting to generate estimates of risk uncertainty, it is important not to neglect the contribution from consequence. Consequence is often no easier to assess and assign a value to than likelihood, and the effect upon the risk calculation is exactly the same. In this section, we discuss the factors affecting consequence uncertainty and its effect upon assurance.

Many factors contribute to consequence uncertainty. Since most of the more worrisome events have never occurred, the full consequences remain incompletely known. A fully described event (a threat-vulnerability pair) will typically specify the who, what, and how of an event, but would probably not specify a time or place. Yet, the consequence associated with an event can vary greatly depending upon when the event takes place. Time of day, time of year, temporal association with other enterprise occupations, can all greatly influence the severity of the same event's consequence. For example, power outages or denial of service attacks would probably be felt much more by an enterprise during its normal working day than in the middle of the night. An enterprise whose business is seasonal would likely suffer greater consequences during its peak months than during the business' off-season. And consequences to organizations could be much greater during critical periods—during a war for a military organization, during a custody battle for a large business, in the middle of a major competitive procurement proposal effort for a consulting firm, etc. By definition, the range of uncertainty (i.e., confidence interval) must include these variations.

In order to consider how the uncertainty surrounding consequence values might be reduced, it is necessary to understand how these values are calculated in the first place. Usually, consequence values are determined through the use of techniques that solicit and harmonize the independent judgments of a number of persons knowledgeable about the mission and survival limits of the enterprise. Knowledge of the mission is important because the evaluation of consequences should always be made from a mission perspective [7]. Understanding the enterprise's survival limits is also important, since, from the perspective of the enterprise itself, the total demise of the enterprise is usually considered the ultimate consequence. Considering the enterprise's mission, these persons develop a set of consequences that they feel most threaten the enterprise. This list is then arranged in priority order. From the prioritized list, and considering specific threat and vulnerability data, a postulated set of events that would produce these consequences is then generated.

Prioritizing the consequences, employing some kind of consensus process, is usually not particularly difficult, but gaining agreement on a numerical value for this consequence can be quite daunting. Many of the most dire consequences are extremely difficult to evaluate. What value does one place on the loss of a human life, for example? At best, several assumptions have to be made in order to produce a meaningful number. Fortunately, for most purposes, it is not necessary to obtain a number that has any real world significance. In the majority of cases, some arbitrary value, like "10," can be assigned to the most serious consequence, and all other consequences can be assigned numbers relative to that arbitrary value.

One of the general approaches that we outlined for evaluating uncertainty—namely, the best case-worst case approach—can be used to judge the uncertainty surrounding consequence. Consider the statement, "The loss that would result from a total shutdown of an enterprise's main computer network would be approximately $1.5M per day." To make such a statement, a number of assumptions, at least partly backed up by data, are required. Assumptions might involve such items as expected business per day, access to backup data, availability of key employees, etc. In order to produce a value for uncertainty, it would be possible to first evaluate such a statement under universally optimistic assumptions to generate a best case value, and then to evaluate the same statement under universally pessimistic assumptions to produce a worst case figure. The difference between them provides a measure of consequence uncertainty. And, assuming that one can compute best case and worst case values for both likelihood and consequence, the computing of a value for assurance amounts to multiplying the best case consequence and likelihood together to yield a best case value for risk, multiplying worst case consequence and likelihood together to yield a worst case value for risk, and then subtracting one from the other to obtain a confidence interval for risk, which is our measure of assurance.

4. The Role of Assurance in Risk Management

People make decisions about security risks all the time. Some decisions amount to "bet the company" choices, while others have much smaller potential consequences. These decisions are often made without considering all the factors because they are either unknown or simply too complex to understand. Organizations in this situation may have a "false confidence" that they are secure, when in fact this confidence is based on an inadequate understanding of the risks. This section describes how the analysis of assurance described above provides some of the information necessary to make a more informed decision about security risks.

There is, of course, a large body of knowledge about risk management, which deals with this issue in great detail. The point of this section is merely to show the role that assurance can play in the risk management process. The approach described here only touches on how the costs associated with investing in security safeguards factor into the decision to accept the risk or not.

4.1 The risk plane

A popular way of displaying different risk-causing events is by way of a *risk plane*. In a risk plane, unfavorable events are plotted on a two-dimensional graph in which consequence serves as one axis and likelihood as the other (see Figure 3). The figure also shows how the consequence uncertainty interacts with the likelihood uncertainty to define an area of risk uncertainty.[4] By

[4] A slightly different method of displaying virtually the same data appears in John Carroll's book on computer security. His book

plotting consequence and likelihood as ranges, and thus risk as an area, a much better intuitive understanding of this uncertainty is conveyed.

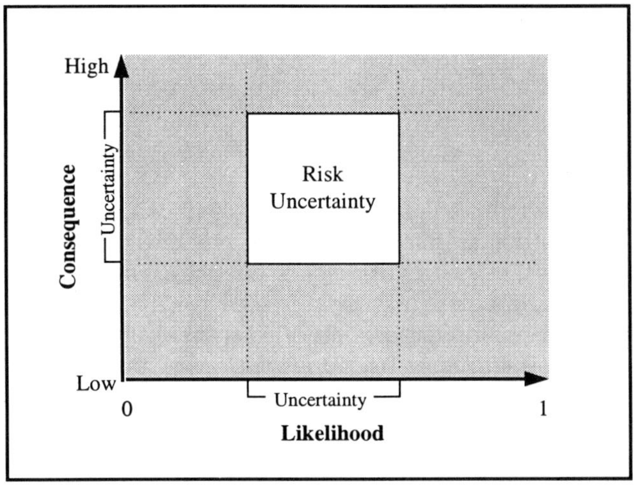

Figure 3: Combining Consequence and Likelihood Uncertainty

4.2 Factors involved in decisions

This paper emphasizes the role that uncertainty plays in making the decision to take some action to reduce a risk. The risk uncertainty is by no means the only factor that must be considered. Cost, schedule, complexity, and even practicality are other important considerations; but the lower the risk uncertainty, the easier it is to balance these other factors.

Figure 4 shows a very simplistic approach to making risk decisions for the purpose of describing the role of uncertainty in the process. A decision-maker could simply select a value of R representing a threshold value above which risks become unacceptable. This results in drawing a constant risk curve through the risk plane. Events below the curve are then ignored while events above the curve are accorded some action (as described in Section 5).

Another approach is to prioritize the risks in terms of overall risk (calculated as the product of consequence and likelihood). Starting at the top of the prioritized list, the decision-maker can then deal with as many of the most serious risks as possible and can look to other factors, such as cost, to decide whether or not to address them.

In this paper, however, events are not simply plotted as points on the risk plane, but as areas of uncertainty. In cases where the risk threshold curve passes through the uncertainty rectangle, as in Figure 4, there is no way to be certain whether the actual risk falls above or below the threshold. In such cases, it is often unclear whether it would be more useful to collapse the rectangle by adding security mechanisms or by obtaining more assurance evidence.

includes a figure containing what he calls a "Plane of Uncertainty," in which severity uncertainty is plotted against frequency uncertainty. See [8], p. 482.

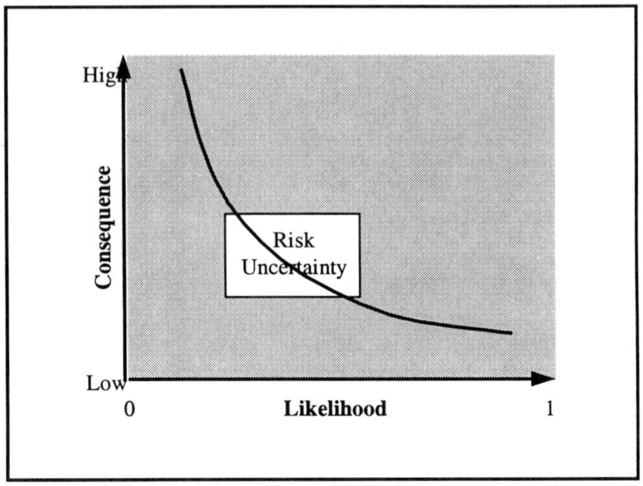

Figure 4: A Simplistic Approach to Risk Decisions

5. Deciding a Course of Action

Consider the decision-maker who must decide whether to accept a risk or make the investment to mitigate the problem. The usual approach for dealing with risks judged to be unacceptable is to identify an appropriate safeguard and implement it. This action will often reduce the risk to an acceptable level.

If the risk can be expressed in monetary units, i.e., dollars, then the risk, which is now equivalent to expected loss, can be compared with the cost of the safeguards necessary to mitigate the expected loss. So long as the mitigation cost is less than the expected loss (probability of loss or likelihood, multiplied by the severity of the loss or consequence), then the reasonable decision is to invest in mitigation. When the mitigation cost is greater than the expected loss, the sensible decision is to accept the risk. It makes sense, then, to invest in safeguards until the expected loss is reduced to the point that it becomes less than the mitigation cost. All of this assumes that the decision-maker has sufficient information on which to base her decision.

However, there are some situations in which the uncertainty associated with a risk is so large that there is no way to tell what effect an additional safeguard would have. In practice, these situations occur frequently. For example, consider a company that is concerned about its susceptibility to the risk of a virus attack. The company employs an undocumented shareware virus tool, so there is a great deal of uncertainty associated with estimates of their residual risk. If the uncertainty is so great that the company decides that the risk of viruses is still unacceptable, they are forced to take some action.

In these cases, the decision-maker is left with two choices for trying to deal with the risk. She could add security mechanisms, such as well documented virus checkers, procedures, or training. Alternatively, she might decide to improve assurance by obtaining more detailed information about the particular virus checker in question. Either method should result in a reduced confidence interval, 2δ, and greater assurance. Adding a security mechanism can do this by raising at least the best case risk value; and adding assurance, by narrowing the gap between best case and worst case estimates. These two alternatives are further explained and contrasted below.

5.1 Adding mechanisms

The most common way of dealing with unacceptable risks is to add another security mechanism, which attempts to reduce the likelihood or consequences of that event. This approach is certainly appropriate when the risk is reasonably well known, i.e., when the uncertainty associated with a particular event is very small. For example, if a disk drive manufacturer has measured the mean time to failure of the devices experimentally, there will be little question about the assurance related to the risk assessments, since the uncertainty has been well established.

In this type of situation, there is little value in gathering additional information to provide the risk assessor with a better basis of estimate. No amount of additional information will reduce the risk to an acceptable level. Therefore, adding a mechanism seems to be the best approach. Of course, adding a mechanism may introduce new uncertainty if there is little information about it, and this new additional uncertainty may negate any benefit gained by adding the mechanism.

5.2 Adding evidence

There are other situations in which the uncertainty associated with a risk estimate is very large. Here, the appropriate action may be different since the assessors do not have good estimates of threat, vulnerability, and consequence. This section discusses ways to reduce this uncertainty.

The uncertainty results from the assessor's lack of relevant information on which accurate estimates of threat, vulnerability and consequence can be based. Sometimes it merely requires assembling the evidence that is already available. This can be quite inexpensive and yet provide a great deal of information to the assessor. In other cases, it is necessary to seek additional information or evidence. Adding evidence serves to increase an assessor's confidence in his risk estimates. For example, a risk assessor provided with details of the track record of a firewall may decide that the worst case is not really as bad as previously thought. This lowers R_{max}, shrinking the confidence interval from the high end. This, in turn, shifts the midpoint of the confidence interval, R^*, representing the best estimate of overall risk, to a lower value.

However, increasing assurance is not always a cause for rejoicing. If a risk assessor is provided with "negative" evidence that a firewall has been successfully penetrated many times, he will conclude that his earlier best-case estimates were too high and lower them. This acts to shrink the confidence interval from the low end, raising R_{min}. In effect, he will be more certain that the risk is greater than originally thought. Although perhaps discouraging, this is useful information that helps the decision-maker make an informed choice.

Having done all this, the decision-maker probably still does not know how much assurance she may have needed, but she is now in a position to decide whether or not the amount of assurance she has is sufficient, and this we claim is quite good enough.

5.3 Case studies

To better illustrate the dilemma often faced by the decision-maker, Figure 5 plots six extreme, stylized event classes on a risk plane. Each event class is represented as a rectangle whose vertical and horizontal dimensions represent, respectively, the uncertainty surrounding the consequence and likelihood of the event. For the purpose of this illustration, we will assume that, in each case, the consequence associated with each event is known fairly well, and that any uncertainty or lack of assurance is attributable to the likelihood factor. By displaying events in this manner, the appropriate action on the part of a decision-maker is much clearer.

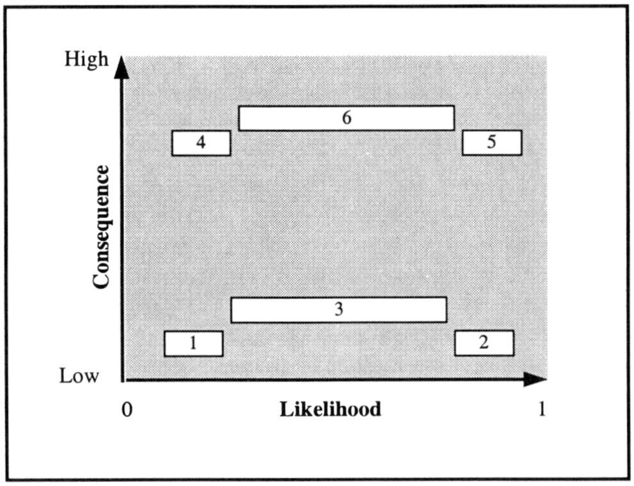

Figure 5: Example Events Plotted on a Risk Plane

Case 1 represents a situation in which both the consequence and likelihood of the event are known, with high assurance, to be low. Any example of this case tends to sound silly as soon as it is voiced, precisely because it is highly unlikely and of low consequence, even if it were to occur. An example might be a passing comet. Since both the consequence and likelihood are known to be low, the risk is very low and no mitigation action is warranted.

Case 2 is similar to Case 1 except that, in this case, the likelihood of the event is high. An example of an event of this class might be an occasional power interruption in an enterprise that is very disciplined in its practice of backing up its files. Since the consequence is low, there is little incentive to spend very much on additional safeguards, but if there were a moderately effective safeguard that could be put in place at low cost, such as an uninterrupted power supply (UPS), it might be worth doing.

Case 3 is different. Here, as before, the consequence is low, but the likelihood could be anywhere. An example of this case might be a hardware failure of a key subsystem that is covered by warranty. If the likelihood were known to be low, one would ignore the problem, as with Case 1, and if the likelihood were known to be high, as in Case 2, one would only invest in relatively inexpensive safeguards. One reasonable approach in this case would be to assume the worst case, act as if the likelihood were high, and invest in cheap fixes if there are any. Another defensible approach, particularly if there are no cheap fixes, would be to gather more evidence in an effort to shrink the confidence interval, i.e., raise the level of assurance. Which decision is the more appropriate would depend upon the relative costs of additional evidence vs. safeguards.

Case 4 presents a similar situation to Case 2, except that in this case, it is the likelihood that is low and the consequence that is high. An extreme example might be the risk of the enterprise being hit by a meteor. Clearly, if this happened, the result would be disastrous, but the odds of its occurring during the lifetimes of the next several generations are small. In this particular example, one would almost certainly take no action whatsoever, but in more normal examples, one might invest in some inexpensive safeguards.

Case 5 represents the situation in which the event in question is known, with high assurance, to be of high consequence as well as high likelihood, implying very high risk. An example of this situation might be a virus attack against an open, unprotected network containing all of the enterprise's information assets. In a case such as this, mitigation is clearly called for, and would be avoided only if the "fix" were either prohibitive in cost or technically unfeasible.

Finally, Case 6 represents the situation for which the consequence of the event is high but the likelihood is not known. Harm caused by a malicious insider is an example of this situation, since, clearly if there were one, the consequence would be quite high because almost any insider, if intending to do harm, can do a great deal. The problem is in knowing whether or not you have or will have such a person. In this case, mitigation efforts may be in order, either to reduce the probability that one exists—i.e., reduce the threat, or to limit the harm that such a person could perpetrate—i.e., reduce the vulnerability. But it probably makes equal sense, since the consequence and risk are so high, to expend some additional effort at narrowing the assurance interval and thus more precisely determine the true likelihood. These examples and the indicated actions for each case are summarized in Table 1.

Case	Likeli-hood	Conse-quence	Assur-ance	Example	Action
1	Low	Low	High	Passing comet	Ignore
2	High	Low	High	Power interruption	Fix if cheap
3	Unk	Low	Low	Warranty-protected HW failure	Get more informa-tion or fix
4	Low	High	High	Meteor	Fix if cheap
5	High	High	High	Unknown Virus	Fix if at all possible
6	Unk	High	Low	Malicious Insider	Get more informa-tion or fix

Table 1: Summary of Different Risk Cases

6. Summary

In this paper, we have presented a case for a somewhat modified view of assurance—one that is orthogonal to the concept of security and risk, and closer to the intuitive notion implying the absence of uncertainty. This, we have argued, has the advantage of better accommodating "negative evidence" and of providing a means of expressing the situation in which low security is accompanied by great certainty. We have also presented a practical method of generating some rough measure of assurance given some means of determining risk. Finally, we have shown how a richer understanding of assurance and its basis can be used in the every-day risk management decisions that decision-makers are called upon to make.

Acknowledgments

No paper is the sole product of its authors: this one is the result of many discussions with many people over several years, whose contribution we gratefully acknowledge. We wish particularly to thank the reviewers of our original version who offered cogent comments and several helpful suggestions, most of which we attempted to apply. We feel that the paper has benefited greatly as a result. Finally, we wish to acknowledge and thank the National Security Agency without whose funding support this paper would never have been written.

References

[1] Jeffrey R. Williams and George F. Jelen, *A Framework for Reasoning about Assurance*, Document Number ATR 97043, Arca Systems, Inc., 23 April 1998.

[2] National Institute of Standards and Technology, Invitational Workshop on Information Technology (IT) Assurance and Trustworthiness, March, 1995.

[3] David R. Wichers, Joel E. Sachs, and Douglas J. Landoll, "What Color Is Your Assurance?"

[4] Idaho State University, Glossary of INFOSEC and INFOSEC Related Terms, Vol. II, Version 6, dated August 1996.

[5] Harald Cramér, *The Elements of Probability Theory*, (New York: John Wiley & Sons, 1955).

[6] Jeffrey R. Williams and Marvin Schaefer, "Pretty Good Assurance," *Proceedings of the New Security Paradigms Workshop*, (IEEE Computer Society Press, 1995).

[7] George F. Jelen, "A New Risk Management Paradigm For INFOSEC Assessments and Evaluations," *Proceedings of the 11th annual Computer Security Applications Conference*, (Los Alamitos, CA: IEEE Computer Society Press, 1995), pp. 261-267.

[8] John M. Carroll, Computer Security, 3rd ed. (Boston: Butterworth-Heinemann, 1995).

Track C

Secure Transactions

Chair

J. McDermott, Naval Research Laboratory

A Certified E-Mail Protocol

Bruce Schneier
Counterpane Systems
schneier@counterpane.com

James Riordan
IBM Zurich Research Laboratory
rij@zurich.ibm.com

Abstract

Protocols to facilitate secure electronic delivery are necessary if the Internet is to achieve its true potential as a business communications tool. We present a protocol for secure e-mail that protects both the sender and the receiver, and can be implemented using current e-mail products and existing Internet infrastructure.

1 Introduction

Electronic mail, or e-mail, has become an essential communication tool for business. The ease of communicating over e-mail, as opposed to traditional tools such as physical mail, fax, or telephone, makes it the communications medium of choice for many people. As more people and businesses move on-line, and Internet access becomes more commonplace, e-mail will be used for even more communications.

In order for e-mail to be used for important communications, some notion of certified delivery must be provided for users. Not all e-mail needs to be certified. Just as in the physical world, conventional mail is sufficient for most communications, but some important communications needs to be sent via certified mail.

A certified e-mail protocol must have the following security properties:

1. Alice (the sender) must have some way of proving that Bob (the receiver) received the mail, should Bob later try to deny it.
2. Bob must have some way of proving that Alice did not send the mail, should Alice later try to claim that she did.

Certified paper mail uses the notion of a signed receipt. When Alice sends Bob certified mail, the Post Office will not release the mail to Bob unless he signs a receipt. This signed receipt is returned to Alice, and acts as a proof of delivery. If Alice does not have this receipt, Bob can claim that the certified mail was never sent. Here the Post Office is acting as a Trusted Third Party. Of course, this protocol only certifies that Alice sent Bob *some piece of mail* and not a particular piece of mail. This weak binding between the certification and the contents being certified is pervasive through all paper authentication protocols, and a problem that digital signature protocols solve easily.

In this paper we present a certified e-mail protocol that both satisfies all the security requirements of a protocol of this type, and is simple to implement and requires no specialized infrastructure. The rest of the paper is organized as follows. In Section 2 we describe previous work on certified delivery and related cryptographic problems. In Section 3 we describe our protocol and the message exchanges involved. In Section 4 we present a security analysis, and in Section 5 we describe the protocol's security properties. Section 6 discusses implementation details, in in Section 7 we offer some conclusions.

2 Previous Work

Several protocols for certifying electronic delivery have been proposed in the literature. The earliest

0-8186-8789-4/98 $10.00 © 1998 IEEE

[Blu81, EGL85] use the notion of oblivious transfer [Kil90]: sending someone a message, with only a probabilistic guarantee of receipt. These protocols, while they have nice provable properties, are extremely computationally intensive and require many communications exchanges between the sender and receiver.

Many protocols, especially those implemented by companies attempting to make a business out of certified delivery, rely on trusted software to provide the security. Alice sends Bob an encrypted message via a certified-delivery software program, which will not allow Bob to read it until he sends Alice back a receipt. These protocols are susceptible to reverse-engineering and hacking, and cannot provide any real assurance of delivery.

Some protocols require a Trusted Third Party. The protocol in [BT94], for example, uses a trusted "Postmaster" to mediate between Alice and Bob. Aside from the logistical (and liability) problems of setting this Postmaster, the Postmaster needs to know the message Alice is sending to Bob. Alice cannot send a certified message to Bob without the Postmaster being able to read it. (Alice could always encrypt the message outside this protocol, but then all the Postmaster could certify is that Bob received an unintelligible bucket of bits.) Similar protocols appear in [Mic96, Mic97a, Mic97b].

Protocols requiring a Trusted Third Party are said to be optimistic [ASW97, ASW98] if the third party is only required in the exceptional case (e.g. one of the parties cannot or will not follow the protocol to its normal conclusion).

In all cases requiring a Trusted Third Party, it is highly desirable to minimize trust and complexity requirements on that third party.

Still other protocols ignore the problem of non-repudiation. The above protocol ends with the Postmaster sending Alice a certified receipt at the same time it sends Bob a key so that he can read the message, but no provisions are made for network transmission errors.

Another similar protocol [ZG96a, ZG96b], specifically does not try to solve the non-repudiation problem. ((more about this))

The system in [PA96] is similar in design.

3 The Protocol

Alice wishes to send Bob a certified message. Bob wants to receive a certified message. We need to build a protocol to facilitate this exchange. That is, we want to build a protocol to allow Alice to be able to prove to an arbiter that Bob has received her message if and only if he did receive it.

We assume that Bob has a public key [RSA78, ElG85] in some commonly recognized format (e.g. X.509 [CCITT89]), that there exists some public-key infrastructure (e.g. PKIX [?]) that Alice can use to verify the public key, that an arbiter can verify the key was valid at the time of the transaction using the public key infrastructure, and that there exists some timed stamped public forum whose contents are publically available (e.g. *The New York Times*, a World Wide Web kiosk service, or a Usenet newsgroup).

Let M be the message, K a key, E_K an encryption method using K and some standard symmetric cipher [NBS77, LMM91, Sch94], and H a message digest, or hash, function [NIST93, Riv95].[1]

1. Alice chooses a random key, K, and sends Bob the encrypted message $E_K(M)$.

2. Bob returns to Alice a digitally signed message with the form:

   I would like Alice to publish the key for the E_K– encrypted message, whose digest is $H(E_K(M))$, by date T at location X. — /s/ Bob

3. Alice publishes the pair $H(E_K(M)), K$ in X on or before date T.

4. Bob retrieves the key and decrypts the message.

If Alice is called upon to prove that Bob received the e-mail, she presents her copies of M, K, $E_K(M)$, and Bob's signed message from Step (2), along with the public record of her publishing them in Step (3) in accordance with Bob's request. The arbiter confirms that $E_K(M)$ is correct and conforms to what was

[1] Details on the cryptographic primitives used in this protocol, including symmetric cryptography, public-key cryptography, message digest functions, and public-key infrastructures, can be found in [Sti95, Sch96, MOV97].

published in Step (3), and also that the publication was in accordance to Bob's request in Step (2).

If Bob is called upon to prove that Alice did not send him the e-mail, he challenges Alice to present the body of evidence listed above. If she cannot, or if any of the evidence does not conform to the rules of the protocol (e.g. the pair $H(E_K(M)), K$ published in X in Step (3) does not match the $H(E_K(M))$ of the message Alice claims to have sent Bob), the arbiter has no choice but to believe Bob.

4 Analysis

The protocol is secure against cheating attempts by either Alice or Bob:

- If Bob refuses to comply in Step (2) or gives an unreasonable date or location, then he does not receive the key for the encrypted message and hence does not receive the message. This is conceptually equivalent of Bob's refusing certified mail at his doorstep.
- If Alice refuses to comply in Step (3) and claims that Bob has received the message when he has not, then Bob can show that Alice did not publish the key by calling upon the public records of location X. This is conceptually equivalent to Alice not sending the message but then claiming she had.
- If Bob refuses to comply with Step (4), then he loses because has claimed that he will comply in Step (2). This is conceptually equivalent of Bob's accepting and signing for the certified mail but refusing to open it.

5 Security Properties

The protocol has a few properties which are worth explicitly noting.

- The signed message of Step (2) must make clear how and when to retrieve the key and how to use it to decrypt the message. This prevents Bob from claiming that Alice has waited unduly in publishing the key while preventing Alice from publishing the key several months late in the East Podunk Quarterly for the message which was encrypted using AC5 (Alice's Code 5).
- Bob may wish to include with his message of Step (2) a description of what he expects from the contents of decrypted message. Doing so greatly reduces Alice's ability to deliver bogus information.
- So long as neither Alice nor Bob attempt to cheat, their identities need never be revealed to a third party. That is, this whole protocol could be conducted anonymously, through anonymous remailers [Sch95, TG96].
- This method does not offer privacy in that an eavesdropper has access to both $E_K(M)$ and K. If privacy is required, the exchanges at Steps (1) and (2) should be conducted using a method providing adequate privacy. There are several e-mail security protocols that could suffice: e.g., PGP [Zim95, Sch95, Gar95, Sch96], PEM [Lin93, Ken93, Bal93, Kal93, Sch95, Sch96], S/MIME [RSA96, Dus96], and others [SH97].
- Alice must retain a copy of T, K, and Bob's key request message for as long as she wishes to be able to prove receipt. This is conceptually equivalent to Alice keeping a copy of the certified-mail receipt.

6 Implementation

Unlike other certified-delivery protocols, the one presented in the paper can be implemented using the current Internet infrastructure. Any of the e-mail security programs mentioned above could be used to provide certified e-mail in this manner. While the integration of this protocol into secure e-mail clients would make it easier to use, it is not required.

A commercial certified-delivery service would necessarily have to combine the delivery protocol with some sort of payment protocol. The NetBill protocol [CTS95], for example, includes a certified- delivery mechanism as part of the protocol. The protocol presented in this paper could easily be augmented with a payment mechanism: a commercial entity could accept payment from Alice is exchange for providing a common public forum for Alice to use in Step (3).

The public kiosks of such commercial certified-delivery services are easily distributable; this stands in sharp contrast to several other schemes involving a third party which require Byzantine agreement [LSP82]. Different kiosks could included time stamped hashes of one anothers contents to improve security. An anonymous access method could be used to minimize trust requires placed upon the service.

Alternately, the protocol could be used in the absence of any commercial provider, simply by using the already-public Usenet newsgroups and a public archiving mechanism such as DejaNews.com.

Similarly, this protocol could be easily used within fair-exchange protocols [Blu81, Ket95, KG95, ASW97, ASW98] to certify delivery of information.

Finally, we note that if Alice has a reliable connection to the public channel, we can render the protocol optimistic [ASW97] by adding steps between 2 and 3:

- Alice gives Bob K directly
- Bob gives Alice a receipt for k

If Bob gives Alice the receipt for K, she need not publish as required by step 3 (thus reducing network traffic). If Bob fails to give Alice the receipt, Alice may continue with step 3.

7 Conclusions

We have presented a protocol allowing certified mail and an optimistic variation on that protocol. These protocols have the features of minimizing trust and complexity requirements on parties external to the two players. The minimization of trust results in greater security. The minimization of complexity results in resilience, ease of deployment, and the possibility of distributing the external party without difficulty.

8 Acknowledgments

References

[ASW97] N. Asokan , Matthias Schunter , and Michael Waidner, "Optimistic protocols for fair exchange", *ACM Computer and communications security*, 1997, pp. 7.

[ASW98] N. Asokan , Victor Shoup , and Michael Waidner, "Optimistic fair exchange of Digital Signatures", *Proceedings of Research in Security and Privacy, Oakland, CA*, May 1998, IEEE Computer Society Press.

[BT94] A. Bahreman and J.D. Tygar, "Certified Electronic Mail," *Proceedings of the Internet Society Symposium on Network and Distributed System Security*, Internet Society, 1994, pp. 3–19.

[Bal93] D. Balenson, "Privacy Enhancement for Internet Electronic Mail: Part III—Algorithms, Modes, and Identifiers," RFC 1423, Feb 1993.

[Blu81] M. Blum, "Three applications of the oblivious transfer: Part I: Coin flipping by telephone; Part II: How to exchange secrets; Part III: How to send certified electronic mail," Department of EECS, University of California, Berkeley, CA, 1981.

[CCITT89] CCITT, Recommendation X.509, "The Directory–Authentication Framework," Consultation Committee, International Telephone and Telegraph, International Telecommunications Union, Geneva, 1989.

[CTS95] B. Cox, J.D. Tygar, and M. Sirbu, "NetBill Security and Transaction Protocol," *The First USENIX Workshop on Electronic Commerce*, USENIX Association, 1995, pp. 77–88.

[DGLW96] R.H. Deng, L. Gong, A.A. Lazar, and W. Wong, "Practical Protocols for Certified Electronic Mail," *Journal of Network and Systems Management*, v. 4 n. 3, 1996.

[Dus96] S. Dusse, "S/MIME Message Specification: PKCS Security Services for MIME," IETF Networking Group Internet Draft, Sep 1996.

[ElG85] T. ElGamal, "A Public-Key Cryptosystem and a Signature Scheme Based on Discrete Logarithms," *IEEE Transactions on Information Theory,* V. IT-31, n. 4, 1985, pp. 469–472.

[EGL85] S. Even, O. Goldreich, and A. Lempel, "A Randomized Protocol for Signing Contracts," *Communications of the ACM*, v. 28, n. 6, Jun 1985, pp. 637–647.

[Gar95] S. Garfinkel, *PGP: Pretty Good Privacy*, O'Reilly & Associates, 1995.

[Kal93] B.S. Kaliski, "Privacy Enhancement for Internet Electronic Mail: Part IV—Key Certificates and Related Services," RFC 1424, Feb 1993.

[Ken93] S.T Kent, "Privacy Enhancement for Internet Electronic Mail: Part II—Certificate Based Key Management," RFC 1422, Feb 1993.

[Ket95] S. Ketchpel, "Transaction Protection for Information Buyers and Sellers," in Proceedings of the Dartmouth Institute for Advanced Graduate Studies '95, 1995.

[KG95] S. Ketchpel and H. Garcia-Molina, "Making Trust Explicit in Distributed Commerce Transactions," Stanford Digital Library Project Working Paper SIDL-WP-1995-0018, October 12, 1995.

[Kil90] J. Kilian *Uses of Randomness in Algorithms and Protocols*, MIT Press, 1990.

[LMM91] X. Lai, J. Massey, and S. Murphy, "Markov Ciphers and Differential Cryptanalysis," *Advances in Cryptology—CRYPTO '91*, Springer-Verlag, 1991, pp. 17–38.

[Lin93] J. Linn, "Privacy Enhancement for Internet Electronic Mail: Part I—Message Encipherment and Authentication Procedures," RFC 1421, Feb 1993.

[LSP82] L. Lamport, R. Shostak, and M. Pease "The Byzantine Generals Problem" *ACM Transactions on Programming Languages and Systems*, Vol. 4, No. 3, July 1982, pp. 382-401.

[Mic96] S. Micali, "Simultaneous electronic transactions with visible trusted parties," U.S. Patent 5,553,145, 3 Sep 1996.

[Mic97a] S. Micali, "Simultaneous electronic transactions with visible trusted parties," U.S. Patent 5,629,982, 13 May 1997.

[Mic97b] S. Micali, "Simultaneous electronic transactions," U.S. Patent 5,666,420, 9 Sep 1996.

[MOV97] A.J. Menezes, P.C. van Oorschot, and S.A. Vanstone, *Handbook of Applied Cryptography*, CRC Press, 1997.

[Mue84] C Mueller-Scholer, "Method and apparatus providing registered mail features in an electronic communication system," U.S. Patent 4,458,109, 3 Jul 1984.

[NBS77] National Bureau of Standards, NBS FIPS PUB 46, "Data Encryption Standard," National Bureau of Standards, U.S. Department of Commerce, Jan 1977.

[NIST93] National Institute of Standards and Technology, NIST FIPS PUB 180, "Secure Hash Standard," U.S. Department of Commerce, May 1993.

[PA96] C.J. Petrie Jr. and W.P. Allen, "Electronic Proof of Receipt," U.S. Patent 5,509,071, 16 Apr 1996.

[PC93] D. Pinkas and P. Caille, "Method for obtaining a securitized cleartext attestation in a distributed data processing system environment," U.S Patent 5,214,700, 25 May 1993.

[Riv95] R.L. Rivest, "The RC5 Encryption Algorithm," *Fast Software Encryption, 2nd International Workshop Proceedings*, Springer-Verlag, 1995, pp. 86–96.

[RSA78] R. Rivest, A. Shamir, and L. Adleman, "A Method for Obtaining Digital Signatures and Public-Key Cryptosystems," *Communications of the ACM*, v. 21, n. 2, Feb 1978, pp. 120–126.

[RSA96] RSA Data Security, Inc., "S/MIME Implementation Guide Interoperability Profiles, Version 2," S/MIME Editor, Draft, Oct 1996.

[Sch94] B. Schneier, "Description of a New Variable-Length Key, 64-Bit Block Cipher (Blowfish)," *Fast Software Encryption, Cambridge Security Workshop Proceedings*, Springer-Verlag, 1994, pp. 191-204.

[Sch95] B. Schneier, *E-Mail Security,* John Wiley & Sons, 1995.

[Sch96] B. Schneier, *Applied Cryptography, Second Edition*, John Wiley & Sons, 1996.

[SH97] B. Schneier and C. Hall "An Improved E-Mail Security Protocol," *Thirteenth Annual Computer Security Applications Conference*, IEEE Computer Society, 1997, pp. 227–230.

[Sti95] D. Stinson, *Cryptography Theory and Practice*, CRC Press, 1995, pp. 138–145.

[TG96] G. Tsudik and C. Gulcu, "Mixing E-Mail with BABEL," *ISOC Symposium on Network and Distributed System Security*, IEEE Computer Society Press, 1996, p. 2–16.

[ZG96a] J. Zhou and D. Gollman, "A Fair Non-Repudiation Protocol," *Proceedings of the 1996 IEEE Symposium on Security and Privacy*, IEEE Press, 1996, pp. 55–61.

[ZG96b] J. Zhou and D. Gollmann "Certified Electronic Mail," *Computer Security — ESORICS '96 Proceedings*, Springer-Verlag, 1996, pp. 160–171.

[Zim95] P. Zimmermann, *The Official PGP User's Guide*, MIT Press, 1995.

Electronic Submission Protocol Based on Temporal Accountability

Michiharu Kudo
Tokyo Research Laboratory, IBM Japan Ltd.

Abstract

This paper describes various possible attacks on temporal properties such as temporal records of payment times and declarations of the closing times for electronic submissions, and explains defense measures that use a trusted third party to provide temporal accountability. We propose a secure electronic submission protocol as a typical time-sensitive application and a temporal accountability logic, which is an extension of Kailar's work. We analyze the proposed protocol by applying our temporal accountability logic, and describe some modifications of the protocol, which reduce the total number of flows while keeping the protocol as logically secure as the original one in terms of temporal accountability.

1 Introduction

Electronic commerce is becoming increasingly common on the Internet, and many security-related electronic payment systems have been built on the basis of various cryptographic methods and standards. These applications are designed to protect important properties of solutions from anticipated types of attack such as eavesdropping, forgery, and espionage. We think that one such important property is a temporal one. For example, an electronic payment server verifies whether the system clock of the end user's computer is within a permitted range of time-drift, because the shopping date measured in the server and the user's record created in the client must be in agreement. In practice, there are many time-critical applications other than payment applications. To use public facilities such as tennis courts in Japan, we usually apply for a lottery ticket by mailing an application form to the appropriate office. Since the application can be received only during a specified period, applicants must pay attention to such temporal constraints. In most cases, the postmark is used as official proof of the application. In a few cases, the arrival time of the application form is used. However, the former seems to be more acceptable to applicants, because there is no official proof in the latter case. We think that the importance of the postmark lies in the provability it provides for temporal activities such as time-critical submissions. In other words, this important temporal property should be protected from adversaries who may forge or alter it. This paper explains the danger of such attacks and a defense strategy. Then we propose a secure electronic submission protocol that uses a trusted third party to provide temporal accountability. We also propose a temporal accountability logic, which is an extension of Kailar's work [K96]. The proposed logic, unlike Kailar's, is capable of representing the provability of temporal activities. We analyze the proposed protocol by applying our temporal accountability logic, and describe some modifications of the protocol, which reduce the total number of flows while keeping the protocol as logically secure as the original one in terms of temporal accountability.

1.1 Related Work

Kailar proposed an accountability logic [K96] for electronic commerce protocols such as payment protocols and public key distribution protocols. He defines accountability as a property whereby the association of a unique originator with an object or action can be proved to a third party. Provability has an important role in the analysis of accountability. Since time-critical applications require proofs that guarantee the temporal activities of each principal, we think that Kailar's accountability logic can be extended for use in analyzing such applications. Although the original logic allows some temporal context such as a During and Until property to be added to represent the validation period of security-related information such as a time-critical delegation key, we extend the original logic so that the logic can represent the temporal accountability. Much work has been done on

0-8186-8789-4/98 $10.00

belief logic in the analysis of key management protocols. Burrows, Abadi, and Needham proposed a belief logic for authentication, which is used for reasoning about authentication protocols and for detecting redundancies and security flaws [BAN90]. In belief logic, each party is said to have a belief when he/she is convinced of a statement after several communications. There is a difference between belief logic and accountability logic as regards provability to other principals. Stubblebine extended the previous belief logic and proposed the notion of recent-secure authentication [S95], which is based on the work of [LABW92], [ABLP93], and [SO94]. The statement has three time properties: at, notbefore, and notafter. These temporal properties were created to represent the secure channel of a principal and freshness constraints for entity authentication. Our method assumes the existence of a trusted third party and the absence of clock synchronization among principals. On the other hand, Stubblebine's work does not assume a trusted third party and requires clock synchronization. Stubblebine and Wright extend BAN logic in order to reach a more precise temporal notion [SW96]. Their logic has three temporal properties: at a certain time t, at a certain time between t1 and t2, and at all times between t1 and t2. They also assume that all principals have their own local times and need to synchronize them. While the primary purpose of their logic is to reason about the soundness of protocols that use certificates which include security-related information with a validation period, our method is to reason about the soundness of protocols that use trusted timestamps which can offer temporal proof. Haber and Stornetta proposed a hash-based timestamp method [HS90]. Since their method can prove the time at which data were received, it is possible to combine their protocol and ours; however, we omit the explanation.

In this paper, we analyze various types of attack, including conspiracy attacks, described in Section 2. Section 3 describes a secure electronic submission protocol that uses a trusted third party. We propose a temporal accountability logic in Section 4. In Section 5 we analyze the proposed protocol by applying the temporal accountability logic. In section 6, we describe further considerations related to protocol analysis.

2 Attacks and Defense Measures for Temporal Transactions

In this section, we describe various types of attack on secure temporal transactions, and propose defense measures. We also explain why a trusted third party that guarantees the accuracy of the current time is required.

2.1 Difficulties

In Internet credit-payment systems, a buyer can easily verify a purchase statement by comparing the price on the receipt and the amount paid later from his/her bank account. However, how can he/she verify that the merchant's system clock is always exact? Such verification becomes important if the merchant engages in temporal transactions such as discount selling during a limited period. If an order is sent by electronic mail, the mail server's system clock is trusted, and the buyer receives a distribution acknowledgement from the mail server. In this way, the buyer can verify that the discount rate on the purchased item is correct. However, we must handle the situation in a more general way. We list several situations that can be more general or less secure:

- The user directly connects to the application server (not via a trusted third-party agent).
- The application server's system clock is not trusted, and may therefore be slow or fast.
- The user's system clock is not trusted, and may therefore be slow or fast.
- A malicious party may alter or forge temporal records stored in the user's machine or server.

With these assumptions, we describe possible malicious attacks on temporal transactions.

2.2 Attacks

We divide possible attacks against temporal transactions into two categories:

A) *Adjustment of the system clock forward or backward by the user, the server, or both in conspiracy*

B) *Forgery, alteration, or removal of temporal records by the user, the server, or both in conspiracy*

One example of an attack on a server by putting forward the system clock is as follows. If the user sends an application form to a public facility office close to the deadline, and the server clock is set a little fast, the application will not be received owing to its late arrival. Another example of a conspiracy attack involving forgery of temporal records concerns paper submission. If an author cannot complete his/her paper by the due date, he/she may request one of the program editors to include the paper even if it is not received by the due date. If the postmark on the envelope is not used as a proof of the submission, the editor can easily add the requested paper to the officially received submissions. In this case, the author and program editor mount a conspiracy attack that involves forging temporal records so that the paper appears to have arrived before the due date.

2.3 Solutions

Some countermeasures against the above attacks are as follows:

A1) Periodic adjustment of the system clock

A2) Distribution of temporal transactions on multiple machines

A3) Use of a trusted third party that offers a correct timestamp

B1) Distribution of temporal transaction records to all principals

B2) Registration of temporal transaction records with another trusted third party

B3) Timestamping of temporal transaction records by a trusted third party

For **A1**, the system clock can be automatically adjusted by running the Network Time Protocol (NTP) [M91] or by running a Global Positioning System driver that provides accurate information on the current time. However, we think that this solution is not sufficiently secure against attacks of type **A**, because the person with the highest administrative access rights can easily change the system clock at any time. For **A2**, Franklin and Reiter presented a distributed server group computation that ensures the integrity of temporal transactions for sealed-bid auction [FR95]. However, this solution still suffers from the above access right problem. For **A3**, a trusted timestamp server is assumed. For **B** categories, note that temporal transaction records must be published outside the server; otherwise, there is no way of preventing forgery, alteration, or removal of records inside the server through attacks of type **B**. For **B1**, all principals must monitor the server's temporal transactions synchronously. For **B2**, a trusted third party for registration must provide a huge amount of storage space for the expected transactions. For **B3**, a trusted timestamp server is assumed. We previously presented an auction protocol in which the temporal transaction records are timestamped by a trusted server [K98].

For reasons of feasibility and trustability, we adopt measures **A3** and **B3** in this paper. We assume the existence of a trusted timestamp server that adds a correct timestamp to the temporal transaction data, that cannot be altered or forged. In this way, we can protect the security of temporal transactions from attacks of types **A** and **B**. Transaction records that contain time-sensitive information are accompanied by temporal proofs generated by the timestamp server. The advantage of this method is that application servers do not have to provide a correct time service even though they provide time-sensitive services to the users. In other words, the timestamp and timestamp server have the same roles as a postmark on a physical envelope and a post office, respectively.

We define the accurate time in this paper as Coordinated Universal Time (UTC), because the latter is used in Stratum 1 of the NTP. The UTC is calculated from both the International Atomic Time (TAI) and corrections for small changes to the TAI determined by the U.S. Naval Observatory and other observatories [M91].

3 Secure Electronic Submission Protocol

We think that the most typical application involving temporal transactions is electronic submission of an application that is permitted within a certain period of time. Note that it is not as easy to design a submission protocol as might be imagined. If an applicant takes a timestamp from the timestamp server for his/her application before the closing time for submission and sends it to the submission server, can it be satisfactorily proved that the submission is correct? Some people may suspect the applicant of sending the application before the opening time for submission. Others may suspect the applicant of sending the application after the closing time for submission, even though his/her submission was generated before the closing time. Therefore we begin by stating the general requirements for the electronic submission protocol:

R1) The receiver must not receive any applications except during the permitted period.

R2) The applicants must submit application data during the permitted period.

R3) The receiver cannot forge, alter, or remove any application once it has been received

R4) The receiver must receive applications that arrive during the permitted period.

3.1 Notation

We use the following notation. Principals are denoted by capital letters $\{A, B, \cdots\}$. We use A to denote *Alice*, who is an applicant, B for *Bob*, who is the receiver of the application forms sent by multiple applicants, and T for *Trent,* who is the trusted timestamp service provider.

Messages are denoted by small letters $\{x, y\}$ except for t. We use t as a time parameter. The predefined time parameters are t_s, which denotes the opening time for submission, and t_e, which denotes the closing time for submission. K_A and K_A^{-1} denote the public key and private key, respectively, for the principal A. $\{x\}K_A^{-1}$ denotes the signature value for a message x calculated by A's private key. *desc* denotes a submission description that consists of t_s, t_e, and *id*. *id* denotes an index number specified for a call for submission. x_i denotes the i-th submission from A_i, which denotes the i-th A. y_i denotes $\{x_i, A, B, \{t_s, \{desc\}K^{-1}_B\}K^{-1}_T\}K^{-1}_{Ai}$. "," denotes an operation for concatenating parameters.

3.2 General Assumptions

The general assumptions for this protocol are as follows:

N1) The time stamp service provider is trusted to provide the current time accurately and to generate correct timestamps. We assume the existence of another function to send notification to other entities at previously specified times.

N2) The applicant's system clock and receiver's system clock are not trusted, and may be fast or slow. We do not assume any clock synchronization for them. We consider another situation in section 6, in which the receiver's clock is accurate.

N3) The receiver is assumed to offer submission services to all applicants fairly.

N4) The computing resources for the receiver and the timestamp server are assumed to be unlimited. It takes only a short time to communicate or execute the protocol.

N5) The digital signature algorithm is based on public key cryptography, and it is impossible to forge or alter a signature owing to the computational complexity.

N6) It is assumed that no denial-of-service attack by a malicious party occurs.

N7) The channel for communication among the principals is assumed to be secured in order to preserve the confidentiality of each message.

3.3 General Flow

The submission protocol consists of four steps: a preliminary step, an opening step, a submission step, and a closing step. In the preliminary step, *Bob* asks *Trent* to notify *Bob* at the opening time and closing time for submission. In the opening step, which is taken when notification is received from *Trent*, an opening timestamp is used to guarantee that the applicant generates an application after the opening time for submission. In the submission step, one or more applicants, *Alice*, send applications to *Bob* and receive timestamps in acknowledgment of their submissions. In the closing step, *Bob* acquires a closing timestamp and sends it back to *Alice*.

We explain the meaning of each protocol flow step by step. In the Preliminary step, *Bob* requests *Trent* to notify *Bob* at the opening time and closing time for submission because *Bob* may not have the accurate time, from assumption **N2**. "NR" denotes a notification service request and "NA" denotes a notification acknowledgment, which is different from a timestamping service. We discuss another scenario, which assumes that *Bob* has the accurate time and does not require the notification service. *Bob* receives acknowledgment of the notification in message 2. *Trent* notifies *Bob* at the opening time for submission in message 3. *Bob* sends a description of a call for submission to *Trent*, which means that *Bob* declares the opening of the period for electronic submission at that time. *Trent* returns a timestamp, that is, a signature on *Bob*'s message with a correct current time value t_s without verifying the contents of the message, *desc*. Instead of using messages 4 and 5, we can also apply the Time Stamp Protocol [ACPZ98] with some modifications. The purpose of this timestamp is to provide a proof that meets requirement **R2** in message 8. *Alice* retrieves *Trent*'s timestamp in message 7 by making a query with *id*, which is the index number of the call for submission. *Alice* sends an electronic submission to *Bob* in message 8. The message consists of application data x_i, the origin, the destination, the timestamp, and the applicant's signature on them. Since the timestamp, which is *Trent*'s signature, can only be generated at the opening time for submission, *Alice* and *Bob* can prove that the applicant's submission was sent after time t_s. If it is before the closing time for submission, *Bob* makes *Trent* issue a timestamp on each application in messages 9 and 10, and returns the timestamp to each applicant in message 11. If *Bob* receives the application after the closing time for submission, *Bob* returns message 15 instead of 9, 10, and 11, which means that the submission period is closed. After receiving message 11, *Alice* verifies that *Bob* received message 8. When the closing time for submission comes, *Bob* is notified by *Trent* in message 12, and *Bob* sends *Trent* a hashed value calculated from all successfully received submissions, and receives a timestamp to declare that the period for electronic submission is closed, in messages 13 and 14, respectively.

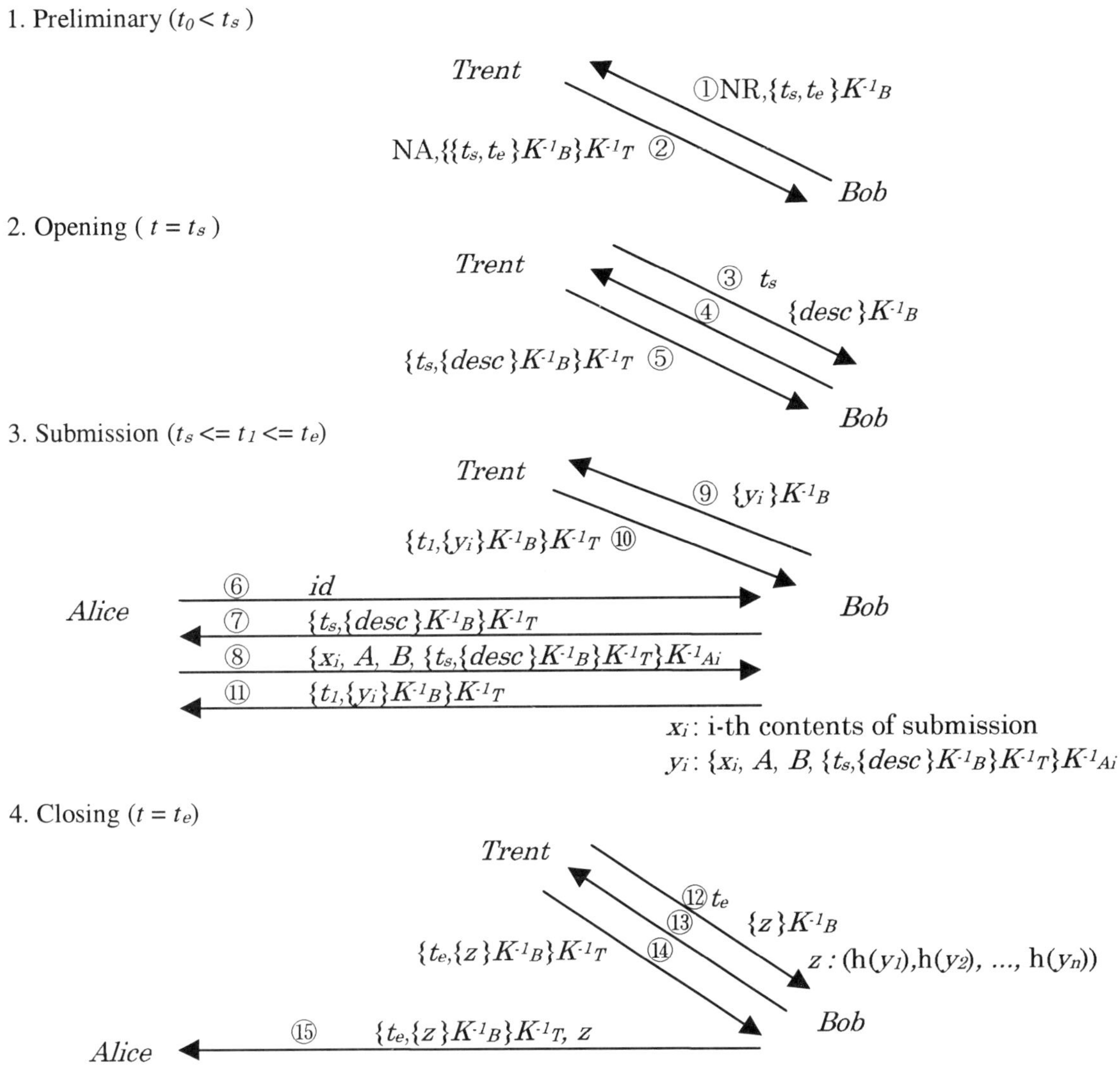

Figure 1. Protocol Flow

Alice receives message 15 and verifies that his/her submitted data are included in it by reconstructing the hashed value, z, from his/her submission data and other applicants' hashed values h(y_i). This implies that each applicant does not have to know about other applicants' data when verifying submissions. The timestamp guarantees the validity of all submissions received by *Bob*, so forging operations on submissions after the closing time can easily be detected. In the case of a subsequent dispute, each applicant and the requester can prove that they followed requirements **R1** , **R2**, and **R3** correctly by showing message 15 and all successfully submitted data, y_i. As for **R4**, we assume that the requester is not malicious and able to receive all submissions, since we have assumptions **N4** and **N6**. Alternatively, some notary service must be used for this purpose.

4 Temporal Accountability Logic

In this section, we present a temporal accountability logic that is an extension of Kailar's framework. The original work is capable of analyzing payment protocols and key distribution protocols, and consists of logical constructs, analysis assumptions, and logical postulates. We add nine new logical constructs and ten new postulates to allow analysis of temporal accountability, which is not possible in the original framework. After briefly explaining the original framework, we describe the proposed logic. We review most of the original constructs and postulates but not all of them.

4.1 Original Logical Constructs

The *Strong Proof* construct is denoted as A CanProve x , which means that a principal A can prove statement x to any principal B. After the sequence of operations, B is convinced of x without any secret y being revealed to B. The *Signature Authentication* construct is denoted as K Authenticates A, which means that key K can be used to authenticate the signature of principal A or to associate principal A unambiguously with any statement encrypted with K^{-1}. The *Message Interpretation* construct is denoted as x in m , which means that x is an interpretation of a field, or a combination of fields in message m. The *Signature Interpretation* construct is denoted as $x \Rightarrow m$, which articulates the interpretation of a signed message; this interpretation is defined by protocol designers and assumed to be evident to all principals involved. The *Statement* construct is denoted as A Says x, which means that principal A is accountable for making the statement x, and for anything that x implies. The *Message Receipt* construct is denoted as A Receives m SignedWith K^{-1}, which means that a principal A receives message m ,which is signed with K^{-1}. The construct m SignedWith K^{-1} means the same as $\{m\}K^{-1}$. The *Trust* construct is denoted as A IsTrustedOn x, which means that a principal A is trusted with regards to statement x. Thus, A has the authority to endorse statement x, and is liable for making statement x.

4.2 Original Postulates Used in the Analysis

The original work uses a notation for the postulates similar to that of [BAN90].

$$\frac{P; Q}{R}$$

means that if statements P and Q hold simultaneously, then statement R holds. ";" denotes conjunction and not temporal ordering. We use the following postulates in this paper. The *Inference* postulate

$$\frac{A\ \text{CanProve}\ x;\ x \Rightarrow y}{A\ \text{CanProve}\ y}$$

means that, if a principal A can prove that x holds, and if x implies y, then it follows that A can prove that y holds.

The *Accountability of Digital Signatures* postulate

$$\frac{A\ \text{Receives}\ (m\ \text{SignedWith}\ K^{-1});\ x\ \text{in}\ m;\quad A\ \text{CanProve}\ (K\ \text{Authenticates}\ B)}{A\ \text{CanProve}\ (B\ \text{Says}\ x)}$$

means that, if a principal A receives a message m signed with the key K^{-1}, the message m contains statement x, and A can prove that the key K authenticates principal B, then A can prove that B is accountable for x. The *Message Receipt* postulate

$$\frac{A\ \text{Receives}\ (m\ \text{SignedWith}\ K^{-1});\ x\ \text{in}\ m;}{A\ \text{Receives}\ (x\ \text{SignedWith}\ K^{-1})}$$

means that, if a principal A receives a message m signed with the key K^{-1}, and the message m contains statement x, then A can prove that x is also signed with K^{-1}. From the definition, $(m$ SignedWith $K^{-1})$ includes all contents and signatures associated with the message. Then, we can also say A Receives x if the above conditional statement holds.

4.3 Temporal Logical Constructs

We propose the following temporal logical constructs:

- The *Generation Before* construct is denoted as x GeneratedBefore t, which means that the message x was generated before or at time t, and therefore x exists at time t and also continues to exist after t according to the usual temporal causal relation. Note that we use the words "after" and "before" in the construct names a little differently from the usual meaning, which does not include a terminal point of time literally.
- The *Generation At* construct is denoted as x GeneratedAt t, which means that the message x is generated at time t. GeneratedAt differs from GeneratedBefore in that the former represents the generated time of x explicitly whereas the latter cannot.
- A *Generation After* construct is denoted as x GeneratedAfter t, which means that the message x is generated at or after time t. This construct is weaker than GeneratedAt, because it conveys no information about when x is generated.
- A *Timestamp* construct is denoted as x TimestampedWith t With K^{-1} , which means that the message x is timestamped with t with the key K^{-1} at time t. This construct has the similar meaning as $(t,\ x)$ SignedWith K^{-1}. x TimestampedWith t With K^{-1} includes all contents and signatures associated with the message.
- A *Timestamp Signature* construct is denoted as x TimesignWith t With K^{-1}, and is used for representing only a signature value of x TimestampedWith t With K^{-1}. It does not include any plain text contents such as t and x.
- A *Says At* construct is denoted as A Says x At t,

which means that a principal *A* is accountable for making the statement *x* at time *t*.

- A *Reception Before* construct is denoted as *A* Receives *x* Before *t* From *B*, which means that a principal *A* receives a message *x* from a principal *B* before or at time *t*.
- A *Reception After* construct is denoted as *A* Receives *x* After *t* From *B*, which means that a principal *A* receives a message *x* from a principal *B* at or after time *t*.
- A *Reception During* construct is denoted as *A* Receives *x* During $[t_s, t_e]$ From *B*, which means that a principal *A* receives a message *x* from a principal *B* during the closed interval $[t_s, t_e]$. We assume $t_s < t_e$.

4.4 Temporal Postulates

We propose the following temporal postulates:

- *Generation Before*

The *Generation Before* postulate relates the provability of a timestamp and the *Generation Before* construct. If a principal *A* receives a message *x* that is timestamped with *t* with a private key K^{-1}, and the timestamp is issued by a principal *T*, and *T* is trusted as regards the accuracy of his/her time, then *A* can prove that message *x* is generated before or at time *t*.

A Receives (*x* TimestampedWith *t* With K^{-1});
A CanProve (*K* Authenticates *T*);
A CanProve (*T* IsTrustedOn *t*)
____
A CanProve (*x* GeneratedBefore *t*)

- *Generation At*

The *Generation At* postulate relates the provability of a timestamp and the *Generation At* construct. If a principal *A* receives a message *x* that is timestamped with *t* with a private key K^{-1} at time t, and the timestamp is issued by a principal *T*, and *T* is trusted as regards the accuracy of his/her time, then *A* can prove that *T*'s signature itself, which is denoted by (*x* TimesignWith *t* With K^{-1}), is generated at *t*.

A Receives (*x* TimestampedWith *t* With K^{-1});
A CanProve (*K* Authenticates *T*);
A CanProve (*T* IsTrustedOn *t*)
____
A CanProve ((*x* TimesignWith *t* With K^{-1}) GeneratedAt *t*)

- *Generation Relation1*

Generation Relation1 postulate describes a relation between the *Generation At* construct and the *Generation Before* construct. If a principal *A* can prove that *x* is generated at *t*, and that *x* is a component of *y*, then *A* can prove that *y* is generated at or after *t*.

A CanProve (*x* GeneratedAt *t*);
x in *y*
____
A CanProve (*y* GeneratedAfter *t*)

For example, suppose there are two messages, *x1* and *x2*, and *x1* is generated at *t1*, and *x2* at *t2*. If we think of a combination of the above messages, *x1* and *x2*, the combined message cannot be generated before *t2*, because *x2* is generated at *t2*. This implies that combined messages must be generated at the latest time for the generation of each components. Therefore *Generation Relation1* holds whatever *x* and combinations we take.

- *Generation Relation2*

The *Generation Relation2* postulate describes a feature of the *Generation After* construct. If a principal *A* can prove that *x* is generated at or after *t*, and *x* is a component of *y*, then *A* can prove that *y* is generated at or after *t*.

A CanProve (*x* GeneratedAfter *t*);
x in *y*
____
A CanProve (*y* GeneratedAfter *t*)

- *Generation Relation3*

The *Generation Relation3* postulate describes a relation between the *Generation At* construct and the *Generation Before* construct. If a principal *A* can prove that *x* is generated at *t*, and *y* is a component of *x*, then *A* can prove that *y* is generated before or at *t*.

A CanProve (*x* GeneratedAt *t*);
y in *x*
____
A CanProve (*y* GeneratedBefore *t*)

- *Generation Relation4*

The *Generation Relation4* postulate describes a feature of the *Generation Before* construct. If a principal *A* can prove that *x* is generated before or at time *t*, and *y* is a component of *x*, then *A* can prove that *y* is also generated before or at time *t*.

A CanProve (*x* GeneratedBefore *t*);
y in *x*
____
A CanProve (*y* GeneratedBefore *t*)

- *Says At*

The *Says At* postulate defines a principal's statement at a certain time. If a principal *A* can prove that *x* is generated before or at *t*, where *x* includes *B*'s signature on *y*, then *A* can prove that *B* says *y* at *t*.

A CanProve (*x* GeneratedBefore *t*);
(*y* SignedWith K^{-1}) in *x*;
A CanProve (*K* Authenticates *B*)
____
A CanProve (*B* Says *y* At *t*)

- *Reception Before, After, During*

Reception postulates define reception accountability

that represents when the message is received. These postulates are domain-specific provability properties.

- *Reception Before*

The *Reception Before* postulate means that if a principal A receives y, which includes a message with the origin and the destination, C's signature on them, and B's signature on all, and if A can prove that y is generated before or at t, and that K_C and K_B authenticate C and B, respectively, then A can prove that B receives x before or at t from C.

A Receives y;
$(((x,C,B)$ SignedWith $K^{-1}_C)$ SignedWith $K^{-1}_B)$ in y;
A CanProve (y GeneratedBefore t);
A CanProve (K_C Authenticates C);
A CanProve (K_B Authenticates B);
―――――――――――――――――――――
A CanProve B Receives x Before t From C

From the second, fourth, and fifth statements of the *Reception Before* postulate, the *Message Receipt* postulate, and the *Accountability* postulate, we obtain A CanProve B Says (x SignedWith K^{-1}_C) and A CanProve C Says x. We think that it is intuitively reasonable that if someone says something - for example, x - that has been already said by a different person, then the former person must have received the contents from the latter beforehand. Although we cannot reason whether the sender sent the message directly to the receiver or not, the contents with the delivery information, such as (x,C,B), can show the original sender and the final destination. We use the word From as the origin of the message.

- *Reception After*

The *Reception After* postulate means that if a principal A receives the message x with the origin and the destination, which is signed by C and B sequentially, and if A can prove that y is generated at or after t, and that K_C and K_B authenticate C and B, respectively, then A can prove that B receives x at or after t from C.

A Receives $(((x,C,B)$ SignedWith $K^{-1}_C)$ SignedWith $K^{-1}_B)$;
A CanProve (x GeneratedAfter t);
A CanProve (K_C Authenticates C);
A CanProve (K_B Authenticates B);
―――――――――――――――――――――
A CanProve B Receives x After t From C

This postulate is intuitively reasonable, because if a component of the original message can be proved to be generated at or after time t, the receiver cannot receive the whole message before time t. Therefore the receiver must receive the message at or after time t.

- *Reception During*

The *Reception During* postulate is intuitively introduced on the basis of the *Reception After* and *Reception Before* postulates.

A CanProve B Receives x After t_1 From C;
A CanProve B Receives x Before t_2 From C;
$t_1 < t_2$
―――――――――――――――――――――
A CanProve B Receives x During $[t_1, t_2]$ From C

5 Protocol Analysis

In this section, we analyze the electronic submission protocol by applying the proposed temporal accountability logic. We apply the same analysis framework as that used in Kailar's work. It consists of stating the protocol's accountability goals, interpreting protocol messages, articulating the initial state assumptions, and analyzing each message. After analyzing the protocol, we can verify that all accountability goals can be obtained from the initial state assumptions and protocol message interpretations.

5.1 Accountability Goals

We present accountability goals for submission transactions according to the requirements stated in section 3. Although the following goals are neither necessary nor sufficient, they seem reasonable as general goals.

G1) *receiver, applicants* CanProve *(opening time and closing time are accurate)*
G2) *applicants* CanProve *(receiver will receive applications sent during the permitted period)*
G3) *receiver* CanProve *(applicants send their applications during the permitted period)*
G4) *applicants* CanProve *(receiver received application during the permitted period)*
G5) *applicants* CanProve *(no application is forged or removed once received)*

5.2 Protocol Interpretation

Since an unsigned message has no effect on the achievement of goals in accountability logic, the following flows can be interpreted:

1) T Receives $((t_s,t_e)$ SignedWith $K^{-1}_B)$
2) B Receives $(((t_s,t_e)$ SignedWith $K^{-1}_B)$ SignedWith $K^{-1}_T)$
4) T Receives ($desc$ SignedWith K^{-1}_B)
5) B Receives (($desc$ SignedWith K^{-1}_B) TimestampedWith t_s With K^{-1}_T)
7) A Receives (($desc$ SignedWith K^{-1}_B)

TimestampedWith t_s With K^{-1}_T)

8) B Receives ((x_i, A, B, ($desc$ SignedWith K^{-1}_B) TimestampedWith t_s With K^{-1}_T)SignedWith K^{-1}_{Ai})

9) T Receives (y_i SignedWith K^{-1}_B)

10) B Receives ((y_i SignedWith K^{-1}_B) TimestampedWith t_l With K^{-1}_T)

11) A Receives ((y_i SignedWith K^{-1}_B) TimestampedWith t_l With K^{-1}_T)

13) T Receives (z SignedWith K^{-1}_B)

14) B Receives ((z SignedWith K^{-1}_B) TimestampedWith t_e With K^{-1}_T)

15) A Receives ((z SignedWith K^{-1}_B) TimestampedWith t_e With K^{-1}_T)

5.3 Initial State Assumptions

The initial state assumptions required in the analysis are as follows:

A1) A,T CanProve (K_B Authenticates B)

A2) B,T CanProve (K_A Authenticates A)

A3) A,B CanProve (K_T Authenticates T)

A4) A,B CanProve (T IsTrustedOn *time*)

A5) (B Says (t_s,t_e)) =>
(*B requests notification at time* t_s *and* t_e.)

A6) (T Says (t_s,t_e)) =>
(*T guarantees that T will notify B at times* t_s *and* t_e.)

A7) (B Says $desc$ At t_s) =>
(*the opening time is accurate and B guarantees that it will receive all applications sent during the permitted period.*)

A8) (B Says z At t_e) =>
(*the closing time is accurate and B guarantees that no submissions can be forged or removed after closing time.*)

A9) (B Receive x During [t_s, t_l] From A) =>
(*B received A's submission sent during the permitted period if* $t_s < t_l < t_e$ *holds.*)

The assumption **A1** denotes that the principal A and T can prove that B is accountable for any statement signed with K^{-1}_B. This assumption is made when the principal can acquire a certificate for the receiver that includes K_B. **A2** and **A3** have similar meanings to **A1**. Note that A denotes not one but multiple applicants. **A4** is from the general assumption **N1**. The last five assumptions are implications of accountability goals.

5.4 Protocol Analysis

- *Message 1*:

This preliminary flow is required when the general assumption **N2** is made. When T receives message 1, T sees a notification service request tag (NR) and can prove the following statement by applying the *Accountability* postulate and the assumption **A1**.

T CanProve (B Says (t_s,t_e))

This statement can be transformed by applying **A5** and the *Inference* postulate.

T CanProve (*B requests notification at time* t_s *and* t_e.)

- *Message 2*:

T sends a notification service acknowledgment in response to Message 1. When B receives message 2, B can prove the following statement by applying the *Accountability* postulate, **A3**, and **A6.**

B CanProve (*T guarantees that T will notify B at times* t_s *and* t_e.)

- *Message 4*:

When notified by T at t_s, B instantly sends a description of the call for submission with his/her signature to T to be timestamped. Although we need a nonce value in the timestamp request message, we omit it for the readability purpose in this paper.

- *Message 5*:

When B receives message 5, B can prove the following statement by applying the *Generation Before* and *Says At* postulate:

B CanProve (B Says $desc$ At t_s)

First, variables x and t in the *Generation Before* postulate are instantiated as $\{desc\}K^{-1}_B$ and t_s, respectively. Next, variables x, y, and t in the *Says At* postulate are instantiated as $\{desc\}K^{-1}_B$, $desc$, and t_s, respectively. Finally, the following statement can be obtained by applying the assumption **A7**:

B CanProve (*the opening time is accurate and B guarantees that it will receive all applications sent during the permitted period.*)

- *Message 7*:

When A receives message 7, A can obtain the following statement in a similar manner to message 5.

A CanProve (B Says $desc$ At t_s)

This can be further transformed by applying **A7**.

A CanProve (*the opening time is accurate and B guarantees that it will receive all applications sent during the permitted period.*)

Then the goal **G2** can be achieved.

- *Message 8*:

When B receives message 8, B can prove the statement that A generated his/her submission after the opening time for submission t_s. Message 8 can be transformed as follows:

B Receives v

where

y : ($desc$ SignedWith $K^{-1}{}_B$)

w : (y TimesignWith t_s With $K^{-1}{}_T$)

u : (y TimestampedWith t_s With $K^{-1}{}_T$)

v : (x_i, u)

Using the above variables, **A3**, and **A4**, the statements

B Receives w

B CanProve (K_T Authenticates T)

B CanProve (T IsTrustedOn t_s)

hold, and we can obtain the following from the *Generation At* postulate.

B CanProve (w GeneratedAt t_s)

We can obtain the following statements from the *Generation Relation1* and *2* postulates since w in u, and u in v.

B CanProve (u GeneratedAfter t_s)

B CanProve (v GeneratedAfter t_s)

The final statement is used in reasoning in message 10.

- *Messages 9* and *10*:

B requests a timestamp with the value of message 8 in message 9. When B receives message 10, the following statement can be proved by applying the *Generation Before* postulate and the *Reception Before* postulate.

B CanProve B Receives v Before t_l From A

We can also obtain the following result from the result obtained in message 8 and the *Reception After* postulate:

B CanProve B Receives v After t_s From A

We obtain the following result from the *Reception During* postulate if $t_s < t_l < t_e$:

B CanProve B Receives v During $[t_s, t_l]$ From A

This means that v, the combination of the application x_i and the timestamp u, is received by B. Finally, we obtain the accountability goal **G3**.

- *Message 11*:

When A receives message 11, from the *Reception During* postulate,

A CanProve B Receives v During $[t_s, t_l]$ From A

can be obtained. Finally, we obtain the following from **A9**:

A CanProve (*B received A's submission sent during the permitted period if* $t_s < t_l < t_e$ *holds)*

This is the accountability goal **G4**.

- *Messages 13* and *14*:

When notified by T at the closing time for submissions, B instantly sends a hashed value calculated from all applications which are successfully received. When B receives message 14, The following statement;

B CanProve (*the closing time is accurate and B guarantees that no submissions can be forged or removed after the closing time)*

can be obtained from **A8**, the *Accountability* postulate, and the *Says At* postulate.

- *Message 15*:

When A receives message 15, A can prove the following statement from the *Says At* postulate and **A8**.

A CanProve (*the closing time is accurate and B guarantees that no submissions can be forged or removed after closing time)*

Therefore, goals **G1** and **G5** can be finally achieved in messages 5, 7, 14, and 15.

6 Discussion

We further discuss on the protocol refinement by using temporal accountability logic and the accuracy of the receiver's clock.

6.1 Protocol Refinement

In the proposed protocol, the receiver has to acquire timestamps in proportion to the number of applicants. If the general assumption **N4** is not made and the number of applicants increases greatly, the possibilities of a performance bottleneck problem at the timestamp server should be considered. By making some modifications to the original protocol, we can avoid this problem while protecting the security of the temporal transactions. We remove messages 9 and 10, and modify message 11 to $\{y_i\}K^{-1}{}_B$. Then, we can reduce the required number of timestamps per call for submission from n+2 to 2 (where n denotes the number of applicants), while maintaining the original security level in terms of temporal accountability. The difference lies in the time at which **G3** is achieved for the receiver and **G4** for applicants. After refinement, the receiver can acquire the proof of **G3** in message 14, and the applicant can acquire the proof of **G4** in message 15, at the closing time for submissions, because the *Reception During* postulate holds at that time. We think that this is a tradeoff problem between efficiency and usability. By adding one more modification to the previous refinement, applicants can acquire the proof of the goal **G3** immediately after receiving the modified message 11 by executing an additional timestamping protocol with the timestamp server, which is similar to messages 9 and 10. We think that the last protocol is more optimal in terms of efficiency than the previously proposed one, because the applicants can decide when they should obtain the goal **G3**. As we have stated, the temporal accountability logic is effective for analyzing protocol and modifying messages, so that we can reduce the number of flows and improve protocol efficiency.

6.2 If the Receiver's Clock Is Accurate

We assume here that the general assumption **N2** is not made and that the receiver is capable of synchronizing his/her local clock with another accurate clock. We can then omit the preliminary step, message 3 in the opening step, and message 12 in the closing step, because the receiver can begin the opening and closing steps without being notified by the timestamp server. Note that a verifier can still verify the temporal accuracy of the submission process by checking the values of the timestamps. If the requester's time is accurate, the verifier can reason that the receiver's clock is accurate and the whole process has been carried out correctly. Otherwise, the verifier can detect that the receiver's clock is not accurate or that the submission-receiving process has been carried out incorrectly. In the latter case, the accountability goal **G1** cannot be obtained.

7 Conclusion

We have explained that electronic commerce applications are closely related to the security of temporal properties. We described possible attacks on temporal properties and proposed a defense measurement that assumes the existence of a trusted third-party of a timestamp server. We presented a secure electronic submission protocol as the most typical electronic commerce application that has a feature for temporal transactions. We also proposed the temporal accountability logic, which is capable of representing the provability of temporal activities, and analyzed the proposed protocol. We explained that the protocol can be refined by making some modifications to the original protocol while maintaining the original security level in terms of temporal accountability. Although the proposed logic does not attempt to solve all problems through temporal accountability, the logic is effective in analyzing protocol, and modifying messages, to improve the number of flows and improve protocol performance.

Acknowledgments

I would like to thank Anish Mathuria for the numerous useful comments on earlier versions of this paper.

References

[ABLP93] M. Abadi, M. Burrows, B. Lampson, and G. A. Plotkin, "A Calculus for Access Control in Distributed Systems," ACM Trans. Program. Lang. Sys., 15(4), Sep. 1993, pp. 706-734.

[ACPZ98] C. Adams, P. Cain, D. Pinkas, and R. Zuccherato, "Time Stamp Protocols," Internet Draft, ftp.ietf.org.

[BAN90] M. Burrows, M. Abadi, and R. Needham, "A Logic of Authentication," ACM Trans. on Computer Systems, Vol. 8, No. 1, Feb. 1990, pp. 18-36.

[FR95] M. K. Franklin and M. K. Reiter, "The Design and Implementation of a Secure Auction Service," IEEE Trans. on Software Engineering, Vol. 22, No. 5, 1995, pp. 302-312.

[HS90] S. Haber and W. S. Stornetta, "How to Time-Stamp a Digital Document," Proceedings of Crypto '90, Lecture Notes in Computer Science, 537, Springer-Verlag, 1991, pp. 437-455.

[K96] R. Kailar, "Accountability in Electronic Commerce Protocols," IEEE Trans. on Software Engineering, Vol. 22, No. 5, May, 1996, pp. 313-328.

[K98] M. Kudo, "Secure Electronic Sealed-Bid Auction Protocol with Public Key Cryptography," IEICE Transactions on Fundamentals of Electronics, Communications and Computer Sciences, Vol. E81-A, No. 1, Jan. 1998, pp. 20-27.

[LABW92] B. Lampson, M. Abadi, M. Burrows, and E. Wobber, "Authentication in Distributed Systems: Theory and Practice," ACM Trans. Computer Systems, 10(4), Nov. 1992, pp. 265-310.

[M91] D. L. Mills, "Internet Time Synchronization: The Network Time Protocol," IEEE Transactions on Communication, Vol. 39, 1991, pp. 1482-1493.

[S95] S. G. Stubblebine, "Recent-Secure Authentication: Enforcing Revocation in Distributed Systems," 19th IEEE Symposium on Research in Security and Privacy, 1995, pp. 224-235.

[SO94] P. F. Syverson, and P. C. van Oorschot, "On Unifying Some Cryptographic Protocol Logics," 18th IEEE Symposium on Research in Security and Privacy, 1994, pp. 14-28.

[SW96] S. G. Stubblebine, and R. N. Wright, "An Authentication Logic Supporting Synchronization, Revocation, and Recency," 3rd ACM Conference on Computer and Communications Security, Mar. 1996, pp. 95-105.

Author Index

— *Notes* —

— *Notes* —

IEEE COMPUTER SOCIETY

Press Activities Board

IEEE Computer Society Publications

The world-renowned Computer Society publishes, promotes, and distributes a wide variety of authoritative computer science and engineering texts. These books are available in two formats: 100 percent original material by authors preeminent in their field who focus on relevant topics and cutting-edge research, and reprint collections consisting of carefully selected groups of previously published papers with accompanying original introductory and explanatory text.

Submission of proposals: For guidelines and information on Computer Society books, send e-mail to cs.books@computer.org or write to the Project Editor, IEEE Computer Society, P.O. Box 3014, 10662 Los Vaqueros Circle, Los Alamitos, CA 90720-1314. Telephone +1 714-821-8380. FAX +1 714-761-1784.

IEEE Computer Society Proceedings

The Computer Society also produces and actively promotes the proceedings of more than 130 acclaimed international conferences each year in multimedia formats that include hard and softcover books, CD-ROMs, videos, and on-line publications.

For information on Computer Society proceedings, send e-mail to cs.books@computer.org or write to Proceedings, IEEE Computer Society, P.O. Box 3014, 10662 Los Vaqueros Circle, Los Alamitos, CA 90720-1314. Telephone +1 714-821-8380. FAX +1 714-761-1784.

Additional information regarding the Computer Society, conferences and proceedings, CD-ROMs, videos, and books can also be accessed from our web site at http://computer.org/cspress

4/16/98